V *The Research Paper*

17 The Research Process 321
17a Thinking about assignment
17b Thinking about a subject
17c Thinking about reader
17d Planning

18 The Library 333
18a Card catalog
18b Reference works
18c Periodicals
18d *Essay & General Literature Index*
18e Data-base searches
18f Government documents

19 Working with Sources 357
19a Working bibliography
19b MLA Works Cited forms
19c Taking notes
19d Assessing sources
19e Assessing subject

20 Composing the Research Paper 388
20a Organizing & writing
20b Avoiding plagiarism
20c Citing sources
20d Formatting the research paper

21 Student Research Paper A: MLA Documentation 413

22 Student Research Paper B: APA Documentation 432

23 Student Research Paper C: Endnote Documentation 480

VI *Grammatical Usage 517*

24 Sentence Structure 536
24a Elements of a sentence
24b Types of sentences

25 Agreement 549
25a Subject & verb
25b Pronoun & antecedent

26 Case of Pronouns and Nouns 549
26a Compounds
26b *Who, whom* in dependent clauses
26c *Who, whom* in interrogatives
26d Reflexive & intensive pronouns
26e After *than, as,* & *but*
26f With linking verbs
26g With infinitives
26h With gerunds

27 Adjectives and Adverbs 558
27a Comparative & superlative forms
27b Adjectives with linking verbs
27c Nouns as adjectives
27d Compound adjectives
27e Colloquial forms

28 Verbs 567
28a Verb forms
28b Irregular verbs
28c Tenses
28d Sequence of tenses
28e Auxiliary verbs
28f Voice
28g Mood

29 Sentence Fragments, Comma Splices, Fused Sentences 587
29a Types of fragments
29b Acceptable uses
29c Comma splices
29d Acceptable splices
29e Fused sentences

VII *Punctuation, Spelling, Mechanics*

30 Punctuation 605
30a Period
30b Question mark
30c Exclamation point
30d Comma
30e Semicolon
30f Quotation marks
30g Apostrophe
30h Colon, dash, parentheses, brackets

31 Spelling 640
31a Trouble spots
31b Similar words
31c Rules
31d Hyphenation
31e Word list

32 Mechanics 658
32a Manuscript
32b Capitals
32c Numbers
32d Abbreviations
32e Italics
32f Syllabication

VIII *Special Writing Situations*

33 Writing Business Letters 677
33a Business correspondence
33b Parts of a letter

34 Composing Résumés and Job Applications 684
34a Designing a résumé
34b Letters of application

35 Writing under Pressure 690
35a Preparing
35b Reading
35c Writing
35d Sample essays

36 Writing with a Word Processor 698
36a Word processing
36b Getting the most out of word processing

Glossary of Usage 707

Grammatical Terms 729

Index 748

The
Heath
Handbook

Gerald P. Mulderig
DePaul University

Langdon Elsbree
Claremont McKenna College

The
Heath
Handbook

Twelfth Edition

D. C. Heath and Company
Lexington, Massachusetts   Toronto

Acknowledgment: Excerpt on page 411 was reprinted with permission from the June 1989 issue of *Trains* magazine. Copyright © Kalmbach Publishing Co.

Acquisitions Editor: Paul Smith
Developmental Editor: Holt Johnson
Production Editor: Karen Wise
Designer: Alwyn Velásquez
Production Coordinator: Lisa Arcese
Text Permissions Editor: Margaret Roll

Published simultaneously in Canada.

Printed in the United States of America.

International Standard Book Number: 0–669–17859–4

Library of Congress Catalog Card Number: 89–85075

10 9 8 7 6 5 4 3 2 1

Preface

When Edwin C. Woolley published the first edition of *The Heath Handbook* in 1907, he established a new standard for composition textbooks in the twentieth century. Though Woolley's tone was dogmatic and his approach to correctness uncompromising, the unprecedented comprehensiveness of his book and its clear organization—350 numbered rules, beginning with a definition of good usage and ending with the proper placement of a postage stamp on a letter—made it an immediate success.

Our understanding of the writing process, and of the way writing should be taught and learned, has changed dramatically in the more than eight decades since Woolley's first handbook appeared. But comprehensive coverage and clarity of organization remain desirable features in a handbook. This twelfth edition of *The Heath Handbook*, the most thorough revision of the book in more than twenty years, represents the most complete and, we believe, the most accessible edition ever published. Every chapter of the book has been revised; many have been greatly expanded or completely rewritten; several others are new to this edition. Throughout the book, moreover, new headings and subheadings break up the text within chapters, making them easier to consult for quick reference.

Past users of *The Heath Handbook* will notice in particular the following major changes:

1. Increased attention to the writing process.

Chapter 1, "Understanding the Writing Process," has been enlarged to include discussion of the recursive and idiosyncratic nature of the writing process. Chapter 2, "Exploring Ideas," includes a new section on keeping a journal and several new examples of student writing. Chapter 3, "Considering Your Audience," and Chapter 4, "Choosing a Voice," both feature expanded exercises. Chapter 10, "Revising the Essay," has been totally rewritten; it includes a new discussion of the nature of revision, a new student essay in the process of being revised, and an extended new section on participating in a peer editing group.

2. Greatly expanded treatment of grammatical usage, punctuation, and mechanics.

Most of the nine chapters in Part VI, "Grammatical Usage," and Part VII, "Punctuation, Spelling, and Mechanics," have been completely rewritten to provide more thorough coverage of usage than was available in any previous edition. Our emphasis in rewriting these sections of the book has been on clear explanations, carefully chosen examples, and an organization that enables the reader to locate information quickly and easily.

3. Expanded treatment of the research paper, including three complete student research papers illustrating MLA, APA, and endnote documentation.

Chapter 17, "The Research Process," has been more than doubled in length; it now includes greater discussion of the process of identifying a subject for research and planning the research project. Chapter 18, "The Library," includes an enlarged section on data-base searches—a change that reflects the increasing availability of both on-line and CD-ROM data bases since the last edition was published in 1986. The number of sample MLA Works Cited entries in Chapter 19, "Working with Sources," has been increased to forty-four and now includes examples of entries for every print and nonprint source that students are likely to encounter. Chapter 19 also includes new sections on evaluating sources and assessing one's subject. Chapters 22 and 23, new to this edition, offer comprehensive discussions of APA documentation and endnote documentation, along with fully annotated student research papers illustrating each of these documentation methods in practice.

4. More complete coverage of the art of writing effective sentences.

Chapter 8, "Writing Effective Sentences," combines material that was scattered among several different chapters in previous editions; it also includes such new topics as avoiding nominalizations and eliminating wordy connectives. The result is a unified and comprehensive discussion of effective sentence writing in a single chapter.

5. A new section on avoiding sexist language.

Chapter 13, "Revising Diction," now includes thorough discussion of the types of sexism too often found in English and suggestions for avoiding them.

6. A new chapter on writing with a word processor.

Chapter 36, "Writing with a Word Processor," is also new to this edition; it surveys the capabilities of word processors and shows students how to use word processing in the planning, drafting, and revising of a paper.

7. More than fifty new exercises.

All exercises that call for the revision of sentence-level errors now consist of sentences that fit together to form brief expository or narrative essays on topics ranging from astronomy to surgery, from Gertrude Stein to Thomas Edison, from the Harlem Renaissance to the Chicago Fire, from traveling by train to writing with a word processor. We think students will find these exercises far more interesting than exercises composed of random, unrelated sentences; these exercises also make it possible for students to consider usage and mechanical errors in a context larger than that provided by a single isolated sentence.

8. An entirely new design.

The typeface has been enlarged and the pages have been reformatted to give students a more readable, accessible text. In addition to the new headings and subheadings, the amount of second color has been increased to make information easier to locate.

9. A full supplement package.

The *Workbook, Diagnostic Tests,* and *Instructor's Edition* provide teachers with support materials that make *The Heath Handbook* a useful classroom tool. In addition, Grammatik III software (a style analysis program) and a variety of word-processing programs and user manuals are available to give students ample help in writing with computers.

Other supplements include copies of the eighth edition of Wilbert J. McKeachie's *Teaching Tips,* an ideal book for beginning instructors, and, through a special arrangement, student subscriptions to *Newsweek* magazine.

We enjoyed the support and assistance of many colleagues and friends as we prepared this edition of *The Heath Handbook.* Specific thanks are due to Robert Acker of the DePaul University Libraries, who shared his expertise in on-line information systems; to Celia Burkhalter of the American Psychological Association, who resolved some thorny questions about APA documentation; to James Catano and Michelle Massé of Louisiana State University, Baton Rouge, who made helpful comments on many portions of the manuscript; to Dusky Loebel of Tulane University, whose contributions to the exercises were invaluable; and to the students who allowed us to use their writing for the first time in this edition: Janet Lively, Cyndi Lopardo, Nancy McClure, Kathleen Mulkerrin, and Brad Olson.

Reviewers of the eleventh edition provided us with many valuable suggestions that helped to shape this revision. We are grateful to Richard R. Bollenbacher, Edison State Community College; David Fuller, Northern State College; Owen W. Gilman, St. Joseph's University; Douglas Hunt, University of Missouri, Columbia; David M. Kvernes, Southern Illinois University, Carbondale; Janet Madden-Simpson, El Camino Community College; Barbara G. Merkel, Cazenovia College; Susan B. Norton, Trident Technical College; and Jeff Watkins, Mt. Hood Community College.

Our copy editor, Roberta H. Winston, read the manuscript with care and insight, making innumerable wise suggestions and saving us from many errors; her contribution to the book has been immeasurable. Finally, no words are sufficient to thank our editors at D. C. Heath and Company—Paul Smith, Karen Wise, and Holt Johnson—for their dedication to this project, and for their advice, assistance, and endless patience.

G. P. M.
L. E.

Contents

PART I Planning

1 Understanding the Writing Process 3

1a Why write? 4
  1. Writing and perception 4
  2. Writing and thinking 4
  3. Writing and self-discovery 5
1b A writer's purpose 5
1c The writing process 7
  1. The recursiveness of writing 7
  2. Avoiding frustration when you write 9
1d About this book 10

2 Discovering Ideas 15

2a Unstructured methods of discovery 15
  1. Brainstorming 16
  2. Free writing 20
  3. Keeping a journal 24
2b Structured methods of discovery 28

3   Considering Your
        Audience   **33**

 3a The rhetorical situation 33
 3b Analyzing audiences 34

4   Choosing a Voice   **39**

 4a A writer's voice 39
 4b Voice and subject 40
 4c Voice and audience 42

PART
II

Writing

5   Organizing an Essay   **53**

 5a Limiting your subject 53
  1. Consider what you know about
   yourself 54
  2. Consider what you know about your
   readers 55
  3. Consider what you know about your
   subject 55
 5b Formulating a thesis statement 56
  1. Components of a thesis statement 56
  2. Precision in a thesis statement 57
  3. Placement of the thesis statement 59
 5c Organizing ideas 59
 5d Writing an introduction 62
  1. Beginning with the thesis
   statement 62
  2. Beginning with a quotation 62
  3. Building up to the thesis
   statement 63
 5e Shaping the body of an essay 64
 5f Writing a conclusion 65
  1. Ending with a sense of finality 65

2. Ending by echoing the introduction   66
3. Ending by bringing ideas together   66

5g   Constructing outlines   67
1. Uses of outlines   67
2. Types of outlines   68
3. Conventions of topic and sentence outlines   71

5h   A sample essay   74

6   Constructing Paragraphs   82

6a   Recognizing paragraphs   82
6b   Using topic sentences   87
1. Formulating a topic sentence   87
2. Positioning a topic sentence   88

6c   Adjusting paragraph length   93
1. Using a short paragraph for emphasis   94
2. Paragraphing dialogue   95

6d   Controlling paragraphs within an essay   96

7   Developing Paragraphs   99

7a   Development by specific detail   100
7b   Development by narration   102
7c   Development by examples   103
7d   Development by definition   104
7e   Development by classification   107
7f   Development by comparison or contrast   109
7g   Development by analogy   111
7h   Development by cause and effect   113

7i A more typical case: combined
methods of development 114

8 Writing Effective Sentences 119

8a Writing unified sentences 119
1. Too many ideas 120
2. Faulty coordination and
subordination 122

8b Writing concise sentences 127
1. Redundant words, phrases, and
clauses 128
2. Nominalizations 129
3. Wordy connectives 130
4. Unnecessary repetition 131
5. Overuse of the passive voice 131
6. *There is* and *it is* constructions 134

8c Creating parallelism 136
1. Coordinate pairs 140
2. Elements in a series 142
3. Repetition of words 142
4. Correlatives 143
5. Subordinate clauses 145
6. Sequence of ideas 146

8d Writing cumulative and periodic
sentences 148

8e Varying sentence length 150

8f Varying sentence openers 152
1. Single modifiers 152
2. Prepositional phrases 152
3. Inversions 153
4. Appositives 153
5. Verbal phrases 153
6. Absolute phrases 154
7. Adverbial clauses 154

9   Choosing Words   157

9a   Using the dictionary   157
  1. Unabridged dictionaries   157
  2. Abridged dictionaries   158
  3. Dictionary abbreviations and
     symbols   159

9b   Levels of usage   164
  1. Edited English   165
  2. Formal English   165
  3. Colloquial English   166
  4. Regional English   167
  5. Dialect and nonstandard
     English   167
  6. Slang   168

PART
III

Revising

10   Revising the Essay   173

10a   Understanding revision   173
  1. Recognize the two types of
     revision   173
  2. Leave time after finishing a draft before
     you revise   174
  3. Analyze your draft
     systematically   174
  4. Be open to possible changes in your
     draft   175

10b   Using your instructor's suggestions in
       revision   175

10c   Using your peers' suggestions in
       revision   184
  1. Participating in a peer editing
     group   184
  2. Using a peer editing worksheet   186

11 Revising Paragraphs 190

11a Inadequate development 190
   1. Recognizing vagueness and generalities 190
   2. Using concrete diction and specific detail 192
   3. Revising an underdeveloped paragraph 193

11b Lack of coherence 196
   1. Transitional words 197
   2. Linking pronouns 198
   3. Repetition of key words 198
   4. Parallel structure 199
   5. Maintaining coherence between paragraphs 200

12 Revising Sentences 203

12a Unclear pronoun reference 204
   1. Ambiguous reference 204
   2. Remote reference 205
   3. Broad pronoun reference: *this, that, which* 206
   4. Indefinite use of *it, they, you* 207

12b Dangling modifiers 210
   1. Dangling participial phrases 211
   2. Dangling gerunds 212
   3. Dangling infinitives 212
   4. Dangling elliptical clauses 213
   5. Permissible dangling constructions 213

12c Misplaced modifiers 214
12d Split constructions 215
12e Confusing shifts 217
   1. Confusing shifts of voice or subject 218

2. Confusing shifts of person or
number   218
3. Confusing shifts of mood or
tense   219

12f Mixed constructions   221

1. Dependent clauses misused as subjects
and complements   221
2. Adverbial clauses misused as
nouns   222
3. Unidiomatic comparisons   222

12g Incomplete constructions   223

1. Incomplete verb forms   223
2. Omitted prepositions   223
3. Incomplete comparisons   224

13 Revising Diction   228

13a Experiencing words   229
13b Denotation and connotation   229

1. The importance of context   230
2. The value of a dictionary   230

13c Abstract and concrete   231

1. The abstraction ladder   231
2. The value of concrete diction   233

13d Idiom   234
13e Figurative language   236

1. Metaphor and simile   236
2. Analogy   238
3. Allusion   239

13f Special diction problems   239

1. Sexist language   239
2. Weak verbs   243
3. Clichés   245
4. Mixed figures of speech   246
5. Empty intensives   247
6. Jargon   247

7. Pretentious diction   249
8. Euphemism   250

PART
IV

Critical Reading and Thinking

14 Thinking Critically   **257**

14a The structure of an argument   258
14b Key assumptions   260
14c The differences between fact and judgment   264
  1. Facts   264
  2. Judgments   265
  3. Using facts and judgments   267
  4. Evaluating authorities   268
14d Believability and tone   270

15 Avoiding Errors
in Reasoning   **273**

15a Legitimate versus hasty generalizations   273
  1. Establishing valid generalizations   273
  2. Criteria for valid generalizations   274
  3. Hasty generalizations   276
15b Mistaken causal relationships   277
  1. Post hoc, ergo propter hoc   278
  2. Reductive fallacy   278
15c Reasoning by analogy   279
  1. Uses of analogies   279
  2. False analogy   280
15d Avoiding the question   280
  1. Begging the question   280
  2. Ad hominem   281
  3. Dummy subject   281

15e False alternatives   281
15f Non sequiturs   282

16 Writing about Literature   **288**

16a Inhibiting assumptions   288
    1. A special logic?   289
    2. Only one correct interpretation?   290
    3. All interpretations equally valid?   290
    4. Implications for the study of
       literature   291

16b Productive questions   293
    1. Interpretive questions   293
    2. Evaluative questions   298
    3. Integrative questions   301

16c A sample student essay   303
16d Useful strategies   307
    1. Keeping a journal   307
    2. Summarizing   308
    3. Working with the words   310

PART V

The Research Paper

17 The Research Process   **321**

17a Thinking about your
     assignment   322
    1. The informative report   322
    2. The researched argument   324
    3. Shared features   326

17b Thinking about a subject   327
    1. Be genuinely interested in your
       subject   327
    2. Be willing to search for a good
       subject   328
    3. Be prepared to make changes in your
       subject   328

17c Thinking about your reader   329
17d Planning the long paper   330
   1. Leave enough time   330
   2. Understand the research process   331
   3. Be prepared for the recursiveness of the research process   332

18 The Library   333
18a The card catalog   333
   1. Reading catalog cards   334
   2. Locating books   335
   3. Using an on-line catalog   335
18b Standard reference works   336
18c Indexes to periodicals   344
18d A special index: the *Essay and General Literature Index*   348
18e Data-base searches   349
   1. On-line searches   349
   2. CD-ROM searches   351
18f Government documents   354

19 Working with Sources   357
19a The working bibliography   357
   1. Assembling a working bibliography   358
   2. Recording bibliographic information   358
19b MLA Works Cited forms   359
19c Taking notes   375
   1. Note cards   375
   2. Types of notes   376
   3. Recognizing a potential "note"   379
19d Assessing your sources   380
   1. How current?   380
   2. How authoritative?   380
   3. How objective?   381

19e Assessing your subject   381
    1. Signs of a good subject   381
    2. Signs of a poor subject   381

20 Composing the Research Paper   **388**

20a Organizing and writing a research paper   388
    1. Know when to stop taking notes   389
    2. Organize your notes   390
    3. Compose a tentative outline   391
    4. Segment your writing   391
    5. Leave time for rethinking and revising   392
20b Avoiding plagiarism   392
    1. Quoting accurately   393
    2. Paraphrasing accurately   395
20c Citing sources   397
    1. Quotations   399
    2. Paraphrases   404
    3. Content notes   406
20d Formatting the research paper   407
    1. Paper   408
    2. Spacing and margins   408
    3. Title page   408

21 Student Research Paper A: MLA Documentation   **413**

22 Student Research Paper B: APA Documentation   **432**

22a Using APA documentation   432
22b APA reference list forms   433

22c Citing sources in APA style   445
  1. Quotations   446
  2. Paraphrases   451
22d Formatting a paper in APA style   452
  1. Paper   452
  2. Spacing and margins   453
  3. Title page   453
  4. Abstract page   454
  5. Text pages   454
  6. References page   454
  7. Footnotes page   454
22e Sample student paper   455

23 Student Research Paper C: Endnote Documentation   480
23a Using endnotes   480
  1. Features of endnotes   481
  2. Features of the endnote page   481
23b Endnote forms   482
23c Sample student paper   492

PART VI

Grammatical Usage

24 Sentence Structure   517
24a Elements of a sentence   517
  1. Subject and predicate   519
  2. Modifiers   519
  3. Identifying subject and verb   520
  4. Complements   523
  5. Phrases   525
  6. Clauses   528
24b Types of sentences   532
  1. Simple sentences   532

2. Compound sentences   533
3. Complex sentences   534
4. Compound-complex sentences   534

25 Agreement   536

25a Agreement of subject and verb   537
    1. Modifying phrases after the subject   538
    2. Compound subject   539
    3. Collective nouns   539
    4. Nouns ending in *s*   540
    5. Linking verbs   540
    6. Inverted sentence order   541
    7. *Or/nor*   541
    8. Indefinite pronouns   541
    9. Relative pronouns as subjects   542

25b Agreement of pronoun and antecedent   544
    1. Compound antecedents   544
    2. Collective nouns as antecedents   545
    3. Indefinite antecedents   545
    4. Demonstrative pronouns   547

26 Case of Pronouns and Nouns   549

26a Compound constructions   549
26b *Who* and *whom* in dependent clauses   551
26c *Who* and *whom* in interrogatives   552
26d Reflexive and intensive pronouns   552
26e Pronouns after *than, as,* and *but*   554
26f Pronouns with linking verbs   554
26g Pronouns with infinitives   555

26h Pronouns and nouns with
       gerunds   555

27 Adjectives and Adverbs   **558**

27a Comparative and superlative
       forms   559
    1. Comparative and superlative forms of
          adjectives   559
    2. Comparative and superlative forms of
          adverbs   559
    3. Irregular comparative and superlative
          forms   560
    4. Adjectives and adverbs without
          comparative and superlative
          forms   560
    5. Correct use of comparative and
          superlative forms   561
27b Adjectives with linking verbs   562
27c Nouns used as adjectives   563
27d Compound adjectives   563
27e Colloquial forms   564

28 Verbs   **567**

28a Verb forms   567
28b Irregular verbs   568
28c Verb tenses   572
    1. Present tense   572
    2. Past tense   572
    3. Future tense   573
    4. Present perfect tense   573
    5. Past perfect tense   573
    6. Future perfect tense   574
    7. Progressive forms   574
28d Sequence of tenses   575
    1. Sequence of tenses in dependent
          clauses   575

2. Sequence of tenses with infinitives 577
3. Sequence of tenses with participles 578

28e Auxiliary verbs 579
1. *Do* 579
2. Modal auxilliaries 580

28f Voice 581
1. Forming passive verbs 582
2. Using active and passive verbs 582

28g Mood 584
1. Indicative mood 584
2. Imperative mood 584
3. Subjunctive mood 584

29 Sentence Fragments, Comma Splices, Fused Sentences 587

29a Types of sentence fragments 587
1. Dependent clause as fragment 588
2. Participial phrase as fragment 589
3. Infinitive phrase as fragment 590
4. Prepositional phrase as fragment 590
5. Appositive phrase as fragment 591

29b Acceptable incomplete sentences 591

29c Comma splices 594
1. Use a period to divide the clauses into separate sentences 594
2. Use a semicolon to connect the clauses 595
3. Use a coordinating conjunction to connect the two clauses 597

4. Use a subordinating conjunction or a relative pronoun to subordinate one clause   598

29d Acceptable comma splices   598
29e Fused sentences   599

PART
VII

Punctuation, Spelling, Mechanics

30 Punctuation   **605**

30a The period   606
1. Period after a declarative or mildly imperative sentence   606
2. Period after an indirect question or a polite request   607
3. Periods with abbreviations   607
4. Periods with ellipses   607
5. Periods in dialogue   608

30b The question mark   608
1. Question marks after direct questions or questions in a series   608
2. Question mark indicating doubtful information   609

30c The exclamation point   609
30d The comma   610
1. Comma with a coordinating conjunction to separate independent clauses   610
2. Comma to set off an introductory element   611
3. Commas to separate elements in a series   612
4. Comma with coordinate modifiers   613

5. Commas to set off a nonrestrictive modifier   614
6. Commas to set off parenthetic elements   616
7. Commas to set off absolute phrases   617
8. Commas in comparative and contrastive constructions   617
9. Commas with interjections, direct address, and tag questions   618
10. Commas with dates, addresses, place names, and numbers   618
11. Commas with direct quotations   619
12. Misuse of the comma   620

30e The semicolon   622
1. Semicolon to connect independent clauses not linked by a coordinating conjunction   622
2. Semicolon to separate independent clauses with internal punctuation   623
3. Semicolon to separate elements in a series   623

30f Quotation marks   625
1. Quotation marks to enclose direct quotations   625
2. Quotation marks to enclose verse quotations   628
3. Quotation marks to indicate titles   628
4. Quotation marks to enclose words defined in the text   629
5. Misuse of quotation marks   629

30g The apostrophe   630
1. Apostrophe to indicate the possessive case   630

2. Apostrophe to form
contractions   631

3. Apostrophe to form the plurals of letters
and numerals   631

* 30h Other punctuation marks: colon, dash,
parentheses, brackets   632

1. The colon   632
2. The dash   634
3. Parentheses   635
4. Brackets   636

31 Spelling   **640**

31a Trouble spots   641
31b Similar words frequently
confused   642
31c Spelling rules   643

1. Final silent *e*   644
2. Doubling the final consonant   645
3. Words ending in *y*   645

31d Hyphenation   646

1. Compound adjectives   647
2. Prefixes   647
3. Numbers   648
4. Suspensive hyphen   648

31e Words commonly misspelled   649

32 Mechanics   **658**

32a Manuscript preparation   658

1. Format   658
2. Quotations   659
3. Manuscript corrections   661

32b Capital letters   661

1. Proper nouns   662
2. Titles of works   664
3. Sentences and quotations   664

32c Numbers   665
32d Abbreviations   667
32e Italics   669
32f Syllabication   671

PART
VIII *Special Writing Situations*

33 Writing Business Letters   **677**

33a The rhetoric of business
correspondence   677
1. Consider your reader   677
2. Consider your form   678
33b Parts of a business letter   678
1. The heading   678
2. The inside address   679
3. The saluation   679
4. The body   680
5. The close   680

34 Composing Résumés and Job Applications   **684**

34a Designing a résumé   684
1. Format   684
2. Content   685
34b Letters of application   685
1. Introduction   685
2. Body   686
3. Conclusion   686

35 Writing under Pressure   **690**

35a Preparing for the essay
examination   690

1

35b Reading the examination 691
   1. Understand the directions 691
   2. Plan your answer 693
35c Writing the essay 693
   1. Start briskly 694
   2. Respond to the question 694
   3. Be analytical 694
   4. Provide specific evidence 695
   5. Review what you have written 696
35d Two sample essays 696

36 Writing with a Word Processor 698

36a Understanding word processing 698
   1. Basic word-processing functions 699
   2. Basic formatting functions 700
36b Getting the most out of word processing 701
   1. Planning your paper on a word processor 702
   2. Writing with a word processor 703
   3. Revising with a word processor 704
   4. Editing with a word processor 706

Glossary of Usage 707

Grammatical Terms 729

Index 748

PART I

1 *Understanding the Writing Process*

2 *Discovering Ideas*

3 *Considering Your Audience*

4 *Choosing a Voice*

Planning

I Under-standing the Writing Process

As you begin this book on writing, it may surprise you to know that no less a person than Plato had serious doubts about the value of learning to write. More than 2,300 years ago, the Greek philosopher argued in one of his works on rhetoric that a person's education is better served by oral discussion and debate than by writing. Unlike a speaker or teacher, he pointed out, a printed book cannot answer its readers' questions, nor can it in turn pose questions to make sure that readers have correctly understood what they have read. According to Plato, those who become dependent on the written word will gradually lose their powers of memory and the ability to think on their own. Believing their knowledge greater than it actually is, they will become conceited and complacent, a burden rather than an asset to their society.

No matter what we think of Plato's doubts about the value of writing, we shouldn't overlook the important fact that he used writing to express those doubts. If he had not, his ideas would probably be unknown today. Plato's written attack on writing suggests in a paradoxical way the inevitability of written communication in the exchange and transmission of ideas. During the centuries since he lived, technological advances ranging from the development of inexpensive paper to the invention of the desktop laser printer have continued to underscore the central role of writing in our civilization. Indeed, our lives would be unimaginable without the written word. Try to picture a world with no books or newspapers, no greeting cards or instruction manuals, no bills, recipes, advertisements, or love letters, and you will realize that we write, quite simply, because we must.

1a Why write?

For a moment, though, let us suppose that writing was not essential to communication in our culture but was instead an activity that we could choose to engage in or not, as we wished. What value could we assign to writing under such circumstances? What benefits does it offer the writer as an activity pursued for its own sake?

1. Writing and perception

In the first place, writing heightens our awareness of the way in which language shapes reality. Writing brings us into contact with language in an especially direct way, demanding that we make deliberate choices from among many alternative ways of identifying, and hence perceiving, the features of our world. Consider, for example, the different implications of the following similar statements:

> Deborah is a *loyal* supporter of the president.
>
> Deborah is a *devoted* supporter of the president.
>
> Deborah is a *zealous* supporter of the president.
>
> Deborah is a *fanatical* supporter of the president.

At what point does loyalty shade into devotion? Devotion into zeal? Zeal into fanaticism? Writing forces us to take positions on such questions, to decide how we will describe, and therefore understand, the world we inhabit. Whenever we choose one label ("zealot") and reject another ("fanatic"), we further define for ourselves the nature of that world. No wonder that respect for the power of language has been the cornerstone of Western education for 2,500 years. We participate in that intellectual tradition, increasing our consciousness of the links between language and perception, each time we write.

2. Writing and thinking

By forcing us to give our ideas concrete form, writing also leads us to understand those ideas more fully. Unlike an impromptu debate with friends over a late-night pizza, a written argument makes us attend to the quality and reasonableness of our ideas; the logical leaps that pass unnoticed in conversation show up in writing as glaring fallacies. When we write, we enter naturally into a kind of internal dialogue with ourselves as we search for the words and sentences that will best capture our elusive thoughts. Because it requires such precision, the act of writing is a uniquely powerful means of discovering and refining our ideas about any subject.

3. Writing and self-discovery

Writing not only leads us to the discovery of new ideas, but also offers opportunities for discovery of the self. When we commit ourselves in writing to an idea, a perspective, a belief, or an argument, we also come to understand ourselves better. Bound up with the intellectual growth that accompanies writing is the personal growth that results from taking a firm position on an issue, from deciding to see the world in one way rather than another. The commitment that is part of every important writing act forces us to come to terms with what we really believe, with who we really are.

1b A writer's purpose

When we use writing not only to explore our ideas, but to communicate those ideas to others, we place ourselves in a configuration of elements often referred to as the **communication triangle.**

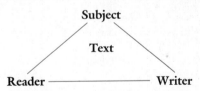

The Communication Triangle

It would be difficult to imagine an act of writing that did not include these four components. Writing obviously presumes a subject, a specific selection from the writer's fund of experiences. Virtually all writing, moreover, is addressed to a reader of some sort. (Even a private journal has at least a single reader: what writer of a journal does not go back and review entries written weeks, months, or years before?) And linking writer, reader, and subject is the written text itself, whether in the form of a letter, an essay, a memo, a novel, or a poem.

1b

These elements, which surround us whenever we attempt to communicate through writing, vary endlessly and thus demand great adaptability from us as writers. When our audience of readers changes, so must the style and content of our writing. No one would use the same language to address a child, an intimate friend, and a senior business colleague. Our approach to writing also changes when our subject or our closeness to the subject changes. The personal tone of an autobiographical essay differs from the more formal tone of a research paper partly because of a writer's different relationship with the material in each case. Finally, our writing changes as the form in which we write changes. Business letters, for example, require that we follow conventions different from those that govern the writing of term papers or of sonnets.

When we speak of a "purpose" in writing, we mean an awareness of the complex ways in which the components of each new communication triangle affect the content, style, tone, and form of what we write. As you will see, this broad concept of a writer's purpose informs much of what we will say about writing in this book. In the next six chapters, for example, we will develop the notion of purpose in writing by considering the following questions that the communication triangle suggests:

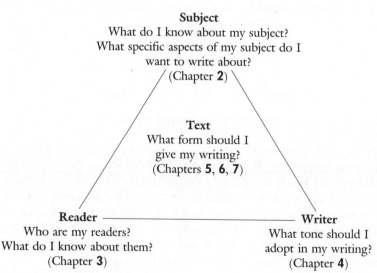

Subject
What do I know about my subject?
What specific aspects of my subject do I
want to write about?
(Chapter **2**)

Text
What form should I
give my writing?
(Chapters **5**, **6**, **7**)

Reader —————————————— **Writer**
Who are my readers?   What tone should I
What do I know about them?   adopt in my writing?
(Chapter **3**)   (Chapter **4**)

1c   The writing process

Rarely do any of us begin a writing task prepared with complete answers to these questions about our purpose. The act of writing is partly deliberate, but partly intuitive as well; intention and inspiration mingle when we write. We clarify and define our purpose as we participate in the scratch-it-out, stop-and-go process that writing always entails.

Some people try to avoid writing, or at least to postpone it, because they find this process frustrating and discouraging. They make the mistake of believing that writing should be a clean and smooth act, word following word until all of their thoughts have been translated neatly onto the page before them. But writing isn't a matter of simply translating ideas into words on a page. Instead, as we suggested above, it involves the far more complex process of discovering the meaning and implications of one's ideas. No matter how clearly you may think you have formulated your thoughts in your mind, putting them down on paper has a way of revealing new angles for you to consider, new questions for you to answer. It's by searching for ways to secure our free-floating thoughts in writing that we find out what we really understand and believe. If this process is often a slow and uncertain one, we shouldn't be surprised.

1.   The recursiveness of writing

For most of us, writing involves frequent stops and starts, the outward signs of our minds at work. The fact that you don't effortlessly fill page after page with your writing doesn't mean that you're not getting anywhere; most writers stop to revise and rethink what they have written well before they get to the end. That's what has happened in the handwritten draft reproduced on the following page—our original draft of the paragraph you just read. As you can see, we began revising—adding and deleting words, phrases, and whole sentences—even before moving on to the next paragraph. And if you compare this draft with the final version of the paragraph above, you'll see that we made many more changes before we finished.

Some writers work more neatly and methodically than this, others much less so. Most writers, though, move forward only by repeatedly

~~Many~~ Some people try to avoid or at least to postpone writing because they find it frustrating & discouraging. They mistakenly persist in believing that the art of writing should be ~~neat &~~ clean & direct, word inevitably following word until all of their thoughts have been translated neatly onto the page before them. But writing ~~is not~~ isn't the translation of ideas into words on a page; it's the discovery of the meanings and the implications of these ideas ~~By finding~~ as ~~it~~ you ~~first~~ search for ways to fix ~~our ideas~~ your thoughts into written words. ~~we discover what they mean to us and to others. When we write,~~ ~~we~~ you also find out what ~~we~~ you really ~~mean~~ intend to say. We shouldn't be surprised to discover that ~~it~~ writing is often a slow, uncertain, unpredictable task.

No matter how clearly ~~you~~ we may think ~~you~~ that we have formulated ~~your~~ our ideas in ~~your~~ our mind, the art of writing them down on paper has a way of ~~raising new questions,~~ revealing new perspectives & raising new questions.

Original Draft of a Paragraph on Page 7

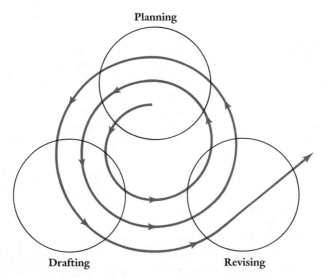

Planning

Drafting   **Revising**

The Recursiveness of the Writing Process

going back to an earlier point and rethinking what they have written, as we did here. For that reason, writing is sometimes described as a **recursive** process, one in which thinking, writing, and revising are not sequential steps but rather stages in a cycle that a writer repeats many times. Each portion of a draft may reveal possibilities for revision, each revision prompting the writer to consider anew his or her subject and purpose, each reconsideration of the subject leading to a new tentative draft.

2.   Avoiding frustration when you write

The difficulty of expressing ideas in writing is frustrating to all of us at one time or another. But you can minimize that frustration if you anticipate—and then, perhaps, even enjoy—the recursiveness of the writing process. Before you begin, prepare for the fact that you may eventually delete and discard much of what you write, replacing it with ideas that you don't yet have, ideas that will come to you only after you have immersed yourself in your writing. Take pleasure in observing how your ideas change and evolve as you commit them to writing, and pay attention to your own distinctive behavior as a

1d

writer. For example, how do you cope with being stuck? Do you reread what you have just written in an attempt to recapture some of the momentum that got you as far as you are? Do you try to refocus your thoughts on your subject? Get up and walk around for a while? Or just daydream until inspiration strikes again? Becoming a writer is partly a matter of identifying the habits that make you most productive and sticking to them whenever possible. Still, that won't necessarily make writing easy. Even experienced writers prepare to spend more time wandering through deserts of mental blankness than luxuriating in pools of creative energy.

1d   About this book

This book is about many elements of the writing process. As we have already suggested, that process varies greatly from person to person. Indeed, though convention governs some aspects of writing, like punctuation and grammatical usage, many others are so idiosyncratic that it's impossible for us to prescribe the best procedures for you to follow. If you have not done so already, you'll have to decide for yourself where and when you are most productive as a writer, which writing materials you're most comfortable with, and what strategies of composition are most fruitful for you.

What we offer in this book is advice that you may find helpful to incorporate into your own writing process. We devote the remainder of this first section to some methods of exploring a subject before you begin to write, to the concept of audience and its relation to the writing process, and to the nature and varieties of a writer's "voice." Later chapters on the form that writing takes will consider topics that range from composing effective sentences to organizing research papers. We'll also present some strategies for revising prose, we'll consider some principles of critical reading and thinking, and we will close by outlining conventions of grammar, usage, and mechanics. Remember, though, that the form of this book forces us to present these subjects in a linear order that is not true to the actual process of writing. Subject, audience, form, and purpose are interrelated, inseparable elements. Planning, writing, and revising are components of the process that overlap and blur.

1d

Make a list of the materials and circumstances that you find most conducive to writing. Consider, for example, the following questions:

1. Where do you write most easily (at a desk, in a comfortable chair, in bed)?
2. When are you most productive as a writer (early morning, midday, late at night)?
3. What kind of paper do you prefer to use (legal paper, unlined typing paper, notebook paper)?
4. What instrument do you usually write with (pencil, ball-point pen, keyboard)?
5. What surroundings do you prefer (silence, conversation, music)?

Compare your list with the lists of others in your class. What do the results reveal about the idiosyncratic nature of writing?

Read the following professional writers' descriptions of the way in which they go about writing. What aspects of their writing processes are also part of your writing process? What differences do you find between their methods of writing and yours?

1. I write when I feel like it and wherever I feel like it, and I feel like it most of the time: day, night, and during twilight. I write in a restaurant, on a plane, between skiing and horseback riding, when I take my night walks in Manhattan, Paris, or in any other town. I wake up in the middle of the night or the afternoon to make notes and never know when I'll sit down at the typewriter.

   —Jerzy Kosinski

2. I like [writing] at home [best] because . . . it's the only place where you can really promise yourself time and keep out interruptions. My ideal way to write a short story is to write the whole first draft through in one sitting, then work as long as it takes on revisions, and then write the final version all in one, so that in the end the whole thing amounts to one long sustained effort. . . . I can correct better if I see [my work] in typescript. After that, I revise with scissors and pins. Pasting is too slow, and you can't undo it, but with pins you can move things from anywhere to anywhere, and that's what I really love doing—putting things in their best and proper place.

   —Eudora Welty

1d

3. Now everything [I write] finds its initial expression in longhand and the typewriter has become a rather alien thing—a thing of formality and impersonality. My first novels were all written on a typewriter: first draft straight through, then revisions, then final draft. But I can't do that any longer. . . . I haven't any formal schedule, but I love to write in the morning, before breakfast. Sometimes the writing goes so smoothly that I don't take a break for many hours—and consequently have breakfast at two or three in the afternoon on good days.

—Joyce Carol Oates

4. Whenever I get up in the morning, I write for about three hours. I write novels in longhand on yellow legal pads. . . . For some reason I write plays and essays on the typewriter. The first draft usually comes rather fast. One oddity: I never reread a text until I have finished the first draft. Otherwise it's too discouraging. Also, when you have the whole thing in front of you for the first time, you've forgotten most of it and see it fresh.

—Gore Vidal

5. I ordinarily write three or four handwritten pages and then rework them for two hours. I can work for four hours, or forty-five minutes. It's not a matter of time. I set a realistic objective: How can I inch along to the next paragraph? Inching is what it is.

—Joseph Heller

6. When I am between books, as I am now, I sit in an armchair and think and make notes. Before I start a book I've usually got four hundred pages of notes. Most of them are almost incoherent. But there's always a moment when you feel you've got a novel started. You can more or less see how it's going to work out. After that it's just a question of detail.

—P. G. Wodehouse

7. The following are some of the things I have had to do to keep from going nuts. . . . Abandon the idea that you are ever going to finish. Lose track of the 400 pages and write just one page for each day, it helps [sic]. Then when it gets finished, you are always surprised. . . . Write freely and as rapidly as possible and throw the whole thing on paper. Never correct or rewrite until the whole thing is down. Rewrite in process is usually found to be an excuse for

not going on. It also interferes with flow and rhythm which can only come from a kind of unconscious association with the material.

—John Steinbeck

8. I write slowly because I write badly. I have to rewrite everything many, many times just to achieve mediocrity. Time can give you a good critical perspective, and I often have to go slow so that I can look back on what sort of botch of things I made three months ago. Much of the stuff which I will finally publish, with all its flaws, as if it had been dashed off with a felt pen, will have [been] begun eight or more years earlier, and worried and slowly chewed on and left for dead many times in the interim.

—William Gass

9. The most important [of my writing rituals] is that I need an hour alone before dinner, with a drink, to go over what I've done that day. I can't do it late in the afternoon because I'm too close to it. Also, the drink helps. It removes me from the pages. So I spend this hour taking things out and putting other things in. Then I start the next day by redoing all of what I did the day before, following these evening notes. When I'm really working I don't like to go out or have anybody to dinner, because then I lose the hour. If I don't have the hour, and start the next day with just some bad pages and nowhere to go, I'm in low spirits.

—Joan Didion

10. If I'm stuck, I try to get myself unstuck before I sit down again [to write] because moving through the day surrounded by people and music and air it is easier to make major motions in your mind than it is sitting at the typewriter in a slightly claustrophobic room. It's hard to hold a manuscript in your mind, of course. You get down to the desk and discover that the solution you had arrived at while having insomnia doesn't really fit.

—John Updike

EXERCISE 3

Use your answers to Exercises 1 and 2 to write a short essay on your writing process. Be as specific as you can about the strategies you ordinarily follow to plan, draft, and revise a piece of writing. What aspects of your writing process are you particularly comfortable with? Are there others that you would like to change or improve? If so, why?

1d

EXERCISE **4**

Write an essay in which you compare the strategies you use to compose two different types of writing, such as a letter to a friend and a paper for a class. What elements of your writing process are common to both? How do you account for whatever differences you find?

2 *Discovering Ideas*

Why is one writer able to create a substantial, convincing essay, while another, working with a similar subject, produces writing that is thin and stale? Good subjects don't alone guarantee good essays; the successful writer also knows how to probe a subject for interesting and important angles to develop in writing. In this chapter, we will describe several such strategies for making your thinking more productive and creative.

You can use the methods of discovery that we discuss here no matter what kind of paper you are working on. If your assignment is an autobiographical paper or a personal experience essay, these techniques should help you recall aspects of your life that you can use as the basis for your paper. If you are writing in an academic discipline such as art or political science or psychology, you may expect these procedures to raise issues that you will want to explore with additional reading or research. In either case, you will have discovered ideas to build on as you write.

You don't need to master every one of these strategies. In fact, because writing is such an idiosyncratic activity, they won't all be equally useful to every writer. Experiment with several of these approaches, and then concentrate on using the ones that seem to work best for you.

2a Unstructured methods of discovery

We can define an **unstructured approach** to discovering ideas for writing as one in which you let your mind go in whatever direction it chooses. The important thing, however, is that you pay attention

15

2a

to your mind's activity and make note of all the ideas it turns up. Only at the end of the discovery process, as you begin to shape your paper, should you go over your notes to decide which ideas you will use and which you will discard. (For suggestions about organizing your raw material, see **5a, 5b, 5c,** and **5g.**)

1.   Brainstorming

Brainstorming is the free and uncontrolled play of the mind with any idea. When we engage in brainstorming, we let our mind's natural powers of association direct the discovery process. The difference between brainstorming and mere random thought is that in a brainstorming session we *write down* all the ideas that come to us so that we finish with a concrete record of our thoughts. The very act of noting each idea, moreover, often prompts the mind to generate still more related ideas.

You may jot down the ideas that occur to you through brainstorming in a simple list like the one below. In this case, a student began to consider writing about some aspect of the subject "gymnastics."

Nick's brainstorming

```
Gymnastics

  --many people think gymnastics is boring

  --they're right

  --practice boring, especially stretching,

      warm-up exercises

  --setting up and breaking down equipment

      monotonous

  --leg lifts are very boring

  --very painful

  --how you do them

  --flat on your back

  --if you do them wrong you get extras
```

```
--leg lifts for punishment as well as exercise
--gymnastics is good for you, though
--getting a high score is worth the effort
--one of the top sports
--becoming increasingly popular thanks to the
     Olympics
--more people beginning training . . .
```

When you brainstorm, you should not "edit" your thoughts in order to produce a neat, orderly list of ideas. Brainstorming, as its name suggests, is a wild, intense activity; its initial results are supposed to be chaotic and disorganized. The time to edit, to look over the ideas you have generated and select those that seem most promising, will come later, as you plan the structure and development of your paper.

Some writers like to use a mapping diagram like that on page 18, rather than a straight list, in the brainstorming process. At the center they place the main idea that they wish to explore. Then, as new ideas come to mind, they write them down on connecting lines drawn out from the center of the page, grouping related ideas together and extending the subgroups as far as possible. One advantage of mapping is that it connects related ideas. Like a straight list, though, the mapping diagram is also tentative and exploratory, and like any method of discovery, it should be expected to generate much more material than you can use in a single well-focused essay. Only when you have extended your ideas as far as possible should you go back to decide which ones might work in your paper.

The illustrations above both involve a subject drawn from the writer's personal experience, but you can also use brainstorming techniques when you are writing a paper based on your reading. In this case, your brainstorming notes will probably fall into two categories: ideas *from* the readings that strike you as important, and ideas *about* the readings that occur to you as you read. In such notes you may be able to discover the focus and basic content for your paper.

Consider this assignment from an introductory sociology course:

2a

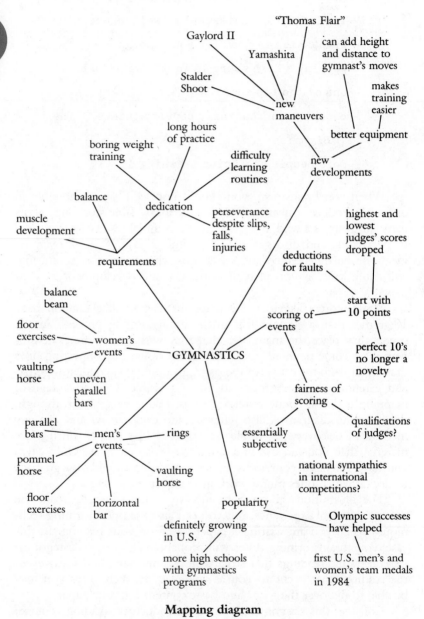

Mapping diagram

Compare the structure and the functions of the family and the values surrounding children and community in modern China and the Israeli kibbutz. Refer to assigned readings by Melford E. Spiro ("Is the Family Universal?") and Bruce Dollar ("Child Care in China"). Length: 2–4 pages, typed.

2a

After reading the two articles, one student jotted down these preliminary notes:

Ellen's brainstorming

```
"Is the Family Universal?"
     Murdock: four functions of nuclear family
          1. sexual
          2. economic
          3. reproductive
          4. educational
     Kibbutz one such group
          --an agricultural collective in Israel:
          communal living, collective ownership of
          all property, communal rearing of children
     Education & socialization function of "nurses"
          and teachers, not parents
     Parents are important to psychological develop-
          ment of child

"Child Care in China"
     Several major ideas about child rearing
          --subordination of personal to social
          needs, respect for productive labor, al-
          truism, cooperation, integration of physi-
          cal w/intellectual labor--tend to develop
          kind of citizen China wants--values
     Importance placed on group activities
     Toys too heavy for one child
     "Multiple mothering" of Chinese tradition
```

Reflecting on these notes, she then sketched out the following more organized thoughts about the two articles:

```
Likenesses
     both value children
     both emphasize group rather than individual
```

2a

> both separate economic and educational function
>   from others
> cooperation preferred over individual action
> both provide psychological security for the
>   child
> family life strong
> both altruistic

Why important?
>   family is institution that guarantees future of
>   society
>   I see this now better than before—all values
>   are focused on children
>   society's way of life and values are impressed
>   in the way children are treated—socializa-
>   tion isn't just education; it's the whole
>   atmosphere of the society in its attitude
>   toward children

The notes Ellen had made about her readings led her to a perspective on the material and to a possible focus for her paper—the similar ways in which cultural values are impressed on children in Israel and China. Formal research, of course, would require much more thoroughness in note taking and documentation (see Part V, *The Research Paper*). But for this shorter, more informal paper, brainstorming offered a valuable first step.

2. Free writing

When you brainstorm, you jot down bits and pieces, fragments of ideas that occur to you as you let your mind roam freely. Another way of capturing your thoughts in flight is free writing. Free writing differs from brainstorming in that you attempt to catch the flow of your thoughts by writing them not as a list of fragmentary ideas, but as a continuous thread of sentences.

Free writing often begins with an idea or question that sparks your thought. Your opening question may be as vague as "What can I say that's worth reading?" or as specific as "What were the principles of the Chicago school of architecture?" Once you have written your

2a

question down, follow it by quickly writing or typing whatever comes to mind as you think about your reply to it. Remember that your question is merely a starting point. Don't attempt to answer it fully, or even to focus your writing around it; let your thoughts take you in whatever direction they will. Try not to pause at all as you write, particularly not to consider such matters as correct punctuation or spelling. If you think you have run out of things to write or are not able to think of words for what you want to say, try rewriting your last five words again and again until something new comes to mind. Your object is to fill your pages with writing, not to compose a coherent essay on the spot.

Some writers actually time themselves when they engage in free writing, trying to get as many words as possible on the page in ten- or fifteen-minute intervals. The idea behind free writing is that our minds will come up with many good ideas if we simply give our thought processes free rein. As in brainstorming, though, it is important that you write down all your ideas as they come to you. It's the written record of your thoughts that distinguishes free writing from daydreaming and that provides concrete material for writing later on.

Here is a brief sample of one student's free writing on the topic of Eastern religions:

Kathleen's free writing

I've been thinking about a bunch of the "ism's" we
talked about in history yesterday. Most are confusing
to me--how to achieve the desired effect? For example, Confucianism stresses that the believer must
achieve inner harmony. What exactly does that mean?
You are at peace with yourself and others, I assume,
but how do you go about it? This brings me to the
next "ism"--Taoism. This one has a more definite
approach--become one with Tao, the force which

2a

permeates the universe, by withdrawing from society
and doing nothing. But without more instruction, I
am lost just as with the first. Both seem to concentrate on inner peace, but seem rather impractical.
These ideas are just too abstract for my taste. I
think I prefer the third religion we talked about,
Buddhism. One Buddhist sect relied on the compassion
of the Buddha in order to gain salvation. This faith
in Buddha seems similar to that of Western religions.
Another sect practiced meditation in order to achieve
enlightenment. Somehow these sects of Buddhism seem
more comprehensible to me—something I can relate
to and understand better. But I guess I need to learn
more about all three religions before I draw conclusions about them.

In this free-writing sample, Kathleen has correctly been more concerned
with getting her ideas down on the page than with structuring her
sentences precisely. By the end of the piece, she has not only explored
her initial reactions to Confucianism, Taoism, and Buddhism, but has
also defined a direction for further research—research that could lead
to a more sophisticated comparison of the three religions. As in this
example, free writing will often point you in interesting directions if
you give it the opportunity.

Like brainstorming, free writing also works with writing based
on reading assignments. In this case, you may find it useful to begin
with rough notes that you have already taken on your sources. With
your notes before you, simply let your mind and your pen or keyboard
take over. Below, for example, is some of the free writing that Ellen
did after jotting her notes on child rearing in China and on the Israeli
kibbutz.

Ellen's free writing

Emphasizes group rather than individual. What does this mean? The community values of the society are focused on communal success not on the individual. Best illustrated by the way children are brought up —most activities occur in groups not in individuals —examples of the building blocks that are too heavy for children to pick up. This forces (Chinese teachers said) group cooperation. More than one child was needed to pick up blocks—whole Chinese society is focused on group effort. Thus we see that children are taught values they will live by for the rest of their lives, thus maintaining the society's values (maybe this should be part of the introduction). Well, it's not really teaching— the blocks are designed to force students to learn to cooperate. It's the whole atmosphere that is in- tended to reinforce the values.

How is this related to the family? Family is the institution that guarantees the future of a society. In China the family has three of the four functions that Murdock mentions: economic, sexual, reproduc- tive, not education—also one that Spiro mentions, affection. This means that the family is not fully part of educational system because the family would tend to individualize—in a society that emphasizes

```
group identity you would have to take children away

from the family, but even the substitute family is

very loving. Do not punish, only correct.
```

Neither of these two "paragraphs" is perfectly coherent, nor should we expect them to be. More important in free writing is maintaining the rapid flow of thought. What Ellen has sketched out here are ideas that she can develop further in other, more deliberately planned paragraphs. After some additional free writing, she will begin to reflect on the best way of organizing her ideas. She may underline sentences in her free writing that seem especially important; she may copy key sentences onto another sheet of paper; she may even group ideas together in a rough sort of outline. With pages of written notes before her, she is in a good position to think about the content and structure of the essay she is going to write.

3. Keeping a journal

Scientists record their observations and ideas in journals—and so do poets. The fact that journal writing has proven a useful tool to people across the intellectual spectrum should lead writers of every type to consider the value of keeping an ongoing record of their responses to the world they live in.

The kind of journal we're speaking about is not one that simply records the events of your daily routine—whom you saw, what classes you went to, what tests you studied for, whom you ate dinner with, what magazine you browsed through, what time you went to bed. What we're describing instead is a journal of ideas—your thoughts and questions about the people, issues, and events in your world. Such a journal is probing and speculative rather than simply factual. And it is also personal, not because its contents are private (they don't necessarily have to be), but because it reflects your unique outlook on the world. The journals of two different people will be as different as the people themselves.

Journal writing differs from free writing in several ways. Whereas free writing is a rapid, almost unconscious activity, writing in a journal is a more leisurely, more reflective, more thoughtful activity, conscious rather than automatic. And while free writing is a technique that writers use sporadically to generate material on specific subjects, journal writing is a sustained, ongoing activity. A journal presumes a kind of continuity; you collect entries together, whether in a notebook or on a computer disk, so that you can go back to reread and reconsider what you have written earlier. Such rereadings may in turn spark new journal entries.

Journals offer opportunities for freedom and experimentation, but they also call for a degree of discipline. Nothing about a journal can ever be labeled "right" or "wrong"; its format and contents are whatever you want them to be. Consequently, you should use a journal to play with ideas, to ask questions that you can't fully answer, to be serious and silly, outraged and outrageous. Experiment with different styles of writing; use your journal to explore not only different aspects of your world, but different sides of yourself. One of the benefits of such a journal should be increasing your feeling of ease when you write—both physical ease (the act of putting words on a page) and intellectual ease (the process of grappling with ideas). But you will achieve such benefits only if you have the discipline to make writing in your journal a regular habit. Plan at the outset to write at least a paragraph or two in your journal several times a week, and provide a record of your journal's development by dating each entry.

In the following journal entry, notice how the student writer has gone beyond a mere listing of events to include commentary on Henry James as a novelist, reflections on himself as a reader, and even some fun with terminology learned in his psychology class.

Brad's journal entry

September 23

Last week I picked up The Portrait of a Lady, by Henry James. I remembered that I enjoyed The American, and I thought that The Portrait of a Lady might also be good, considering it was written by the same author. I sat down to read it, and thought that I didn't mind it being slow, because I had only started. Something was bound to happen soon. I was reading about forty pages a day, and each time I sat down I expected at least one slightly entertaining thing to occur. Four days later I was trying to tell myself that this was not an idiotically boring story. "Something will surely interest me soon." "This is how British women were in those days." "She's not really disgustingly snobbish."

But eventually I got really mad and began to attack Henry James: "I'm surprised anyone could stand to read this stuff." Then I fought with myself: "Well, The American was pretty enjoyable. I must be missing something good here." I had been fighting like this all the time I was reading. At least I knew I was trying to keep an open mind. But finally my id got a choke hold on my superego and started dragging him around by his hair. When my superego gave in, my ego suggested that I drop the book, go to the library, and check out a good Follett spy novel.

Of course this isn't literary analysis, and it isn't supposed to be; it's a record of an immediate personal response. What makes this passage a good journal entry—besides the genuineness of Brad's voice as a writer and his obvious sense of humor—are the provocative questions it suggests. Why exactly does he react so negatively to Isabel Archer, the title character in *The Portrait of a Lady*? Why does this novel appeal to him so much less than *The American* did? What's different about James's handling of the two books? All of these are good topics for

Brad to consider when he writes in his journal again. Journal entries that raise such interesting questions not only inspire additional journal entries, but may also be the genesis of a more formal piece of writing.

EXERCISE 1

Using either listing or mapping, explore one of the general subjects below, or another subject of your choice. Generate as many ideas as you can in one sitting. Wait at least a few hours and then come back to the same subject. Can you add some new ideas to those you wrote down earlier? Repeat this procedure several times, and then review all the ideas you have jotted down. Which ideas interest you? Which do you think you could make interesting to someone else?

1. Fitness
2. Learning to drive
3. Children
4. Jealousy
5. Music

6. Personal computers
7. Television commercials
8. Solitude
9. The environment
10. City life

EXERCISE 2

Select a chapter from one of your textbooks, and use the brainstorming method described on pages 16–20 to explore its contents. What key ideas in the chapter did you identify? What ideas of your own were you able to generate in response to the chapter you read?

EXERCISE 3

Write steadily for ten minutes on one of the topics below, or on another subject of your choice. At the end of ten minutes, select what you consider to be the most important idea in your free writing, copy it onto the top of a clean page, and write again for ten minutes without stopping. When you have finished, underline the best ideas from your two sessions of free writing and try to rewrite them into a single coherent paragraph.

1. My greatest accomplishment so far in life has been _____.
2. The most important person in my life is _____.
3. Television would be much better if _____.
4. I always feel good when _____.
5. The most important decision I will have to make this year is _____.

2b Structured methods of discovery

We described previous approaches to discovery as "unstructured" because they follow no predetermined pattern. The results of brainstorming, free writing, and journal writing depend solely on the unpredictable way in which ideas surface in your mind. In contrast, **structured approaches** to discovery follow an orderly plan, usually a fixed set of questions to answer or a checklist of topics to consider. Like the methods of discovery described above, structured methods demand mental alertness and concentration. For some writers, though, the direction provided by structured methods of discovery makes them more productive than brainstorming, free writing, or journal writing.

One of the simplest—and most effective—structured approaches to discovery is the set of questions learned by every novice journalist:

Who?

What?

When?

Where?

Why?

How?

Armed with these questions, a journalist is expected to be able to assemble the essential information about any subject that he or she is investigating. By expanding this formula with additional questions under each of these main headings, we can create a useful structured approach for examining any subject for writing.

Before we do that, however, a few words are in order about the most effective way of using such a set of questions. Many students trying such a discovery procedure for the first time mistakenly believe that their task is to come up with a single answer for each of the questions involved. Two things are wrong with that conception of structured discovery procedures. First, if this approach is to be successful, your goal must be to produce *as many responses as possible* to each question. You should not treat these questions like examination questions for which there is only one correct answer; instead, reflect on each one carefully, using it to squeeze from your mind as much information about your subject as you can. Second, you must recognize that not every question will be relevant to every topic. Don't feel that this approach is not working if you don't have an answer for every question.

Remember, too, that the answers you get from asking these questions are not themselves topics for a variety of different papers, but raw material that you will eventually refine into a single essay. As with brainstorming and free writing, your initial objective is to collect as much diverse information about your subject as possible. Later, as you begin to organize your paper (see Chapter **5**), you will be able to pull out the best ideas from your notes and consider how they can be most effectively organized, and whether they can be further developed. Like brainstorming and free writing, therefore, structured methods of discovery are useful only if you work through them with pen in hand, jotting down all the ideas that occur to you and assembling pages of working notes on your subject.

Now let's look at an expanded version of the journalist's set of questions. In the questions below, *X* represents the subject you are thinking of writing about.

Who?

Who is involved in X?
Who benefits from X?
Who suffers because of X?

What?

How is X defined?
How would you describe X?
What is X similar to?
What parts make up X? How are they related to each other?

When?

When did X occur?
How long did X last?
What events preceded X?
What events followed X?

2b

Where?

> In what setting did X occur? What were the physical surroundings?
>
> What other circumstances made X possible?
>
> How might X have been different if the circumstances had been different?

Why?

> What are the causes of X?
>
> What are the consequences or effects of X?

How?

> How did X come to be?
>
> Who made X?
>
> How does X work?

To see the versatility of these questions, consider the way in which one student used them to generate ideas about her hobby, photography. Reflecting on the questions above yielded several pages of notes, among which she was gradually able to find a controlling idea for an essay on the subject. Here is just a portion of Julie's notes, those that she made in response to the second set of questions, under the heading "What?"

Excerpt from Julie's discovery questions

What?

> How is photography defined?

> A chemical process involving light, an image, and a light-sensitive material.

> How would you describe photography?

> As a knack or gift.

As a hobby—but photography requires more
equipment than most hobbies—can be expensive (film,
developing)—takes time for photographer to become
really skilled.

As a talent.

As a profession.

As an art form—photography is more highly technical than most art forms—also, the artist is restricted by many conditions beyond her control.

As a form of personal expression.

What is photography similar to?

Painting—but the photographer's imagination
is limited by lighting, setting, subjects, equipment.

Writing—photographs can tell a story—either
a single picture, or a series of photographs—images
and setting establish mood—subjects' faces can
convey emotion.

What parts make up photography? How are they related to each other?

Photographer herself.

Equipment: camera (more than one?), lenses
(normal, telephoto, zoom, wide-angle—necessary
for maximum creativity); filters (UV, skylight,

2b

```
polarizing, star-effect, colored--for effective

color reproduction and special effects); tripod;

flash; camera case and equipment bag.

    Subjects: human (posed, candid), landscapes,

animals (hard to control).

    Experts for developing, printing, enlarging

(without first-rate processing, all the photogra-

pher's efforts are futile).   .

    Purchasers of photographs: magazines, news-

papers, friends.
```

Working through these and the other questions, Julie recognized for the first time the conflict that existed between her attraction to photography as a medium of creative expression and the many elements of photography that she could not control—equipment limitations, unpredictable conditions for work, unreliable processing, and the like. In the opposition that she discovered between her natural abilities and the inescapable restrictions imposed on those abilities, she was able to find a central idea for a paper: balancing the rewards of photography against its intrinsic frustrations.

Exploring a subject in this systematic way takes concentration, persistence, and imagination. But by enabling you to think carefully about many sides of your topic, such a procedure can help make you a writer with something worth saying.

EXERCISE 4

In Exercise 1 (page 27) you used brainstorming to explore a possible subject for writing. Now examine the same subject using the set of questions on pages 29–30 above. Are you able to generate new information?

EXERCISE 5

Choose another subject and explore it first with free writing (follow the directions in Exercise 3, page 27) and, a day later, with the set of questions presented in this section. Which approach to discovery—unstructured or structured—seems to work better for you?

3 *Considering Your Audience*

The term **rhetoric** has long been associated with the concept of persuasion. The politician seeking the votes of his constituents is practicing rhetoric, as is the courtroom attorney arguing for her client's innocence. But *rhetoric* may also refer more broadly to the use of language in order to produce any effect—sympathy, anger, euphoria, contempt—in an audience of hearers or readers. If we think of rhetoric in this larger sense, we can see that virtually every act of human communication contains a rhetorical element. We may not spend our days asking for votes or pleading for the lives of clients, but at the very least we usually want the people around us to believe that we are worth listening to. Inspiring that belief in our friends and associates is itself a rhetorical act, no matter what the subject under discussion may be.

3a The rhetorical situation

The relationship between your audience and yourself—whether in conversation or in writing—is called the **rhetorical situation.** In spoken dialogue, you can easily see whether or not other people understand what you are saying, and their expressions and comments will let you know immediately that they approve or object. The case is much different when you write. Alone with your thoughts and your keyboard, you can only imagine how readers will react to what you write. Whenever you pause to think about the best arguments to use or to consider how a sentence will sound to your readers, you are demonstrating your sensitivity to the rhetorical situation in which you find yourself.

Good writers are able to alter their writing to suit widely different audiences and rhetorical situations. All of us, in fact, make similar adjustments of tone and style every day. If you are explaining a suspension bridge to a small child, you don't use the vocabulary of a civil engineer. If you are showing a campus visitor through your college library, you don't use the familiar tone that is suitable with close friends or family members. If you are embroiled in a heated debate, you don't use arguments that you know will only further antagonize your opponent. The person who is sincerely trying to communicate makes every effort to find language appropriate to his or her audience.

In a writing course, students are often directed to consider others in the class as their audience. In most business and professional writing, however, your readers may not be as familiar to you as your fellow students are. To cope with writing tasks in the real world—with business letters and office memoranda, for example—you will need to be able to adapt your writing to the specific rhetorical situations at hand. And such adaptation will require that you know how to analyze and understand your audiences.

3b Analyzing audiences

Many beginning writers like to think that they are writing for the "general reader." In fact, such a person doesn't exist. Few subjects, after all, can realistically be said to interest all people, or even most people. If you think carefully about any paper you have written in the past, you will realize that no matter how broad its appeal, you can imagine readers for whom it would be inappropriate or simply uninteresting. Even the members of your composition class—the audience you may consider most like yourself—come from different geographical areas, ethnic and religious backgrounds, and family situations, and those differences may profoundly affect their reactions to what you write.

Once you recognize that your audience is never people in general, but always a particular selection from humanity, you must consider ways of identifying and understanding that audience, for only if you understand the disposition of your readers can you write effectively for them. Every complex argument has several sides, and no single approach will satisfy all possible audiences. Do your readers already understand your subject, or must you provide background information? Do they already share your beliefs, or must you persuade them to see

3b

your subject as you do? The answers to such basic questions will necessarily affect the content and tone of your writing.

Some writers try to visualize an individual member of the audience they are addressing. But this strategy will not be of much value if you lack specific knowledge about your audience. Instead, you might try posing a series of specific questions about your readers. Such questions, like those below, take some of the guesswork out of understanding your audience.

Questions for analyzing audiences

Audience's background

What do I know about my audience's

1. age?
2. social status?
3. level of education?
4. political positions?
5. moral beliefs?

Audience's relation to subject and writer

1. What does my audience already know about this subject?
2. What else do I want my audience to know?
3. What do I want this audience to think of me as a person?
4. What evidence or arguments will be convincing to this audience?

Of course, not all of these questions will be relevant in every case. But for most writing tasks this checklist will provide a helpful way of reflecting systematically on your audience and rhetorical situation.

As you respond to these questions, you must consider how your answers will shape the writing you are about to do. For example, if you are writing in a technical field such as architectural engineering, you will freely use the specialized vocabulary of the field if your readers share your expertise, but not if they are laypeople. Neglecting to consider your audience would be disastrous in either case: you'd be incomprehensible to nonspecialists if you used technical language, but if you failed to do so with an audience of engineers, you'd look like a rank amateur rather than a professional. Similarly, if your subject is politics, the strategies you use to mobilize readers who already share your beliefs

3b

will be utterly different from the approach you would take to convert opponents to your position.

In the following audience analysis, note how one student's use of the questions above leads him to a fuller understanding of his audience and hence to a clearer conception of his purpose in writing. In this case, the student had decided to write a letter to be published in his campus newspaper about damage to furnishings in the university library. Should such a letter be directed to the students responsible for the damage, or should it be directed to the rest of the students on campus, the indirect victims of the vandalism? The writer's analysis of these two groups of readers helps him decide which audience to address and what approach to take in his letter.

Marc's analysis of his audience

Audience's background

1. Age
    —all students on campus approximately my age
    —vandals act younger than they are
    —socially immature?

2. Social status
    —most students from middle-class backgrounds
    —about a third have part-time jobs
    —some paying entire university tuition without help from parents

3. Level of education
    —academically speaking, same as mine
    —but what about social education, i.e., respecting other people's property and rights?

4. Political positions
    —not relevant

5. Moral beliefs
    —wrecking furniture a kind of stealing: steals from university, which must pay to replace damaged items; steals from other students, who are deprived of good study conditions
    —do vandals see matter this way, as a moral issue?
    —probably not
    —if they do, then little apparent sense of guilt

3b

Audience's relation to subject and writer

1. What does my audience already know about this subject?
      —students who use the library to study know about extent of damage to chairs, couches, and study carrels
      —other students may not know about issue at all
      —vandals know what has been done *and* who's responsible

2. What else do I want my audience to know?
      —if my audience is student body at large, I want them to know the seriousness of the problem, and to know that there are students like me who are angry, who feel that something should be done to stop vandalism
      —if audience is vandals, I want them to know that there are students who condemn their actions
      —which approach will be more effective in stopping vandalism?
      —which audience should I address?

3. What do I want this audience to think of me as a person?
      —reasonable—or outraged?
      —is it possible to be sympathetic to vandals?—I don't see how
      —so should I appear angry?
      —is any approach going to matter if my audience is the vandals themselves?
      —do they care what I think?—probably not

4. What evidence or arguments will be convincing to this audience?
      —if audience is vandals, could try to appeal to their respect for others' rights—but do they have any such respect?
      —can I realistically expect to change such people's actions with a single letter?
      —better possibility: try to persuade other students that vandalism can be stopped if students mobilize against it
      —examples from other campuses available?
      —also, present vandalism as an attack on their rights
      —their tuition pays for damage
      —vandals are stealing from them
      —no one is more directly concerned than students themselves
      —their responsibility to take action

3b

By systematically examining two possible audiences—the vandals and their victims—Marc was able to define both his audience and his purpose more clearly. The vandals, he gradually realized, represented an audience whose actions he could not possibly hope to affect with a single letter to the college newspaper. On the other hand, such a letter might be able to mobilize the majority of the student body against the few who were guilty of the destruction.

As this example suggests, analyzing your audience must be an early step in the writing process, since an understanding of your audience's background and needs will inevitably shape the content of your writing. The more complete the notes you can make about your audience, the better prepared you will be to make decisions about the content, organization, and tone of your writing.

EXERCISE 1

Examine the role that awareness of audience has played in shaping a letter to the editor or an opinion column published in a recent edition of your local newspaper. Consider the following issues about writer and audience that we have discussed in this chapter:

1. How does the writer's choice of subject define the audience for whom he or she is writing? What readers would be *outside* that audience?
2. How does the writer demonstrate his or her understanding of the audience's background? What can you conclude about the age, social status, level of education, political positions, or moral beliefs of the reader whom this writer seems to be addressing?
3. How much knowledge about the subject does the writer presume? What background information does he or she supply for the reader?
4. How does the writer wish to be regarded by the reader? What kind of person does he or she seem to be? Rational? Emotional? Serious? Witty?
5. What evidence or arguments does the writer use to support his or her position? Can you imagine a reader for whom this evidence would *not* be convincing?

EXERCISE 2

Using the questions on page 35, write out an analysis of the next audience for whom you intend to write. Underline what you consider to be the most important points in your analysis. How will these points influence what you write?

Choosing a Voice

W riting begins as dialogue; it is one person speaking to another about something important to both. We write because we wish to extend this one-to-one relationship to a larger number of persons. One of the pleasures of writing is discovering that we do not as writers have to give up the sense of self that enlivens conversation, for we can create in our writing the many different voices we use in speaking.

4a A writer's voice

In spoken dialogue, your facial expression, gestures, and tone of voice determine to a great extent the way your audience responds to what you say. The pitch, volume, and pace of your speech tell your listeners whether you are serious or mocking, decisive or doubtful—in short, how you feel about your subject matter. In writing, you must translate these physical and auditory signals into visual symbols so that the eyes of your readers will hear the tone of your voice. The more proficient you become as a stylist, the more voices you will have at your disposal. Your written voice—like your speaking voice— can vary in tone from ironic to passionate, from annoyed to outraged, from humorous to grim.

Of course, developing a personal voice in writing is complicated by the fact that our language comes from a public stock. We cannot each invent a new language; no one would understand us. Yet the linguistic symbols that limit us also enable us to be who we are. We assert our identity by choosing from the language we find around us the words and styles that best suit our personalities and our purposes.

The first step in developing your writer's voice, therefore, is recognizing that you can make choices. If you carefully examine the voice in your past writing, you may be surprised by how often you have surrendered your power of choice and unconsciously borrowed the phrasing and tone of people around you. The language of parents and friends, of the media and the bureaucratic world, inevitably creeps into the writing that most of us do. In some situations, though, you have no doubt found yourself writing with genuine feeling and power. The composition of a letter to someone you care for or the assertion of a value you believe in can move you to choose your words carefully, to rewrite sentences again and again until you feel certain that what you have written will move your reader. In such a creative act you can almost hear your voice in the words on your page and see the look of recognition on the face of the person you are addressing. Making this experience a part of every writing act is the goal of all serious writers.

To a large extent, the voice in our writing—what we might also call the *tone* of our writing—depends on two relationships: our attitude toward our subject, and our attitude toward our reader. We will consider both of these relationships in the sections that follow.

4b   Voice and subject

Before you can write with any distinguishable voice, you must first decide for yourself how you feel about your subject. In the broadest terms, writers might be said to regard their subjects either positively or negatively. But the range of possible attitudes within each of these large categories is enormous, limited only by each writer's range of emotional responses. The city council's plan to reduce funding for public transportation may *concern* one citizen, *disturb* another, *anger* a third, *outrage* a fourth. An act of kindness between acquaintances may inspire appreciation, affection, admiration, or devotion, depending on the people involved.

To convey our attitude toward our subject in writing, we must rely on carefully chosen words and details. In the passage below, for example, the writer does not explicitly state his attitude toward nurses, but his admiration and respect are nonetheless clear because the details he includes emphasize efficiency, sensitivity, and personal concern.

Details convey attitude toward subject

The nurses, the good ones anyway (and all the ones on my floor were good), make it their business to know everything that is going on. They spot errors before errors can be launched. They know everything written on the chart. Most important of all, they know their patients as unique human beings, and they soon get to know the close relatives and friends. Because of this knowledge, they are quick to sense apprehensions and act on them. The average sick person in a large hospital feels at risk of getting lost, with no identity left beyond a name and a string of numbers on a plastic wristband, in danger always of being whisked off on a litter to the wrong place to have the wrong procedure done, or worse still, *not* being whisked off at the right time. The attending physician or the house officer, on rounds and usually in a hurry, can murmur a few reassuring words on his way out the door, but it takes a confident, competent, and cheerful nurse, there all day long and in and out of the room on one chore or another through the night, to bolster one's confidence that the situation is indeed manageable and not about to get out of hand.

—Lewis Thomas, *The Youngest Science:
Notes of a Medicine Watcher*

In the same way, May Sarton helps us to understand her feelings about the life she lives by presenting details from her daily routine:

Details convey attitude toward subject

For me the most interesting thing about a solitary life, and mine has been that for the last twenty years, is that it becomes increasingly rewarding. When I can wake up and watch the sun rise over the ocean, as I do most days, and know that I have an entire day ahead, uninterrupted, in which to write a few pages, take a walk with my dog, lie down in the afternoon for a long think (why does one think better in a horizontal position?), read and listen to music, I am flooded with happiness.

—May Sarton, "The Rewards of Living
a Solitary Life," *New York Times*

Sarton's paragraph might perhaps be reduced to the assertion "My solitary life is satisfying." But without the details with which she has described her day, we would not fully understand her sense of satisfaction. As writers, we must remember that merely asserting our attitude toward our subject is insufficient. If we want our readers to understand our feelings, and perhaps even to share them, we must rely on carefully chosen diction and details that will show our readers why we feel as we do.

All of this is not to suggest that every writer's attitude toward his or her subject can be precisely labeled, or even that every piece of writing will always reveal its writer's attitude. Many writing situations call for the objective reporting of information, such as we find in the following passage.

Objective reporting

If low-income and working-class nonvoters suddenly appeared at the polls, would they change American politics? According to careful studies of the question, the answer is no. Pollsters find that the political views of nonvoters—at least on matters that appear on the ballot—are not terribly different from those held by voters. Careful analysis by political scientists suggests that if nonvoters were to vote, they would shift the electorate slightly to the left on economic issues, such as jobs, government spending, public works, and the like, but slightly to the right on social issues, such as busing, abortion, and other life-style questions.

—David Osborne, "Getting Out the Vote," *Atlantic*

Of course, we should remember that apparent objectivity in writing is also the result of a writer's choice—the decision *not* to reveal one's attitude toward the subject.

4c Voice and audience

If we have clearly defined our attitude toward our subject, we have laid the groundwork for writing with an honest voice. But equally important to a writer's tone is the relationship that the writer seeks to establish with his or her readers. Just as we easily shift our spoken language to suit the many different people whom we address throughout the day, from family members to strangers, we must be ready to adapt our written language to each rhetorical situation that we confront as writers.

Some writing situations naturally require that we use language that suggests a personal relationship with our readers. In letters to

4c

close friends, for example, we tend to use the simplified sentence structure of conversation, the diction of colloquial speech (including contractions and slang), and the first-person and second-person pronouns *I*,
we, and *you*. If we did not, our writing would seem stilted and artificial.
For other writing tasks, however, such as the writing of a research
paper, distance between writer and reader is more suitable than intimacy.
In such writing, we strive to create polished sentences that will suggest
our careful thinking; we adopt a more formal diction (including, perhaps, specialized words appropriate to the discipline in which we are
writing); and we tend to avoid the first-person and second-person
pronouns.

It is important to realize, however, that no absolute rules will
help us in determining how to approach our readers when we write.
"Never use *I*" might be an acceptable guideline for formal academic
writing, but in other writing situations it would be as absurd as a
rule like "Always use slang." Instead, we must think carefully about
the kind of relationship with our audience that is appropriate to our
rhetorical situation, and about the means available to us for creating
this relationship in our writing.

The examples of a letter to a friend and a formal research paper
are just two points on a vast continuum of potential writer/reader
relationships. Along the continuum are an infinite number of degrees
of closeness between writer and reader, ranging from the greatest distance to the greatest intimacy. At one end, for example, is the writing
found in many professional journals, which uses distance between writer
and reader as one means of suggesting the writer's authority:

Great distance between writer and reader

This paper has shown that a direct generalization of assumptions
that Davis and Hinich have shown to be sufficient for multidimensional
median voter results in *deterministic* voting models is sufficient for multidimensional median outcomes in *probabilistic* voting models. Among other
things, this is an indication of just how strong the assumptions that they
originally studied are. The generalization that was studied here is similar
in spirit to the original assumptions of Davis and Hinich—both in its
explicit use of pseudo-norms and scaling functions and in its retention
of symmetry for the distribution of the voters' ideal points in the society.
As a consequence, it should be recognized that this generalization itself

4c

is also highly restrictive—and could easily fail to hold in a specific economy that is of interest.

—Peter J. Coughlin, "Davis-Hinich
Conditions and Median Outcomes in
Probabilistic Voting Models,"
Journal of Economic Theory

The distance between writer and reader in this passage results partly from the writer's highly technical vocabulary—"multidimensional median voter results," "probabilistic voting models," "pseudo-norms and scaling functions"—which places the passage outside the realm of ordinary conversation between two individuals. This distance is reinforced by the writer's deliberate avoidance of personal pronouns. In the first sentence, for example, he has chosen to write "This paper has shown . . ." rather than "I have shown. . . ." Similarly, he later uses the passive voice to remove both himself and his reader from the text:

"The generalization that was studied here. . . ."
[rather than "The generalization that I studied here. . . ."]

"As a consequence, it should be recognized that. . . ."
[rather than "As a consequence, you should recognize that. . . ."]

In this case, as in much writing intended primarily to report or inform, the writer's main interest is his subject rather than his reader. The formal voice of a scholar is more appropriate to such a writing situation than the familiar voice of a friend.

Informative writing need not be impersonal, however, even when the subject is a grand one. In the following passage, for example, Kenneth Clark compares two major artists of the Middle Ages, the painter Giotto and the poet Dante, yet his tone borders on the informal.

Moderate distance between writer and reader

Although I think that Giotto was one of the greatest of painters, he has equals. But in almost the same year that he was born, and in the same part of Italy, was born a man who is unequalled—the greatest philosophic poet that has ever lived, Dante. Since they were contemporaries and compatriots, one feels that it should be possible to illustrate Dante by Giotto. They seem to have known each other and Giotto may have painted Dante's portrait. But in fact their imaginations moved on very different planes. Giotto was, above all, interested in humanity: he sympathised with human beings and his figures, by their very solidity, remain on earth. Of course there is humanity in Dante—there's everything in Dante. But he also had certain qualities that Giotto lacked: philosophic power, a grasp of abstract ideas, moral indignation, that heroic contempt for baseness that was to come again in Michelangelo; and, above all, a sense of the *un*earthly, a vision of heavenly radiance.

—Kenneth Clark, *Civilisation: A Personal View*

On the whole, Clark's diction here is as lofty as his subject. Phrases like *philosophic power* and *heroic contempt for baseness* are not part of most people's everyday conversation. But Clark pulls the tone of this passage toward the informal by interjecting himself in its first sentence ("I think"), by using a contraction ("there's everything in Dante"), and by starting several sentences with the conjunction *but,* often regarded as a somewhat colloquial sentence opener.

These features, sparingly used in Clark's passage, are among the characteristics that we usually expect to dominate less formal writing. In the paragraph below, for example, written as an introduction to a personal essay, the writer combines the personal pronouns *I* and *you* with generally informal diction to draw the reader into the world of his experience.

Moderate intimacy between writer and reader

The solid vibration that goes through your arms and body when you perfectly connect a wooden bat with a leather-covered baseball is a feeling of pure exhilaration. My love affair with hitting baseballs began with stickball games on my street, continued through Little League, junior high, and high school, and persists even now when I go to the Revere batting cages, where occasionally some Boston Red Sox players hit. I've consistently been a good hitter through the years, with the exception of a period of steady decline from the end of my sophomore year in high school through half of my junior year. During this batting slump, I wondered whether I had completely lost the ability to hit a baseball well. What was I doing wrong? Was I striding too soon? Were my hands coming around too fast? Was I rotating my hips improperly? I consulted every book on hitting to check the mechanics of my swing. I changed my stance a hundred times. But still my batting slump hung on.

—David A. Miller [student]

4c

In the language of advertising and popular journalism we often see an attempt to establish an even closer bond between writer and reader. Notice the especially direct appeal to the reader in the following magazine announcement, soliciting suggestions for new articles. Here the writer creates an extremely informal tone by liberally using personal pronouns, contractions, colloquial diction, and slang.

Great intimacy between writer and reader

Our Eyes and Ears

"Frontlines" needs you, the legions of *MJ* faithful and faithless, the fifth column in the war for irreverence and investigation. Send us your troubling and bubbling items, yearning to breathe free.

Although we can't acknowledge every item sent in, we do acknowledge those we use. What's more, if we use something you tip us off to, we'll rush you $15 and a *Mother Jones* T-shirt.

—Mother Jones

The tone of all writing results from choice. Effective writers are so conscious of their writing voice that they bring a distinctive touch even to routine writing situations. If you resolve to be personally committed to any act of writing, to care about what you say and how you say it, such involvement will compel you to write vigorous prose. Writing becomes a mechanical task only when we fail to listen to our voice and to the imagined response of our reader.

EXERCISE 1

Analyze the writer's voice in each of the passages below. What is the writer's subject? In which cases do details or diction reveal the writer's attitude toward that subject? Does the writer's relationship with the reader tend toward distance or intimacy? How does the writer create this relationship?

1.   It is time for the baby's birthday: a white cake, strawberry-marshmallow ice cream, a bottle of champagne saved from another party. In the evening, after she has gone to sleep, I kneel beside the crib and touch her face, where it is pressed against the slats, with mine. She is an open and trusting child, unprepared for and unaccustomed to the ambushes of family life, and perhaps it is just as well that I can offer her little of that life. I would like to give her more. I would like to promise her that she will grow up with a sense of

her cousins and of rivers and of her great-grandmother's teacups, would like to pledge her a picnic on a river with fried chicken and her hair uncombed, would like to give her *home* for her birthday, but we live differently now and I can promise her nothing like that. I give her a xylophone and a sundress from Madeira, and promise to tell her a funny story.

—Joan Didion, "On Going Home,"
Slouching towards Bethlehem

2.   In England, until the end of the fourteenth century, the government, the business community, the courts, the towns, kept their records in French or Latin; lords and knights conducted their correspondence in French, when they corresponded at all. Then with amazing suddenness, in a span of less than fifty years during the first decades of the fifteenth century, French well nigh disappeared and Latin faded. The rolls of Parliament, chronicles, letters, town records, were cast in the vernacular. The Englishness of England had arrived. At this same time there developed the impulse not only to enjoy with keener awareness the flavor of living, the drama of character, but also to record these manifestations.

—Paul Murray Kendall,
The Art of Biography

3.   I think the observable reluctance of the majority of Americans to assert themselves in minor matters is related to our increased sense of helplessness in an age of technology and centralized political and economic power. For generations, Americans who were too hot, or too cold, got up and did something about it. Now we call the plumber, or the electrician, or the furnace man. The habit of looking after our own needs obviously had something to do with the assertiveness that characterized the American family familiar to readers of American literature. With the technification of life goes our direct responsibility for our material environment, and we are conditioned to adopt a position of helplessness not only as regards the broken air conditioner, but as regards the overheated train. It takes an expert to fix the former, but not the latter; yet these distinctions, as we withdraw into helplessness, tend to fade away.

—William F. Buckley, Jr., "Why
Don't We Complain?" *Esquire*

4.   If you have never attempted to trace your lineage, and would enjoy an interesting and fascinating adventure that may well develop

4c

into a family project, and lead to a lifetime avocation, I heartily recommend that you inaugurate a search for your very own family tree which is located somewhere in the great forest of humanity. I can almost hear you ask: "Where do I start?" Start right in your own home, where you will find evidences of family history all about you.

There is no magic formula to follow in tracing family history because each search presents different problems, and the solution of one problem usually leads to several new and unsolved ones. You simply take a logical approach, as in any other field of research, and work from the known facts to the unknown. *Time* and *place* are the basic factors in the solution of all genealogical problems.

—Ethel W. Williams, *Know Your Ancestors:*
A Guide to Genealogical Research

5.   For the Northern Plains, it was a year plagued by disasters. First came the drought, the result of sparse rainfall in the spring and summer. Then came the grasshoppers, great brown clouds that descended on crops of wheat, barley, oats, and finally the grasslands. What the grasshoppers left behind, the hailstorms battered to the ground. In August, lightning from a dry thunderstorm struck randomly across the state, igniting rotten logs, brush, and needles in Montana's forests. As strong winds fanned the tiny flames, the fire rose like an angry dragon, sucking in air, heating it, and blasting it through the trees at speeds of up to sixty miles an hour. Herds of elk and deer raced ahead of the wall of fire. Coyotes scampered on singed feet into nearby canyons. For days, the flames crowned the tops of Ponderosa pine and Douglas fir, leaping from ridge to ridge in a brilliant nighttime spectacle of soaring embers that could be seen thirty miles away.

—Carol Ann Bassett, "After the Big Fire
in Next-Year Country," *American West*

6.   In our time it is broadly true that political writing is bad writing. Where it is not true, it will generally be found that the writer is some kind of rebel, expressing his private opinions, and not a "party line." Orthodoxy, of whatever colour, seems to demand a lifeless, imitative style. The political dialects to be found in pamphlets, leading articles, manifestos, White Papers and the speeches of Under-Secretaries do, of course, vary from party to party, but they are all alike in that one almost never finds in them a fresh, vivid, home-made turn

4c

of speech. When one watches some tired hack on the platform mechanically repeating the familiar phrases—*bestial atrocities, iron heel, blood-stained tyranny, free peoples of the world, stand shoulder to shoulder*—one often has a curious feeling that one is not watching a live human being but some kind of dummy: a feeling which suddenly becomes stronger at moments when the light catches the speaker's spectacles and turns them into blank discs which seem to have no eyes behind them.

—George Orwell, "Politics and the
English Lanugage," *Collected Essays*

7.   Now, if I, as a black man, profoundly believe that I deserve my history and deserve to be treated as I am, then I must also, fatally, believe that white people deserve their history and deserve the power and the glory which their testimony and the evidence of my own senses assure me that they have. And if black people fall into this trap, the trap of believing that they deserve their fate, white people fall into the yet more stunning and intricate trap of believing that they deserve *their* fate, and their comparative safety; and that black people, therefore, need only do as white people have done to rise to where white people now are. But this simply cannot be said, not only for reasons of politeness or charity, but also because white people carry in them a carefully muffled fear that black people long to do to others what has been done to them. Moreover, the history of white people has led them to a fearful, baffling place where they have begun to lose touch with reality—to lose touch, that is, with themselves—and where they certainly are not happy. They do not know how this came about; they do not dare examine how this came about. On the one hand, they can scarcely dare to open a dialogue which must, if it is honest, become a personal confession—a cry for help and healing, which is really, I think, the basis of all dialogues—and, on the other hand, the black man can scarcely dare to open a dialogue which must, if it is honest, become a personal confession which, fatally, contains an accusation. And yet, if we cannot do this, each of us will perish in those traps in which we have been struggling for so long.

—James Baldwin, "Unnameable Objects,
Unspeakable Crimes," *Black on Black*

8.   A number of curious experiences occur at the onset of sleep. A person just about to go to sleep may experience an electric shock, a

4c

flash of light, or a crash of thunder—but the most common sensation is that of floating or falling, which is why "falling asleep" is a scientifically valid description. A nearly universal occurrence at the beginning of sleep (although not everyone recalls it) is a sudden, uncoordinated jerk of the head, the limbs, or even the entire body. Most people tend to think of going to sleep as a slow slippage into oblivion, but the onset of sleep is not gradual at all. It happens in an instant. One moment the individual is awake, the next moment not.

—Peter Farb, *Humankind*

PART II

5 *Organizing an Essay*

6 *Constructing Paragraphs*

7 *Developing Paragraphs*

8 *Writing Effective Sentences*

9 *Choosing Words*

Writing

5 *Organizing an Essay*

Our preceding discussion of the initial planning that you should do as a writer focused on the three points of the communication triangle—discovering ideas about your *subject,* drawing conclusions about your *reader,* and making decisions about your own voice as a *writer.* This section of our book considers the choices you must make as you draft an essay, and thus it focuses on the fourth element of the communication triangle—the written *text* that links writer, reader, and subject. We begin with the overall structure of an essay. Chapters **6**, **7**, **8**, and **9** will then examine in greater detail its component parts—unified and well-developed paragraphs, effective sentences, and precisely chosen words.

5a Limiting your subject

Effective writing often depends on the writer's ability to limit the scope of a subject appropriately. We are never able to write everything that could be said about a topic, simply because all writing tasks have length limits of some kind. In the case of college writing, this limit is usually imposed by the instructor to whom the paper is submitted. Your instructor is probably not going to count the number of words in your paper, but he or she may not be pleased by a paper that is several pages longer than what was assigned. When you write an essay exam in class, the limits are even more absolute. Once class time is up, you will be expected to have isolated the important points in the questions you answered and to have discussed them adequately.

One of the purposes of college writing in all disciplines is to provide you with such practice in deciding what is really important about your subject. You practice limiting a subject in college writing because the writing situations you will confront in the world after graduation impose similar strict limits. Business reports, advertising copy, magazine articles, dissertations, books—all of these force writers to limit their subjects according to the time and interests of their readers. A business report must be thorough and complete, but it must also get to the point; its readers should not be expected to wade through pages of tangential background material and piles of preliminary observations. A book in any field, similarly, interests its intended readers by appealing to their desire to know something new about the subject at hand. No one wants to find a new book padded with information that is readily available elsewhere.

As these examples suggest, limiting a subject is principally a writer's response to fundamental questions of purpose and audience, the inevitable constraints in every writing situation. Consequently, there are no easy procedures for limiting a subject that will work in all situations. But recognizing the role of purpose and audience in this process makes it possible for us to construct some useful questions to pose as we approach any writing task.

Suppose, for example, that you have been concerned about the importance of conserving the world's natural resources. When you begin to consider this large subject, you may be tempted to despair over the number of important topics that you could write about: the threats to natural wilderness areas; the diminishing amount of agricultural land available to grow food for the world's population; the limited supplies of oil and natural gas; the use of other sources of energy (solar, geothermal, nuclear) and their potential advantages and hazards; the pollution of the air by exhaust gases from factories and cars; the pollution of rivers and lakes by industrial wastes, sewage, and acid rain; the production of pure drinking water in urban areas; the necessity of controlling population growth. All of these are certainly important subjects, yet they could not all be treated adequately even in a book-length study.

How do you start? You might use the following guides, based on the three points of the communication triangle, to help you narrow your topic.

1. Consider what you know about yourself

What aspect of your subject is most interesting or important to you? Why? If you have lived in America's farming belt, then you are probably concerned about such issues as the increasing urbanization of rural land, the erosion of topsoil, and the potential dangers of long-term pesticide use. If you live in a large urban area, then you have no doubt experienced the effects of smog and read about sewage treatment and waste disposal. You may have grown up near one of the nation's massive nuclear power plants; in that case, you have certainly formed opinions, favorable or unfavorable, about the use of nuclear reactions to produce electricity. If you enjoy outdoor activities like boating or backpacking, then you have probably been grateful for the existence of clean lakes and unspoiled mountain trails. There's a simple point here: choose an angle on your subject that genuinely interests you. All successful writers care about their subjects; they use their backgrounds and natural inclinations to steer them toward the kinds of subjects that they will be able to write about with genuine interest and concern. You should too.

5a

2.   Consider what you know about your readers

If you could tell your readers only one thing about your subject, what would it be? Why? As we said in Chapter **3**, a thorough consideration of your audience can lead you to a clearer sense of your purpose in writing. A clear sense of purpose, in turn, helps you limit your subject. Suppose, for example, that your essay is to be duplicated and distributed for comments to the members of your writing class. What can you say about your subject that is new to them? What aspect of your subject might they identify with? What might they consider important about your subject? You can narrow a paper on any topic by regarding it as an essay with a specific point that you want your readers to carry away with them.

3.   Consider what you know about your subject

What aspect of your subject could you develop best with the material you have at hand? Behind this question is the simple fact that you can't write effectively without something to say; thus, you should not limit your subject to an area in which you have only scanty knowledge. For some topics, you will be able to use the discovery methods discussed in Chapter **2** to generate information from your own personal experience; on other occasions, you will think of potentially interesting approaches to your subject that can be researched in a library. But don't try to take on a narrow subject without adequate information about it; doing so will invariably make the writing process exasperating and will result in a finished essay that is thin and unconvincing. Always select from among the many possible aspects of your subject the ones about which you have substantial and important knowledge.

5b   Formulating a thesis statement

Like all stages of the writing process, the process of limiting a subject cannot be described by rigid rules or formulas. Sometimes, the suggestions above may immediately lead you to see how your subject should be focused; at other times, you may fully understand what you want to say only after you have begun to draft a paper. Regardless of your method, as your understanding of your precise subject evolves, you should try to formulate your controlling idea in a single sentence or two known as a **thesis statement.**

1.   Components of a thesis statement

A thesis statement may begin as a tentative expression of your paper's main point, subject to change as your idea's work themselves out on your page. In its final form, however, the thesis must be specific and unambiguous, for it establishes a kind of contract between writer and reader, a promise about the content of the paper that is to follow. Typically, a thesis contains two elements: the precise subject of the essay, and a word or phrase that even further limits this subject. The importance of that restricting word or phrase is illustrated in the following example, which shows how a single subject may be limited in different ways:

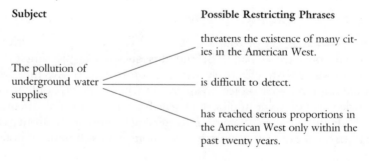

Subject	Possible Restricting Phrases
	threatens the existence of many cities in the American West.
The pollution of underground water supplies	is difficult to detect.
	has reached serious proportions in the American West only within the past twenty years.

A clear thesis often implies a method of development. Though the subject in each of these thesis statements is the same, the different ways in which it is restricted will produce three quite different essays. The first thesis will lead to a paper that explores the threat that underground water pollution poses to human life, examining its effect on the health and livelihood of Americans in western states. The paper that develops from the second thesis statement will be much more technical in nature; we might expect it to deal with such matters as the engineering difficulties involved in reaching underground water supplies and the scientific process of testing them for pollution. In the third case, we might anticipate a paper that takes a historical perspective, examining the causes of underground water pollution and explaining why this phenomenon is a relatively recent one.

5b

2. Precision in a thesis statement

Much of a thesis statement's potential usefulness is lost if either its subject or its focus is vaguely stated. Sometimes a writer may believe that he or she has composed a thesis with a clear subject, when in fact the thesis contains only a generalized topic, not the actual subject that the writer intends to develop:

Vague subject   Many experiences help a person develop a respect for the rights of others.

This general statement may perhaps provide a kind of background for a paper, but notice that it does not contain a specific subject. What experiences does the writer intend to describe? Compare the thesis statement above with this one, which substitutes the writer's specific subject:

Precise subject   *Sharing a college dorm suite with five other students* helps a person develop a respect for the rights of others.

Sometimes the problem with a thesis is not that its stated subject is too vague, but that the thesis does not limit the subject adequately. In each of these thesis statements, for example, the writer begins with a sufficiently specific subject but fails to restrict it in a way that makes the paper's point clear:

| **Vague restriction** | Climbing Long's Peak as a teenager was a very important experience for me. |
| **Vague restriction** | The Vietnam War years had a great impact on this country. |

In what ways was climbing Long's Peak important? What effects of the war in Vietnam have endured in America today? Without such information, these thesis statements merely announce a subject; they do not commit the writers to anything specific, nor do they help the reader to anticipate what will follow. In contrast, the thesis statements below add to the same subjects a more precise restriction:

| **Precise restriction** | Climbing Long's Peak as a teenager *restored my faith in my ability to set and accomplish goals.* |
| **Precise restriction** | The Vietnam War years *created divisions in American society that have lasted into the 1990s.* |

In both of these thesis statements, the subject is focused in a way that provides the writer with direction and that arouses expectations in the reader about the paper's development.

A writer who uses a thesis statement merely to announce what he or she plans to do in a paper often neglects to include any restriction of the subject at all:

| **Announcement of subject with no restriction** | In the following paper, I will discuss my decision to spend my senior year in high school as an exchange student in Ireland. |

Avoid thesis statements that rely on this and similar formulas, such as "I will use my essay to consider . . ." and "This paper will examine. . . ." In the case above, the writer's subject—his decision to attend school abroad—is clear, but his dependence on a formulaic announcement of this subject has obliterated any trace of the way he intends to develop his paper. Revised by the addition of a precise restriction, the thesis statement reveals the writer's plan to the reader.

| **Precise subject and restriction** | I decided to spend my senior year in high school as an exchange student in Ireland *because I wanted to learn about my family's roots.* |

3.   Placement of the thesis statement

Typically, a thesis statement is placed near the beginning of an essay, often in the opening paragraph. In that position, it serves both the reader and the writer in several important ways. For the reader, it provides a way of focusing attention that will make the task of reading easier. Some beginning writers mistakenly feel that a precise thesis near the beginning of a paper gives away too much of the paper's point and may therefore cause readers to lose interest in an essay from the very start. What such writers forget is that readers need to know where a paper is leading if they are to follow its development and evaluate its arguments. Your readers, after all, do not have the same familiarity with your subject that you do. They do not begin to read with an understanding of the connections between points that you have worked out for yourself, nor will they necessarily grasp the logic of your organization immediately. A clear, specific thesis gives the reader a head start in comprehending the ideas that follow.

5c

A well-formulated thesis is of as much value to the writer as to the reader. For the writer, it serves as a constant reminder of the direction that the paper should be taking. Every new argument, each specific detail, should in some way advance the focus of the thesis statement. Once a draft of the paper is complete, you can check its development against the idea stated in the thesis. Does the paper stick to the subject and focus that you established in the thesis? Does it develop these ideas completely and specifically? A good thesis provides an important standard for evaluating a paper's development and logic.

Theoretically, a thesis may be placed anywhere in an essay, as long as it is prominent enough to be recognized as the thesis by the reader. In an inductive argument, for example, the thesis—the main idea being argued—is often held until the end, after all the relevant evidence has been presented. A thesis placed in the concluding paragraph may also provide a dramatic turn to an essay and give the reader a sense of discovery. But no matter where the thesis occurs, it should offer your readers a clear and precise statement of your paper's focus.

5c   Organizing ideas

Sometimes the subject of a paper will itself determine the best arrangement of the ideas to be used in developing a thesis. A student explaining how to install a new tile floor, for example, might naturally organize her paper around the steps involved in the process:

```
Steps in installing a tile floor
      --assemble tools and materials
      --remove old flooring
      --prepare surface
      --cut and lay new tile
```

Most topics for writing, however, are more complicated than this example suggests. Moreover, writers who have used methods of discovery like those we described in Chapter **2** will usually have more material at hand than they can fit into a single paper and will need to select from among the ideas they have noted. When your material doesn't clearly determine the organization of your paper, begin by formulating as precise a thesis statement as you can, and then experiment with several ways of arranging your supporting ideas, each based on a different approach. Sketch out your ideas on paper, so that you will be able to spot opportunities for adding, deleting, and rearranging your material. A writer who wishes to argue the thesis "Grades in college are an obstacle to education" might start by selecting from his notes all the arguments that fit logically under the heading of grades and students:

```
Effects of grades on some students
      --become an end in themselves
      --lead students to select easy courses
      --sometimes provoke cheating or plagiarizing
      --limit students' attention to material for
          tests
      --cause anxiety
```

Among the remaining notes he might find some that address the subject from the standpoint of teachers:

```
Effects of grades on teachers
      --sometimes force teachers to make difficult
         distinctions among students
      --change teacher's role from instructor to
         judge
      --force teacher to develop distance from
         students
```

With both lists before him, the writer might see that his thesis could be developed by presenting the effects that grades have on students' attitudes toward teachers and courses:

```
Students' attitude toward teacher
      --see teacher primarily as judge rather than
         instructor
      --develop reluctance to consult teacher outside
         class

Students' attitude toward course
         --avoid challenging courses to protect average
         --concentrate only on what is required for tests
         --ultimately develop narrow intellectual range
```

Remember, of course, that such preliminary organizing is temporary and can be changed as the paper begins to take shape. Don't take your headings so seriously that they become a straitjacket instead of a support. The actual process of writing may suggest new material, or reveal a lack of material, and may thus lead you to modify your original thesis and plan of development.

Section **5g** will consider formal outlining as an aid to arranging ideas, and Chapter **7** will examine some basic patterns for arranging ideas within paragraphs. The point to be made here is that you must consciously search for an effective pattern, experimenting with different arrangements until you discover one that makes sense. Look for natural divisions in your subject, and trust your instinctive sense for logic and clarity.

5d   Writing an introduction

Few rules of writing are binding, but it is ordinarily desirable that an essay's introductory paragraph (1) attract and hold the reader's attention, (2) indicate the subject matter of the paper, and (3) reveal in some way the writer's attitude toward the subject. As these guidelines suggest, you can usually write an effective introduction only *after* you have formulated your thesis statement. In fact, since the success of an introductory paragraph depends on a writer's understanding of the complete essay, many writers work on their introductions after they have written everything else for a paper.

1.   Beginning with the thesis statement

If you remember that any beginning can be changed, or even discarded, you should not be hesitant about starting an introduction. One way of getting started, especially for short papers, is to begin with your thesis statement:

> *The so-called generation gap of the 1960s and 1970s was replaced in the 1980s by feelings of open, deep indifference.* In the 1960s youth was attacked for its involvement in political and peace movements and its rebellion against sterile education and the war-as-usual. In the 1970s it was criticized for its preoccupation with careers, its apathy about social issues, and its interest in "doing one's own thing." Knowing that earlier generations were denounced for contradictory reasons, many students of the 1980s saw no reason at all why they should listen to adult America.

2.   Beginning with a quotation

If your subject is a published work, you might try opening with a key quotation from the text you are going to discuss, as the student writer of the following example did.

> It is the "quick, compact imagery of a single statement that forms the basis of Navajo poetry," says Oliver LaFarge. *This remark can well be*

illustrated in LaFarge's own story of Navajo life, Laughing Boy, *a novel in which things are perceived and identified through "quick, compact imagery."* The first image of the novel ties the protagonist, Laughing Boy, to his environment: "His new red headband was a bright color among the embers of the sun-struck desert, undulating like a moving graph of the pony's lope"—a simple statement, but a "compact image" of the movement of a man on his horse over flat ground.

In this paragraph, the writer has used a quotation from LaFarge to provide the focusing phrase for the thesis statement: *"Laughing Boy* [is] a novel in which things are perceived and identified through 'quick, compact imagery.' "

3. Building up to the thesis statement

Perhaps the most sophisticated introduction is one that gradually builds up to the thesis statement. Placing the thesis at the end of an introduction enables you to begin with background information that establishes a context for your main point. Moreover, a thesis in this position leads smoothly into the first paragraph of the body of the paper. In the following introductory paragraph, for example, notice how the student writer uses a brief historical survey to frame her thesis.

Beginning in the 1960s, the United States saw a growing militancy among Native Americans. During this time, these people began to put aside their intertribal difficulties and feuds, and to unite and support each other's causes. The American Indian Movement (AIM), with its militancy and activism, soon drew national attention to the oppression and discrimination of Indian peoples. AIM, however, worked outside the established system, battling for Indian rights on the streets. *Now Native Americans have gone beyond this strategy and are waging battle from a new front—the courtroom.*

Without the perspective provided by the opening sentences of this introduction, we would not understand the significance of the writer's thesis, which focuses on the new legal action being taken by Native Americans.

In the following introductory paragraph, another student writer has used the same strategy to establish a context for his analysis of a short story.

It's often difficult for us to pause and analyze our relationships with other people. Instead, we find it easier to live each day as it comes without forming personal commitments or attachments. Sooner or later, though, everyone realizes that it is impossible to live with a person and not really care whether he or she will be there tomorrow. *The two characters in Dan Jacobson's short story "Led Astray" come to this realization and discover that no relationship can exist without feeling.*

5e

To appreciate the effectiveness of this approach, notice that the thesis statement and the introductory sentences in this paragraph could not simply be flipped around in the reverse order. The thesis is not merely attached to the introductory sentences; rather, it appears to develop out of them.

In the following student paragraph, the writer uses his opening sentences for a different purpose—to create an informal tone and to establish himself as an authority on his subject.

The Hawaiian Islands are anchored in a position where they receive sea swells the year round. The contour of the ocean floor and the structure of the reefs turn these swells into beautiful breaking waves, which make Hawaii a surfer's paradise. I have been surfing in this paradise every day for the last seven years, and I can tell you that there is probably no more purely natural act than surfing. You are at one with nature's most basic element—the living sea. *But as changing times bring "progress" to the islands, surfing in Hawaii will also be forced to change.*

No matter what form of introduction you use, remember that confidence, authority, and solid content characterize the most successful opening paragraphs. Stay clear of any beginnings that sound trite and obvious: "Our modern world is an ever-changing one." "It is obvious to everyone that today's children watch too much television." Such beginnings discourage even the most determined reader.

5e   Shaping the body of an essay

The section on outlining later in this chapter and the discussion of paragraphing in Chapters **6** and **7** offer the fullest treatment of the material that comes between the introduction and the conclusion— the body of your paper. But this is an appropriate place to mention the principle of **emphasis** and its role in shaping the body of an essay.

The more space you give an idea, the more important it will appear to your reader. As you begin thinking about how to present your ideas in the body of your paper, therefore, plan to develop points that are approximately equal in importance with roughly equal amounts of evidence and discussion, and devote more space to any ideas that you wish to stand out above others. Keep in mind the distinction between what your readers already know about your subject and what else you want them to know (see **3b**). Commonly accepted judgments or matters of fact, for example, can be stated briefly, but your position on a controversial issue may need the support of concrete evidence presented in one or more fully developed paragraphs with tight logical structure.

5f

You can achieve appropriate emphasis in an essay through arrangement as well as balance. Whenever you use several facts, examples, or arguments to establish a point, consider arranging them in order beginning with the weakest argument or the least important fact and moving to the strongest and most important. Evidence organized in this way gives you the chance to convince a skeptical reader through what seems to be the accumulating of solid proof. If you use your best evidence first, the rest of your paper will seem anticlimactic, and the force of your entire argument may be undercut.

5f   Writing a conclusion

Not every paper requires a conclusion. A particularly short essay, for example, may not need the added sense of completeness that a conclusion provides. When a conclusion is called for, however, it should be more than a sentence or paragraph attached to the end of an essay with a mechanical transition like "Therefore . . ." or "In conclusion. . . ."

1. Ending with a sense of finality

Rather than merely summarizing what has gone before, the best conclusions mark the arrival of the essay at the destination announced in its introductory paragraph. An essay should end with the ease and authority of a musical composition that brings its themes to a unified, harmonious resolution, giving the reader a sure sense of finality. For example, consider this ending to a student's seven-hundred-word essay on Chekhov's play *The Seagull*.

When the curtain falls on *The Seagull,* one has the feeling that the story is not at all ended, that the action continues behind the curtain. Reflecting on this, one may find that the secret of Chekhov's effect lies in avoiding the overly dramatic, the play in which everything builds to one climax centered in one character. Chekhov has allowed the themes of love and death, of dreams and reality, to unfold in the random, senseless way that they occur in our lives.

2. Ending by echoing the introduction

Often the feeling of completeness that a well-written conclusion conveys can be created by recalling a word or phrase from the introduction. The student surfer whose introduction we quoted above went on to argue that the increasing number of surfers in Hawaii would either have to discipline themselves to share the waves or have to expect state regulation of the sport, and he concluded by emphasizing the concept of the living sea and the inevitability of change—two key ideas from his opening paragraph:

> Unless we treat the sea with the consideration that it deserves as a source of wonder, pleasure, and life, sacrificing our own selfish desire to catch the big wave regardless of who or what is in the way, we can look forward to the regulation of surfing. Police patrolling the beaches, floodlights stuck into the sand for day and night surfing, licenses, permits, tickets—these are not pleasant prospects. But neither are the fights, the racial name-calling, the indifference to another surfer's safety that one encounters all too often in Hawaiian waters. To live in a world of change we must learn to change ourselves.

3. Ending by bringing ideas together

A writer may also conclude strongly by making connections between ideas explored earlier in the paper. In the following student example, an analysis of Robert Pirsig's *Zen and the Art of Motorcycle Maintenance* and Ralph Ellison's *Invisible Man,* note how the writer links Phaedrus and the Invisible Man, the protagonists of the two novels.

> Participation in life and the celebration of its possibilities are what both Phaedrus and the Invisible Man finally affirm. They are able to do so as a result of their personal quests. Yet they both set out in ignorance,

not knowing the direction they are actually headed in. At the end, when the Invisible Man says, "Who knows but that, on the lower frequencies, I speak for you?" it is a warning that most of us are still back at the very beginning simply because we think we're not or, worse yet, because we don't even think about it.

No competent writer dashes off a conclusion at the last moment. When we finish reading an essay we should feel that it had to end as it did. Writing that creates this sense of completion is the result of careful thought and painstaking revision, but its effectiveness justifies the effort.

5g Constructing outlines

For many writers, one of the most effective means of planning and revising papers is outlining, the systematic listing of an essay's main points. Even the most experienced writers usually begin with some kind of informal outline, however much they may modify it or deviate from it as they expand upon their subject. For less experienced writers, outlining can be an essential tool.

1. Uses of outlines

Outlines serve several purposes. Perhaps the most important use of the formal outline is to help a writer organize ideas generated during the discovery stage of the writing process (see Chapter **2**). The visual model of an essay's structure that an outline provides can help the writer anticipate the logical divisions of a topic, decide on appropriate supporting evidence and detail, and consider connections between the paper's main points. The more complex the topic and the more elaborate its supporting evidence, the more essential outlining becomes.

A second use of the formal outline is to assist in the revision of a rough draft or an unsatisfactory final version. When a paper seems to lack coherence, balance, or tight logical structure, a formal outline of the paper's contents can help to diagnose its problems. An outline enables you to translate the vague feeling that something is wrong with a paper into specific knowledge about which points need further development and where stronger transitions would improve coherence.

5g

Finally, outlines often provide a fruitful way of examining another writer's plan and structure. Suppose, for example, that you have read three essays on Lincoln's use of power during the Civil War and are to write on the authors' differing assumptions about the presidency. By constructing three accurate outlines and thereby highlighting in visual form the crucial differences among the essays, you can save yourself from skimming over and over the same paragraphs and snatching at random phrases or details. Formal outlining is also useful when you are asked to refute another writer's argument. By outlining his or her essay, you can isolate the key issues and examine the evidence and logic that support them. Outlining your reading, in short, enables you to discover someone else's views as you clarify your own.

2. Types of outlines

Informal outlines may follow any pattern that a particular writer finds helpful, but formal outlines fall into three groups: the paragraph outline, the topic outline, and the sentence outline. Each has its particular uses and limitations.

The first of these, the **paragraph outline,** is a list of sentences numbered so that sentence one summarizes paragraph one, sentence two summarizes paragraph two, and so on. For example:

1. Outlining is a systematic listing of an essay's most important points.
2. The first use of a formal outline is to help the writer anticipate the main divisions of the topic and connect ideas and evidence.
3. The second use of the formal outline is in the revision of a rough draft. . . .

The paragraph outline helps you review the progression of major ideas in a paper. For that reason, it is often a good starting point in planning an essay. What the paragraph outline does not show clearly, however, are the kinds of evidence used to develop the paragraphs in an essay or the precise logical relationships between them. As you become more certain about your paper's probable organization and development, you may want to rely more heavily on the outline forms that do indicate this material—the topic and sentence outlines.

The **topic outline** begins with the entire thesis statement, the main idea being developed in the paper. After the thesis, though, its entries are words or brief phrases, numbered and lettered to show the relative importance of the paper's supporting ideas. (For notes on the scheme of numbers and letters used in constructing outlines, see the next section.)

For brief papers in class, tests, and short analyses or reports, the topic outline is useful and usually sufficient. Carelessly used, however, with headings like "Introduction," "Main Body," and "Conclusion" and subheadings like "Example," "Reasons," and "Results," it does nothing to counteract vague thinking. Consider the following example:

5g

Vague topic outline

The Change from School to College

I. Introduction
   A. High-school ideas
   B. Reasons for these ideas

II. What my first impressions were
   A. Two examples
   B. Results

III. Conclusions
   A. Why I have changed my mind
   B. Advice to high-school seniors

The vague entries here largely undercut the potential value of outlining. Though they suggest the paper's general direction, they do little to help the writer organize his ideas or consider his supporting evidence.

For long papers, a **sentence outline** may be even more valuable than a good topic outline. Since each entry in a sentence outline is a complete sentence, this form of outline makes possible a thorough consideration of a paper's contents. Note how a good topic outline can be expanded into a sentence outline:

Effective topic outline

The Complexity of Experience of Laughter

Thesis: Although there are several theories of laughter, no single one accounts for the quite distinct emotions that cause it.

I. Single explanation theories of laughter
   A. Social punishment
      1. Mocks differences
      2. Shows feeling of superiority

    B. Defense against social taboos
       1. Relies on dirty jokes
       2. Is relief of tension
    C. Sudden surprise
       1. Stimulated by the unexpected act
       2. Is delight in being startled
  II. Complex experience of laughter
    A. Descriptions of feelings
       1. "To have the last laugh"
       2. "To laugh at"
       3. "To laugh off"
    B. Descriptions of vocal expressions
       1. "To chuckle"
       2. "To giggle and titter"
       3. "To snicker"
       4. "To guffaw"
 III. Inadequacies of theories of laughter to experience of laughter
    A. Failure to account for description of feelings
       1. No sudden pleasurable surprise in social punishment theory
       2. No sense of superiority in social taboo theory
       3. No self-embarrassment in pleasurable surprise theory
    B. Failure to account for sheer joy
       1. No explanation of lovers' spontaneity by any theory
       2. No explanation of delight in success by any theory

Expansion to sentence outline

The Complexity of Experience of Laughter

Thesis: Although there are several theories of laughter, no single one accounts for the quite distinct emotions that cause it.

  I. The theories tend to explain laughter by a single emotion or cause.
    A. Laughter is social punishment inflicted by the majority.
       1. It mocks differences in dress, behavior, and belief.
       2. It is a feeling of superiority and satiric awareness.
    B. Laughter is a defense against social taboos.
       1. It is stimulated by the dirty joke and obscene remark.
       2. It is a safety-valve response relieving tension.
    C. Laughter is the expression of pleasure in the sudden surprise.
       1. It is stimulated by the unexpected physical or verbal act.

       a. The physical is often the sudden fall or thump.
       b. The verbal is usually a witty remark.
    2. It is delight in being startled.
II. The experience of laughter is not a simple one.
  A. Our feelings while laughing vary.
    1. Vindictively we "have the last laugh."
    2. In amusement we "laugh at" something.
    3. In embarrassment we "laugh it away."
  B. The vocal expressions of laughter vary.
    1. We "chuckle" in a low tone when inwardly satisfied.
    2. We "giggle and titter" in rapid, high-pitched sounds when silly.
    3. We "snicker" in sly, half-suppressed tones at another's plight.
    4. We "guffaw" in loud tones when heartily enjoying ourselves.
III. The theories are inadequate to the experience of laughter.
  A. No theory accounts for the ways we describe our feelings.
    1. The theory of laughter as social punishment neglects the laugh of sudden pleasurable surprise.
    2. The theory of laughter as a defense against social taboos minimizes the laugh of punishment and mockery.
    3. The theory of laughter as pleasurable surprise slights the laugh of self-embarrassment.
  B. All theories omit the laughter of sheer joy of being and doing.
    1. They do not account for the spontaneous laughter of children, lovers, and parents.
    2. They do not account for the triumphant, delighted laugh of the successful artist or athlete.

Notice that the sentence outline contains far more information and reveals a more detailed analysis than the topic outline. The sentence outline has the advantage of compelling you to formulate more explicitly the material you intend to use. For longer papers on complex topics— say, 1,500 words on the effects of automation on unions or 2,000 words on methods of crime prevention—a sentence outline may be the best help.

3. Conventions of topic and sentence outlines

    The following system of alternating numbers and letters is nearly universal in outlines:

Thesis:
- I.
  - A.
    - 1.
    - 2.
      - a.
      - b.
  - B.
- II.
  - A.
  - B.
  - C.

5g

In topic outlines, capitalize the first letter of the word beginning each heading, but do not punctuate the end of the entry, since it is not a sentence. In sentence outlines, start with a capital letter and end with a period or other appropriate punctuation.

An outline begins with the thesis statement, the main idea to be developed in the paper. Roman numerals indicate the major *subdivisions* of the idea stated in the thesis. Capital letters, Arabic numbers, and small letters mark further and further subdivisions. The key to the logic of every outline is coordination and subordination. Coordinate points—those of equal importance—are indented the same distance from the left margin; under them, farther from the left margin, come subordinate, or supporting, points. In the outline above, for example, I and II are main points of equal importance, A and B are points of equal importance supporting I, and 1 and 2 are points of equal importance supporting A.

If an outline is to function as a tool for analysis, these conventions must be taken seriously. A writer who divides material like this negates the whole reason for outlining:

Illogical and confusing

- I. Advantages of outboard motors
  - A. Relatively inexpensive
  - B. Attachable to any small boat
- II. Easily transportable

"Easily transportable" is logically a subtopic under I, "Advantages of outboard motors." It should be made parallel with A and B:

Revised to clarify coordination and subordination

I. Advantages of outboard motors
    A. Relatively inexpensive
    B. Attachable to any small boat
    C. Easily transportable
II. Disadvantages of outboard motors
    A. Troublesome to repair on the water
    B. Limited fuel capacity

5g

When one subheading includes material covered in other parallel headings, the subdivisions are said to overlap. Overlapping subdivisions suggest that the writer has not analyzed his or her material fully.

Poorly analyzed—overlapping

I. Organized welfare groups
    A. Early relief organizations
    B. Red Cross
    C. Community Chest
    D. Relief organizations today

Logically, "Relief organizations today" *includes* the Red Cross and Community Chest. If the pattern of development is to be chronological, the writer should stick to it consistently and make Red Cross and Community Chest subdivisions under modern welfare agencies:

Clearly subdivided

I. Organized welfare groups
    A. History of early relief organizations
    B. Relief organizations today
        1. Red Cross
        2. Community Chest

One last word about subdivisions: convention demands that each subdivided topic must have at least two headings. The argument runs that dividing something must produce at least two parts. Occasionally, however, a lone subhead is a useful means of *reminding yourself* of an example, illustration, or reference to be included when you are writing:

Examples noted

    I. Extension of Mohammedan power under the early caliphs
       A. Eastward and northward
          1. For example, Persian and Greek lands
       B. Westward
          1. For example, Syria, Egypt, and northern Africa

5h Though they may be useful in working outlines, such lone headings should be eliminated from the final version of an outline.

5h   A sample essay

We close this chapter with a student paper illustrating the elements of a successful essay that we have discussed here—an appropriately limited subject, a precise thesis statement, a smooth introduction, well-balanced development, and an effective and substantial conclusion. This paper was inspired by E. B. White's frequently reprinted essay "Once More to the Lake," in which he describes a week-long vacation with his son at a lake in Maine where his own family had spent the month of August each year when he was a boy. For White, the experience vividly brought back childhood memories that kept him eerily suspended between youth and adulthood. "I began to sustain the illusion that [my son] was I, and therefore, by simple transposition, that I was my father," he writes. "I would be in the middle of some simple act, I would be picking up a bait box or laying down a table fork, or I would be saying something, and suddenly it would not be I but my father who was saying the words or making the gesture. It gave me a creepy sensation." Watch how this student analyzes a similar experience in her own life.

Breaking the Chain

Janet's opening sentences establish a clear context for the essay by succinctly but vividly describing her baby-sitting duties. We learn

Jenny was six, Marcia was eight, and I was sixteen when we spent the summer together. Although the pay was terrible, baby-sitting for those brown-eyed, skinny little girls was by far the best summer job

I ever had. They lived just down the block and therefore played on the same playground, explored the same forbidden creek bottom, and rode bicycles over the same bumpy paths that I had known intimately as a child. Simultaneously supervising and sharing in their activities, I felt emotions similar to those that E. B. White expresses in his essay "Once More to the Lake." "[I]t would not be I but my father who was saying the words or making the gesture," writes White of his memory-filled vacation with his son. Like White, I startled myself more than once that summer by echoing my mother's words and phrases to Marcia and Jenny. White's experiences gave him a "creepy sensation"; mine made me wonder for the first time what kind of parent I would be.

At sixteen, I was still under the authority of my parents, who in my estimation were unreasonably protective. Each time I left the house, I would have to detail to my mother exactly where I was going, who I was going with, when I would be back. Walking out the door, I was invariably told to wear

who was involved, and when and where the events that she describes occurred. By including the phrase *best summer job*, Janet also prepares us to share her favorable attitude toward her subject.

A key quotation from White's essay leads Janet to her thesis statement, which presents a precise subject (her baby-sitting experience) and a clear restricting phrase ("made me wonder . . . what kind of parent I would be").

Janet organizes her second paragraph around what she felt was her mother's unreasonable protectiveness— background that we need to understand the point she wants to

5h

5h

make about her own behavior as a baby-sitter.

Notice the well-chosen, specific details with which she makes her point.

my seat belt, check for fire escapes, cross only at stoplights, stay clear of public rest rooms, and leave a phone number that I could be reached at. Even at Marcia and Jenny's age I had thought my mother's perpetual admonishments ridiculous, but as a teenager I deeply resented them. Specifically outlining my every plan to my parents was particularly irritating, and I had vowed repeatedly to myself that I would never place such demands on my own children.

In this paragraph, Janet begins to develop the idea raised in her thesis: what did the restrictions that she imposed on Marcia and Jenny—so much like the protectiveness of her mother—predict about her own future as a parent?

Again, specific details make the situation convincingly real.

Nonetheless, my tiny, energetic wards never left the house that summer until I had found out where they were going and when they would return, and had extracted a promise from them that they would not ride their bicycles around the block. Marcia and Jenny argued as fervently against the restrictions I placed on them as I had protested against my mother's rules. Why couldn't they walk half a mile alone to visit a friend? Why should they stay out of Coleen's pool just because her mother wasn't home? To my surprise, I usually responded with the precise phrases I had so often heard my mother use with me. That frightened me. My mother's words were filled with genuine concern, never harshness, but they were <u>her</u> words, and I scared myself by spewing them out so automatically. Even though I felt that my mother worried needlessly and restricted me unnecessarily, I found myself worrying about and limiting my girls to the same degree. I was "raising" Marcia and Jenny in the same manner that my parents had raised me, which was most likely similar to the way they had been raised. Was I destined to raise my own children in the same way? It seemed to me suddenly that I was trapped in an unbreakable chain of parental behavior from which I would never be able to escape.

But at the same time that I felt and acted like my mother out of concern for Marcia and Jenny's safety, I also closely identified with the freedom they wanted and understood the resentment they felt at the rules I laid down. Thus, like White, I experienced the startling sensation of living a dual existence. Down deep, I knew how difficult it was for the two of them to pinpoint their play areas, because summer days

5h

Here's the sentence that gave Janet the idea for her title ("Breaking the Chain").

Against the sternness of her parental role, developed in the preceding paragraph, Janet now balances an effective description of the way in which Marcia and Jenny's games reminded her of her own childhood.

5h

weren't meant to be planned. They lived
their vacation as spontaneously as my
friends and I had, waking each morning with
the wonderful knowledge that they had the
whole day before them with nothing, but
everything, to do. A typical day might begin
by playing "Barbies" in a friend's cool
basement, followed by a game of jump rope
in someone else's front yard; after lunch,
they'd reassemble, perhaps to construct a
fort behind still another friend's garage.

Specific details and
diction (*scamper,
high-pitched
giggles*) bring the
scene to life.

Sitting on the porch, watching them scamper
from yard to yard and listening to their
high-pitched giggles, I became one of their
group and reexperienced the carefree feeling that had come with summer before camps
and jobs occupied my summer days. I couldn't
let them play kickball in the street or walk
unaccompanied to the Dairy Spot, but I hated
to put any kind of limits on their glorious
freedom.

Janet effectively
links her conclusion
to her introduction
by again
mentioning E. B.
White's essay, her
starting point.

Despite my worries about those little
girls that summer, and about my future as
a parent, I truly enjoyed those three
months. Spending time with Marcia and Jenny
allowed me to relive the pleasures and free-

dom of my early summers on Maplewood Street, just as White's vacation with his son enabled him to relive his childhood summers at the lake. The experience of acting out the dual roles of parent and child was unsettling to me that summer, much as it had been for White, but I've since been able to resolve the conflict it created within me. Now that I've been away from my parents' authority, I realize that the "chain" of parental behavior is not as unbreakable as I had thought. As I grow older, I realize that I am different from my mother after all. I can raise my children with fewer restrictions—if I'm able to recall, as I did that summer, how it feels to be a child.

She then connects the major ideas of the paper by explaining how she has resolved the conflict that she described above.

5h

The rhythm of Janet's last sentence creates a satisfying sense of finality.

—Janet Lively [student]

Our marginal notes on Janet's essay not only highlight the principles of essay organization that we have discussed in this chapter, but also point out the clear organization of its paragraphs and the specificity of its details and diction. Those are subjects that we will examine further in the chapters that follow.

EXERCISE 1

The suggestions for narrowing a subject (pages 53–56) will work best *after* you have explored a subject and considered your intended audience (see Chapters **2** and **3**). But to test their effectiveness, try using them to limit one or more of the following broad subjects, or another equally general subject of your choice. Which of the suggestions seem to be most helpful?

1. Family relationships
2. Music
3. Science
4. Your hometown
5. International relations

6. Religion
7. Transportation
8. Animals
9. Space exploration
10. Peace

5h

EXERCISE 2

Complete each of the following thesis statements in two *different* ways by adding two different restricting phrases. Make a list of the main points you might use to develop a paper for each of the thesis statements you produce.

Example

The campus radio station . . .

Thesis #1: The campus radio station gives students firsthand experience with sophisticated broadcasting equipment.

Thesis #2: The campus radio station plays a blend of music that fails to attract either students on campus or the public at large.

1. My best friend . . .
2. Extracurricular activities in high school . . .
3. Outstanding teachers . . .
4. College math [or English or biology] courses . . .
5. Having [or not having] a car on campus . . .

EXERCISE 3

On which of the subjects below do you already have a reasonably firm position? For each such case, formulate a thesis statement that would be the foundation for an essay of between five hundred and seven hundred words. How might you develop your essay?

1. Violence in television
2. The appeal of science fiction
3. Sex education in schools
4. The role of the SAT in the college admissions process
5. The death penalty
6. Defense spending
7. The study of foreign languages
8. The eating habits of American young adults
9. Prayer in public schools
10. Drunk driving

EXERCISE **4**

Write two *different* introductions for a paper that would develop *one* of the thesis statements that you produced in Exercise 2 or Exercise 3 above. Which introduction do you like better? Why? Would the essays that followed these introductions be likely to differ? If so, how?

EXERCISE **5**

5h

Examine an article in a magazine such as *Scientific American, Atlantic Monthly,* or *Natural History,* and consider the following points about its organization and development:

1. Is the conclusion of the article related to its introduction? How?
2. Does the article have a clear thesis? Where is it stated?
3. What are the main points with which the author develops the thesis?
4. What kind of evidence or support does the author present for each of these main points?

6 *Constructing Paragraphs*

The concept of a paragraph is no doubt familiar to you. Just about everything we read—from novels to newspapers, from textbooks to cookbooks—is printed with indentations that mark new paragraphs. And in most of your writing, you also probably adopt the tradition of using paragraphs to divide what you write into separate chunks. At the same time, you no doubt recognize that such divisions are not arbitrary, that paragraphs have a certain logic behind them. But how can we define more precisely what paragraphs are? And can we determine some principles for writing good paragraphs? These are among the questions to be explored in this chapter. Later chapters will consider two other aspects of paragraphing: methods of developing paragraphs (Chapter **7**) and points to keep in mind as you revise paragraphs (Chapter **11**).

6a Recognizing paragraphs

Try to imagine, for a moment, a world with no paragraph indentations. Every book, every newspaper, every magazine would present a solid page of type, with no white spaces inviting you to pause and rest, even momentarily. Reading under these circumstances would be tedious and tiring. But would paragraphs exist, even if the indentations that signaled them did not? To find out, try reading the following short magazine article, printed without its original paragraph indentations. In particular, consider this question: without the indentations, has this text now become a single long paragraph, or are the original separate paragraphs still here, and still perceptible, with a little extra work on your part?

> In the course of almost four decades of research, Dr. Paul MacLean of the National Institute of Mental Health has determined that there is a

zoo in the human brain. More precisely, there are in the human brain evolutionary holdovers from our animal origins, he says, that influence our behavior and thinking. In its evolution, the human forebrain has expanded in size while retaining three basic formations that reflect our ancestral relationship to reptiles, early mammals, and recent mammals. Radically different in size as well as chemistry, and in an evolutionary sense countless generations apart, the three formations constitute a hierarchy of three brains in one—a triune brain. The reptilian core, or "biological brain," which MacLean calls the R-complex, is involved in basic social behavior and preservation of the self and of the species. It contains built-in formats for the instinctual behavior of dominance and territoriality. As an example of human behavior that reflects that protoreptilian impulse, MacLean offers the "place preference" of lizards, which is no different, he says, from Archie Bunker's territorial attitude about his favorite chair. The limbic system, or "emotional brain," is a holdover from early mammals. Its integration of internal and external experiences accounts for the ineffable affective feelings required for self-preservation and for perpetuation of the species. Without the limbic system (a term that MacLean coined) there wouldn't be the kinds of behavior that distinguish mammals from reptiles—namely, nursing in conjunction with maternal care, vocalization for the purpose of maintaining contact, and play. The neomammalian formation, or "intellectual brain," is found only in the higher mammals. It makes language and rational thought possible for man and fosters cultural life. According to MacLean, the triune brain obliges us to view ourselves from three perspectives. As a further complication, there is evidence that the two older formations lack the necessary neural machinery for verbal communication. Despite [this] built-in incompatibility of the three brains, MacLean is not without hope for man. The continuing influence of our animal origins, millions of years strong, will not be easily transcended, but it can be, MacLean says in his forthcoming book, *The Triune Brain*.

—John White, "On the Brain," *Esquire*

Despite the way in which this passage is printed, you probably approached it by mentally dividing the text into separate chunks, in order to follow it more easily. When the author tells us in the introductory sentences that the human brain retains traces of three earlier formations, we expect him to discuss these three brains in the rest of the article. And that is indeed what he does in three middle paragraphs, each devoted to a different brain formation. After describing the three, he concludes with a paragraph commenting on the necessary conflict among them.

We look for these kinds of divisions whenever we read because, in order to read with understanding, we need to be able to identify the main ideas in the text before us and to perceive their relationship to one another. If we lived in a world where paragraphs were never marked, we would have to find them on our own as we read. To put it another way, if paragraphs were unknown in our world, we would simply have to invent them.

6a

We might say that paragraphs have a primarily *rhetorical* function. That is, they are intended by a writer to affect a reader in some way—in this case, to help a reader identify and follow the writer's principal ideas. Underlying this concept of a paragraph are two principles. First, a paragraph should ordinarily be unified around a single thought. If the function of paragraphing is to help point out a writer's main ideas, then it follows logically that separate ideas should be developed in separate paragraphs. Second, if the reader is to make sense of the text, all the paragraphs in a given piece of writing must be related to one another in some clear way.

Sometimes, of course, we create paragraphs almost unconsciously. When we are writing well, we find ourselves deeply involved in our subject and able to discover new ideas and connections as we go along. On such lucky occasions, we usually paragraph by the instinctive feeling that one section is complete and that we are ready to begin a new one. At other times, we may become aware of the proper places for paragraph breaks only gradually, as we make slow progress through the cycle of writing and revising discussed in Chapter 1. As a writer, you should be prepared to discover paragraphs in your writing where you had not previously seen them. Look for opportunities to combine short paragraphs, be ready to divide longer ones, and don't hestitate to move a sentence from one paragraph to another. Paragraphs are molded out of clay, not carved in stone; experienced writers expect to reshape them as they work toward a final draft.

EXERCISE 1

Each of the following passages has been formed by printing two consecutive paragraphs without indentation. Separate each passage into two paragraphs again, and explain your reason for dividing them where you did. What is the main idea in each of the paragraphs you identified? Is the relationship between those ideas clear?

1. Whoever said that people who do the least complain the most must have known my boss, Miss Eleanor. By hiding behind paperwork that takes the other store managers only a fraction of the time to finish, she is able to push the jobs she should be doing on whoever else is within earshot. Across the entire store one can hear her yelling for a clerk to bring her a file folder or a cash register tape lying only a few feet away. Her voice, fierce and commanding, together with her stony face and dark eyes, freezes everyone around her in fear. Eleanor is as vain as she is fearsome. In front of her desk she has a three-foot square mirror in which we see her constantly making faces, admiring herself, and talking to herself. In her nearby "private" cabinet she has two cans of hair spray, a box of bobby pins, several combs and brushes, a set of electric curlers, enough makeup to make Frankenstein look acceptable, and half a dozen issues of *Vogue* magazine. It's no wonder Miss Eleanor is always so busy.

    —Cathy Kwolik [student]

2. The first thing you have to know, if you are going to be serious about Panama hats, is that genuine Panamas are not made in Panama at all and never have been. They are made in Ecuador—that is, the raw body of the hat is made in Ecuador, handwoven out of very thin strips of jipijapa palm leaves. Nor are they woven underwater, as many people seem to think; the leaves are simply woven while moist. The hat body is then sent off to hat makers around the world to be sized, blocked, and trimmed. But the important part, the weaving, has already happened in Ecuador. The misnomer is understandable: Sailors and traders first encountered the hat when they went ashore in Panama more than 150 years ago. Naturally, they called it a Panama hat, and the name they gave it stuck. All the more so when Teddy Roosevelt was photographed wearing a Panama hat at the construction site of the Panama canal. In the ensuing rush to buy Panama hats, no one took the trouble to straighten out the name, not even the Ecuadorians who had made Roosevelt's hat.

    —John Berendt, "The Panama Hat," *Esquire*

3. Medieval courtiers saw their table manners as distinguishing them from crude peasants; but by modern standards, the manners were not exactly refined. Feudal lords used their unwashed hands to scoop food from a common bowl and they passed around a single goblet from which all drank. A finger or two would be extended while eating, so as to be kept free of grease and thus available for the

6a

next course, or for dipping into spices or condiments—possibly accounting for today's "polite" custom of extending the finger while holding a spoon or small fork. Soups and sauces were commonly drunk by lifting the bowl to the mouth; several diners frequently ate from the same bread trencher. Even lords and nobles would toss gnawed bones back into the common dish, wolf down their food, spit onto the table (preferred conduct called for spitting under it), and blow their noses into the tablecloth. By about the beginning of the sixteenth century, table manners began to move in the direction of today's standards. The importance attached to them is indicated by the phenomenal success of a treatise, *On Civility in Children,* by the philosopher Erasmus, which appeared in 1530; reprinted more than thirty times in the next six years, it also appeared in numerous translations. Erasmus' idea of good table manners was far from modern, but it did represent an advance. He believed, for example, that an upper-class diner was distinguished by putting only three fingers of one hand into the bowl, instead of the entire hand in the manner of the lower class. Wait a few moments after being seated before you dip into it, he advises. Do not poke around in your dish, but take the first piece you touch. Do not put chewed food from your mouth back on your plate; instead, throw it under the table or behind your chair.

—Peter Farb and George Armelagos,
Consuming Passions

4.   Until 1883 a Chicagoan asked to tell what time it was could give more than one answer and still be correct. There was local time, determined by the position of the sun at high noon at a centrally located spot in town, usually City Hall. There was also railroad time, which put Columbus, Ohio, six minutes faster than Cincinnati and 19 minutes faster than Chicago. Scattered across the country were 100 different local time zones, and the railroads had some 53 zones of their own. Typically, a traveler journeying from one end of the U.S. to another would have to change his watch at least 20 times. To do away with the inevitable confusion, the railroads took the matter into their own hands, holding a General Time Convention in the fall of 1883 at the Grand Pacific Hotel at LaSalle Street and Jackson Boulevard, the site of the present Continental Bank Building [in Chicago]. Its purpose: to develop a better and more uniform system of railroad scheduling. The convention secretary, William F. Allen, editor of the *Official Railway Guide* in New York, proposed that four equal time zones be established across the country. Five

were actually adopted—Intercolonial (now Atlantic, including Nova Scotia and New Brunswick in Canada), Eastern, Central, Mountain and Pacific.

> —June Sawyers, "The End to Falling Back and Forth in 100 Time Zones," *Chicago Tribune*

6b Using topic sentences

Writers separate their ideas into paragraphs so that readers will be able to follow those ideas more easily. Sometimes a writer also succinctly states the main idea of a paragraph in a sentence known as a **topic sentence.** Just as a thesis statement directs the reader's attention to the central idea in an essay, a topic sentence, when it exists, aids the reader in more readily grasping a paragraph's point. Like a thesis, it usually introduces both a subject and a specific aspect of that subject, or focus. Like a thesis, too, a topic sentence is in some sense an arguable statement, one that leads to, or even demands, specific support or proof in the rest of the paragraph.

1. Formulating a topic sentence

Which of the following two sentences meets the criteria for a topic sentence that we have just described?

a. Abraham Lincoln was born in what is now Larue County, Kentucky.

b. A food processor, as more and more good cooks are discovering, is an indispensable kitchen tool.

Because it does not raise an idea that requires further comment, but instead simply states a fact, the first sentence could not be a strong topic sentence. This sentence presents a clear subject—Lincoln's birthplace—but it does not contain a focusing idea about that subject that could be developed further. In contrast, the second sentence has both a clear subject, *food processor,* and a controlling focus, *indispensable.* When we read this sentence, we naturally expect it to be followed by discussions that will explain why a food processor is in fact indispensable in one's kitchen. What tasks does it do well? Does it save time? Or eliminate waste? Such a topic sentence, with a clearly stated subject and focus, prepares the reader for the direction the paragraph is going to take.

A well-formulated topic sentence offers benefits to the writer as well, by providing a kind of blueprint that directs the development of the rest of the paragraph. Organizing paragraphs around topic sentences in your first draft can help you generate content for each paragraph by focusing your attention on the specific point that you must develop. And keeping your topic sentences in mind as you revise an essay is a way of checking that all the sentences in a paragraph really belong there.

6b

EXERCISE 2

Which of the following could make good topic sentences? Identify the subject and the specific focus of each. How might you develop those sentences into paragraphs?

1. Sunspots, magnetic storms on the sun's surface, are responsible for a number of important phenomena on earth.
2. Acquiring an inexpensive metal detector can be the start of a profitable hobby.
3. In most of the United States, the average annual rainfall is between 15 and 45 inches.
4. Montreal, the largest city in Canada, is also the second-largest French-speaking city in the world.
5. The most important requirement for a successful long-distance runner is not endurance but concentration.
6. Last July two friends and I went backpacking in the Smokey Mountains.
7. A person suffering from heatstroke must receive correct treatment swiftly.
8. The plays of Hrotswitha von Gandersheim, a tenth-century German nun, often suggest that she had a lively sense of humor.
9. Airmail service in the United States began in 1918.
10. *The Grapes of Wrath* is John Steinbeck's novel about dispossessed Oklahoma farmers.

2. Positioning a topic sentence

Topic sentences are often found near the beginnings of paragraphs. In this position, a topic sentence arouses expectations in the reader about the paragraph's development. A good paragraph satisfies those expectations with relevant, specific, convincing information.

The following paragraph, from the student essay at the end of Chapter **5**, illustrates the way in which a topic sentence placed at the beginning of a paragraph predicts the paragraph's development.

Topic sentence first

> *At sixteen, I was still under the authority of my parents, who in my estimation were unreasonably protective.* Every time I left the house, I would have to detail to my mother exactly where I was going, who I was going with, when I would be back. Walking out the door, I was invariably told to wear my seat belt, check for fire escapes, cross only at stoplights, stay clear of public rest rooms, and leave a phone number that I could be reached at. Even at Marcia and Jenny's age I had thought my mother's perpetual admonishments ridiculous, but as a teenager I deeply resented them. Specifically outlining my every plan to my parents was particularly irritating, and I had vowed repeatedly to myself that I would never place such demands on my own children.

6b

The focusing phrase here is *unreasonably protective,* and the writer goes on to develop that idea by clustering specific details from her experience around three main points:

Topic sentence: Parents were unreasonably protective

- Information she had to provide before leaving house
- Warnings her parents gave her as she left
- Her growing resentment as a teenager

Although the beginning of a paragraph is a natural place for focusing our thoughts, there is nothing sacred about starting a paragraph with a topic sentence. A topic sentence may be placed anywhere—after a transitional sentence, in the middle of a paragraph, or at the end as a kind of conclusion. When a topic sentence comes in the middle of a paragraph, it usually links the sentences that precede it with the material that follows it, as in this example.

Topic sentence in middle

> In the Western world, the person is synonymous with an individual inside a skin. And in northern Europe generally, the skin and even the clothes may be inviolate. You need permission to touch either if you are a stranger. This rule applies in some parts of France, where the mere touching of another person during an argument used to be legally defined

6b

as assault. *For the Arab the location of the person in relation to the body is quite different.* The person exists somewhere down inside the body. The ego is not completely hidden, however, because it can be reached very easily with an insult. It is protected from touch but not from words. The dissociation of the body and the ego may explain why the public amputation of a thief's hand is tolerated as standard punishment in Saudi Arabia.

—Edward T. Hall, *The Hidden Dimension*

This paragraph's opening sentences on Western ideas about personhood provide the context for the writer's subsequent explanation of the Arab conception of the person. The topic sentence—the fifth sentence—introduces the writer's main idea, the contrast between Western and Arab attitudes, with the focusing phrase *quite different.* We might outline the development of this paragraph in the following way:

- Western world views "person" and "body" as the same
- Even superficial physical contact may be considered a violation of the person

Topic sentence: Arab conception of "person" is different

- Person is deep inside the body
- Punishment of the body does not threaten the person within

When the topic sentence concludes a paragraph, it usually pulls together sentences that have led up to it. In these cases, the subject and focus of the paragraph are left implied until the reader reaches the topic sentence, as in the following paragraph.

Topic sentence last

Seen from an aeroplane high in the air, even the most gigantic skyscraper is only a tall stone block, a mere sculptural form, not a real building in which people can live. But as the plane descends from the great heights there will be one moment when the buildings change character completely. Suddenly they take on human scale, become houses for human beings like ourselves, not the tiny dolls observed from the heights. This strange transformation takes place at the instant when the contours of the buildings begin to rise above the horizon so that we get a side view of them instead of looking down on them. The buildings pass into a new stage of existence, become architecture in place of neat toys—for *architecture means shapes formed around [people], formed to be lived in, not merely to be seen from the outside.*

—Steen Eiler Rasmussen, *Experiencing Architecture*

This topic sentence could have been placed at the beginning of the paragraph, but by reserving it until the end the writer creates an effective sense of climax. We might outline the paragraph's structure like this:

6b

- Buildings are merely sculptural forms when viewed from far above
- Buildings become architecture when viewed in human scale, from the side

Topic sentence: Architecture means shapes formed to be lived in by human beings

The practice of constructing a paragraph around a focusing sentence is a useful one, but it's possible for a paragraph to be well unified even though it does not contain an explicit topic sentence. The important thing, though, is that its main idea must be evident to the reader. The following student paragraph, for instance, has no stated topic sentence, but its central idea is still clear.

Implied topic sentence

Classes at the medieval University of Paris began at 5 A.M. First on the agenda were the ordinary lectures, which were the regular and more important lectures. After several ordinary lectures and a short, begrudged lunch hour, students attended extraordinary lectures given in the afternoon. These were supplementary to the ordinary lectures and usually given by a less important teacher, who may not have been more than fourteen or fifteen years old. A student would spend ten or twelve hours a day with his teachers, and then following classes in the late afternoon, he had sports events. But after sports, the day was not over. There was homework, which consisted of copying, recopying, and memorizing notes while the light permitted. Nor was there much of a break. Christmas vacation was about three weeks, and summer vacation was only a month.

If we were to formulate a topic sentence for this paragraph, it might be something like, "The long school day at the medieval University of Paris made heavy demands on students." That's the idea clearly implied by the paragraph's development:

Implied topic sentence: Medieval school day made heavy demands

- Ordinary lectures from 5 A.M. till lunch
- Extraordinary lectures after lunch
- Sporting events in late afternoon
- Tedious homework until darkness fell

As you can see, an implied topic sentence works only when the development of your paragraph leaves no room for doubt about its point. Most of the time, you should probably make an effort to include a topic sentence somewhere in your paragraph, rather than risk leaving your reader uncertain about your main idea.

6b

EXERCISE 3

Identify the topic sentence in each of the following paragraphs. What subject and specific focus does it introduce? How do the rest of the sentences in the paragraph develop that idea?

1.   Violence as a way of achieving racial justice is both impractical and immoral. It is impractical because it is a descending spiral ending in destruction for all. The old law of an eye for an eye leaves everybody blind. It is immoral because it seeks to humiliate the opponent rather than win his understanding; it seeks to annihilate rather than to convert. Violence is immoral because it thrives on hatred rather than love. It destroys community and makes brotherhood impossible. It leaves society in monologue rather than dialogue. Violence ends by defeating itself. It creates bitterness in the survivors and brutality in the destroyers.

—Martin Luther King, Jr., *Stride toward Freedom*

2.   Commercial interruption is most damaging during that 10 per cent of programming (a charitable estimate) most important to the mind and spirit of a people: news and public affairs, and drama. To many (and among these are network news producers), commercials have no place or business during the vital process of informing the public. There is something obscene about a newscaster pausing to introduce a deodorant or shampoo commercial between the airplane crash and a body count. It is more than an interruption; it tends to reduce news to a form of running entertainment, to smudge the edges of reality by treating death or disaster or diplomacy on the same level as household appliances or a new gasoline.

—Marya Mannes, "The Splitting Image," *Saturday Review*

3.   All is not well for caves or cave dwellers in Missouri. Many serious problems now exist in the effort to preserve caves in their

original condition. Casual visitors often turn into vandals, breaking formations and chasing off the easily scared bat populations. In addition, holes and pits on the surface caused by natural cave collapses are being used as dumps, resulting in contamination of water systems in the caves. Another increasingly serious problem is the growing contamination of caves by septic tank drainage. The contamination of Devil's Icebox Cave by septic tanks, for example, has caused national groups such as the Sierra Club to organize a cave preservation program. Finally, the Army Corps of Engineers has been responsible for flooding hundreds of caves with its river-damming projects in the state.

—Scott Stayton [student]

6c

4.   Children often transform what should be a matter of nutrition into a question of self-determination. For some youngsters the benevolence of their parents' assertions that carrots are good for you, that they help you see in the dark, is lost in the suspicion that they are being tricked into tasting something nasty. Distrust flavors the carrots, they *do* taste unpleasant, and the child is even more adamantly opposed to eating them. The parents insist, the child resists, and battle lines are drawn. The issue is no longer whether vegetables are indeed good for you, but whose will power is to prevail. The ability to sustain her refusal becomes a matter of survival for the child. I recall that the longer I held out, the more I feared that giving in would topple my tower of autonomy. Those who would suggest that my parents simply were not authoritative enough underestimate the depth of my young conviction.

—Susan Young [student]

6c Adjusting paragraph length

Just as the structure of a paragraph is designed for the reader's benefit, so also the length of a paragraph is determined by its helpfulness to the reader. Indeed, we might say that the appropriate length of a paragraph is directly related to its structure. The key question is always: *How much evidence do you need to develop the idea in your topic sentence?* Pages consistently cluttered by short, underdeveloped paragraphs scatter the reader's attention and give the impression of a writer unable to think an idea through completely. On the other hand, if too many sentences are combined without paragraph indentations, the reader will have a difficult time isolating the writer's main ideas. Paragraphs that run consistently to more than a page are little better than no paragraphing at all, since they force the reader to do work that is the writer's responsibility.

Ordinarily, then, we might say that a paragraph should be longer than one sentence but shorter than a page. But note that the length of paragraphs varies considerably in different kinds of writing. In formal, scientific, or scholarly writing, paragraphs may be four hundred words or longer. In magazine articles, the average length is below two hundred words. In newspapers, paragraph breaks occur even more frequently— every fifty words or so—in order to maximize white space in the narrow columns of text. If you're in doubt about the length of a paragraph you're working on, ask yourself the questions about structure that we discussed above:

1. What is the main idea in this paragraph?
2. Have I provided enough evidence, detail, or discussion to develop it to my reader's satisfaction?
3. Have I included irrelevant material that should be moved to another paragraph or discarded?

1.   Using a short paragraph for emphasis

Occasionally, you may want to use a very short paragraph to call attention to an important shift in the line of thought or to emphasize a crucial point. Such paragraphs are effective but should be used carefully and sparingly. Notice in the following example that the student might have joined his short paragraph to either of the others. He chose instead to make the two sentences into a separate transitional paragraph and thus to stress the importance of his early training and the shock he was to receive.

Brief transitional paragraph for emphasis

. . . I know from personal experience the truth of Erich Fromm's criticism that the American male is forced to repress his feelings. Our society does tend to suspect emotional outbursts in a man as signs of "abnormality." From childhood onward, I was taught to "control" my emotions. I was told constantly that good little boys don't cry; they act like big strong men. The little boy who fell off his tricycle and got up with a smile was admired and recommended as a model to be emulated by the rest of the tricycle set. Nor were feelings of pain the only emotion I was encouraged to suppress. Anger, hostility, envy, and melancholy were all taboo, and this training was almost impossible to resist.

By the age of thirteen, I was a true believer in this Spartan code. It was at this age that I was first startled into doubting it.

My uncle had been ill but had kept this fact secret from . . .

2. Paragraphing dialogue

6c

In a narrative, any direct quotation, together with the rest of a sentence of which it is a part, is paragraphed separately. The reason for this convention is to make immediately clear to the reader the change of speaker.

Speakers paragraphed separately

"But 'glory' doesn't mean 'a nice knock-down argument,'" Alice objected.

"When *I* use a word," Humpty Dumpty said, in a rather scornful tone, "it means what I choose it to mean—neither more nor less."

"The question is," said Alice, "whether you *can* make words mean so many different things."

"The question is," said Humpty Dumpty, "which is to be master—that's all."

—Lewis Carroll, *Through the Looking-Glass*

The same convention is usually observed in cases where the speaker is not named each time.

Unidentified speakers paragraphed separately

"Would you like to go to South America, Jake?" he asked.

"No."

"Why not?"

"I don't know. I never wanted to go. Too expensive. You can see all the South Americans you want in Paris anyway."

"They're not the real South Americans."

"They look awfully real to me."

—Ernest Hemingway, *The Sun Also Rises*

However, brief dialogue that is closely related to the narration may be included within a paragraph.

Short dialogue included in paragraph

> Now and then Mr. Bixby called my attention to certain things. Said he, "This is Six-Mile Point." I assented. It was pleasant enough information but I could not see the bearing of it. I was not conscious that it was a matter of any interest to me. Another time he said, "This is Nine-Mile Point." Later he said, "This is Twelve-Mile Point." They were all about level with the water's edge; they all looked alike to me; they were monotonously unpicturesque. I hoped Mr. Bixby would change the subject.

> —Mark Twain, "Old Times on the Mississippi"

6d

6d Controlling paragraphs within an essay

Rarely are we called on to write a single, isolated paragraph. More often, we have to be able to develop and control individual paragraphs in the context of a longer composition. In the following essay, the student writer demonstrates just such a firm sense of paragraph unity and appropriate paragraph length. Considered separately, each paragraph here makes a clear point, developed with specific details that interest and satisfy us. But the paragraphs of this essay also fit together neatly, leading us as readers through the writer's experiences and his reflections on them. The result is an effective piece of writing, well organized and complete. (The paragraphs in this essay have been numbered for easy reference in Exercise 4.)

I Surrendered

1. Social order, it is said, can only be maintained through the restriction and prohibition of our often whimsical impulses (taking off from school or work, swimming nude, indulging in casual sex). Thus we find ourselves inhibited by a civilization that was supposed to ensure our well-being. Parents, public opinion, and the law condition us to keep the lid tightly clamped on our drives for free and outward expression of inner needs: we are made to stop and evaluate our actions and thoughts and to feel guilty when they are not acceptable. And because this guilt often makes us tense and ill at ease, we give up and submit. This guilt is what I understand Freud to be describing in *Civilization and Its Discontents,* and it is what I learned to be a melancholy truth when I went hitchhiking up the West Coast with my sleeping bag and thoughts of being free to do what I wanted.

2.   My hitchhiking trip with a white friend from Long Beach to Canada was plagued by social pressure even before it began. Two weeks before we started, reports over the news about hitchhikers being axed in their sleeping bags, as well as drivers being robbed, beaten, or killed, did not make our trip sound like a good idea to my family. My family was also concerned that reports like these make drivers hesitant to stop for anyone unless they have a gun under the seat. That was just the beginning, though. I could have handled the fears others had for me, but the guilt I was made to feel was harder to cope with.

6d

3.   My brother-in-law and I had a long discussion about the dangers of hitchhiking. The list was a frightening one that included the possibility I might be hassled and jailed by the police or be robbed and stranded. I felt quite guilty about running off and frolicking around while everyone worried about me, and this guilt took some of the pleasure—the thrill, day-to-day suspense, and excitement—out of the trip. Instead, it made me wary and insecure.

4.   My brother-in-law and I also discussed the fact that very few blacks hitchhike in the live-on-the-road manner I was about to, which means sleeping in forests, communes, or freeway shrubbery, or going into strange towns and meeting all kinds of people. He suggested that if tension in any given situation forced a serious racial confrontation, my friend would surely turn to the safe side and against me. This kept me wondering all through the trip, and to my dismay, kept me looking for hints of racism in him. My new suspicions cast a shadow over the trip and added to the guilt I was already feeling.

5.   Hitchhiking is illegal in California, but the law is not usually enforced if the hitchhikers stay on the curb. We carefully heeded this policy and had no problems at all until just south of San Luis Obispo, where we were searched for weapons. There we were insulted by a pair of California Highway Patrol officers while they went over us. Among the many insults was the one directed at me, asking me who I was going to rape next. But, knowing how public opinion would side with the police if we retaliated, we kept our mouths closed. We knew that if the police reported subduing a couple of wandering, violent hippies, then the stereotype of the hippie (shiftless young bums begging for food and for money to buy drugs with) would justify the police in the public's view and set people's minds at ease. So we checked our natural impulse to fight back, but we were angry with ourselves for having to do so. We felt guilty for not standing up for our rights.

6. Even with that episode behind us, the rest of the trip didn't bring me the sense of freedom I'd hoped for. The possible presence of dope in the cars of the young people who picked us up made me uneasy. But not my friend. He indulged heavily in marijuana all the way up the coast whenever he could get some. I knew that if we were arrested for dope it would go on my record, damage my chances in the future, and hurt my family badly. One morning, near Eureka, California, my friend and another hiker who joined up with us smoked as much marijuana as they could hold. I was fearful that a band of night-roaming vigilantes would swarm on us and take us away. Later, in Canada, I felt guilty the very first time I got in line for a feed-in. I was self-conscious because the food was paid for by Canadian taxpayers and was meant for needy people. We had enough money to buy food.

7. It now seems that everything we did, beginning with the very thought of hitchhiking, was meant to prove we weren't as trapped as the people we left behind. But when it came to the wild, free expression of inner drives, I couldn't throw off the wet blanket of society. I couldn't even go skinny-dipping in the Russian River because there were people around and I was afraid of what they might think if I stripped. We loved Canada and its forests, but we came back. Even though the air and water were like nectar in comparison to those of Los Angeles, we returned to the smog and noise and people. We discarded the forests, rivers, and meadows for the benefits and security of our social surroundings. I surrendered.

—Samuel Reece [student]

EXERCISE 4

Reread Samuel Reece's essay "I Surrendered" (above) and consider the following questions.

1. What is Reece's thesis statement?
2. How do the final sentences of paragraph 2 provide a transition to paragraph 3?
3. Why has Reece separated paragraphs 3 and 4, both of which involve his brother-in-law's advice?
4. What is the topic sentence in paragraph 5? In paragraph 6? How does Reece develop each of these topic sentences?
5. How does Reece link his concluding paragraph with his introduction?

7 *Developing Paragraphs*

What happens in a paragraph—the form that its contents assume—is often determined by the subject itself. If you are writing out a description of an automobile accident for your insurance company, you will probably let chronological order dictate the structure of your material (signaled left turn, waited for traffic light to change, started across intersection, suddenly saw other car coming through red light). On the other hand, if you are discussing two political candidates in your school newspaper, you might find your paragraphs taking shape around comparisons of the candidates' positions on several key issues. In short, in words that the great American architect Louis Sullivan wrote a century ago, "Form follows function."

Sometimes, however, the subject you are writing about may not arrange itself on your page with inevitable clarity and logic. For these occasions, it's useful to be acquainted with a number of basic patterns of paragraph development. Readers unconsciously expect to be able to discern such patterns and may be confused by a paragraph whose sentences seem to be pointed in no clear direction. Controlling patterns of paragraph development, therefore, is another way of making your writing more effective by satisfying your readers' expectations.

Before we consider some widely used methods of paragraph development, though, a caution and a hint. The important caution to keep in mind about these strategies is that, in actual practice, they are rarely used independently of one another. Instead, they naturally and inevitably overlap; development by examples, for instance, also implies development by detail. Thus, you should probably regard these patterns less as a set of alternatives than as a master list of techniques to select from and combine freely.

The hint: you should consider these approaches not simply as ways of *arranging* the contents of a paragraph, but also as ways of *generating* content both for paragraphs and for entire essays. In this sense, these strategies resemble the methods of discovering ideas that we discussed in Chapter **2** (indeed, you'll probably recognize occasional overlap with the structured methods of discovery in **2b**). Phrased as questions, they can help you reveal new and potentially interesting angles of your subject to write about:

- With what specific details can I describe X?
- In what order did the events surrounding X occur?
- What examples of X do I have?
- How can I define X?
- How can I classify types of X?
- What components or examples of X can I compare?
- What is X analogous to?
- What are the causes and consequences of X?

7a   Development by specific detail

A paragraph lacking specific detail may strike a reader as dull and uninspired, even though its central idea is clear. Part of every writer's obligation is to supply the details necessary to support a paragraph's main idea. As a writer, you need to be able to distinguish between paragraphs that make effective use of detail and paragraphs that only seem to be developed specifically, but in reality offer little precise information that would move a reader to accept your argument or share your perspective.

Writing with specific detail begins with recalling as precisely as possible the event to be described and then re-creating the taste, touch, sound, and sight with carefully chosen words. Often a paragraph can be dramatically improved by the simple substitution of specific details for generalities, without further revision. For example, in the two versions of the paragraph below, taken from a student essay about a senior class trip to Florida, notice how the writer has increased the effectiveness of his writing without adding significantly to its length, just by substituting specific details. The italicized passages indicate where changes have been made.

Vague original

When we left our high-school parking lot that Saturday morning, no one was prepared for the discomforts of the trip ahead. We did a variety of things to pass the time, but monotony soon crept in. Also, I became cramped from sitting for long periods of time. When night finally came, we slept sitting up in our seats. Some slept on the aisle floors, where food and drinks had been spilled.

7a

Topic sentence: No one was prepared for the discomforts of the trip

- Unsuccessful attempts to overcome monotony
- Uncomfortable seats
- Poor sleeping conditions

Revised with detail

When *the Greyhound bus roared out* of our high-school parking lot *at 6:30* that Saturday morning, no one was prepared for the discomforts of the trip ahead. For a while we *sang songs and played cards* to pass the time, but monotony soon crept in. Also, after *seven or eight hours of sitting in the same seat,* I became stiff and cramped. When night finally came, most of us *dozed restlessly* sitting up in our seats, while others *huddled* on the *narrow* aisle floors where *potato chips* and *Coke* had been spilled.

Of course, specific details in a paragraph must also be relevant to the writer's purpose. They must be *selected,* not merely inventoried. Details become boring—mere padding—when the writer confuses quantity with quality. For example, if an American student were asked by his Polish correspondent what a "drugstore" is, the American should not try to explain it by listing every type of cold tablet, sleeping pill, foot powder, lipstick, face cream, shaving lotion, writing implement, cigarette, candy, and magazine that it sells. But neither would it be helpful for him to write back simply that a drugstore fills prescriptions and sells medical supplies and cosmetics. Instead, the American might begin with such a definition and then explain that "medical supplies" *range from* cough syrups to allergy tablets, and that cosmetics *include* eye shadow, fingernail polish, and cologne. Such an approach would effectively suggest the variety and specialization of items available in a drugstore without the tedium of an exhaustive list.

7b   Development by narration

Narrating events—reporting what happened, and in what sequence—is part of our daily interaction with other people. Effective written narration depends on the exact selection of details, arranged in such a way that a reader can easily follow the order of the events in question.

Sometimes a paragraph of narration includes a topic sentence that focuses its development around a specific idea. In the following paragraph, for example, the focusing word is *grandiose.*

> In fourth grade I embarked upon a grandiose reading program. "Give me the names of important books," I would say to startled teachers. They soon found out that I had in mind "adult books." I ignored their suggestion of anything I suspected was written for children. (Not until I was in college, as a result, did I read *Huckleberry Finn* or *Alice's Adventures in Wonderland.*) Instead, I read *The Scarlet Letter* and Franklin's *Autobiography*. And whatever I read I read for extra credit. Each time I finished a book, I reported the achievement to a teacher and basked in the praise my effort earned. Despite my best efforts, however, there seemed to be more and more books I needed to read. At the library I would literally tremble as I came upon whole shelves of books I hadn't read.
>
> —Richard Rodriguez, *Hunger of Memory*

Topic sentence: I embarked upon a grandiose reading program

- Startled teachers by requesting important books
- Refused to read anything written for children
- Reported achievements and basked in praise
- Trembled at shelves of books remaining to be read

But a paragraph developed by narration doesn't always need a thematic focus, or even a topic sentence, to hold it together. Chronology alone may be sufficient. The paragraph below, describing the Battle of Hastings between King Harold of England and William of Normandy in 1066, has no topic sentence; its unity and coherence arise from the precise time markers that the writer has inserted to orient us to the sequence of events.

> Bringing his troops south again with all possible speed, Harold arrived in London on October 6. Five days later, having collected all the reinforce-

7c

ments he could muster under his banner, he marched south for the Sussex Downs, where he hoped to take William by surprise and to cut him off from his ships, which lay at anchor at Hastings. As it happened, it was Harold who was caught by surprise. Riding out of Hastings early on the morning of October 14, William and his knights came in sight of Harold's infantry near Telham Hill at nine o'clock. The Normans advanced on the attack immediately, before the small English army was even drawn up in battle array. It was a hard-fought battle, in which the Normans had to throw in one mounted attack after another against the English front, but at the end of the day Harold was killed, and his remaining followers fled from the field.

—Christopher Hibbert, *Tower of London*

[No topic sentence]

- October 6: Harold arrived in London
- Five days later: marched south toward Sussex Downs
- October 14, nine o'clock: surprised by William and his knights near Telham Hill
- At end of day: killed after hard-fought battle

7c Development by examples

An example is a member of a larger class or category, chosen to illustrate the class to which it belongs. Typically, the topic sentence of a paragraph developed by examples introduces the class that the writer wishes to develop. In this paragraph, for example, the class to be illustrated is "sources of contaminants."

Many contaminants contribute to air pollution inside offices, and they have a variety of sources. The worst offender, for smokers and non-smokers alike, is ambient cigarette smoke, which contains benzene, formaldehyde and other carcinogens. Wet-process copiers give off odorless hydrocarbons, causing fatigue and skin irritations. Dry-process copiers leak ozone, an irritant to the eyes and respiratory tract. Computer screens exude low levels of radiation.

—Susan Gilbert, "Hazards of the Toxic Office," *Science Digest*

Topic sentence: Contaminants in office air have a variety of sources

- Cigarette smoke contains benzene, formaldehyde, and other carcinogens

- Wet-process copiers give off odorless hydrocarbons
- Dry-process copiers leak ozone
- Computer screens exude radiation

The four sources of office air pollution mentioned here are not all that could be cited. Rather, they are typical members of the class, presumably selected in this case because of their prevalence and importance.

Often examples are introduced in a paragraph with the transitions *for example* or *for instance*. But even without these transitional markers, the structure of a paragraph developed by examples should be evident to a reader if the category that the examples illustrate is clearly stated at the outset. In the following paragraph, the illustrated category is "remedies [that] meet the test of modern scientific medicine."

> Undoubtedly many of the witch-healers' remedies were purely magical, such as the use of amulets and charms, but others meet the test of modern scientific medicine. They had effective painkillers, digestive aids, and anti-inflammatory agents. They used ergot for the pain of labor at a time when the Church held that pain in labor was the Lord's just punishment for Eve's original sin. Ergot derivatives are still used today to hasten labor and aid in the recovery from childbirth. Belladonna—still used today as an antispasmodic—was used by the witch-healers to inhibit uterine contractions when miscarriage threatened. Digitalis, still an important drug in treating heart ailments, is said to have been discovered by an English witch.
>
> —Barbara Ehrenreich and Deirdre English, *For Her Own Good: 150 Years of the Experts' Advice to Women*

Topic sentence: Some witch-healers' remedies meet the test of modern scientific medicine

- Ergot used for the pain of labor
- Belladonna used to prevent miscarriage
- Digitalis discovered by an English witch

7d   Development by definition

In informal logic, definition involves referring a term to a general class of related elements (its genus), and then distinguishing it from others in that class. Before examining definition as a method of paragraph development, we should perhaps explain this basic use of the term.

To take a simple example, we would begin defining a pen by classifying it as a "writing instrument." However, since the class "writing instrument" also includes a number of other elements—pencils, felt markers, typewriters, to name just a few—we would have to go one step further and differentiate it from these and other members of the class. A pen, we might therefore continue, is "a writing instrument that makes use of a hard point and a colored fluid."

7d

Term	Class	Differentiation
pen	writing instrument	makes use of a hard point and colored fluid
pencil	writing instrument	with a core of solid-state material like graphite inside a wooden or plastic case

A description of an object can include all kinds of specific details— the pencil has a chewed end and is coated with yellow paint embossed with the motto "Quinn's Lumber Yard"—but these details are irrelevant to the definition of the term. Similarly, examples do not by themselves constitute a definition, although they may help to clarify one. To say that a Dixon Ticonderoga No. 2 Soft is an example of a pencil is not the same as specifying what the meaning of the term *pencil* is.

You may be able to define an unfamiliar term in a sentence by apposition, that is, by following the term with a word or phrase that clarifies its meaning:

Simple definition by apposition

The x-ray showed a crack in the *tibia,* or *shinbone.*

Please analyze the importance of the *denouement—the final unraveling or outcome of the plot*—in Lord Jim.

Tonight the moon will be in *apogee,* that is, *at the point in its orbit farthest from the earth.*

But when you are dealing with complex terms or terms used in a special sense, you may have to devote a paragraph or more to definition. The following student paragraph illustrates such an **extended defini-**

7d

tion. The writer first classifies Sarah Woodruff and Clarissa Dalloway as belonging to the class of people whom she labels "heroic." Then, to differentiate her subjects' heroism from that of others in the class, she rejects one set of meanings for the term (control and domination) and presents another (sensitivity, endurance, independence.) She closes the paragraph with examples that show how each of her subjects meets this definition of "heroic."

> The central characters in John Fowles's *The French Lieutenant's Woman* and Virginia Woolf's *Mrs. Dalloway* are women who embody certain heroic qualities that set them apart from what one character calls "the great niminypiminy flock of women in general." These two women, Sarah Woodruff and Clarissa Dalloway, are not heroic in the traditional masculine, aggressive sense of the word. They do not seek to control or to dominate but to cultivate a sensitivity, to endure, and to remain free of masculine narrow-mindedness. They possess a power that allows them to remain open to the compelling vitality of life. Their heroism is their ability to be responsive to reality, to feel even if it entails suffering and uncertainty; and this heroism spurs others on to live in the presence of life, with all its beauty and terror. Sarah is a free woman, and through her sensitivity, forbearance, and courage, she liberates Charles, a man caught in the petrifying forces of Victorian society, preoccupied with duty and piety. Clarissa Dalloway's radiant, vital presence at her party, a ritual of community, helps to liberate her guests from their shells of individual solitude and memory. It is in this sense and these ways that they are heroic.

Topic sentence: Sarah Woodruff and Clarissa Dalloway embody heroic
    qualities
- Not in the masculine, aggressive sense of the word
- But in their sensitivity and openness to the compelling vitality
  of life
  - Sarah Woodruff liberates Charles from duty and piety
  - Clarissa Dalloway liberates party guests from shells of solitude
    and memory

A few rules apply to the writing of all definitions, simple and extended. First, avoid circular definitions, that is, the use of the term being defined in the definition itself. "Democracy is the democratic process" and "An astronomer is one who studies astronomy" are both circular definitions. When words are defined in terms of themselves, no one's understanding is improved.

Second, avoid definition composed of long lists of synonyms. When a paragraph begins, "By education, I mean to give knowledge, develop character, improve taste, draw out, train, lead," the readers know they are in for the shotgun treatment. The writer has indiscriminately blasted a load of abstract items at them, hoping one will hit. Precision and thoughtfulness are more important to a good definition than sheer volume.

7e

Third, avoid loaded definitions, definitions that rely on evocative or inflammatory language. Their purpose is usually emotional impact rather than clarity. The negative phrasing of a definition like "Euthanasia is the outright murder of a helpless human being" makes the writer's bias unmistakable. Conversely, "By euthanasia I mean merciful intervention in a fellow human being's suffering" is a definition heavy with positive suggestions. Such judgments—for that is what they are—are sometimes used for powerful effect in persuasion but they do not lead toward clarification if offered as definitions.

7e   Development by classification

A writer using classification to develop a paragraph enumerates and describes the main divisions of a subject, either for clarification or as an introduction to further discussion. Underlying classification is the notion that the elements of any large group—classic cars, college students, home computers—can be divided into a number of subgroups ("There are three basic types of X"), and that the classification will better help us understand the category as a whole. In the following paragraph, for example, the noted anthropologist Margaret Mead uses classification to lead us to a new perspective on the concept of "culture."

The distinctions I am making among three different kinds of culture— *postfigurative*, in which children learn primarily from their forebears, *cofigurative*, in which both children and adults learn from their peers, and *prefigurative*, in which adults learn also from their children—are a reflection of the period in which we live. Primitive societies and small religious and ideological enclaves are primarily postfigurative, deriving authority from the past. Great civilizations, which necessarily have developed techniques for incorporating change, characteristically make use of some form of cofigurative learning from peers, playmates, fellow students, and fellow apprentices. We are now entering a period, new in history, in which the young are taking on new authority in their prefigurative apprehension of the still unknown future.

—Margaret Mead, *Culture and Commitment*

Topic sentence: Cultures may be divided into three types

- In postfigurative cultures, authority derives from the past
- In cofigurative cultures, learning is exchanged among peers
- In prefigurative cultures, the young apprehend a still unknown future

Mead's paragraph illustrates a number of the principles of classification. First, a classification makes sense only if the things being classified are grouped according to some clearly understood principle or feature. For ease in record keeping, a college typically classifies its students according to a number of different principles: year of study, major, place of residence (dormitory, fraternity/sorority house, off-campus apartment, parents' home, etc.), to name just a few. Such classifications provide a useful means of organizing data, but a classification is usually worth writing about at length only if it also helps us understand something more fully or more clearly. Margaret Mead classifies cultures according to the sources of their members' education, and by doing so she gives us an important new perspective on some differences between our own culture and others that have preceded us.

The second feature of a successful classification is that it is exhaustive; that is, all the members of the larger group must fit into one or another of the categories of the classification. A college's students could not be classified sensibly as history majors, psychology majors, and music majors unless the college offered only these three fields of study. The three categories in Mead's paragraph illustrate the exhaustiveness necessary to a successful classification: societies are either postfigurative, cofigurative, or prefigurative; there are no other possibilities.

You routinely use classification every time you sort your laundry, plan a shopping trip, or organize the papers on your desk. Classification also becomes an important pattern of organization for writing when it helps you lead your readers to a new understanding of a complex subject.

7f Development by comparison or contrast

When we wish to point out the similarities or differences between two subjects, comparison or contrast is the logical method of development. The writer of an effective comparison/contrast paragraph indicates at the start the two subjects that will be treated and organizes the details related to each in a way that is easy for the reader to follow.

Comparisons are usually structured in one of two basic ways. In the first, known as an **alternating comparison,** the writer switches back and forth between two subjects throughout the paragraph, creating for the reader a point-by-point comparison based on specific aspects of the two subjects. The writer of the following paragraph, for instance, uses an alternating structure to compare books and films.

> There are other ways in which our freedom of choice is more limited with respect to film. While reading a book, we can imagine things quite freely even within the limits set by the description of the writer. Before *Gone with the Wind* was adapted to film, readers could picture Rhett Butler however they wished, although presumably basing that picture on the descriptions provided by Margaret Mitchell. But from the release of that movie on, Rhett Butler will always look like Clark Gable; indeed, that will be hardly less so even for readers who have never seen the film, so famous has that portrayal become. When we read Mary Shelley's novel *Frankenstein,* we may or may not be able to overcome the visual image imposed by all the movie *Frankenstein* monsters. But when we see the film *Frankenstein,* it is impossible for us to overcome the visual image; that is all there is, it is right in front of us, and we cannot make it any different. Moreover, a film can only show us what can be shown; the eye can only see what can be seen by the eye, a limitation not shared by the mind's eye.
>
> —Morris Beja, *Film and Literature: An Introduction*

Topic sentence: Film limits our imagination more than books do

- Book version of *Gone with the Wind* allowed readers to picture Rhett Butler however they wished
- Film version of *Gone with the Wind* has forever linked Rhett Butler and Clark Gable

- Book version of *Frankenstein* may enable us to create our own visual image of the monster
- Film version of *Frankenstein* limits our imagination to the image on the screen

7f

The first two sentences in this paragraph indicate that a comparison between films and books is to follow, and the words *more limited* and *imagine* specify the basis of the comparison. Beja alternates between books and films in the rest of the paragraph because his point—that films impose limitations on the imagination that books do not—can best be illustrated by juxtaposing specific books and their film adaptations.

In the second type of comparison, called **divided comparison,** a writer deals fully with the first subject before turning to the second, thereby dividing the paragraph approximately in half. This approach works well when the subjects cannot be compared on a point-by-point basis and the writer is more interested in describing each at length. In the following divided comparison, the beginning of a longer paragraph, E. B. White reflects on one of the changes that have occurred at his favorite lake since he visited the place as a boy.

> Peace and goodness and jollity. The only thing that was wrong now, really, was the sound of the place, an unfamiliar nervous sound of the outboard motors. This was the note that jarred, the one thing that would sometimes break the illusion and set the years moving. In those other summertimes all motors were inboard; and when they were at a little distance, the noise they made was a sedative, an ingredient of summer sleep. They were one-cylinder and two-cylinder engines, and some were make-and-break and some were jump-spark, but they all made a sleepy sound across the lake. The one-lungers throbbed and fluttered, and the twin-cylinder ones purred and purred, and that was a quiet sound, too. But now the campers all had outboards. In the daytime, in the hot mornings, these motors made a petulant, irritable sound; at night, in the still evening when the afterglow lit the water, they whined about one's ears like mosquitoes. . . .
>
> —E. B. White, "Once More to the Lake," *Collected Essays*

[Implied topic sentence: The new outboard motors were less agreeable than the earlier inboard ones]

- Inboard motors
  - Made a sleepy sound
  - Throbbed, fluttered, purred
- Outboard motors
  - Made a petulant, irritable sound
  - Whined like mosquitoes

Although this paragraph lacks an explicit topic sentence, White's opening sentences introduce the subject of the paragraph, outboard motors, and clearly suggest the comparison that is to follow ("only thing that was wrong now," "unfamiliar nervous sound"). Structurally, the paragraph hinges on the transition *but* at the beginning of the seventh sentence, which divides it into two parts, the first describing the agreeable sounds of the old inboard motors, the second expressing White's mild annoyance with the newer and noisier outboards.

7g

7g Development by analogy

One special type of comparison is analogy, a comparison between two essentially unlike things, one familiar to the reader, the other unfamiliar. As a method of illustration, a clever analogy can sometimes make a difficult concept easier to understand. In the following student paragraph, for example, the writer was faced with the problem of showing how the characters in William Faulkner's short story "Spotted Horses" could continue to admire and tolerate a man who continually fleeced them. To solve this problem, the student used the apt analogy of a game of pool with Willie Hoppe, for many years the world champion.

"That Flem Snopes," says the narrator. "I be dog if he ain't a case now." The townspeople had respect for a good horse trader and Flem Snopes was that. Since money was of grotesque importance to these people who had to dig for every penny, they admired a man who could come by it easily and cleverly. Ironically, when Flem skinned someone of his last nickel and kept the fact to himself, the people would interpret Flem's silence as sheer modesty, while the victim laughed off as hopeless any thought of retribution. Their admiration for and toleration of Flem is not hard to understand. It was like a game of pool in which you lose so decisively to Willie Hoppe that you feel no bitterness—merely a sense of pride and awe at having played the master at all. After Willie has beaten you and quietly taken off the stakes, you admit sheepishly to others you were licked before you started and put the cue back on the rack instead of taking it into some dark alley to wait for Willie. Most people didn't even try to beat the time-honored master, Flem Snopes, at his game of swindling.

- Townspeople admired Flem's ability to acquire money so easily
- His victims laughed off any thought of retribution

Topic sentence: The people's admiration for and toleration of Flem was like the attitude of someone who had lost a game of pool to Willie Hoppe

- You feel pride and awe at having played the master at all
- You admit sheepishly that you were licked before you started

Professional writers often use analogy to make difficult technical or abstract ideas accessible to the average reader, and they take care, while developing their paragraphs, to be sure that the readers regard the analogies as illustrations, not proofs. In developing the following paragraph on theories of gravitation, for example, Lincoln Barnett refers to his analogy as "this little fable."

The distinction between Newton's and Einstein's ideas about gravitation has sometimes been illustrated by picturing a little boy playing marbles in a city lot. The ground is very uneven. An observer in an office ten stories above the street would not be able to see these irregularities in the ground. Noticing that the marbles appear to avoid some sections of the ground and move toward other sections, he might assume that a [semimagnetic] "force" was operating which repelled the marbles from certain spots and attracted them toward others. But another observer on the ground would instantly perceive that the path of the marbles was simply governed by the curvature of the field. In this little fable Newton is the upstairs observer who imagines that a "force" is at work, and Einstein is the observer on the ground, who has no reason to make such an assumption. Einstein's gravitational laws, therefore, merely describe the field properties of the space-time continuum. . . .

—Lincoln Barnett, *The Universe and Dr. Einstein*

[Implied topic sentence: The difference between Newton's and Einstein's ideas about gravity is like the difference between two perspectives on a game of marbles]

- Newton's perspective: from ten stories up
  - Attributes movement of marbles to unseen forces repelling and attracting them
- Einstein's perspective: at ground level
  - Recognizes that path of marbles is governed by curvature of playing surface

7h   Development by cause and effect   7h

In a paragraph developed by cause and effect, a writer stresses the connections between a result or results and the preceding events. Some cause-and-effect paragraphs are primarily persuasive. Their purpose is to make the reader feel the forcefulness of the writer's conclusions, or at least see the grounds for those conclusions. Other cause-and-effect paragraphs are essentially explanatory. They are intended to help a reader understand a necessary relationship between causes and effects.

A cause-and-effect paragraph may begin by stating an effect and then explaining its causes, or it may open with a cause and go on to explore its various effects.

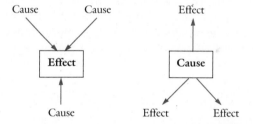

More often, however, causes and effects are intermingled in a subtler way, as in the following paragraph about television's influence on politics.

While the public and politicians are often blamed for being more concerned with images than with issues, the image bias may be inherent in the way we now get political information. Through television, we come to feel we "know" politicians personally, and our response to them has become similar to our response to friends and lovers. Just as we would not marry someone on the basis of a résumé or a writing sample, so are we now unwilling to choose Presidents merely on the basis of their stands on the issues. We want, instead, to know what they are "really like." However, the current drive toward intimacy with our leaders involves a fundamental paradox. In pursuing our desire to be close to great people or to confirm their greatness through increased exposure, we destroy the distance that enabled them to appear great in the first place.

> —Joshua Meyrowitz, "Politics in the Video Eye:
> Where Have All the Heroes Gone?" *Psychology Today*

7i

Topic sentence: The emphasis on image is inherent in the way we get political information

- Television has made us feel that we "know" politicians personally
  - We want to know more than their stands on issues
  - We want to know what they are "really like"
- This intimacy has replaced the distance that enabled our leaders to appear great

Two pairs of causes and effects are explored in this paragraph. The first sentence states an effect (the emphasis on political "image") whose cause (television's ability to make us feel close to politicians) is explained in the three sentences that follow. The last two sentences introduce a related issue: our desire for intimate knowledge of our leaders, Meyrowitz points out, is a cause whose ultimate effect is the collapse of their appearance of greatness. Such sophisticated analysis demands careful thinking as well as precise control of a paragraph's structure and organization.

7i A more typical case: combined methods of development

As we said at the start of this chapter, most writers find themselves using a combination of the methods of development that we have been discussing. To illustrate this point, we have separated the following long paragraph into segments developed in turn by definition, contrast, and example.

Topic

I never have much confidence in people who talk a great deal about "their image" or "so-and-so's image"; they make me wonder if they even care about what the real thing is.

Definition

By image, I don't mean an accurate copy or truthful likeness. I mean, rather, the same thing that PR types, bureaucrats, and political managers too often mean: a counterfeit, a phony projection, a manipulated picture intended to give the illusion of actuality.

Contrast

7i

In daily situations where actual performances can be judged and experienced firsthand, rather ordinary ones like house painting or plumbing, no one spends much time worrying about the image of the performer. These performers are very different from the rigged ones on TV: either the walls are smoothly rolled and the faucets are fixed, or they aren't; the painter or plumber is competent or not so competent. But in some parts of our society, we are not even supposed to think about the reality as long as the image is "good."

Example

Recently, while watching a talk show, I was struck by one guest, a candidate for office, who kept harping on our need for "the image of strong leadership." The more he dwelled on his opponent's failure to project such an image, the more I wondered what policies the speaker stood for, what he would do if elected. And when he defended his expensive media blitz as part of "getting my image across" to the voters . . .

A good paragraph is a "bounding line" that encloses its own distinct material. The phrase belongs to the artist and poet William Blake: "The great and golden rule of art, as well as of life, is this: That the more distinct, sharp, and wirey the bounding line, the more perfect the work of art. . . . How do we distinguish the oak from the beech . . . one face or countenance from another, but by the bounding line and its infinite inflexions and movements? . . . Leave out this line, and you leave out life itself: all is chaos again."

EXERCISE 1

Write two different paragraphs on one of the topics below. In the first, make the diction as vague and general as you can. In your second paragraph on the subject, substitute specific detail to make your description vivid and interesting.

1. An ideal campsite
2. A teacher who cannot sit still or stay in one place

7i

3. Subway or bus passengers late at night
4. A public swimming pool on a hot day
5. The amusement section of a fair or carnival
6. A student trying to stay awake in class
7. Your best friend's room
8. A persistent salesperson
9. A man or woman shopping for clothes
10. A college dining room at noon

EXERCISE 2

Write a paragraph developed by narration on one of the subjects below, or another subject of your choice. Begin by listing points you might include and, if possible, formulating a topic sentence.

1. The process by which you selected your college or university
2. The way you usually go about writing a paper
3. The stages in which your friendship with another person developed
4. The last time you found yourself in an embarrassing situation
5. The last time you were pleased with what you had accomplished

EXERCISE 3

Write a paragraph developed by examples on one of the subjects below, or another subject of your choice. Begin by listing points you might include and formulating a topic sentence.

1. The sameness of fast-food restaurants
2. A new trend in popular music
3. Lack of understanding among people
4. Overlooked problems in our society
5. Creativity

EXERCISE 4

Write a paragraph developed by definition on one of the subjects below, or another subject of your choice. Begin by listing points you might include and formulating a topic sentence.

1. Satisfaction
2. Commitment
3. Masculinity
4. Femininity
5. Concern for others
6. Propaganda
7. Caution
8. Neatness
9. Challenge
10. Anxiety

EXERCISE **5**

Write a paragraph developed by classification on one of the subjects below, or another of your choice. Begin by listing points you might include and formulating a topic sentence.

1. Relatives
2. Summer jobs
3. Extracurricular activities
4. Desires
5. Decisions

EXERCISE **6**

Write a paragraph developed by comparison or contrast on one of the subjects below, or another of your choice. Begin by listing points you might include and formulating a topic sentence.

1. Discussing and arguing
2. Two close friends
3. Photography and painting
4. High-school and college computer courses
5. Yourself and your brother or sister

EXERCISE **7**

Write a paragraph developed by cause-and-effect analysis on one of the subjects below, or another subject of your choice. Begin by listing points you might include and formulating a topic sentence.

1. Why I am frustrated by _____.
2. Why I prefer _____ to _____.
3. Why I usually refuse to _____.
4. Why I am always willing to _____.
5. Why I don't believe _____.

EXERCISE **8**

Choose one of the subjects that you wrote about in the exercises above and write a paragraph on the same subject developed by a different method. For exámple, if you defined "commitment" (Exercise 4), now try *contrasting* it with a slightly different concept such as "fanaticism." If you classified summer jobs (Exercise 5), now try *describing* a particularly satisfying or distasteful summer job that you have had. If you analyzed the cause of one of your frustrations (Exercise 7), now try *classifying* all the things that frustrate you. Pay attention to the way in which the choice of a method of development may determine how you think about a subject.

Closely examine the paragraphs of several articles in a magazine such as *The New Yorker, Psychology Today, Rolling Stone,* or *Scientific American.* What methods of paragraph development can you identify? How often do the paragraphs seem to be developed by a combination of methods? Based on your findings, write a paragraph about paragraph development in published writing.

7i

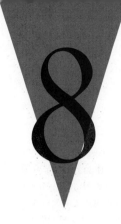

Writing Effective Sentences

What qualities make one sentence "strong," another "weak"? Answering that question brings us to the subject of style in writing. Although the precise sources of a writer's style may be as difficult to isolate as the components of a professional basketball player's style or the elements that characterize the style of service at a fine restaurant, the study of writing style does repay our effort. Through it a writer is able not only to appreciate more fully the mastery of other writers but also to enlarge his or her own repertoire of stylistic skills.

Our specific focus in this chapter is sentence style. We begin with two qualities that are always virtues in a sentence—unity and conciseness. From there we move on to consider strategies that can enhance the rhythm, emphasis, and smoothness of your sentences.

If concentrating on your sentence style is a new experience for you, you may at first find it difficult to break old habits and to experiment with new patterns. But you cannot increase your stylistic fluency if you are not willing to take a few risks. Like proficiency in all skills, stylistic skill comes with practice and experience. Seek out opportunities to use the following strategies in your prose, and you may be surprised by the new confidence and sophistication of your writing.

8a Writing unified sentences

A unified sentence makes its point clearly and unambiguously. This is not to suggest that a unified sentence must be a short one; it may in fact contain many details if their relationship to one another and to the sentence's main idea is clear. Below we discuss two impediments to the kind of sentence unity that we are talking about, together with some ways of overcoming them.

1. Too many ideas

A sentence is not a container designed to hold all the available information on a subject, though some sentences read as if their authors had that impression. To create unity in a sentence that rambles on from point to point, first isolate the various ideas that the sentence includes and then look for ways to divide the sentence into two sentences or to eliminate less important information.

8a

Divide the sentence

The simplest way to achieve unity with a rambling sentence is to divide it into two or more separate sentences. The following sentence is a candidate for such revision. As it stands, it tries to cover too much ground, from the first cries for woman's suffrage to the passing of the Nineteenth Amendment.

Ununified sentence Many people objected when the cry for woman's suffrage was first heard, and the opposition continued for decades, until finally men began to realize that women were entitled to the vote, and in 1920 the Nineteenth Amendment was ratified.

Revise this sentence by identifying the separate ideas it contains and grouping them in different sentences.

Sentence 1 Many people objected when the cry for woman's suffrage was first heard.

Sentence 1 The opposition continued for decades.

Sentence 2 Finally men began to realize that women were entitled to the vote.

Sentence 2 In 1920 the Nineteenth Amendment was ratified.

Revised as two sentences Many people objected when the cry for woman's suffrage was first heard, and the opposition continued for decades. Finally, however, men began to realize that women were entitled to the vote, and in 1920 the Nineteenth Amendment was ratified.

In this revised version, the first sentence is now unified around the idea of opposition to woman's suffrage, the second around the granting of suffrage to women.

Eliminate less important information

Sometimes an ununified sentence can be revised simply by eliminating unimportant ideas that intruded when the sentence was first drafted. That's what has happened in the following case.

8a

Ununified sentence	Inexpensive word processors, which first became available to the public in the late 1970s and which, like other technological innovations such as computer chips and digital recording, are part of what sociologists call the postindustrial revolution, have made a significant dent in the electric typewriter market, which includes secretaries, students, and teachers, among others.

Again, revise by listing the distinct ideas in this sentence and considering their importance to its main point.

Keep	Inexpensive word processors first became available to the public in the late 1970s.
Eliminate	Inexpensive word processors, like computer chips and digital recording, are part of what sociologists call the postindustrial revolution.
Keep	Inexpensive word processors have made a significant dent in the electric typewriter market.
Eliminate	The electric typewriter market includes secretaries, students, and teachers, among others.

The information about computer chips, digital recording, sociologists, and the postindustrial revolution is only tangentially relevant to the point that word processors are cutting into the sale of electric typewriters. And most readers would probably not need to have the members of that market listed for them.

Revised with less important information eliminated	Inexpensive word processors have made a significant dent in the electric typewriter market since they first became available to the public in the late 1970s.

Combine strategies

Neither of the strategies above may alone be sufficient to unify some disorganized sentences. In these cases, you may need both to divide the sentence and to scrutinize its contents for extraneous ideas to delete.

8a

Ununified sentence	The earliest known examples of sculpture date from the Paleolithic period, which ended about twenty thousand years ago and is sometimes called the Old Stone Age, making sculpture one of the oldest arts, many pieces of sculpture having been found in caves or old burial grounds in various parts of the world.

The point here seems to be the great antiquity of sculpture, but it is obscured by the sentence's rambling structure and excessive detail.

Sentence 2	The earliest known examples of sculpture date from the Paleolithic period.
Sentence 2	The Paleolithic period ended about twenty thousand years ago.
Eliminate	The Paleolithic period is sometimes called the Old Stone Age.
Sentence 1	Sculpture is one of the oldest arts.
Eliminate	Many pieces of sculpture have been found in caves or old burial grounds in many parts of the world.
Revised as two sentences with less important information eliminated	Sculpture is one of the oldest arts. The earliest known examples of sculpture date from the Paleolithic period, which ended about twenty thousand years ago.

In this revised form, the first sentence succinctly makes the main point, and the second sentence supports it with specific detail.

2.   Faulty coordination and subordination

The Latin roots of the words *coordination* and *subordination* make their difference in meaning clear:

co, "with"

sub, "under"

ordinare, "to arrange in order"

Coordinate constructions, most of which are formed with the coordinating conjunctions *and, but, for, or, nor, yet,* and *so,* define two or more sentence elements as equally important. They rank elements *with* each other. *Sub*ordinate constructions, on the other hand, present elements in a sentence as unequal in importance, focusing the reader's attention on one at the expense of others. They rank some elements *under* others in the sentence. Subordinating words fall into two categories:

8a

Relative pronouns

that	which	whom
what	whichever	whomever
whatever	who	whose
	whoever	

Subordinating conjunctions

after	before	than	where
although	even though	though	whereas
as	how	unless	wherever
as if	if	until	whether
as though	since	when	while
because	so that	whenever	

Sometimes you can use either a coordinate or a subordinate construction to combine separate ideas into a single unified sentence. The choice will depend on the relative importance of the ideas. Do you wish the reader to perceive them as equal or unequal in importance?

Ideas to be combined into one sentence	Matthew checked the spelling in the report. Theresa checked the calculations.
Coordinate construction balances Matthew's work and Theresa's	Matthew checked the spelling in the report, and Theresa checked the calculations.

In this sentence, the coordinating conjunction *and* directs the reader to regard Matthew's work and Theresa's as equally important. The two clauses in the sentence receive equal emphasis and are called **coordinate clauses.** But if you connect these ideas by placing a subordinating conjunction before either clause, you shift the focus of the sentence and the reader's attention to the opposite one:

8a

Subordinate construction shifts attention to Theresa	While Matthew checked the spelling in the report, *Theresa checked the calculations.*
Subordinate construction shifts attention to Matthew	While Theresa checked the calculations in the report, *Matthew checked the spelling.*

The clause that follows the subordinating conjunction is called the **subordinate clause;** the other clause, on which the sentence's emphasis falls, becomes the **main clause.**

These three versions of the same sentence illustrate alternative ways of combining ideas to create sentence unity: giving equal weight to ideas by connecting them with a coordinating conjunction, or singling out one idea for emphasis by placing the other in a subordinate construction. If used incorrectly, though, coordinate and subordinate constructions undermine sentence unity by misdirecting the reader's attention.

Faulty coordination

Sentence unity collapses when a writer uses a coordinating conjunction to connect ideas that are either unrelated or unequal in importance:

Faulty coordination creates disunity	Elizabeth Michaels chaired yesterday's meeting and is the company's newest computer whiz.

Using the coordinating conjunction *and* to link the two ideas in this sentence—that Michaels chaired the meeting and that she is the company's newest computer genius—makes them seem somehow comparable. But these ideas are not related, at least not in any sense that the sentence makes clear, and their dissimilarity produces an unfocused, ununified sentence. A subordinate construction, such as a relative clause, would enable the writer to focus the sentence on either of these ideas by subordinating the other:

Subordinate construction focuses attention on the meeting   *Elizabeth Michaels,* who is the company's newest computer whiz, *chaired yesterday's meeting.*

Subordinate construction focuses attention on computer skill   *Elizabeth Michaels,* who chaired yesterday's meeting, *is the company's newest computer whiz.*

Faulty subordination

As we have said, when one idea in a sentence is placed in a subordinate construction, the emphasis in the sentence automatically shifts to the *other* idea. A writer who forgets this principle may accidentally place the sentence's main idea in a subordinate construction. This error, sometimes called **upside-down subordination,** creates disunity in a sentence by erroneously directing the reader's attention to the less important idea.

Upside-down subordination   As Mr. Boardman drove off the road, *he tried to kill a bee inside the car.*

Correct subordination   As Mr. Boardman tried to kill a bee inside the car, *he drove off the road.*

The main idea here is clearly driving off the road, not killing the bee, but the pattern of emphasis is reversed in the first sentence, where the writer has mistakenly placed the main idea in a subordinate clause introduced by the subordinating word *as.*

EXERCISE **1**

Improve the unity of the following sentences by dividing them into separate sentences, by eliminating unnecessary information, and/or by using coordinate or subordinate constructions.

1. Anyone who writes would profit from learning how to use a word processor, and a computer at first might seem intimidating to someone

who has no background in electronic technology, which has reshaped so much of modern life.

2. Although composing on a word processor is much more efficient than writing on a typewriter, using a word processor requires little more skill than typing does.

3. A writer does not have to know how to program computers or even understand how they work, but once he or she learns a few simple operations, the writer can begin composing.

4. A writer needs to learn the procedure for beginning a file, which varies depending on the word-processing program being used, such as WordStar, WordPerfect, MultiMate, or Word, and the procedure for moving the text around on the screen.

5. Many writers find that they can compose more efficiently with a word processor, and revision with a word processor can take place constantly.

6. Changes that a writer might be reluctant to make during typing, because such changes are so complicated, particularly if one's typewriter does not have a correction feature, can be accomplished on the computer screen in seconds.

7. Because working on a word processor can be fun, it offers immediate rewards, and the only problem is endless revising.

8. Revising is so easy, and the writer needs to learn when to stop.

EXERCISE 2

Improve the unity of the following sentences by dividing them into separate sentences, by eliminating unnecessary information, and/or by using coordinate or subordinate constructions.

1. Black Kettle, who was a chief of the Cheyenne, who lived primarily in eastern Colorado, believed that fighting the white settlers would be futile, and he hoped to find safety for his tribe.

2. Major E. W. Wynkoup assured Black Kettle that his tribe would be safe at Sand Creek, and he commanded the troops at Fort Lyon, thirty miles away.

3. Wynkoup's efforts, which did not suit his superiors, led to his being recalled from his post in November of 1864, and his replacement, who was Major Scott Anthony, agreed to the promise Wynkoup had made to the Cheyenne.

4. On the basis of this assurance, Black Kettle's tribe settled at Sand Creek, and along with them settled a band of Arapaho under Chief Left Hand, and altogether the settlement numbered about seven hun-

dred, which included five hundred women, children, and elderly people.

5. Near the end of November, a former minister, who was Colonel Chivington, arrived at Fort Lyon with a cavalry troop.
6. Anthony sent Chivington and a hundred soldiers to Sand Creek, and they attacked the settlement at dawn on November 29, 1864.
7. Left Hand was killed, Black Kettle escaped the massacre, the soldiers killed between four hundred and five hundred Indians, and most of the dead were women and children.
8. The soldiers took a hundred scalps, and these were displayed in a Denver theater several weeks later.

8b Writing concise sentences

Superfluous words weaken a sentence. But in saying this, we need to distinguish between brevity in writing, which is sometimes a virtue, and conciseness, which always is. Any sentence can be made brief by paring words and details; the difficulty is knowing what to strike out and what to retain. Concise writing manages to include all the essential information without wasting words.

Too wordy	By the time trading ended on Wall Street yesterday, the stock market had fallen down forty points, which was significant because it was the sharpest decline since a similar drop seven months ago.
Too brief	The market plummeted yesterday.
Appropriately concise	The stock market fell forty points yesterday, the sharpest decline in seven months.

Answering a young man's question about how to become a good stylist, the English writer Sydney Smith once said, "You should cross out every other word. You have no idea what vigor it will give your style." Though exaggerated, Smith's advice makes an important point. Notice how the deadwood in the following passage blocks the reader's way:

Because *of the fact that* I wanted to major in *the field of* business, I *proceeded to* take several courses in *the area of* accounting in *the period of* my sophomore year. *During the time* when I was a junior, I *was* still *of the belief* that business was my best choice for *the purpose of* making a living.

When we eliminate the words that contribute nothing to this passage, the sentences make their simple point more directly:

> Because I wanted to major in business, I took several courses in accounting in my sophomore year. As a junior, I still believed that business was my best choice for making a living.

8b

To help you identify and eliminate wordiness, we have grouped wordy constructions into six main categories.

1.   Redundant words, phrases, and clauses

The word *redundancy* comes to us from the Latin word meaning "to overflow." In writing, redundancy is a flood of words that repeat the same ideas. Redundancy does not clarify; it merely bores.

Redundant	When the poet writes *in his poem* that the character was never "odd in his views," he means that the man was a conformist, *accepting the standards of his society in all respects.*
Concise	When the poet writes that the character was never "odd in his views," he means that the man was a conformist.

Redundant phrasing often results from needlessly spelling out the meaning of a word that can stand alone. Poets, as we know, write poems; we do not need to be reminded of that fact in the sentence above. Nor do we need a definition of the word *conformist.* Notice similar duplication in the following sentences.

Redundant	Over the years, she began to suspect that she was being exploited by her relatives, *that they wanted to take advantage of her and use her.*
Redundant	The criticisms I want to make are major ones *that you ought to consider carefully because of their importance.*
Redundant	We like to be appreciated for our talents *that we possess,* and we hope to be praised for our achievements *that we have attained as individuals.*

In these sentences, the italicized words provide superfluous definitions of the simple concepts "exploitation," "major," and—in the last example—"our."

Common redundant phrases to be on the watch for include the following:

attractive *in appearance*	complete *entirely*
cooperate *together*	perplexing *in nature*
red *in color*	refer *back* to
repeat *again*	round *in shape*
several *in number*	small *in size*
tall *in height*	young *in age*

8b

2. Nominalizations

The noun form of a verb is called a **nominalization.** We need nominalizations in our language—words like *argument, explanation,* and *life*—in order to talk about abstract concepts. Nominalizations weaken a writer's style, though, when they are pressed into service in place of more direct verbs. When a writer uses a verb phrase containing a nominalization instead of a verb, the result is almost always a wordy sentence.

Wordy nominalizations   *It is the* city council's *intention* to *make a decision about* the future of the Maple Street park at tomorrow's meeting.

Concise   The city council *intends* to *decide* the future of the Maple Street Park at tomorrow's meeting.

As the sentences above illustrate, nominalizations not only generate useless, extra words; they also mask the action being described and hence deprive a sentence of the punch that only a strong verb can deliver.

Nominalizations are one of the hallmarks of what is occasionally called the bureaucratic style, the style of some writers in business and government who mistakenly persist in believing that more words are better than fewer, that indirectness is better than directness. We encounter this style so often that it is sometimes difficult to recognize, let alone resist. Below is a list of common nominalizations to watch out for, together with their more direct equivalents.

Nominalization	More concise verb
I am of the belief that . . .	I believe . . .
She reached the conclusion that . . .	She concluded . . .
He will make a determination of . . .	He will determine . . .
We held a discussion of . . .	We discussed . . .
She provided an explanation of . . .	She explained . . .
He has the intention of . . .	He intends to . . .
We are in need of . . .	We need . . .
They made a recommendation that . . .	They recommended . . .
I will conduct a study of . . .	I will study . . .

The key to improving a sentence containing a nominalization is recognizing the nominalization and identifying the action that it conceals. Once you state that action as a verb and the actor as its subject, the other elements in the sentence will usually fall into place. Your new sentence will always be more direct, more economical, and more forceful than the original.

3. Wordy connectives

Join elements in your sentences as directly and economically as possible.

Wordy connective	The most prolonged cold spell of the century occurred *during the time in which* Jerry was living in Iowa.
Concise	The most prolonged cold spell of the century occurred *while* Jerry was living in Iowa.
Wordy connective	Sarah continued to study German *because of the fact that* she hoped to become an interpreter.
Concise	Sarah continued to study German *because* she hoped to become an interpreter.

Below are some examples of wordy connectives and their more concise equivalents.

Wordy connective	Concise
at this point in time	now
because of the fact that	because
due to the fact that	because
during the period when	when or while
for the purpose of providing	to provide
in order to prove	to prove
in the event that	if
in a great many cases	often
the majority of	most
on the occasion when	when
the way in which to	how to

8b

4. Unnecessary repetition

Repetition is not always a flaw in writing. In fact, as you will see when we discuss parallel structure in **8c**, the artful repetition of syntactic structures can please the ear and enhance the meaning of a sentence. But repetition that creates awkwardness rather than emphasis should be eliminated.

Repetitious The *problem* of the homeless is a formidable *problem*.

Concise The problem of the homeless is formidable.

Repetitious If *you* read the *story* carefully, *you* will find a pattern of imagery in the *story* that makes the *story* mean more than *you* first thought the *story* did.

Concise If you read the story carefully, you will find a pattern of imagery that enlarges its meaning.

The best way to isolate cases of unnecessary repetition is to read your writing out loud, trusting your ear to detect the jarring sound of a word or phrase that occurs too frequently.

5. Overuse of the passive voice

A verb is said to be in the **active voice** when the grammatical subject of a sentence does the action presented in its predicate:

Active verb   She *wrote* the book.

Active verb   He *read* the book.

Active verb   The critics *praised* it.

Who wrote the book? *She* did. Who read it? *He* did. The subjects of these sentences do the actions that their verbs describe.

Occasionally, though, the person or thing *acted upon* in a sentence is more important than the one who acts; in this case, the sentence can be written with the object or recipient of the action placed in the subject position. The verb in such a sentence is said to be in the **passive voice:**

Passive verb   Her book *was nominated* for the Pulitzer Prize.

Passive verb   Only exceptional books *are selected* for this award.

The actions here—nominating and selecting—were performed by people not important to the sentences, hence not identified in them. If we wanted to insist on using only active verbs, we could write *A jury nominated her book for the Pulitzer Prize,* but doing so would radically shift the emphasis of the sentence, mistakenly directing the reader's attention to an anonymous group of people and away from the real point of the sentence—the book and the honor it received.

A passive verb is not only appropriate but necessary when the doer of the action in the sentence is unknown:

Passive verb   My car *was* apparently *stolen* during the night.

The conventions of scientific and technical writing dictate the frequent use of the passive voice as well, since it is the experiment and not the experimenter that is important:

Passive verbs   A cubic centimeter of water *was added* to the solution, and the test tube *was heated.* No reaction *was observed.*

Problems with passive verbs

Even in these cases where passive verbs are legitimate and necessary, they present one disadvantage over active verbs: because they are always formed by combining a past participle with some form of the verb *be,* passive verbs are always less concise than active verbs. Add to that the fact that in most writing the doer of an action is more important than the recipient of the action, and you have two reasons to avoid using passive verbs unnecessarily.

Unnecessary passive   After my first draft *has been completed* and the paper *has been set* aside for a day or two, revising *is begun* by me.

Unnecessary passive   Classics like Charles Dickens's novels *will* always *be appreciated* by readers.

Unnecessary passive   "Who ever reads an American book?" *was asked* by an English critic in the nineteenth century.

8b

Rewritten in the active voice, these sentences become more concise and forceful. Not only can the active verbs be expressed in fewer words, but the prepositional phrases needed to identify the actors here—*by me, by readers, by an English critic*—can be dropped when those actors are placed in the subject position:

More concise active   After I *have completed* my first draft and *have set* the paper aside for a day or two, I *begin* revising.

More concise active   Readers *will* always *appreciate* classics like Charles Dickens's novels.

More concise active   "Who ever reads an American book?" an English critic *asked* in the nineteenth century.

Passive constructions often obscure the true actor in a sentence, making it confusing as well as wordy:

Confusing passive   The changes that *had been made* in the conservation bill by the committee *were accepted* by the Senate, which voted to pass the bill.

One can hardly tell what happened here. Who did what? The actors are the committee and the Senate; active verbs make their roles easier to perceive:

Clearer active   The Senate *passed* the conservation bill that the committee *had amended*.

The point is to be able to distinguish between active and passive verbs and to use passives only when they are necessary and appropriate. Be especially sensitive to those wordy passive constructions that, like the nominalizations we discussed above, often surface in bureaucratic prose, sometimes as a deliberate means of concealing the actor or actors in a sentence:

8b

Passive conceals actor   It *has been determined* that a tax increase, however unpopular, offers the only solution to the budget deficit.
[*Who* has determined this?]

Passive conceals actor   It *was thought* that the world's natural resources were inexhaustible.
[*Who* thought this?]

Writing in the active voice demands more careful thinking and more exact phrasing:

More exact active   Only a handful of the few people who seriously considered the question thought that the world's natural resources were inexhaustible.

6.   *There is* and *it is* constructions

There is/are . . . and *It is* . . . constructions are common, and in many cases acceptable, sentence openers:

Idiomatic   There is no reason to doubt her honesty.
[*There* is called an expletive; the grammatical subject of the sentence is *reason*. A more formal version of the sentence might be *No reason exists to doubt her honesty*.]

Idiomatic   It is true that he had been drinking before the accident.
[In this construction, the expletive *it* anticipates the actual grammatical subject, the clause *that he had been drinking before the accident*. The construction suggests that the writer is making a concession.]

But carelessly used, these constructions merely add words that contribute nothing to the meaning of the sentence:

Wordy   It was in 1927 that Virginia Woolf published her novel *To the Lighthouse.*

Wordy   There are many readers who consider this book her finest work.

A simple way to revise such sentences is to delete the expletive and begin with the true subject:

8b

Concise   Virginia Woolf published her novel *To the Lighthouse* in 1927.

Concise   Many readers consider this book her finest work.

EXERCISE 3

Revise the following sentences to make them more concise. Be prepared to explain which of the types of wordiness discussed above you have identified and eliminated.

1. Today most people in our modern world are familiar with science fiction, but it may not be known by them that a long history has been had by science fiction.
2. In the nineteenth century, there were great technological developments that were beginning to develop, and early science fiction was in large part a response to these changes.
3. There are many people who are of the belief that Mary Shelley's book, *Frankenstein; or, The Modern Prometheus,* a novel published in 1818, is the first science-fiction novel.
4. An important early influence on SF was H. G. Wells, whose novels were many in number, including *The Invisible Man* and *The War of the Worlds,* both published in the period of the late 1800s.
5. The nineteenth century also saw the first beginnings of what was to become a major SF publishing market, magazines.
6. Although often these magazines frequently contained stories inferior in quality from a literary standpoint, it is a fact that many articles by many well-known writers were published in them, including the writer Edgar Rice Burroughs, the originator and creator of Tarzan.
7. The term *science fiction*—abbreviated SF, never "sci-fi"—didn't come into general, widespread use until the 1930s.
8. Due to the fact that science fiction includes many different and various types of literature, it is difficult to define.

9. Writers of SF are characterized by an insistence that the events they portray are possible.
10. Over the years, SF has continued to grow and develop; among many recent trends are more radical political themes and the trend toward more work by women writers.

EXERCISE 4

Revise the following sentences to make them more concise. Be prepared to explain which of the types of wordiness discussed above you have identified and eliminated.

1. In some way, shape, or fashion, everyone laughs.
2. But as individuals, we each laugh at those things that we each individually find amusing.
3. In intellectual humor, people use their minds; in order for a person to laugh at a pun, for example, there must first be a realization by a person that a single word may have two different and distinct meanings.
4. In contrast, slapstick humor, on the other hand, is visually humorous.
5. In other words, what that means is that something that is seen by a person appears to be funny, like a man slipping on a banana peel and slipping and falling.
6. Unfortunately, it is true that one person's humor may be another person's pain.
7. There are in-jokes, which belong to a certain group or clique, and which reinforce a listener's feeling of inclusion and belonging only in the event that he or she is a member of the group.
8. But if a joke refers to something that is not understood by the listener, such a joke can be a way and means of making the person feel excluded.
9. Ethnic jokes, too, can also be painful on the occasion when it is one's own ethnic origin that is the target of the humor.
10. Despite these problems, humor is still needed by each and every one of us as a necessary, enjoyable, pleasurable release from the everyday tension of our daily lives.

8c Creating parallelism

The human eye and the human ear lean toward balance and harmony. We like matchings and pairs, equity, pattern, order. Once a major chord is struck in a piece of music, we expect to hear it again, just as we appreciate looking at surfaces where planes and colors complement one another. In writing, this ordering of like element with like element is called **parallelism,** or **parallel structure.** Parallel structure balances word with word, phrase with phrase, subordinate clause with subordinate clause. It is one of the most basic of stylistic devices, one that is appropriate in many writing situations.

Parallel words and phrases

It is often the failure who is the pioneer in   new lands,
                                                 new undertakings,
                                          and   new forms of expression.

—Eric Hoffer

8c

We are joined by   highways,
                    networks,
            and   slogans,
          not by   imaginative acts.

—Wright Morris

And he yearned to package for   each of the children,
                                 the grandchildren,
                          for   everyone,
          that   joyous certainty,
          that   sense of mattering,
                      of moving and being moved,
                      of being one and indivisible
                          with   the great of the past,
                          with   all that freed, ennobled man.

—Tillie Olsen

Parallel clauses

Where She Danced is the story of two generations of American dancers:
                how they were educated,
                what gave them the courage, the insight, the
                    foolhardiness to say they had found a new art form,
          and   what gave them the drive to insist on its ultimate
                    seriousness.

—Elizabeth Kendall

The *Iliad* is only great because all life is a battle,
          the *Odyssey* because all life is a journey,
  and   the Book of Job because all life is a riddle.

—G. K. Chesterton

Parallel sentences

Children begin by loving their parents.
After a time they judge them.
Rarely, if every, do they forgive them.

—Oscar Wilde

8c

The scientist anatomizes, someone must synthesize; the scientist withdraws, someone must draw together. The scientist particularizes, someone must universalize.

—John Fowles

Although the following sentences are a rather extreme example of parallel structure, they offer a good illustration of the effects that can be created with parallelism. To appreciate the way in which parallel structure works in this passage, try reading it slowly out loud:

The cunning and attractive slave women disguise their strength as womanly weakness, their audacity as womanly timidity, their unscrupulousness as womanly innocence, their impurities as womanly defencelessness; simple men are duped by them, and subtle ones disarmed and intimidated. It is only the proud, straightforward women who wish, not to govern, but to be free.

—Bernard Shaw

The first independent clause of Shaw's compound sentence states its subject and predicate simply. The phrases functioning as the direct objects of the verb (*what* do these slave women disguise?) have exactly the same construction because they are grammatical equals in the sentence. We might illustrate their parallel relationship by diagramming them like this:

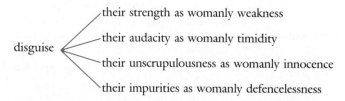

disguise
their strength as womanly weakness
their audacity as womanly timidity
their unscrupulousness as womanly innocence
their impurities as womanly defencelessness

The parallelism of Shaw's sentence does not end there. In the independent clause following the semicolon, *simple men* are balanced against *subtle ones*, and *disarmed* and *intimidated* form parallel elements in the predicate of the second clause:

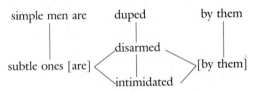

The sections of the sentence on either side of the semicolon are themselves contrasted in parallel fashion. The active voice of the verb in the first clause (*disguise*) is balanced against the passive voice of the verbs in the second (*are duped . . . disarmed and intimidated*); aggression is balanced against passivity.

The brisk second sentence introduces parallel objects of the verb *wish* with the correlatives *not . . . but.*

    the . . . women who wish   not to govern
                                but to be free

The initial pair of adjectives (*cunning* and *attractive*) defining the subject of the first clause (*slave women*) is here paralleled by a new pair of adjectives that describe the different women in this second sentence (*proud, straightforward*). Shaw ingeniously suggests the inequality between the two types of women by replacing the *and* that connects the adjectives in the first sentence with a comma in the second. A new rhythm is established.

This analysis of just two sentences suggests the concentration of ideas and the range of effects that a writer can create using parallel structure. Parallelism both compares and contrasts, affirms (*both . . . and*) and negates (*neither . . . nor*) by putting like or different elements in similar constructions. Perhaps the fact that we have two eyes, two legs, two sides of the brain, two hands (*on the one hand . . . on the other hand*) accounts for our pleasure when elements in a sentence are balanced, and our dissatisfaction when they are askew. Whatever the reason for our attraction to equality and balance, parallelism is indispensable for good writing. Below are some guidelines for fashioning parallel sentences.

8c

1. Coordinate pairs

All sentences joined by the coordinating conjunctions *and, or, nor, for, but* should be in like grammatical structures. Balance nouns with nouns, phrases with phrases, clauses with clauses.

Faulty   He likes reading all the books he can lay his hands on and to write whenever the mood strikes him.

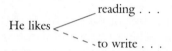

The reader is jarred by the faulty parallelism of the gerund *reading* with the infinitive *to write*. Rewriting the sentence with two infinitives or two gerunds creates parallel structure.

Parallel   He likes *to read* all the books he can lay his hands on and *to write* whenever the mood strikes him.

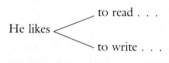

Parallel   He likes *reading* all the books he can lay his hands on and *writing* whenever the mood strikes him.

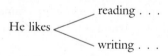

In the first sentence below, the conjunction *and* connects an infinitive phrase and a subordinate clause beginning with *that*—two structures that are not parallel. The second sentence presents one way of revising for parallelism.

Faulty   Students in composition classes learn to read with attention and that coherent essays must be written.

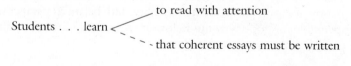

Parallel   Students in composition classes learn *to read* with attention
and *to write* coherent essays.

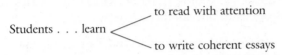

The sentence could be rephrased to emphasize the parallelism even
more.

8c

Parallel   Students in composition classes learn *to read attentively*
and *to write coherently*.

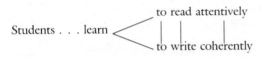

Sometimes the part of a sentence that should be parallel to another
part is so far away that the writer forgets to balance both.

Faulty   I try to stay awake in chemistry class, fortifying myself
with coffee, pinching myself at intervals, hanging by my
fingernails on the professor's every word, but falling asleep
nonetheless.

Falling is not parallel to the three other participles in this sentence,
which describe the writer's strategies for staying awake. The parallel
pair of ideas is *trying to stay awake* and *falling asleep*. The sentence
should be rewritten with parallel independent clauses.

Parallel   *I try* to stay awake in chemistry class, fortifying myself
with coffee, pinching myself at intervals, hanging by my
fingernails on the professor's every word, but *I fall asleep*
nonetheless.

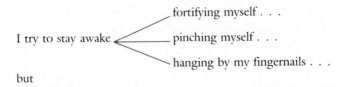

2. Elements in a series

Like coordinate pairs, three or more elements in a series must be grammatically parallel to one another.

8c

> **Faulty** I concluded that she was intelligent, witty, and liked to make people feel at home.

The first two elements after the verb *was* are adjectives; the third is another verb. The lack of parallelism is clearly revealed if we construct a diagram of the sentence:

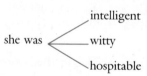

The faulty parallelism can be corrected by making all three elements adjectives:

> **Parallel** I concluded that she was *intelligent, witty,* and *hospitable.*

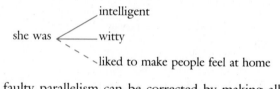

The sentence might also be rewritten by inserting another *and* to create two parallel noun clauses.

> **Parallel** I concluded *that she was* intelligent and witty, and *that she liked* to make people feel at home.

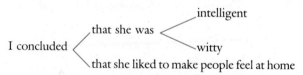

3. Repetition of words

Sometimes it is necessary to repeat a conjunction, preposition, or other preceding word to make a parallel construction clear.

Unclear   My adviser told me that I spent far too much time worry-
         ing about what was expected of me and I needed more
         confidence in myself.

Clearer   My adviser told me that I spent far too much time worry-
         ing about what was expected of me and *that* I needed
         more confidence in myself.

My adviser told me ⟨ that I spent . . .

that I needed . . .

8c

Unclear   Because she had been teaching for twenty years and she
         could remember being a student herself, I listened to
         her advice.

Clearer   Because she had been teaching for twenty years and *because*
         she could remember being a student herself, I listened
         to her advice.

Because she had been teaching. . . ⟩ I listened to her advice

because she could remember . . .

Occasionally, the absence of such a preceding word can significantly
distort the meaning of a sentence:

Unclear   The vineyard is often visited by tourists who sample grapes
         and connoisseurs of wine.

. . . tourists who sample ⟨ grapes

connoisseurs of wine

Clearer   The vineyard is often visited by tourists who sample grapes
         and *by* connoisseurs of wine.

The vineyard is often visited ⟨ by tourists who sample grapes

by connoisseurs of wine

4. Correlatives

Conjunctions that occur in pairs are called **correlatives:** *either
. . . or, neither . . . nor, not only . . . but also, both . . . and.* The

rule to follow when you use correlatives is that the parts of speech immediately following each conjunction must be identical.

Faulty   William Blake is not only famous for his poetry but also for his illustrations.

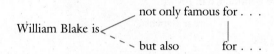

Not only in this sentence is followed by the adjective *famous; but also,* however, is followed by a prepositional phrase beginning with *for.* In this case, the faulty parallelism can be corrected simply by rearranging the words in the sentence:

Parallel   William Blake is famous *not only for* his poetry *but also for* his illustrations.

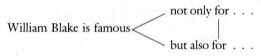

Consider the following similar case.

Faulty   He either is a liar or a remarkably naive person.

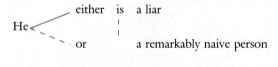

This sentence can be revised in three different ways to create parallelism around the correlatives *either . . . or:*

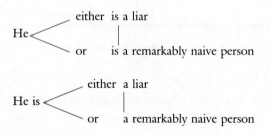

8c

Either he is a liar,

or   he is a remarkably naive person

In the final example below, the faulty parallelism could be corrected by inverting *both* and *to*, but doing so would produce the awkward split construction *to both raise*. A better solution is to add another *to* after *and:*

8c

> **Faulty**   The legislature hoped both to raise taxes and stimulate business.

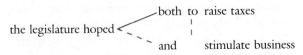

the legislature hoped　　both to raise taxes

　　　　　　　　　　　and　　　stimulate business

> **Parallel**   The legislature hoped *both to* raise taxes *and to* stimulate business.

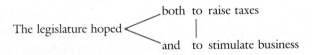

The legislature hoped　　both to raise taxes

　　　　　　　　　　　and　　to stimulate business

5. Subordinate clauses

A subordinate clause is never parallel to the main clause in a sentence, and it should not be connected to the main clause by *and* or *but*.

> **Faulty**   She is a woman of strong convictions and who always says what she thinks.

The clauses can be put into proper relationship to one another by omitting the coordinating conjunction:

> **Correct**   She is a woman of strong convictions who always says what she thinks.

An alternative is to rewrite the sentence with two parallel subordinate clauses:

> **Parallel**   She is a woman *who has* strong convictions and *who* always *says* what she thinks.

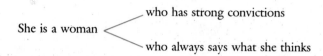

She is a woman ─── who has strong convictions
                    who always says what she thinks

Faulty parallel constructions like those in the following sentences are corrected in a similar way.

8c

Faulty	In the middle of the sleepy village is a statue dating from 1870 and that depicts General Lee on horseback.
Parallel	In the middle of the sleepy village is a statue *that* dates from 1870 *and that* depicts General Lee on horseback.
Faulty	He appeared before the committee with a long written statement, but which he was not allowed to read.
Parallel	*He* appeared before the committee with a long written statement, *but he* was not allowed to read it.

6. Sequence of ideas

Elements that are parallel in grammatical structure should also be parallel in sense. Used carelessly, a parallel construction can lead to an illogical series or an awkward sequence of ideas, as in the following sentence.

Illogical	Her many friends, her recent marriage, and her slumping business could not offer Amy the happiness she had known while in college.

The items in this series are not parallel in meaning. A person might reasonably be expected to find happiness in friends and marriage, but not in a slumping business. Only the first two of these ideas can be expressed in a parallel construction.

Correct	Neither her many friends nor her recent marriage could offer Amy the happiness she had known while in college.

A similar juxtaposition of positive and negative ideas in the following sentence creates a puzzling effect:

Illogical	During his last year in law school, David rose to the top of his class, worked on the law review, and decided not to enter law practice.

Correct   During his last year in law school, David rose to the top of his class and worked on the law review. However, he decided not to enter law practice.

8c

EXERCISE 5

Revise the following sentences to correct faulty parallelism.

1. The earliest astronomers used the stars to make calendars and also in order that they could mark the time of religious rites.
2. Stonehenge, the ancient circle of stone monuments in southern England, was apparently used for religious, practical, and for astronomical purposes.
3. Hipparchus, who lived around 150 B.C., was the first astronomer to attempt classifying stars and to map their paths.
4. His successor, Ptolemy, is credited with having cataloged more than a thousand stars and with the fact that he firmly established the theory that the universe revolves around the earth.
5. The Ptolemaic system not only influenced the ancient world but also it dominated thinking about the cosmos until the sixteenth century.
6. Until quite recently, astronomy, religion, and the subject of philosophy were connected in people's minds.
7. For centuries, people clung to the Ptolemaic theory and as they resisted the idea that the earth might not be the center of the universe.
8. A hundred years after Copernicus proposed this theory in the sixteenth century, the idea was still considered heretical and to be dangerous.
9. More recently, Edmund Halley, famous for the comet he discovered and that he tracked, helped to dispel some of the myths surrounding the solar system and its workings.
10. Today, the occasional confusion of astronomy and astrology remains as a sign of the blending of the rational and mysterious ideas—a mixture some people are unwilling to give up.

EXERCISE 6

Create at least one parallel construction in each of the following sentences by adding appropriate words, phrases, or clauses. Change the original sentence slightly if necessary.

Example

The afternoon sunlight filtered through the trees.

Parallel words added: The afternoon sunlight filtered through the *leaves and branches* of the trees.

Parallel phrases added: The afternoon sunlight filtered through the trees, *casting shadows* on the blanket *and making reading* difficult.

Parallel clause added: The afternoon sunlight filtered through the trees, *and a light wind brushed across the grass.*

1. Vince's pictures of the Bradley Warehouse fire were the start of his career as a professional photographer.
2. The fire occurred after all the employees had left for the day.
3. Vince had just started working as a night security guard at the warehouse.
4. Of course, no matter where he was, Vince kept his camera handy.
5. When he smelled smoke, he immediately called the fire department.
6. While he waited for the fire trucks to arrive, he took pictures of the blaze.
7. Once he was nearly injured when a burning beam fell close to him.
8. At that point, Vince decided that he had enough pictures.
9. The newspaper offered to buy the best of his shots.
10. Vince's pictures were good enough to get him a job at the newspaper.

8d Writing cumulative and periodic sentences

Sentences are sometimes characterized as **cumulative** or **periodic,** depending on where their main ideas occur. A cumulative sentence states its main idea first and then follows it with modifying words, phrases, or clauses.

Cumulative sentences

> *I began to keep a journal* when I discovered that my life was interesting, my dreams colorful, and my thoughts rather remarkably profound.

> *My brother stared at the unopened letter,* trembling, pale, oblivious of the students who crowded past him in the stairwell.

Both of these cumulative sentences open with the main idea, to which are added phrases and clauses that provide supplementary information. Cumulative sentences offer a writer two advantages. First, they are clear, direct, and relatively easy to control. We generally speak in cumulative sentences, making a statement and then elaborating on it with details or qualifications. Every writer who can identify the main idea of a sentence has the beginning of a possible cumulative sentence. Second, such sentences are wonderfully flexible. Once the main idea of a sentence is on the page, a writer can freely arrange modifiers after it, varying its length and rhythm.

Periodic sentences are opposite in structure from cumulative sentences. In a periodic sentence, the main idea is held until the end—until the period—and the sentence begins instead with all the subordinate details. A periodic sentence can very effectively engage the attention of the reader, who is made to continue reading until the point of the sentence is revealed.

8d

Periodic sentences

When I discovered that my life was interesting, my dreams colorful, and my thoughts rather remarkably profound, *I began to keep a journal.*

Trembling, pale, oblivious of the students who crowded past him in the stairwell, *my brother stared at the unopened letter.*

Periodic sentences are suspenseful and conclusive, since the weight of their statement falls on the long-awaited predication. And because they are artful and deliberate, such sentences give the reader an impression of thoughtful arrangement. Placed strategically after a series of cumulative sentences, the periodic sentence, surprising the reader by reversing the expected pattern, has an emphatic effect.

But periodic sentences also present a writer with certain hazards. For one thing, since they are less characteristic of contemporary prose than cumulative sentences are, periodic sentences used excessively give writing a slightly old-fashioned ring. Moreover, a periodic sentence whose main idea is not important enough for the emphasis that it inevitably receives may sound anticlimactic or even ridiculous:

As the rainy night grew darker and the mysterious banging and howling in the attic stairway increased, I decided to make a peanut-butter sandwich.

No one can prescribe when to use a cumulative sentence, when a periodic one. Such a choice must grow out of your subject, the surrounding sentences in your prose, and your instinctive sense of appropriateness. But only when you have mastered both forms will you be able to choose between them consciously and deliberately.

8e

EXERCISE **7**

By adding different sets of appropriate modifiers, rewrite each of the following sentences first as a cumulative sentence and then as a periodic sentence. Do you prefer one version of your sentence over the other?

Example

No one seemed to be living in the house.

Cumulative version: No one seemed to be living in the house, which loomed darkly against the stormy sky, its broken window panes and rotten siding suggesting years of neglect.

Periodic version: Although the grounds were neatly cared for and lights burned within the curtained windows on the second floor, no one seemed to be living in the house.

1. The college faced a serious financial crisis.
2. Most of its residence halls needed renovation.
3. Another top priority was expansion of the library.
4. The last fund-raising campaign had fallen millions of dollars short of its goal.
5. The president reached a decision.
6. Some academic programs would have to be eliminated.
7. Students and faculty were outraged.
8. Many felt that cutbacks should be made in other areas.
9. A faculty committee began to look into the matter.
10. The committee's role was only advisory.

8e Varying sentence length

When the sentences in a passage are all approximately the same in length and structure, as in this opening passage from a published article, the result can be tedious reading.

Monotonous sentences

Nonsense bears the stamp of paradox. The two terms of the paradox are order and disorder. Order is generally created by language, disorder by reference. But the essential factor is their peculiar interplay. Elizabeth Sewell, in a penetrating analysis of nonsense, stresses the idea of dialectic. Yet her analysis deals almost exclusively with the formal structure of order. . . .

No reader can be expected to maintain interest in such prose for very long. Most of us, after all, read for pleasure as well as for information, and we expect writers to appeal to our desire for prose that satisfies and delights. The kind of monotonous prose in the example above can be revised effectively simply by varying the length and structure of the sentences.

8e

Varied sentences

> Nonsense bears the stamp of paradox, whose two terms are order and disorder. Although order is generally created by language and disorder by reference, the essential factor is their peculiar interplay. Elizabeth Sewell stresses the idea of dialectic in a penetrating analysis of nonsense, yet her analysis deals almost exclusively with the formal structure of order. . . .

The six sentences of the original, each approximately ten words long, have here been combined into three sentences of thirteen, eighteen, and twenty-five words. Related ideas are joined more clearly, and the second sentence's opening adverbial clause (*Although order* . . .) eliminates the monotony caused by a series of sentences that all begin with their subjects. Moreover, the progressively increasing length of these three sentences leads the reader more smoothly into the rest of the article. Variety, in short, has the same beneficial effects on writing that it has on life itself.

Becoming familiar with the English sentence structures described in Chapter **24** is the first step toward developing variety in your writing. Experiment with prepositional and verbal phrases; look for opportunities to use subordinate clauses; try to mix simple, compound, complex, and compound-complex sentences in your prose. At the same time, vary the length of your sentences. Remember that a string of long sentences is just as tiring to a reader as a series of short ones. It's the mixing of sentences of different lengths that keeps most readers engaged in a text.

8f Varying sentence openers

One important way of giving your prose new sophistication is by varying the first elements in your sentences. Many of us think of the main idea in a sentence first and are therefore inclined to place it first in the sentence. But when every sentence in a piece of writing begins with its subject, as in the first passage quoted above, the effect is wearying dullness. Try experimenting with some of the alternative ways of opening sentences described below. (See Chapter **24** for further information about each of these constructions.)

1. Single modifiers

When a modifying word is placed at the start of a sentence, rather than buried somewhere else, it inevitably draws attention. The result is an emphatic sentence opening.

Fay checked through the reports carefully, despite distracting noises coming from the office next door.

Carefully, Fay checked through the reports, despite distracting noises coming from the office next door.

The exhausted street musician began to pack up his collection of instruments.

Exhausted, the street musician began to pack up his collection of instruments.

2. Prepositional phrases

Like single modifiers, prepositional phrases can often be pulled from a later position in a sentence and placed at its beginning for variety and greater emphasis.

The weather in this city is completely unpredictable.

In this city, the weather is completely unpredictable.

U.S. auto manufacturers have begun to reestablish their credibility with American consumers during the past five years.

During the past five years, U.S. auto manufacturers have begun to reestablish their credibility with American consumers.

3. Inversions

An inverted sentence reverses the normal word order (subject-verb-complement) by placing the complement before the verb. Use this effective construction sparingly.

8f

Judy's red hair was barely visible behind the piles of paper on her desk.

Barely visible behind the piles of paper on her desk *was* Judy's red hair. **[positions of subject and predicate adjective reversed]**

I consider international peace the most important issue of our time.

International peace I consider the most important issue of our time. **[direct object placed before subject and verb]**

4. Appositives

Though usually placed after the nouns they refer to, appositives can precede them and may be used to begin a sentence.

Those stained-glass windows, a gift of the college's first graduate, are irreplaceable.

A gift of the college's first graduate, those stained-glass windows are irreplaceable.

David, an unwilling partner in the scheme, feared that he would lose more money than he would make.

An unwilling partner in the scheme, David feared that he would lose more money than he would make.

Some readers would say that both of these sentences have been improved by beginning with the appositive, which in each of the original versions interrupts the flow of the sentence in its position between the subject and predicate.

5. Verbal phrases

Look for opportunities to convert verbs in a sentence into participial or gerund phrases as beginning elements.

Alina was worried about the legal implications of the document and refused to sign it.

Worried about the legal implications of the document, Alina refused to
sign it. **[participial phrase]**

I considered many ways of using my medical training and finally
decided to work in the field of public health.

After considering many ways of using my medical training, I finally
decided to work in the field of public health. **[preposition with
gerund phrase]**

6. Absolute phrases

An absolute phrase—usually made up of a noun plus an adjective or participle—is a distinctive sentence opener. Use it for emphasis
and economy.

Mark tried to attract Julie's attention by waving his arms wildly.

His arms waving wildly, Mark tried to attract Julie's attention.

Jill's patience was exhausted, and she began to raise her voice.

Her patience exhausted, Jill began to raise her voice.

7. Adverbial clauses

Moving an adverbial clause from the end of a sentence to its
beginning shifts emphasis, and changes a cumulative sentence into a
periodic one.

The mayor refused to sign the proclamation, because most of the
city council members advised against it.

Because most of the city council members advised against it, the mayor
refused to sign the proclamation.

Sometimes an independent clause can be reduced to an adverbial clause
and used as a sentence opener.

Service at the oldest restaurant in town has been declining, but the
prices have steadily risen.

Although service at the oldest restaurant in town has been declining, the
prices have steadily risen.

Ultimately, you must decide which of these strategies best suit
your writing. Read your prose aloud, experiment with new stylistic
techniques, and work toward developing a style that reflects your own
personality.

8f

EXERCISE 8

The following sentences all begin with the subject. Rewrite each so that some other element functions as the sentence opener.

1. Frank Lloyd Wright, perhaps the greatest of American architects, studied engineering briefly at the University of Wisconsin, but he never completed his degree.
2. Wright arrived in Chicago in 1887 and found work as a draftsperson for the architect Joseph Lyman Silsbee.
3. Wright was hired after less than a year as assistant to Louis Sullivan, the most famous architect of his day.
4. Wright married Catherine Tobin in 1889 and built his now-famous house in the Chicago suburb of Oak Park.
5. Wright and Sullivan argued soon afterward because of Wright's violation of an agreement not to accept independent commissions, and they parted company.
6. The Oak Park house was enlarged and extensively remodeled as Wright's family grew.
7. Wright added a studio and office to the house in 1895, and from this point until about 1910, Oak Park was the hub of his professional career.
8. The strikingly innovative houses that Wright designed for his neighbors were among the first of his so-called prairie houses, and they startled the conservative community of Oak Park.
9. Wright raised the main living area of his houses to the second floor to increase the sense of privacy, but he eliminated the attic to maintain the horizontal appearance of his design.
10. The interiors of Wright's houses are dramatically open, because one can always see at least a portion of the adjacent rooms.

EXERCISE 9

Most of the sentences in the paragraph below are of about the same length, and all begin with the subject. Rewrite the paragraph to increase variety in sentence structure and sentence length. Add new material as necessary.

Selecting an apartment in a strange city is a task full of unknowns. The first step is finding the apartments you want to inspect. You will probably need a recent city map to guide you. A city map, however, doesn't give you all the information you need. It doesn't tell you that there's a noisy factory across the street from the apartment

8f

you saw advertised. You have to arrive at the apartment to discover that. The reliability of your new landlord is another very important question. Your landlord may seem friendly when you first meet. He or she must be available when your pipes begin to leak. Acquiring information about your new neighbors may also be difficult. An apartment complex may be quiet when you visit it during the day. You may not meet your neighbors until after you have moved in. They may have a state-of-the-art stereo system that keeps you awake nights. It may even rattle the dishes in your cupboard. Your signature on a lease may condemn you to a year of frustration.

Choosing Words

Like all languages, English is constantly changing. New words are added as names are required for new inventions, discoveries, and ideas: *laser, transistor, fax, meson, tagmeme.* Old words acquire new meanings as they are used in new ways: *half-life* (physics), *snow* (television), *hardware* (computers), *cartridge* (stereo recording). And some words disappear as the need for them vanishes; such is the case, for example, with a whole vocabulary dealing with horse-drawn vehicles. Words gain or lose prestige: *strenuous* and *mob,* once considered slang, are now in standard usage. As all of these examples suggest, an important part of being a writer is developing a genuine curiosity about words.

9a Using the dictionary

A dictionary is an attempt to record the current uses and meanings of words. Although many people believe that a dictionary tells them what a word *ought* to mean or how it *should* be used, a modern dictionary tries to be an accurate and objective record of what is actually being said and written. It discriminates among the current meanings of a word and tries to indicate the ways in which each is used. Since words and constructions differ in prestige value, a conscientious lexicographer will also try to record the current status of words, usually by usage labels such as *Dialectal* or *Regional, Obsolete* or *Archiac, Informal, Colloquial, Nonstandard,* or *Slang.*

1. Unabridged dictionaries

Unabridged dictionaries seek to be comprehensive guides to the language. Containing hundreds of thousands of entries, they typically trace not only the origins of each word but also the history of its usage. Large, often multivolume works, unabridged dictionaries are invaluable sources of information about the development and present status of the language. They are found in a library's collection of reference works.

9a

The Oxford English Dictionary. 2nd ed. 20 vols. Oxford: Clarendon, 1989.
[Commonly known by its initials, the *OED* is the standard historical dictionary of the language, tracing and illustrating the development of each word from its earliest recorded appearance to the present. This new edition of the *OED* supersedes the earlier thirteen-volume edition of 1933 and its four supplements.]

Webster's Third New International Dictionary of the English Language. Springfield: Merriam-Webster, 1986.
[Controversial when it first appeared in 1961 because of its minimal inclusion of labels to designate nonstandard and disputed usage, *Webster's Third* is second only to the *OED* in comprehensiveness.]

The Random House Dictionary of the English Language. 2nd ed. New York: Random House, 1987.
[Though smaller in scope than the dictionaries cited above, the *Random House* is recently revised and up to date.]

Webster's New Twentieth Century Dictionary of the English Language. 2nd ed. New York: Collins, 1979.

2. Abridged dictionaries

Abridged, or condensed, dictionaries provide a selection of the data contained in their unabridged counterparts. Often called *desk* or *college* dictionaries, they combine convenience, low cost, and thoroughness adequate for almost all writing tasks. The following abridged dictionaries, frequently updated, are all reliable reference tools:

The American Heritage Dictionary
The Random House College Dictionary
Webster's Ninth New Collegiate Dictionary
Webster's New World Dictionary

Note that these abridged dictionaries are not the same as so-called pocket dictionaries. Those smaller, paperbound volumes may be useful for checking spelling and pronunciation, but their information about what words mean and how they are used is insufficient for serious writers.

3.   Dictionary abbreviations and symbols

9a

To use a dictionary effectively, you must understand the abbreviations and symbols it uses. You will find them explained in its introductory section. Below are entries from four college dictionaries, followed by notes on the information they provide.

---

spelling & syllabication   etymology

¹**im·ply** (im plī′) *vt.* **-plied′, -ply′ing** ⟦ ME *implien* < OFr *emplier* < L *implicare,* to involve, entangle < *in-,* in + *plicare,* to fold: see PLY¹ ⟧ **1** to have as a necessary part, condition, or effect; contain, include, or involve naturally or necessarily [drama *implies* conflict] **2** to indicate indirectly or by allusion; hint; suggest; intimate [an attitude *implying* boredom] **3** [Obs.] to enfold; entangle —*SYN.* SUGGEST

reference to discussion of synonyms   usage label

---

² **im·ply** \im-′plī\ *vt* **im·plied; im·ply·ing** [ME *emplien,* fr. MF *emplier,* fr. L *implicare*] (14c) **1** *obs:* ENFOLD, ENTWINE **2:** to involve or indicate by inference, association, or necessary consequence rather than by direct statement < rights ~ obligations > **3:** to contain potentially **4:** to express indirectly < his silence *implied* consent > *syn* see SUGGEST *usage* see INFER

illustrations of use

---

¹ With permission. From *Webster's New World Dictionary.* Third College Edition. Copyright © 1988 by Simon & Schuster, Inc.

² By permission. From *Webster's Ninth New Collegiate Dictionary* © 1988 by Merriam-Webster, Inc., Publishers of the Merriam-Webster® Dictionaries.

9a

pronunciation   part of speech   meanings
↓   ↓   ↓

³ **im·ply** (im·plī′) *v.t.* **·plied, ·ply·ing 1.** To involve necessarily as a circumstance, condition, effect, etc.: An action *implies* an agent. **2.** To indicate or suggest without stating; hint at; intimate. **3.** To have the meaning of; signify. **4.** *Obs.* To entangle; infold. —**Syn.** See INFER. [< OF *emplier* < L *implicare* to involve < *in-* in + *plicare* to fold. Doublet of *EMPLOY.*]
—**Syn. 1.** *Imply* and *involve* mean to have some necessary connection. *Imply* states that the connection is causal or inherent, while *involve* is vaguer, and does not define the connection. **2.** *Imply, hint, intimate, insinuate* mean to convey a meaning indirectly or covertly. *Imply* is the general term for signifying something beyond what the words obviously say; his advice *implied* confidence in the stock market. *Hint* suggests indirection in speech or action: our host's repeated glances at his watch *hinted* that it was time to go. *Intimate* suggests a process more elaborate and veiled than hint: she *intimated* that his attentions were unwelcome. *Insinuate* suggests slyness and a derogatory import: in his remarks, he *insinuated* that the Senator was a fool.

full discussion of synonyms

---

inflected forms
↓

⁴ **im·ply** (ĭm-plī′) *tr.v.* **-plied, -ply·ing, -plies. 1.** To involve or suggest by logical necessity; entail: *His goals imply a good deal of hard work.* **2.** To say or express indirectly: *His tone implied a malicious purpose.* **3.** *Obs.* To entangle. —See Usage note at **infer.** [ME *implien,* to enfold < OFr. *emplier* < Lat. *implicare.* —see IMPLICATE.]

reference to —
discussion of
usage

---

³ From *Funk & Wagnalls Standard College Dictionary,* Updated edition (Funk & Wagnalls). Copyright © 1977 by Harper & Row, Publishers, Inc. Reprinted by permission of the publisher.

⁴ © 1985 by Houghton Mifflin Company. Reprinted by permission from *The American Heritage Dictionary, Second College Edition.*

Spelling and syllabication

When more than one spelling is given, the one printed first is usually preferred. Division of the word into syllables follows the conventions accepted by printers.

Pronunciation

A key to the symbols used to indicate pronunciation of words is usually printed on the front or back inside cover of the dictionary. Some dictionaries also run an abbreviated key to pronunciation at the bottom of each page or every other page. Word accent is shown by the symbol (′) after the stressed syllable or by (') before it.

Parts of speech

Abbreviations (explained in the introductory section of the dictionary) are used to indicate the various grammatical uses of a word: for example, *imply, v.t.* means that *imply* is a transitive verb.

Inflected forms

Forms of the past tense and past and present participles of verbs, the comparative or superlative degree of adjectives, and the plurals of nouns are given whenever there might be uncertainty about the correct form or spelling.

Etymology

The history of each word is indicated by the forms in use in Middle or Old English, or in the language from which the word was borrowed. Earlier meanings are often given.

Meanings

Different meanings of a word are numbered and defined, sometimes with illustrative examples. Some dictionaries give the oldest meanings first; others list the common meanings of the word first.

Usage labels

Descriptive labels, often abbreviated, indicate the level of usage: *Archaic, Obsolete, Colloquial, Slang, Dialectal, Regional, Substandard,*

Nonstandard, and so on. Sometimes usage labels indicate a special field rather than a level of usage: for example, *Poetic, Irish, Chemistry.* If a word has no usage label, it may be assumed that, in the opinion of the editors, the word is in common use on all levels; that is, it is *Standard English.* Usage labels are often defined and illustrated in the explanatory notes in the front of a dictionary. We discuss a number of the more common ones in the section that follows (see **9b**).

9a

Synonyms

Many words have closely related or nearly identical meanings and require careful discrimination. A full account of the distinctions in meaning among synonyms (for example, *suggest, imply, hint, intimate,* and *insinuate*) may be given at the end of the entry for each word, or cross-references to its synonyms may be provided.

EXERCISE 1

In looking up the meanings of words, try to discover within what limits of meaning the word may be used. Read the definition as a whole; do not pick out a single synonym and suppose that this and the word defined are interchangeable. After looking up the following words in your dictionary, write a sentence for each one that will unmistakably illustrate its meaning.

anachronism	innocuous	precocious
eminent	materiel	sinecure
fetish	misanthropy	sophistication
hedonist	nepotism	taboo
imminent	philanthropy	travesty

EXERCISE 2

Look up each of the following words in the *Oxford English Dictionary,* in another unabridged dictionary, and in an abridged one, and write a one-page report explaining how the larger dictionaries explain the use of each word more carefully and clearly than the smaller one. Give the title, the publisher, and the date of each dictionary.

Bible	color	idealism
catholic	court	liberal
Christian	evolution	

9a

EXERCISE 3

How may the etymologies given by the dictionary help one to remember the meaning or the spelling of the following words? Look up their origins in an abridged dictionary, or for more information, in a dictionary of etymology like *The Barnhart Dictionary of Etymology,* ed. Robert K. Barnhart (N.p.: Wilson, 1988). (Note that when a series of words has the same etymology, the etymology is usually given only with the basic word of the series.)

alibi	insidious	privilege
capitol	isosceles	sacrilegious
cohort	magnanimous	sarcasm
concave	malapropism	subterfuge
denouement	peer (noun)	thrifty

EXERCISE 4

Most dictionaries put abbreviations in the main alphabetical arrangement. Locate the following abbreviations and their meanings.

at. wt.	Ens.	LL.D.
CAB	ff.	OAS
colloq.	K.C.B.	PBX
e.g.	l.c.	Q.E.D.

EXERCISE 5

Consult the dictionary for the distinction in meaning between the members of each of the following pairs of words:

neglect—negligence	instinct—intuition
ingenuous—ingenious	nauseous—nauseated
fewer—less	eminent—famous
admit—confess	criticize—censure
infer—imply	increment—addition

EXERCISE 6

In each sentence, choose the more appropriate of the two italicized words. Be able to justify your choice.

1. Many in the class were *disinterested, uninterested* and went to sleep.
2. His charming innocence is *childlike, childish.*
3. The problem is to assure the farm workers of *continuous, continual* employment.

4. She is *continuously, continually* in trouble with the police.
5. I am quite *jealous, envious* of your opportunity to study in Europe.
6. She is so *decided, decisive* in her manner that people always give in to her.
7. If we give your class all of these privileges, we may establish *precedents, precedence* that are unwise.
8. She always makes her health her *alibi, excuse* for her failures.

EXERCISE 7

Find the precise meaning of each word in the following groups, and write sentences to illustrate the differences in meaning among the words in each group.

1. abandon, desert, forsake
2. ludicrous, droll, comic
3. silent, reserved, taciturn
4. meager, scanty, sparse
5. knack, talent, genius
6. anxious, eager, avid

9b Levels of usage

Every good dictionary tells you the contexts in which the use of a word is appropriate, its customary usage. **Standard English** includes the great majority of words and constructions that native speakers would recognize as acceptable in any situation or context, whether spoken or written. All words in a dictionary that are not otherwise labeled are, in the judgment of the editors, Standard English and acceptable for general use. A good many other words and constructions, which for various reasons have a more limited use, are commonly labeled in various ways. For example, words used in some sections of the country but not in all, such as *carry* in the sense of "escort" ("He carried his sister to the movies") will be labeled *Regional* or *Dialectal*. If the usage is even more localized, the label will be more specific: *Southwestern U.S., New England*. Other labels—such as *Archaic, Obsolete,* and *Rare*—identify words that are not in common use.

Appropriateness of usage depends upon a number of interacting factors. Some words and phrases are associated only with particular groups, whether ethnic (for example, black English), professional (legal language), generational (the speech of teenagers), or economic. Dictionaries use terms like *nonstandard, substandard, colloquial, jargon,* and *slang* to distinguish such words and phrases from Standard English.

Level of formality is another factor that affects usage. We use some constructions solely with intimate friends and relatives, others only on the most formal of occasions. Thus most people would find it as out of place to greet a family member with "May I help you, sir?" as to ask a customer, "What do you want, darling?"

1. Edited English

9b

Edited English, the usual written form of the language, is relatively formal Standard English. It is the language of books from reputable publishers, good magazines, and most newspapers. Edited English is defined not merely by choice of words, but by widely accepted conventions of spelling, punctuation, grammatical usage, and sentence structure. The general subject of this book is Edited English, the normal means of official communication in the professions and in business and industry.

Authorities on language often differ among themselves, particularly where the language seems to be changing. For example, many handbooks deplore the use of *contact* as a verb meaning "to get in touch with." But the most recent editions of five leading dictionaries differ widely: two accept the usage, with no label, as Standard English; one accepts it but labels it an *Americanism;* two others label it *Informal* and discourage its use in Edited English.

Faced with such disagreement, what practical conclusion can we draw? If you use *contact* as a verb and someone challenges it, you can certainly defend yourself by citing *Webster's Ninth New Collegiate Dictionary* or the *Random House College Dictionary,* both of which make no objection to it. Of course, being challenged is a nuisance, and controversial usages may be distracting for readers. If the main purpose of your writing is to get something said, be wary of usages that need lengthy defense.

2. Formal English

Formal English appears in scholarly or scientific articles, formal speeches, official documents, and any context calling for scrupulous propriety. It makes use of words and phrases, such as *scrupulous propriety,* that rarely occur in conversation and that would seldom appear in casual writing. As another example, consider the verb *endeavor.* This is a perfectly good word that everyone knows, but its use is limited almost entirely to formal, written English, and even there it is not common. It is likely to give a bookish flavor to casual writing, and it is almost never used in speech. (Try to imagine yourself handing a friend a piece of writing with the request, "Endeavor to read this.") Formal English also includes technical language—the specialized vocabularies (sometimes called *jargon*) used in such professions as law, medicine, and the sciences. Technical language can be very precise and economical, but it is Greek to the ordinary reader and out of place in most Edited English, except in such special circumstances as legal documents, medical reports, and scientific papers. The basic principle of good usage is to fit the level of your language to the situation and to the expected reader. The most formal English is for the most formal occasions, such as a commencement or a funeral, or for official personages, such as college presidents in their public speeches and writing. In the most formal English, one might *endeavor to assuage one's consternation;* less formally the writer might say *attempt to calm* (or even *try to end*) *your fears.*

Levels of usage, like the language itself, undergo changes from generation to generation. Such changes have been especially rapid in recent decades. During the past seventy years, the center of Edited usage has moved away from the formal level toward greater informality. Especially in magazines and newspapers, good writers are more likely to use *colloquialisms* and even *slang* rather than risk the stilted pomposity of Formal English in a commonplace context.

3. Colloquial English

Colloquial English means, literally, conversational English. Everyone's language is more casual and relaxed among friends than in public speech or writing. Examples are adjectives such as *steep* for "expensive," verbs like *get away with* something, and adverbs such as *sure* in the sense of "certainly" (*I sure would like* . . .). When words and constructions are labeled *Colloquial* (some dictionaries use *Informal* for the same purpose), you should consider whether they may be jarringly out of place in the context of your writing. If in doubt, look for accepted synonyms.

4. Regional English

The label **Regional** refers to usage that is common only to speakers in a limited geographical area. These words are often standard in speech and informal writing in the regions where they are found, and sometimes they are useful additions to the local vocabulary. But for general public writing, including most college writing, they should be avoided when equivalent words in national currency are available. Some examples of regional words and expressions are *gumband* for *rubber band*, *yuz* and *y'all* for *you*, and *stand on line* for *stand in line*.

9b

5. Dialect and nonstandard English

A **Dialect** is a variety of a language spoken in a particular region of the country or by a socially identifiable group of persons. Speakers of a dialect may use not only special vocabulary, but also distinct grammatical structures that differ from those of Standard English. All dialects—including Standard—retain words and linguistic rules that have died out in other dialects (*reckon* and *yonder*, for example, in the Southeast). Other dialect forms are new to the language, as when the Southeasterner says *You might could say that* rather than *Maybe you could say that*, or the Midwesterner *Tom smokes a lot anymore* where most speakers of English would say *Tom smokes a lot these days*. Speech forms that are restricted to a particular social dialect are often labeled *Nonstandard* (sometimes *Substandard*) in dictionaries. The use of *learn* for *teach* or *she don't* for *she doesn't* are Nonstandard in this sense.

To the modern linguist, all the dialects spoken by different groups in American society are equally expressive varieties of English, even though many of their most obvious forms are not appropriate in Edited English. However, the social prestige and broad acceptability associated with Standard English make it important for educated persons to be able to distinguish this form of English from other types. Since a regional or social dialect's grammatical rules may differ from the rules of Standard English, students who are bidialectal have two sets of grammatical rules to keep in mind. They must be aware of those areas where their spoken English and written English conflict, and they may have to proofread their written work with special care to make certain that it follows the conventions of Edited English.

The labels *Nonstandard* and *Substandard* are also used to indicate a wide variety of usages not accepted by most educated readers but not necessarily associated with dialects at all: misspellings, unconventional punctuation, idiosyncratic grammatical constructions, and certain widespread usages that educated people have qualms about writing. Examples are words such as *irregardless* for *regardless, imply* for *infer,* and *flaunt* for *flout,* and grammatical errors such as *between you and I* (where *me* is correct). Many other common problems of this nature are listed in the Glossary of Usage at the end of this book. Expressions labeled *Nonstandard* have no place in serious Edited English, unless in direct quotation.

6. Slang

Slang is the label given to words with a forced, exaggerated, or humorous meaning used in extremely informal or colloquial contexts. To call a man whose ideas and behavior are unpredictable and unconventional *a kook* or to describe his ideas as *for the birds* satisfies some obscure human urge toward irreverent, novel, and vehement expression. Some slang terms remain in fairly wide use because they are vivid ways of expressing an idea that has no exact standard equivalent: *stooge, lame duck, shot* of whiskey, card *shark.* Such words are becoming accepted as Standard English. *Mob, banter, sham,* and *lynch* were all once slang terms. It is quite likely that, eventually, such useful slang words as *honky-tonk* and *snitch* will also be accepted as Standard.

A good deal of slang, however, reflects nothing more than the user's desire to be colorful, outrageous, or part of a particular in-group, and such slang has little chance of gaining complete respectability. Sports commentators and disc jockeys, for example, often use a flamboyant jargon intended to show off their ingenuity and cleverness and to establish their credentials as members of a select group or inner circle who keep up with the times. For centuries criminals have used a special, semisecret language, and many modern slang terms originated in the argot of the underworld: *gat, scram, squeal* or *sing* (confess), *push* (peddle).

Slang should be used with discretion in writing, since most slang terms fit only uncomfortably into Edited English. Furthermore, much slang goes out of fashion very quickly, and dated slang sounds more quaint and old-fashioned than Formal English. *Smashed* has worn well, but *tight, crocked, bombed,* and *plastered* may soon be museum pieces. In the 1950s, to call someone a *square* identified the speaker as a youthful, up-to-date person; today, a person who uses this term seems stuck in a bygone era.

9b

The chief objection to the use of slang is that it so quickly loses any precise meaning. Calling a person a *nerd,* a *twerp,* or a *bozo* conveys little more than your feeling of dislike. *Cool* and *bummed out* are the vaguest kind of terms, lumping all experience into two crude divisions, pleasing and unpleasing. Try to get several people to agree on the precise meaning of *nerd* and you will realize how vague and inexact a term it is. The remedy is to analyze your meaning and specify it. What exactly are the qualities that lead you to classify a person as a *twerp* or a *nerd?*

If, despite these warnings, you must use slang in serious writing, do it deliberately and accept the responsibility for it. Do not attempt to excuse yourself by putting the slang term in quotation marks. If you must apologize for a slang term, do not use it.

EXERCISE **8**

With the aid of a dictionary and your own linguistic judgment (that is, your ear for appropriateness), classify the following English words as *Formal, Informal, Colloquial,* or *Slang.*

1. crank, eccentric, [a] character
2. hide, sequester, sneak
3. irascible, cranky, grouchy
4. increase, boost, jack [up the price]
5. decline, avoid, pass [up]
6. pass [out], faint, swoon
7. necessity, [a] must, requirement
8. inexpensive, [a] steal, cheap
9. snooty, pretentious, affected
10. crib, steal, plagiarize, pilfer

9b

For each of the following Standard English words, supply one or more slang terms and, to the best of your ability, judge which are so widespread that they have already begun to creep into highly informal writing (for example, letters to friends, college newspaper columns) or seem likely to do so in the near future.

Example: to *sleep* [to *crash,* slang]

1. money
2. to relax
3. a skilled performer
4. to be going steady or to be in love
5. failure
6. to tell off
7. pleasant or enjoyable
8. to vomit
9. liquor
10. to ignore or disregard
11. complaint
12. a dull person
13. an unconventional person
14. to be unfairly treated
15. puzzling

Pick five or six slang terms widely used around campus and ask at least five people to define the meaning of each term in Standard English. How much agreement do you find? Now look up the same words in the *New Dictionary of American Slang,* ed. Robert L. Chapman (New York: Harper, 1986). How accurate are this dictionary's definitions of those words? What new information about their origins does the dictionary provide?

PART III

10 *Revising the Essay*
11 *Revising Paragraphs*
12 *Revising Sentences*
13 *Revising Diction*

Revising

10 *Revising the Essay*

Few
rom childhood on, we learn to ask others
what they think and to pay attention to the opinions they express.
Serving on committees in school or in our community, exchanging
views on a recent film, sorting out tangled relationships with friends,
relatives, or lovers—in these and dozens of other situations we depend
on the opinions of others to deepen our understanding or guide our
actions. We count on others to help us test and focus our ideas, to
make us notice what we might otherwise have overlooked. At our
best, when our egos do not intrude, when we don't feel threatened,
we realize how vital the insights of other people can be, how much
we can gain by collaborating. Such moments are possible in writing,
too, particularly in the stages of revision.

10a Understanding revision

Revision, as the Latin roots of the word suggest, is "seeing
again"—the chance to rethink an argument, reconsider evidence, rearrange ideas, rephrase sentences. As we observed in Chapter **1**, many
writers revise as they compose. But most writers also take time after
completing a draft to review their work. Because revision at this stage of
the writing process is just as idiosyncratic as every other aspect of composing, we cannot prescribe rules for revising that will always work
for you. We can, however, suggest a few general principles for you to
keep in mind as you look for ways to revise a draft of an essay.

1. Recognize the two types of revision

Some students become so preoccupied with making sentence-
level changes in their writing (substituting words and correcting punctuation, for example) that they overlook larger matters. Experienced writ-

ers, in contrast, recognize that effective revision occurs on two different levels. **Macro revision** involves the larger elements that make an essay successful: the sharpness of its focus, the clarity of its organization, the appropriateness and specificity of its supporting evidence. **Micro revision,** on the other hand, deals with smaller changes, like those ensuring that sentences are clear and concise, diction is specific, and punctuation is correct.

This chapter and the next will deal with macro revision—revision that focuses on the design of the essay as a whole and the strength of its paragraphs. In Chapters **12** and **13** we will turn to micro revision—revising sentences and diction. We think that separating the levels of revision in this way makes them easier to discuss, and we hope that this division will remind you to focus on large matters as well as small ones when you revise. But by organizing our discussion of revision in this way, we do not mean to suggest that these two levels of revision are unrelated, or that you should revise at only one level at a time. In actuality, most writers constantly move back and forth between larger and smaller elements as they revise their work.

2.   Leave time after finishing a draft before you revise

This is perhaps the most frequently given—and most frequently ignored—piece of advice about revising. All of us occasionally find ourselves writing against the pressure of a deadline, and in such circumstances we compress writing and revising into a single, continuous process. When possible, though, it's a good idea to allow some time—at least a few hours, ideally a few days—to elapse between drafting an essay and revising it. You need such time to detach yourself from your work, to put some distance between yourself and your enthusiastic first efforts. Returning to an essay after such a break, you bring a degree of objectivity that will help you spot weaknesses in your writing and a fresh perspective that will help you find better ways of communicating what you want to say.

3.   Analyze your draft systematically

Sometimes we are prompted to revise by the instinctive feeling that a passage doesn't sound right, or that it doesn't say what we wanted it to. Intuition is a valuable guide; a passage that sounds wrong to you after you've written it probably won't sound any better to your readers. Still, we can't always depend on intuition alone to identify opportunities for revision. It's also a good idea to examine a draft systematically, considering its main elements one at a time. If you don't already have such a system, you might try using the Checklist for Writing and Revising that we have printed inside the back cover of this book. Addressing both macro and micro revision, the questions in this checklist can help you reflect on the plan of your paper as well as on the strength of its constituent parts.

4. Be open to possible changes in your draft

No revision will succeed, though, if you are so committed to the words on your page that you resist considering significant changes in what you have written. One of the hardest tasks that any writer faces is deleting lines, perhaps even paragraphs, that took hours to put down on paper and starting afresh to find a better way to get the point across. And yet, unless we are prepared to make such changes, there is little point in reviewing a draft at all.

Genuine revision demands your willingness to reconsider not just the phrasing of your essay, but its purpose and design. It requires that you be ready to let go of passages that may have seemed acceptable when you originally composed them and to search for stronger evidence and more effective patterns of organization. No wonder that professional writers usually expect to spend as much time revising a paper as they did writing it in the first place. They know that the small changes they make in a draft have a way of leading them to larger ones, and they approach revision prepared to discover new ways of shaping the composition as a whole.

10b Using your instructor's suggestions in revision

The written comments that an instructor makes on a draft of your essay are your most obvious source of assistance as you consider how to revise. Your instructor may make several different kinds of marks on your paper: short correction symbols like those printed inside the back cover of this book; numerical references to specific sections of this book (5a, 12d, and the like); brief notes or questions in the margins of the paper; and a slightly longer final comment on the paper's strengths and weaknesses. All such marks will be helpful, but you shouldn't necessarily expect them to provide a step-by-step plan for revising your paper. Revision, after all, is not simply a matter of following someone else's directions; rather, it's a creative process, a process through which you make your own discoveries about what you have written. Thus you should plan to use your instructor's comments not as a blueprint for revision but as a guide to reflecting on what you have accomplished in your paper and thinking about improvements that you might make.

As you read the following preliminary draft of a student paper, notice how the instructor's comments focus the writer's attention on problems and suggest (but don't prescribe) ways of solving them.

10b

Social Insecurity

Young people today hold high hopes for their futures, and why not? We live in Amer-

⌃ ica—the land of opportunity. If one

⌃ speaks with a factory worker or with a yuppie

though, it quickly becomes apparent that

agr a major concern in everyone's mind is what

will happen when they reach retirement

age. It certainly is in mine. Politicians

awk *sent* would respond with Social Security as the

promise of retirement. But the majority of

us are not politicians, and do not believe

Social Security will be there once we reach

cliché our golden years. Nothing I heard in the

last presidential campaign concerning this

issue served to (reassure) me otherwise.   *ww*

    There is little doubt that Franklin   *trans?*
Roosevelt was one of our greatest Presi-
dents. When he conceived Social Security   *thin ¶-how is*
in the New Deal era of the 1930s, he had a   *it related to*
breakthrough idea. Until then, working-   *your introduction?*
and middle-class retirement security was
virtually nonexistent.

10b

    A vexing problem in Washington these
days is, however, that Social Security
in the 1990s ("ain't what it used to be.")   *avoid slang*
(Designed) to provide reasonable "secu-
rity" for the elderly, the current amount   *dm*
received monthly does not come close to
meeting the basic costs of the recipients. Barely being able to keep gas turned
on and food on the table does not foster a   *awk*
sense of security for most Americans.   *sent*

    Social Security was begun in order to
provide for America's working-class re-   *again, no clear*
tired persons. The scope of the program has   *connection with*
grown considerably since the 1930s to where   *previous ¶*
it now includes retarded persons, disabled
persons, some single parents, and other se-   *vague—explain*
lected individuals singled out for inclu-   *or delete*
sion. These people do indeed need governmental support, but the Social Security

jargon   machine and its (in-place infrastructure)

agr →   <u>has</u> seemed to be the vehicle of choice, rather than creating new, more specialized programs.

very thin
¶ — expand,
or combine
with another?   Another problem with Social Security is that it lags behind the changes in America's economy. Inflation has consistently outpaced the cost-of-living adjustments made to the Social Security program.

?   Social Security is an agreement (in kind) between a person and the government. I pay into the program all my working years and help to take care of today's elderly. Then when I reach retirement age, the workers of tomorrow will be paying into the program and supporting me. This all-for-one-and-one-for-all attitude seems logical and simple

doesn't add
much —
explain or
delete   enough. But with the problems cited and (many others not touched on,) the program is quickly heading for an (all-for-one-and-

could be →
clearer   none-for-all conclusion. (Social Security is nothing more than a governmental program

ww — overhaul?   in need of a major (facelift.)

another under-
developed ¶   Perhaps I am being presumptuous in assuming a program I started paying into before I even understood what it was for should

support me in my later years. What right
do I have to the thousands of dollars I will
have paid into it?

Conscientious adults must look at the
reality of the situation. We cannot count
on Social Security being there. At its *unclear—*
when?
present rate the program will never survive. Through individual retirement accounts, certificates of deposit, and the
like, we must plan on our own for supporting *same cliché*
ourselves in our golden years. *as #1*

10b

We all need to realize the truth of the
matter; Social Security has not always been *shouldn't this*
historical back-
in such a dismal state. When it was created *ground come*
it worked beautifully, because the birth- *earlier? Combine*
rate was high and contributors far outnum- *with #2?*
bered recipients. Since 1964 and the end
of the so-called baby boom, America's popu- *Combine this*
lation has begun to age rapidly. Today *material with*
there are almost three contributors for ev- *earlier #s on*
ery recipient. Projections into the *SSA's problems?*
twenty-first century estimate a time when
recipients will nearly equal contributors
and eventually outnumber them if present
trends continue. The mathematics here is
not difficult, and yet our leaders in Wash—

What *is* its
purpose? Not
clear.

ington continue to ignore it. Why they do
is not the purpose of this essay. The fact
is they do, and we as concerned citizens must
realize the gravity of the situation and
prepare ourselves accordingly.

Disappointingly
vague. What
exactly do you
want readers
to do?

10b

Your subject is an important one, and you seem to
have given it considerable thought. But as I suggest
above, the focus and organization of this paper are
not very clear. When you revise, I think you should
(1) decide what point you want to make and state
it explicitly, and (2) improve the coherence of
your analysis by combining some of the short
paragraphs that deal with the SSA's history and
current problems.

The instructor has used some of his marginal comments to point
out problems that call for micro revision—for example, the agreement
errors in paragraphs 1 and 4, the vagueness and jargon in paragraph
4, the inexact diction in paragraph 6. But as his final comment indicates,
this paper's most serious weaknesses demand revision at the macro
level. To revise the paper successfully, the student will have to be
willing to reorganize its contents, pulling together related ideas that
are scattered throughout this draft of the essay, deleting material that
confuses the paper's structure, and discovering a focus for her analysis.

In the revised version below, notice above all the clearer structure
that the writer has imposed on her material. With the short paragraphs
combined and extraneous information eliminated, the paper now more
clearly presents the growing problems with Social Security and ends
more conclusively with the writer's opinion about the changes that
are needed.

Social Insecurity

Young people today hold high hopes for their futures, and why not? We live in America, the land of opportunity. Yet looming in the back of most of our minds is worry about what will happen to us when we reach age sixty-five. To this concern, politicians respond that Social Security is the promise of retirement. But those of us who are not politicians are unconvinced that Social Security will be there when we need it. Regrettably, nothing I heard in the last presidential election persuaded me otherwise.

The problems facing Social Security today have not always existed. Conceived during the New Deal era of the 1930s, Social Security worked well at its onset At that time, the birthrate was high and contributors far outnumbered recipients. Social Security provided a guaranteed income for millions of working- and middle-class retired persons where none had existed before.

In recent years, however, problems

10b

This revised paragraph, focusing on the origins of the Social Security Administration, draws on material from the second and ninth paragraphs of the original draft.

This paragraph, on

10b

the Social Security Administration's growing problems, unites material from paragraphs 4, 5, and 9 in the earlier draft. Transitional phrases make the main points clear: *In the first place, Moreover, A final problem. . . .*

have arisen in the Social Security Administration. In the first place, the scope of the program has grown considerably since the 1930s. Now those receiving benefits from the retirement account include retarded persons, disabled persons, and some single parents. Moreover, with the end of the so-called baby boom, America's population has begun to age rapidly, while the number of working contributors to the Social Security program declines. As a result, today there are only about three contributors for every recipient, and projections into the next century point ominously to a time when the number of recipients will equal and then exceed the number of contributors. A final problem with Social Security is that it lags behind changes in America's economy. Inflation has consistently outpaced the cost-of-living adjustments made to the Social Security program, and consequently the amount that most people receive each month does not come close to meeting their basic expenses.

This transitional paragraph, a shortened and

Social Security was supposed to be an agreement between each citizen and the government. I pay into the program all my working years to help take care of today's elderly. Then when I reach retirement age, the workers of tomorrow will be paying into the program and supporting me. In theory this plan seems simple enough, but the realities of the 1990s indicate that it cannot continue to function in this way for long.

If the Social Security Administration is to survive into the twenty-first century, we need to replace elected officials who refuse to acknowledge the program's precarious condition with others who realize that decisive action to correct its ills is needed now. And we must be willing to reconsider the program's goals. I believe that we must return Social Security to its original purpose, retirement security for the elderly. For others who have been receiving Social Security benefits, we will need to initiate new programs, along with new methods to fund them. Unless we are prepared to undertake such reform, more and more elderly Americans in the years ahead will find that "Social Security" is just a broken promise.

clarified version of the original paragraph 6, leads the writer to the recommendations that she wants to make in her final paragraph.

10b

The closing paragraph of the revised essay is much more specific than the conclusion of the earlier version. Here the writer makes two precise recommendations: that we elect officials who are prepared to deal with the problems facing Social Security, and that we consider restructuring the program.

In contrast to the inconclusive ending of the first draft, the final line of this essay powerfully suggests the urgency of the problem.

10c Using your peers' suggestions in revision

Professional writers almost always ask their colleagues to comment on the writing that they do before completing a final draft. If you have a friend or roommate who is willing to read your drafts with a critical eye, you should consider enlisting that person's advice for your revising too. Make it clear that you are not simply looking for compliments on what you've written; instead, you want to know about parts of your paper that the reader considers unclear, weakly developed, hard to follow, or just dull. Ask your reader to make brief comments in the margins of your draft, and then talk over his or her reactions to it. You may find that discussing your paper with someone who has read it will help you not only to understand its problems but also to think of ways to correct them.

1. Participating in a peer editing group

Your instructor may assign you to a group of four or five students who read and comment on early drafts of one another's papers throughout the academic term. If you haven't been in such a group before, you may not be sure what kind of advice to give to the other writers in your group. In fact, you may not feel that your advice is very valuable at all. But it is. You don't have to be an accomplished writer to offer useful advice on someone else's paper; you simply have to be a careful, sympathetic, honest reader. Here are some guidelines to consider as you look for appropriate comments to make.

Be considerate

Most of us feel that we have invested some part of ourselves in what we write, particularly if the paper deals with a subject from our experience or an issue that we care strongly about. To avoid hurting another writer's feelings, therefore, you should avoid making sweeping negative judgments about an essay, such as "This paper bored me," or "I don't know why you'd want to write about *this* subject." Such comments can wound the writer without helping him or her to see how the paper might be improved.

Be honest

On the other hand, a host of purely positive comments won't be of much value to another writer either. If everyone in the group says, "I thought your paper was great—I wish mine were that good," the writer may briefly feel gratified, but later, when he or she sits down alone to try to revise the essay, such compliments won't be very helpful. The best advice here is also the simplest: say what you really feel after reading the paper, touching on both its strengths and its weaknesses. Always begin with something that you think the writer has done well, but then go on to discuss elements of the paper that could perhaps be handled better.

10c

Be specific

Although most writers will be interested in your general reactions to their papers, the only really useful suggestions for revision are specific ones. Use your comments, whether oral or written, to point to the precise parts of the paper that you think the writer should reconsider. Don't say, "I think some of the evidence in this paper is weak"; instead, identify the places where the evidence doesn't convince you: "The examples that you give in paragraph 3 don't seem to support your thesis." Don't say, "Sometimes your paragraphs are hard to follow"; instead, specify the places where you have difficulty: "I get lost after the third sentence in paragraph 2."

Be prepared with comments on both the micro and the macro levels

We have made the point that revision proceeds on two levels, a macro level that focuses on large issues like purpose, organization, and evidence, and a micro level concerned with sentence-level matters. The revision suggestions made by a peer editing group should also address both kinds of issues. Observations about word choice and comma usage can be useful, but they alone won't help a writer make a badly organized paper coherent, or an unfocused paper clear. Everyone in a peer editing group should also be prepared to make comments on the macro level—for example, comments about the clarity of the paper's focus and organization, about the appropriateness of the writer's tone, or about the strength of the evidence that the writer has cited to support the paper's main points.

2.   Using a peer editing worksheet

You can use the Checklist for Writing and Revising inside the back cover of this book not only to examine your own drafts, but also to consider papers produced by other writers in your peer editing group. Or you might find it easier to talk about another student's paper after you and the other members of your group have filled out a Peer Editing Worksheet like the one below.

10c

Don't think of the Peer Editing Worksheet as a scorecard; rather, use it as a way of opening up a discussion of the paper under consideration. Using the Peer Editing Worksheet, members of the group individually evaluate the paper. Then, with the help of the paper's author, they compare and discuss their written responses.

Peer Editing Worksheet

Writer's name _____   Evaluator's name _____

1. What does this paper's introduction accomplish? Does it introduce the writer's subject? Does it arouse your interest in the paper? _

   _____

   _____

   _____

2. What is the thesis statement in this paper? _____

   _____

3. Briefly state the paper's main points, and then comment on how effectively each of these points supports the paper's thesis.

Main Point	*Effective Support for Thesis?*
(a) _____	(a) _____
(b) _____	(b) _____
(c) _____	(c) _____
(d) _____	(d) _____

---

4. If you were writing this paper, what other points might you use to support its thesis? _____
_____
_____

5. Identify the most successful and the least successful paragraphs of the paper, and explain why you selected them. Consider such matters as the following: Is the paragraph's main idea clearly indicated? Is the paragraph's development effective? Is the paragraph's organization easy to follow?
Most successful paragraph: _____
Reason: _____
_____
Least successful paragraph: _____
Reason: _____
_____

10c

6. Identify two or three of the strongest sentences in the paper, and explain why you selected each (for example: vivid diction, effective use of parallel structure, good sense of the writer's voice).

Strongest Sentences (give paragraph number and sentence number)	Reasons
(a) _____	_____
(b) _____	_____
(c) _____	_____

7. Identify two or three of the weakest sentences in the paper, and explain why you selected each (for example: confusing syntax, vague diction, awkward phrasing).

Weakest Sentences (give paragraph number and sentence number)	Reasons
(a) _____	_____
(b) _____	_____
(c) _____	_____

8. What does the paper's conclusion accomplish? Does it bring the paper to a strong close? _____
_____
_____
_____

Both agreement and disagreement among the group's members can be useful to the writer of the paper. Strong agreement—for example, about the effectiveness of a certain paragraph or the awkwardness of a specific sentence—provides either reassuring evidence of the paper's strengths or convincing proof of its weaknesses. Disagreements can be equally valuable. For example, when several readers formulate a paper's thesis statement in sharply different ways, the writer has probably failed to make clear the focus of the paper. The group members' next step in such a case should be to determine why they were unable to agree on the writer's main point. Perhaps the thesis statement should be reworded so that its subject or restriction is more precise. Or perhaps it needs to be moved to a more prominent position in the paper. By highlighting areas where at least some readers failed to grasp the writer's intentions, disagreements among group members should provoke a discussion of the paper that will help the writer to identify opportunities for effective revising.

10c

The completed Peer Editing Worksheets are valuable not only as starting points for the discussion of a writer's paper, but also as aids to the writer when he or she begins to revise the paper. At the close of the discussion, all the members of the group should give their completed worksheets to the writer, so that he or she may draw on their comments and advice while revising the essay. The written observations that peer editors have made about the effectiveness of the paper's introduction and conclusion, about the strength of its supporting evidence, about its most successful and least successful paragraphs, and about its strongest and weakest sentences can help to guide the writer's reshaping of the essay long after the group has finished talking about it.

If you haven't engaged in such collaborative efforts before, or if you don't know the other members of your group very well, you may at first feel a bit uncomfortable with small-group work. Be patient. As the group begins to jell, you'll find it easier to join into discussions of other writers' papers and of your own. Such experience, you'll discover, will sharpen not only your powers of careful reading, but your writing skills as well.

EXERCISE 1

Use the Checklist for Writing and Revising inside the back cover of this book to analyze the first draft of your next essay. To be certain that you give proper attention to the topics that the checklist covers, write out brief answers to each of the first nine questions.

EXERCISE 2

Look over several papers that your instructor has marked and returned to you. Do the instructor's comments point mainly to the need for micro revision, or to opportunities for macro revision? Do similar problems, at either level, turn up in more than one paper? Use your instructor's marks to make a personal checklist of things to keep in mind when you revise your next essay.

EXERCISE 3

Many writers fail to revise effectively because they feel too closely tied to the structure and language of their first draft. If you sometimes hesitate to tamper with the early draft of an essay, try the following procedure. After completing a draft of your paper, put it aside for a day or more, and then write a new version of the essay without looking at the original draft. Compare the two versions. Do you find that the changes you made in the second version were more substantial than the changes you ordinarily make when you revise?

10c

EXERCISE 4

Ask two friends to read a draft of your next essay and to record their reactions on a Peer Editing Worksheet like the one on pages 186–187. How much correlation do you find between their responses? If possible, bring both friends together to discuss their reactions to your paper.

II Revising Paragraphs

Paragraphs are the timber writers use to construct papers. Depending on the writer's blueprint, they can be cut into various sizes and shapes and planed down or nailed together, and they can serve as doors, joists, or flooring. Problems occur, however, when a beam is too thin to support the weight it must bear, or when it is cracked and knotty, or when the tongue and groove do not match. To put it another way, effective paragraphs have the thickness of evidence needed to sustain their ideas, they are unsplintered and intact, and they are firmly joined together. Here, we will discuss two of the most common weaknesses in paragraphs—lack of development and lack of coherence—and some means of repair. (To be sure that you understand the main characteristics of effective paragraphs, you may wish to read or review Chapters **6** and **7**.)

11a Inadequate development

Although its central idea may be clear, an underdeveloped paragraph is too brief, general, thin, or dull. Developing a paragraph does not mean padding out a simple statement or repeating the same idea in different words. It means taking the time to be clear, accurate, and specific.

1. Recognizing vagueness and generalities

As you read the following student essay, about a group of freshmen meeting their adviser and having dinner together, pay particular attention to what you *don't* find out about the event:

Mr. Miller was not what I had expected of a faculty member. He was not over fifty years old. He was not wearing thick glasses. He was, in contrast, about twenty-six, rather athletic looking, and a very interesting conversationalist, not only in his own field, but in every subject we discussed.

My classmates, most of whom I had not met before, were also a surprise. There were no socially backward introverts, interested only in the physical sciences, as I had feared. I found instead some very interesting people with whom I immediately wanted to become friends. Some were interested in sports, some in music, some in politics. Each individual had something to offer me.

The Millers did a marvelous job of preparing the dinner. We did a marvelous job of eating it. However, the real purpose of the dinner was to become acquainted with at least one of our faculty members and about ten of our fellow students. In this endeavor we were also quite successful, for the discussions begun during the meal lasted for a long time after and as a matter of fact, some of them were continued the next day.

This year's adviser dinner was very rewarding, and I believe it should remain a tradition. The students really get to know each other, and a few of the faculty are pleasantly surprised.

11a

A reader might well wonder why the dinner should be continued as a tradition. Nothing the writer says carries real conviction because nothing is developed concretely. These paragraphs raise more questions than they answer: (1) Why should the writer have expected his adviser to be an ancient, nearsighted bore? (2) What was Mr. Miller's "field" and what did he talk about as a "very interesting conversationalist"? (3) What exactly did his classmates' various interests "offer" him? (4) If the meal was so memorable, what was it and how many servings did he have? (5) What was talked about so enthusiastically and "for a long time after" the meal?

What has gone wrong here? The writer has substituted jargon (*very interesting conversationalist, socially backward introverts*), vague generalities (*some were interested in sports, some in music, some in politics*), and unexplained events (the dinner discussion) for specific detail. The paragraphs are not developed; they merely repeat the same idea unconvincingly—that the adviser's dinner was a good chance to discover that faculty and students were in some vague way "interesting," not what the writer "had expected."

2. Using concrete diction and specific detail

Concrete diction cuts out fuzziness and gives a paper sharpness and depth. Consider these sentences from the essay above: *The Millers did a marvelous job of preparing the dinner. We did a marvelous job of eating it.* Do they mean that the Millers barbecued two dozen hamburgers and tossed a spicy bean salad for a delicious buffet meal on paper plates? Or do they mean that the Millers gave a sit-down dinner, complete with white linen, silver setting, and candlelight, and served roast turkey, hot rolls, and two vegetables? Either of these alternatives is better than the empty generality of the original. A buffet dinner for thirteen people implies relaxed hosts, students going for several helpings, and comfortable informality. A sit-down dinner for thirteen people implies busy hosts, reserved freshmen, hushed requests for the gravy, and long, earnest discussion as the coffee lingers in cups and the candles melt. Whatever the case was, specific wording would help readers see the event and prepare them for the point that the writer wants to make about it.

11a

Specific detail comes from recalling the taste, touch, sound, and sight of an event as clearly and precisely as possible. In the following two paragraphs, for example, the student writer has improved her original by re-creating the incident more specifically and thus providing her readers with the information they need to picture it in their minds. The italicized passages indicate the places where she has made her major changes.

Vague original

Though the air was *uncomfortable,* the sand was *soothing* and warm, and I dug a *hole* into it and piled it up *until it half-covered* me from the air. I sat there, shivering in the *air,* until the sand *began falling away* from me. I tried to *bury my legs* again, but the sand *was dry and it would not stay in place. I tried to find* damp sand near me, but in a short time it also dried out and *wouldn't stay in place.* So I rested for *a while* and watched the sea rise and fall and the various objects it threw onto the beach. *Seaweed* and *other things* were washed up, then carried back in a regular rhythm.

Revision for detail

Though the air was *cold,* the sand *felt soft* and warm, and I dug a *damp trough* in it and piled it up around my *legs until I had a body only from the waist up.* I sat there, shivering in the *cool mist,* until the sand began to *crumble* down around me. I tried to *gather it back up* on my legs, but it *had dried* and *kept slithering down again in little shifting rivers. I dug with my hands beside me* until I came to damp sand that I piled on my legs, but in a short time it too *dried and slipped away.* So I rested *my head on my knees* and watched the sea rise and fall and *rise and fall, bringing with it,* to the beach, something new each time: a *loop of rust-colored* seaweed, *a shell, a rock, a small jellyfish. And falling away,* it would *often take with it* what it had *just brought.*

11a

The revised version is not much longer than the original, but it tells much more. It's the choice of words, not the number of words, that makes the difference.

3. Revising an underdeveloped paragraph

If your instructor comments that your paragraphs are inadequately developed, try using either of the following strategies as you revise.

Identify generalities

Examine the paragraph carefully for vague generalities, needlessly abstract words, and clichés, and underline them. For instance:

When they are young, children are free and can be themselves. They are protected from nature's hardships by our modern-day society and by our complex technology. They only have to keep out of trouble. Mostly they are free to do whatever they want. But as they get older, they have more and more duties and responsibilities put upon them. They begin to lose their freedom and become conformists.

When they are young may be changed to *Before they start elementary school; free and can be themselves* to *playful, spontaneous, and imaginative; protected from nature's hardships* to *protected from hunger, disease, and the weather.* Underlining may also reveal that certain generalities, if they mean anything at all, are untrue or need extensive qualification: Do children who bike to school, who roam where they wish afterward, and who spend time in the evenings with their friends really "lose their freedom and become conformists"? Or, to take a very different view, is it true that our "modern-day society" and our "complex technology" "protect" a ghetto child from rats, crime, poverty, sickness, and dilapidated firetraps?

11a

Construct lists of supplementary details

Make a list of all the possible details or examples you could add to the paragraph. You won't be able to use all of these, of course, without drowning your reader in specifics, but a written list of details offers you a starting place for making judicious and effective additions to your paragraph.

In the following example, notice how the student has identified places where he might insert additional details and has made a preliminary list of the kinds of items that he could include:

Working as a door-to-door salesperson in and
around St. Louis last summer gave me more than just
extra spending money. It gave me a chance to meet
types of people* I might otherwise never have known,
and some practical experience* I am glad I had.

* *construction workers living in trailers —
retired jazz musicians living in
boarding houses — young couples renovating
inner-city duplexes — retirees in
suburban condos*

* sizing up a person's interests and tastes — keeping my temper when insulted — making friends with hostile dogs — thinking on my feet

The successful writer is able to choose from the details at hand those that will best support the point that he or she wants to make. In this paragraph, for example, note how the general statement asserted in the topic sentence and the specific details included in the rest of the paragraph unite to form a clear and convincing argument:

11a

Details support an argument

One section of Golding's *The Inheritors* demonstrates how science fiction can incorporate the materials of ritual. *The journey of Lok's primitive people to their summer home on the cliff is a model of the rite of renewal and contains many of the themes associated with it in religious traditions* [Topic sentence]. Mal, as leader, makes the choice of direction when faced with a fork on the trail, picking the harder but quicker way in order to reach the comfort of the terrace cave sooner. Lok, not concentrating on the path but preoccupied with food, slips and falls when he turns to what he thinks is the smell of the fire the old woman is carrying. Along the trail, the tribe stops and stands in awe of an "ice woman," frozen snow that resembles their mother earth goddess Oa. All these images—the ageless choice between two paths, the stumbling caused by wordly hunger, and yet the knowledge that deity is ever-present—portray components of the ritual passage witnessed for thousands of years, as for example in the Judeo-Christian tradition. Once the people arrive at the terrace, they believe they are protected and safe, like travelers who have passed through the guarded gates. And to complete their journey, they must sanctify their home by rekindling the fire the old woman has carried as coals. The transport and the revival of the hearth fire by Lok's people are just as necessary as the transport of the Ark of the Covenant and the building of an altar were to the Hebrew people as they moved. For Lok and his people believe they have reached their promised land.

11b Lack of coherence

Within every paragraph, the sentences should be arranged and linked in such a manner that readers can easily follow the thought. It isn't enough for readers to know what each sentence means; they must also see how each sentence is related to the one that precedes it and how it leads into the one that comes next. Without transitional devices to indicate such relationships, even a reasonably well-unified paragraph can be difficult to follow:

Disjointed

In Tillie Olsen's story "I Stand Here Ironing," a young woman attempts to love and help her oldest daughter, Emily. The mother's own problems and responsibilities prevent her. The mother was young. Her husband abandoned her. She was forced to work. This separated her from Emily. Emily had to be left with others, and the mother lost touch with her. The mother was able to find a new husband. She was soon forced to concentrate on her other children. Her other daughter, Susan, is the most notable example. Susan became everything Emily was not. Susan was blonde, pretty, quick, and articulate. Emily was dark, slow, and sickly. The mother looks back with guilt. She says, "I was a young mother, I was a distracted mother."

Although it has unity and development, this paragraph lacks coherence; the writer too often leaps and jumps erratically from one sentence to the next, as reading aloud will make especially clear. Revised by slight rephrasing and the addition of connecting words, the paragraph becomes easier to follow:

More coherent

In Tillie Olsen's short story "I Stand Here Ironing," a young woman attempts to love and help her eldest daughter, Emily, *yet* her own problems and responsibilities prevent her from fulfilling *these goals. As a young mother, abandoned by her husband,* she had to work, *and was thus separated from her daughter. Forced to leave* Emily with others, the mother lost touch with her. *Although* the mother was able to find a new husband, she was soon forced to concentrate on her other children, *most notably* her other daughter, Susan. Susan became everything Emily was not—blonde, pretty, quick, and articulate. Emily was dark, slow, and sickly. *Looking back in guilt,* the mother says, "I was a young mother, I was a distracted mother."

In the revised passage, the writer is no longer thinking in single sentences only. Instead, he has looked for the continuity among his ideas and for the most accurate means of showing this continuity in each case.

Most writers rely on four devices for achieving coherence: transitional words, linking pronouns, the repetition of key words, and parallel structure.

1. Transitional words

Transitional words and phrases help to indicate relationships between sentences:

Cause or Effect	Contrast	Addition
as a result	but	also
because	however	besides
consequently	in contrast	furthermore
hence	nonetheless	in addition
since	on the contrary	moreover
so	on the other hand	next
therefore	still	too
thus	yet	

Example	Comparison	Conclusion
for example	in the same way	in conclusion
for instance	likewise	in short
specifically	similarly	to conclude
		to sum up

Notice how carefully used transitional words help us follow the writer's argument in this passage:

Transitional words provide coherence

Past and future are two time regions which we commonly separate by a third which we call the present. *But* strictly speaking the present does not exist, *or* is at best no more than an infinitesimal point in time, gone before we can note it as present. *Nevertheless* we must have a present; *and so* we get one by robbing the past, by holding on to the most recent events and pretending that they all belong to our immediate perceptions. If, *for example,* I raise my arm, the total event is a series of occurrences of which the first are past before the last two have taken place; *yet* I perceive it as a single movement executed in one instant of time.

—Carl Becker, *The Heavenly City of the Eighteenth-Century Philosophers*

11b

2. Linking pronouns

Sentences may also be connected by pronouns that have clear antecedents. This technique is an effective way of avoiding needless repetition. Notice in the following example how Henry James substitutes *it* for *symbolism* and later for *this suggestion,* and how he uses the phrase *this suggestion* to point back to the entire preceding sentence.

Linking pronouns provide coherence

In *The Scarlet Letter* there is a great deal of symbolism; there is, I think, too much. *It* is overdone at times, and becomes mechanical; *it* ceases to be impressive, and grazes triviality. The idea of the mystic *A* which the young minister finds imprinted upon his breast and eating into his flesh, in sympathy with the embroidered badge that Hester is condemned to wear, appears to me to be a case in point. *This suggestion* should, I think, have just been made and dropped; to insist upon *it,* and return to *it,* is to exaggerate the weak side of the subject. Hawthorne returns to *it* constantly, plays with *it,* and seems charmed by *it;* until at last the reader feels tempted to declare that his enjoyment of *it* is puerile.

—Henry James, *Hawthorne*

3. Repetition of key words

Paragraph coherence may also be maintained by the repetition of key words that are related to a central idea. In the following passage, notice the key words *darkness, deep sea,* and *blackness* and the words related to them by contrast, such as *sunlight, red rays,* and *surface:*

Repeated key words provide coherence

Immense pressure, then, is one of the governing conditions of life in the *deep sea; darkness* is another. The unrelieved *darkness* of the *deep waters* has produced weird and incredible modifications of the *abyssal* fauna. It is a *blackness* so divorced from the world of the *sunlight* that probably only the few men who have seen it with their own eyes can visualize it. We know that *light fades out rapidly with descent below the surface*. The *red rays* are gone at the end of the first 200 or 300 feet, and with them all the *orange and yellow warmth of the sun*. Then the *greens* fade out, and at 1,000 feet only a *deep, dark, brilliant blue* is left. In *very clear waters* the *violet rays* of the spectrum may penetrate another thousand feet. Beyond this is only the *blackness* of the *deep sea*.

—Rachel Carson, *The Sea Around Us*

11b

4. Parallel structure

Continuity can also be sustained by parallel structure, which calls attention to similar ideas. This coordination of equally important ideas is often useful with introductory or summary paragraphs, although its use is by no means confined to such paragraphs. In the following example, the first paragraph is taken from the beginning of a chapter, the second from near its conclusion.

Parallel structure provides coherence

To "become a pueblo" *meant to adopt* many of the ways and political forms and ambitions of townspeople. *It meant to accept* the tools, leadership, and conceptions of progress which were then being offered to the villagers of Yucatan by the leaders of Mexico's social revolution. *It required* the inhabitants *to give up* some of the isolation which was theirs in the remote and sparsely inhabited lands that lay apart from the goings and comings of city men. In future they would be a part of the political and economic institutions of Yucatan, of Mexico, and—though of course they would not have put it so—of the one world that was then in the making.

• • •

Chan Kom had attained its loftiest political objective. *It had become* the head of its own municipality. *It had made* itself into a pueblo, a community of dwellers—some of them—in masonry houses. *It had* a municipal building, with a stone jail; a school building, also of masonry;

a masonry church—and a masonry Protestant chapel. *It had* two gristmills and four stores. *It had* two outdoor theatres and a baseball diamond.

—Robert Redfield, *A Village That Chose Progress: Chan Kom Revisited*

Notice how the parallel structure in the first three sentences of the second paragraph restates what it meant for Chan Kom to achieve its "loftiest political objective." Notice how the parallel structure in the last three sentences of the second paragraph lists equally important features in a "community of dwellers." And notice how the parallel structure of the second paragraph harks back to the parallel structure of the first paragraph—from what Chan Kom "had attained" to what "it required" to become a pueblo.

5. Maintaining coherence between paragraphs

The main devices for maintaining coherence between paragraphs are the same as those for providing coherence within a paragraph—transitional words, linking pronouns, repeated key words, and parallel structure. Equally important is the *arrangement* of the material so that a paragraph begins with some reference to the idea that has come before, or ends with some reference to the idea that is to be taken up next. In the following example, notice how the writer typically begins a paragraph by referring to the main idea developed in the previous one. Such a strategy enhances the clarity and logic of his essay.

Up to our own day **[1893]** American history has been in a large degree the history of the colonization of the Great West. The existence of an area of free land, its continuous recession, and the advance of American settlement westward, explain American development **[thesis]**.

Behind institutions, behind constitutional forms and modifications, lie the vital forces that call these organs into life and shape them to meet changing conditions. The peculiarity of American institutions is the fact they have been compelled to adapt themselves to the changes of an expanding people—to the changes involved in crossing a continent, in winning a wilderness. . . . **[omission of the rest of the paragraph]**

In this advance, the frontier is the outer edge of the wave—the meeting point between savagery and civilization. . . . **[omission of the rest of the paragraph]**

The American frontier is sharply distinguished from the European frontier—a fortified boundary line running through dense populations. The most significant thing about the American frontier is that it lies at the hither edge of free land. . . . **[omission of the rest of the paragraph]** In the settlement of America we have to observe how European life entered the continent, and how America modified and developed that life. . . . The frontier is the line of the most rapid and effective Americanization. . . . **[rest of paragraph suggests how, and concludes]** And to study this advance, the men who grew up under these conditions, and the political, economic and social results of it, is to study the really American part of our history.

—Frederick Jackson Turner, "The Frontier in American History"

11b

EXERCISE **1**

This exercise is for practice in working with concrete detail and diction.

1. List as many details as you can for describing one of the following subjects. Then write two paragraphs about the subject, the first as complete as you can make it, the second edited to include only the most relevant details.

   A cat stalking a moth or grasshopper

   A crowded airport terminal

   Runners in a marathon

   A college party

   An audience at the late showing of a horror film

2. Plan a tentative outline for an upcoming paper and list as many concrete examples or details as you can for each major idea or stage in the analysis. Write a rough draft using all of your evidence. Then study your rough draft with the following questions in mind: Do all the examples and details warrant inclusion? If some are more effective than others, why are they? Do some of the examples or details bring others to mind that you had not included? If so, is any of the new material more effective than your original evidence? How or why?

EXERCISE **2**

This exercise is for practice in improving paragraph coherence.

1. Analyze the paragraphs of a recent paper you have written to determine what specific devices you have used most frequently for coherence.

If you still have the rough draft, compare it with the final version. What changes, if any, did you make to improve coherence? If you made changes, were they to improve the order used (for example, making time sequence clearer), to supply more specific links, or to sharpen up the thrust of the whole argument? Or were they a combination of these?

2. Exchange rough drafts for an assigned paper with a classmate and go over each other's work for paragraph coherence. Mark every passage that lacks coherence and suggest revisions. Then discuss these proposed changes. Which do you find helpful? Why? Which do you reject? Why?

EXERCISE 3

This exercise is for practice in improving paragraph development and coherence.

1. Pick a topic below and write *one* paragraph on it as rapidly as you can for about twenty minutes. Then revise the paragraph by adding, expanding upon, or trimming detail as needed, and by using whatever devices you decide will improve coherence. If you find that you need more than one paragraph in revising, make the necessary transitions and division(s).

A case for or against banning smoking in public places

A case for or against instituting an import quota on foreign cars

A film or book you especially liked or disliked

A singer or musical group you especially like or dislike

A person you are glad you met, or wish you had not

A place you would like to return to or never visit again

A skill you wish you had learned or don't care to learn

2. Revise the revision you produced above. Then compare all three revisions and answer the following questions: What are the most noticeable improvements in paragraph development and coherence, especially between the first and third drafts? While writing the revisions, did you change your mind or modify your views? Is the last version the best you can do? Or would still another revision improve the detail and coherence?

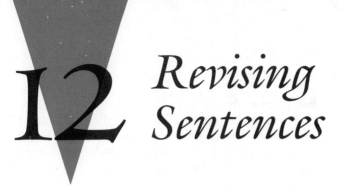

12 Revising Sentences

If paragraphs are the timber for building papers, then by analogy sentences are the kinds of wood chosen for the paragraph. Each kind of wood has its own texture, color, and strength; some are harder to work with than others; some are more likely to warp than others. Pine is soft, common, cheap, and serviceable, rather like the ordinary sentence using the verb *to be*. Maple is hard, close-grained, and highly finished, like the complex sentence with parallel elements. Most oak is heavy, durable, and strong, like the long, formal periodic sentence. Each kind has its own qualities and advantages. Problems occur, however, when one uses unseasoned or wet wood or oversized nails, or when one tries to cut against the grain. The flooring buckles or cracks; the board splits or splinters. So, too, with sentences—unseasoned or handled wrongly, they can warp or fracture.

Sentences are often crudely shaped during the preliminary stages of writing. Trying to maintain the creative flow of ideas, we slap down the words as they come. Fragments and fused sentences, mixed constructions and faulty parallelism—these may be the rough materials that confront us when we begin revising. And because revising entails rethinking, the job is challenging. For rethinking demands that we examine each statement to see if it says exactly what we want it to say. Few sentences will survive this scrutiny intact. Testing what we think, we grope for words and stumble over structures, but in rethinking we cross out and rearrange, shift parts, polish and hone.

Revising sentences entails more than repairing them for coherence and clarity, however. Because different words—like different woods—have their particular textures, colorings, and associations, experienced writers also pay attention to their diction as they reshape their sentences. For convenience, we have placed these two aspects of revision in separate

203

chapters. The first chapter, this one, stresses ways that you can revise *structures* that are awkward, confusing, or misleading. Chapter **13,** "Revising Diction," stresses ways you can revise to *name* more concretely and felicitously. But our division is for convenience only: both elements are part of an effective strategy for sentence revision.

12a Unclear pronoun reference

A pronoun is a substitute for a noun. The noun it stands for is called the **antecedent** because it usually goes (Latin: *cedere*) before (*ante*) the pronoun.

> antecedent   pronoun
> *Rita Martinez* lives in Boulder, but *she* has relatives in San Diego.

> antecedent   pronoun
> When the *plane* left O'Hare, *it* was already behind schedule.

Note, though, that the antecedent—despite its literal meaning—may *follow* the pronoun in some constructions.

> pronoun   antecedent
> Although *it* was behind schedule, the *plane* finally took off.

As you read over your sentences with an eye to revising them, examine every pronoun to make sure its antecedent is clear.

1. Ambiguous reference

When persons of the same sex are mentioned in the sentence, confusion may occur about which person the pronoun refers to:

Unclear The novelist Virginia Woolf assured her sister Vanessa, who was a painter, that *she* was a great artist. **[We cannot be sure whether Woolf was assuring her sister that she (Woolf) or Vanessa was a great artist.]**

Revised The novelist Virginia Woolf told her sister Vanessa, who was a painter, "You are a great artist."

Do not use a pronoun in such a way that it might refer to either of two antecedents. If there is any possibility of doubt, revise the sentence to remove the ambiguity.

Unclear   In *Nostromo,* Conrad's style is ironic and his setting is
highly symbolic, so that *it* sometimes confuses the reader.
**[Does *it* refer to *Nostromo,* Conrad's style, his setting,
or a combination of these? Clarify the sentence by eliminating the pronoun.]**

Revised   Conrad's ironic style and highly symbolic setting in *Nostromo* sometimes confuse the reader.

Revised   In *Nostromo,* Conrad's style is ironic, and his highly symbolic setting sometimes confuses the reader.

Both of these sentences are now clear, though each says something
different.

12a

2. Remote reference

A pronoun too far away from its antecedent may cause misreading. Either repeat the antecedent or recast the sentence.

Unclear   By 1890, architects in Chicago had perfected the floating
raft foundation, a thick mat of concrete with embedded
steel rails that would evenly distribute the weight of a
heavy structure. *It* could support a building of sixteen
or more stories—an unheard-of height.
**[The pronoun *It* is too far removed from its antecedent,
foundation, and seems instead to refer to the noun *structure.*]**

Revised   By 1890, architects in Chicago had perfected the floating
raft foundation, a thick mat of concrete with embedded
steel rails that would evenly distribute the weight of a
heavy structure. *Such a foundation* could support a building
of sixteen or more stories—an unheard-of height.
**[The antecedent has been repeated in the second sentence
for clarity.]**

Revised   By 1890, architects in Chicago had perfected the floating
raft foundation. This thick mat of concrete with embedded
steel rails could support a building of sixteen or more
stories—an unheard-of height.
**[The sentences have been recast to eliminate the pro-
noun.]**

3. Broad pronoun reference: *this, that, which*

In speech we often use the pronouns *this, that,* and *which* to refer broadly to the idea expressed in a preceding clause or sentence. In writing, however, such loose pronoun reference can be misleading or confusing. If the preceding clause contains a noun that might also be mistaken for the antecedent, the reference may be ambiguous as well. In such cases, revise the sentence to eliminate the pronoun or to give it a definite antecedent.

12a

> **Unclear**   The beginning of the book is more interesting than the conclusion, *which* is unfortunate.
>
> **[On first reading, the pronoun *which* seems to refer to *conclusion,* even though conclusions are not usually described as fortunate or unfortunate. The writer wants the *which* to refer to the whole idea of the main clause, but the noun at the end gets in the way.]**

Revised, the sentence might read:

> **Revised**   Unfortunately, the beginning of the book is more interesting than the conclusion.
>
> **[The pronoun has been eliminated and the sentence is crisper.]**

In the following sentence, the *which* is being made to stand for more than it can clearly express.

> **Unclear**   In the eighteenth century, more and more land was converted into pasture, *which* had been going on to some extent for several centuries.

The inclusion of a noun in the revised version both defines and reiterates the idea.

> **Revised**   In the eighteenth century, more and more land was converted into pasture, *a process that* had been going on to some extent for several centuries.
>
> **[The vague pronoun reference has been cleared up by adding *process,* a noun that summarizes the idea of the main clause and gives the pronoun *that* an antecedent.]**

The pronoun *this* should not stand alone as the beginning word in a sentence that follows another sentence of great length and complication.

Unclear   The Japanese fugu, or puffer, is one of the most lethal
                fishes in the world, its poison 275 times deadlier than
                cyanide, yet it is considered a choice dish in Tokyo, Kyoto,
                and other cities, where it sells for more than $200 a
                plate. *This* means that its preparation must be controlled
                and supervised.

"This *what?*" the reader may well ask, since the idea serving as the
antecedent of *This* is unclear. The revision will depend on what the
writer means:

Revised   This *toxicity* means that its preparation must be controlled
                and supervised.

Revised   This *costliness* means that its preparation must be controlled
                and supervised.

4. Indefinite use of *it, they, you*

English contains a number of idiomatic expressions using the
impersonal pronoun *it: It is hot, It rained all day, It is late.* The pronoun
it is also used clearly in sentences like "It seems best to go home at
once," in which *it* anticipates the real subject, *to go home at once.* Avoid,
however, the *it* that needs a clear antecedent and has none.

Unclear   The Tzotzil Indians are only nominal Catholics, using
                its symbols and adapting them to the traditional Mayan
                religion.
                **[The antecedent of *its* has to be inferred from the noun
                Catholics, which means people who belong to a church
                and not the institution itself.]**

Revised   The Tzotzil Indians are only nominal Catholics, using
                the symbols and the names *of the Church* and adapting
                them to the traditional Mayan religion.

Unclear   Lewis Thomas, author of *Lives of the Cell,* is a physician
                and writer who spends his spare hours practicing *it.*
                **[The sentence lacks an activity that could be the anteced-
                ent of *it.*]**

Revised   Lewis Thomas, author of *Lives of the Cell,* is a physician
                who spends his spare hours practicing writing.

The indefinite use of *they* can sound childish or paranoid.

12a

> **Unclear** If intercollegiate sports were banned, *they* would have
> to develop an elaborate intramural program.

Who, the writer should rigorously ask, are *they?* The answer should
appear in the revised sentence:

> **Revised** If intercollegiate sports were banned, *each college* would
> have to develop an elaborate intramural program.

Watch out for the vague, accusatory *they,* which can swell to dark
proportions.

12a

> **Unclear** At registration *they* made us line up on the outside of
> the gymnasium and wait until *they* called the first letter
> of our last names; *they* made some of us stand in the
> rain for hours.

Be exact in describing the event and in assigning responsibility:

> **Revised** At registration *we* had to line up on the outside of the
> gymnasium and wait until *a monitor* called the first letter
> of our last names; *some of us* had to stand in the rain
> for hours.

The indefinite use of the pronoun *you* to refer to people in general
is widespread in conversation and frequent in informal writing: *Around
here, you never know what the neighbors will say.* Formal usage, however,
still restricts *you* to mean *you, the reader,* as in *You can use these review
questions to enhance your understanding of the poems,* and requires the
substitution of the pronoun *one* or of a noun.

> **Informal** Small classes give *you* a chance to take part in discussions.
> **Formal** Small classes give *one* a chance to take part in discussions.
> **Formal** Small classes give *the student* a chance to take part in
> discussions.

While the impersonal or general use of *you* is both natural and appropriate in certain informal contexts, it is clearly inappropriate in other
contexts:

> **Inappropriate** During the American Revolution *you* were forced
> to choose sides.
> **[The pronoun *you* cannot mean *you, the reader* in
> this context.]**

Revised   During the American Revolution *colonists* were forced to choose sides.

If the pronoun *one* seems stilted, try recasting the sentence.

Awkward   In proofreading, *one* should catch all of *one's* careless errors.

Better   In proofreading, *writers* should catch all of *their* careless errors.

12a

EXERCISE 1

Revise the following sentences to correct unclear pronoun reference.

1. The amount of cholesterol in an egg is admittedly high, but it is an excellent source of protein.
2. Many people like to cook eggs because you can prepare them so easily.
3. With only a little practice, one can also prepare fancy dishes, which makes eggs a versatile food.
4. Before cooks beat eggs for meringues, they should be at room temperature; this makes them fluff.
5. A cook should put the egg mixture into a bowl, turn the mixer on high, and slowly add sugar to it.
6. Baking a meringue successfully requires low humidity, which explains why meringues don't always come out right.
7. A soufflé is even trickier to prepare; you have to fold the yolks gently into fluffy egg whites without breaking them.
8. Once the soufflé is put into the oven, it should not be opened until it is done.
9. This ensures that it will rise.
10. One cook told her apprentice that she had to learn to be patient.

EXERCISE 2

Revise the following sentences to correct unclear pronoun reference.

1. Socrates, the self-appointed critic of ancient Athens, made many enemies, which resulted in his being brought to trial in 399 B.C.
2. The charges against him were behaving impiously and corrupting the young people of Athens, but they were ridiculous.
3. Socrates might not have received the death penalty from the court had he not mocked it openly.

4. They sentenced him to imprisonment until he poisoned himself by drinking hemlock.
5. Socrates accepted the cup of poison calmly, which was the way he had lived his life.

12b Dangling modifiers

A **modifier** is a word or phrase that functions in a sentence to limit or describe another word or group of words. If there is no word or group of words in the sentence for the modifier to describe or limit, the modifier is said to *dangle,* as in the following sentence.

12b

Dangling   *Having eaten our lunch and waited an hour to digest our food,* the lake felt cool and pungent on that first hot afternoon of summer.

The literal syntax of this sentence states that the lake, well fed and well digested, felt cool on a summer afternoon. Of course, that is not what the writer meant, but the subject the modifying phrase is intended to limit—*we* or *the picnickers* or *the class of ninety-two?* (there is no way of knowing)—is not in the sentence. *Lake,* then, is the only possible body, even if it is of water, for the participial phrase *having eaten our lunch and waited an hour to digest our food* to modify.

Almost all dangling modifiers occur at the beginning of the sentence, and almost all result from oversight. Once detected, they can be mended in either of two ways.

1. Supply the noun or pronoun that the phrase logically modifies:

                    modifier
Revised   *Having eaten our lunch and waited an hour to digest our food,*

           word modified
           we plunged into the lake, which was cool and pungent on that first hot afternoon of summer.

2. Change a dangling phrase into a complete clause:

                clause replaces modifying phrase
Revised   *After we had eaten our lunch and waited an hour to digest our food,* we swam, that first hot afternoon of summer, in the cool and pungent lake.

1. Dangling participial phrases

Participial phrases are verbal modifiers that function in the sentence as adjectives do. When a participial phrase begins a sentence, it must be followed by the word it modifies, that is, by the person or thing doing the action expressed by the participle or being described by it.

Dangling *Analyzing Joan Didion's style, her essay* seemed to me to be cool, detached, and uncommitted to purpose or point of view.
[This sentence says, erroneously, that the *essay* is doing the analyzing, not the reader.]

12b

Revised *Analyzing Joan Didion's style, I* discovered that the writing, especially in this essay, was cool, detached, and uncommitted to purpose or point of view.

Dangling *Supported by a wide majority of voters, smoking* will be banned in public buildings by the new ordinance.
[Contrary to what this sentence seems to say, it is not smoking, but the ordinance banning smoking, that has wide public support.]

Revised *Supported by a wide majority of voters, the new ordinance* will ban smoking in public buildings.

Dangling modifiers at the end of a sentence are less frequent than those at the beginning, but they are equally confusing and awkward.

Dangling The mountains were snow-covered and cloudless, *flying over the Rockies.*

Revised *Flying over the Rockies, we* saw snow-covered, cloudless mountains.

Revised *When I flew over the Rockies,* the mountains were snow-covered and cloudless.

A dangling participle should not be confused with an absolute phrase, which is an acceptable construction. Such a phrase consists of a participle *and* a subject; it is grammatically unconnected to the rest of the sentence.

His mind preoccupied with his marital problems, William forgot his lunch date with the chancellor.

The dinner for the new athletic director started late, *the guest of honor having been caught in the five-o'clock traffic.*

For more on absolute phrases, see **8f** and **24a**.

2. Dangling gerunds

A **gerund** is a verb form ending in -*ing* that is used as a noun. A gerund phrase dangles when the subject of the gerund—the doer of the action—is not apparent to the reader.

12b

Dangling   *After explaining my errand to the guard,* an automatic gate swung open to let me in.
[Obviously, a gate cannot explain an errand to a guard, or to anyone else, but the sentence fails to say who the true actor is.]

Revised   *After explaining my errand to the guard,* I drove through the automatic gate, which had opened to let me in.

Revised   *After I had explained my errand to the guard,* an automatic gate swung open to let me in.

Dangling   *In doing research,* notes should be entered on separate index cards.
[Because the sentence does not say *who* is doing research, the gerund phrase dangles.]

Revised   *In doing research, a writer* should enter notes on separate index cards.

Revised   *When you do research,* you should enter notes on separate index cards.

3. Dangling infinitives

An **infinitive,** a verb preceded by the word *to,* is said to dangle when the subject of its action is not expressed. Always look carefully at an infinitive phrase to make certain that *who* is doing the action is clearly expressed.

Dangling   *To develop a lively writing style,* a variety of sentence structures should be used.
[*Sentence structures* cannot develop a lively writing style; only people can.]

Revised	*To develop a lively writing style, one* should use a variety of sentence structures.
Revised	*If you want to develop a lively writing style,* you should use a variety of sentence structures.
Dangling	*To be considered for law school, the LSAT* must be taken. **[Who is being considered? That person, the subject of the infinitive *to be considered*, must appear in the sentence.]**
Revised	*To be considered for law school, an applicant* must take the LSAT.
Revised	*If a person wishes to be considered for law school,* he or she must take the LSAT.

12b

4. Dangling elliptical clauses

Sometimes we omit the subject and main verb from a dependent clause and write *while going* instead of *while I was going*, or *when a child* instead of *when he was a child*. Such shorthand phrasing results in an **elliptical clause,** which is perfectly acceptable as long as its subject is made clear in the rest of the sentence. If the subject of an elliptical clause is not clear, the construction dangles.

Dangling	*When six years old,* my grandmother died. **[The omission of the subject *I* here results in a confusing—even ludicrous—sentence.]**
Revised	*When I was six years old,* my grandmother died.
Dangling	Do not add the beans *until thoroughly soaked.* **[Who or what is about to get wet? Clarify the sentence by expanding the elliptical clause.]**
Revised	Do not add the beans *until they have been thoroughly soaked.*

5. Permissible dangling constructions

Some idiomatic verbal phrases, such as *to begin with, judging from past experience, considering the situation, granted the results,* or *to sum up,* have become well established and need not be attached to any particular noun.

Judging from past experience, he is not to be trusted.

Granted the results, what do they prove?

To sum up, all evidence suggests that the decision was a fair one.

12c Misplaced modifiers

A modifier is **misplaced** if it is not near enough to the word it is intended to modify. In English, word order is crucial to meaning. Adjectives, adverbs, and phrases or clauses that function as modifiers must be placed close to the words they are intended to limit or define. The difference that the placement of a modifier makes in a sentence becomes clear if we observe what happens in the following sentence when the adverb *only* is moved about:

The notice said *only* [**said *merely***] that clients were invited to see the exhibit on the third floor.

The notice said that *only* clients [**clients *alone***] were invited to see the exhibit on the third floor.

The notice said that clients were invited *only* [**invited for the *one* purpose**] to see the exhibit on the third floor.

The notice said that clients were invited to see the exhibit on the third floor *only* [**the third floor *alone***].

Some modifying phrases and clauses can be moved around to various positions in the sentence. An introductory clause, for example, can often be shifted from the beginning of a sentence to the middle or the end.

Whatever the public may think, I am sure that Picasso will be remembered as one of the greatest artists of our times.

I am sure, *whatever the public may think,* that Picasso will be remembered as one of the greatest artists of our times.

I am sure that Picasso will be remembered as one of the greatest artists of our times, *whatever the public may think.*

This freedom, however, has its dangers. Movable modifiers may be placed so as to produce misreadings or real ambiguities. Unlike the dangling modifier, which cannot logically modify any word in the sentence, the misplaced modifier may seem to modify the wrong word or phrase in the sentence:

Misplaced   She wrote the full story of her recovery from drug
                  addiction *in only a month.*
                  **[This sentence says that the recovery took only a month.
                  Compare the revised version, which says what the
                  writer actually intended.]**

Revised   *In only a month,* she wrote the full story of her recovery
                  from drug addiction.

Be especially careful to place adverbs exactly where they belong
in the sentence.

Misplaced   He scolded the student for cheating *severely.*
Revised   He *severely* scolded the student for cheating.

Misplaced   I have followed the advice *carefully* given by the manual.
Revised   I have *carefully* followed the advice given by the manual.

Modifiers are said to *squint,* or to look two ways at once, when
they are placed so that they might refer to either a preceding word
or a following word in the sentence.

Squinting   The tailback who injured his knee *recently* returned
                  to practice.
                  **[Is the injury recent, or the player's return to practice?
                  The modifier must be moved to eliminate ambiguity.]**

Revised   The tailback who *recently* injured his knee returned
                  to practice.

Revised   The tailback who injured his knee returned to practice
                  recently.

12d Split constructions

Avoid splitting the parts of a verb phrase with a long modifying
phrase or clause.

Split   I *have,* more than the rest of the class, *been* in a panic
                  since the term paper was assigned.

Revised   More than the rest of the class, I *have been* in a panic
                  since the term paper was assigned.

Split infinitives—that is, infinitives with a modifier between the *to* and the verb—are also usually considered awkward and should be avoided.

> **Split**   Stunned by the accident, we found it difficult *to* accurately *describe* the other car.
>
> **Revised**   Stunned by the accident, we found it difficult *to describe* the other car accurately.

However, if eliminating a split infinitive would result in even clumsier phrasing, let it stand.

12d

> **Acceptable split**   To avoid insolvency, the city's transit system will have *to* nearly *double* ridership during the coming year.

Most readers would find the only alternative—*have nearly to double*—more objectionable than the split infinitive in this sentence.

EXERCISE **3**

Revise the following sentences to eliminate dangling and misplaced modifiers and split constructions.

1. Derived from Vulcan, the Roman fire god, glowing rivers of molten lava are suggested by the word *volcano.*
2. Some volcanoes continue to be associated with myth and ritual. For example, Hawaii's Kilauea Volcano is, by many villagers, said to be the home of Pele, the goddess of volcanoes.
3. To appease Pele and bring good luck, flowers and gin are sometimes offered to the volcano.
4. Erupting frequently, scientists have paid a great deal of attention to Kilauea.
5. The eruptions usually there are mild ones, though; spurting lava and steam, tourists sometimes get quite a show.
6. Not all volcanoes are, unfortunately, so benign.
7. Burying people under almost fifty feet of ash, A.D. 79 saw the deadly eruption of Mount Vesuvius, which wiped out Pompeii.
8. Producing deadly gas as well as giant tidal waves, tens of thousands of lives were lost in 1883 when Krakatoa erupted.
9. While destroying acres of forestland, few people were killed by the more recent eruption of Mt. St. Helens in Washington state.

10. Described as dormant, active, or extinct, geologists continue to be fascinated and awed by volcanoes.

EXERCISE 4

Revise the following sentences to eliminate dangling and misplaced modifiers and split constructions.

1. Begun in 776 B.C., the Greek god Zeus was honored by the original Olympic games.
2. Though at first consisting only of footraces, new events like boxing and chariot racing were gradually added to the games.
3. To qualify for competition, ten months of training had to be completed.
4. Athletes who won Olympic contests heroically returned to their home city-states.
5. The games were held every four years until they were discontinued in A.D. 394, considered too pagan by the Christian emperor of Rome.
6. The Olympic games were, in 1896, revived in Athens.
7. For merely attending the games in ancient times, death was the punishment for women.
8. In 1912, however, fifty-seven women were present to fully participate in the Olympics.
9. By shattering world records in the two-hundred-meter race and the broad jump, Hitler's attempts to make the 1936 Berlin games a tribute to Aryan superiority were thwarted by Jessie Owens, the black American track star.
10. The Olympics were struck by tragedy in 1972 when Arab terrorists in Munich took Israeli athletes hostage, ending in seventeen deaths.

12e

12e Confusing shifts

Shifts in sentence structure often lead to confusion. If the first clause of a sentence is in the active voice, the second clause should not be in the passive voice unless there is a good reason for the change. Similarly, a sentence that begins in the present tense should not switch to the past tense halfway through, and one that starts with the first-person *I* point of view should not shift to *you*. Revise sentences to ensure consistency in mood, tense, voice, and person.

1.   Confusing shifts of voice or subject

A shift from the active to the passive voice almost always involves a confusing change in the subject as well, and thus makes a sentence doubly awkward.

12e

Shift	After *I* finally *discovered* an unsoldered wire, the *dismantling* of the motor *was begun*.
Revised	After *I* finally *discovered* an unsoldered wire, *I dismantled* the motor. **[The subject of this sentence shifts from the *I* of the dependent clause to the *dismantling* of the independent one; the voice shifts from active in the first clause to passive in the second. The sentence would be logically consistent if both verbs were in the passive voice: *After an unsoldered wire was found, the motor was dismantled.* But the passive voice is not required by the sense of the sentence. Repeating *I* as the subject of the independent clause produces subject and voice consistency.]**

Confusing shifts from the active to the passive voice can also lead to questions about agency.

Shift	He *left* the examination after his answer *had been proofread*.
Revised	He *left* the examination after he *had proofread* his answer. **[The passive second clause of the faulty sentence leaves us wondering who proofread the answer. The repeated subject and active voice of the revised sentence clarify the meaning.]**

2.   Confusing shifts of person or number

A writer who fails to concentrate on the pronouns in a sentence may create a shift in person—for example, from the third person (*he, she, one*) to the second person (*you*). The result is almost always a fuzzy, unfocused sentence.

Shift	When *one* tries hard enough, *you* can do almost anything.
Revised	When *you* try hard enough, *you* can do almost anything.
Revised	When *a person* tries hard enough, *he or she* can do almost anything.

Revised   When *we* try hard enough, *we* can do almost anything.

Revised   When *people* try hard enough, *they* can do almost anything.

A shift in number from singular to plural confuses the reader and results in faulty pronoun agreement.

Shift   If a *customer* is ignored or kept waiting, *they* should complain to the management.

Revised   If a *customer* is ignored or kept waiting, *he or she* should complain to the management.

Revised   If *customers* are ignored or kept waiting, *they* should complain to the management.

3.   Confusing shifts of mood or tense

12e

A sentence should end in the same mood with which it begins. If the opening mood is an order or a command, the sentence is an imperative and should not shift without good reason to the indicative mood.

Shift   First, *locate* the library on the campus map; then *you should find* the card catalog and the reference section.

Revised   First, *locate* the library on the campus map; then *find* the card catalog and the reference section.
[The first clause is an order, a command addressed in the imperative mood to an understood *you*. The second clause, which is a statement giving advice, is in the indicative mood. The revision puts both clauses in the imperative mood.]

A sentence that begins in the past tense should not change to the present tense.

Shift   *I stood* on the starting block and *looked* tensely at the water below; for the first time in my life *I am* about to swim the fifty-yard freestyle in competition.

Revised   *I stood* on the starting block and *looked* tensely at the water below; for the first time in my life *I was* about to swim the fifty-yard freestyle in competition.

Revised   *I stand* on the starting block and *look* tensely at the water below; for the first time in my life *I am* about to swim the fifty-yard freestyle in competition.

Remember that it is a convention to use the historical present in writing about literature: *Hamlet stabs Laertes. Isak Dinesen writes about South Africa.* Be careful in this case not to lapse by habit into the past tense.

Shift   At the beginning of the *Divine Comedy,* Dante *finds* that he has strayed from the True Way into the Dark Wood of Error. As soon as he *realized* this, Dante *lifted* his eyes in hope to the rising sun.

Revised   At the beginning of the *Divine Comedy,* Dante *finds* that he has strayed from the True Way into the Dark Wood of Error. As soon as he *has realized* this, Dante *lifts* his eyes in hope to the rising sun.

12e

EXERCISE **5**

Revise the following sentences to correct shifts in voice, person, number, and tense.

1. If a visitor went to Harlem in the 1920s, you would find a place of sharp contrasts.
2. This section of New York City was a ghetto, and yet it is a center for black artists, writers, and intellectuals.
3. A black artist could come to Harlem from another part of the country and find an audience for their work.
4. The movement that came to be called the Harlem Renaissance produces such important writers as Claude McKay and Jean Toomer.
5. Langston Hughes was perhaps the best-known writer of the Harlem Renaissance; poetry, plays, novels, and children's books were published by him.
6. What most white people knew about Harlem, though, was limited to the jazz clubs you found there, places like the Cotton Club that catered to white "slumming parties."
7. When a white person talked about these places, they used terms like *exotic* and *sensual.*
8. This perception of blacks as mysterious Africans was just as distorted as the earlier one of blacks as contented slaves is.
9. Unfortunately, the plays and books about blacks that reached a large white audience tended to be those that perpetuate prevailing stereotypes.
10. The Great Depression settled over the country in the 1930s, and Harlem's period of intellectual and artistic activity was ended by it.

12f Mixed constructions

A sentence that begins with one grammatical structure and then shifts to another is called a **mixed construction.** For example, when a modifying phrase begins a sentence, a reader expects a noun to follow; if it doesn't, as in the case below, a garbled sentence results.

Mixed   *By requiring* drivers to have their cars periodically inspected *is one way* to cut down on accidents.

Revised   *By requiring* drivers to have their cars periodically inspected, *we can* cut down on accidents.

Revised   *Requiring* drivers to have their cars periodically inspected *is one way* to cut down on accidents.
              [In the first revision, the prepositional phrase at the beginning of the sentence is given a subject, *we*, to modify. In the second revision the preposition *by* is dropped and the construction becomes a gerund phrase, subject of the verb *is*.]

12f

1. Dependent clauses misused as subjects and complements

A dependent clause, by definition, stands beside an independent clause for support. Using a dependent clause as the subject or the complement of a verb can produce a badly mixed construction.

Mixed   *Because they installed solar heating* when they remodeled their house *made their fuel bills lower.*

Revised   *Because they installed solar heating* when they remodeled their house, *their fuel bills were lower.*

Revised   *Installing solar heating* when they remodeled their house *made their fuel bills lower.*
              [The first revision subordinates dependent to independent clause in a fully formed complex sentence. In the second revision, the gerund phrase is the subject of the verb *made*.]

Common to speech, *the reason . . . is because . . .* construction is redundant, since *because* means *for the reason that.* Use one word or the other in a sentence, but not both.

Mixed	*The reason* their fuel bills were lower *is because* they installed solar heating when they remodeled their house.
Revised	Their fuel bills were lower *because* they installed solar heating when they remodeled their house.
Revised	*The reason* their fuel bills were lower *is that* they installed solar heating when they remodeled their house.

2. Adverbial clauses misused as nouns

A common mixed construction is the illogical use of *when* or *where* as part of the complement of *is*—the "is when" or "is where" error.

12f

Mixed	One *thing* that keeps me from driving to the city *is when* I think of the traffic jams.
Revised	One *thing* that keeps me from driving to the city *is the thought* of the traffic jams.
Revised	I won't drive to the city because of the traffic jams.
Mixed	*Symbiosis is where* dissimilar organisms live together in a mutually advantageous partnership.
Revised	*Symbiosis is a state where* dissimilar organisms live together in a mutually advantageous partnership.
Revised	*Symbiosis is the* mutually advantageous *partnership* of dissimilar organisms living together.
	[The faulty sentences are mixed constructions that link a noun with an adverbial clause. They are revised by retaining the *is* verb and linking the noun with another noun (*One thing . . . is the thought; Symbiosis is a state*), or by recasting the sentence without *is*.]

3. Unidiomatic comparisons

Be careful not to mix idiomatic ways of making comparisons.

Mixed	Erasable paper is easier *to type on than on bond.*
Revised	*Erasable paper is easier* to type on *than bond is.*
Revised	It is *easier to type on* erasable paper *than* **[to type]** *on* bond.

12g Incomplete constructions

Do not omit words necessary for grammatical completeness, particularly in compound constructions.

1. Incomplete verb forms

When both verbs in a compound construction are in the same tense, the second auxiliary verb can be omitted:

> Information will be sent to all students who *have signed* up for the Education Abroad program and **[who have]** *paid* the fee.

However, when the verbs in a compound construction are in different tenses, the grammatical sense of the sentence usually requires that they both be written out in full.

12g

Incomplete	Modern languages *have* and always *will be* an important element in the college curriculum. **[One could not say that languages *have be an important element*. The verb form *been* is needed to complete the sentence.]**
Revised	Modern languages *have been* and always *will be* an important element in the college curriculum.

2. Omitted prepositions

English idiom requires that certain prepositions be used with certain adjectives and verbs. We say, for example, *interested in, aware of, devoted to*. We expect others to *agree with,* or to *object to,* or even to *protest against* our plans. When the verbs or adjectives in a compound construction take different prepositions, both prepositions must be included. If you are in doubt about the right preposition to use, a standard college dictionary will guide you. (See also **13d**.)

Incomplete	He was *oblivious* and *undisturbed by* the noise around him.
Revised	He was *oblivious to* and *undisturbed by* the noise around him.
Incomplete	No one could have been more *interested* or *devoted to* her constituents than Senator Chong.

Revised   No one could have been more *interested in* or *devoted to* her constituents than Senator Chong.

3. Incomplete comparisons

In comparisons, do not omit words necessary to make a complete idiomatic statement.

Incomplete   She is as witty, if not wittier, than her brother.

Revised   She is as witty *as,* if not wittier *than,* her brother.

Revised   She is as witty as her brother, if not wittier.
[If we delete *if not wittier* from the faulty sentence, the statement says *She is as witty than her brother,* which makes no sense.]

Incomplete   Leonardo da Vinci had one of the greatest, if not the greatest, minds of all time.

Revised   Leonardo da Vinci had one of the greatest minds, if not the greatest *mind,* of all time.
[No one, not even Leonardo, can have *the greatest minds.*]

Incomplete   Robert's expectations were more modest than his brother.

Revised   Robert's expectations were more modest than *those of* his brother.

Revised   Robert's expectations were more modest than *his brother's.*
[The first sentence erroneously compares Robert's expectations and Robert's brother. Each of the revised versions correctly expresses a comparison between the two men's *expectations.*]

Incomplete   The food here costs no more than any other restaurant in town.

Revised   The food here costs no more than **[it does]** *at* any other restaurant in town.
[The first sentence mistakenly compares the cost of food and the cost of restaurants. Adding the preposition *at* to the sentence clarifies its meaning.]

12g

Avoid the illogical use of *any* and *than*.

Incomplete   For many years the Empire State Building was taller than any building in New York.

Revised   For many years the Empire State Building was taller than any *other* building in New York.
[*Any building in New York* includes the Empire State Building, and a building cannot be taller than itself.]

Make sure the reader can tell what is being compared with what.

Incomplete   Claremont is farther from Los Angeles than Pomona.

Revised   Claremont is farther from Los Angeles than Pomona *is*.

Revised   Claremont is farther from Los Angeles than *it is* from Pomona.
[In the two revisions, both terms of the comparison are completely filled in, and there is no ambiguity about what is being compared.]

12g

Many commercials and advertisements make claims that rest on incomplete comparisons. Both the student of language and the consumer should challenge ungrammatical and empty statements.

Incomplete   Philsoc Gas gives more and better mileage for the dollar.
[We should ask, *more and better* than what? Than a team of mules? Than another kind of gasoline? If so, which one?]

Incomplete   Buy the bigger, crunchier, crisper, better-tasting breakfast cereal.
[Again: than what?]

Note that the words *so*, *such*, and *too* when used as comparatives are completed by a phrase or clause indicating the standard of comparison.

I am *so* tired *that I could drop*. I had *such* a small breakfast *that* I was starving by noon, and when we stopped for lunch, I was *too* tired *to eat*.

EXERCISE **6**

Revise the following sentences to eliminate mixed and incomplete constructions.

1. Because our facial expressions show emotion makes us think that their only purpose is to communicate with others.
2. However, by making these expressions actually controls the flow of blood to the brain.
3. The reason we touch our faces may be because we need to stimulate our minds.
4. So it makes sense that rubbing our foreheads has and always will be a sign of thought.
5. Just because we are not conscious of our facial movements does not mean that there is no reason for them.
6. When we are in pain, we are unaware and oblivious to the way our faces contort.
7. In contracting our facial muscles diverts blood from the face, and that is why we turn pale.
8. Crying, on the other hand, may be as good if not better than tranquilizers, because it actually numbs the brain.
9. Israel Waynbaum, the French physician who investigated this topic many years ago, claimed that when we smile actually creates happiness.
10. Being conscious and alert to our expressions may have an effect on others and on ourselves.

EXERCISE **7**

Revise the following sentences to eliminate mixed and incomplete constructions.

1. The development of the Motion Picture Production Code in 1930 was when the film industry began to be censored.
2. By censoring movies reduced their sexual content.
3. A movie could include adulterers if they were essential to its plot, but they had to end up less happy than any characters in the film.
4. The demand and popularity of gangster movies is where violence became an issue.
5. When James Cagney became as big if not a bigger star than Mae West, the censors began to worry about violence in movies.
6. One reason the censors looked at gangster movies was because they wanted to make Americans aware and committed to the saying, "Crime does not pay."

12g

7. Revealing the method of committing a crime was a violation as serious, if not more serious, than depicting violence, for the censors felt that people might imitate crimes they saw in the movies.
8. Because censors were worried about the authority of police meant that all law-enforcement officers had to be portrayed as honest.
9. The reason censorship exists in a society is because some people believe it can control the society's ills.
10. Different things will be censored in different generations, but censorship has and always will be a controversial issue.

12g

Revising Diction

> *The great archetypal activities of human society are all permeated with play from the start. Take language for instance—the first and supreme instrument which man shapes in order to communicate, to teach, to command. Language allows him to distinguish, to establish, to state things; in short, to name them and by naming them to raise them into the domain of the spirit.*
>
> —Johan Huizinga

Language is a link between self and other: in playing with language, we experience the world; in sharpening our words, we make the world manageable. Our discovery of these powers begins early and unselfconsciously. If, for example, we move back to our childhood games (or perhaps the games of our parents and friends), we may rediscover these powers. We may live once again in the child's jeering or shame of "Tattle-tale, tattle-tale,/Stick your head in the garbage pail"; the ritual oath of "Cross my heart and hope to die/Drop down dead if I tell a lie"; or the gleeful celebration of "Made you look, you dirty crook,/Stole your mother's pocketbook!" We distinguish the "tattle-tale" (what naming could be more specific?); we establish our laws ("Cross my heart"); we state the victory of "Made you look." We communicate, teach, command.

But, looking back, it appears that we did more. We twisted our tongues with "She sells seashells by the seashore"; mocked authority with "Teacher, teacher, I declare/I spy a hole in your underwear"; and counted off with "One potato, two potato, three potato, four." We *tested* words for their sounds, their shock value, their rhythmic combinations. In playing (often very intently) with language, we did not merely master the different ways of naming and therefore of making the world inhabitable; we learned that the emotional colors, the sounds, and the contexts of particular words belong to their meaning as much as a deep, insistent voice belongs to the Siamese cat or the horny rings of warning belong to the rattlesnake. We learned a fundamental lesson about **diction,** or word choice: not only that different words name different realities but that the ways by which they name are as curious and as complicated as the reality itself.

13a Experiencing words

Each word has a long history behind it, a fascinating ancestry of origins, of slowly changing meanings, of curious and forgotten uses as well as current, living ones—in short, an *etymology*. For instance, the word *diction* is derived from the Latin *dicere*, "to say," and ultimately from the Indo-European root *deik*, "to show or to point out," as its kinship with the Latin word for finger, *digitus,* and the English *digit* reveals. To know the root or roots of a word is to know something valuable about the source of its power to name.

The more fully we understand the ways in which words "name" the features of our world, the more precise and effective our diction can be. Granted, no word can ever duplicate the reality of the thorn that pierces our thumb, the sunset that moves us to silent joy, or the turbulence of first infatuation. Recognizing this limitation of language, however, writers who are attentive to diction achieve precision and depth by selecting words that most nearly approximate their thoughts and feelings. Too often the complaint "You know what I mean" or "You know what I'm saying" is actually a sign of someone in too much of a rush to learn about words.

13b Denotation and connotation

The first of the complex ways by which words name is through their denotations and connotations. Their **denotations** are their most literal meanings. For instance, to take a stark example, *body, corpse,* and *cadaver* can all have the same denotation—a dead human being. **Connotations,** on the other hand, are a word's overtones, echoes, emotional colorings, and associations. Thus we would hardly speak of going to a funeral home to view the *corpse* of a friend, let alone the *cadaver. Body* is the most intimate in its connotations, expressing the sad acknowledgment that someone we care for is no longer there

13b

and that those familiar features will soon be gone forever: the word, in this context, connotes a commonly shared grief over an irrevocable reality. By contrast, *corpse* and *cadaver* connote the coldly impersonal, the anonymous, the institutional, as when police officially speak of finding an unknown corpse in a field or when medical students speak of dissecting a cadaver.

1.   The importance of context

The connotation of each word must be appropriate to the context. For instance, *to compliment* and *to flatter* may denote the same action—giving praise to another person—but note the differences in their connotations. Usually, *to compliment* (or *compliments*) is used in the context of generous, justified praise given publicly or freely: "I'd like to compliment you on (or pass on a compliment about) your performance." In contrast, *to flatter* (or *flattery*) connotes excess, even deception. Sometimes it may be harmless enough, as when we speak of "a photographer who flatters his subjects," or innocent, self-admitted smugness as when we say, "I flatter myself that. . . ." More often, though, it connotes gratifying vanity, favor seeking, blandishments. Still, if forced to choose between being called a *flatterer* and an *apple-polisher,* most of us would probably elect the former. The context in which *apple-polishing* is used is unmistakable: blatant insincerity and favor seeking that are obvious to everyone, except perhaps the recipient.

Some connotations stem from our deep, often unconscious associations. When, for example, Phyllis Thompson concludes a poem "When I die, I will turn to bone/like these. And dust of bone. And then, like God/to stone," she draws on these associations in rhyming *bone* and *stone:* hardness, dryness, gray-whiteness, inertness. Drawing on equally deep but different associations, the poet Andrew Marvell three centuries ago praised "a green thought in a green shade." He knew very well that readers of English after his lifetime would bring to the phrase the positive associations of grass, trees, growth, life, and tranquility.

2.   The value of a dictionary

In short, context—the relevant environment of speaker, audience, and subject—is all. But the context in which a given word is appropriate may not always be as evident as in the examples we have used above. It's easy to decide whether you want to describe your best friend as *slender, slim,* or *skinny.* However, deciding when to use such similar terms as *reparation, redress, restitution,* and *indemnity* may give almost any writer pause. For cases like these, you will need to rely on a good desk dictionary, such as those discussed in Chapter **9.** Many of these dictionaries not only provide the precise meaning of a word, but also discuss the subtle differences in connotation among terms that have similar denotations. You can't become a truly confident writer without such a book at your side.

13c Abstract and concrete

The second of the complex ways by which words name is through their abstractness and their concreteness. Words that name specific, tangible things are **concrete;** words that designate general qualities, categories, or relationships are **abstract.** A general term like *food* is a name for a whole group of specific things: tomato soup, fried chicken legs, chilled lettuce and alfalfa sprouts, sliced applies, cheesecake, and so forth.

1. The abstraction ladder

Note, though, that *abstract* and *concrete* are relative, not absolute, terms. In his influential book *Language in Thought and Action,* the linguist S. I. Hayakawa used what he termed an "abstraction ladder" to show how a concrete object can be perceived at greater and greater levels of abstraction. To understand Hayakawa's point, consider our example below, which offers increasingly abstract perspectives on a specific ancient oak tree known as "Charter Oak":

1. The tree *Charter Oak* that exists at the atomic and subatomic level, incredibly complex and changing.
2. The tree *Charter Oak* that we experience, not the word but only the limited number of features our nervous system selects from the complex reality.
3. The word *Charter Oak* itself, which is the name we give the particular perceived object but which is not the object itself, already tremendously simplified.
4. The word *oak,* which stands for what *Charter Oak$_1$,* and oak$_2$,

oak₃, and so on share in common—in short, thousands of oaks of different ages, sizes, conditions, and so on.

5. The word *tree,* which stands for the traits we have abstracted that oaks, palms, pines, and so on share in common and which, of course, omits much, much more.
6. The word *plant,* which includes any living organism that cannot move voluntarily and usually makes its own food by photosynthesis—trees, flowers, bushes, and so on.
7. The word *organism,* which includes any living thing.

And so on up the ladder, as far as we choose to go.

13c

The point, then, is not just that *abstractness* and *concreteness* are relative as terms, but also that we need general words as well as specific ones. For certain subjects or in certain contexts, we have to generalize, abstract, deal in whole categories. And at its own level of generality such prose can have great precision. The English philosopher John Stuart Mill, writing on *The Subjection of Women* in the late 1860s, is as intelligible to us now as he was to his contemporaries because of such precision:

Effective abstract diction

> For what is the peculiar character of the modern world—the difference which chiefly distinguishes modern institutions, modern social ideas, modern life itself, from those of times long past? It is that human beings are no longer born to their place in life, and chained down by an inexorable bond to the place they are born to, but are free to employ their faculties, and such favorable chances as offer, to achieve the lot which may appear to them most desirable. Human society of old was constituted on a very different principle. All were born to a fixed social position, and were mostly kept in it by law, or interdicted from any means by which they could emerge from it.

He continues, with the same forceful generalities, to argue that what is becoming true for the men of Western Europe and America should also be true for women. Discussing the slaveries that have vanished and "the subjection of women," which still remains, he is necessarily well up the abstraction ladder: long historical periods and change, abuses of one-half of humanity, and the huge social costs are all part of his argument.

But even writers as skillful as Mill is at this "rung" come down the ladder at some point because abstract terms eventually have to be given the substance of concreteness by comparisons or examples. In the following passage, for instance, Jonathan Swift makes us see and feel what the term *war* meant in the eighteenth century:

Effective concrete diction

> And being no stranger to the art of war, I gave him a description of cannons, culverins, muskets, carabines, pistols, bullets, powder, swords, bayonets, battles, sieges, retreats, attacks, undermines, countermines, bombardments, sea-fights; ships sunk with a thousand men, twenty thousand killed on each side; dying groans, limbs flying in the air, smoke, noise, confusion, trampling to death under horses' feet; flight, pursuit, victory; fields strewed with carcases left for food to dogs, and wolves, and birds of prey; plundering, stripping, ravishing, burning and destroying. I assured him that I had seen them blow up a hundred enemies at once in a siege, and as many in a ship, and beheld the dead bodies drop down in pieces from the clouds, to the great diversion of all the spectators.

13c

The abstract term *war* is translated into the realities it too often obscures: massive cruelty, pain, and dying—pieces of human bodies dropping "from the clouds, to the great diversion of all the spectators."

2. The value of concrete diction

This passage from Swift should suggest why teachers of writing urge their students to be specific, to be concrete. Concrete language compels our attention by its immediate appeal to the world of our experience. While the best writing shifts gracefully between abstract and concrete, overdependence on colorless abstractions makes for tediously dull reading. Consider the following:

Abstract	For dinner we had some really good food.
Concrete	For dinner we had barbecued steaks and sweet corn.
Abstract	She liked to argue about controversial subjects.
Concrete	She liked to argue about religion and politics.
More concrete	She liked to argue about God's existence and the merits of socialism.

In paragraphs, or entire papers, that settle for "really good food" and "controversial subjects," no real thought is taking place; like an unfocused camera, the writer is not registering anything in particular.

When you examine the diction of your sentences, remember that a specific statement often requires no more space than a vague one, yet it can communicate much more information:

> **Vague**   One member of my family has recently begun her professional career.
>
> **Concrete**   Last week my sister Lynn joined the law firm of Bailey, Harney, and Johnson.

13d You will achieve only as much reality in your papers as your words actually name; you may find that the effort to think concretely takes time and imagination, but it's the only way you have of discovering and sharing your meaning.

13d Idiom

Still another of the complex ways by which words name is through **idiom,** an expression peculiar to itself within a language, not explainable by the ordinary meaning of its individual words. Idioms, in short, are arbitrary, as when we say *make out* (succeed), *make up* (reconcile), and *make do* (be satisfied with). They are as fixed as the Spanish *Hace frío* ("It's cold"), which literally and unaccountably to one learning the language translates as "It makes cold."

In English, we often rely on prepositions to indicate subtle but essential relationships. To take a stand *on* an issue, to be *in* a quandary, *out* of luck, *off* your rocker—these idiomatic expressions make a kind of spatial sense as figures of speech: we can, if we stop to visualize it, imagine standing on an issue, defending our point of view, planting our feet firmly on an ideological turf we call our own. Some verbs, however, require prepositions that are arbitrary and unexplainable. How can persons who are learning English and know the words *take, in, up, down,* and *over* deduce the meaning of the following: *take in* (comprehend), *taken in* (fooled); *take up* (begin to do something), *take down* (humiliate), *take over,* and *overtake?* They can't, any more than they could figure out the differences among *put up with* (tolerate), *put on* (assume), *put away* (deposit, renounce), and *put down* (suppress).

Each of these idioms has to be learned separately. Here are some additional idiomatic uses of prepositions:

abide *by* a decision

agree *with* a person; *to* a proposal; *on* a procedure

angry *at* or *about* something; *with* a person

argue *with* a person; *for* or *about* a measure

compatible *with*

correspond *to* or *with* a thing; *with* a person

differ *from* one another in appearance; differ *with* a person in
   opinion

independent *of*

interfere *with* a performance; *in* someone else's affairs

listen *to* a person, argument, or sound; listen *at* the door

with regard *to*

stand *by* a friend; *for* a cause; *on* an issue

superior *to*

wait *on* a customer; *for* a person; *at* a place; *in* the rain; *by*
   the hour

13c

Idiom demands that certain words be followed by infinitives, others by gerunds. For instance:

Infinitive	Gerund
able to go	capable of going
like to go	enjoy going
eager to go	cannot help going

How can you be certain, as you revise a paper, that you've used idiomatic phrases correctly? Again, any good desk dictionary will guide you. Under the word *stand*, for example, the *American Heritage Dictionary* provides meanings for such combinations as *stand down, stand for, stand in, stand off, stand out,* and *stand up,* as well as for such additional idiomatic phrases as *stand a chance, stand one's ground, stand on one's own feet,* and *stand to reason.* Other desk dictionaries do the same.

13e Figurative language

The last broad category to be discussed is that of **figurative language.** When we speak figuratively, we speak nonliterally: we compare one quite distinct thing with another for some quality we think they have in common, or identify one thing by another in terms of a common quality. Figurative language is a complex and powerful means of creating, showing, or limiting relationships. Thus, when we speak of costs being *cut,* of price *gouging,* or of a state *draining* its taxpayers, we use implied comparisons to intensify and vivify our point. Of course, a merchant charged with price gouging has not, in fact, taken a chisel and scooped grooves on his or her customers any more than we have made a chest incision and inspected the right auricle and right ventricle when we speak of *getting to the heart of the subject.* These phrases are economical and precise: price *gouging* says how we feel when we think we have been defrauded (we speak of the "chiseler"); *getting to the heart of the subject* names our intent to discover the source of its life, the vital center. The right figure of speech can turn an otherwise pedestrian phrase into an arresting observation that bears the stamp of your personality and imagination.

1. Metaphor and simile

A **metaphor** is a direct comparison of two things on the basis of a shared quality. The word *metaphor* is itself a buried metaphor, since it means *to transfer* or *carry across:* when we compare, we are carrying a trait from one thing to another as if over a bridge or road. Metaphor says that one thing is another: *All the world's a stage; Snow blanketed the ground; The road of excess leads to the palace of wisdom.* A *dead metaphor* has, so to speak, become so common in usage that it has lost its life, its capacity to startle us with the aptness of the comparison; but it is not really "dead," only moribund, and can be brought back to life, as when we complain, "The beer was all head and no body."

Metaphor is one of the most powerful causes of linguistic growth, change, and vitality. To speak of large, expensive, inefficient automobiles as *gas-guzzlers,* a sharp decline in the value of currency and a sharp rise in prices as *runaway inflation,* or citizens receiving inadequate services for their money as *the public's being shortchanged*—to employ these and other metaphors that have come into general use is to be conveniently brief, exact, and vivid. In fact, whether we realize it or not, we organize whole categories of our experience through certain metaphoric structures. For example, we systematize our concepts of vitality and power through metaphors of upwardness, our concepts of debility and weakness through metaphors of downwardness: she is at the *peak* of her fame, or she *fell* from the public's favor; he is *on top* of the situation, or he is *under* the control of others. Language is always vitally metaphoric because our realities—our hopes, desires, circumstances, and fears—change. The relevant issue is not whether metaphors are employed but whether they pinpoint accurate relationships, or whether they are forced, mixed, or trite. We will return to these abuses later.

13e

One final, positive word about metaphors, and some advice: begin to feel their presence; make a practice of looking for them not only in nouns (the *heart* of the subject) but also in verbs. Metaphorical language gives nourishment in ways that the junk food of needlessly abstract phrasing never can—the difference between saying "Avoid repetitious or unnecessary phrasing" and "*Cut* out the *deadwood.*" American English has been wonderfully rich fare for our writers, as the following passage from Mark Twain's *The Adventures of Huckleberry Finn* may suggest:

> Once or twice of a night we would see a steamboat slipping along in the dark, and now and then she would *belch* a whole world of sparks up out of her chimbleys, and they would *rain* down in the river and look awfully pretty; then she would turn a corner and her lights would *wink* out.

Granted, Twain's prose is in a dialect that only a gifted writer could imitate, but the presence of metaphor here is clear enough. In more standard English, F. Scott Fitzgerald's metaphors deepen the vision of Long Island and America as a lost Eden at the end of *The Great Gatsby:*

> Most of the big shore places were closed now and there were hardly any lights except the shadowy, moving glow of a ferryboat across the Sound. And as the moon rose higher the inessential houses *began to melt away* until gradually I became aware of the old island here that *flowered* once

for Dutch sailors' eyes—a fresh, green *breast* of the new world. Its vanished trees, the trees that had *made way for* Gatsby's house, had once *pandered in whispers* to the last and greatest of all human dreams; for a transitory enchanted moment man must have *held his breath* in the presence of this continent, compelled to an aesthetic contemplation he neither understood nor desired, face to face for the last time in history with something commensurate to his capacity for wonder.

Like a metaphor, a **simile** states a comparison between two things, but unlike a metaphor, it uses the words *like* or *as* to do so:

13e

Simile "I sensed a wrongness around me, *like* an alarm clock that has gone off without being set."

—Maya Angelou

Simile ". . . her tepid, sluggish nature, really *like* something eating its way through a leaf."

—Katherine Anne Porter

Simile [a muddy sow that would] "stretch out and shut her eyes and wave her ears whilst the pigs was milking her, and look as happy *as if* she was on salary."

—Mark Twain

2. Analogy

A comparison can be extended into an **analogy,** which not only illustrates a point but also suggests an argument or point of view (Chapter **7** discusses the use of analogy in building paragraphs; Chapter **15**, its use and abuse in reasoning). Consider, for instance, Mary Ellman's startling analogy between astronauts and pregnant women:

The astronaut's body is awkward and encumbered in the space suit as the body of a pregnant woman. It moves about with even more graceless difficulty. And being shot up into the air suggests submission too, rather than enterprise. Like a woman being carted to a delivery room, the astronaut must sit (or lie) still, and go where he is sent. Even the nerve, the genuine courage it takes simply not to run away, is much the same in both situations—to say nothing of the shared sense of having gone too far to be able to change one's mind.

3. Allusion

In an **allusion** the comparison is made between some present event, situation, or person and an event or person from history or literature. Usually, the allusion is a brief reference to something the reader is assumed to know, as when journalists allude to a recent scandal as "another possible Watergate." Sometimes the writer may employ several allusions, as when Adrienne Rich says of a woman who reads about women in books written by men:

> She finds a terror and a dream, she finds a beautiful face, she finds La Belle Dame Sans Merci, she finds Juliet or Tess or Salome, but precisely what she does not find is that absorbed, drudging, puzzled, sometimes inspired creature, herself, who sits at a desk trying to put words together.

13f

A sense of audience should determine what allusions, if any, are appropriate. There is no point in throwing away allusions or in alienating your readers by appearing to be more knowledgeable than they. An allusion can deepen the meaning of a statement for those who recognize the comparison, but the statement should still make perfectly clear sense without it.

13f Special diction problems

We turn now from the ways in which words name to some of the ways in which they may obscure and weaken prose. The disciplined writer, the one who considers and cares about words, is able to recognize these types of inappropriate and ineffective diction and knows how to revise prose in order to eliminate them.

1. Sexist language

At the beginning of Chapter **9** we pointed out that English, like all languages, is constantly changing. One of the most important changes to occur recently in English is an increased sensitivity to sexist language—usages that treat men and women unequally or that betray stereotypes about what it means to be female or male. Unfortunately, inequality and stereotyping persist in our culture; the point is that language should not be used in a manner that serves to perpetuate this condition. To put it another way, language that refers to women and men should be *inclusive* rather than *exclusive*.

Publishers, professional organizations, broadcasters, and the general public have become steadily more concerned with avoiding language that fosters notions of inequality between women and men. As a result, writers who are not alert to the kinds of sexism that we describe below increasingly run the risk of alienating their readers.

Avoid using "man" in a generic sense

13f

Writers and speakers who attempt to defend the traditional use of the word *man* to mean "all human beings" argue that its connotation is generic, that it does not suggest individual men but people in general. In phrases such as "the average man" or "every man for himself," they say, *man* simply means "person."

In reality, the notion that *man* has a generic connotation rather than a sex-specific one is easy to disprove. One need only consider a sentence like the following:

> On this campus, unfortunately, any man who wants an active social life has to be a member of a fraternity or a sorority.

Why does this sentence jar? The ending startles us precisely because we do not read the word *man* in the beginning of the sentence in a generic sense, but instead attach to it a male connotation that subsequently clashes with the word *sorority* at the sentence's end. A number of alternative wordings, each with a different meaning, are possible:

Acceptable	On this campus, unfortunately, any man who wants an active social life has to be a member of a fraternity. **[*Man* is not used here as a generic noun; the sentence is now *about* men only.]**
Acceptable	On this campus, unfortunately, any woman who wants an active social life has to be a member of a sorority. **[The sentence is now about women only.]**
Acceptable	On this campus, unfortunately, any student who wants an active social life has to be a member of a fraternity or a sorority. **[The language is now sex neutral; it includes both women and men.]**

Avoiding the allegedly generic *man* is easy. For *man*, substitute "person" or "human being" or whatever other noun fits the context (like "student" in the example above). For *mankind,* use "humanity" or "human beings."

Exclusive   We are committed to hiring the best man for the job.
Inclusive   We are committed to hiring the best *person* for the job.

Exclusive   Since the beginning of history, man has been an inventor and an innovator.
Inclusive   Since the beginning of history, *human beings* have been inventors and innovators.

Exclusive   AIDS is the most recent example of mankind's struggle against the mystery of disease.
Inclusive   AIDS is the most recent example of *humanity's* struggle against the mystery of disease.

13f

The same principle applies to compounds with the word *man*. A reasonable sex-neutral substitute is always available: for *manmade,* use "synthetic"; for *manpower,* use "work force." Finally, also avoid using the word *man* as a verb:

Exclusive   Representatives of the senior class will man the information booth during freshman orientation.
Inclusive   Representatives of the senior class will *staff* the information booth during freshman orientation.

Avoid using the pronoun "he" in a generic sense

Like *man,* the pronoun *he* (together with *his, him,* and *himself*) has often been used in a generic sense to refer to people in general when its antecedent is indefinite. But also like the noun *man, he* is demonstrably not a sex-neutral pronoun. If it were, the following sentence would make sense:

> Everyone who attended last year's meeting of the National Organization for Women increased his understanding of the organization's agenda for the 1990s.

When the context clearly implies women as well as men, the pronoun *he* immediately seems out of place. Why? Because, despite traditionalists' claims to the contrary, *he, his,* and *him* are inevitably sex-specific terms. And if *his* excludes women in the sentence above, it does the same in each of the sentences below as well. Indeed, the personal pronouns in these sentences *define* their contexts as exclusively male.

Exclusive   Each participant in the race should take his place at the starting line by nine o'clock.

Exclusive   A good writer often does his best work in solitude.

Exclusive   Every attorney in the firm understood himself and his colleagues better after the meeting.

13f   Avoiding the sexist use of the pronoun *he* is simply of matter of substituting "he or she." When that alternative seems awkward, recast the sentence using plural nouns and pronouns.

Inclusive   Each participant in the race should take *his or her* place at the starting line by nine o'clock.

Inclusive   A good writer often does *his or her* best work in solitude.

Inclusive   *All the attorneys* in the firm understood *themselves* and *their* colleagues better after the meeting.

Use sex-neutral language to identify people's roles

With few exceptions, all roles in our society are occupied by women and men. The language used to refer to people in their roles should therefore be free of references to gender like the suffix *-man.*

Sex specific	Sex neutral
businessman	businessperson
chairman	chair, chairperson
congressman	representative, member of Congress
fireman	firefighter
housewife	homemaker
mailman	mail carrier
male nurse	nurse
policeman	police officer
salesman	salesperson
woman judge	judge
workman	worker

The same rule applies in the case of words that were formerly given the feminine endings *-ess* or *-trix*, which suggest that women are occupying roles defined by men and that they should be distinguished from their male counterparts.

Sex specific	Sex neutral
authoress	author
aviatrix	aviator
poetess	poet
sculptress	sculptor
stewardess	flight attendant

13f

Use parallel language to discuss women and men in parallel contexts

Perhaps the most insidious variety of sexist language involves the unequal treatment of men and women in the same context. When women and men are discussed in parallel contexts, the terminology that designates them should also be parallel. Consider the following examples.

Nonparallel   Two students and a coed were accosted at knifepoint while walking across the campus last night.

Parallel   Two *male students* and a *female student* were accosted at knifepoint while walking across the campus last night.

Nonparallel   That company has a history of hiring more men than girls.

Parallel   That company has a history of hiring more *men* than *women*.

Nonparallel   The only guests who have not yet arrived are Hank Evans and his wife.

Parallel   The only guests who have not yet arrived are *Hank* and *Patricia* Evans.

2. Weak verbs

Anemic writing almost always results when, rather than using a vigorous verb, we connect subject and complement with the verb *be.* So-called **linking** (or **copulative**) **verbs** also include *become, seem, appear,* and *remain.* We cannot, of course, write entirely without linking verbs, especially when indicating logical equivalents:

> The commission's downtown development plan *was* disappointingly vague.
>
> Most physicians in the Soviet Union *are* women.

In cases such as these, the linking verb functions like an equal sign, equating the subject and complement in a sentence. But used excessively, linking verbs make for bland and monotonous prose:

13f

Weak verbs

> William LeBaron Jenney *was* the nineteenth-century Chicago architect who *was* the inventor of the skeletal-frame skyscraper. Jenney's Home Insurance Building of 1884 *was* apparently the first tall building in which an iron-and-steel frame *was* the main support, rather than load-bearing exterior walls of brick or stone. But if Jenney *was* a technical innovator, he *was* not a man with a clear aesthetic vision. His early buildings *are* often collections of discordant elements and eclectic ornamentation. Jenney's Manhattan Building of 1891, for example, *seems* to be a number of separate buildings set on top of each other. There *is* a lack of unity in its design that *is* immediately evident.

Linking verbs like those in the passage above are not the only verbs that create dull prose. *Occur, take place, prevail, exist, happen,* and other verbs expressing a state of affairs also make for needlessly colorless writing.

Weak	In the afternoon a sharp drop in the temperature *occurred*.
Stronger	The temperature *dropped* sharply in the afternoon.
Weak	Throughout the meeting an atmosphere of increasing tension *existed*.
Stronger	As the meeting progressed, the tension *increased*.

Make your verbs work. Good writers enliven their observations by selecting sharp verbs and by using verbals as modifiers. Consider these sentences from an essay by the naturalist Edward Hoagland:

Strong verbs

> Mountain lions spirit themselves away in saw-toothed canyons and on escarpments, and when conversing with their mates, they coo like pigeons, sob like women, emit a flat slight shriek, a popping bubbling growl, or mew, or yowl. They growl and suddenly caterwaul into falsetto—the famous scarifying scream functioning as a kind of hunting cry close up, to terrorize the game. They ramble as much as twenty-five miles in a night, maintaining a large loop of territory which they cover every week or two.

The verbs that assert, *spirit away, coo, sob, emit, growl, caterwaul,* and *ramble,* and the infinitive *to terrorize* are reinforced by the action of the verbals, *conversing, popping, bubbling, scarifying, functioning, hunting,* and *maintaining.* Even the nouns *shriek, growl, mew, yowl, scream,* and *loop* contribute to the energy of the passage, since in other contexts they function as verbs and carry these active connotations with them. Action verbs and verbals make us feel, see, hear, smell; they appeal to our senses and body knowledge, our primary ways of knowing and understanding.

13f

For some further advice on using verbs effectively, see **8b**.

3. Clichés

   In "Politics and the English Language," George Orwell writes: "Modern writing at its worst does not consist in picking out words for the sake of their meaning and inventing images in order to make the meaning clearer. It consists in gumming together long strips of words which have already been set in order by someone else, and making the results presentable by sheer humbug." Much of the time these "long strips of words" are the tritest of metaphors and similes. No thought is involved, no feeling evoked; thus we get the *all-American family* lucky to live in the *land of opportunity, working like the devil* to *make their dreams come true.* This string of stock phrases, or **clichés,** as they are called, is admittedly ludicrous, but even a single cliché in a sentence suggests that the writer has not cared enough to seek out an original way of presenting his or her thoughts.

   Clichés are an insidious weakness in writing precisely because they are so common in speech. Here is a list of the kinds of phrases that we are talking about:

acid test
agony of suspense
all boils down to
as luck would have it
beat a hasty retreat
bitter end
bolt from the blue
breathless silence
checkered career
cool as a cucumber
deep, dark secret
depths of despair
doomed to disappointment
few and far between
gone off the track
green with envy
growing by leaps and bounds
heave a sigh of relief
hit the nail on the head
in this day and age
jumping on the bandwagon

more than meets the eye
moving experience
other side of the coin
out in the cold
poor but honest
proud possessor of
quick as a flash
rotten to the core
slow but sure
straight from the shoulder
tempest in a teapot
trials and tribulations
undercurrent of excitement
uphill battle
walking on air
water under the bridge
wave of optimism
work hand in hand
worth its weight in gold
young in spirit
youthful glee

13f

Enclosing a cliché in quotation marks does not make its use acceptable in writing, any more than deliberately tripping an alarm system would exculpate a burglar from his or her crime. If you rely on the language's ready-made phrases, you can't escape the charge of unoriginal thinking.

4. Mixed figures of speech

Mixed figures of speech result when writers have stopped thinking about the logical and visual sense of what they're saying. Used deliberately, they make their point by comic incongruity, as in this sentence:

Whenever he saw a spark of genius, he watered it.

Most of the time, however, they are confused, bizarre, or both:

Mixed   I know it sounds like sour grapes, but that's the whole kettle of fish in a nutshell.

Mixed   The southern states, being completely agricultural, hinged around the barn.

Mixed   He was saddled with a sea of grass-roots opinion that his campaigners had ferreted out for him.

5. Empty intensives

Intensives, such as *really, very, so,* and *much,* may give emphasis to conversation, but they weaken written language. They are often cover-ups for the fact that the writer lacks a vocabulary with a wide range of emphatic words.

13f

Weak   The major was *really* angry over the city council's refusal to approve her proposed budget for the new fiscal year.

Weak   I was *so* happy to hear about David's new job.

Weak   Marcelle believes that proponents of medical experimentation on live animals are *very* bad people.

Why settle for *really angry* when there are *enraged* and *furious,* for *so happy* when there are *pleased* and *delighted,* for *very bad* when there are *wicked, detestable, rotten, vile*? Every time you are tempted to place a "very" before a word, look that word up in a good college dictionary and try to discover a stronger equivalent that will convey the meaning you want in all its intensity. Or else just leave out the intensifier. In most cases, your sentence will be stronger without it:

Weak intensive   The evidence points to only one conclusion—the company was engaging in *very* deliberate fraud.

Stronger   The evidence points to only one conclusion—the company was engaging in deliberate fraud.

6. Jargon

To quote Orwell once again: "The great enemy of clear language is insincerity." Sincerity implies candor, trust, unaffectedness. **Jargon,** in contrast, obfuscates and boasts.

There are two kinds of jargon: the technical language used by certain professionals and the empty generalities that are the bluff of the insincere or incompetent writer. Here, we are not concerned with necessarily technical language: even handbook writers and readers need terms like *dangling modifier, comma splice,* and *faulty subordination* to name specialties of the trade. We are concerned, rather, with ponderous, wordy, inflated prose that obscures the obvious. This is the jargon that most readers object to—the language of bureaucrats, publicists, politicians, college professors, and students when they hope the inflation of their prose will raise the commonplace to the significant.

Our minds are befogged every day by phrases like *capability factor, career potential, divergent life-styles, socio-personal development, decision-making process, social interaction, holistic learning procedures, methodologies, technical implementations,* and *fundamental value structures.* We cannot easily escape from this publicized network of confused language, but if we learn to recognize the stylistic flavor of jargon, we may avoid it in our own writing. Jargon words are, by and large, abstract rather than concrete, and contain more than one syllable (as if the jargon writer assumed that the addition of a syllable would add weight to the word). Jargon words are often nouns masquerading as verbs: *concretize, finalize, interiorize.* Sometimes nouns are turned into adverbs or adjectives by the addition of the suffix *-wise: languagewise, subjectwise, moneywise, weatherwise.*

Jargon is best deflated by a translation into clear English:

Obscured by jargon

> The leader-follower relationship must be looked upon as a field situation and such a field will be structured and sustain its structure only when the views of the leader are acceptable to the followers. The leader-follower field will be extended to the degree that the leader is seen to have authority to assume the leader role. As the relation of the leader's apparent right to authority is moved progressively away from the problem area confronting the group, there will be an increasing tendency for the leader-follower field to disintegrate.

This specimen, while not the worst, typifies the habits of jargon— inflated prose and overuse of the passive voice. Thus *leader* and *group* become *the leader-follower relationship* in a *field situation,* and the leader's interfering becomes a movement *away from the problem area confronting*

13f

the group. Stripped of their jargon, these sentences mean no more than this:

Clarified

> A group will fall apart when its members no longer agree with the views of their leader. Whatever degree of authority a leader has is gained from the group's willingness to grant it. The more the group feels its leader is interfering, the less likely it is to follow.

In addition to being obscure and tiresome, jargon, when it conceals or distorts the reality it describes, can be dangerous, even deadly. The phrase *antipersonnel detonating devices* obscures the chilling reality of bombs that kill men, women, and children. Similarly, the deviousness of official statements like "The United States cannot foreclose any option for retaliation" distracts us from the protest we might register had the writer said what he meant: "The United States will use nuclear weapons if necessary."

13f

7. Pretentious diction

Pretentious diction, like the pretentious person, is stiff and phony—in short, a bore. Our diction becomes pretentious if we always choose the polysyllabic word over the word of one syllable, a Latinate word when an Anglo-Saxon one will do, flowery phrases in place of common nouns and verbs. Writing should be as honest and forthright as plain speech. And since we have the opportunity to revise and edit what we write, it should be even more economical, direct, and to the point.

Sometimes, ordinary words seem inadequate to carry the weight we want our thoughts to have, so we decorate statements with ornate language:

Pretentious   His vigilant attention to the well-being of others profoundly influences the personal life-styles of all those fortunate enough to bear the appellation of "his friends."

This sentence says little more than, "His thoughtfulness influences the way his friends live." The fancy language is out of proportion to the statement it makes.

To guard yourself against this sort of thing, read your papers aloud, listening for phrases that you cannot imagine ever speaking to a friend or classmate. Be wary of words that dress up simple facts: *charisma* for *popularity, interface* for *meet, utilize* for *use, profitable enterprise* for *money-maker, purchase* for *buy, decision-making process* for *leadership.* As you consult your college dictionary to develop your vocabulary, note the fine distinctions among synonyms and consider whether the words you choose will strike your reader as counterfeit or genuine. Keep in mind Samuel Johnson's advice: "Read over your compositions and, when you meet a passage which you think is particularly fine, strike it out."

13f

8. Euphemism

Often when we want to avoid harsh facts we resort to a particular kind of circumlocution, the **euphemism.** The Greek word means "good speech," but euphemisms seldom are good for writers. Too often they are cosmetics to cover up painful realities. To avoid facing the finality of death, for example, people have always used euphemisms: *passed on* or *passed, gone west, met his Maker, gone to her reward.* The *dear departed* rests in his casket in the *slumber room,* often having been *prepared* by the *funeral director,* who today is likely to preside at a *memorial service* instead of a funeral. Ultimately, the *loved one* is not buried but *laid to rest,* not in a graveyard but in *The Valley of Memories.* Such sentimental wordiness is intended to comfort the bereaved by pretending that death is sleep, but its effect—like that of all euphemistic language—is one of stilted insincerity.

EXERCISE 1

Pick one or two words that interest you (nouns, verbs, adjectives, and adverbs are your best bet) and consult the *Oxford English Dictionary* in your library. The *OED* (its familiar title) is the indispensable reference for anyone curious about our language: it gives a word's first known appearance in print, its changing uses (with historical examples), and the fullest record we have of its connotations and denotations. Write a full paragraph in which you (1) note the word's primary shifts in meaning, and (2) indicate what you take to be its primary connotations and denotations now.

EXERCISE 2

With the help of a dictionary (and perhaps a dictionary of Roman and Greek mythology) discover the concrete particular in which each of these words originated. Write a brief explanation of why and how you think some of these words came to mean what they mean today.

cereal	cupidity	hackneyed	panic
chapter	erotic	infant	paradise
comma	genius	language	surgery

EXERCISE 3

13f

Choose three words that have similar denotations: for example, *to please, to gratify, to delight; concerned, involved, committed; fame, celebrity, stardom.* Then write a paragraph on the differing connotations of each word, and compose a sentence or two to show how the word is used in context.

EXERCISE 4

Choose three concrete nouns and take them up three or four rungs on the abstraction ladder, beginning above the atomic and subatomic rung.

EXERCISE 5

Choose three abstract nouns (for example, *wealth, humanity, art*) and take them down four or five rungs on the abstraction ladder.

EXERCISE 6

Analyze the following paragraphs for jargon, pretentious diction, and clichés. Translate the paragraphs into Standard English if you can, and if not, be prepared to say why.

1. A corollary of reinforcement is that the consequences of responding may be represented exhaustively along a continuum ranging from those that substantially raise response likelihood, through those that have little or no effect on response likelihood, to those that substantially reduce response likelihood. An event is a positive reinforcer if its occurrence or presentation after a response strengthens the response. Sometimes good grades, words of praise, or salary checks act as positive reinforcers. An object or event is a negative reinforcer if its withdrawal or termination after a response strengthens the response. Often bad grades, shame, or worthless payments act as negative reinforcers. The above notion sounds complex and difficult to apply but is indeed extremely simple.

2. All courses (process or outcome) in the University system that are judged to contain written or oral communication goal statements should constitute a set of courses from which a student must select some number. This client-oriented marketplace approach to core requirements is a solution. Enrollment determines which courses will survive and which will not. However, academic tradition is rife with distrust of student judgment; and it can result in a self-fulfilling prophecy where faculty compete in playing to the "house" because they are convinced that ultimately only those who do will survive. This solution is usually condemned without trial.

EXERCISE 7

13f

Analyze the following paragraphs for clichés, pretentious diction, and jargon. Translate the paragraphs into Standard English if you can, and if not, be prepared to say why.

Henry

As human beings, each of us grows and benefits in some way from ordinary experience each day. For the past five years I have sought a higher understanding of human attitudes, especially those of a positive nature, and of the mental processes that underlie and reinforce them. By listening to people, I have gained much wisdom; by seeking out those who have much to share, I have grown. I have begun the arduous but satisfying search for maturity.

One individual who has given me special insights is Henry. A married, older person who has had much experience in diverse walks of life, he is a special person. One day he joined a group of us after classes while we were sitting on the grass. I immediately felt his desire to communicate some special aspect of his life—something that was preoccupying him very deeply.

Henry began to relate the experience of his recent separation from his wife. It bothered me at the time that someone with such an understanding nature as his would have such a deep personal problem, and I questioned him regarding the reasons for his trouble. At the time I was involved in a personal relationship and wanted our communications to be open. What Henry told me became one of the most valuable teachings of my life. He told how he and his wife had stopped making a conscious effort to work at their relationship. Their life had become a burden and a sorrow.

My own relationship has grown into a beautiful experience, but it is one I have to work at and strive to improve. Henry made me realize that we have to lose our selfishness. I feel that I have matured, and we have grown together, and I am a better person for it. Today is the first day of the rest of my life.

List all the clichés, weak verbs, and examples of jargon you can find in several of your recent papers. Review these lists with the following questions in mind: Are there significant differences among the lists in the frequency of clichés, weak verbs, examples of jargon? Can you see some connection between the topic and the frequency of your ineffective diction? If so, what seems to be the connection? Are there any particular clichés, weak verbs, or jargon words you use often?

13f

Select one of the papers used for Exercise 8 and rewrite it, or at least the offending passages. Revise the diction by making it as concrete and fresh as you can.

Analyze the diction of the following sentences. Be prepared to say what words or figures of speech would more effectively express the writer's meaning.

1. Our balloons of egotism filled with the air of freshman knowledge were soon to be pricked by the pinpoints of self-awakening.
2. As the town grew, the theater obtained a foothold in the hearts of the citizens.
3. Drinking seems to have its claw in the economy of San Francisco.
4. Poring through *Paradise Lost* was like wading in deep water.
5. A good education is the trunk for a good life, for it is the origin of all the branches that are your later accomplishments.
6. His immaturity may improve with age.
7. The basic objective of the indoctrination program is to build strong class spirit and to weed out those who are leaders in the class.
8. Darwin's *Origin of Species* began an epic of materialism.
9. Margaret Mead's book had a great success because Americans are grossly interested in sex.
10. Jefferson and Madison were two of the most prolific characters our nation produced at that time in history.
11. Because he did not follow the code, he was blandished from society.
12. He was a male shogunist pig.

13. She succeeded in deleting her flaw and, in doing so, became a stronger, ursine being.
14. In Tillie Olsen's story "I Stand Here Ironing," the mother paradoxically loves her child but has to farm it out to a day-care center.
15. Sarty does not realize that his father is the noose around his neck until Sarty gets his feet planted firmly on the ground to stop his mutation into a passive being.
16. He reflects on the way Sarah has been ostersized.
17. O'Neill seems to be saying that alcohol and narcotics are not helpful devices in problem solving.
18. He has a vicarious relationship through his son.
19. His trip around the world is a soul search.
20. She is still young and arouses bodily disturbances in Robert.

13f

PART
IV

14 *Thinking Critically*
15 *Avoiding Errors in Reasoning*
16 *Writing about Literature*

Critical Reading and Thinking

14 *Thinking Critically*

Any expository writing that is more than just a summary of dates and events involves critical reading and thinking: interpreting evidence, making generalizations, arriving at conclusions. You may be discussing a book that you find persuasive or unpersuasive; you may be arguing for or against some new policy; you may be explaining your actions or beliefs. In each case, you are trying to convince your readers, and if you credit them with intelligence, you will want to convince them by your reasonableness.

In this section, we are using the phrases *critical reading* and *critical thinking* in the broad sense of sound and adequate reasoning. Our treatment is necessarily brief, ignoring many technicalities more suitably examined in a full course in logic. It also omits discussion of certain specific writing strategies that aid clear reasoning but are more properly taken up elsewhere. These techniques include the *definition of terms,* the ways of achieving *sentence unity,* and the ways of achieving *paragraph coherence.* You may wish to review these techniques in conjunction with this section (see **7d**, **8a**, **11b**).

We start with a principle that underlies all that follows in these chapters. It is this: *unsound reasoning is often the result of ignorance rather than intentional deception or incurable bigotry; the person has not known enough, and perhaps has not cared enough, about the subject and has generalized hastily.* Consider a commonplace example—the difference between an uninformed driver and a skilled mechanic. The car suddenly stalls and won't start. What does this driver frequently do? He (or she) checks the gas, finds the tank half full, opens the hood, and pokes around. With luck, he happens upon the fan belt and finds it intact. Now stuck, he concludes the battery must be dead because that's what happened last time. While looking for a phone and hoping that someone will stop, he again vows to himself to take a course in auto maintenance offered at the community college and to read through the manufacturer's manual, lying unopened these past months.

With skilled mechanics, it is quite otherwise. Taking their time, they proceed systematically, checking various possibilities until they find the source of trouble. Drawing on their knowledge, they reason from known effect to probable cause until they solve the problem. Because they are informed, they do not generalize rashly; because they care, they are not hasty.

The point of this rather ordinary example is, first of all, our need to recognize what we don't know and to do whatever is necessary to become knowledgeable. When our information is scanty, we cannot see complexity, nuance, or difference. We do not know how to proceed, and we risk the impulsive conclusion. (The skilled mechanic can be as foolish as anyone else on subjects he or she is ignorant about.) But most college subjects do demand that we recognize complexity, nuance, difference—as, indeed, do many of the things we study outside the academy. Presently, we will discuss some guidelines for evaluating and shaping complex data into complex arguments and for judging among authorities in particular fields. Here, before looking at some more specific principles of critical reading and thinking, we simply wish to reiterate in slightly different terms the principle we began with: *to enhance sound reasoning, take the time necessary to do research and to be informed about your subject.*

14a The structure of an argument

The preliminaries of an argument are usually definitions. Having defined *capital punishment* as "execution, the death penalty for a crime," you can then argue for or against it. One "argument," or "reason," you might give for capital punishment is that it deters murder. A "reason" or "argument" against it might be that it does not deter murder. Note that the words *argument* and *reason* are interchangeable and that they imply an identical process of thinking.

In most discussions of logical analysis, the word *argument* signifies any two statements connected in such a way that one is based on the other. The argument has two parts: a premise (or evidence) and an inference (or immediate conclusion):

14a

premise or evidence

Capital punishment deters murder.

inference or immediate conclusion

Therefore, it should be continued.

Because capital punishment does
    not deter murder,

it should be abolished.

We use arguments constantly in writing and in speaking, and we recognize them by the actual or implied presence of connectives such as *because, so,* and *since,* and by auxiliaries such as *ought, should,* and *must.* The structure of an argument, then, is an observed fact or set of facts, or else a generalization presumably based on facts (the premise), leading to a conclusion (the inference). And usually we intend, though we may not always state explicitly, a final conclusion or point:

inference ◄──────── **premise**

I'm tired out *because* I've been studying too
hard.

final conclusion

► So I'll take a
break now.

14a

final conclusion ◄──────── **inference** ◄──────── **premise**

She wasn't angry. She didn't mean it, *since* she was joking about it
    later.

Usually, a final conclusion has several arguments, not simply one, to support it. The inference of one argument may be the premise for the next, and so on in a chainlike pattern to the final conclusion, the clasp:

premise 1 and . . .

National prestige is fostered by
success in the Olympic games.

premise 2

Successful countries
use professional athletes.

[inference from premises 1 and 2 becomes premise 3]

Since we wish to be successful in maintaining our prestige,
[inference from premise 3 becomes premise 4]

we cannot afford to field amateurs.

final conclusion

Consequently, we should begin a program of national recruiting and
    full-time support for our Olympic athletes.

Several distinct strands of argument may be knotted into the one final conclusion, itself often the beginning of a conversation or a paper:

final conclusion
There is no good reason for our starting a program of national recruiting and full-time support for our Olympic athletes.

first argument introduced   **premise 1**
To begin with, the modern games were not founded to foster nationalism. Professionalism is contrary to the intent of the games **[inference from premise 1]**.

second argument introduced   **premise 2**
In the second place, nationalistic rivalries have made the protection of the athletes difficult and costly. This politicizing has made the games a great burden for the host country **[inference from premise 2]**.

third argument introduced   **premise 3**
Moreover, if one looks at the remarkable record of success that amateurs have had . . .

14b

Just as a paragraph can develop several arguments to support one conclusion, so several paragraphs can each develop one or more arguments to support a thesis, itself a final conclusion.

If you are required to identify the premises and inferences of an argument—your own or someone else's—try an outline (see **5g**). Outlining assists critical reading by isolating the major issues and evidence, and it assists critical writing by systematically pinpointing areas of disagreement.

14b Key assumptions

So far, we have considered an argument's structure, not its truthfulness. An argument's structure may be quite consistent, yet its premises and conclusions may be unsound. One of the commonest causes of unsound arguments is the writer's failure to examine the key assumptions.

A key assumption is a connection between the premise and the inference that is *taken for granted before* the argument is advanced; and it is a *presupposed* relationship between the argument and the final conclusion. Consider the following:

premise 1 and . . .   **premise 2**
Beth has an A− average   Sharon has a B− average
[inference from premises 1 and 2 becomes premise 3]

Since Beth is obviously a better student
[inference from premise 3 becomes premise 4]

she should do better work in a creative writing course.

final conclusion
Consequently, she certainly should be given preference over Sharon.

Clearly, unless you *took for granted* that grades and creativity are related, you couldn't very well argue that Beth's superior average was proof that she would do better work in the writing course than Sharon. The argument assumes *beforehand* that grades and creativity are connected. Nor could you *conclude* that Beth ought to be given priority unless you had *presupposed* this relationship. Key assumptions frequently operate in deductive logic, in which one moves from the general to the particular:

If   Academic success and success in creative writing are connected
                                                         Premise
If   Beth has a better grade average than Sharon   **Premise**
Then   Beth will be more successful as a creative writer.
                                                         Conclusion

Like the premises in deductive logic, the key assumptions underlying an argument must be sound before they are built on. If the assumptions are false or only partly true, the whole argument collapses. Writers who blithely rely on unexamined assumptions risk overlooking evidence that might undermine their conclusions. For example, if you were to assume that academic success and creativity are related (the key assumption), you would have to overlook those students with mediocre or even poor averages who are gifted painters, dancers, or poets, and you would have to ignore those intelligent honor students who seem to lack imagination, or at least seldom do more than safe, competent work.

Key assumptions occur all the time, in all kinds of arguments and contexts—letters to the editor, talk-show controversies, reviews

14b

of films and books, political campaigns. Consider the following arguments, for example. Each (in one variation or another) is popular; each has one or more key assumptions. We need to ask two questions about each of these arguments: (1) What are the key assumptions? (2) Do these assumptions require explaining or defending? The first argument:

Argument: A great many of the movies that Hollywood makes give an unfair picture of American life because they show mainly its violence and its obsession with sex.

Assumptions: 1. That movies should give a "fair" picture of whatever they are picturing.
2. That there is such a thing as a "fair picture."
3. That violence and obsession with sex are not "typical" of American life.

Question: Are these self-evident assumptions?

14b   The second argument:

Argument: Enriched courses for gifted students are a valuable addition to the high-school curriculum because such courses offer these students a chance to fulfill college requirements and to begin specializing earlier.

Assumptions: 1. That college students should choose their major and specialize as soon as possible.
2. That the purpose of enriched high-school courses is to satisfy college requirements, not to master a subject for its own sake.
3. That gifted students are particularly deserving of special attention.

Question: Are these self-evident assumptions?

There are at least a couple of things you can do to help protect yourself against unsound assumptions and arguments built on them. First, *make it a habit* to ask what other people are taking for granted in their arguments. If their key assumptions need challenging, challenge them. Second, *make it a habit* to ask yourself what you have taken for granted in your argument. If these assumptions need explaining, explain them; if they need defending, defend them. The exercises that follow are designed to give you this kind of practice.

EXERCISE 1

Consider each of the following arguments. Each (in one form or another) is widespread; each has one or more key assumptions. Analyze the argument to determine the key assumptions it makes and which of these, if any, would need to be explained or defended. If you find the assumptions shaky or untenable, specify your reasons for challenging them.

1. Politicians who take an unpopular stand during an election are foolish because they simply increase their chances of losing.
2. Civil rights laws are useless because morality can't be legislated.
3. Arguments about artistic merit or performance are pointless because all such judgments are based merely on personal likes and dislikes.
4. Nuclear policy should be left to the experts because the average person doesn't have enough information to know what's best.
5. It's a mistake to argue with teachers because they'll only mark you down; just give them what they want and take a good grade.

EXERCISE 2

14b

Choose one of the topics below (or one of the arguments in Exercise 1) and write one paragraph of two hundred words or so, as rapidly as you can, and take a firm stand. Then analyze your paragraph with the following questions in mind: (1) What are the key assumptions? (2) Do they need defending? (3) What kinds of arguments or evidence would support them? Then *rewrite* the paragraph in the light of your analysis and compare it with your original. Have you made significant changes in your case?

1. Colleges should (should not) have required courses for all freshmen.
2. The major television networks should (should not) be left to themselves in matters of programming and censorship.
3. Public universities should (should not) impose fixed quotas on the number of out-of-state students they will admit.
4. Ticket scalping at popular events should (should not) be prohibited.
5. Drunk drivers should (should not) automatically be deprived of their licenses for a fixed period of time on their first arrest.

EXERCISE 3

Analyze the argument in a paper that you or your instructor found unsatisfactory, focusing on the following questions: (1) What key assumptions underlie your argument? (2) Do these assumptions require explaining or defending? (3) If so, how would you explain or defend them?

Ask the questions in Exercise 3 about an argument that you've identified in a published letter to the editor of your local newspaper.

14c The differences between fact and judgment

As the preceding exercises may have suggested, what can be proved and what one approves of do not always coincide. The differences between fact and judgment, though not always easy to determine in a given case, are important.

1. Facts

14c

A **fact** may be defined as any statement, any declarative sentence, that can be proved true. The definition says nothing about who does the proving or what method of proof is used. It merely stipulates the possibility of verifying the statement. It rules out commands, questions, and exclamations as provable assertions—no one will try to prove or disprove utterances like "Shut the door!" "How old is she?" "Wow!"

The definition eliminates more than these obvious examples. "Water is wet"; "A yard has 3 feet"; "New York has more people than Chicago"; "Shakespeare was born in 1564"—most people would agree that such statements are all "facts." But saying "Water is wet" isn't the same as saying "The paint on the door is wet." The first sentence is either a *tautology*, a needless reputation of an idea to anyone familiar with the qualities of "waterness," or else instructions to a very young child on how to identify the feeling of liquid on his or her fingers. To say "A yard has 3 feet" is also to state a truth-by-definition—quite different from saying "The track was only 99 yards long." We can touch the paint and measure the track and thereby answer "Yes, it is" or "No, it isn't" to the assertion. But what point is there in responding "Yes, it is" or "No, it isn't" to statements like "Water is wet" or "A yard has 3 feet" except to agree with definition?

Some statements are verifiable facts because they are stated in quantifiable terms, that is, in such a way that what is asserted can be weighed, measured, or counted: "Jean weighs 90 pounds," "The last discus throw was 147 feet," "There are 36 people ahead of me in line." Even in these cases, of course, you assume that the scale or the tape measure is accurate, and that your index finger has not pointed at the same head twice. Other facts presuppose greater faith: If you believe that "New York has more people than Chicago" and "Shakespeare was born in 1564" are factual statements, you are not simply accepting the authority of an almanac and an encyclopedia. You are trusting the accuracy and conscientiousness of every census taker hired in these cities by the Bureau of the Census and the reliability of scholars who have inspected the parish records of baptism in Stratford-on-Avon.

Admittedly, life is too short for anyone to verify personally more than a fraction of the "facts" he or she learns, and many things have to be taken on authority. Still, you ought to cultivate the habit of skeptical analysis in reading and writing. It can help you detect those judgments that are unverifiable—those that are often "proved" in writing by heavy underlining and double exclamation marks and in conversation by rising voices and tempers. How, for instance, can one prove (or disprove) such statements as "You can't change human nature" or "Materialism is the greatest threat to our way of life"?

14c

2. Judgments

A **judgment** is a conclusion expressing some form of approval or disapproval. The term should not be dismissed because it is taken to connote "mere opinion." There are, after all, reasonable grounds and confirming facts for "good judgment" as well as the arbitrary assumptions and disregarded facts in "poor judgment." Sometimes the judgment is a fairly simple, safe inference from the facts, as in the judgment "Helen Wills Moody was one of the finest tennis players in the game's history," which is based on her winning the Women's National Singles seven times, the Women's National Doubles three times, and the Women's Singles at Wimbledon eight times. The phrase *one of the finest* is a judgment of her record. Sometimes, a judgment is a complicated inference from many facts, none of which is immediately clear. Consider three propositions, in which the judgments are italicized:

1. In 1940, there were 131,669,275 Americans, averaging 44.2 people per square mile; by 1980, *the population was larger and denser,* 226,545,805 people, averaging 64 per square mile.

[This first statement contains the terms *larger* and *denser,* which denote a factual inference. The statement is clearly factual and the inference results from a simple computation.]

2. Between 1940 and 1980, as the country *became more urbanized and heavily populated,* the American farm *became more efficient through increased mechanization and specialization.*
[This second statement, a judgment, presupposes the first statement in the judgment *more urbanized and heavily populated.* But it assumes much more. To prove *more efficient through increased mechanization,* the writer would need figures showing the increased use of electricity and various kinds of power machinery. To prove *specialization,* the writer would need data showing the increased percentage of farms that raise only crops of livestock, or produce only dairy goods. The evidence exists, of course, to defend the judgment that the American farm has become more efficient.]

14c

3. *Profit-seeking specialization and mechanization are destroying the small, self-sufficient family farm in America and the deep attachment to the land and tradition that are so much a part of the family farm.*
[In this third statement, the judgment is far more conspicuous than in the first two, and the facts are less immediately evident. To prove, for example, the existence of *the small, self-sufficient family farm* with its *deep attachment to the land and tradition* would require detailed information. This information would have to include data about income, expenses, size of family, acreage worked, period of ownership without tenancy, length of political and religious affiliations, and a study of attitudes toward marriage, education, and the like. Such information might take the form of statistics or the extensive observations of qualified observers, or both. It would have to include the New York family raising some sheep and a few cows, some acres of wheat and garden tomatoes; the North Carolina family raising a hillside of tobacco and corn, supplemented by hogs and hunting; the Illinois family running a small dairy and orchard; the Colorado family raising grain and beef near the foothills of the Rockies; and the California family raising grapefruit and oranges near the desert's edge. Then the information about all of these families would have to be analyzed to see whether there is such a type as *the small, self-sufficient family farm* with distinct values or whether there are sharply different regional variations.]

You can no more help making judgments about human actions and goals than the writer of the third statement could help feeling strongly about the changes taking place in the American farm. In fact, the writer might say that information about income and attitudes toward marriage had little to do with her judgment, that she was talking about qualities that could only be experienced personally. The grounds for this judgment might be her own life on a small Iowa farm or New Mexico ranch; novels like Willa Cather's *O Pioneers!,* Steinbeck's *The Red Pony,* or Harriette Arnow's *The Dollmaker;* short stories like those in Hamlin Garland's *Main-Travelled Roads;* movies like *Country;* or the memories of a country doctor. The question would then be what other qualities are slighted. Do the films, fiction, and memoirs show only loyalty, belief, the close-knit family, and hard work? What of the fatigue and boredom, the bigotry and blighted vision, the drudgery and failure they reveal? Fiction, films, and memoirs present possibilities, not facts: they can make us see, feel, and share the intensity and variety of human life in a particular time and place, but they cannot offer statistical certainty.

14c

3. Using facts and judgments

When you make judgments, then, express your facts clearly and accurately and show clearly the way in which the facts warrant your judgment; when you don't know the facts or have reason to suspect their authority, suspend judgment. And don't be reluctant to ask others to do the same. Try to distinguish between those judgments that involve personal preference and are not provable and those that may be supported by evidence and arguments. For your college writing, this advice implies your willingness to do research; to distinguish among facts, statements that may be factual, and judgments; and to tolerate uncertainty. The last is especially hard to do: often the experts in specialized fields are so much at odds that you either are tempted to give the matter up entirely or else arbitrarily decide "one side *must* be right, the other wrong, so I will choose."

If, for example, you were to look up the statistics on capital punishment, you would find no clear-cut agreement among the criminologists, psychologists, and various law-enforcement officials about what the figures prove—and no agreement among the statisticians, either. But the issue is too important to be ignored simply because you cannot prove conclusively that capital punishment is or is not a deterrent to crime. There are other factual grounds that may help you form a judgment: How many innocent men or women have been executed, or how many saved at the last minute? Do minorities, the poor, and the uneducated receive the death sentence more frequently than others convicted of murder?

4. Evaluating authorities

As has been pointed out, we cannot verify personally more than a fraction of the "facts" we learn, and necessarily we have to take many things on authority. Still, when experts disagree about their facts and their judgments, there are a few helpful guides.

The first guide is to be sure that a supposed expert is an authority on the subject at hand. If a famous physicist and a chemist differ about disarmament, you may have to suspend judgment as far as their argument about the technical issues is concerned, but you don't have to feel that either of them is an expert on American and Soviet foreign policy. Other writers and scholars have made that subject their life's work, and you should turn to them.

A second guide is to consider the experts' probable motives in relation to their testimony. An executive for a major car manufacturer who testifies that "all reasonable steps have been taken to make safe, energy-efficient cars" may well not be as reliable an authority as a writer for an independent trade magazine or engineering firm.

A third guide is to see what others in the field say about the strengths or weaknesses in an expert's research. Suppose that you are doing a project on drug use among high-school students. If book reviews generally praise a husband-and-wife team for their studies of suburban students but criticize their failure to study inner-city students as thoroughly, you would want to confine yourself to the couple's discussion of suburban students only, and look elsewhere for evidence about inner-city students.

14c

EXERCISE 5

Determine which parts of each of the following statements are facts and which parts are judgments. For each judgment, decide what kind(s) of facts or evidence, if any, could be cited to support the judgment.

1. Smoke Cigarmellos! They last longer, burn cooler, and are easier on you than cigarettes. They are cleaner and cheaper than pipes.
2. Julius Caesar, Rome's greatest general and ruler, was assassinated in 44 B.C. by Cassius, Brutus, and other personal enemies.
3. A meter equals 39.37 inches.
4. A kilometer contains 1,000 meters.
5. Michael Jordan is one of the finest offensive players in professional basketball today.
6. If one compares the number of talented women now entering law schools with the number twenty years ago, one sees how wasteful of abilities those sexist admissions policies were.
7. The concern over "computer literacy" is just another educational fad, largely promoted by manufacturers rather than by genuine demand.
8. Real mastery of a foreign language means the ability to think in the language, not simply to translate headlines and signs, word by word.
9. There is no clear evidence one way or another about the effectiveness of strict gun laws in preventing crime.
10. The early bird catches the worm—but who wants the worm?

14c

EXERCISE **6**

Pick a controversial issue you feel strongly about and summarize your views in two or three sentences. Then analyze your sentences with the following questions in mind: What evidence can you cite to support your judgments? Do you make judgments that are difficult to support?

EXERCISE **7**

Choose two of your papers—preferably a good one and a weaker one—and analyze each to determine how well the judgments are supported by evidence. Is the weaker paper characterized by unsupported judgments or unsupportable judgments? Try revising a paragraph or two to make the judgments more convincing.

EXERCISE **8**

Choose a paper to be revised (either a rough draft for a paper due or an essay that has been returned for rewriting) and go over it carefully, marking every judgment. If you find judgments that are unsupported, try revising them to make them more convincing.

EXERCISE 9

Choose a piece from the editorial page—a signed opinion column, a letter, an editorial—and underline its judgments. Are they supported? If not, draft an answer in which you show how or why they are unreasonable or unconvincing.

14d Believability and tone

14d

The aim of most writers is believability. Novelists usually strive to make their stories realistic. Dramatists usually contrive to make their plots and characters credible. Even authors who play with the fantastic and the imaginary want to gain the reader's consent. A satirist like Jonathan Swift in *Gulliver's Travels,* a fabulist like J. R. R. Tolkien in *Lord of the Rings,* or a science fiction writer like Ursula K. Le Guin in *The Left Hand of Darkness* tries to make a fictional world that is internally consistent and that obliquely refers to our world. In applying the term *believability* specifically to argumentation, we mean the reader's belief that the writer's reasoning can be trusted.

Several factors contribute to your reader's trust in your case, including the orderliness of your argument, the plausibility of your assumptions, the persuasiveness of your evidence, and the accuracy of your logic. But these factors may not be enough to earn the reader's confidence. Even if the assumptions are defended, the conclusions supported by detail, and the arguments free of obvious errors, the tone may offend. Quite rightly, readers become skeptical when they feel the writer is trying to crowd them or compel their assent by vehement or dogmatic insistence. Consider the following paragraph:

Excessive vehemence distances reader

Lurking behind the walls of trailers and apartments, concealed by the privacy of homes, suppressed by the terror of its helpless victims, domestic violence is destroying the integrity of the American family! It shatters children and marriages; it releases the most hideous emotions and feelings humans are capable of. It is the most sordid display of depravity one can imagine. No social evil is more vicious! Domestic violence threatens the very foundations of our society.

What offends here is not the writer's choice of subject (the destructiveness and prevalence of domestic violence can be documented) but his choice of tactics. He assaults his topic and reader with exclamation marks, unqualified statements, and highly charged words like *hideous, sordid,* and *vicious.* He leaves no room for honest differences of opinion and judgment; for example, readers who might feel that drug addiction or alcoholism poses as great a social problem as domestic violence does. However reasonable the rest of his case, he has risked losing the reader's trust by a lack of moderation. Now consider the same paragraph rewritten to earn credibility:

More moderate tone engages reader

> One of the serious social problems in America is domestic violence. Because its victims, usually women and young children, are often frightened and silent, the magnitude of this problem is not always recognized. The privacy of the home—whether trailer, apartment, or house—too frequently conceals its consequences. But the bruised child, the battered wife or lover, and the angry, confused male all find themselves trapped, the law and social agencies unable to intervene until violence has already occurred, and not always easily even then.

14d

The revision solicits concern, not unquestioning acceptance or submission.

A believable tone is a moderate one. It allows for other viewpoints and alternatives without compromising the writer's basic conviction. For instance:

> For many Americans, domestic violence may seem a deplorable but less acute social disorder than alcoholism. The effects of domestic violence are not, perhaps, as visibly publicized and dramatic as certain effects of alcoholism—the televised image of the totaled car and the paramedics arriving, and the escalating rates of injury and death. But its long-term results are, far too often, the battered child who becomes the battering adult. Although it receives less attention and less research funding than alcoholism, its consequences are not less tragic.

A moderate tone also recognizes connections where connections exist and concedes what is unknown:

In reality, domestic violence and alcoholism are not wholly separate social disorders. Each frequently contributes to the other, and neither is fully understood in its causes.

In short, a moderate tone trusts its evidence and the reader's intelligence. The argument is believable because the writer invites—not compels—belief.

EXERCISE 10

Choose one of the following topics and write a paragraph in which you make the tone as dogmatic and as vehement as you can. Then rewrite the paragraph to make the tone moderate and believable.

1. A case for or against athletic scholarships.
2. A case for or against a minimum legal drinking age.
3. A case for or against prayer in public schools.
4. A case for or against police roadblocks to catch drunken drivers.
5. A case for or against the use of animals in medical research.

14d

Avoiding Errors in Reasoning

The failure to examine key assumptions and the confusion of fact with judgments—discussed in the previous chapter—are not the only causes of faulty reasoning. Other reasoning errors, commonly known as **logical fallacies,** also lead to conclusions that will not stand up to scrutiny. Those faulty patterns of thinking, and the best ways of avoiding them, are our focus in this chapter.

15a Legitimate versus hasty generalizations

To generalize is to draw conclusions about a whole class or group after studying some members of the group. Suppose, for instance, that after meeting two bright, articulate, and friendly freshman counselors who are also English teachers, you are convinced that the English department must be outstanding for its teaching. Do you have reasons to question this generalization? Yes, because your sampling may be quite unrepresentative and in any case is quite small. The counselors were probably chosen for this job because they are so effective. But even so, suppose you still have a hunch that the English department is outstanding for its teaching. How would you establish such a generalization?

1. Establishing valid generalizations

Arriving at an accurate generalization usually requires several steps. First, you would have to identify the group "outstanding department" by defining it as, say, the one whose members consistently receive the highest ratings on student evaluations. Otherwise, the generalization is no more than a vague judgment. You would then have to show that a higher percentage of members of the English department rated at the top of the evaluations than members of other departments did.

In such cases, where all the relevant facts about a limited group are available, one may indeed generalize by simply counting or checking accurately—a parking attendant inspects each car on the lot and generalizes that all headlights are off; a dean reviews all the high school transcripts and generalizes that every freshman has had at least a year of foreign language before entering the college. But much of the time it is not possible to do a complete check. Necessarily, therefore, one also generalizes by **induction,** that is, by observing a number of specific examples of the group and then concluding that other examples will *probably* be like those observed. Young children use induction when, after grabbing at two or three cats, they conclude that all cats scratch. Later, when they understand what grabbing is and when they have seen more cats, they learn to generalize that most cats will not scratch unless they are grabbed. Pollsters use induction when they question a representative sample of voters to determine how all voters feel or will probably vote. A consumers' research organization uses induction when it purchases samples of all the different brands of washing machines, tests them carefully, and then generalizes about which brands are likely to be most efficient.

2. Criteria for valid generalizations

Like most other valid arguments, then, legitimate generalizations rest on sound evidence. To generalize accurately, you need to consider how well your evidence will support the conclusions you wish to draw from it.

Typical evidence

Since generalizations are made about classes or groups, the first criterion of generalizations is that the evidence be typical of the class or group. An argument using freshmen on the debate team as the basis for generalizing about the speaking abilities of all members of the freshman class would not be very convincing, because the evidence being cited (a small number of articulate debaters) does not fairly represent the larger group (the freshman class).

Often, though, the untypicality is less crude, more a question of interpretation than of outright error. Are Hemingway's male and female heroes in *A Farewell to Arms* and *The Sun Also Rises* "typical" of the period in their disillusionment with World War I and its aftermath? Before arguing for this point, you would need to investigate prevailing social attitudes at the time. Perhaps you would also want to examine the characters who appear in other contemporary novels, those by F. Scott Fitzgerald, John Dos Passos, and Ford Madox Ford, for example. The point is this: Do not attempt to generalize about a group unless you can demonstrate in a reasonable way that your sample is in fact typical of the larger group.

Adequate evidence

The second criterion of generalizations is that the evidence be adequate. Americans spending a few days in London or Europeans touring the United States for two weeks will acquire many superficial impressions, some of them probably accurate. But this sampling of evidence will be far too limited to support a generalization like "The English are reserved" or "Americans are friendly but ignorant." Other examples of inadequate evidence are an essay citing the two police officers who were reprimanded for roughness as proof that the city's thousands of police officers are brutal, or a term paper citing the suicide of one rock star to show that all rock stars are deeply unhappy, tormented people. Like typicality, adequacy is sometimes difficult to judge— anthropologists finding only a jaw fragment and a few bones or archaeologists finding only a faded temple painting may have to infer what they can and hope for more evidence. But you can assist yourself and your reader by explaining why you think your evidence is adequate, if there is likely to be doubt. If only a quarter of the 250 freshmen vote for class officers, you have adequate evidence that "something" is wrong with morale, though you would have to talk with many of the nonvoters to find out precisely what it is.

15a

Relevant evidence

The third criterion of generalizations is that the evidence be relevant. Figures showing that all fraternity students on campus have a C average or better would not be proof that fraternities produce outstanding students. At best, such data would suggest only that fraternities help their members to remain in good academic standing—a far more modest claim. Similarly, when researchers at a consumers' organization test washing machines, their results will enable them to generalize only about how well different brands will wash, not about other factors such as the likelihood of costly repairs during the life of each machine. To arrive at generalizations on that subject, they will have to turn to a different body of evidence, such as reports from current owners of each brand of machine.

Accurate evidence

The fourth criterion of generalizations is that the evidence be accurate. This standard seems self-evident, yet if you were to read through the long, careful book reviews in such publications as *Scientific American,* the *American Historical Review,* or the *Journal of American Folklore,* you would find two common criticisms: that the writer has been careless about checking facts, and indiscriminate about sources. In cases of extreme carelessness, the reviewer legitimately questions the author's right to be trusted, regardless of how original the ideas are. The most helpful guides you have are the ones for expert testimony: Does the information come from a recognized source? What are the person's motives in relation to the evidence? What agreement is there among others in the field about strengths or weaknesses in the researcher's work?

3. Hasty generalizations

A generalization based on atypical, inadequate, irrelevant, or inaccurate evidence is called a hasty generalization. A few types of hasty generalizations are so common that they deserve special mention here.

Stereotype

A **stereotype** is a sweeping, unfounded generalization about an ethnic group, a profession, or a social role. The writer who suggests that all politicians are crooked, all mothers-in-law are bossy, all athletes are dumb, all accountants are dull, or all city dwellers are unfriendly is indulging in stereotyping, and any arguments founded on such false generalizations will be worthless. Stereotypes are crude caricatures that deny the variety and diversity of individuals.

Oversimplification

Oversimplification is another form of hasty generalizing. Usually, it entails making a question seem easier than it is. Statistics, especially, can lead to oversimplifying. For example, if two classes have markedly different averages on a reading comprehension test, you could not generalize that everyone in the first class outperformed everyone in the second class. Since a few very high scores might have pulled up some mediocre ones in the averaging, you would have to compare all the individual scores to reach such a conclusion. Still less would you be entitled to simplify the results by generalizing that those in the first class were "better students" than those in the second. What would the vague phrase *better students* mean in this context? And how would the results of this single test support such an assertion?

Unqualified generalization

The **unqualified generalization** is a third form of hasty generalization, a claim whose exaggerated inclusiveness belies the scanty evidence that supports it. Unqualified generalizations are easy to recognize; they typically contain such blanket terms as *all, every, none,* and *no one:* "All the freshmen think Orientation Week is a waste of time" or "Not one woman student at this college trusts the dean." To the questions "How do you know? Have you talked with every freshman or every woman?" the writer usually answers: "Of course not, but I know several people who feel. . . ." A responsible writer more accurately identifies the evidence for his or her assertions: "All the freshmen *I have spoken with* feel that . . ." or "None of the women *on my floor* believe. . . ."

15b Mistaken causal relationships

Mistaken causal relationships are errors in reasoning about cause and effect. Perhaps the two most frequent kinds are the post hoc, ergo propter hoc fallacy and the reductive fallacy.

1. Post hoc, ergo propter hoc

The **post hoc, ergo propter hoc fallacy** is the error of arguing that because B follows A, A is the cause of B. (In Latin, *post hoc, ergo propter hoc* means "after this, therefore because of this.") Sequence is not proof of a causal relationship. The fact that B follows A is not proof that B was caused by A. Primitive beliefs like a full moon "causing" pregnancy and their modern equivalent in the television commercial linking love with a change in toothpastes are easy enough to laugh at. But clear thinking on serious social problems can be obscured by this fallacy. For example, those who complain that high-school test scores have dropped during the six months since the new mayor took office may have found a convenient scapegoat for their frustration over the state of public education, but such fallacious reasoning may cause them to overlook the real—and potentially remediable—causes of declining student performance.

15b

2. Reductive fallacy

The **reductive fallacy** occurs when simple or single causes are given for complex effects, creating a generalization based on insufficient evidence. Such generalizations as "Athens fell because of mob rule" and "Luther caused the Reformation" are reductive. That is, instead of specifying the mob or Luther as only one important condition, these assertions make Luther or the mob the single agent of causation. In 1964, when the U.S. surgeon general announced a high correlation between cigarette smoking and lung cancer, he indicated that one was probably a contributory cause of the other. But since not all heavy smokers die of lung cancer and since there is evidence that industrial fumes and car exhaust are also injurious in this regard, he did not say that smoking is the only cause of lung cancer or that every smoker will develop lung cancer. Insofar as they cannot directly isolate, identify, and control each factor in a sequence, scientists, like historians, usually observe the test of sufficiency: only if A alone is sufficient to produce B can it be called the cause of B.

To let your readers judge the sufficiency of your argument, define its conditions and limitations as clearly as you can. With complex relationships, remember that there is a significant difference between saying "It is caused by" and "It has been helped by," just as there is between saying "Luther caused" and "Luther contributed to" or "The reason for the revolution" and "One reason for the revolution." The limited statement can be more exact because it is more tentative: it implies that other conditions, other contributing factors, may be as important as the one singled out for discussion.

15c Reasoning by analogy

An **analogy** is a comparison between two different things or events that shows the way or ways in which they are similar. For example, to explain how the novelist works, one could draw the analogy between the writer and the potter: both begin with a rough idea or image, but discover the particular shape of the plot or vase as they work with their materials, often modifying the outlines several times before they are satisfied.

1. Uses of analogies

Analogies can vividly illustrate and clarify difficult ideas. In the following student paragraph, for example, the writer has used her analogy skillfully to describe the complex techniques of a satirist:

> The sight of a monkey pushing through the jungle, leaping from tree to tree, seems "natural" and, perhaps, graceful. However, when a monkey is placed in a small cage or zoo, his boundings from side to floor to side to ceiling seem antic and "unnatural." The satirist employs the same techniques of limitation. He confines his subject, as it were, to a small cage, or at least one tree, for purposes of close observation. The setting in which he moves his object is limited and its barriers are precisely drawn. The satirist, in effect, traps the victim in his most ridiculous positions and does not allow him to wander off or in any way escape an intensely mocking portrayal.

Analogies have been fruitful in science because they have suggested new lines of research and testing. Benjamin Franklin saw a similarity between lightning and electric sparks; the similarity between x-rays and the rays emitted by uranium salts raised questions about the source and nature of this energy, and eventually led Marie Curie to discover radium; mathematicians such as John von Neumann, instrumental during the early development of computers, saw an analogy between the way the human nervous system works and the way a relay of vacuum tubes can be made to work.

2. False analogy

An analogy can be illustrative or suggestive, but it cannot be conclusive. It may introduce an intriguing hypothesis or possibility, but it cannot offer proof. Consequently, you would do well to suspect any conclusions that are supported only by an analogy, particularly when the differences between the two things being compared are equal to or greater than their similarities. To argue, for example, that the countries of Africa should have federated into a United States of Africa to solve their political and economic problems, one would have to ignore some obvious dissimilarities with the American colonies. The latter, unified by language and a common foe, had in most cases a long tradition of local self-government. African countries, in contrast, are separated from one another by deep linguistic and cultural differences and in several cases are inwardly divided by tribal rivalries. An argument based on this false analogy does not have much hope of success.

False analogies obscure and prevent clear thinking about serious and difficult questions. To detect analogies used as proof, examine the argument to see if any evidence is offered other than a comparison between two different things or events. In your own writing, if you think an analogy is essential to your argument, rethink your entire case: don't allow yourself to frame an argument solely around deceptive similarities.

15d Avoiding the question

When writers fail to give relevant evidence for their arguments, they are said to be avoiding the question.

1. Begging the question

Begging the question is one such common failure. A question is begged when writers use as a proven argument the very point they are trying to prove. For example, a person who argues that the poor are lazy and points to families on welfare as "evidence" is assuming without proof that only lazy opportunists receive government assistance—the very point to be demonstrated.

2. Ad hominem

The **ad hominem argument**—the argument, as the Latin phrase says, "to the man"—is a second common form. Here, the tactic is to condemn the morals, motives, friends, or family of one's opponent and hence to divert attention from the substance of the opponent's argument. For instance: "How could you possibly agree with Berloff about the school bond? I hear from some people he's a real snob." The issue is the school bond, not Berloff's alleged snobbery.

The evaluation of expert testimony should not be confused with the ad hominem argument: in the former, you ask what a person's professional credentials are and the reasons for his or her position—that is, you attempt to distinguish between fact and judgment; in the latter, you insinuate by sarcasm or similar means that a case is unsound because there is something wrong with the person making it.

3. Dummy subject

The **dummy subject** is another device commonly used for avoiding the question. As the label implies, the technique is to stuff, set up, and knock down a dummy issue that is substituted for the real issue. For example: "You say that drilling for oil in wilderness areas threatens the environment. But answer this: do you expect American industry and transportation to function without oil products?" The issue is not whether we are to continue to produce oil and gasoline for heating buildings and fueling cars; for the foreseeable future, at least, there cannot be any argument on this point. The dummy subject set up in this statement obscures the real issue at hand: whether the possibility of locating oil in wilderness areas outweighs the damage that may be done to the landscape and the wildlife. That's a much more complicated question than the one posed here.

15e False alternatives

The false **either/or** argument assumes that there are only two alternatives in a given situation. If parents tell a child, "You must be lazy, because the only reasons for poor schoolwork are laziness or stupidity, and I know you aren't dumb," they commit this error. They ignore other alternatives: the child may be bored with easy work, or he may lack adequate academic preparation, or he may be unhappy for a variety of reasons. The either/or fallacy often surfaces in arguments intended to mobilize people to act: "If we don't elect Helen Fabian mayor, our public schools will continue to decline!" As careful writers know, few issues can actually be reduced to such an either/or proposition.

15f Non sequiturs

In Latin, *non sequitur* means "It does not follow." A **non sequitur** occurs when there is no connection between the premise and the conclusion, as in the following: "Carolyn likes algebra, so she ought to be a good treasurer." The connection between liking algebra and taking care of money is entirely unclear.

15f

EXERCISE 1

Analyze each of the following generalizations by the four criteria for valid generalizations discussed in **15a**. Be prepared to explain *which* generalizations are defective and in what ways.

1. From a recent faculty committee meeting: "Students are making a farce out of the government's low-interest loan program for college financing. The percentage of students who deliberately default is steadily rising, and there's no reason to think it will drop or that students will begin to feel responsible for paying the money they owe. The whole program is just a waste of the taxpayer's money."

2. From a recent "Letters to the Editor" column: "How can your editorial writer deny that Americans are the most wasteful, extravagant consumers of gas in the world! Drive along any expressway or freeway at rush hours and count all the cars with only one passenger and look at the miles of bumper-to-bumper traffic."

3. From a recent college newspaper: "This school has the worst meals of all the state colleges. Any athlete or debater can tell you the meals you get at other colleges make the ones we get look awful."

4. From the *Guinness Book of World Records:* "The only admissible evidence upon the true height of giants is that of recent date made under impartial medical supervision. Biblical claims, such as that for Og,

King of Bashan, at 9 Assyrian cubits (16 feet 2½ inches) are probably due to a confusion of units. Extreme mediaeval data from bone measurements refer invariably to mastodons or other nonhuman remains. Claims of exhibitionists, normally under contract not to be measured, are usually distorted for the financial considerations of promoters. There is an example of a recent 'World's Tallest Man' of 9 feet 6 inches being in fact an acromegalic of 7 feet 3½ inches."

EXERCISE 2

Analyze each of the following statements of causal relationship to determine which ones are guilty of the post hoc, ergo propter hoc fallacy or the reductive fallacy.

1. More than two-thirds of the people in our state voted for the limitation on the state property tax and deliberately deprived local communities of all kinds of services. The only explanation is sheer selfishness; they were afraid of higher taxes.
2. All the children in the remedial reading class watch at least twenty hours of television a week. With all that passive sitting, no wonder they can't read.
3. It is not surprising that the divorce rate is climbing; all those young couples splitting up now grew up during the chaos of the 1960s; they never had a chance at a stable environment.
4. Since 1940, the government has gotten bigger and bigger, and taxes have gone higher and higher. The conclusion is obvious.

15f

EXERCISE 3

Analyze each of the following analogies to determine whether it is used as an illustration, a hypothesis suggesting further investigation, or proof.

1. From a pamphlet: "Pornographic literature is arsenic that poisons the system. It's not enough to label it and put it on the shelf. Just as some children can't read the label on the bottle and others want to experiment, some juveniles and adults can't discriminate and others are tempted by the warning. Such books should be locked up in libraries where only scholars with reason for using them can get at them, in the same way druggists only sell arsenic from behind the counter by special permission."
2. From a composition handbook: "Many of the rules in this book, making no mention of exceptions or permissible alternatives, are dogmatic—purposely so. If a stranger is lost in a maze of city streets

and asks for directions, one doesn't give him the several possible routes, with comments and cautions about each. He will simply become more confused and lost. One sends him arbitrarily on one route without mentioning equally good alternative ways. Likewise, the unskilled writer can best be set right by simple, concise, stringent rules."

3. From a student editorial: "The administration never gets tired of telling us that the state college is part of society as a whole. It harps on student responsibility for 'good taste' in plays and publications, student responsibility to obey state laws about drinking and driving, and student responsibility for property. By the same line of reasoning, then, how can the administration claim it has the final right to approve of campus organizations and their speakers? If the state university is part of 'society as a whole,' it ought to recognize our rights as well as our obligations. We aren't asking for the privilege of being subversive; we are asking for the civil rights we have in 'society as a whole'—the rights to hear whom we wish and join the groups we wish."

4. From a student theme: "The college has the same obligation to satisfy the student that a store does to satisfy the customer. Students and their parents pay the bills, and they ought to have a much freer say about what courses they take. No clerk would think of telling a customer she had to buy several things she didn't want before she could buy the item she came for. And no store would keep as clerks some of the men and women the college keeps as professors. They can't even sell their product."

5. From a medical journal: "If you place a number of mice together in fairly close quarters and then systematically introduce an increasing variety of distractions—small noises, objects, movements—you increase the probability of neurotic behavior. Cannot something like this process help explain the growth of neurotic behavior in our ever more crowded, complex society? The possibility is worth considering."

EXERCISE 4

Pick one of the following analogies and write a paragraph using the analogy as proof. Then, in a second paragraph, show precisely how the analogy is false or misleading, as you have developed it.

1. The family budget and the federal budget
2. The referee in boxing and the arbiter in labor disputes
3. The captain of a ship and the president of a democracy

4. Packaging the goods well and giving a lecture well
5. Determining the warnings on chemicals and determining the ratings of films

EXERCISE 5

The following statements contain unsound reasoning. Identify the different kinds of fallacies and specify what change, if any, would improve the argument.

1. Either you trust a person or you don't. And you don't do business with someone you don't trust. The same principle ought to be observed in foreign affairs; you don't do business with countries you can't trust.
2. Anyone with a grain of sense would have known that the county didn't need to buy land for a park. But those officials don't learn easily. It wasn't proof enough for them that a majority voted against the purchase in the election. They had to go to the state legislature and get voted down, too.
3. Freshman "Hell Week" is one of the oldest and dearest traditions of the college. Many of us alumni can remember having our heads shaved and getting up at midnight for roll calls and jogs around the track. Those of us on the Alumni Board oppose the abolition of the custom. We find the arguments for doing away with "Hell Week" childish and tiresome. We were good enough sports to go along with the sophomores in our time.
4. I don't see why I received such a low grade on this term paper. I put in hours of work on it and did several rough drafts. And I followed the format you asked for. It doesn't seem fair.
5. Any man who supports an Equal Rights Amendment either has been brainwashed by feminists or else has no guts.
6. To be an actor, you have to be on a real ego trip. That's why people become actors. All you have to do is look at any famous star and you'll see the living proof.
7. Laws against smoking on trains, in restaurants and theaters, and in other public places discriminate against my right of free choice. If I want to take the risks with my health because of the pleasure I get, that's my business. I'm not trying to tell others how to live their lives.
8. "Reflection on Ice-Breaking"
   Candy
   Is dandy

15f

But liquor
Is quicker
—Ogden Nash

EXERCISE 6

To sharpen your eye for others' fallacies, take a newspaper and turn to the editorial and opinion section. Go through it carefully, isolating and analyzing any errors you find. Better still, if there's a column you find particularly objectionable, write a letter to the editor pointing out how the reasoning is unsound.

EXERCISE 7

The following is a satire, written by a student, of the arbitrary assumptions, unexamined generalizations, and misleading analogies that are all too often found in print. In analyzing the argument, see how many of these logical errors you can find.

15f

Why Have Teachers?

In the early days of America, before the establishment of compulsory schooling, moral standards were high. People were contented with the simpler virtues. Girls learned to sew, cook, and keep house; men, to farm or work at some trade. Marriages were stable and happy; there was no such thing as divorce. Today this happy scene has changed—the morals of modern America are corrupted. Every newspaper carries stories of murder, embezzlement, adultery, and divorce. What has caused this shocking situation? Is it possible to regain the happy state of early America?

The most influential institution during the formative years of each American is the school, governed and dominated by the teachers. From these teachers children learn the human faults of blind obedience, prejudice, and the betrayal of one's kind in the form of tattling. These early sown seeds bear the bitter fruit of low morality. Clearly, teachers do much to undermine the morality of American children, and through them, that of society.

The obvious solution is to eliminate the teacher as much as possible. Modern children are increasingly capable of educating themselves. There are more college students today than ever before, a fact which proves that youth today possess superior intelligence. By educating themselves, they would not be subjugated to the influence of teachers. They would share their knowledge willingly, each gaining from the other, with no one person dominating the others.

Cynics will sneer that this system is impractical, that students need guidance and even indoctrination in fundamentals before they can think on their own. Nothing could be further from the truth! One of the most clear-thinking, intelligent men in this nation's history, Abraham Lincoln, was almost entirely self-educated. Think of the effect on our society of an entire generation with the training and characteristics of Lincoln. The present immorality would disappear; a high moral standard would be developed. The group that is undermining morality would be minimized in its influence, and the education of American youth placed where it belongs—in the hands of these same youth.

15f

16 *Writing about Literature*

I know noble accents
And lucid, inescapable rhythms;
But I know, too,
That the blackbird is involved
In what I know.

From "Thirteen Ways of Looking
at a Blackbird," by Wallace Stevens

Like the speaker in Stevens's poem, we as readers have known "noble accents" and "lucid, inescapable rhythms" in the poems, plays, and stories we have read. And, like the speaker reflecting on the blackbird, we have perhaps reflected on our involvement with the work. Stevens's lines suggest several major challenges in writing about literature. How to understand our relationship to the work? How to share our experience of it most effectively with other readers? How to convince others that ours is a valid way of looking at the work?

Obviously, in this short chapter we can offer only a few guidelines for thinking and writing about literature. These are complex subjects, certainly not to be reduced to rules such as those for the uses of the apostrophe. Nevertheless, we can say some things about the questions posed above that will make your writing about literature more effective and more pleasurable. For convenience, we will divide our discussion into three broad categories: Inhibiting Assumptions, Productive Questions, and Useful Strategies.

16a Inhibiting assumptions

By *inhibiting assumptions,* we mean those preconceptions and attitudes students often bring to the academic study of literature that block clear thinking and writing. Such assumptions make students distrust their abilities, or make them defensive and dogmatic, or both.

1. A special logic?

You are probably familiar with one of these inhibiting assumptions: the notion that writing about literature requires some esoteric technique or special logic, mastered only by the gifted few. You may have heard friends say (and felt yourself) something like the following: "What does she want me to say? I don't know how to write about poetry." "How am I supposed to put this essay together? I don't know what to do with the novel."

These and similar remarks frequently assume that reasoning about literature is different from, say, reasoning about history, psychology, or biology. Clearly the materials being reasoned *about* do differ. Literary characters and events are not the same as actual persons and historical events, or the theories of perception and personality studied in psychology. But a little reflection should suggest that the principles of clear exposition—defining and developing a topic, observing and describing evidence accurately, supporting generalities by detail—do *not* change. Consider your own experience of discussing a film or novel with friends outside class. You agree or disagree that a character or event was or was not significant and say why (stating a topic and its implications). You recall your impressions of the character or event as fully as you can; sometimes you are corrected by your friends, and sometimes you correct them (observing and describing evidence). And you connect the details you remember to the judgment you are defending (supporting generalizations).

In short, we question the assumption that thinking and writing about literature require a special logic, because we often do make sense about it to each other. Usually, such discussions occur naturally and spontaneously, without our worrying self-consciously about method. The belief that there must be some arcane technique for discussing literature probably results, in part at least, from the way subjects are divided by the curriculum—literature in one room, history in another, and biology in a third, each subject with its own procedures and terminology, none apparently related to the other. But this division of labor (and that is mainly what a curriculum is) can unduly inhibit us. It can make us question our ability to communicate effectively in the academic setting, even though we have talked intelligibly about a variety of works in more informal settings.

16a

2.   Only one correct interpretation?

Another inhibiting assumption concerns the authority of interpretations: the belief that there must be a single, unambiguous, "correct" interpretation of a given work. You recognize this view in the simple way it is often stated. In effect, it says, "Well, what *is* the right interpretation of the poem? There must be one."

Now this assumption is not entirely unwarranted. We have been taught that right answers exist. But, again, if we turn to our experience outside the classroom, we probably find that we are more discriminating. Experience has very probably taught us that right answers may be found in some areas but not in others. In matters that involve simple calculation or measurement—arithmetic, chemistry labs, and the like— we reasonably expect to find the correct solution. In matters of human choice, motive, and action (the substance of literature), however, we have to master the demanding discipline of tolerating ambiguity and perplexity. The poet John Keats called this discipline "negative capability" and described it as one's ability to accept "uncertainties, mysteries, doubts, without any irritable reaching after fact and reason" (letter of December 27 [?], 1817). However strongly we may wish otherwise, we learn that adulthood involves the recognition that certain situations and differences have to be accepted and lived with. So, too, with plays, poems, and stories: because they so often are complex explorations of human motive and actions, they cannot be reduced to a single "correct" statement of the author's "message." In simple terms, what is *the* meaning or "message" of *Hamlet, Pride and Prejudice,* or the *Iliad?* If you sometimes find yourself irritably wanting to simplify the meaning of a work, resist the temptation. The assumption that such a single, correct statement of its meaning exists can inhibit your response to the work's depth and power, transforming it into a formula, a slogan, at best a ten-word telegram.

3.   All interpretations equally valid?

At the other extreme is the belief that since all interpretations are wholly subjective and individual, none is better than any other. "I don't see what's wrong with my interpretation," says the person who holds this view. "After all, it's just a matter of personal opinion."

But this, too, is an assumption that is frequently contradicted by our behavior outside the classroom. If, for instance, we are discussing the history of science fiction or the achievements of its major writers, we are unlikely to accept all views equally. We know that some friends have read widely and deeply, while others have narrow views based on limited exposure and knowledge. The same holds true in dozens of other interests we may have—gymnastics, interior decorating, chess, country music, whatever. We don't usually insist that others share our interests, only that they not make snap judgments and offer facile interpretations out of ignorance while claiming the right to do so because "it's just a matter of opinion." By contrast, we often give heed to those we know to be sensitive and informed. While not compelled to treat them as experts, we have learned that they see, feel, and grasp more; that they can make more connections; that they make us understand more fully than we can by ourselves. We don't necessarily assume that their judgments and interpretations are always right but rather that their views are probably more inclusive and penetrating than other opinions—in short, better.

16a

4. Implications for the study of literature

What does all of this imply about the study of literature? Most immediately, it implies your need to prepare and to be informed—to use dictionaries for unfamiliar words and allusions, to consult a glossary of literary terms for the meanings of such terms as *irony* and *dramatic monologue,* to reread shorter works several times and at least parts of the longer ones. Beyond such preparation, it implies an open attitude, a readiness to consider varying interpretations (including your own) as rough approximation. Consider them as hypotheses about a work's meaning. In the natural sciences, hypotheses are tested against all the facts and, other things being equal, those with the greatest explanatory power are judged better. That is, those hypotheses uniting the most features into a coherent pattern with the least complication are considered the more probably true. Admittedly, the analogy between literary interpretations and scientific hypotheses is only partial, because literature often depends on the kinds of irreducible paradoxes and ambiguities that science tries to avoid. Nevertheless, the analogy points out certain shared characteristics. Hypotheses are subject to frequent review in the light of new data, just as interpretations may be reviewed in the light of new evidence found in the text. Hypotheses are provisional and sometimes modified, just as interpretations may be tentative and sometimes revised. We urge you to think of interpretations as resembling hypotheses, because such an attitude increases the likelihood of greater understanding of the work. This attitude can shift the reader's attention away from defensiveness about an entrenched view and toward what he or she shares in common with other readers—the evidence of the text. Consider the following example.

Two students in a class discussion take different viewpoints on Mark Twain's *The Adventures of Huckleberry Finn*. One interprets the novel as essentially the story of Huck's coming of age and learning he cannot trust the adult world. As evidence, the student points to Pap's abusiveness and selfishness, the unthinking violence of feuds and mobs, the barbarity of the small towns, and the duplicity of the King and the Duke. The other student interprets the novel as essentially Twain's attack on slavery. As evidence, the student points to Huck's experiences with Jim, their growing friendship, and Huck's crisis of choice when he decides he would rather go to hell by helping Jim escape than return him to slavery. If the two students construe the different interpretations primarily as differences of opinion or as mutually exclusive alternatives, they risk becoming locked into their positions and ignoring what they might learn from each other. If, however, they construe their interpretations as tentative explanations—as hypotheses—they enhance their chances of improving their understanding. They can rethink their analyses to include what they have omitted. Thus, they might find they can synthesize their separate arguments into a more comprehensive one. They might conclude that as Huck comes of age he learns he cannot trust the adult world but can trust only his personal feelings, especially in his relations with Jim. This revised interpretation is richer than the two originals because it incorporates the evidence of *both*. But it is only provisional, not final. Interpretations, like hypotheses, are approximations, not absolute and unchanging truths.

So far, we have been questioning a few assumptions that impede full responses to and clear thinking about literature. You might call these the "negative factors" and still wonder about some positive ones. What are the kinds of questions and strategies that will sharpen your focus in thinking about poetry, drama, and fiction?

16b Productive questions

In one of her poems, Emily Dickinson says,

Tell all the Truth but tell it slant—
Success in Circuit lies
Too bright for our infirm Delight
The Truth's superb surprise

We may read her lines to identify three major kinds of questions to be asked. The first concerns the "slantness" and the "circuit" the writer has chosen. How is the work put together? What are the resulting effects and meanings? Why this particular direction or slant? These we will call questions of **interpretation.** The second kind of question concerns our "Delight," infirm or otherwise. How well do we judge the work to have succeeded? By what standard? For what sort of audience? These we will call questions of **evaluation.** The third kind of question concerns the "Truth," all or partial, surprising or familiar. How can the individual work or writer be related to some larger context or perspective? What religious, social, or artistic ideas does the work contain? What aspects of human experience in general? These we will call questions of **integration.**

Now clearly a given essay may address all three kinds of questions, though it will usually emphasize one kind more than the others. Normally, writers don't ask themselves whether they are interpreting, evaluating, or integrating, any more than they worry about which method of paragraph development they are using. Nevertheless, good criticism in the arts is primarily the act of pointing—of singling out important details or features, specifying how a particular effect is achieved, noticing resemblances among works. And effective pointing depends on asking the relevant questions to *focus* attention. We begin with questions that focus attention on interpretation.

1. Interpretive questions

To ask *what* a work means, you will find it helpful to begin with a prior question: *How* does it mean? How is it constructed? How are the parts—the stanzas, the chapters, the scenes and acts— related to one another? Through whose eyes is the story told? Why? Is there a dominant image throughout? How is it developed or modi-

16b

fied? Any or several of these questions will help answer the fundamental question interpretation tries to answer: How are we to understand the work?

Begin with the title

If you find your impressions are vivid but difficult to verbalize, begin with the work's title and its chapters or subtitles if it has any. Effective titles are frequently *governing images* of meaning. They are a condensed shorthand of the direction in which the writer intends to go—what Emily Dickinson means by the "slant" or "circuit." For instance, Joyce Carol Oates has written a fine novel set largely in mid-twentieth-century American cities and mainly focused on women whose lives are for the most part shaped by suffering and pain they do not understand; she has entitled the novel *them* and its first section "Children of Silence." If you were to read the novel, you would soon discover how powerfully the title unifies aspects of the work: "them" are the powerless, anonymous, marginally poor not usually written about; "them" are the losers in the pursuit of the American dream; and "them" are those other faceless figures and forces the losers blame for their suffering. Similarly, if you were to read the first section, set in the Great Depression and war years when older men were often broken by unemployment and younger men depressed and even violent, and when women endured as best they could, you would realize that these are indeed "Children of Silence." Their lives warped by historical forces they have no words for, the men turn inward and sullen, the women to the empty clichés of romance or domesticity, and to vague hopes for a better life they cannot precisely describe.

Consider who tells the story

Consider the question of who tells the story and why. What does Twain gain by having Huck tell his own story in his own words? Surely one major result is that we come to know Huck's sweetness and shrewdness, his untutored decency and wit, better than we know most people's qualities in actual life. We realize that Huck *is* his word in every sense. His arguments with and caring for Jim, the inventive lies he tells to save the two of them, his acute perceptions about the fraudulence of others, his ignorance of history and culture, and his

16b

knowledge of immediate realities—all of these elements Twain renders in Huck's words, which reveal his essential character. And, on reflection, we may raise other questions: What else has Twain made us experience through the colloquial, seemingly spontaneous language of this largely natural boy? How have we been made to feel about Pap's drunken brutality and vulgarity? About the Widow Douglas's gentility? About Tom's zeal for adventure at Jim's expense? Eventually, we may conclude that Huck's words are the ones by which we measure all else in the novel—the characters; the events; what it means to be a slave, a piece of disposable property; the possible cost of civilization itself, a loss of a vision like Huck's.

Identify a meaningful image or pattern

Another way of organizing your impressions is to identify, review, and analyze a repeated image or a recurrent pattern of action the author has charged with meaning. In the following passage, a student is discussing Doris Lessing's novel *The Golden Notebook* and its heroine, Anna Wulf, a writer whose personal and professional life is in shambles:

16b

> During the time Anna is seeing Mother Sugar, a Jungian psychoanalyst, she has her first dream, a nightmare, about "the joy in spite." She tells Mother Sugar, "It mocked and jibed and hurt, wished murder, wished death. And yet it was always vibrant with joy." In Anna's dreams, the embodiment of this principle progresses from a jug, to a grotesque dwarf, a deformed creature, a half-human, to a person: the progression of terror of an object, to terror of the dream as myth, to terror of Saul, her actual lover. Anna must work through her fears of the principle of destruction if she is to write again. Her fear of the cruelty that destruction brings helps cause her inertia, her writer's block. She must learn to turn that force into a creative one.

Here, the student has chosen to concentrate on an image. In this next example, another student has chosen a recurrent pattern of action in Ralph Ellison's novel *Invisible Man*.

> *Invisible Man* begins with a prologue that informs the reader that the black narrator is an invisible man who lives in a hole. He is invisible "simply because people refuse to see me." But he is also invisible because he has fled from seeing himself and has allowed others to manipulate

him. Throughout most of the novel, the narrator is kept running by different authority/father figures or systems, submitting to each though he unconsciously rebels against them, repressing his own anger, tension, despair, and humiliation. What Ellison shows (to me, at least) is that the narrator flees not only because other people can't see beyond his blackness but also because the narrator can't accept his own humanity and his responsibility for himself.

These two examples of student writing demonstrate the value of isolating a significant image or action and asking yourself *what it adds up to*. We have used novels as illustrations so far, but you can often do the same with poems, short stories, and plays. By questioning a part and teasing out its meanings and effects, you begin to see the larger pattern of the work. In fact, the resonant part may be no more than a line or two, a sentence that you marked while reading because it gave shape to your own impressions. Frequently, such lines occur near or at the end of the work as thematic summaries. The journey completed, the writer looks back to see *what* the direction has meant. For instance, at the end of Arthur Miller's play *Death of a Salesman,* Linda, the wife of Willy Loman, the salesman of the play's title, stands next to his grave and sobs, "I made the last payment on the house today. Today, dear. And there'll be nobody home. We're free and clear. We're free. We're free." Reading these lines, we may feel that Miller is a bit insistent but we also certainly perceive his dramatic intent: to make us realize how unfree Willy was, how trapped by a certain American ideal of success, and how damaging and difficult it may be to achieve freedom from this ideal, not only for Willy's family but for us, "we," the audience.

16b

Examine the tone

Still another question you can pose concerns the tone of the work. What *is* the tone, the speaker's emotional stance toward the subject? This question is especially appropriate for (though not confined to) lyric poetry, in which there is no story, or only a vaguely suggested situation. By recognizing the tone, you can locate the cluster of feelings and attitudes that have moved you, not by the plot and events but by the curve and motion of the speaker's voice. Reading aloud, you can retrace the rises and the falls, the beckonings and the separations, the reaching outward and the drawing inward that affected you on

silent reading. In a frequently reprinted essay, the poet and critic
R. P. Blackmur wrote of "Language as Gesture," and this is the essence
of lyric poetry—language *as* gesture. The speaker's voice gestures by
greeting, by rejecting, by embracing. And as you perceive the tone,
you may recall other lines or poems that echo it, that make similar
gestures. One might, for instance, begin with Edward Fitzgerald's translation of *The Rubaiyat of Omar Khayyam:*

> Come fill the Cup, and in the fire of Spring
> Your Winter-garment of Repentance fling:
> The Bird of Time has but a little way
> To flutter—and the Bird is on the wing.

In turn, these lines might bring to mind Christopher Marlowe's "The
Passionate Shepherd to His Love" and his invitation:

> Come live with me and be my love,
> And we will all the pleasures prove
> That valleys, groves, hills, and fields,
> Woods, or steepy mountain yields.

16b

Catching the tone of both poems, one would discover differences as
well as similarity. Both passages are a call to life, to test the joy of
living in the body and through the senses; they both gesture by implor-
ing. But Fitzgerald's lines contain a reminder, almost a warning, not
found in Marlowe's—that the moment is brief, that "The Bird of Time"
is "on the wing." Marlowe's tone, by contrast, is seductive in its promise
of timeless youth. In fact, Sir Walter Raleigh answers Marlowe in
"The Nymph's Reply to the Shepherd" with the speaker's skepticism
of the young man on the make. Raleigh begins,

> If all the world and love were young,
> And truth in every shepherd's tongue,
> These pretty pleasures might me move
> To live with thee and be thy love.

and concludes,

> But could youth last and love still breed,
> Had joys no date nor age no need,
> Then these delights my mind might move
> To live with thee and be thy love.

As you may have decided by now, interpretive questions probe by comparison and contrast. They investigate the ways titles unify diversities, parts resemble or differ, images evolve or change, voices agree or disagree. Remember that the most important thing you know about a poem or a story is what you were thinking and feeling while reading the work. Begin by asking what elements in the work help account for whatever you felt and thought. Select a feature that has lingered with you; reason from effects to causes. As you move from particular to particular, you will necessarily compare and contrast. And as you find likeness and difference, you will integrate your feelings about and understanding of the work. You will become the interpreter of meaning, the negotiator between the work and your reader.

2. Evaluative questions

In a broad sense, anyone who writes about literature evaluates continually. The scenes, characters, and lines to be discussed or omitted, the themes and ideas to be stressed or minimized, the works themselves to be singled out for analysis—all of these represent choices about what is significant or insignificant. Similarly, readers have likes and dislikes, preferences for certain writers or kinds of literature and aversions to others. Different readers have different needs and expectations. For certain readers, the romance, detective story, or historical novel is a pleasant narcotic, used to kill time, escape, or doze off with. For others, fairy tales and fantasy offer a kind of substitute world where good and evil, high adventure and vivid conflict are found undiluted. And so on. The uses readers make of literature are varied and personal and often changeable. The stories that we loved as children sometimes disappoint us when we reread them as adults; the best-seller we enjoyed four years ago may bore us when we browse through it again.

We mention these familiar facts for three reasons. The first is that it makes no more sense to quarrel about the reality of different tastes in literature than it does in clothing or music. One may admire some tastes and deplore others, but that is another issue. The second reason is that people usually become better readers by exploring a variety of genres, works, and writers on their own and at their own rate. What is right for one person at a given age or stage of development may not be for another. Individual growth cannot be computer programmed.

16b

The third reason is that the academic study of literature differs in important ways from one's own leisure reading. Teachers hope that the works they have chosen will prove challenging, stimulating, and pleasurable, but they cannot guarantee these rewards for any given student. Rather, what teachers can promise is a more systematic examination of certain significant works, techniques, ideas, and genres than most people are likely to undertake on their own. For these reasons, we have stressed interpretive questions. Interpretive questions are the ones the academic study of literature can most effectively ask students to think and write about. The evaluative questions we will look at are, therefore, limited to those that most frequently arise in class.

Judging a work's success

One of the most common questions you will be asked is "How successful do you think the work is?" This is *not* the same as being asked "Did you like the work?" You can like or dislike a novel or poem for many reasons, some of which may have little to do with the work itself—wishing to please a respected teacher, having fixed ideas about what literature should be, being burdened with too much work for thoughtful reading, and so forth. The question "How successful do you think the work is?" is usually asked in relation to specific criteria or in a specific context—or should be. The most productive question *you* can ask is "Successful in relation to what?" Discussable judgments and evaluations require a framework, a stipulation of terms or assumptions. In this respect, evaluating literature is no different from evaluating paintings, films, or other works of art.

16b

Assumptions are particularly important. If they are not clear, they should be clarified. If they seem questionable, they should be scrutinized. For instance, one popular assumption—not always explicitly stated as such—is a play or novel should be well made, with a decisive beginning, middle, and end. But what does one mean by a *decisive* ending? Is it in fact true that important novels and plays always have such endings? Some important works—especially modern ones—do not end decisively; they simply stop. Ralph Ellison's *Invisible Man*, for instance, ends with the narrator finally understanding more about himself and the world but still living in a hole. In fact, many contemporary works close with the survivors disabused of illusions or pretenses but with their futures quite uncertain—Albee's *Who's Afraid of Virginia Woolf?* and Golding's *Lord of the Flies,* to mention but two. We simply don't know what the characters are going to do after the end of the text.

Taking chances with the unfamiliar

Be clear about standards and assumptions, including your own, and be willing to take chances with the unfamiliar. Like certain acquaintances, some poems, novels, and plays will seem difficult, strange, sometimes even threatening, when you first encounter them. They have to be lived with for a while. Here, for instance, is what one student found after living with Tillie Olsen's fiction long enough to be moved by it:

16b

> Raised in affluent, upper-class America, I have rarely come in contact with the poverty Tillie Olsen describes in her short stories. But her treatment of suffering powerfully conveys the despair, the broken lives, the caring, and sometimes even the hope that poverty entails. I found that Ms. Olsen develops an intensity of pain, resentment, love, and understanding that simply does not exist in more privileged communities. She made me realize the terrible destruction of human potential and personality that poverty can cause, but she also made me see how easily one can become hardened by comfort. At the end of *Tell Me a Riddle,* I had some hope that poverty can be overcome, but I found this hope tempered by the realization that as one gains affluence, one too easily loses intensity of emotion and the ability to understand.

Notice what the writer has done. Rather than hurrying to make up her mind about whether Olsen's stories are good or bad, she has taken the time to ask an entirely different kind of question, something like "What have I felt and understood that I had not before?" We suggest that this type of question is the most productive for works you find unfamiliar or unsettling.

We read texts, but texts also "read" us. Certain writers and works, that is, disturb our habitual ways of thinking and feeling and our conventional notions about what literature should be. If we remain open, they make us feel our own limitations. If, as happens occasionally, you find you are expected to write about such a work, try beginning with the following questions: Why do I find this book strange or discomforting? Is there something about myself or my beliefs I resist coming to terms with? After thinking about these questions as honestly as you can, you are always free to decide that what you have discovered was not worth the bother. It is also possible, however, that you will discover some things about yourself that take you on a far more interesting journey than safer, more familiar works have.

3. Integrative questions

By *integrative questions,* we mean those that ask about the individual writer's or work's relationship to some larger context. Such questions may concern the connections between the work and the writer's life or times; the work and philosophical, political, or religious ideas; the work and certain artistic movements or forms; the work and human experience in general. To be specific: What does the fiction of Toni Morrison, Alice Walker, and Toni Cade Bambara say about the lives of black women in America? What did T. S. Eliot learn from Ezra Pound about poetry? What political and social ideas was Swift satirizing in *Gulliver's Travels?* How does Virginia Woolf's criticism illuminate her major novels? What are the relationships between Shelley's interest in philosophy and his poetry? How does Dickens's humor differ from Fielding's? Why were the Beat poets called *Beat?*

Integrative questions are often the most exciting ones you can ask. They encourage wide reading, research, and concentrated thinking. They invite you to pursue a line of inquiry in depth and to sustain it until you have found the answers that make the most sense. Courses that center on a historical period, one or two authors, a movement or theme, or a genre quite naturally provoke such questions—the instructor's, your own, or both. Even introductory and broad survey courses lend themselves to such questions. The satisfaction of answering these questions is that they allow you to interpret individual works and then to connect what you have found to a larger argument or thesis—in short, *to integrate.* Integrating is the discovering of significant relationships among things.

Defining your question

What is a good integrative question? To begin with, it should be one that is answerable. To ask "What did Salinger really have in

16b

mind when he wrote *Catcher in the Rye?*" is to ask a question that is probably unanswerable: nobody but Salinger could know, and he's not saying. A more manageable question is "What central themes of *Catcher in the Rye* are found in Salinger's other works?" It is answerable because the texts are available. Effective integrative questions are essentially the same as those you ask in preparing to write any paper involving research and critical thinking. (See also Chapter **17** on the research process.)

Unless your instructor assigns the topic, your first question is the hardest: What more do I want to know about the work or writer? The period or society that shaped the work or writer? Some philosophical, religious, or artistic idea that permeates the work or influenced the writer? Other similar works or writers? Even if the topic is assigned, you can normally sharpen it by posing your own question and checking with the instructor to be sure it's relevant.

16b Clarifying your interest

The second question is closely related to the first: Why do I want to know more about this? Of course it's because you are interested, but *why in terms of the topic?* For instance, suppose you wanted to know more about some recent feminist writers. Why? Because of their treatment of women? Of men? Of women and men? Of women's sexuality? Of mothers and daughters? Sometimes, especially at the beginning, it won't be easy to answer why, and often your interests will change as you get into the topic. But the more you can at least *tentatively* answer this question, the more you clarify your focus.

Planning your research

The third question is also crucial: What more do I need to know to answer my question? Here your primary and secondary reading and your conversations with the instructor are essential. Occasionally, you may find that you need to know too much, that the question is too vast or complicated to be manageable. For instance, if you were to ask seriously "What are the differences between the treatment of World War I and that of World War II in American fiction?" you would be committing yourself to a very long program of reading and research. More frequently, though, what you will need to know involves not only the extensive reading but also the relevant concepts. We stress the importance of concepts because they represent your larger intellectual stake in the question; they provide the boundary lines of your chosen turf. For example, if you wondered how Achilles in the *Iliad* differs from Odysseus in the *Odyssey* as an epic hero, you would have to master the concept of "epic hero" to answer your question.

Avoiding oversimplification

Like interpretive questions, integrative questions are usually answered by making significant comparisons and contrasts. In doing so, you should keep two more stock questions in mind. Both questions concern the danger of oversimplification. The first is "Have I tried to make the concept do too much work or expanded it too widely?" Be wary of broad, catchall ideas such as "search for identity," "crisis of faith," and "Romanticism." Clearly defined and given a specific context, they can be extremely useful, but they can easily become pigeonholes into which everything is shoved. In a loose sense, for example, most novels probably do dramatize "the search for identity," but how does that help one understand the differences between Huckleberry Finn's flight and Hester Prynne's remaining on the scene of her disgrace in *The Scarlet Letter* as "searches"?

The second question is "Have I looked at important differences as well as important similarities?" Difference is as vital as similarity. Writers sometimes do change their themes, subject matter, or techniques and style. History does affect and modify beliefs, artistic conventions, individual lives. To echo the philosopher William James, every difference that is a difference makes a difference.

16c A sample student essay

We have emphasized questions because they give momentum to thinking. They nudge you to move from effect to cause, impression to source, individual case to general principle. To close this discussion, we include a student essay that effectively blends interpretive and integrative questions into one unified argument. The essay concerns the function of Old Hilse, a character in Gerhart Hauptmann's play *The Weavers,* a dramatization of a revolt by impoverished Silesian weavers

in central Europe during the 1840s. The writer's central question is
"Why is Old Hilse even in the play?" His answer is a persuasive demonstration of *how* Old Hilse changes our understanding of the play, the
effect he has upon us.

Why Old Hilse?

**What Old Hilse
does *not* cause or
influence**

If one were to examine the contribution
of Old Hilse to the plot of The Weavers, one
would be hard put to find any excuse for his
being in the play. He neither alters the
course of the main action nor initiates any
new actions. His speeches to the main characters are unheeded. He does not join the
rebel weavers, nor does he come to the defense of the manufacturers. He remains
neutral in the battle, in no way affecting
its outcome. His only connection with the
action of the play is to be an unintentional
and all-but-unnoticed casualty.

Focusing question

Then why are his unheeded lines ever
spoken? Why is this character brought into
the play at all?

The play begins with a dispute between
the younger weavers and the manufacturer's
buyer, builds up the weavers' discontent
with their poverty and fatigue, and reaches
a climax with their open rebellion. It

16c

roars toward what we hope will be its trium-
phant conclusion. But it runs head-on into
Old Hilse. Here is a man whom we fully expect
to jump on the bandwagon, or at least act
as a dramatic counterpoint by siding with
the manufacturers. But Old Hilse just
states his contempt for this particular
uprising, reiterates his belief in duty,
and goes back to his daily weaving. For a
moment the rapidly moving picture of a
community in revolt is frozen. The logic
that has been leading up to the great truth
of why all the weavers must kill all the
owners is stopped just short of a final
conclusion. The almost cornily beautiful
victory of good over evil, already fore-
shadowed in the impoverished mass's sack-
ing of a manufacturer's estate, falters.
Old Hilse, the most respected weaver, the
one most representative of simple devotion to weaving, will not join the rebellion.

In a moment the machine starts to rum-
ble again. The drunken and possessed leaders of the rebellion rush out of Hilse's
house to battle the government troops. The

Old Hilse's action—his refusal to join the rebellion—and its immediate effect on our involvement in the plot

16c

16c

Further effects on the reader—the meaning(s) of Old Hilse's choice

Initial statement of what Old Hilse does cause—our seeing the plot from a new perspective

Summary and strong restatement of Old Hilse's function—final answer to "Why Old Hilse?"

plot starts up again. But the reader left behind begins to question the rebels. Why won't Old Hilse join? Why does his refusal, although not altering the plan of the rebellion one bit, alter the meaning of it so greatly? Hilse is certainly not afraid. He is a wounded veteran of a much greater war. As he starts to talk about the war, the rebellion raging outside begins to shrink. It is nothing to him. What's more, it is nothing to anyone except those who are inside of it. Suddenly the story of the young weavers battling for their rights and the older ones gradually joining them becomes a pathetic example of the pattern we see in the papers almost daily, the local rebellion. This is Hilse's contribution. He is the only character who stands far enough outside the battle to see it as the futile effort it is, not as the glorious rebellion that the other weavers think it is. He has seen it all before. He can even predict jail terms for the leaders. Hilse takes us far enough from the story to see it clearly. Hilse, who is nothing to the plot's outcome, is everything to its meaning: he makes

```
the plot change from a story in which we are
as personally wrapped up as the characters
into a dismal pattern of the universality
of revolt born by suffering and hunger,
doomed to be led astray by its own excesses,
and thus defeated.
```

16d Useful strategies

Apart from the questions we have discussed, you have other ways to assist your thinking and writing about literature. The most important of these, of course, is your paying close attention to the terms, themes, and techniques of analysis that your instructor stresses. We know of no substitute for the student's participating in class, asking questions, and keeping up with the reading. The more actively responsible you become for your own education, the more likely you are to get what *you* want from it. The strategies we will suggest should help you achieve this end.

16d

1. Keeping a journal

A time-proven strategy for increasing one's pleasure in and understanding of literature is keeping a journal or reading log. Many students who have kept journals find they do best to set aside two or three periods a week for writing about their class reading. Length of entry and format often vary: some students write several hundred words on each novel, play, or poem; others jot down short notes, impressions, or references to specific pages they wish to return to. The subject matter can also take varying forms: some students pursue a theme or two from work to work; some explore their personal feelings and thoughts and connect the work to their own experience; some isolate key passages, images, or characters and reflect on these; and others, depending on the work, may try a combination of these approaches. Unless assigned and collected by the instructor, such journals are entirely private. Journals allow the student to write about any aspect of the reading in whatever way is most congenial. That is part of the journal's value: its freedom.

The advantages of keeping a journal are several. To begin with, it allows you to explore your own reactions to the works at greater length and in greater depth than class sessions may permit. By doing so, you make the poem or story more fully your own. Moreover, the journal encourages you to sort out your impressions while they are still fresh. Sometimes, a few weeks after reading a work, you may recall having had some wonderful insights but have no idea now what they were. Journals help you remember. Finally, journals can assist your reviewing in either of two ways. Looking over your journal, you may find some topic you have discussed several times; this topic may be a subject for a paper. Or, reviewing your journal for in-class tests or essays, you may rediscover evidence and ideas that you might otherwise overlook.

If you have not kept a journal before, you may want to review our suggestions for keeping a journal in **2a**. Don't be concerned if you find yourself a bit self-conscious and awkward when you begin. These feelings are entirely natural and usually diminish as you become more experienced. At the very least, we encourage you to try one for a few weeks: it's an excellent way of making the academic study of literature a more personal inquiry.

16d

2. Summarizing

Another useful strategy is summarizing. While this can take a number of forms, the summarizing technique we especially recommend is best suited for scenes or acts of plays, the sections or chapters of prose fiction, and the divisions of longer poems. Briefly, such summaries consist of a few phrases or sentences that set down the *primary* events, themes, and images; the summary is a record of the dominant impressions the section has made. Here, for instance, is the summary of a chapter called "Pastoral," from V. S. Naipaul's moving novel *A House for Mr. Biswas,* based on the life of Naipaul's father, an Indian journalist growing up in Trinidad:

```
Brief pastoral. Mr. B's birth curse, death of calf
and father: family dispersed; no home.
```

And here is the summarizing note for the next chapter, entitled "Before the Tulsis":

```
Beyond childhood: school, beatings, work with Pundit
(& disgrace), liquor store, sign painter. This novel
goes in real stages; youth-adolescence, concluding
with sex, hopes of love and romance, à la Samuel
Smiles.
```

At first, you may wonder of what possible value these summaries are to anyone but the writer. That is their point: they are the *writer's* record of his key impressions on first reading. They are not intended as a total synopsis of the plot, still less as the novel's "message." Rather, *they organize the passages that have been marked throughout the chapter into significant units to be examined more fully later.* They are, so to speak, mile markers on the road of meaning.

16d

The value of this kind of summarizing is most obvious for long, complex works when you are reading them for the first time. Summaries help you retrace what you have read and sort out the central developments and ideas from the lesser ones; they map the major features of the territory you have just explored. Reviewing the territory later, you can inspect the details more analytically because you already have a tentative framework into which they fit. In a somewhat different fashion, summarizing can help unravel the knotty strands of shorter but nevertheless complex pieces. Though only 204 lines, Browning's poem "Childe Roland to the Dark Tower Came" is one of his most mysterious works. Here is one reader's summary of the poem that at least served as a start toward understanding it:

```
Strange poem in several ways: dreams, snatches of
memory of picture and verse, not B's usual control;
the wasteland where all effort is futile, things
mysterious and pointless--world does not mean
intensely and mean good. Note poem filled with images
```

```
of failure, betrayed strength, weakness, aging and
decay without honor——memory no help.
```

The main use of this note for the writer was that it highlighted several ways this poem differed from others by Browning and therefore highlighted what needed to be thought about.

Rather like some journal entries, the summarizing note is your own record in your own words of your primary conclusions. And like its journal equivalent, such a note is best used as an aid for further, more carefully detailed analysis. It is another means of engaging yourself more actively with the reading.

3. Working with the words

16d

Plays, poems, and fiction are made out of words, not clay or copper. When you are caught up in a short story or sonnet, you are enmeshed in the *effects* of words—their connotations and denotations, their plasticity and firmness, their freshness and familiarity. And when you think and write critically about the story or poem, you are partially disengaging yourself from the words in order to look at them. Themes, images, and events do not exist in the abstract; they are embedded in and realized through the words, the stuff of language. Whatever "happens" in literature happens because of the patterns that have been made out of words. Whatever "happens" in analysis and criticism happens usually because these patterns have been *explicated*.

Explication

To explicate is to unfold. To explicate a piece of literature is to unfold the ways the words have been shaped into larger units of meaning—couplets, lines, scenes, chapters, completed works. As we will presently see, even a short poem may include *layers* of suggestiveness and *strands* of imagery. Explication, the unfolding of these layers and strands, is essential to critical thinking about literature. And while critical thinking and writing do not end with explication, they usually begin with it. Before you can go on to larger questions—How does this writer differ from that writer? This epic compare with that epic?— you have to work with the words. Even if you do not write about the language as such, you at least have to think about it as such.

How do you think about "language as such"? To begin with, you will need to look up unfamiliar words and allusions and see how they are used in context. Beyond that, you should, at least with shorter poems and sections of plays, try reading aloud to catch the sounds, rhythms, intonations, and other elements that compose the body language of words. These are essentially preliminaries, however. Your main activity is more easily illustrated than described. To give you an idea of what's involved, we suggest you first read the poem that follows, written in the last years of Walt Whitman's life. After you have read the poem aloud a couple of times and looked up words like *hawser'd,* try answering these questions: (1) How is the picture of old age embedded in particular images? (2) Why is the unifying image "The Dismantled Ship," rather than, say, "The Forgotten Ship"? (3) How can the poem be read as a picture of human loss and decay, particularly Whitman's?

16d

The Dismantled Ship

In some unused lagoon, some nameless bay,
On sluggish, lonesome waters, anchor'd near the shore,
An old, dismasted, gray and batter'd ship, disabled, done,
After free voyages to all the seas of earth, haul'd up at last and hawser'd
    tight,
Lies rusting, mouldering.

Now compare your analysis with the following, an extract from a student essay:

> Whitman views a perishing man as a model for suffering and loss: the victim loses his strength and abilities, is helpless, alone, neglected. His central image, a rotting ship, helps develop this theme because it is easily associated with a weakening body, an aging man, or even, as the editors hint, the elderly Whitman himself. The image conveys not just the idea of a decaying object or thing, but a decaying person. It invites the reader to empathize, to imagine the analogy between ship and human being, both now impotent and forgotten.
>
> Whitman's diction develops his theme. It makes the reader feel the tragedy of a man or ship perishing, of an outcast weak and abandoned. Like a ship rotting in "some unused lagoon," mired in stagnant water and cut off from the "seas of earth," so an aging man may be shut up in a nursing home or live alone, confined, separated from life. He is "anchor'd

near the shore," cut off by time, space, and thought from the ships and men sailing the wide oceans. He is "dismasted . . . disabled, done"; like a "mouldering" ship that has lost its source of power, his age has cost him his Freudian source of energy—his libido. He is "dismantled," unmanned. He is unable to make "voyages" of life and love from person to person and country to country, "free" to choose and "free" from cost or worry. The ship is no longer freshly painted and intact; the old man's skin is weathered, his body weakened. The "good gray poet" has become a "gray and batter'd ship."

Nor is there any returning to the days of old, for time has him "hauled up at last and hawser'd tight." The inevitable price of the years of "free voyages to all the seas of the earth" is to become worn out, an empty hull to be dragged aside and secured to prevent drifting. Yet what is perhaps still worse about his decay is the lack of concern by others, for while his person cries out to be cared for—to stop the "rusting" and "mouldering"—he is alone. He is lonely but no one comes; he is feeble, but no one helps. The sluggish waters lapping against the hull are all that is heard.

16d

Layers of meaning

Notice *how* the student's explication above proceeds. It finds three possible layers of meaning in the words—the image of the ship, of an aging man, and of the poet Whitman. It does not say the poem "is" one layer only or has one "message," but instead tries to find correspondences and similarities among these layers. And it argues for such correspondences by finding them embedded *in* the words. To put it in different terms, the explication unfolds each image to see *how* it may be read in relation to the ship, an aging man, and, on occasion, the poet Whitman. Still, the explication does not claim to be the complete or only interpretation of the poem. Explications are rarely if ever "complete." Here, for instance, the student could have done more with the sounds: Whitman's diminuendo in "dismasted . . . disabled, done" or his finality in "haul'd up at last and hawser'd tight," to mention but one possibility. Nor does this explication preclude other readings with a somewhat different emphasis. Another student, having read about Whitman's last years, might unfold these meanings more fully than the writer of the essay has. And in fact, if a second student were to interpret the poem mainly as a picture of the poet's old age, this reading would supplement, not contradict, the first reading. The two readings would constitute hypotheses about the poem to be compared in relation to the evidence—the words of the text.

Poems for comparison

Now, having read a poem, an explication, and our comments, try working with the words of another of Whitman's poems. This one is concerned with youth, beginnings, fullness of power, and experience. Read it aloud and analyze it first for its own layers of meaning—its playfulness with motion and speed, light and color, water and wind. Then juxtapose it to "The Dismantled Ship": what is the composite picture, and how is it composed by the contrasting images?

The Ship Starting

Lo, the unbounded sea,
On its breast a ship starting, spreading all sails, carrying even her
    moonsails,
The pennant is flying aloft as she speeds she speeds so stately—below
    emulous waves press forward,
They surround the ship with shining curving motions and foam.

16d

This composite picture of youth and age, beginnings and endings, could just as easily be developed in a single work quite unlike Whitman's two poems. We will close with such a poem, one by Emily Dickinson. In working with her words, you might begin by explicating *quiet dust* and the connections between *Gentlemen and Ladies* and *Lads and Girls*. Then try to visualize how *Bloom and Bees/Exist an Oriental Circuit,* that is, live out a full cycle. After you have finished with Dickinson's poem, compare it with Whitman's two poems: what are the significant contrasts in the imagery and meanings?

This quiet Dust was Gentlemen and Ladies

This quiet Dust was Gentlemen and Ladies
And Lads and Girls—
Was laughter and ability and Sighing
And Frocks and Curls.

This Passive Place a Summer's nimble mansion
Where Bloom and Bees

Exist an Oriental Circuit
Then cease, like these—

To conclude, let us recall the questions posed at the chapter's beginning and make a final suggestion. The questions: How to understand our relationship to the work? How to share our experience of it most effectively with others? How to convince others that ours is a valid way of looking at the work? The suggestion: Begin with the words. In and through them alone you have experienced "the noble accents" and "lucid, inescapable rhythms" you have known.

EXERCISE 1

This first group is designed to give you a chance to question inhibiting assumptions.

1. Write a paragraph on Whitman's "The Dismantled Ship" in which you reduce the poem to one meaning, that is, make all the images show only the loneliness of old age, *or* its feebleness, *or* its absence of activity. Then write another paragraph in which you show how much you have had to leave out of the poem in order to achieve a single meaning. Now compare the two paragraphs: How radically did you simplify the poem's imagery? What was the greatest reduction in meaning you made? How was it the greatest reduction?

2. Write a paragraph on Whitman's "The Ship Starting" in which you interpret the poem as, say, a reader beginning an absorbing novel, a crowd moving across a field, or a rocket accelerating off its pad. Then write a paragraph that questions the plausibility of your interpretation as a hypothesis. Now compare the two paragraphs: What is the most telling evidence you cited to question the interpretation? How is it the most telling?

EXERCISE 2

This second group is designed to give you practice with interpretive, evaluative, and integrative questions.

1. Pick a work—a poem, play, or piece of fiction—that you like and know well and that has an effective title. Write several paragraphs in which you show *how* the title acts as a governing image to unify elements of the work—its plot and characters, themes and development, images and details, and so on. Make as many connections as

16d

you can, even if a few of them seem a bit strained or farfetched. When you have finished, reread the paragraphs critically and revise them by concentrating on the most important connections that should be made. Now compare the two sets of paragraphs: How much of the first version did you discard? What elements of the first version became more unified in the second?

2. Choose a short story or novel and write several paragraphs in which you imagine how the work would be different if told from another point of view—for instance, *The Adventures of Huckleberry Finn* through Jim's eyes, or *Heart of Darkness* through Kurtz's eyes. Then write an analysis of what changes you have had to make, what new aspects of the story you have discovered or highlighted, and what modifications in meaning and theme your version entails.

3. Do the same with a short poem, for instance, Thomas Hardy's "Had You Wept" from the woman's point of view, Frost's "Mending Wall" through the neighbor's eyes, or Robinson Jeffers's "Hurt Hawks" through the "terrible eyes" of the bird or "the wild God."

4. Write a paragraph on Dickinson's "This quiet Dust" in which you visualize as fully as you can *how* dust permeates the poem. For instance, how does cloth ("Frocks") look, feel, and smell as it turns to dust, or how do summer flowers ("Bloom") fade and dry?

16d

5. Choose some type of literature you read purely for pleasure—mass-market romances, science fiction, sports stories, fantasy, whatever. Then evaluate by describing as precisely as you can the kind(s) of pleasure you look for and make a case for such reading by specifying the ways it can be successful.

6. Thumb through the editor's headnotes or introductions to the authors and selections in your literature anthology and find some critical judgment that you disagree with. Try to choose one that points to some limitation or failure in the work or writer—for instance, remarks like "Hardy's novels and poems are too often marred by pessimism" or "Sylvia Plath's poetry is too painful for most readers." Then write a thoughtful response in which you perhaps concede part of the criticism but find other grounds for valuing the writer or work.

7. Jot down three or four integrative questions that you might be interested in answering. For example: What connection is there between a writer's work and life? Between a historical period or event and a work? Between a religious or philosophical idea and a work? Then review your questions critically with the following in mind: (1) Is the question, as worded, answerable? If not, can it be rephrased to become so? (2) What more would you have to know to answer the

question? (3) What significant similarities and differences might an educated guess lead you to expect?

8. Using the student paper "Why Old Hilse?" as a model, write an essay in which you analyze how a character is used primarily to provide some larger perspective on or understanding of a play, poem, or novel.

EXERCISE 3

16d

This third group is designed to give you practice in working with useful strategies.

1. Keep a journal faithfully for at least a month, making at least two entries a week of 150 words each. Write on whatever aspects of the literature you wish—how it's related to your experience, what ideas you find most interesting, why you like or dislike a particular work: whatever you find most congenial. At the end of the month, reread your entries with the following questions in mind: (1) Did you have any new insights or make any discoveries while writing? (2) Did writing about the literature increase your pleasure in it?

2. For an assigned work (preferably a longer one) try summarizing its parts, sections, or chapters at the end of each division. Then, after you have finished the work, reread your summaries with the following questions in mind: (1) Did the summarizing help you understand the whole section more clearly? (2) As you review your summaries, do you find you have a firmer grasp on the entire work?

3. Choose two poems that deal with the same theme—love and loss, men and women misunderstanding each other, delight in a natural setting or living creature, suffering and recovery, the passage from adolescence to adulthood, and so on. Write an analysis in which you first explicate each work and then compare and contrast the two as treatments of the theme.

4. Choose a short poem (of no more than twenty-five lines) you like. Then write as complete an explication of it as you can, unfolding every image as fully as possible and looking for the ways the images support and develop the theme. After you have finished, read your analysis with the following questions in mind: (1) Can you find images you want to do still more with? (2) How much has your explication changed your understanding of or feelings about the poem? Why?

5. Follow the instructions in number 4, above, but use the lyrics to a popular song (rock, country, folk, whatever). Pose yourself one ques-

tion in addition to those listed in number 4: What happens to the lyric when you consider the words without the music?

6. Choose a page of a short story or novel you like and analyze it carefully with the following in mind: Do you find the kinds of images that you expect in poetry? If so, what are they and how are they used? If not, what evidence of craft or technique do you find? How, as best you can determine, are these effects achieved? How do they affect you as a reader?

16d

The Research Paper

17 The Research Process

18 The Library

19 Working with Sources

20 Composing the Research Paper

PART V

21 Student Research Paper A: MLA Documentation

22 Student Research Paper B: APA Documentation

23 Student Research Paper C: Endnote Documentation

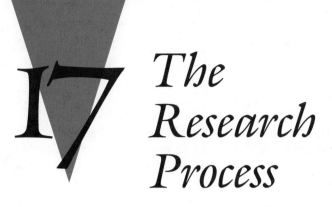

17 *The Research Process*

When we open a newspaper at the end of a busy day, we may not think that we are doing research, but we are. We are doing research as we scan the paper for reports about the mayor's latest conflict with the city council, or about the response of the stock market to the Federal Reserve Board's new monetary policy. We are doing research when we copy a recipe out of the food section, check the standings of our favorite team, read a movie review, or hunt through the classified ads for a good used lawn mower. Research is part of the texture of our lives. It answers one of our deepest needs as thinking human beings—our need for information.

Gathering information is not a mechanical task; on the contrary, it constantly calls forth our powers of judgment and evaluation. After we have seen a baseball game or a new movie, we seek out friends to discuss it with, newspaper accounts or reviews to read. Why? By considering the opinions of people around us, we come to understand our own judgments better. Which play was really the turning point in the game? Which actor's performance was central to the film's success? We question and rethink our ideas not only during a debate in a noisy cafeteria or a crowded bar, but also in our silent interaction with the printed opinions of others.

The urge to do research, then, is rooted not simply in our curiosity but in our desire to understand. Behind every fact that engages our attention lies our natural wish to comprehend its meaning, our impulse to fit it into a context or pattern. Writing papers based on research satisfies that impulse, but it does something more: through the process

321

of gathering and evaluating information, it calls the writer into a kind of conversation with researchers who have preceded him or her. A research paper assignment is thus an invitation to become part of a far-flung community of thoughtful men and women, sharing their concerns, agreeing and disagreeing with their opinions, reflecting and expanding upon their conclusions.

17a Thinking about your assignment

The starting point in planning a research project is understanding what your instructor wishes you to do. We begin, therefore, by distinguishing between two different kinds of research papers, the **informative report** and the **researched argument**.

1. The informative report

The first type of research project, the informative report, attempts to describe, explain, or shed new light on a specific aspect of a subject. The writer of an informative report asks a question about this subject—a question, perhaps, that is somehow different from those that other people have asked—and answers it by collecting facts and viewpoints from various sources, by selecting out what seems to be particularly significant or interesting, and by assimilating this information into a paper that focuses and presents it in an original way. The informative report is never a mere summary of what someone else has said. Instead, it strongly bears the stamp of the researcher, both in the assertion that he or she makes about the subject and in the evidence that he or she chooses to support that assertion.

You will find an example of such a paper—Emmet Geary's "Recovery from the Florence Flood: A Masterpiece of Restoration"—in Chapter **23**. In this case the writer's assignment was to research any event from the 1960s and develop a paper that explored some specific aspect of that event. Like all researchers, Emmet began with a large subject—natural disasters—and only slowly zeroed in on a precise and manageable subject for investigation. The diagram on page 323 shows the stages by which he narrowed his subject.

Browsing among entries in the volumes of the *Readers' Guide to Periodical Literature* that span the 1960s (see **18c**), Emmet first moved from "disasters" to the narrower subject of "floods." One of the most

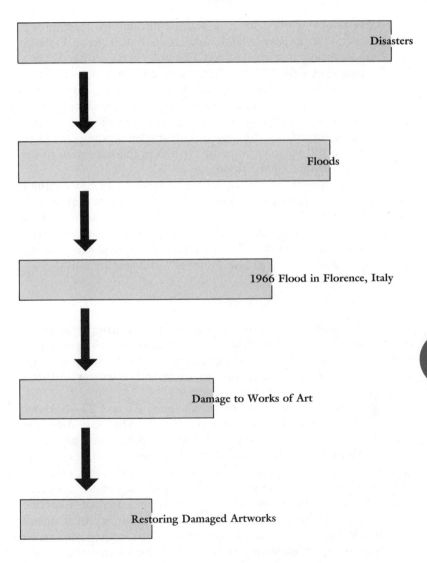

17a

Emmet Focuses a Subject for Research

destructive floods of the decade, he learned through his reading, was the flood of the Arno River that devastated the Italian city of Florence in 1966. Realizing that this subject was too broad to handle in a comprehensive or original way, Emmet posed a question about it: Was any aspect of this flood unusual? What caught his attention as he read articles about the flood were reports about the damage done to Florence's unique collection of art treasures from the Renaissance. But even this subject, he discovered with further reading, could be focused into a still narrower one for his paper: the *restoration* of the works of art damaged by the flood.

Having arrived at this narrow subject, Emmet could now continue his research more efficiently, looking only for sources that dealt specifically with this topic and taking notes with a new sense of purpose and direction. The ultimate result was his tightly organized paper, which focuses on the unusual steps taken by professional restorers and concerned volunteers to save Florence's damaged treasures.

2. The researched argument

The second type of research paper uses evidence to shape an original argument. Rather than collecting and assembling materials to describe or explain a subject, the researcher who is writing an argument uses his or her research first to arrive at a judgment and then to defend that judgment before a reader.

The research papers reprinted in Chapters **21** and **22**—Suzanne Conlon's "Anne Bradstreet's Homespun Cloth: The First American Poems" and Cyndi Lopardo's "Career versus Motherhood: The Debate over Education for Women at the Turn of the Century"—are examples of this second type of paper. Cyndi wanted to write about women and education, but beyond those ideas she had not defined a subject. Like Emmet, she began by reading broadly in search of a specific topic that would interest her. An article on the history of women's education in *The Encyclopedia of Education* (see **18b**) aroused her interest in American higher education at the end of the nineteenth century, and particularly in the debate then raging over the appropriateness of rigorous academic programs for women. A bibliography at the end of the encyclopedia article sent Cyndi to two book-length histories of women's education in America, Thomas Woody's *A History of Women's*

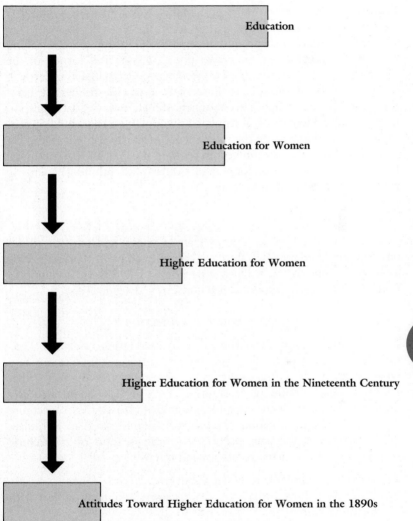

Cyndi Focuses a Subject for Research

Education in the United States and Mabel Newcomer's *A Century of Higher Education for Women.*

Armed with the background information she acquired from reading the relevant portions of these two books, Cyndi next turned to the *Nineteenth Century Readers' Guide* (see **18c**) in search of a list of articles from the 1890s on the subject. Based on the articles she located there, she drew her own conclusions about the debate over higher education for women and tentatively formulated the argument she would present in her paper: that despite the increasing educational opportunities for women at the turn of the nineteenth century, much of society continued to regard higher education for women primarily as a means of enhancing roles within the home and family.

3. Shared features

Our summary of Emmet's and Cyndi's research procedures has oversimplified the often slow and complicated process of identifying a workable subject, but it illustrates two features that are common to both the informative report and the researched argument.

A research paper makes an assertion

17a   First, a good research paper is focused around a central assertion. You needn't panic if, as you start your research, you're not sure what your paper's central assertion is going to be, for the fact is that it's impossible to know what assertion you can make about a subject until you have done a considerable amount of reading. As you acquire more and more information, though, you should begin to formulate *possible* assertions for your paper. After each session of researching your subject, ask yourself the following questions:

1. What am I *now* able to assert about my subject?
2. What do I think I *might* be able to assert about my subject with further research?

Use the answers to these questions to assess your progress and to direct your next research efforts. The final assertion that you make about your subject—the assertion that unifies your paper—will take the form of a thesis statement with a precise subject and restriction. (For a review of the components of an effective thesis, see **5b**.)

A research paper reflects its writer's originality

The second feature common to both the informative report and the researched argument is originality. You may think there is little room for your own originality as a writer in a paper that is based on what other people have written about a subject, but that isn't true. Every good research paper owes its success to the researcher's unique talents as a thinker and investigator. The more creatively you have thought about your subject, the more distinctive your paper's focus will be. The more thoroughly you have researched your subject, the more diverse the sources of information that your paper will bring together. In its final form, your research paper will gather and present information about your subject in a way not duplicated by anyone else who has written on it.

17b Thinking about a subject

If doing research is new to you, your first impulse may be to choose a topic that you already know well. Such a choice, however, is almost certain to rob your research of any interest or satisfaction, leaving you only with tedious and meaningless busywork. The purpose of research, after all, is not to document what you already know, but to discover what you do not know. As disturbing as it may sound at first, you are doing real research only if you do not know where it will lead.

17b

1. Be genuinely interested in your subject

The fundamental requirement for a topic to research is the same as that which should guide the choice of any subject for writing: your true interest in it. In a freshman writing course, your instructor may leave the subject for your research paper entirely up to you, or may allow you to choose from a list of subjects or a general subject area. Even if your instructor limits the range of subjects more narrowly, you should seek out a specific angle or focus that for some reason appeals to you. Research is a process of discovery. You can participate in this process fully only if you select a subject that is a genuine question for you—a problem, a mystery, a tantalizing unknown quantity.

2. Be willing to search for a good subject

You may have been able to find a good subject for the other papers you have written in freshman composition by turning to your personal experiences, your reading, or your entries in a journal. That will not be the case for a research paper. You will not be able to define a workable subject by sitting quietly at your desk and thinking deeply about the assignment. Instead, as our descriptions above of Emmet's and Cyndi's research procedures suggested, the process of identifying a potentially good subject for research begins with serious work in the library.

Although they were writing different kinds of papers, both Emmet and Cyndi began their hunt for a good subject in the same way: by looking for ideas and inspiration first in general sources of information. Emmet, searching for a topic from the 1960s, browsed through articles in the *Readers' Guide* until something in the titles he read attracted his attention. He did not complete the process of narrowing his subject—from disasters, to floods, to Florence, to the destruction of artworks, to the restoration of those works—in a single session in the library; instead, that process extended over several days of reading articles and thinking about them.

17b Cyndi, too, started with general reading—in her case, an encyclopedia in the field of education. When the topic of women's education in the nineteenth century caught her eye, she pursued it first by examining two general histories of women's education and then by looking at specific articles on the topic that were published at the turn of the century. Only after reading a number of these articles was Cyndi certain that there was enough material here to support an entire paper on the attitudes toward women's education in the 1890s.

The point is this: a good topic for a research paper doesn't fall ready-made into one's lap; instead, it evolves slowly, as the researcher becomes more and more familiar with the subject area. The process of finding such a topic demands patience and persistence.

3. Be prepared to make changes in your subject

In Chapter **1**, we observed that the very process of writing alters a writer's conception of his or her topic. Sometimes the topic becomes narrower, as the writer becomes aware of the need to balance completeness with limitations on length. Sometimes it changes focus, as the writer thinks of related subjects and ideas. In research, many of these modifications of your topic will occur before you begin writing, during the research process itself.

As you start to explore a tentative subject, you must be ready to accept changes in your original plan. You should expect your research to lead in directions you had not anticipated, to new sources of information and new ideas that will inevitably affect your original conception of your topic. The opinions of others will modify your early ideas, leaving you with new perspectives to consider. On other occasions, unfortunately, you may find that the libraries available to you do not have enough material on your subject from which to construct a serious research paper, and you will be forced to modify your original subject radically or to abandon it altogether. Such is the life of the dedicated researcher—a combination of excitement and frustration, of discovery and disillusionment.

17c Thinking about your reader

Professional researchers write with a keen awareness of their potential readers. Typically, scholars begin a research project with a specific journal in mind to which they plan eventually to submit the finished project for publication. They know what sorts of people read that journal and what those people probably already know about the subject. They also know whether they are elaborating on someone else's research or contradicting it, and as a result they have a fair sense of the extent to which their work will be regarded as innovative, controversial, or revolutionary.

17c

It's very possible that your own professional work after college will place you in a similar situation. Whether you do research for publication in a professional journal or for in-house distribution to colleagues in a business setting, you will be writing for a community of readers whose potential reactions to your research will be constantly in your mind. For this assignment, however, your sole audience is likely to be your instructor. How can awareness of this audience affect what you write?

The key questions about audience that we outlined in Chapter **3** apply here as well: What does your reader already know about this subject? What else do you want your reader to know? If, in the case of your instructor, you're unsure about how to answer these questions, you should plan to discuss your paper with him or her as it evolves. Find out what your instructor knows about your subject, and what aspects of your research he or she finds particularly intriguing. Use such discussions to direct your research efforts and to shape your paper, so that in its final form it responds to your instructor's interests and questions.

17d Planning the long paper

Perhaps the most disconcerting requirement of a research paper is its length—often five or more times longer than most of the other papers you have written in freshman composition. Writing a long paper that draws on material from different sources is good practice in the kinds of writing tasks that people in many professions are called on to complete—business reports, legal briefs, case histories, and feature articles, to name just a few. But such writing makes demands that shorter, less formal essays do not.

1. Leave enough time

The finest library facilities and the best ideas for a research paper will not be of much use to you if you do not leave enough time to work on your paper. You may have been able to write a first draft of your other essays in freshman composition in just a few sittings—one devoted to exploring the subject, one to outlining and planning, one to composing. That approach, however, will not be sufficient for a serious research paper, which usually involves at least a few weeks of preliminary work even before you begin writing, and several composing sessions as you assimilate and structure the material you have accumulated.

You can never begin researching too early, for you must be prepared for all the setbacks that accompany research, ranging from the topic that grows increasingly complex (or that fails to develop at all) to the crucial book that you discover is missing from your library. And the task of fusing your final set of notes into a coherent whole may also be more difficult than you expect. The most important rule for research,

17d

then, is to plan ahead, leaving yourself plenty of time to gather information and several sessions for writing and revising. The research paper completed in a single coffee-soaked night is not likely to be very successful, no matter how thorough the research on which it is based.

2. Understand the research process

As we have already suggested, the research process involves a number of steps, including identifying a subject, collecting information, selecting the material you want to use, assimilating it into a coherent, focused piece of writing, and accurately documenting your sources. To work efficiently in each of these stages, you should understand their relation to one another and to the research process as a whole. We suggest, therefore, that you at least skim through the six chapters that follow before you begin to work on your paper.

Locating information and taking notes

The first step in composing a research paper, of course, is gathering information. For your purposes, that will mean doing substantial research in a library. You can't understand or focus your topic until you have a firm grasp of what others have written about the subject. In Chapters **18** and **19** we will discuss some important sources of information in the library and some strategies for taking effective notes from the material you find.

17d

Assimilating materials and avoiding plagiarism

By definition, research draws on the work of others. One of the keys to composing a successful research paper is being able to integrate the fruits of research into your paper, smoothly incorporating the information you have collected into your own prose. A second key to successful writing based on research is distinguishing between the legitimate and illegitimate use of other people's ideas and words in your paper. Presenting such material as your own, whether deliberately or accidentally, is a serious offense known as plagiarism. In Chapter **20** we will deal with the artful—and accurate—use of these materials in your paper.

Using standard methods of documentation

Your instructor will no doubt specify which style of documentation he or she would prefer that you use to indicate your sources of information. In this book, we present three of the most widely used documentation methods. The first, discussed in Chapter **19**, is the method advocated by the Modern Language Association and used in literary study and many other humanities fields. The second, described in Chapter **22**, is prescribed by the American Psychological Association and widely used in the social sciences. The third method, involving endnote citations, is less widely used today than formerly but is still the norm in some disciplines; it is presented in Chapter **23**. Each of the sample student research papers in Chapters **21**, **22**, and **23** illustrates one of these methods.

3. Be prepared for the recursiveness of the research process

In our first chapter, we described writing as a recursive rather than a linear process, that is, a process whose stages are often cyclical rather than sequential. The same is true for the research process. You can avoid some of the frustration of doing research by preparing for the fact that composing a research paper inevitably involves backtracking: abandoning an unworkable subject and beginning anew; discarding notes that prove worthless and searching for better ones; rethinking your paper's focus again and again; returning to the library, even after you have begun writing the paper, to verify a quotation or to look for just one more source. When you feel caught in a dizzying whirl of contradictory note cards, half-completed paragraphs, citations to still unexamined sources, and maddeningly arbitrary documentation rules, you'll know that you have become a true researcher at last.

17d

The Library

When most people think of libraries, they think of books—and with good reason, for books are the most visible of any library's holdings. When you use a library for serious research, however, you need to be familiar with the many other kinds of materials available—especially with standard reference works, magazines, journals, newspapers, and government publications. Since most American libraries use the same basic system for filing and organizing materials, we can offer some guidelines below that will apply to almost any library that you have access to. But we should perhaps stress that this is only an introduction to library use. To get the most out of your library, you will have to discover its own particular strengths—its large microfilm holdings, for example, or its outstanding record collection. You will need to know where various holdings are kept and what library policies govern their use. You can learn about these and other features of your library through the official tours that many college libraries offer at the beginning of the semester. Or you can give yourself a tour. Ask at the main desk for a map of the building and its features, or simply wander from floor to floor at a leisurely pace, identifying the materials available and noting their locations. Becoming familiar with the arrangement and system of your library is your first task as a serious researcher, one that will help to make your work more efficient and satisfying.

18a The card catalog

The card catalog in a library is the major index to its holdings. Usually, all the books, reference works, indexes, and periodicals received by a library are indexed alphabetically here on three-by-five-inch cards.

Each book is ordinarily listed in at least three different places: under its author's name (under each author's name if there are more than one); under its title; and under the subject or subjects it covers. In some university libraries, author and title cards are collected in a single alphabetical catalog, while subject cards are filed separately, also in alphabetical order.

1. Reading catalog cards

Catalog cards contain a good deal of potentially important information, including the publication date of a book, the number of

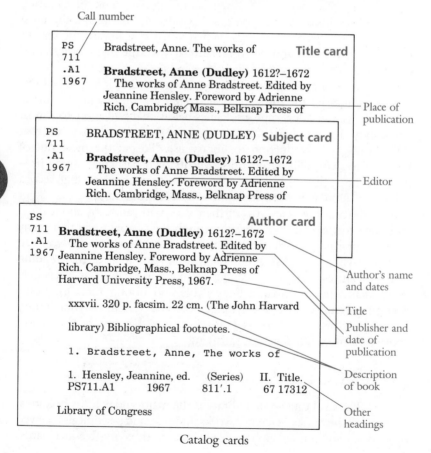

Catalog cards

its pages, and notes about such features as indexes and illustrations in the book. The more you use the card catalog, the more skilled you will become in assessing this information before you actually examine the book itself. When you identify a book that you wish to look at, make a note of its *call number,* also found on the catalog card. The call number, which is based on a nationally used classification system, is your guide to the location of the book in your library. Two principal systems of classification are used by American libraries: the Dewey Decimal System (a numerical system) and the Library of Congress System (an alphabetical classification). At your library's main desk, you can get further information about the system your library follows. If your library has open stacks—that is, if library patrons are allowed to browse through the shelves and select books themselves—you will also find information there about the location of books throughout the library.

2.   Locating books

When you want to know where a specific book is located in your library, the author or title card will lead you to it fastest. When you don't know authors or titles, look through the cards under the subject you are interested in. Since both the Dewey Decimal System and the Library of Congress System are based on subject matter, you will usually find that the books your library has on a particular subject are shelved together. You can use the subject cards, therefore, not only as a listing of the library's holdings on a subject but also as a guide to the appropriate section of the book stacks. If your library has open stacks, some browsing around in this area will usually lead you to a number of useful books. Feel free to pull down from the shelves any books that look interesting, but respect your library's policies about reshelving books. To avoid the chaos created by accidental mis-shelving, many libraries ask that you do not put books back yourself, but instead leave them on a table or at some other designated place for library staff members to reshelve.

3.   Using an on-line catalog

Increasingly, libraries are developing computer systems that enable patrons to bypass the card catalog and locate books and other materials simply by typing the author or title into a computer terminal,

18a

which then displays all of the information normally found on a card in the card catalog. Some such systems also make it possible to search for books by subject. If your library has put its holdings "on line" with such a system, you should definitely learn how to use it, for it will save you valuable time. However, because subject searches on these systems can sometimes be hard to use effectively and because a library may not have all of its holdings on line, you will probably also want to be sure that you know how to locate books through the card catalog if you have to.

18b Standard reference works

You can use the card catalog to locate not only individual books by a specific author or on a particular subject, but also the standard reference works owned by your library—encyclopedias, dictionaries, indexes, and bibliographies. Your personal library no doubt includes a number of reference books, such as a dictionary and a desk encyclopedia; a college or public library, however, may own hundreds of specialized and useful reference works. These works fall into two general categories: books that offer facts (usually in the form of compact essays on various subjects), and books that provide bibliographies (lists of other books and articles on a given subject). As we explained in Chapter **17**, reference books in the first category are a good starting place for your research efforts, for the overview of a subject that they provide will often include references to a host of interesting subtopics ideal for further exploration. Reference books in the second category will lead you to further sources of information as your research efforts begin in earnest.

Reference works, like other books, are shelved according to call number, but most libraries conveniently place their reference books together in a single section of the library, or even in a separate reference room. (The catalog card will indicate whether that is your library's practice.) As you become familiar with the reference works in your library, you may want to keep your own list or card file of the ones that you have found especially useful, so that you can locate them quickly for future research work. Skill in using your library's reference collection, like skill in most other areas of life, will come from frequent practice.

What follows is a list of some standard reference works, grouped by type and subject. You will no doubt find many more in your library.

Guides to reference books

Guide to Reference Books.
Guide to the Use of Books and Libraries.
The Reader's Adviser.

General information

Collier's Encyclopedia.
Dictionary of the History of Ideas.
Encyclopedia Americana.
Encyclopaedia Britannica.
New Columbia Encyclopedia.

Gazetteers and atlases

Columbia-Lippincott Gazetteer of the World.
National Geographic Atlas of the World.
Rand McNally Atlas of World History.
The Times Atlas of the World.

18b

Reference books for special subjects

Art and architecture

Bryan's Dictionary of Painters and Engravers.
Encyclopedia of World Art.
Haggar, Reginald C. Dictionary of Art Terms.
Hamlin, T. F. Architecture through the Ages.
Myers, Bernard S., ed. Encyclopedia of Painting.
Zboinski, A., and L. Tyszynski. Dictionary of Architecture and
    Building Trades.

Biography

American Men and Women of Science. Includes scholars in the
    physical, biological, and social sciences.

Current Biography. Monthly since 1940, with brief bibliographic entries and an annual cumulative index.

Dictionary of American Biography. 20 vols. and supplements;
bibliographic entries at the end of each article.

Dictionary of National Biography (British). 22 vols. and supplements; each article accompanied by a bibliography.

Directory of American Scholars.

James, Edward T., and Janet W. James, eds. *Notable American
Women, 1607–1950.* Has bibliographic entries.

National Cyclopedia of American Biography. Includes supplements.

Webster's Biographical Dictionary.

Who's Who (British), *Who's Who in America, International
Who's Who.* Brief accounts of living men and women;
frequently revised.

Who's Who of American Women. 1958–.

Classics

Avery, C. B., ed. *New Century Classical Handbook.*

Hammond, N. G. L., and H. H. Scullard, eds. *Oxford Classical
Dictionary.*

Harvey, Paul, ed. *Oxford Companion to Classical Literature.*

Current events

Americana Annual. 1923–. Annual supplement to the *Encyclopedia Americana.*

Britannica Book of the Year. 1938–. Annual supplement to
the *Encyclopaedia Britannica;* some entries have a brief bibliography.

Facts on File. 1941–.

Statesman's Year Book. 1864–. A statistical and historical annual
giving current information (and brief bibliographies) about
countries of the world.

World Almanac. 1968–.

Economics and commerce

Coman, E. T. *Sources of Business Information.* A bibliography.

Greenwald, Douglas, et al. *McGraw-Hill Dictionary of Modern Economics.* Has bibliographic references.

Historical Statistics of the United States: Colonial Times to 1970. Includes indexes and bibliographies.

International Bibliography of Economics. 1952–.

Munn, Glenn G. *Encyclopedia of Banking and Finance.* Has bibliographic entries.

Sloan, Harold S., and Arnold Zurcher. *A Dictionary of Economics.*

Statistical Abstract of the United States. 1897–.

Wyckham, Robert G. *Images and Marketing: A Selected and Annotated Bibliography.*

Education

Burke, Arvid J., and Mary A. Burke. *Documentation in Education.*

Deighton, Lee C., ed. *Encyclopedia of Education.* Has bibliographic entries.

Husen, Torsten, and T. Neville Postlethwaite, eds. *International Encyclopedia of Education.*

Knowles, Asa S. *International Encyclopedia of Higher Education.*

Mitzel, Harold E., ed. *Encyclopedia of Educational Research.*

World Survey of Education.

Film

Bawden, Liz-Anne, ed. *Oxford Companion to Film.*

International Encyclopedia of Film.

History

Adams, James T., ed. *Dictionary of American History.* A bibliography accompanies each article.

American Historical Association: Guide to Historical Literature.

Cambridge Ancient History. Bibliographic footnotes.

Cambridge Medieval History. Bibliographic footnotes.

Langer, William L., ed. *Encyclopedia of World History.*

Martin, Michael R., et al. *An Encyclopedia of Latin-American History.*

Morris, Richard B., and Graham W. Irwin, eds. *Harper Encyclopedia of the Modern World.*

New Cambridge Modern History. Bibliographic footnotes.

Literature

American

Hart, J. D. *Oxford Companion to American Literature.*

Leary, Lewis. *Articles on American Literature.*

Spiller, Robert E., et al. *Literary History of the United States.* Entries include bibliographic essays.

British

Baugh, A. C., et al. *A Literary History of England.* Has bibliographic entries.

Drabble, Margaret, ed. *Oxford Companion to English Literature.*

Sampson, George. *Concise Cambridge History of English Literature.*

Watson, George, ed. *New Cambridge Bibliography of English Literature.*

Wilson, F. P., and Bonamy Dobree, eds. *Oxford History of English Literature.* Excellent bibliographic essays at the end of each volume.

General

Fleischmann, Wolfgang Bernard, ed. *Encyclopedia of World Literature in the Twentieth Century.* Brief bibliographies.

Grigson, Geoffrey. *The Concise Encyclopedia of Modern World Literature.* Brief bibliographic entries.

8b

Leach, Maria, and Jerome Fried, eds. *Funk & Wagnall's Standard Dictionary of Folklore, Mythology, and Legend.*

MacCulloch, John A., et al. *Mythology of All Races.* Bibliography at end of each volume.

Preminger, Alex, F. J. Warnke, and O. B. Hardison, eds. *Princeton Encyclopedia of Poetry and Poetics.* A brief bibliography accompanies each article.

Toye, William, ed. *Oxford Companion to Canadian Literature.*

Music and dance

Apel, Willi. *Harvard Dictionary of Music.* Has brief bibliographic entries.

Beaumont, Cyril W. *A Bibliography of Dancing.*

De Mille, Agnes. *The Book of the Dance.*

Ewen, David. *The World of Twentieth Century Music.* Brief bibliographic entries.

Grove, George. *Dictionary of Music and Musicians.* This work and the *Harvard Dictionary of Music* are the authorities in the field. Excellent bibliographies.

Hanna, Judith Lynne. *To Dance Is Human.*

Orrey, Leslie, ed. *Encyclopedia of Opera.*

Scholes, P. A. *Oxford Companion to Music.* Includes bibliographies.

Thompson, Oscar. *International Cyclopedia of Music and Musicians.* Brief bibliographies.

Westrup, J. A., ed. *New Oxford History of Music.* Includes bibliographies.

Philosophy

Copleston, Frederick. *A History of Western Philosophy.* Bibliography at end of each volume.

Edwards, Paul, ed. *Encyclopedia of Philosophy.* Bibliographies.

Urmson, J. O. *Concise Encyclopedia of Western Philosophy and Philosophers.* Brief bibliography at end of volume.

Political science

Levy, Leonard W., ed. *Encyclopedia of the American Constitution*.

Morgenthau, Hans. *Politics among Nations*.

Political Handbook of the World. 1927–.

Smith, Edward C., and A. J. Zurcher, eds. *Dictionary of American Politics*.

White, Carl M., et al. *Sources of Information in the Social Sciences*.

Psychology

Beigel, Hugo. *Dictionary of Psychology and Related Fields*.

Corsini, Raymond J., ed. *Encyclopedia of Psychology*.

Drever, James. *Dictionary of Psychology*.

Gregory, Richard L., ed. *Oxford Companion to the Mind*.

The Harvard List of Books in Psychology. Annotated.

Psychological Abstracts. 1927–.

Wolman, Benjamin B., ed. *International Encyclopedia of Psychiatry, Psychology, Psychoanalysis, and Neurology*.

8b Religion

Buttrick, G. A., et al. *Interpreter's Dictionary of the Bible: An Illustrated Encyclopedia*. Has bibliographic entries.

Cross, F. L., and Elizabeth A. Livingstone. *Oxford Dictionary of the Christian Church*. Has brief bibliographies.

Eliade, Mircea, ed. *Encyclopedia of Religion*. Brief bibliographic entries.

Encyclopedia of Islam.

Encyclopedia Judaica.

Hastings, James, ed. *Encyclopedia of Religion and Ethics*.

Jackson, S. M., et al. *New Schaff-Herzog Encyclopedia of Religious Knowledge*.

Malalasekera, G. P., ed. *Encyclopedia of Buddhism*.

New Catholic Encyclopedia.

Science

General

McGraw-Hill Encyclopedia of Science and Technology.

Meyers, Robert A., ed. *Encyclopedia of Physical Science and Technology.*

Newman, James R., et al. *Harper Encyclopedia of Science.* Brief bibliographic entries.

Van Nostrand's Scientific Encyclopedia.

Life sciences

Benthall, Jonathan. *Ecology in Theory and Practice.* Includes bibliographic references.

De Bell, Garrett, ed. *The Environmental Handbook.* Bibliography at end of volume.

Gray, Peter, ed. *Encyclopedia of the Biological Sciences.* Brief bibliographic entries.

Reich, Warren T., ed. *Encyclopedia of Bioethics.*

Smith, Roger C., and W. Malcolm Reid, eds. *Guide to the Literature of the Life Sciences.*

18b

Physical sciences

International Dictionary of Physics and Electronics.

Kemp, D. A. *Astronomy and Astrophysics: A Bibliographical Guide.*

Larousse Encyclopedia of the Earth: Geology, Paleontology, and Prehistory.

Universal Encyclopedia of Mathematics.

Van Nostrand's International Encyclopedia of Chemical Science.

Sociology and anthropology

Biennial Review of Anthropology.

International Bibliography of Sociology. 1951–.

Sills, David L., ed. *International Encyclopedia of the Social Sciences.* Each article followed by a bibliography.

Social Work Year Book. 1929–. Includes bibliographies.

Theater

Bordman, Gerald M. *Oxford Companion to American Theatre.*

Encyclopedia of World Theater.

Gassner, John, and Edward Quin, eds. *Reader's Encyclopedia of World Drama.*

Hartnoll, Phyllis, ed. *Oxford Companion to the Theatre.* Bibliography accompanies each article.

18c Indexes to periodicals

Many students new to research rely heavily—or even exclusively—on books as their sources of information. Such a strategy has its pitfalls. For one thing, books are not usually as well focused as a narrowly defined research topic, and finding the precise information you need in a towering stack of general books on a subject can become an exercise in frustration. Moreover, the time involved in producing a book means that current information—the most recent developments in Middle Eastern politics, for example, or the latest advances in AIDS research—may not be available in book form. To find such information, in addition to material on virtually any other kind of topic, you can turn to articles in periodicals.

Just as the card catalog provides an author, title, and subject index to your library's book holdings, periodical indexes offer a fast and easy way of locating articles in magazines, journals, and newspapers. Usually, you will find your library's periodical indexes grouped together in the reference collection. It is important to know the scope of at least the major indexes described below, because they cover different kinds of periodicals. However, since many of these indexes are produced by the same publisher in similar formats, you will discover that after you have become familiar with the layout of one, you can move easily to the others. For example, note the similarities in form of the indexes illustrated on page 345. The distinguishing feature of each of these

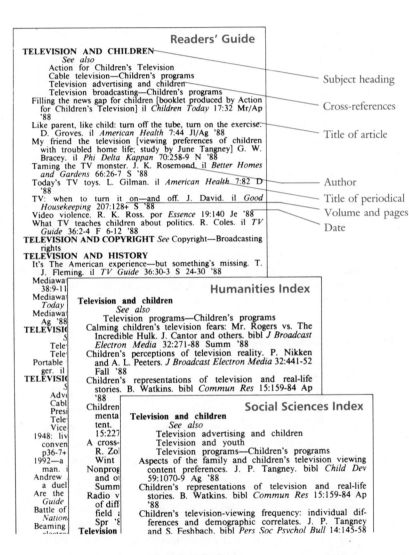

Periodical Indexes

indexes is not the way it arranges its contents, but the distinctive type of periodical it covers.

Once you have used the indexes below to locate potentially useful articles on the subject you are researching, determine whether or not your library subscribes to the journals you need by looking them up in the card catalog. Most libraries bind back issues of periodicals like books and shelve them together in a periodical room or by call number among books in the stacks. Current issues are usually on display in a periodicals reading room. For assistance in locating the periodicals you need, ask at your library's main desk.

If your library does not have a specific periodical that you need, ask at the Interlibrary Loan department about acquiring a photocopy of the article you're interested in from another library. Most libraries offer this service for a small charge. However, you should try not to depend on articles that you must order in this way. Unless your library can obtain copies of articles by fax, the ordering process can take several weeks, and the article, when it arrives, may turn out to be of less value to you than its title promised.

General periodical indexes

18c

Readers' Guide to Periodical Literature. 1900–.
> An author and subject index to more than two hundred magazines of general interest, such as *Consumer Reports, Ms., Newsweek, Sports Illustrated,* and *Popular Electronics.* Bound volumes cover a year or more; paperback supplements keep the index current usually to within a few weeks.

Humanities Index and *Social Sciences Index.* 1974–. Formerly a single index, published as the *Social Sciences and Humanities Index* from 1965 to 1974, and as the *International Index* from 1907 to 1965. The major general index to professional journals in the humanities (for example, *American Literature, Harvard Theological Review, Journal of Philosophy, New England Quarterly*) and the social sciences (for example, *Crime and Delinquency, Geographical Review, Journal of Economic Theory, Political Science Quarterly*). Same format as the *Readers' Guide,* though usually somewhat less current.

New York Times Index. 1913–.

An invaluable subject and author index to one of the world's great newspapers. Provides a brief summary of most articles, together with a citation to issue date, section, and page. Most libraries carry the *New York Times* on microfilm; for the location of microfilms in your library and instructions on their use, ask at the main desk or in the reference room. If you live in an area served by another major newspaper, your library may also have an index for it that will help you find information on significant current and past events in your community.

Nineteenth Century Readers' Guide. 1890–99.

A two-volume supplement to the *Readers' Guide,* produced in the same format.

Poole's Index to Periodical Literature. 1802–1906.

A six-volume index of nineteenth-century periodicals by subject only. For authors, consult the *Cumulative Author Index for Poole's Index to Periodical Literature,* ed. C. Edward Wall (Ann Arbor: Pierian Press, 1971).

Biography Index. 1946–.

A subject index to articles and sections of books that are biographical in character. Note that an effective search requires consulting every volume. Same format as the *Readers' Guide.*

18c

Subject periodical indexes

Many disciplines produce thorough indexes to a variety of specialized journals in the field. Whenever your research is within a specific academic discipline, you should check to see whether such an index exists. The indexes that follow, and others like them, can be located through the library's card catalog; you will usually find them shelved near the general periodical indexes described above. Most use the same format as the *Readers' Guide.*

Applied Science and Technology Index. 1957–.

Art Index. 1929–.

Biological Abstracts. 1926–.

Business Periodicals Index. 1958–.

Current Anthropology. 1960–.
Economic Abstracts. 1953–.
Education Index. 1929–.
Engineering Index. 1884–.
General Science Index. 1978–.
Historical Abstracts. 1955–.
Music Index. 1949–.
Philosopher's Index. 1940–.
Modern Language Association International Bibliography. 1956–.
 Formerly the *MLA American Bibliography,* 1921–55.
 The major bibliography of articles on English, American,
 and foreign language and literature.
Psychological Abstracts. 1927–.
Public Affairs Information Service. 1915–.
 A valuable index of articles, books, pamphlets, government
 documents, and other reports on public administration,
 international relations, and a broad range of economic
 and social issues.
Religious Index One: Periodicals. 1973–.
Sociological Abstracts. 1955–.
Zoological Record. 1864–.

18d A special index: the *Essay and General Literature Index*

This is an appropriate place to mention one other unusual index—not an index to periodicals, but an index to *sections* of books. The *Essay and General Literature Index* (1900–), whose location you can find in the card catalog, is a semiannual subject and author index to collections of essays on different subjects, often written by different authors. This index is usually the only way to locate such essays, since the title and subject classification of these books in the card catalog will ordinarily not be specific enough to help you.

Suppose, for example, that you are interested in the subject of women and art. If you look under the two headings "Women" and

"Art" in the card catalog, you will find dozens of books on each subject, but you might spend days—or even weeks—looking through the books on women for those that also deal with art, and searching in the books on art for material on women artists. A few minutes of browsing in a recent issue of the *Essay and General Literature Index,* however, will lead you to the heading "Women in Art," and under it, entries like the following:

> Withers, J.   Judy Chicago's Dinner party: a personal vision of women's history. *In* Art the ape of nature, ed. by M. Barasch and L. F. Sandler p789–99

What this entry means is that an essay by J. Withers entitled "Judy Chicago's Dinner Party: A Personal Vision of Women's History" is included on pages 789–99 of the book *Art, the Ape of Nature,* edited by M. Barasch and L. F. Sandler. The complete publication information for any book that you find listed is included at the back of the volume of the *Essay and General Literature Index* that you are using. With this information, you can go to the card catalog and determine whether the book is available in your library. The library in which we located this book listed it in the card catalog only under its title, the names of its two editors, and the broad subject heading "Art—Addresses, Essays, and Lectures." Without the *Essay and General Literature Index,* we would have had no easy way of finding Withers's essay.

18e Data-base searches

An increasing number of libraries offer their patrons computerized access to lists of articles, unpublished papers, and other sources of information on a wide variety of subjects. Such computerized files are known as **data bases.** Many college and university libraries provide access to such data bases in one or both of the following ways.

1. On-line searches

Libraries may subscribe to the services of a data-base "vendor," a company that makes available by computer the contents of many different data bases compiled and updated by independent companies and associations. For example, DIALOG, one of the largest such vendors, currently offers access to nearly two hundred separate data bases in business, technology, the humanities, the social sciences, and the natural sciences. In all, a DIALOG subscriber may search through more than seventy-five million records for titles relevant to a specific subject.

Conducting an on-line search

To perform a data-base search in most libraries, you will be asked by the reference librarian to complete an information form on your subject. The librarian will then enter one or more "descriptors," or relevant subject headings, into a computer terminal, and the computer will search through all of the data bases on the system and compile a list of appropriate sources. On some systems, moreover, you can order a printed copy of the full text of an article. Some libraries also subscribe to simplified searching systems that library patrons can use directly, without the intermediary help of a librarian.

The only drawback to such on-line searching is the cost, which is usually calculated according to the length of time you are connected to the computer system. Although a ten-minute computer search may cost only a few dollars, a search that takes considerably longer can become an unrealistically expensive proposition for undergraduate research. On the other hand, data-base searches offer enormous savings of time. In just a few minutes, a computer can scan bibliographies that might take weeks to examine by hand. On-line data bases are also more current than printed reference works can be. The Wilsonline data bases, for example, which offer computerized access to the Wilson family of periodical indexes (*Readers' Guide, Humanities Index, Social Science Index, Biography Index, Education Index,* etc.), are updated twice each week, whereas the corresponding bound indexes usually lag several weeks to several months behind the current date.

Additional on-line data bases

Below is a list of some other widely used on-line data bases. Check with your reference librarian to determine whether these or similar on-line data bases are available at your library.

Arts and Humanities Search
Indexes more than thirteen hundred journals in the humanities, beginning in 1980.

Dissertation Abstracts Online
Indexes American dissertations in all disciplines, beginning in 1861.

PsycINFO
Indexes more than a thousand journals in psychology, beginning in 1967.

Scisearch
Indexes a variety of journals in science and technology, beginning in 1974.

Social Scisearch
Indexes more than fifteen hundred social science journals, beginning in 1972.

2. CD-ROM searches

Many data bases are also available on laser-read compact discs, similar to the compact discs used for recording and playing back music. Libraries that receive data bases on such discs (referred to as *CD-ROM,* for "compact disc, read-only memory") often make them directly available to patrons at no charge.

For example, most of the Wilson periodicals, including the *Readers' Guide,* the *Humanities Index,* and the *Social Sciences Index,* are available for CD-ROM searches. All the records contained in each of these indexes since 1983 (or in some cases 1984) have been recorded on a single compact disc that is replaced with an updated version four times a year. The disc's contents are read by laser and displayed on an ordinary computer terminal. But a CD-Rom search is more than a computerized version of the browsing you might do in the printed volumes of one of these indexes. Using a command called Wilsearch, you can perform a very powerful kind of subject search that is possible only on a computer.

Using Wilsearch

The Wilsearch request menu asks you to enter up to eight descriptive words covering the topic you are interested in. The more terms you enter, the more precise—but also the more limited—your search will be. The computer then searches all of the records on the compact disc (that is, all of the articles indexed since 1983 or 1984), looking for any articles that have in common all the terms you've

18e

Wilsearch
request
menu

```
Enter your search request for HUM

Subject words: education
  2nd subject: women
  3rd subject:

  Author/name:
  Title words:

  Journal name:
  Organization:
  Dewey number:

    Press Enter key to perform search

   ┌─────────────────────────────────────────────────────┐
   │ You do not need to fill out the entire screen. Use  │
   │ only those lines appropriate to your search request.│
   └─────────────────────────────────────────────────────┘
```

Search identifies
eighty articles
on women and
education

```
                  WILSONDISC - WILSEARCH
    FILE:HUM - Humanities Index 2/84-06/30/89        READY
    --------------------------------------------------------
    SEARCH                                        NUMBER of
    SET  | STEP | FORMULATION                    | POSTINGS
    --------------------------------------------------------
     1   |  1   | FIND EDUCATION(BI)             |   1055
     2   |  2   | FIND WOMEN(BI)                 |   3506
     3   |  3   | FIND 1 AND 2                   |    80
         |      |       (ss #1)... 1055 Postings |
         |      |       (ss #2)... 3506 Postings |

       ┌──────────────────────────┐
       │  80 CITATIONS FOUND       │
       │ HIT ─┘ ENTER              │
       └──────────────────────────┘
```

18e

Publication
information
for one entry

```
 1 HUM
Book Review
  Arnold, Lois
Four lives in science; women's education in the
nineteenth century
reviewed by McGrath, Sylvia Wallace
The Journal of American History 72: 416 S '85
```

Searching a CD-ROM Data Base with Wilsearch

indicated. If it finds any matches, it displays the full citations one at a time and gives you the opportunity to print out a copy of any entries that interest you.

Suppose, for example, that you, like Cyndi, are interested in women's education in the nineteenth century. Using the Wilsondisc for the *Humanities Index,* you might begin by entering just two of your key terms, *education* and *women.* (See the illustrations on page 352.) The computer then reads the disc and in this case identifies a total of eighty articles indexed since February 1984 that involve both of these subjects. To narrow the search, you could enter a third key word, *nineteenth century.* The computer would then identify and display the titles of articles that include all three key terms, like the one shown in the illustration.

Additional CD-ROM data bases

Similar searching capabilities are available on a variety of other CD-ROM data bases, such as those listed below. To determine whether your library subscribes to these or other CD-ROM data bases, check with your reference librarian.

Academic Index

Indexes nearly four hundred journals and magazines considered likely to be used in undergraduate research. Includes citations to periodicals in the humanities, the social sciences, business, education, psychology, and biology, as well as citations to general interest magazines. Some citations begin as early as 1985. Also includes citations to the *New York Times* for the most recent six-month period. Updated monthly.

ERIC

An index of materials available through the Educational Resources Information Center, including published journal articles and unpublished research reports.

Infotrac Magazine Index Plus

Indexes more than four hundred widely read magazines such as those indexed in the *Readers' Guide,* beginning in 1983. Includes citations to the *New York Times* for the most recent three-month period. Updated monthly.

18e

Newspaper Abstracts Ondisc
An index to the *New York Times,* the *Chicago Tribune,* the *Wall Street Journal,* and the *Christian Science Monitor,* beginning in 1985.

18f Government documents

One of the most often overlooked and yet one of the most valuable sources of information on a wide range of subjects is the

18f

Alphabetical Subject Index in
Monthly Catalog of United States Government Publications

Administrative agencies – United States – Bibliography – Periodicals.
Requirements for recurring reports to the Congress : a directory /, 85-14696

Administrative agencies – United States – Directories.
Congressional liaison handbook., 85-14784

Administrative procedure – United States.
Regulatory analyses for severe accident issues : an example /, 85-16090

Adolescence.
Teenage suicide : hearing before the Subcommittee on Juvenile Justice of the Committee on the Judiciary, United States Senate, Ninety-eighth Congress, second session, on oversight on the factors that may lead to teenage suicide, and what may be done to prevent that tragedy, October 3, 1984., 85-16319

Monthly Catalog entry number (keys subject index entries to main entries)

Monthly Catalog Entry

85-16319   **Y 4.J 89/2:S.hrg.98-1262**
United States. Congress. Senate. Committee on the Judiciary. Subcommittee on Juvenile Justice.
Teenage suicide : hearing before the Subcommittee on Juvenile Justice of the Committee on the Judiciary, United States Senate, Ninety-eighth Congress, second session, on oversight on the factors that may lead to teenage suicide, and what may be done to prevent that tragedy, October 3, 1984. –
Washington : U.S. G.P.O., 1985.
iii, 80 p. : 24 cm. – (S. hrg. ; 98-1262) Distributed to some depository libraries in microfiche. Includes bibliographies. "Serial no. J-98-143."
● Item 1042-A, 1042-B (micro-fiche)
1. Suicide – United States – Prevention. 2. Adolescence I. Title. II. Series: United States. Congress (98th, 2nd session : 1984). Senate. S. hrg. ; 98-1262.   OCLC 11895490

Author of document

Title

Publication information

Library cataloging information

Locating Government Documents

U.S. government. Each year, the agencies of the national government publish thousands of pamphlets, booklets, magazines, and books on hundreds of subjects. Many libraries routinely receive and catalog much of this material, which is usually collected together in a single location.

The subject index in the *Monthly Catalog of United States Government Publications* is a good place to begin discovering the range and variety of government documents. The subject headings in one recent issue include everything from "Acid Rain" to "Airplane Inspection," from "Computer Graphics" to "Chippewa Indians," from "Lake Trout" to "Literacy," from "Radioactive Waste Disposal" to "Retirement" to "Rhetoric" to "Rocket Engines." Once you have located some promising titles in the subject index, the government documents librarian in your library can show you how to use the index to the documents on file and how to find items in your library's collection.

EXERCISE 1

Choose several of the subjects below and read the entries about them in *Collier's Encyclopedia,* the *Encyclopedia Americana,* and the *Encyclopaedia Britannica* (check both sections, the *Micropaedia* and the more detailed *Macropaedia*). Which encyclopedia's coverage seems generally most complete? Which one seems most up to date? Which supplies the best bibliographies of additional sources?

1. aging
2. crime
3. cocaine
4. Detroit
5. fencing
6. greenhouse effect
7. humor
8. Jerusalem
9. Navajo/Navaho
10. Normans
11. Frances Perkins
12. sextant
13. surfing
14. Louis Tiffany
15. trademark

18f

EXERCISE 2

Use the *Readers' Guide* to locate the earliest magazine article available in your library on one of the subjects below. Look up the article, read through it, and write a short essay explaining how our conception of the subject has changed since it was published.

1. AIDS
2. microwave cooking
3. Ronald Reagan
4. stereo
5. television

18f

19 *Working with Sources*

A list of books, articles, and other sources of information on a given topic is called a bibliography. Most research papers end with a bibliography or with a list of all the works the writer has referred to in the paper. But the research process also *begins* with the compilation of a "working bibliography," that is, a list of sources that the writer intends to examine. Only after assembling such a preliminary list of sources do most researchers move to the next important stage of research, taking notes.

19a The working bibliography

The working bibliography is valuable for a number of reasons. First, it becomes your master list of sources. Over a period of several weeks of research, you will not be able to remember all of the books and articles that you consulted, some of which were useful and some of which you found irrelevant to your topic. The working bibliography offers a systematic way of keeping track of all of these sources. Because it contains references to sources that you must still check, it provides an outline of the research work that remains for you to do; and since it includes the sources you have looked at, it helps to eliminate accidental backtracking. Second, the working bibliography gives you a place to make potentially useful notes about your sources as you examine them. Later, when you are putting your paper together, you will often find it helpful to be able to recall what an author's main point in an article was, or what your reactions to a book were as you read it.

1. Assembling a working bibliography

Use common sense in choosing items for your working bibliography. Don't waste time, for example, in collecting references to obscure publications not available in your library. Interlibrary loans are possible but may be time-consuming, unpredictable, and expensive; you will usually find it more rewarding to explore the resources of your own library. Look for information in the most likely places. If your topic is a recent event or a living person, for instance, start with newspapers and periodicals rather than with books.

The most sensible way to compile your working bibliography is to enter each potentially important source that you identify on a separate three-by-five-inch card or slip of paper. On the back of each card, make your brief notes about the source. The separate cards can be sorted in any number of handy ways; for example, you might place all the sources remaining to be consulted on the top, all those you have already examined on the bottom. When you are at last ready to prepare your paper's concluding bibliography (or *Works Cited* list, as it is frequently called), you can simply remove cards for the sources not used in the paper, alphabetize the remaining cards, and type the Works Cited list directly from them.

2. Recording bibliographic information

In order to be able to use your working bibliography cards as the basis of your paper's final Works Cited list, you must be careful to include all the information needed for the bibliography entries when you fill out each card. Otherwise, you will find yourself trekking back to the library at the last minute to look up a missing year of publication or to double-check an illegibly written author's name. The best plan, as you fill out each bibliography card, is to use the precise bibliographic *form* described below, in order to expedite typing the Works Cited list from your original cards.

Bibliography forms vary from discipline to discipline, but most systems of citing and listing sources aim for clarity and simplicity. None is inherently superior to another. In this chapter and the next two we will follow the system of documentation and bibliographic (Works Cited) forms prescribed by the Modern Language Association (MLA) and used in many humanities fields. Chapters **22** and **23** will

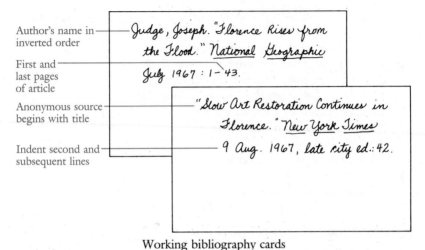

Author's name in inverted order	Judge, Joseph. "Florence Rises from the Flood." National Geographic
First and last pages of article	July 1967 : 1-43.
Anonymous source begins with title	"Slow Art Restoration Continues in Florence." New York Times
Indent second and subsequent lines	9 Aug. 1967, late city ed.: 42.

Working bibliography cards

illustrate two other systems of documentation. The most important thing about using any such system is that you must follow it precisely and consistently. Though its rules are arbitrary, they cannot arbitrarily be broken.

19b MLA Works Cited forms

On the following pages you will find model MLA Works Cited forms for most of the sources you are likely to encounter. Remember to have these samples at hand when you are compiling your working bibliography so that you can refer to them as you fill out your bibliography cards. Note that the author's name is always given last name first for easy indexing. For the same reason, the second and subsequent lines of each entry are always indented. (For additional information about MLA Works Cited forms, see Joseph Gibaldi and Walter S. Achtert, *MLA Handbook for Writers of Research Papers,* 3rd ed. [New York: MLA, 1988].)

Table of MLA Works Cited forms

Books
1. **Book by one author**
2. **Book by two or more authors**

3. Book by a committee, commission, association, or other group
4. Anonymous book
5. Later or revised edition of a book
6. Edited book (*author's work is being cited*)
7. Edited book (*editor's work is being cited*)
8. Translated book (*author's work is being cited*)
9. Translated book (*translator's work is being cited*)
10. Book in more than one volume
11. Republished book
12. Book that is part of a series
13. Book published by a division of a press
14. Book published before 1900
15. Book with incomplete publication information

Parts of books

16. Introduction, preface, foreword, or afterword in a book
17. Essay in a collection of essays by various authors
18. Poem, short story, or other work in an anthology
19. Journal or magazine article reprinted in a collection of essays by various authors

19b   *Articles in journals and magazines*

20. Article in a journal paginated by the volume (*continuous pagination*)
21. Article in a journal paginated issue by issue
22. Article in a journal with issue numbers only
23. Article in a weekly or biweekly magazine
24. Article in a monthly or bimonthly magazine

Articles in newspapers

25. Article in a newspaper
26. Editorial in a newspaper
27. Letter to the editor

Other print sources

28. Abstract in *Dissertation Abstracts International*
29. Book review

30. **Dissertation, unpublished**
31. **Encyclopedia article** (*or article in similar reference work*)
32. **Government document**
33. **Interview, published**
34. **Map**
35. **Pamphlet**
36. **Proceedings of a conference**

Nonprint sources

37. **Computer software**
38. **Film**
39. **Interview, personal**
40. **Lecture**
41. **Microfilm or microfiche**
42. **Recording**
43. **Television program**
44. **Videotape**

Books

1. **Book by one author**

19b

    Novarr, David. The Lines of Life: Theories of Biog-

        raphy, 1880–1970. West Lafayette: Purdue UP,

        1986.

- A colon separates the book's main title and subtitle.
- The abbreviation *UP* means "University Press." For nonaca-
  demic publishers, use a shortened form of the company's name:
  Heath for D. C. Heath and Company, *Knopf* for Alfred A.
  Knopf, Inc., and so on.

2. **Book by two or more authors**

    Scholes, Robert, and Robert Kellogg. The Nature of

        Narrative. London: Oxford UP, 1966.

- When more than one city of publication is given, use only the first in your citation (the title page of this book also lists Oxford and New York).
- In listing the authors' names, follow the same order used on the book's title page.
- Give the second author's name in normal rather than inverted order.
- If there are three authors, list both of the last two authors' names in normal order: Davis, Jane, Lee O'Brien, and Sylvia Mattheson.
- If there are more than three authors, you need give the name only of the first, following it by the Latin abbreviation *et al.* ("and others"), not underlined: Walker, Stephen A., et al.

3. **Book by a committee, commission, association, or other group**

American Automobile Association. <u>Illinois/Indiana/Ohio Tour Book</u>. Falls Church: American Automobile Assn., 1987.

Ground Zero. <u>Nuclear War: What's in It for You?</u> New York: Pocket, 1982.

- A parenthetical text citation for either of these books would begin with the joint author's name: (American Automobile Association 44), (Ground Zero 169). See **20c**.

4. **Anonymous book**

<u>Kodak Guide to 35mm Photography</u>. Rochester: Eastman Kodak, 1980.

- A parenthetical text citation for this book would begin with a shortened form of the title: (*Kodak Guide* 16). See **20c**.

19b

5. Later or revised edition of a book

Miller, Casey, and Kate Swift. The Handbook of Non-

sexist Writing. 2nd ed. New York: Harper,

1988.

Townsend, John Rowe. Written for Children: An Out-

line of English-Language Children's Litera-

ture. Rev. ed. Philadelphia: Lippincott,

1975.

6. Edited book (*author's work is being cited*)

Gaskell, Elizabeth. The Life of Charlotte

Brontë. Ed. Alan Shelston. Harmondsworth:

Penguin, 1975.

Pope, Alexander. The Poems of Alexander Pope. Ed.

John Butt. New Haven: Yale UP, 1963.

19b

• When you are citing the work of the author, put the editor's
name after the title.

7. Edited book (*editor's work is being cited*)

Garber, Frederick, ed. The Italian. By Ann Rad-

cliffe. London: Oxford UP, 1968.

Marshall, Sam A., ed. 1990 Photographer's Market.

Cincinnati: Writer's Digest Books, 1989.

• When you are citing the work of an editor, put the author's
name (if one exists) after the title.

8. Translated book (*author's work is being cited*)

Brumm, Ursula. American Thought and Religious
Typology. Trans. John Hoaglund. New Brunswick: Rutgers UP, 1970.

9. Translated book (*translator's work is being cited*)

Lind, L. R., trans. The Aeneid. By Vergil. Bloomington: Indiana UP, 1962.

10. Book in more than one volume

Sturzo, Luigi. Church and State. 2 vols. Notre
Dame: U of Notre Dame P, 1962.

Johnson, Edgar. Sir Walter Scott: The Great
Unknown. Vol. 1. New York: Macmillan, 1970.
2 vols.

19b

- If you use only one volume of a book published in multiple volumes, indicate the volume you are using after the title, and end the entry with the total number of volumes in the set.

11. Republished book

Shirer, William L. Berlin Diary: The Journal of a
Foreign Correspondent 1934–1941. 1941. Harmondsworth: Penguin, 1979.

- The copyright page of this paperbound book indicates that it was originally issued in 1941 by a different publisher. Information about the first publisher is not required in this citation, but the original publication date is given after the title.

12. Book that is part of a series

Radley, Virginia L. <u>Samuel Taylor Coleridge</u>.

    Twayne's English Authors Ser. 36. New York:

    Twayne, 1966.

- Give the name of the series and, if provided, the number of the volume in the series before you list the publication information.

13. Book published by a division of a press

Ehrenreich, Barbara, and Deirdre English. <u>For Her</u>

    <u>Own Good: 150 Years of the Experts' Advice to</u>

    <u>Women</u>. Garden City: Anchor–Doubleday, 1979.

McDonnell, Thomas P., ed. <u>A Thomas Merton Reader</u>.

    Rev. ed. Garden City: Image–Doubleday, 1974.

19b

- When a book is published by a division of a publishing house, give the name of the division first, followed by a hyphen and the name of the publisher.

14. Book published before 1900

Kellogg, Brainerd. <u>A Text–Book on Rhetoric</u>. New

    York, 1897.

- In citations to books published before 1900, the publisher's name may be omitted. Use a comma, not a colon, between the place of publication and the date.

15. Book with incomplete publication information

```
Marr, George S.  The Periodical Essayists of the
     Eighteenth Century.  London: Clarke, n.d.
```

- The abbreviation *n.d.* means "no date."
- If the place of publication is missing, substitute the abbreviation *N.p.* ("no place"); if the publisher's name is missing, use the abbreviation *n.p.* ("no publisher"). The citation for a book with no publication information would be as follows: N.p. : n.p., n.d.

Parts of books

16. Introduction, preface, foreword, or afterword in a book

```
Miller, J. Hillis.  Introduction.  Bleak House.  By
     Charles Dickens.  Ed. Norman Page.  Harmonds-
     worth: Penguin, 1971.  11–34.
```

19b

17. Essay in a collection of essays by various authors

```
Young, Richard E.  "Concepts of Art and the Teaching
     of Writing."  The Rhetorical Tradition and
     Modern Writing.  Ed. James J. Murphy.  New
     York: Modern Lang. Assn., 1982.  130–41.
```

- Follow the title of the essay with the title of the book in which it appears and the name of the book's editor or editors.
- End the entry with the first and last pages on which the essay is found.

18. Poem, short story, or other work in an anthology

Raleigh, Walter. "The Advice." The Anchor Anthology of Sixteenth-Century Verse. Ed. Richard
S. Sylvester. New York: Anchor-Doubleday,
1974. 330–31.

- End the entry with the first and last pages on which the work in question is found.

19. Journal or magazine article reprinted in a collection of essays by various authors

Fogle, Richard Harter. "The Abstractness of Shelley." Philological Quarterly 24 (1945): 362–
79. Rpt. in Shelley: A Collection of Critical
Essays. Ed. George M. Ridenour. Twentieth
Century Views. Englewood Cliffs: Prentice,
1965. 13–29.

19b

- Provide information about an article's earlier publication when it is noted in the collection you are using. *Rpt. in* ("reprinted in") indicates that the reprinted version of this article is the one being cited.

Articles in journals and magazines

20. Article in a journal paginated by the volume (*continuous pagination*)

Miller, Jerome A. "Horror and the Deconstruction of
the Self." Philosophy Today 32 (1988): 286–98.

- Most periodicals published quarterly or less frequently use continuous pagination for all the issues published in a single year; that is, if the year's first issue ends with page 125, the second issue begins with page 126. The citation to such a periodical includes the name of the journal, the volume number (32), the year of publication (1988), and the first and last pages of the article (286–98).

21. Article in a journal paginated issue by issue

Butterick, George. "Charles Olson's 'The Kingfish-

   ers' and the Poetics of Change." American Po-

   etry 6.2 (1989): 28–59.

- When each issue of a journal begins with page 1, the citation includes the volume (6) *and* the issue number (2), in addition to the year of publication and the first and last pages of the article.
- A title ordinarily enclosed in double quotation marks appears in single quotation marks when it is part of a larger title enclosed in quotation marks.

22. Article in a journal with issue numbers only

Jacobson, Paul. "Temperature and Your Guitar's

   Health." Guitar Review 75 (1988): 17–18.

- When a periodical uses issue numbers but no volume numbers, give the issue number (75) as if it were a volume number. Compare with item 20 above.

23. Article in a weekly or biweekly magazine

Rudolph, Barbara. "Adrift in the Doldrums." Time

   31 July 1989: 32–34.

- Follow the title of the magazine by listing the date in inverted form, a colon, and the first and last pages of the article. Abbreviate months, except for May, June, and July.
- Begin the citation to an anonymous article with the title.

24. Article in a monthly or bimonthly magazine

```
Blakely, Mary Kay. "Coma: Stories from the Edge of

    Death." Life Aug. 1989: 80-88.
```

- For a bimonthly magazine, include both months, abbreviated if possible, connected by a hyphen: Jan.-Feb. 1990: 23-28.

Articles in newspapers

25. Article in a newspaper

```
Donoghue, Denis. "Does America Have a Major Poet?"

    New York Times 3 Dec. 1978, late city ed., sec.

    7: 9+.

"GM Plans Taiwan Office." Wall Street Journal 11

    July 1989: B2.
```

19b

- Specify the edition of the newspaper when it is indicated on the masthead.
- If the newspaper is divided into separately paginated sections, specify the section. If the sections of the newspaper are lettered, the section can be incorporated into the page citation (B2).
- Indicate an article continued on nonconsecutive pages with a plus sign after the first page of the article (9+).
- Begin the citation to an anonymous article with the headline or title.

26. Editorial in a newspaper

"'Restraint' Spurs Terrorists." Editorial. Chicago Sun-Times 3 Aug. 1989: 42.

- A signed editorial begins with the author's name in inverted order.

27. Letter to the editor

Hayden, Lavonna. "Broadway Blues." Letter. Village Voice 28 Feb. 1989: 4.

- The title "Broadway Blues" has been supplied by the editor. Not all published letters are given titles.

Other print sources

19b

28. Abstract in *Dissertation Abstracts International*

Krantz, Susan Ellen. "The First Fortune: The Plays
and the Playhouse." DAI 47 (1986): 189A. Tulane U.

29. Book review

Pettit, Norma. Rev. of American Puritanism: Faith
and Practice, by Darrett B. Rutman. New England Quarterly 43 (1970): 504-06.

- If the review has a title, put it in quotation marks after the author's name.

30. Dissertation, unpublished

Rauff, James Vernon. "Machine Translation with Two-
Level Grammars." Diss. Northwestern U, 1988.

31. Encyclopedia article (*or article in similar reference work*)

"Phonetics." Encyclopaedia Britannica: Micropaedia. 15th ed. 1986.

Dunn, Mary Maples. "Penn, William." Encyclopedia
of American Biography. Ed. John A. Garraty.
New York: Harper, 1974.

- For familiar reference works such as standard encyclopedias, include the name of the author of the article (if the article is signed), the title of the entry, the name of the encyclopedia, and its edition (if given) and year of publication.
- For less familiar reference works, supply full publication information.
- Omit page and volume numbers in either type of citation when the work is organized alphabetically.

19b

32. Government document

United States. Superintendent of Documents.
Poetry and Literature. Washington: GPO,
1978.

- Unless the name of the author of a government publication is given, begin the citation with the name of the government and the name of the agency issuing the document.
- *GPO* is an abbreviation of "Government Printing Office."

33. Interview, published

Drabble, Margaret. Interview. <u>Interviews with
     Contemporary Novelists</u>. By Diana Cooper–
     Clark. New York: St. Martin's, 1986. 47–73.
Stern, Gerald. "A Poet of the Mind: An Interview with
     Gerald Stern." By Elizabeth Knight. <u>Poetry
     East</u> 26 (1988): 32–48.

* Begin citations to interviews with the name of the person
  interviewed.
* Identify the citation as an interview if it is untitled and provide
  the name of the interviewer, if known, together with standard
  publication information.

34. Map

<u>Southeastern States</u>. Map. Falls Church: American
     Automobile Assn., 1988.

35. Pamphlet

Rusinow, Dennison I. <u>Yugoslavia's Muslim Nation</u>.
     Hanover: Universities Field Staff Intl.,
     1982.

* The citation form for a pamphlet is the same as that for a
  book.

36. Proceedings of a conference

Rousseas, Stephen W., ed. <u>Inflation: Its Causes,
     Consequences and Control</u>. A Symposium Held by

the Dept. of Economics, New York U. 31 Jan.

1968. Wilton: K. Kazanjian Economics Founda-

tion, 1968.

- Include the title and date of the conference before the publication information.

Nonprint sources

37. Computer software

Etter, Thomas, and William Chamberlain. Racter.

Computer software. Mindscape, 1984.

- If the software is available in different versions, indicate the version you are citing after the name of the program: Vers. 2.2.

38. Film

Casablanca. Dir. Michael Curtiz. With Humphrey Bo-

gart, Ingrid Bergman, and Claude Rains. Warner

Bros., 1942.

19b

39. Interview, personal

Toulouse, Teresa A. Personal interview. 31 Mar.

1985.

40. Lecture

Catano, James V. "The Paradox Behind the Myth of

Self—Making: Self—Empowerment vs. the Power of

the Academy." Conference on College Composi-

tion and Communication. Seattle, 17 Mar. 1989.

41. Microfilm or microfiche

When citing a publication reproduced on microfilm or microfiche, simply use the ordinary citation form appropriate for that publication.

42. Recording

Friendly, Fred W., and Walter Cronkite, eds. The Way
     It Was: The Sixties. Narr. Walter Cronkite.
     CBS, F3M 38858, 1983.
Barbieri, Gato, tenor sax. Tropico. Audiotape.
     A&M, CS-4710, 1978.

43. Television program

Nightline. ABC. WLS, Chicago. 23 Jan. 1990.
"Baka: People of the Forest." Writ. and prod. Phil
     Agland. National Geographic. PBS. WTTW, Chi-
     cago. 7 Aug. 1989.

- The basic information in a citation to a television program is the title of the program, the network, the local station and city, and the date. For a specific episode of a program, begin with the episode's title.
- Information about the production of a program (writer, producer, director, narrator, etc.) may be included when appropriate.

44. Videotape

The Beggar's Opera. Videocassette. By John Gay.
     Prod. and dir. Jonathan Miller. With Roger
     Daltrey and Carol Hall. BBC-TV/RM Arts, 1985.
     135 min.

19c Taking notes

After you have identified several likely sources of information on your topic, your next impulse may be to arm yourself with packages of loose-leaf paper or piles of legal tablets to be filled up with notes. But remember that you will be writing your paper directly from your notes, not from the books you've consulted (which are hard to refer to), or from the periodicals you've read (which usually cannot leave your library). The basic consideration for note taking, then, is this: how can you take notes that will be most useful and most accessible later, as you compose the paper?

1. Note cards

For most people, the answer to this question is to take notes on separate cards or slips of paper, four by six inches or larger (regular typing paper cut in half works well). The rationale for such a system is simple. Note taking is an exploratory act, not a definitive one; as you are taking notes, you can never be certain which notes you will later use and which you will not need. If your notes are on separate cards, you will later be able to sort them out, clip them together, arrange some, and discard others. You will gain a flexibility that will enormously simplify the task of organizing and writing your paper.

For such a system of note taking to work, though, each note card must be *self-contained*. It must, in other words, contain three pieces of information:

19c

1. *A clear, complete note*
   Be certain that the single note you put on each card is sufficiently complete to make sense to you later, when you no longer have in front of you the article or book that it came from.

2. *A reference to your source*
   To ensure that you will later be able to cite sources accurately in your paper, you must include on each note card a reference to the source from which that note was taken. Don't copy all the publication information for the source onto each note card; instead, develop a system for keying the note cards to the bibliography cards in your working bibliography. For exam-

ple, you might write just the author's last name at the top of each card (but be careful to distinguish between sources if two of them share the same last name).

3. *The page number*

You must be certain that the page number or numbers from which you took the note also appear on the note card, because you will have to cite those page numbers in your final paper.

2. Types of notes

Before we discuss the content of your notes, let's consider the types of notes that you might take. There are four basic types of notes, and a single note card may contain just one or a combination of all four.

Direct quotation

Copying direct quotations onto note cards may at first seem to be the easiest way to take notes, but often it actually creates more work for you later on. Mounds of undigested quotations lacking their original contexts are usually harder to work with as you are writing your paper than incisive and thoughtful notes in your own words (see *Paraphrase,* below). Sometimes, however, you will find a writer who states his or her point so forcefully or cleverly or succinctly that you believe you might want to quote the author's own phrasing in your paper. In such cases, when you copy an author's exact words onto your note card, be certain to enclose them in quotation marks so that later, as you compose your paper, you will be able to distinguish between your own words on your note cards and the words that belong to others.

Be certain, too, that everything within the quotation marks is exactly as it appears in the original quotation; you are not free to omit or add words randomly, or to change punctuation or spelling. If you have to add a word or phrase for clarity, you must enclose the added material in square brackets ([ ]—not parentheses). If you wish to delete part of an overly long quotation, you must show the deletion with three spaced periods (. . .) called ellipses. Quotations, in short, must be handled with precision. If you fail to set them off with quotation marks, you leave yourself open to the serious charge of plagiarism,

19c

Text of source

essentially a struggle for survival. The amenities of gracious behavior could hardly be expected to flourish in the midst of the damp and dirt of the hastily built, overcrowded shelters, the crippling illnesses, and the spiritual disabilities of homesickness, sorrow and discouragement. But the Puritan's code of good manners was an integral part of his standard of Christian conduct, and for these devout colonists, especially those among them who had been privileged to live gently in England, it must have been disheartening to see the formality of every-day communication, the respect for individual privacy, the quick concern for a troubled neighbor, and the dignity of innate self-possession, too often falter and fail under the weight of outrageous circumstance.

Tho
failed
was be

Bibliography card

White, Elizabeth Wade. *Anne Bradstreet:*
"The Tenth Muse." New York :
Oxford UP, 1971.

Note card

Source ——— White, p. 116

Page ———

Paraphrase ——— Crude living conditions particularly hard for Puritan colonists to endure, since

Quotation ——— "the Puritan's code of good manners was an integral part of his standard of Christian conduct...."

Researcher's ——— (another example of moral tone of
note to self   life in Massachusetts Bay Colony)

Source, bibliography card, note card

19c

discussed in the next chapter (see **20b**). If you alter them without indicating the change, your instructor may penalize you for inexact handling of sources.

Paraphrase

A paraphrase is a restatement of another writer's ideas in words that are entirely your own. Paraphrasing takes thought and care, for it must reflect the meaning of the given text but be wholly original in phrasing. You may not simply replace some of the words in another writer's sentence with your own; instead, the very structure of your sentence should be different from your source's. Good paraphrasing takes time when you are doing it, but it can save time later: if you have paraphrased well, you may be able to write your paper directly from material on your note cards (though you will still need to acknowledge the source of the ideas contained in your prose). For advice on paraphrasing properly, see **20b**.

Summary

19c

As you get further and further along in your research, you will be better able to decide when you need to note all of the details given in a passage in one of your sources and when you can simply summarize the passage in a sentence or two. Look for opportunities to use summary effectively as a way of reducing your work without sacrificing important information.

Notes to yourself

Have you found a quotation that might make an attention-getting introduction to your paper? Are you reading a source whose ideas contradict those in other articles you've examined? Is the book in front of you the best survey of your subject that you have located so far? Because you can't expect to remember all the peripheral ideas that occur to you as you do your research, write them down on your note cards as they come to mind. Later, when you review your cards in preparation for outlining the paper, you'll be glad for the clarifying, explanatory, or suggestive notes that you made to yourself while you were deep in the research process.

3. Recognizing a potential "note"

As this description of notes suggests, note taking is far from being a mechanical task. It is a thoughtful, even creative, act that demands your alertness and care.

You may be wondering how you will recognize a "note" when you encounter one in your reading. When you are just beginning to research a topic, after all, almost everything you read about it may be new. Is everything, therefore—every page, every paragraph, every sentence—a note waiting to be jotted down? If that is so, you may be thinking, note taking will mean paraphrasing or summarizing the complete contents of every article or book you pick up.

Although there are no secret tricks that will unfailingly enable you to spot potential notes hidden among the closely packed lines of an article in the *New York Times,* note taking is, fortunately, a more selective process than the description in the previous paragraph suggests. You might keep the following general guidelines in mind as you decide what information to commit to your note cards.

1. A good note will make a clear point. If you can't understand what the author you're reading is saying, copying down a quotation from the article or a paraphrase of the text will not help you later. The notes you take should be clear enough for anyone looking over your note cards—even a person who had not read the original sources—to understand.

2. Good notes often reflect the particular attitudes or opinions of the author whom you are reading. Try to write notes that capture the essence of an author's argument, concisely restate the main point, or indicate his or her biases.

3. Good notes will present specific information—facts, places, descriptions, examples, statistics, case histories. Like all good essays, successful research papers are grounded in specific information, information that must exist on your note cards when you begin to compose your paper.

In the early stages of your work, you should expect to take many notes that you will later discard. This is an inevitable part of research work, since, as we said earlier, it is only through the research process that you will be able to define and focus your subject clearly. Taking

19c

notes and rethinking your original topic go hand in hand. To put it more brutally: you'll have to take many notes that you will ultimately throw away before you'll know which ones to keep.

19d Assessing your sources

Above we made the point that you must approach note taking in a thoughtful way, isolating the key ideas in a source and finding the most accurate and most concise way to record those ideas on your note cards. Effective note taking requires another kind of reflection as well: carefully considering the quality of your sources and their appropriateness to your research project.

1. How current?

How important to your paper is *recent* information about your subject? If you are writing about historical events, you may wish to examine material published over a large span of time. A paper on the San Francisco earthquake of 1906, for example, might well draw both on contemporary accounts of the disaster and on modern assessments of its influence on subsequent city planning. In contrast, if you have chosen a current subject or one that is undergoing continual change, you will need the most up-to-date sources available. In science, politics, and medicine, for example, old information is frequently useless information.

2. How authoritative?

What can you find out about your author's qualifications to write on your subject? Begin by looking at the end of an article or on the jacket of a book for a note that cites the author's professional position or other publications. In addition, be alert for citations to your author's work in other sources, either in textual references or in footnotes. Notice whether your author's name turns up frequently in bibliographies—an indication that he or she has published widely. Finally, consider the evidence that your author uses to support his or her assertions. Is it the kind of specific and substantial information that suggests a thorough acquaintance with the subject? The better qualified the author, the more certain you can be that the information you are reading is accurate and complete.

3. How objective?

Whether or not you have been able to locate information about your author, you should watch for signs of the author's biases within his or her writing itself. Pure objectivity, of course, is rare, since every writer's perspective colors his or her handling of a subject. The question here is whether your author's biases are so strong that they may result in a distorted presentation of the subject. Is your author's work based on facts or on judgments? Does your author make questionable assumptions? (See **14a**, **14b**, and **14c**.) Does he or she satirize or ridicule those who have taken different positions? If you detect hints of bias in your author, you will want to examine the work of a broad range of other sources as well, so that your own perspective on the subject will be as balanced as possible.

19e Assessing your subject

Use your initial note taking as a way of assessing the likelihood that the subject you've chosen will yield a successful research paper. Often, taking notes from just a few of the sources that you expect to be most promising will tell you whether your subject is going to work or not.

19e

1. Signs of a good subject

A good subject will grow richer and more interesting as you research it. You will discover perspectives on the subject that you had not considered and will find yourself caught up in the process of discovering and synthesizing information about the topic. Your reading will suggest a number of possible directions for further research, many of which you may find intriguing.

2. Signs of a poor subject

In contrast, any of the following situations should suggest to you that your subject may be unworkable.

1. All the sources you examine make the same meager points about the subject. There's less to be learned here than you expected.
2. The sources you read suggest that the topic is far more complicated than you initially realized. You begin to feel that you will never be able to comprehend, let alone focus, your subject.
3. Your reading bores you. The subject turns out to be much less interesting than you expected.

Of course, you should give any subject a fair chance of blossoming by investigating all possible types of sources—reference works, books, magazine and journal articles, newspapers, essays in collections. Be certain, moreover, to discuss your research problems with your instructor, who may be able to help you salvage a subject that appears unworkable by suggesting a new focus for your research or specific sources for you to investigate. But don't wait until just days before your paper is due to ask your instructor for help, or for permission to look for another subject. Plan to talk with him or her at the first signs of trouble in your research.

EXERCISE 1

19e

Write a Works Cited entry in correct MLA format for each of the following sources. Note that in some cases you do not need all the information provided.

1. A review of Jane F. Gardner's book Women in Roman Law and Society, published in 1986 by the Indiana University Press in Bloomington. The review, written by Mary R. Lefkowitz, appears on pages 1185 and 1186 of volume 92 of the American Historical Review (1987), a continuously paged journal.
2. An interview with Alvin Ailey entitled Alvin Ailey Celebrates 30 Years of Dance, published in the November 1988 issue of Essence. The article begins on page 64 and continues on nonconsecutive pages later in the magazine. The interviewer is A. Peter Bailey.
3. Sheila A. Egoff's book Thursday's Child: Trends and Patterns in Contemporary Children's Literature, published in Chicago by the American Library Association. The year of publication is 1981.
4. An article entitled Of Time and Mathematics, published by Philip J. Davis in the Southern Humanities Review, volume 18, 1984. It appears on pages 193 to 202. The journal is continuously paged.
5. Frances Gray's essay The Nature of Radio Drama, in a book entitled

Radio Drama and edited by Peter Lewis. The book was published in London by Longman. The year of publication is 1981. The essay appears on pages 48 to 77.

6. Cost Estimate Jumps for Music Center Expansion, an article in the September 12, 1984, issue of the Los Angeles Times. It appears on page 1 of section VI.

7. The article Sleep in the 1983 Encyclopedia Americana. Ian Oswald wrote the article, which appears on pages 31 to 33 of volume 25. No edition is given.

8. An article in the Journal of Broadcasting by Joanne Cantor, Dean Ziemke, and Glenn G. Sparks. The title is Effect of Forewarning on Emotional Responses to a Horror Film. It appears on pages 21 to 31 of volume 28, 1984. The journal is continuously paged.

9. A two-volume book by Joseph N. Ireland entitled Records of the New York Stage from 1750 to 1860. It was originally published in 1866 and was republished in 1966 by Benjamin Blom, Inc., of New York.

10. An anonymous article on page 23 of the August 6, 1984, issue of Business Week. The title is Job Safety Becomes a Murder Issue.

11. C. A. Patrides's article Shakespeare and the Comedy beyond Comedy, published in the second number of volume 10 of the Kenyon Review, a journal that pages each issue separately. The year of publication is 1988. The article appears on pages 38 to 57.

12. A book by Charles J. Maland entitled Frank Capra. It is a volume in Twayne's Theatrical Arts Series and was published in 1980 in Boston by Twayne.

13. Charles Shapiro's afterword to Charles Dickens's novel Hard Times, published in 1961 by the Signet Classics division of New American Library in New York. The afterword is found on pages 293 to 297.

14. The article Dermatology by W. B. Shelley, found on pages 302 to 307 of The Oxford Companion to Medicine, a two-volume reference work arranged alphabetically. The editors are John Walton, Paul B. Beeson, and Ronald Bodley Scott. The book was published in Oxford by Oxford University Press in 1986.

15. A book entitled Life Insurance Companies as Financial Institutions, produced by the Life Insurance Association of America and published in 1962 by Prentice Hall in Englewood Cliffs.

19e

EXERCISE 2

In **19c** we mentioned that a researcher should try to summarize the major points in a source when possible, rather than copying onto a note card a host of small details. For practice in the art of summarizing, write a brief summary in your own words of each of the following passages. Try to capture both the passage's main point and its key details in no more than two sentences.

Example

Text

Babylon—the city and its empire—flourished for almost 2000 years, from about 2225 B.C. until its capture by Alexander the Great in 331 B.C. When the Greek conqueror of the world died there, Babylon could be said to have died too. But up to that time it had been the cultural capital of the civilised world; and even after its site was lost, buried under mounds of rubble, its existence was never forgotten. The very name has always had a magical sound to it. The Hebrews placed the Garden of Eden somewhere nearby. The Greeks wrote that it contained two of the Seven Wonders of the World. The Romans described it as "the greatest city the sun ever beheld." And to the early Christians "Great Babylon" was the symbol of [human] wickedness and the wrath of God. And so it was "by the waters of Babylon" that the history of the Western world could be said to have begun.

Although it seems unbelievable that a metropolis of such size and splendour should have vanished from the earth—its outer defences alone were ten miles in circumference, fifty feet high, and nearly fifty-five feet deep—the fact is that by the first century B.C. nothing remained but its walls. For Babylon had been devastated so often that by this time it was abandoned except for a few refugees who made their homes in the rubble. The royal palaces had been looted, the temples had fallen into ruins, and the greater part of the city inside the walls was overgrown with weeds.

—James Wellard, *Babylon*

Summary

By the first century B.C., little except the massive walls remained of Babylon, the most magnificent city of the world from 2225 B.C. until the fourth century B.C., a city whose reputation earned it a place in Hebrew, Greek, Roman, and early Christian myth.
[The passage's central point—expressed in this summary—is the contrast between Babylon's greatness for two thousand years and its stunning obliteration by the first century B.C.]

1.   Despite the hype, losing weight doesn't always lead to better health. "Seesawers"—those who put on many pounds and then shed them—may nearly double their risk of heart disease, according to a study from the University of Texas School of Public Health. Those who gain little or no weight and those who put on weight but make no effort to lose it may run no additional risk of coronary disease.

Texas researchers, who studied 400 men ages 20 to 40, theorize that seesawers who gained 10% or more of body weight after losing pounds in weight-loss programs created a sharp rise in artery-clogging cholesterol. This apparently wasn't the case with the "no-gain" and "gain-only" groups. The risk for the gain-only group: Their large, continuous gains increased the risk of fatal cancers.

"Avoid fast-loss starvation diets," advises one of the researchers, Peggy Hamm. "If you are comfortable with your present weight, work hard at maintaining it and avoid wide fluctuations. If you're not comfortable with your weight, adjust your life-style and your eating habits so that you take the excess weight off very gradually."

—"The Downside of Dieting," *Changing Times*

2.   The windmill was an inspired answer to the problem of the lack of water power, and was undoubtedly one of medieval Europe's most important inventions. Essentially an adaptation of the watermill to a new source of power, it made use of the familiar mechanism—now inverted so as to be driven by sails mounted high in the building, rather than by a waterwheel at its base. But a more fundamental alteration was also necessary. The difficulty with the windmill, and what presumably delayed its invention, was the problem of how to harness a power source that regularly changed its direction, and which would not be directed or controlled. With the watermill the water always flowed along the same channel, and at a rate the miller could vary by means of sluices; the seemingly intractable problem for the first windmill builders was to contrive a way of keeping the sails facing into the wind. The solution they came up with was to balance the windmill on a single massive upright post, so that the miller could push the whole structure around to face in whichever direction he wanted. The windspeed he could compensate for, like any sailor, by adjusting the spread of canvas on the lattice-work sails.

—Richard Holt, "The Medieval Mill —A Productivity Breakthrough?" *History Today*

19e

3.   Although dreams seem to arise unbidden, you can choose the subjects of your nighttime dramas. One technique you might try is a technique called "incubation," developed by psychologist Gayle Delaney of San Francisco. Choose a problem or question in your life, she suggests, and write down a few sentences about it. Then, just before you go to bed, compose a one-line question that sums up what you want to know, such as "Why do I fight with my spouse?" Lay the paper beside you, repeating the question over and over to yourself as you fall asleep.

When you awaken, write down everything you remember about any of your dreams. Don't reject anything as irrelevant. As Delaney says, "Dreams speak to us in symbols," so even a farfetched image may, after some wide-awake thought, be seen to bear on the incubated problem. If the technique doesn't work the first night, keep trying. Delaney reports a high success rate among her patients.

The tricky part is remembering. About the only way to capture a dream is to write it down immediately upon waking, for dreams vanish within 15 minutes. If you don't remember a dream, write down whatever is on your mind—those thoughts often come from the night's dreams and may be the first clue to retrieving them.

—"A Blueprint for Dreaming," *Newsweek*

19e

4.   Santa Fe style isn't a reference to fashion or popularity. It's a blue sky, spiritual attitude towards life, and an abiding but quiet appreciation for a unique community culture that started in the early 1600s with sun-baked bricks of mud and straw.

Back then in 1610 when the city was officially founded on an empty mesa 7,000 feet above sea level, the rule of law came long distance from the king of Spain—with the tentative acquiescence of the local Pueblo Indians. Seven decades later, the natives revolted, and it was not until 1692 that the "city of holy faith" was reclaimed for Spanish colonialism by Don Diego de Vargas. The Republic of Mexico eventually had its heyday of authority beginning in 1821, after which Anglo traders began arriving in wagons on the old Santa Fe Trail. In 1846 during the War with Mexico, General Stephen Watts Kearny claimed Sante Fe for the Stars and Stripes.

So the city's tradition of tolerance for new faces goes way back. Today that aspect of Santa Fe's culture is perhaps its most appealing. The town is made up of many subgroups that don't mesh, yet don't clash. Among them are Hispanics who trace their local lineage back hundreds of years and world-class physicists working on nuclear re-search at the nearby Los Alamos National Laboratory. There is a huge artistic community and an army of waitresses and desk clerks. Santa Fe being the capital city, its state-government contingent numbers in the thousands. And there's a shockingly large collection of the world's wealthiest individuals who keep very much to themselves.

This is an impossible mix. But the suspension holds—even after they stirred in the New Agers with their vegetarian dream rolfing and herbal acu-massage therapy, and the Sikhs with their turbans and beards. Santa Fe is open to almost all ways of thinking, and that makes for a far more interesting, cosmopolitan city than its size and location would ordinarily suggest.

> —Paul Young, "Santa Fe Style: Impossible
> Cosmopolitan Mix," *American West*

19e

20 *Composing the Research Paper*

20a

Perhaps the most important advice to keep in mind as you organize and write your paper is that the research paper, though it may be longer than other essays you have written, is more similar to than different from a typical expository essay, and its success will depend largely on the same principles of effective writing that we have discussed and illustrated throughout this book. If you have learned how to formulate a thesis and introduction, how to write clearly structured paragraphs, how to use specific diction and development effectively, how to ensure coherence and maintain consistency of tone, then you should be able to write a good research paper.

We won't deny, however, that the matter of integrating other people's ideas and words with your own text complicates the task of composing a research paper. Accordingly, in the section below we present some guidelines to follow as you organize your paper, and in the following two sections we deal specifically with incorporating information from your sources into the paper. We end this chapter by considering some important matters of format for your final draft.

20a Organizing and writing a research paper

The more you learn about your subject from note taking, the more you may feel that you will never be able to stop examining sources without the risk of missing some potentially important new piece of information. Strictly speaking, of course, that's true. But the realities of research—whether in college or in professional life—dictate that you must at some point call a halt to your research and begin shaping into a coherent whole the material that you have collected.

1. Know when to stop taking notes

How will you know when you've collected enough information and can begin writing your paper? It's difficult to be certain that you've done enough research, but you might expect your work to lead to this point in stages something like the following.

Examine your major sources

First, take notes from all of your major sources, that is, all of those that you initially expected to be important sources of information on your topic, either because their titles seemed particularly promising or because you had already skimmed through them. As we noted at the end of the preceding chapter, you should complete this stage of the research process with a reasonably sure sense that your subject is in some way going to provide the basis for a successful paper.

Look for connections among your notes

Once you move beyond your list of major sources and start examining others, you will probably discover a number of the same topics surfacing again and again, and you will begin to see connections among your note cards for the first time. Source Y, for example, has an opinion different from source X's; source B confirms a point made by source A. Recognizing such connections is a good sign that you are mastering your subject. This is usually the point at which you will be able to define a more precise direction for your paper and your additional research. You will have become familiar enough with your subject to identify those aspects of it that seem most worth investigating.

20a

Think about what your research proves

At about this point, you will no doubt realize that you have developed ideas of your own about your subject, based on the reading and note taking you have done. The best researchers, after all, are less interested in mere piles of accumulated data than in ways of using the data they have collected to support their own observations and ideas.

Once you are able to see beyond your separate notes to the ways in which those notes can be used to substantiate a larger argument of your own, a sense of the completeness of your work may begin to grow upon you. You may gradually begin to develop a vague mental outline of some of the key ideas you think your paper should cover. When you reach this point, it may be time to retire from the library— for a while, at least—and have a try at writing your paper.

2. Organize your notes

The first stage in writing your paper is reviewing and sorting out all of the notes you have taken, collecting together notes from different sources that explain, comment on, or give evidence for the same specific points. If you have put your notes on separate cards or slips of paper, you will find this easy to do.

20a

As you read each note card, decide which aspect of your subject it pertains to, and group it with others that address the same issue. Don't be surprised if you have a large "miscellaneous" category made up of notes whose value seems questionable; many of your early note cards may indeed be no longer important, now that you have more clearly focused your subject. Realize, however, that although sorting out your note cards will help you define the main issues to concentrate on in your paper, it may also reveal points that need further research. Some additional trips to the library in search of specific pieces of information may still be necessary before your paper is finished.

Some writers, in sorting out their note cards, attach a "comment card" to each note card, briefly indicating the way they expect to use the note in the paper. Later, when they have begun writing, they can easily expand the comment card into a sentence or two that establishes a clear context for the material on the note cards. This practice helps to guarantee that the finished paper will not be a mere splicing together of facts or quotations; instead, the notes will function as part of a larger argument created by the researcher.

3.   Compose a tentative outline

Few writers can progress beyond this point in composing a long paper without making at least an informal outline. The piles of note cards before you will help. Each of the large piles may be one of the main points in your paper, a main heading in your outline. Within each pile you will find notes that will make up the subpoints to be covered. With your usable notes organized in groups before you, sketch out an outline of your paper on a separate sheet of paper, including all the subpoints that you have notes to support. Some writers like to mark their note cards to correspond with the points in their written outline, so that they will know just which cards to pick up as they compose the paper.

4.   Segment your writing

Even a researcher who begins writing with a firm grasp of his or her subject and a clear conception of the form that he or she wants the final research paper to take may sometimes feel overwhelmed by the amount of material to be assimilated into the paper. For that reason, many researchers view their papers in segments, and they approach the task of writing by thinking about and working on only one segment at a time. For example, you might set as the goal of your first composing session drafting only the introduction to your paper—the opening paragraph or paragraphs that will provide the reader with necessary background on your subject and introduce the paper's thesis. If you have formulated a tentative outline, make drafting just one new section of the outline the objective of each successive composing session. Don't feel that you have to compose the paper's parts sequentially; if you get stuck while writing one segment, leave it temporarily and work on a different one instead.

20a

As in all writing, your goal is to put down on paper a draft, not a final polished essay. Write in any way that will help you move along quickly, whether that means using a soft pencil, a ballpoint pen, a typewriter, or a word processor. Skip lines if you write by hand, so that you will have room for later additions and changes.

In **20c** below, we will discuss ways of incorporating quotation and paraphrasing into your paper. But it is appropriate here to point out that you shouldn't take the time to copy into your draft quotations that you intend to use in your text. Instead, simply clip the note card with the quotation on it to the appropriate page of the draft. The time to worry about smoothly incorporating such material into your text will come later, as you revise.

5.   Leave time for rethinking and revising

When you do begin revising, you should probably be prepared to make more changes than you might have made in other papers you have written. The length of a research paper and the number of different materials on which it is based open up a variety of possibilities for its organization, and you need to be ready to reassemble your material in several ways before you find a satisfactory arrangement. Transitional words, phrases, and sentences will be more important than ever as you attempt to link together smoothly the information gathered from your various sources and your own observations and conclusions.

Be prepared, too, for the possibility that you will have to return to the library to check a source or page number, to make sense of a confusing but important note card, or even to do some additional research. For this reason, the best advice we can offer is to leave enough time to write your earliest draft in several sittings, to put it away for a day or two (or at least overnight), and then to return to it fresh for thorough revision. A research paper is a complex project, and you should not expect to be able to dash off a draft one evening, patch it up the next, and hand it in the following morning. Apart from matters of composition—formidable enough in a paper of this length—you will need time to double-check the accuracy of your citations, type up the paper in the correct format, and proofread carefully. Leave yourself enough time to assemble a paper worthy of the weeks of research you have completed.

20b   Avoiding plagiarism

Although the research paper is similar in many respects to the other writing you have done, it presents you with at least one major new task: accurately citing the sources of your research. If you fail to distinguish between your own words and thoughts and those of your sources, you mislead your reader into assuming that everything in the paper is your own work. Passing off the language or ideas of someone else as your own is a serious violation known as **plagiarism.**

In **20c** we will discuss the proper format for citing sources in your paper. Before we do that, however, we need to look more closely at the concept of plagiarism itself, particularly as it pertains to using quotation and paraphrase in a research paper. Those are the two basic situations in which you must cite your sources in order to avoid plagiarizing, and we will examine them separately.

1. Quoting accurately

You must enclose every direct quotation in quotation marks, and you must cite its source in the paper. This rule is easy enough to understand. If you did not enclose in quotation marks the direct quotations that you take from your sources, your reader would have no way of knowing which words were yours and which were your sources'. And once you do use quotation marks to set off these phrases or sentences, your reader's natural question will be, "Who wrote this?" Your citation of the source answers that question.

A quotation must present the words of your source exactly as they appear in the original text unless you use ellipsis marks or brackets to indicate that you have made changes in the text (see **30a** and **30h**). Be careful not to distort the meaning of the original text by omitting key words or by using the quoted passage in a sense not intended by the original writer. Consider the following examples.

20b

Source

> In a given area the plague accomplished its kill within four to six months and then faded, except in the larger cities, where, rooting into the close-quartered population, it abated during the winter, only to reappear in spring and rage for another six months.
>
> —Barbara W. Tuchman, *A Distant Mirror: The Calamitous 14th Century* (New York: Knopf, 1978) 93.

Inaccurate use of quotation

> In fourteenth–century cities, the plague "rooted
> into the close population during the winter, only
> to reappear in spring and rage for another six months"
> (Tuchman 93).

[The quoted passage in this sentence resembles Tuchman's, but it is not a word-for-word reproduction of her text, and it is therefore unacceptable. This writer has changed the word *rooting* to "rooted," and has omitted the words *quartered* and *it abated*.]

Inaccurate use of quotation

> According to Barbara Tuchman, the great plague of
> the fourteenth century lasted only "four to six
> months and then faded" (93).

20b

[This writer has quoted Tuchman's words accurately but has radically distorted her meaning by ignoring the rest of her sentence, where she refers to the plague's cyclical return in the cities, year after year.]

Accurate use of quotation

> In medieval cities, according to Barbara Tuchman,
> the plague "abated during the winter" but typically
> "[reappeared] in spring and [raged] for another six
> months" (93).

[To make Tuchman's words fit the structure of his sentence, this writer had to change the original text's *reappear* and *rage* to *reappeared* and *raged;* he indicated those changes in an acceptable way, by putting the substituted words in brackets. Otherwise, the quoted passages are faithful to the original.]

2. Paraphrasing accurately

You must cite the source of every paraphrased idea unless that idea would be considered common knowledge. To explain this documentation rule, we need to discuss separately its two key terms, **paraphrase** and **common knowledge.**

Paraphrasing

To paraphrase an idea means to change the words in which it is expressed without materially altering its meaning. Many writers have difficulty grasping the precise point at which the wording of a quotation has been sufficiently altered to constitute an acceptable paraphrase. *In general, several words in succession taken from another source may be said to constitute direct quotation.* Thus you cannot turn a quotation into an acceptable sentence of your own simply by changing a few words in the original. Consider the following examples, based on the same excerpt from Barbara Tuchman that we used above.

Unacceptable paraphrase

In a specific area the plague killed its victims in four to six months and then receded, except in big cities, where it declined in the winter, only to reappear in spring and flourish for another six months (Tuchman 93).

[This writer has merely substituted a few words of his own for words in the source. The structure of the sentence, however, is Tuchman's. The result is plagiarism.]

Unacceptable paraphrase

The plague accomplished its kill within four to six months in most places, but in the cities it abated during the winter and would rage again in the spring (Tuchman 93).

20b

[The structure of this writer's sentence is original, but she has used several phrases taken directly from Tuchman: *accomplished its kill within four to six months, abated during the winter.* Borrowing such phrases without enclosing them in quotation marks makes the writer guilty of plagiarism. Just the word *rage* as used here would constitute plagiarism in most readers' eyes, even though it is not part of a longer phrase taken from Tuchman, because it is such a distinctive verb in Tuchman's original sentence.]

Acceptable paraphrase

In the crowded cities, the plague never completely

disappeared; though relatively dormant in the win-

ter, it returned in full force when the weather turned

warm again (Tuchman 93).

[This writer has captured the exact meaning of Tuchman's passage, but in a sentence that is original in structure and diction. The only major words taken from Tuchman are *cities, plague,* and *winter;* such duplication is acceptable, since it would be impossible to find synonyms for these basic terms.]

20b

Common knowledge

As we indicated above, even a quotation converted into acceptable paraphrase must have its source cited in your paper unless it falls into a category often referred to as "common knowledge." What does common knowledge mean?

In practice, writers often find it simply impossible to give sources for everything they write. Where, for example, did we get these rules for avoiding plagiarism? We really don't know. For years we have heard plagiarism talked about, have read about it, and have recognized examples of it in our students' papers. In short, our knowledge of what the term means is common knowledge, part of our understanding for which we have no single identifiable source.

If you are unsure whether an idea you encounter in your research qualifies as common knowledge, you might keep in mind the following two-step test. An idea is common knowledge and its source need not be cited *only* if

1. you found it repeated in many sources, rather than stated in just one; or
2. you believe it would be familiar to an average educated person, even one who had not researched the subject (a person, for example, like one of your classmates).

For example, the fact that the Olympic games originated in Greece would not need citation, since it fulfills both of the conditions above (it is information that would be found in many books and articles on the Olympics, *and* it is a fact familiar to most people). Nor would the fact that the modern Olympic games were begun in 1896 require citation; although that fact fails the second condition (most people you asked would probably not be able to give you this date), it passes the first (anyone doing research on the Olympics would repeatedly encounter the date in a variety of sources).

In contrast, a single author's opinion about the propaganda value of the 1936 Berlin Olympics in Nazi Germany would probably need a citation, even if the opinion were acceptably paraphrased. Such a statement would not meet either of the conditions above. As a specific writer's opinion, it would appear only in a single source (though if you found a great many writers who shared this opinion, it would then qualify as common knowledge after all). And as the statement of a presumed authority on the Olympics, it would not be information that we could expect others who had not studied the subject to know.

20c

20c Citing sources

Above we described the situations in which you must indicate the sources of the material—whether quoted or paraphrased—that you have used in writing your research paper. In this section, we turn to the method of making such citations in the text of your paper.

The system of documentation adopted by the Modern Language Association of America in 1984 eliminates the elaborate footnotes used for years by both students and scholars. The simplicity of this new system and the academic prestige of its proponent, the MLA, have brought it into widespread use, particularly in the humanities. Keep in mind, however, that preferred methods of documentation vary arbitrarily from discipline to discipline. In Chapters **22** and **23** we present two other widely used forms of documentation, the system of parenthetical citation prescribed by the American Psychological Association and the system of endnote documentation formerly advocated by the MLA. Still other methods of documentation exist as well. The best advice we can offer you is to follow closely whatever model your instructor suggests.

The MLA system reduces documentation to two components. First, at the end of each passage whose source must be noted, the last name of the author and the page or pages on which the material is found are inserted in parentheses:

(Alexander 197–98)

At the end of the paper, on a separate sheet with the heading "Works Cited," a complete bibliographic entry is provided for each of the sources cited in the text (see the sample Works Cited list on page 431). These entries, which follow the forms that we described in **19b**, are arranged alphabetically according to the last names of the authors:

Alexander, Edwin P. On the Main Line: The Pennsylva

nia Railroad in the 19th Century. New York:

Potter, 1971.

If you properly filled out a bibliography card for each of your sources as you took notes, you will be able to alphabetize the cards for the sources you used and copy your Works Cited entries directly from them.

The examples below illustrate this method of citing sources and some ways of smoothly incorporating quoted and paraphrased material into your text.

1. Quotations

Typically, the parenthetical citation in a text comes *after* the quotation marks that close a quotation but *before* the sentence's end punctuation:

Parenthetical citation in text

The definitive biography of Mahatma Gandhi remains
to be written. As one Gandhi scholar has explained,
"Multivolume works written by Gandhi's former colleagues and published in India are comprehensive in
scope, but their objectivity suffers from the authors' reverent regard for their subject" (Juergensmeyer 294).

Citation in works cited

Juergensmeyer, Mark. "The Gandhi Revival--A Review
      Article." Journal of Asian Studies 43 (1984):
      293-98.

20c

What follows are some variations on this basic method of documenting quotations.

Setting off a long quotation

A quotation of more than four lines is set off from the text and indented ten spaces from the left margin. Such a quotation is usually introduced with a colon unless it begins in the middle of a sentence that grammatically continues the sentence that introduces it. The parenthetical citation is placed *after* the end punctuation.

Parenthetical citation in text

One editor suggests that photographers trying to publish their work should aim to surpass--not just
equal--the photographs they see in print:

> Editors know where they can get pictures
> like the ones they've already published.
> If you want to get noticed, you have to take
> pictures better than those. This is espe-
> cially true if you are looking for assign-
> ments rather than to sell existing pic-
> tures. Why take a chance on a new
> photographer who will come up with no bet-
> ter than what you already have, an editor
> might reason? (Scully 33)

20c

Citation in works cited

Scully, Judith. "Seeing Pictures." Modern Photography May 1984: 28-33.

Incorporating the author's name into the text

You can often fit quotations into your text smoothly by introducing the author's name before the quotation or by placing it at
some point in the middle of the quotation. In such cases, only the
page number of the source needs to appear in the parenthetical citation.
The following examples illustrate both of these techniques:

Parenthetical citation in text

The English, notes Richard Altick, are obsessed by
love for their dogs: "Walking dogs is a ritual that

proceeds independently of weather, cataclysms, and
the movements of the planets; they are led or carried
everywhere, into department stores, fishmongers',
greengrocers', buses, trains" (286).

Citation in works cited

Altick, Richard D. To Be in England. New York: Norton, 1969.

Parenthetical citation in text

"After watching a lot of music videos," Holly Brubach
observes, "it's hard to escape the conclusions that
no one has the nerve to say no to a rock-and-roll star
and that most videos would be better if someone did"
(102).

Citation in works cited

Brubach, Holly. "Rock-and-Roll Vaudeville." Atlantic July 1984: 99-102.

20c

Citing a work by more than one author

When two or three persons wrote the material that you wish
to quote, include the names of all. Follow the same order in which
the names are printed in the original source:

Parenthetical citation in text

Selvin and Wilson argue that "a concern for effective
writing is not a trivial elevation of form over content. Good writing is a condition, slowly achieved,
of . . . being what one means to be" (207).

Citation in works cited

> Selvin, Hanan C., and Everett K. Wilson. "On Sharp-
>
>   ening Sociologists' Prose." <u>Sociological</u>
>
>   <u>Quarterly</u> 25 (1984): 205–22.

When your source is a work by more than three authors, give the name only of the first in your parenthetical text citation, followed by the abbreviation *et al.* (Latin for "and others") not underlined. For example:

> (Leventhal et al. 54)

Citing an anonymous work

If the author of the material you are quoting is not given, use the title, or a shortened form of the title, in your parenthetical text citation. Place the titles of articles in quotation marks; underline the titles of books. Remember that, whenever you quote, you may use part of an author's sentence rather than the whole, as long as the section you have chosen fits into the syntax of your own sentence and does not misrepresent the author's original meaning:

Parenthetical citation in text

> Environmentalists protested that a recent study of
>
> the plan to spray herbicides on marijuana "systemati-
>
> cally underestimated the possibility of damage from
>
> such spraying and exaggerated the benefits to be
>
> achieved by a spraying program" ("Marijuana Spray-
>
> ing" 14).

Citation in works cited

> "Marijuana Spraying Opposed." <u>New York Times</u> 22
>
>   Aug. 1984: 14.

20c

In the case of a one-page article like that above, the page number may be omitted in the text citation.

Citing a multivolume work

The parenthetical text citation to a work in more than one volume includes the volume number and a colon before the page citation:

Parenthetical citation in text

> The medieval manor house dominated nearby cottages
> "not only because it was better built, but above all
> because it was almost invariably designed for de-
> fence" (Bloch 2: 300).

Citation in works cited

> Bloch, Marc. Feudal Society. Trans. L. A. Manyon.
> 2 vols. Chicago: U of Chicago P, 1961.

Citing two works by the same author

20c

If your list of Works Cited includes more than one work by the same author, your parenthetical text citations to this author must indicate which work you are referring to. In such cases, add a shortened version of the relevant title. In the list of Works Cited, substitute three hyphens and a period for the author's name in the second citation.

Parenthetical citation in text

> "Of America's eastern rivers," writes one historian,
> "none was longer or potentially more important than
> the one the Indians accurately described as the
> 'Long-reach River'--Susquehanna" (Hanlon, Wyoming
> Valley 17).

Citations in works cited

Hanlon, Edward F. The Wyoming Valley: An American

    Portrait. Woodland Hills: Windsor, 1983.

---. "Urban-Rural Cooperation and Conflict in the

    Congress: The Breakdown of the New Deal Coali-

    tion, 1933-1938." Diss. Georgetown U, 1967.

2. Paraphrases

A successful research paper, as we suggested earlier, is more than a string of quotations. Although a strategically placed quotation can help to focus a paragraph or emphasize a point, an extended series of quotations in a research paper often creates the impression of disjointedness and confusion. Look instead for opportunities to express in your own words the ideas that you have discovered during your research.

As the following examples illustrate, the rules described above for acknowledging the sources of quotations also apply to paraphrased material.

20c

Parenthetical citation in text (author's name in parenthetical citation)

The steadily growing role of television in politics

has helped to shift attention away from the politi-

cians' stands on issues to the way they appear before

the camera (Meyrowitz 51).

Citation in works cited

Meyrowitz, Joshua. "Politics in the Video Eye: Where

    Have All the Heroes Gone?" Psychology Today

    July 1984: 46-51.

Parenthetical citation in text (author's name incorporated into text)

One effect of the microscope's development in the
late 1600s, Paul Fussell points out, was to change
attitudes toward insects. Whereas people in the seventeenth century had considered insects innocuous
creatures, eighteenth-century men and women, exposed for the first time to drawings of magnified insect bodies, regarded them as hideous and contemptible (235-36).

Citation in works cited

Fussell, Paul. The Rhetorical World of Augustan Humanism: Ethics and Imagery from Swift to Burke.
London: Oxford UP, 1965.

Parenthetical citation in text (source with two authors)

Computers may be dominating the modern office, but
architects are beginning to counter this technological takeover by designing comfortable and inviting
office interiors (Davies and Malone 73).

Citation in works cited

Davies, Douglas, and Maggie Malone. "Offices of the
Future." Newsweek 14 May 1984: 72+.

Parenthetical citation in text (anonymous source)

Some airport delays, it appears, can be blamed on government deregulation of the airlines. On at least

20c

one weekday at Kennedy International Airport, for
example, airlines have now scheduled over sixty ar-
rivals between four and five o'clock, even though
the airport can accommodate only forty-nine landings
each hour ("Not Quite Ready" 25).

Citation in works cited

"Not Quite Ready When You Are." Time 9 July 1984:
25.

3. Content notes

Although footnotes have been eliminated from the citing of
sources in the MLA system of documentation, they may still be used
to add supplementary information to the text of a research paper.
Such notes, often referred to as **content notes,** are indicated in the
text with consecutive superscript numerals and are placed either at
the bottom of the appropriate page or together on a separate sheet,
with the heading "Notes," inserted after the text of the paper and
before the Works Cited page. If you collect your notes together on a
separate sheet, as most instructors prefer, double-space between and
within the notes. Indent the first line of each note five spaces.

Content notes offer a convenient means of including explanatory
material or referring the reader to additional sources of information:

Text with superscript

The art of biographical writing in nineteenth-century England has generally been undervalued,[1] with
the result that modern readers tend to regard Victorian biographies with a certain condescension and
smugness.

Note

¹ A few recent authors, however, have recognized the artistic merit of at least some nineteenth-century biographical writing. For useful readings of several major biographies of the period, see Gwiasda and Reed.

The full publication information for sources mentioned in notes is supplied in the Works Cited list:

Citations in works cited

Gwiasda, Karl E. "The Boswell Biographers: A Study of 'Life and Letters' Writing in the Victorian Period." Diss. Northwestern U, 1969.

Reed, Joseph W., Jr. English Biography in the Early Nineteenth Century, 1801–1838. New Haven: Yale UP, 1966.

20d

20d Formatting the research paper

The physical appearance of a research paper makes its own contribution to the paper's effectiveness. A meticulously prepared paper naturally inclines the reader to expect content of equal quality. Haphazard typing, by contrast, can undercut the authority of even the best research and writing by giving a reader the impression of hasty and careless work. Proper format, therefore, is more than a superficial concern.

The format guidelines below are based on those suggested by the Modern Language Association. Your instructor may give you supplementary or alternative instructions to follow.

1. Paper

Using a typewriter or computer printer with a fresh ribbon, type or print out your research paper on standard 8½-by-11-inch white bond. Do not use onionskin paper, which is hard to read, or erasable typing paper, which easily smears. For convenient reading, most instructors prefer that the pages of a research paper be held together with a paper clip rather than stapled or fastened in a folder.

2. Spacing and margins

Double-space everything in your paper—text, long quotations, notes, and Works Cited list. Double-space as well between page headings (such as "Works Cited") and the first line of text on the page.

Leave a one-inch margin on the top, bottom, and sides of each page. Page headings such as "Notes" and "Works Cited" are centered just within this margin, one inch from the top of the page. Page numbers are placed outside the top margin, one-half inch from the top of the page and one inch from the right side of the page. Number all pages, including the first. You should not use punctuation or abbreviations such as *p.* with page numbers; however, to guard against pages becoming separated and misplaced, you may precede the number on the top of each page with your last name: Smith 1, Smith 2, and so on.

20d

3. Title page

Do not include a separate title page unless your instructor specifically requests it. Instead, on four separate double-spaced lines in the upper left corner of the first page, type your name, the name of your instructor, the course number, and the date. Double-space, center the title of your paper, and double-space to begin the text of the paper. Double-space between lines of your title if it runs onto a second line. (See the sample title page on page 415.)

EXERCISE 1

Treat each of the passages below as if it were to become part of a research paper you are writing. In each case, compose the following:

1. A few sentences of your own incorporating an acceptable paraphrase of one or more of the ideas in the passage.
2. A few sentences of your own incorporating a quotation taken from the passage. (Remember that if you quote only part of a sentence, the phrase or clause that you quote must fit into the syntax of your sentence.)
3. A citation of the source in proper form for a Works Cited list.

Remember to include appropriate parenthetical text citations in your sentences for the first two items above.

1. Los Angeles, one might reasonably guess, is the most prodigious user of water in the state of California, if not the entire world. At least 12 million people inhabit the metropolitan region, a sightless sprawl that has filled a basin twice the size of Luxembourg and is spilling into the ultramontane deserts beyond. The climate is semi-arid to emphatically dry, although many people, including Anglenos, seem surprised when you point this out, because enough water comes in by aqueduct each day (about two billion gallons) to have transformed this former stubbly grassland and alkali waste into an ersatz Miami, six times as large. Los Angeles now diverts the entire flow of the Owens River, one of the largest of the eastern Sierra Nevada streams; it appropriates a substantial share of the Colorado River, the largest by far in the American Southwest; it siphons off about a third of the flow of the Feather River, one of the biggest in the state, through an aqueduct 445 miles long. The few meager streams in and around the basin have long since been sucked dry.

20d

   In Los Angeles, even after months of habitual drought (southern California is virtually rainless from April through November), the fastidiously manicured lawns remain green. The swimming pools remain filled, eight million cars well washed. There are verdant cemeteries for humans and their pets. The Palm Springs Chamber of Commerce boasts of more than 100 golf courses, shining like green lakes in that desiccated landscape, where it rains about four inches in a typical year. Los Angeles is a palpable mirage, a vast outdoor Disneyland, the Babylon and Ur of the desert empire that is the American West.

[The opening two paragraphs of an article in the bimonthly magazine Greenpeace. The title of the article is The Emerald Desert; the author is Marc Reisner; the article appears on pages 6 to 10 of the July-August 1989 issue.]

2. What were the Romans like at that time—at the beginning of contact with the older Greeks in the middle of the third century B.C.? They were a small group of a few hundred thousand souls, one group of several that had emerged from barbarous central Europe and pushed their way into Italy in search for land, and they had long plodded on in silence at the dull task of making the soil provide food. For a while they had been subdued by the Etruscans, but taught by their conquerors to use arms in strong masses, they had applied this lesson by driving off their oppressors and re-establishing their old independent town meetings, returning again to the tilling of the soil. A prolific and puritanic folk with a strict social morality, they outgrew their boundaries and began to expand. In the contests that resulted the Romans came off the victors. In [page break] organizing the adjacent tribes into a federal union they revealed a peculiar liberalism—unmatched anywhere among the barbarians of that day—by abstaining from the exaction of tribute; they also betrayed an imagination of high quality in the invention of cooperative leagues, and unusual capacity for legal logic in the shaping of municipal and civic forms.

   [A passage on pages 9 and 10 (note the page break indicated in this excerpt) in Tenney Frank's book Life and Literature in the Roman Republic, originally published in 1930 as volume seven of the Sather Classical Lectures, republished in 1965 by the University of California Press at Berkeley.]

20d

3. In a Boston business district that lately has been overwhelmed by glass and metal office towers, oddly shaped hotels, and an abundance of trendy shops, a few vestiges of the old "Hub City" remain. Paul Revere's house still stands in a neighborhood that is fighting off condominium developers. Faneuil Hall, a revolutionary war meeting-house, is the centerpiece of a burgeoning plaza full of shops and restaurants. Baseballs still fly over the left-field wall at Fenway Park, one of the last surviving stadiums that knew Babe Ruth. And then there's South Station.

   Once South Station dominated its neighborhood in Dewey Square; now it lays in the shadow of several of those new office towers. But at age 90, South Station is nearing the end of a major facelift that will ensure its status as a Boston landmark into the next century. At the same time, South Station remains one of the busiest stations on Amtrak's busiest route, the Northeast Corridor, of which it is the northern anchor.

[From page 38 of an article by Tom Nelligan in Trains, a monthly magazine. The article, entitled Boston South Station Revival, runs from page 38 to page 42 in the June 1989 issue.]

4. In the second half of the seventeenth century, Holland, a term used to describe the seven United Provinces of the Northern Netherlands, was at the peak of its world power and prestige. With its dense, teeming population of two million hard-working Dutchmen crowded into a tiny area, Holland was by far the richest, most urbanized, most cosmopolitan state in Europe. Not surprisingly, the prosperity of this small state was a source of wonder and envy to its neighbors, and often this envy turned to greed. On such occasions, the Dutch drew on certain national characteristics to defend themselves. They were valiant, obstinate and resourceful, and when they fought—first against the Spaniards, then against the English and finally against the French—they fought in a way which was practical and, at the same time, desperately and sublimely heroic.

[Passage is on page 178 of Peter the Great: His Life and World, by Robert K. Massie, published in 1981 in New York by Ballantine Books. The book was first published by Alfred A. Knopf in 1980.]

5. Pity the Pilgrims, who stepped ashore to confront a wall of forest and a cruel joke beneath the trees. New England stands on granite. Except for the silted beaver meadows and alluvial valleys like the Connecticut, the glaciers left the colonists only a thin mantle of hilly, stony soil. The Southeast also was of mineral-poor rock, and it had weathered too long in the rain. Save for the river deltas and the limestone valleys, its old soils were largely pooped out before the first ax rang in the forest.

[Passage is on page 376 of an article by Boyd Gibbons on pages 350 to 388 of National Geographic, September, 1984. The title of the article is Do We Treat Our Soil Like Dirt?]

20d

21 *Student Research Paper A: MLA Documentation*

Suzanne Conlon's research paper, "Anne Bradstreet's Homespun Cloth: The First American Poems," may be a bit shorter than the paper you are working on, but it illustrates well the principles of research that we have been discussing in the last four chapters.

First, Conlon positions and develops her thesis very effectively. It comes at the end of two paragraphs of introduction, paragraphs that give even the reader who knows nothing about Bradstreet and her times enough information to follow the paper's argument. In the rest of the paper, Conlon develops that argument—that Bradstreet's poetry reflects her human rebelliousness as well as her Puritan submissiveness—by interweaving her own analyses of key poems with the observations of other critics.

This deft and unobtrusive use of sources is in fact one of the paper's main strengths. The facts and brief quotations that Conlon inserts here and there add texture to her analysis without overshadowing her own presence in the paper. The paper never becomes a mere summary of other people's ideas; instead, it remains sharply analytical, punctuated by Conlon's subtle reminders of the way in which the points she is making advance her thesis.

For the origin of Conlon's title, see her analysis of Bradstreet's poem "The Author to Her Book" in the fourth paragraph of the paper.

21

Conlon has quoted rather than paraphrased Rich's words because they offer an especially vivid impression of the Massachusetts Bay Colony. The themes of desolation and hardship that the quotation introduces will be important to Conlon's analysis of Bradstreet's poetry.

Compare Conlon's excerpt from Bradstreet's letter to her children with the original text:

> After a short time I changed my condition and was married, and came into this country, where I found a new world and new manners, at which my heart rose. But after I was convinced it was the way of God, I submitted to it and joined to the church at Boston.

Conlon has selected only the passage in these sentences that directly relates to Bradstreet's reactions to the New World and has inserted in brackets the words *in revolt* to clarify the intended meaning in Bradstreet's somewhat ambiguously worded sentence. The ellipses at the end of the quotation indicate the omission of the final words of the original text. The superscript *1*, raised a half-line, refers the reader to the content note after the last page of the paper.

Suzanne E. Conlon

Professor Les Perelman

English 100

February 22, 1990

Anne Bradstreet's Homespun Cloth:

The First American Poems

In 1630 a young Englishwoman sailed for the New World with her husband and parents aboard the <u>Arbella</u>, the flagship of the Winthrop fleet carrying Puritan settlers from Southampton to the Massachusetts Bay Colony (White 103). The voyage was rough and uncomfortable, and the landing was not quite the relief that the eighteen-year-old bride had expected; she had been brought, in Adrienne Rich's words, to "the wild coast of Massachusetts Bay, the blazing heat of an American June, the half-dying, famine-ridden frontier village of Salem, clinging to the edge of an incalculable land-mass" (ix). Forty years later Bradstreet was to write in a letter to her children that she "found a new world and new manners, at which my heart rose [in revolt]. But after I was convinced it was the way of God, I submitted to it . . . ." ("To My Dear Children").[1]

21

The long Richardson quotation has been cut down by the two omissions indicated with ellipses. The omitted words are irrelevant to Conlon's point here. Note that a quotation with ellipses must make grammatical and logical sense without the omitted words.

21

The factual information about the publication of Bradstreet's book is available in many sources and may therefore be considered common knowledge. It does not need specific documentation.

2

The conflict between revulsion and submission
that Bradstreet expresses in these lines can be
traced to her Puritan background. As one scholar explains, "The Puritan was always trying to achieve a
balance between this world and the next. . . . One
could not safely turn one's back on this world, for
the simple reason that God has made it and found it
good; yet one could not rely upon . . . an earthly
life which was, at last, insubstantial" (Richardson
317–18). Anne Bradstreet's dilemma involved a similar conflict between opposite impulses. Instead of
loving the New World, she at first hated the harsh
life it imposed on colonists, but this feeling went
against her conviction that God's will demanded her
to stay there and submit. Eventually she managed to
strike her own balance: despite periods of doubt and
depression, she bore and raised eight children in
the wilderness near Andover, and in intervals stolen
from her scanty leisure time she wrote five long
didactic poems. The poems had been collected in manuscript as a present for her father, Thomas Dudley,
and they were not meant to be published. But her
brother-in-law took the manuscript with him on a
journey to England and had it printed, as a surprise,

Conlon has used her first two paragraphs to establish the background needed for an understanding of Bradstreet—her arrival in America, her conflicting attitudes toward the New World, the essential elements of her Puritan background, and the origins of her book. All of these points converge in Conlon's thesis at the end of paragraph 2—that Bradstreet's poetry combines rebelliousness and submission in an American variation of the Puritan dilemma.

21

Conlon has skillfully fitted the lines of verse that she quotes into the grammatical structure of her sentence. Compare her excerpt with the complete stanza in Bradstreet's poem:

> I am obnoxious to each carping tongue
> Who says my hand a needle better fits,
> A poet's pen all scorn I should thus wrong,
> For such despite they cast on female wits:
> If what I do prove well, it won't advance,
> They'll say it's stol'n, or else it was by chance.

In Conlon's text, a slash (/) indicates the line division, and her citation provides the title of the poem and the lines she has quoted. (See Conlon's content note after the last page of the paper.)

Conlon quotes rather than paraphrases Cotton Mather because his words vividly illustrate the Puritans' distaste for poetry. The citation "qtd. in Hoffman 253" indicates that Mather's words are directly *quoted* by Hoffman on page 253 of his book. Compare with "Hoffman 253," which would indicate that the words were Hoffman's own.

3

under the title The Tenth Muse, Lately Sprung Up in America. In its combination of human rebelliousness and spiritual submission, Anne Bradstreet's poetry represents an American variation of the "Puritan dilemma" (Miller and Johnson 2: 287) as it was experienced by a sensitive, cultivated, and pious woman of early New England.

A good Puritan woman was supposed to base her life on submission to God and to subordinate her own interests to the welfare of her father, husband, and family. Anne Bradstreet was fully aware of "each carping tongue/Who says my hand a needle better fits" ("The Prologue" 27–28). Such critics held that it was an aberration for a woman to write at all. It was even more unseemly, if not actually sinful, for a Puritan woman to write poetry. To the Puritan mind, poetry represented attachment to the things of this world: to words rather than to the dogma that words were meant to communicate, to the natural world rather than to the Heavenly Kingdom, to loved ones rather than to God. Cotton Mather, the great Puritan preacher, announced magisterially that poets were "the most numerous as well as the most venomous authors" in the Devil's Library on earth (qtd. in Hoff-

Anne Bradstreet's poem "The Author to Her Book" is reprinted below. Note that Conlon has selected from it just those phrases she needs and has fitted them smoothly into her own sentence structure to create a concise and effective summary.

The Author to Her Book

Thou ill-formed offspring of my feeble brain,
Who after birth didst by my side remain,
Till snatched from thence by friends, less wise than true,
Who thee abroad, exposed to public view,
Made thee in rags, halting to th' press to trudge,
Where errors were not lessened (all may judge).
At thy return my blushing was not small,
My rambling brat (in print) should mother call,
I cast thee by as one unfit for light,
Thy visage was so irksome in my sight;
Yet being mine own, at length affection would
Thy blemishes amend, if so I could:
I washed thy face, but more defects I saw,
And rubbing off a spot still made a flaw.
I stretched thy joints to make thee even feet,
Yet still thou run'st more hobbling than is meet;
In better dress to trim thee was my mind,
But nought save homespun cloth i' th' house I find.
In this array 'mongst vulgars may'st thou roam.
In critic's hands beware thou dost not come,
And take thy way where yet thou art not known;
If for thy father asked, say thou hadst none;
And for thy mother, she alas is poor,
Which caused her thus to send thee out of door.

Here Conlon is moving from the first main section of her paper, which deals with Anne Bradstreet's earlier poems and the background against which she wrote them, to the second main section, which is concerned with a closer look at Bradstreet's later poetry. Conlon makes her transition effectively, using a quotation from Bradstreet's early work to introduce the point that there is "another voice" in the first volume of poems, "forceful, ironic, intelligent."

4

man 253). Any woman who attempted to join this company was apt to come to a bad end, as had the wife of the governor of Hartford, Connecticut, who had suffered insanity because, it was alleged, of her devotion to reading and writing. There was also the example of the sister of Bradstreet's husband, disgraced in her family for "Irregular Prophecying" and preaching in England, as well as Bradstreet's friend Anne Hutchinson, expelled by the Massachusetts Bay Colony for listening to the inner voice of God rather than to the elders of the Church (White 173–76).

Such consequences of speaking out may have prompted Bradstreet's humility in her early verse, which she describes meekly as the "ill–formed offspring of my feeble brain." She had hoped, she continues, to trim her "rambling brat" in better dress, though "nought save homespun cloth i' th' house I find" ("The Author to Her Book" 1, 9, 19). It is an apt phrase to describe the mixture of pedantic learning, dull moralizing, and poetic cliché that made the book popular in its own time. But another voice also speaks out in this first volume, a forceful, ironic, intelligent voice, as in these lines from "In Honour of Queen Elizabeth":

21

21

Conlon's analyses of "Before the Birth of One of Her Children" and of "Contemplations" focus on the tension between the human and the spiritual in Bradstreet—the point asserted in the paper's thesis.

5

> Now say, have women worth? or have they
>
>> none?
>
> Or had they some, but with our Queen is't
>
>> gone?
>
> Nay masculines, you have thus taxed us
>
>> long,
>
> But she, though dead, will vindicate our
>
>> wrong.
>
> Let such as say our sex is void of reason,
>
> Know 'tis a slander now but once was
>
>> treason. (99–104)

As she set about revising her poems and adding to them
in the second edition, Anne Bradstreet drew upon this
voice. Instead of writing what she thought was expected of a Puritan poet, she now wrote what she felt,
drawing for material on the timeless events of a
woman's personal life. The tension generated by the
persistent conflict between the duty owed to God and
the human concerns of Bradstreet's everyday world
gives strength and vitality to these later poems.

A typical example is "Before the Birth of One
of Her Children," which expresses Bradstreet's
fears, well founded in the seventeenth century, of
dying in childbirth. Her sadness arises not from terror of the afterlife, for she had the Puritan's confi-

In each of these paragraphs, Conlon gives the title of the poem being quoted in the first sentence; citations to the poem later in the paragraph, therefore, need to provide only the appropriate line numbers.

21

6

dence in salvation, but from imagined grief at leaving her husband. The tears that dropped on her manuscript, she writes, fell also for her children, and
she begged her husband to "protect [them] from step-
dame's injury" (26).

"Contemplations," by common agreement the most
successful of her poems, has as its underlying theme
the truth that earth as well as heaven declares the
glory of the Lord. Looking at the autumnal splendor
of the New England landscape, Bradstreet asks:

> If so much excellence abide below,
> How excellent is He that dwells on high,
> Whose power and beauty by his works we
> know? (10-12)

Though the poem unflinchingly faces the passing of
fragile beauty and human life into the everlasting-
ness of God, the poet nevertheless lingers for a long,
loving look by the river's bank with her senses full
and a "thousand fancies buzzing in my brain" (178).
"Contemplations" has been called the first American
nature poem (Waggoner 8).

Another theme that evokes the best in Bradstreet
is the terrible mystery of the early death of children. Three of her grandchildren died within five

Again, ellipses and brackets indicate Conlon's changes in the original text of Bradstreet's poem:

> But plants new set to be eradicate,
> And buds new blown to have so short a date,
> Is by His hand alone that guides nature and fate.

Conlon again returns explicitly to her thesis by pointing out Bradstreet's "submissiveness" and her "protest."

21

7

years, and Bradstreet's protest at this eradication
of "plants new set . . . [a]nd buds new blown" ("In
Memory of My Dear Grandchild Elizabeth Bradstreet"
17-18) is at first bitter, revealing a dark root of
anger and grief. In the end, as always, she submits:

> Such was His will, but why, let's not
> dispute,
> With humble hearts and mouths put in the
> dust,
> Let's say He's merciful as well as just.
> ("On My Dear Grandchild Simon Bradstreet"
> 10-12)

Along with the submissiveness, one hears in such
poems as this the persistent protest of Bradstreet's
heart against the desolate life in this new world.

One of the senseless accidents of life that the
Puritan was bound to accept as part of God's merciful
Providence was the loss of worldly goods. When the
Bradstreet house burned down through the carelessness of a servant, she lost not only her shelter from
the New England weather but all the little personal
possessions that had helped to make her new life tol-
erable. Compared to the modest wealth she had known
in England, her American treasures must have been

Student Research Paper A: MLA Documentation

No colon is needed to introduce the quotation after the word *places*, because the quoted lines are grammatically part of the sentence that introduces them.

If a verse quotation begins in the middle of a line, indent the first line several additional spaces. Again, no introductory colon is needed here, because the quoted lines complete Conlon's own sentence.

21

In the paper's conclusion, Conlon deftly echoes her thesis by stressing the way in which the human concerns of Bradstreet's poetry represent a break from her Old-World Puritan roots.

8

paltry, but losing them was still painful, and her
grief was real as she looked at the places

> Where oft I sat and long did lie:
> Here stood that trunk, and there that
>   chest,
> There lay that store I counted best.
> ("Some Verses upon the Burning of Our
> House" 28–30)

But Bradstreet well knew the Puritan's answer to such
tribulation. She might feel sorrow at the sight of
her treasures now in ashes, but

> when I could no longer look,
> I blest His name that gave and took,
> That laid my goods now in the dust. (17–19)

Bradstreet's later poems, in which the Old World
and its old history are forgotten and the New World
and its trees and small graves are remembered, assure
her a prominent place in the American tradition. The
recognition that came with the publication of her
first poems seems to have freed her to write poetry
about what she saw and touched and lost. These later
poems still stand, more than three hundred years after she wrote them, as honest testaments of the human
condition as one woman saw it.

21

Note

¹ Quotations from Bradstreet's works are taken from the Hensley edition. Line numbers are given for verse quotations.

Works Cited

Bradstreet, Anne. The Works of Anne Bradstreet. Ed.
    Jeannine Hensley. Cambridge: Harvard UP,
    1967.

Hoffman, Daniel G., ed. American Poetry and Poet-
    ics. Garden City: Anchor–Doubleday, 1962.

Miller, Perry, and T. H. Johnson. The Puritans. 2
    vols. New York: Harper, 1963.

Rich, Adrienne. Foreword. The Works of Anne Brad-
    street. Ed. Jeannine Hensley. Cambridge:
    Harvard UP, 1967. ix–xx.

Richardson, Robert D., Jr. "The Puritan Poetry of
    Anne Bradstreet." Texas Studies in Litera-
    ture and Language 9 (1967): 317–31.

Waggoner, Hyatt H. American Poets from the Puri-
    tans to the Present. New York: Dell, 1968.

White, Elizabeth Wade. Anne Bradstreet: "The
    Tenth Muse." New York: Oxford UP, 1971.

21

22 *Student Research Paper B: APA Documentation*

Originally formulated more than sixty years ago to guide psychologists in the preparation of scholarly articles, the American Psychological Association's style of documentation is the norm today for professional publication not only in psychology but throughout the social sciences. In this chapter we will discuss and illustrate the features of APA documentation, explain the formatting of a paper prepared according to APA guidelines, and close with a sample student research paper documented in APA style.

22a Using APA documentation

APA documentation style resembles MLA documentation in its use of brief parenthetical references in the text to a list of full citations—called a reference list—at the end of the paper. But subtle differences distinguish the two methods of documentation. If you are already familiar with MLA documentation style, you will want to keep in mind the following distinctive characteristics of APA reference list citations.

1. Initials are always used in place of an author's first and middle names.
2. The author's name is always followed immediately by the date of his or her publication in parentheses. The remaining publication information comes later in the citation.
3. Not every major word in the title of a book or periodical article is capitalized; only the first word of the title, the first word of a subtitle, and any proper nouns in the title are capitalized.
4. The second and subsequent lines of each citation are indented three spaces, not five.
5. In general, APA documentation uses fewer abbreviations than MLA style; months of the year and names of universities, for example, are written out in full.

22b APA reference list forms

In **22c** and **22d** we will discuss the features of APA parenthetical citations and provide guidelines for formatting the components of a paper prepared in APA style. First, however, we present a list of sample reference citations in APA format for the most frequently used types of source. (For additional information about APA citations, see the *Publication Manual of the American Psychological Association,* cited in item 3 below.)

Table of APA reference forms

Books

1. **Book by one author**
2. **Book by two or more authors**
3. **Book by a committee, commission, association, or other group**
4. **Anonymous book**
5. **Later or revised edition of a book**
6. **Edited book**

22b

7. Translated book
8. Book in more than one volume
9. Republished book

Parts of books

10. Essay in a collection of essays by various authors
11. Journal or magazine article reprinted in a collection of essays by various authors

Articles in journals and magazines

12. Article in a journal paginated by the volume (continuous pagination)
13. Article in a journal paginated issue by issue
14. Article in a weekly magazine
15. Article in a monthly magazine

Articles in newspapers

16. Article in a newspaper
17. Letter to the editor

22b

Other print sources

18. Book review
19. Dissertation, unpublished, microfilm copy
20. Dissertation, unpublished, manuscript copy
21. Encyclopedia article
22. Government document
23. Interview, published
24. Proceedings of a conference
25. Report

Nonprint sources

26. Computer software
27. Film, videotape, audiotape, slides, chart, artwork
28. Lecture, unpublished

Books

1. Book by one author

Hayes, J. R. (1978). Cognitive psychology: Think-

    ing and creating. Homewood, IL: Dorsey Press.

- Capitalize only the first word of the title and the first word of the subtitle (and proper nouns in the title, if any).
- Add the U.S. Postal Service abbreviation for the state if the city of publication is not well known.
- For nonacademic publishers, use a shortened form of the company's name, omitting such terms as *Co.*, *Inc.*, and *Publishers*. However, write out in full the names of university presses (see item 7 below).

2. Book by two or more authors

Clark, H. H., & Clark, E. V. (1977). Psychology and

    language: An introduction to psycholinguistics.

    New York: Harcourt.

Naylor, J. C., Pritchard, R. D., & Ilgen, D. R.

    (1980). A theory of behavior in organizations.

    New York: Academic Press.

22b

- Regardless of the number of authors, give the names of all in inverted order, following each name with a comma and preceding the last name with an ampersand (&).

3. Book by a committee, commission, association, or other group

American Psychological Association. (1963). Pub-

    lication manual of the American Psychological

    Association (3rd ed.). Washington, DC: Author.

- When the author of the book is also its publisher, substitute the word *Author* for the name of the publisher at the end of the citation.
- The first parenthetical text citation to this work would begin with the joint author's name written out in full: (American Psychological Association [APA], 1963). Since the abbreviation of this association's name is a familiar one, subsequent parenthetical text citations may give only the abbreviation: (APA, 1963). See **22c**.

4. Anonymous book

Research in outdoor education: Summaries of doctoral
      studies. (1973). Washington, DC: American Asso-
      ciation for Health, Physical Education, and Rec-
      reation.

- The parenthetical text citation for an anonymous work begins with the first two or three words of the title: (Research in Outdoor, 1973). See **22c**.

5. Later or revised edition of a book

Phelps, R. R. (1986). A guide to research in music
      education (3rd ed.). Metuchen, NJ: Scarecrow.
Jourard, S. M. (1971). The transparent self
      (rev. ed.). New York: Van Nostrand.

- When information in parentheses follows the title of a book, as it does here, no punctuation appears between the title and the parentheses.

6. Edited book

Halebsky, S. (Ed.). (1973). <u>The sociology of the</u>
 <u>city</u>. New York: Scribner's.

Stam, H. J., Rogers, T. B., & Gergen, K. J. (Eds.).
 (1987). <u>The analysis of psychological theory:</u>
 <u>Metapsychological perspectives</u>. Washington,
 DC: Hemisphere.

7. Translated book

Hauser, A. (1982). <u>The sociology of art</u> (K. J.
 Northcott, Trans.). Chicago: University of Chicago Press. (Original work published 1974)

- In parentheses after the title, supply the translator's name in normal order.
- End the citation with a parenthetical note giving the date of the book's original publication. Do not use punctuation within these parentheses.

8. Book in more than one volume

Ford, J. (1975). <u>Paradigms and fairy tales: An</u>
 <u>introduction to the science of meanings</u> (Vols.
 1-2). London: Routledge.

- After the title, indicate which volumes of the work you refer to in your paper; that information may differ from the total number of volumes in the work.

9. Republished book

Cottrell, F. (1970). <u>Energy and society: The rela-</u>
    <u>tion between energy, social change, and economic</u>
    <u>development</u>. Westport, CT: Greenwood Press.
    (Original work published 1955)

- The copyright page of this book indicates that it was originally
  issued in 1955 by a different publisher. Although information
  about the first publisher is not required in this citation, the
  original publication date is given in a parenthetical note at
  the end of the citation.

Parts of books

10. Essay in a collection of essays by various authors

Boskoff, A. (1964). Recent theories of social
    change. In W. J. Cahnman & A. Boskoff (Eds.),
    <u>Sociology and history</u> (pp. 140–157). New York:
    Free Press of Glencoe.

Tawney, J. W. (1977). Educating severely handi-
    capped children and their parents through tele-
    communications. In N. G. Haring & L. J. Brown
    (Eds.), <u>Teaching the severely handicapped</u>
    (Vol. 2, pp. 315–340). New York: Grune & Stratton.

- Follow the title of the essay by the name(s) of the editor(s)
  of the book in which it is contained, the title of the book,
  and the pages on which the essay is found.
- For an essay in a multivolume collection, include the appropriate volume number as shown in the second example.

- Note that when inclusive page numbers are provided in an APA citation, the complete second number is used (not 315–40, but 315–*340*).

11. Journal or magazine article reprinted in a collection of essays by various authors

```
Motokawa, K.  (1965).  Retinal traces and visual

    perception of movement.  In I. M. Spigel (Ed.),

    Readings in the study of visually perceived

    movement (pp. 288–303).  New York: Harper.

    (Reprinted from the Journal of Experimental

    Psychology, 1953, 45, 369–377)
```

- When information about an article's earlier publication is noted in the collection you are using, provide it in parentheses at the end of the citation.

Articles in journals and magazines

22b

12. Article in a journal paginated by the volume (continuous pagination)

```
Webster, G. R.  (1989).  Partisanship in American

    presidential, senatorial, and gubernatorial

    elections in ten western states.  Political

    Geography Quarterly, 8, 161–179.
```

- Most periodicals published quarterly or less frequently use continuous pagination for all the issues published in a single year; that is, if the year's first issue ends with page 125, the second issue begins with page 126. The citation to such a

periodical includes the name of the journal (underlined), the
volume number (separately underlined), and the first and last
pages of the article (without the abbreviation *pp.*).
• Do not enclose the title of the article in quotation marks.

13. Article in a journal paginated issue by issue

Maranto, C. D. (1987). Continuing concerns in music

therapy ethics. <u>Music Therapy</u>, <u>6</u>(2), 59–63.

• When each issue of a journal begins with page 1, include
the issue number (2) in parentheses immediately after the
underlined volume number (6).

14. Article in a weekly magazine

Jaroff, L. (1989, July 3). Fury on the sun. <u>Time</u>,

pp. 46–55.

Running up a global tab. (1989, July 10). <u>Time</u>,

p. 47.

• Give the date with the year first, followed by the month,
unabbreviated, and the day.
• End the citation with the page number or numbers of the
article, preceded by *p.* ("page") or *pp.* ("pages").
• For an anonymous article, begin the citation with the title.

15. Article in a monthly magazine

Hill, J. V. (1989, May). The design and procurement

of training simulators. <u>Educational Technology</u>,

pp. 26–27.

Healthy eating in Europe. (1989, May). <u>World</u>

<u>Health</u>, p. 30.

Articles in newspapers

16. Article in a newspaper

Freitag, M. (1989, August 17). The battle over
   medical costs. New York Times, pp. 25, 28.
U.S. panel weighs birth pill warning. (1989, March
   29). Chicago Sun-Times, p. 2.

- If an article is continued on nonconsecutive pages, give all
  page numbers, separated by commas: pp. 25, 28.

17. Letter to the editor

Capezza, D. (1989, July 13). Of course, oil spills
   can be prevented [Letter to the editor]. New York
   Times, p. A22.

- Follow the editor's title (if one exists) by a bracketed notation
  identifying the piece as a letter.

22b

Other print sources

18. Book review

Kimble, G. A. (1988). Psychology's brief history
   [Review of Historical foundations of modern psychology]. Contemporary Psychology,
   33, 878-879.
Belotti, M. (1988). [Review of The paradox of poverty: A reappraisal of economic development policy].
   Journal of Economic Literature, 26, 1233-1234.

- If the review has a title, give it before the bracketed notation identifying the piece as a review.
- Note that the name of the author of the work being reviewed does not appear in the citation.

19. Dissertation, unpublished, microfilm copy

```
Johnson, T. P.  (1989).  The social environment and
     health.  Dissertation Abstracts International,
     49, 3514A.  (University Microfilms No. 8903561)
```

- Use this format if your source is a university microfilm copy of a dissertation. Note that the date given refers to this volume of *Dissertation Abstracts International,* not the date of the dissertation itself.

20. Dissertation, unpublished, manuscript copy

```
Johnson, T. P.  (1989).  The social environment and
     health (Doctoral dissertation, University of
     Kentucky, 1988).  Dissertation Abstracts In-
     ternational, 49, 3514A.
```

- Use this format if your source is a manuscript copy of a dissertation. When the dates of the dissertation and of the publication of its abstract in *Dissertation Abstracts International* differ, as they do here, the parenthetical text citation includes both: (Johnson, 1988/1989).

21. Encyclopedia article

```
Dashiell, J. F.  (1983).  Behaviorism.  In Ency-
     clopedia Americana (Vol. 3, pp. 469–471).
     Danbury, CT: Grolier.
```

- Treat an encyclopedia article the same as an article in a multi-volume collection of essays by different authors (see item 10 above).

22. Government document

U.S. Women's Bureau. (1975). <u>Handbook on women</u>
<u>workers</u>. Washington, DC: U.S. Government Print-
ing Office.

23. Interview, published

Lyman, F. (1988, January). [Interview with Maggie
Kuhn, founder of the Gray Panthers]. <u>The Pro-</u>
<u>gressive</u>, pp. 29–31.

- If an interview has a title, insert the title before the bracketed notation that identifies the piece and its subject (see item 17 above).

24. Proceedings of a conference

Genaway, D. C. (Ed.). (1983). <u>Conference on inte-</u>
<u>grated online library systems</u>. Canfield, OH:
Genaway & Associates.

Stilson, D. W. (1957). A multidimensional psycho-
physical method for investigating visual form.
In J. W. Wulfeck & J. H. Taylor (Eds.), <u>Proceed-</u>
<u>ings of a Symposium Sponsored by the Armed</u>
<u>Forces–NRC Committee on Vision</u> (pp. 54–64).
Washington, DC: National Academy of Sciences–
National Research Council.

22b

- Use the first form for a citation to the collected proceedings of a conference, the second for a citation to a single article in such a collection.

25. Report

Butler, E. W., Chapin, F. S., Hemmens, G. C., Kaiser, E. J., Stegman, M. A., & Weiss, S. F. (1969). <u>Moving behavior and residential choice: A national survey</u> (National Cooperative Highway Research Program Rep. No. 81). Chapel Hill: University of North Carolina, Center for Urban and Regional Studies.

Price, M. E., & Botein, M. (1973). <u>Cable television: Citizen participation after the franchise</u> (Research Rep. No. R–1139–NSF). Santa Monica, CA: Rand.

- If the report has been given a number, supply it in parentheses after the title.

Nonprint sources

26. Computer software

Etter T., & Chamberlain, W. (1984). <u>Racter</u> [Computer program]. Northbrook, IL: Mindscape.

27. Film, videotape, audiotape, slides, charts, artwork

Messecar, R. (Author & Producer/Editor), & Hales, D. (Author). (1982). <u>Theater of the night:</u>

> The science of sleep and dreams [Film]. Pleas-
>
> antville, NY: Human Relations Media.
>
> Jordan, P. (Producer & Director). (1974). Preju-
>
> dice: Causes, consequences, cures [Videotape].
>
> Carlsbad, CA: CRM Films.

- Identify the functions of major contributors in parentheses after their names.
- Identify the medium in brackets after the title of the work.

28. Lecture, unpublished

> Zappen, J. P. (1989, March). Scientific rhetoric
>
> in the nineteenth and early twentieth centuries.
>
> Paper presented at the Conference on College Com-
>
> position and Communication, Seattle, WA.

- Include the month of the meeting or conference at which the lecture was delivered.

22c

22c Citing sources in APA style

APA text citations, like MLA citations, are inserted into the text parenthetically. But APA parenthetical citations differ from MLA citations in three ways:

1. The APA citation includes the author's name and the year of publication of the source. The page number is added only when a quotation is being cited.
2. The elements in an APA parenthetical citation are separated by commas.
3. The abbreviations *p.* and *pp.* are used with page numbers.

Compare the following examples of parenthetical citations in APA style with the corresponding MLA citations described in **20c.**

1. Quotations

As in MLA format, the parenthetical citation in the text comes *after* the quotation marks that close the quotation but *before* the sentence's end punctuation:

Parenthetical citation in text

The definitive biography of Mahatma Gandhi remains
to be written. As one Gandhi scholar has explained,
"Multivolume works written by Gandhi's former colleagues and published in India are comprehensive in
scope, but their objectivity suffers from the authors' reverent regard for their subject" (Juergensmeyer, 1984, p. 294).

Citation in reference list

Juergensmeyer, M. (1984). The Gandhi revival--A
      review article. Journal of Asian Studies, 43,
      293-298.

Below are some variations on this basic method of documenting quotations.

Setting off a long quotation

A quotation of more than forty words is set off from the text and indented five spaces from the left margin. Such a quotation is commonly introduced with a colon, and the parenthetical citation is placed after the end punctuation:

Parenthetical citation in text

One editor suggests that photographers trying to publish their work should aim to surpass--not just
equal--the photographs they see in print:

22c

Editors know where they can get pictures like
the ones they've already published. If you want
to get noticed, you have to take pictures better
than those. This is especially true if you are
looking for assignments rather than to sell existing pictures. Why take a chance on a new photographer who will come up with no better than
what you already have, an editor might reason?
(Scully, 1984, p. 33)

Citation in reference list

Scully, J. (1984, May). Seeing pictures. Modern
Photography, pp. 28–33.

Incorporating the author's name into the text

If you introduce a quotation by mentioning the author's name
in your text, use only the author's last name, unless first initials are
needed to distinguish between two authors with the same surname.
Follow the author's name immediately with the year of the source's
publication in parentheses. The page number, also in parentheses, comes
after the quotation:

22c

Parenthetical citation in text

The English, notes Altick (1969), are obsessed by
love for their dogs: "Walking dogs is a ritual that
proceeds independently of weather, cataclysms, and
the movements of the planets; they are led or carried
everywhere, into department stores, fishmongers',
greengrocers', buses, trains" (p. 286).

Citation in reference list

> Altick, R. D. (1969). <u>To be in England</u>. New York:
>
> Norton.

Citing a work by more than one author

If your source was written by two authors, include the names of both in the parenthetical text citation, following the same order in which the names are printed in the original source:

Parenthetical citation in text

> Selvin and Wilson (1984) argue that "a concern for
>
> effective writing is not a trivial elevation of form
>
> over content. Good writing is a condition, slowly
>
> achieved, of . . . being what one means to be" (p.
>
> 207).

or

> Two sociologists argue that "a concern for effective
>
> writing is not a trivial elevation of form over con-
>
> tent. Good writing is a condition, slowly achieved,
>
> of . . . being what one means to be" (Selvin & Wilson,
>
> 1984, p. 207).

Citation in reference list

> Selvin, H. C., & Wilson, E. K. (1984). On sharpening
>
> sociologists' prose. <u>Sociological Quarterly</u>,
>
> <u>25</u>, 205–222.

Note the following variations on this rule when more than two authors are involved:

22c

1. When the source was written by three to five authors, give all their names in the first parenthetical text citation, but in subsequent citations include in the parenthetical text citation the name of the first author only, followed by the abbreviation *et al.* (Latin for "and others"; the abbreviation is not underlined): (O'Malley et al., 1990, p. 101).
2. When six or more authors are involved, give the name of the first author only, followed by the abbreviation *et al.*, in all parenthetical text citations.

Note, however, that the reference list citation includes the names of all authors, regardless of the number.

Citing an anonymous work

If you quote an anonymous work, use the first two or three words of the title in your parenthetical text citation. Place the titles of articles in quotation marks (but note that they are not enclosed in quotation marks in the reference list citation), and underline the titles of books. Capitalize all major words of the title in the parenthetical text citation (but not in the reference list citation).

22c

Parenthetical citation in text

Environmentalists protested that a recent study of the plan to spray herbicides on marijuana "systematically underestimated the possibility of damage from such spraying and exaggerated the benefits to be achieved by a spraying program" ("Marijuana Spraying," 1984, p. 14).

Citation in reference list

Marijuana spraying opposed. (1984, August 22). New York Times, p. 14.

Citing a multivolume work

The volume number of a multivolume work appears in the parenthetical text citation only when the reference list citation indicates that more than one volume of the work has been consulted (see item 8 in **22b** above).

Parenthetical citation in text

```
The medieval manor house dominated nearby cottages
"not only because it was better built, but above all
because it was almost invariably designed for
defence" (Bloch, 1961, Vol. 2, p. 300).
```

Citation in reference list

```
Bloch, M. (1961). Feudal society (L. A. Manyon,
    Trans., Vols. 1-2). Chicago: University of Chi-
    cago Press. (Original work published 1939)
```

22c

Citing two works by the same author

If the sources you use include more than one work by the same author, the date that you give in each parenthetical text citation may alone be sufficient to indicate which work is being cited. If more than one work by an author has been published in the same year, however, differentiate among works by adding lowercase letters to the dates in *both* the reference list and the parenthetical text citations:

Parenthetical citations in text

```
(Gilbert, 1985a, p. 112)
(Gilbert, 1985b, pp. 164-165)
```

Citations in reference list

Gilbert, L. A. (1985a). Dimensions of same-gender
   student-faculty role-model relationships. <u>Sex</u>
   <u>Roles</u>, <u>12</u>, 111-123.
Gilbert, L. A. (1985b). Measures of psychological
   masculinity and femininity: A comment on Gaddy,
   Glass, and Arnkoff. <u>Journal of Counseling Psy-</u>
   <u>chology</u>, <u>32</u>, 163-166.

2. Paraphrases

As we noted above, APA documentation style departs from
MLA style significantly in the case of paraphrasing. In APA style the
parenthetical text citation does not include a page number when the
writer is paraphrasing, rather than quoting, a source.

22c

**Parenthetical citation in text (author's name in parenthetical
citation)**

The steadily growing role of television in politics
has helped to shift attention away from the politicians' stands on issues to the way they appear before
the camera (Meyrowitz, 1984).

Citation in reference list

Meyrowitz, J. (1984, July). Politics in the video
   eye: Where have all the heroes gone? <u>Psychology</u>
   <u>Today</u>, pp. 46-51.

Parenthetical citation in text (author's name incorporated into text)

One effect of the microscope's development in the late 1600s, Fussell (1965) points out, was to change attitudes toward insects. Whereas people in the seventeenth century had considered insects innocuous creatures, eighteenth-century men and women, exposed for the first time to drawings of magnified insect bodies, regarded them as hideous and contemptible.

Citation in reference list

Fussell, P. (1965). The rhetorical world of Augustan humanism: Ethics and imagery from Swift to Burke. London: Oxford University Press.

22d Formatting a paper in APA style

The manuscript style described by the American Psychological Association in its *Publication Manual* is intended primarily for authors who are submitting articles for consideration by professional journals. The writers of the manual note, therefore, that its requirements may need to be modified for use in undergraduate classes.

In the guidelines below, we have modified only the APA's title-page requirements, in order to allow for inclusion of the course number and name of the instructor, as well as the date on which the paper is submitted. Check with your instructor for supplementary or alternative instructions.

1. Paper

Using a typewriter or computer printer with a fresh ribbon, type or print out your research paper on standard 8½-by-11-inch white bond. Avoid dot-matrix computer printers unless they print clearly and legibly. Do not use onionskin or erasable paper.

2. Spacing and margins

Double-space everything in your paper—text, long quotations, footnotes, and reference list. Double-space as well between page headings (such as "References") and the first line of text on the page.

Leave a 1½-inch margin on the top, bottom, and sides of each page. In the upper right corner of each page (including the first), about three-quarters of an inch from the top of the page, type a short title, consisting of the first two or three words of the paper's title. The short title guards against pages becoming separated and misplaced. Double-space after the short title, and number the pages consecutively with Arabic numbers typed under its last character; do not use abbreviations such as *p.* with page numbers. Double-space again on each page to introduce a page heading or continue the text. Type a maximum of twenty-five lines of text on each page.

3. Title page

On four double-spaced lines centered on the title page, provide the following information:

22d

1. The title of your paper, not enclosed in quotation marks or underlined. Capitalize only the first letters of important words in the title. Double-space between the lines of a title typed on more than one line.
2. Your name.
3. The course for which the paper is being submitted, followed by a comma and your professor's name: Psychology 100, Professor Sharon March.
4. The date of submission.

Don't forget to include your short title and first page number on double-spaced lines in the upper right corner. See the sample title page on page 456.

4.   Abstract page

In APA style, a paper begins with an abstract, or summary, of its contents, typed on a separate page. The abstract should be about one hundred words long; it should present the purpose or thesis of your paper, indicate the types of sources you investigated, and state the conclusions you arrived at.

Double-space after typing the page number, and center the word *Abstract* on the next line. Double-space again, and type your abstract in block style—that is, without the usual paragraph indentions. See the sample abstract on page 457.

5.   Text pages

The text of your paper begins on page 3. Double-space after typing the short title and page number, and center your title on the page. Double-space again, and begin the first line of the paper.

6.   References page

22d

In APA format, the sources used in a research paper are listed alphabetically on a final page, with the heading "References" centered at the top of the page. Do not underline this heading or enclose it in quotation marks. Double-space after this heading and give the citation for the first source used; double-space between lines of each citation and between citations. Alphabetize an anonymous source by the first significant word in the reference list citation. See the sample reference list on pages 477–478.

7.   Footnotes page

As in MLA format, content notes, if any, are given on a separate page. In APA format, this page *follows* the reference list page or pages. At the top of the page, center the heading "Footnotes" (or "Footnote," if only one note is given); again, do not underline this heading or enclose it in quotation marks. Double-space between this heading and the first footnote. Begin each footnote with a superior number indented five spaces; do not leave a space between the superior number and the first word of each footnote. Double-space between and within footnotes. See the sample footnotes page on page 479.

22e Sample student paper

Cyndi Lopardo's "Career versus Motherhood: The Debate over Education for Women at the Turn of the Century" is a good example of a paper based on what are called primary sources. Primary sources are raw data, documents, or evidence—for example, the results of experiments; original letters and diaries; historical records; and eyewitness accounts of events. Secondary sources, in contrast, are other writers' commentaries on or analyses of primary works. In this paper Cyndi's primary sources are published articles from the 1890s, from which she has acquired a firsthand sense of contemporary ideas about the education of women.

Cyndi's task in the paper is the same one that confronts every researcher whose work is based on primary sources—to analyze the data, draw conclusions about it, and then present and defend those conclusions to her readers. Of course, the final paper does not include every article Cyndi examined. Instead, having used her reading to develop a thesis, Cindi selects the articles that provide the best evidence for the point she wants to make: that while increasing numbers of women had access to higher education by the end of the nineteenth century, there was widespread feeling that colleges should be specifically training women for motherhood rather than for possible professional careers outside the home.

One of the strengths of this paper is Cyndi's handling of her evidence. In the first place, she blends quotation, paraphrase, and summary well, providing just the right amount of detail necessary for the reader to understand each article she cites. Throughout the paper, moreover, she clearly introduces each piece of evidence, indicating the specific point it is intended to illustrate. Cyndi also effectively groups together similar pieces of evidence and points out their similarities to her readers. The result of all these strategies is a well-organized paper that convincingly supports its thesis.

22e

Career versus Motherhood

1

Career versus Motherhood: The Debate over Education

for Women at the Turn of the Century

Cyndi Lopardo

Education 100, Professor Karen J. Blair

March 20, 1990

22e

Abstract

By 1890, the opening of colleges for women and the advent of coeducation had settled the issue of women's access to higher education. But another question remained unresolved: the purpose of a college education in a woman's life. Articles published during the 1890s on the goals of higher education for women suggest that, despite the professional accomplishments of many educated women in the nineteenth century, social forces were at work to keep women's education focused on the enrichment of home and family. A woman's right to a professional career outside the home would not be recognized until the next century.

22e

Lopardo's opening paragraphs effectively provide background and focus for the paper. The first paragraph identifies educational opportunity as a key element in the women's movement of the nineteenth century; the second focuses on the status of higher education for women in the 1890s; and the third isolates a specific issue in discussions about women's education during that decade. Note the effective transitions between these paragraphs: the first sentence of each paragraph smoothly refers to the key idea in the preceding one.

22e

The original text of the passage that Lopardo quotes from the Seneca Falls Declaration is as follows:

> He has denied her the facilities for obtaining a thorough education, all colleges being closed against her.

APA style permits changing the first letter of a quotation from uppercase to lowercase (or vice versa) without brackets. (In MLA style, such a change would have to be indicated: "[h]e has denied. . . .") Lopardo clarifies the quotation by using brackets to substitute *woman* for *her*.

Career versus Motherhood: The Debate over Education

for Women at the Turn of the Century

The origins of the modern women's movement have

frequently been traced to the convention of women

organized by Elizabeth Cady Stanton and Lucretia Mott

in Seneca Falls, New York, on July 19 and 20, 1848.

Besides launching the drive for women's suffrage,

the Seneca Falls Convention produced a major document

in the history of women's rights. The Declaration

of Sentiments and Resolutions, modeled after the Dec-

laration of Independence, listed both the grievances

and the aspirations of politically active women in

the nineteenth century. To this document the begin-

nings of educational opportunities for women can also

be traced, for one of its stated grievances against

man was that "he has denied [woman] the facilities

for obtaining a thorough education, all colleges be-

ing closed against her" ("Seneca Falls Declaration,"

1973, p. 316).

The participants in the Seneca Falls Convention

could not have foreseen how quickly that inequity

would be remedied. By 1890, many of the women's col-

leges that are today associated with excellence in

In APA style, paraphrased material is cited by author and date alone. Page numbers are included only after quotations.

Lopardo's third paragraph introduces the evidence she will present—published articles from the 1890s—and ends with the thesis she will argue.

22e

APA style encourages the use of subheadings to highlight a paper's organization. Double-space before and after a subheading; do not underline or capitalize it. In a more technical paper (for example, one reporting the results of an experiment), the problem being investigated would be introduced in the opening paragraphs and the rest of the paper would be divided with the following headings: Method, Results, Discussion.

education had opened their doors--among them Mt.
Holyoke, Vassar, Smith, Wellesley, Radcliffe,
Bryn Mawr, and Barnard. Even more significant, by
this time nearly two-thirds of all the nation's
colleges and universities were coeducational
(Buckler, 1897).

On the surface, then, the story of women's education in the nineteenth century would seem to be one
of rapidly expanding opportunities. By the end of
the century, however, a new debate was raging--not
over women's access to higher education, but over
the purpose of such an education in a woman's life.
An examination of articles written during the 1890s
on the goals of higher education for women leads one
to conclude that equality of opportunity was not yet
within women's grasp. Higher education did not open
up new spheres of activity for most women at the end
of the nineteenth century; instead, these articles
suggest that powerful social forces were at work to
keep education for women focused on the enrichment
and enhancement of home and family.

Supporters of Opportunities for Women
To be sure, some educators of the time did call

22e

Quotations of more than forty words are set off by indenting five spaces from the left margin. Ellipsis marks indicate omitted material.

Career versus Motherhood

5

for broader educational and professional opportunities for women. Butler (1896), for example, criti-
cized the ways in which women's development was retarded by prevailing attitudes in society—for example, by the belief that girls' elementary and secondary education should not be as rigorous as boys'.
Franklin (1898) agreed that what we today would call
social conditioning was responsible for the gap between the accomplishments of men and those of women.
The "youthful dreams and aspirations of a gifted boy
cluster around high achievement and resounding
fame," he explained, "because all that he hears and
reads tends to arouse in him such ambitions" (p. 46).
In contrast, the girl is taught to focus her life
on "the conquest of men by beauty and charm" (pp. 46–
47). No wonder, therefore, that women's professional accomplishments had not equaled those of men:

> Men who have had the spark of genius or even of
> talent in them have been spurred to effort by
> all their surroundings, by the traditions of
> the race, by rivalry with their comrades, by
> the admiration which the opposite sex accords
> to brilliant achievements. . . . What of all

22e

The superior number *1* refers to a content note, which is found at the end of the paper on the page following the reference list.

22e

Note how the opening sentences of this paragraph organize the material that follows. The first sentence is transitional, contrasting the critics to be presented here with the supporters of opportunities for women discussed above. The second sentence identifies one group of critics, those who attempted to belittle women's professional accomplishments. Since Buckler is then introduced as a member of this group, the reader is prepared for a discussion that illustrates her treatment of women's accomplishments in this way.

this has there been for women? How many have
been so placed as to even think of an intellectual career as a possibility? . . . The very ab-
sorption in a high intellectual interest . . .
was, in the case of girls, up to the last two
or three decades, universally condemned and
repressed and thwarted even in the most cultivated families. (p. 43)[1]

Two Groups of Critics

Such defenses of women's intellectual rights
were, however, far less typical of the 1890s than
criticism of wider educational and professional opportunities for women was. The critics could hardly
ignore women's recent achievements in such previously male fields as science, law, and medicine, but
one group of these critics found ways of denigrating
those accomplishments in order to assert the need
for a college curriculum for women that was focused
on the home and family. Buckler (1897) is representative of this group. On the one hand, she concedes
that "there is no walk of life which, in some quarter
of the globe at least, is not open to [women]" (p.
302). But on the other hand, even as she enumerates

22e

22e

In the quotation from Buckler, Lopardo underlines the phrase *the good of the community* to emphasize the standard by which Buckler is judging women's accomplishments. Following APA style, she inserts the phrase *italics added* in brackets immediately after the underlined phrase to indicate that she has added underscoring (emphasis) not found in the original text.

women's accomplishments in professional life, Buckler concludes that women have never "achieved anything absolutely first-rate, whether as creation or
as discovery" (p. 303), and that there is little
chance they ever will:

> If women were ever intellectually equal to men,
> when and why did they begin to fall behind? And
> if they never were equal, how can they hope to
> catch up now, when masculine education is ad-
> vancing at as great a rate as feminine? (p. 308)

Why should women pursue a professional career if they
are thus doomed to second-rate accomplishments? Or,
as Buckler phrases the question, "Is it for the good
of the community [italics added] that she should engage in these higher branches [of literature, science, and art]?" (p. 296). In Buckler's view, wom-
en's professional accomplishments have been so
meager as to be inconsequential to the community at
large. Instead, she asserts, women should find satisfaction "in assisting and carrying out the creations of men. For it is in this subordinate relation
that women can probably find their truest and widest
sphere, that of Influence" (pp. 308-309).

22e

An effective transitional sentence indicates that Bolton is also included in the first group of critics, those who sought to diminish women's professional accomplishments.

Lopardo now moves to a second group of critics, those who felt that the college curriculum for women should place greater emphasis on domestic issues. Note the transitions within this paragraph that link its main examples: Brown (1896), *for example,* agrees. . . . Backus (1899) *also* praises. . . .

Bolton (1898) approaches the issue of college education for women in a similar way. She begins by cataloging women's accomplishments from biblical times to the present, but in spite of this evidence she concludes, paradoxically, that "[women's] genius has but a limited field; while many have obtained fame through their knowledge of mathematics and its applications to astronomy, they show but little aptitude for the natural sciences, and rarely exhibit any inventive faculty" (pp. 510-511). A life of learning, she claims, can therefore never offer a woman the same fulfillment as being "a happy wife and good mother" (p. 511). Echoing Buckler (1897), Bolton suggests that if women's education is to be put to a worthwhile purpose, it should be to "assist some loved one to perfect his researches" (p. 511).

A second group of critics took pains to praise the new educational opportunities open to women, but warned of the dangers of a college curriculum for women that neglected domestic issues. Brown (1896), for example, agrees with Franklin and Butler that "every human being, man or woman, should have all the education that he can take" (p. 431). But she defends

22e

When citing two works by the same author, include the dates of both works in parentheses, separated by a comma: (Smith, 1895, 1898) or Smith (1895, 1898). If you use a parenthetical citation to cite two or more works by different authors, arrange them in alphabetical order and separate them with a semicolon: (Jones, 1988; Smith, 1990).

women's education only in terms of its usefulness
as preparation for motherhood, and she concludes by
warning that "whatever in the education of girls
draws them away from [the home] is an injury to civilization" (p. 432). Backus (1899) also praises the "new
womanhood" of her decade, citing "mental ambition"
as the "dominating force among intelligent modern
women" (p. 461). But she leaves little room for such
amibition in her conception of women's higher education. Instead, her defense of the current college
curriculum for women rests solely on its contribution
to motherhood:

22e

> Can we not secure better returns from college
> training [of women] if the needs of the family,
> the ideals of wifehood, be kept steadily in the
> view of our daughters—the home be made the cri-
> terion for all mental effort exercised without
> the home? (p. 461)

Increasing Conservatism

At least some critics of higher education for
women during the 1890s became more conservative as
the twentieth century approached. Two articles by
Smith (1895, 1898), for example, illustrate the ap-

The date in parentheses after the second mention of *Smith* indicates which of her articles is being discussed in this paragraph.

22e

As above, Lopardo uses brackets to insert words that make the quoted passage clearer. The original version begins as follows:

> In fact, nobody knew very well what she was there for; it seemed only fair that she should "have a chance too," but a chance for what? . . .

Career versus Motherhood

10

parently increasing pressure for domestic education
at the college level. Like Brown (1896) and Backus
(1899), Smith (1895) applauds the new educational
opportunities open to women whose "distinctive intellectual bent demanded some other outlet than
housekeeping for their energies. They wished to
teach in the higher schools, or to enter the professions of literature, law, or medicine" (p. 27). As
Smith surveys the recent history of higher education for women, however, it becomes clear that her
own vision of women's education is a significantly
narrower one:

22e

> In fact, nobody knew very well what [a woman]
> was [in college] for; it seemed only fair that
> she should "have a chance too," but a chance for
> what? Why, to marry, of course! But nobody
> ever said that aloud, and nobody thought of
> adapting her training to her probable and desir-
> able business in life. (p. 28)

In the future, Smith says hopefully, the "tendency
to emphasize the profession of wifehood and motherhood in its proper relations will be increasingly
controlling in all education of women" (p. 33).

Lopardo effectively summarizes Smith's entire article of 1898 in a single paragraph. Note the key passages from the last paragraph of the article that she has selected to quote (the quoted passages are italicized):

> If to all these practical and utilitarian attainments the mother can add *the graces of culture in music or art or literature,* she may give the child a background for education and a resource in life beyond the power of statistics to estimate. The elevation, enrichment, and sweetening of the family life by these contributions from the mother's own storehouse of culture are a safeguard against temptation from without not to be matched by legislation or training, or even by church influence. To *make the household sweet, wholesome, dignified,* a place of growth, is certainly a profession requiring not merely the best training, but a specific training adapted to those ends.

Lopardo's concluding paragraph returns smoothly to the note on which the paper began—the Seneca Falls Convention of 1848. Here she introduces a second quotation from the Seneca Falls Declaration—a passage demanding equality in career opportunities—to underscore her concluding point, that although women had access to higher education by the end of the century, they had still not gained the right to use that education in a professional career outside the home.

At the end of the decade, Smith (1898) returns to this topic, but in an even more reactionary way. Now she calls the idea of having women pursue the same college curriculum as men an "experiment" (p. 522) that has failed. In its place, she proposes in detail a curriculum that will enable a woman to "make the household sweet, wholesome, dignified" (p. 525)— that is, a course of study emphasizing manual training, hygiene, "standards of honor and honesty," and "the graces of culture in music or art or literature" (p. 524).

Conclusions

22e

Clearly the statistics regarding higher education for women at the end of the nineteenth century do not tell the whole story. It is true that the question of women's access to higher education had been resolved in the half-century since the Seneca Falls Convention, for most of the nation's colleges and universities had opened their doors to women. But another Seneca Falls resolution—one calling for "equal participation with men in the various trades, professions, and commerce" ("Seneca Falls Declaration," 1973, p. 317)—was far from fulfilled. Al-

Career versus Motherhood

12

though the education of women had become socially
acceptable, it remained focused on the enrichment
of home and family life; the intellectual life available to women could be pursued only as a sort of hobby.
The battle for the right to an education that was truly
equivalent to men's and for the right to a career outside the home remained to be fought in the next century.

22e

Career versus motherhood

13

References

Backus, H. H. (1899, February 25). Should the college train for motherhood? Outlook, pp. 461–463.

Bolton, H. I. (1898, August). Women in science. Popular Science Monthly, pp. 505–511.

Brown, H. D. (1896, March 7). How shall we educate our girls? Outlook, pp. 431–432.

Buckler, G. G. (1897). The lesser man. North American Review, 165, 296–309.

Butler, N. M. (1896, April 4). The right training of girls under sixteen. Outlook, pp. 626–627.

Franklin, F. (1898). The intellectual powers of woman. North American Review, 166, 40–53.

The Seneca Falls declaration of sentiments and resolutions. (1973). In H. S. Commager (Ed.), Documents of American History (Vol. 1., pp. 315–317). Englewood Cliffs: Prentice.

Smith, M. R. (1895, November). Recent tendencies in the education of women. Popular Science Monthly, pp. 27–33.

Smith, M. R. (1898, August). Education for domestic life. Popular Science Monthly, pp. 521–525.

22e

Career versus motherhood

14

Woodworth, R. S. (1933). Ladd–Franklin, Christine. In D. Malone (Ed.), <u>Dictionary of American Biography</u> (Vol. 10, pp. 528–530). New York: Scribner's.

Career versus motherhood

15

Footnote

[1]Franklin's liberal perspective on the issue of professional careers for women can perhaps be explained by a biographical detail: he was married to the well-known psychologist Christine Ladd-Franklin. Although Ladd-Franklin fulfilled the doctoral requirements at Johns Hopkins University in 1882 and went on to a distinguished career in teaching and research at Columbia University, Johns Hopkins refused to award her a degree until 1926 because it did not officially recognize women as graduate students (Woodworth, 1933).

22e

23 *Student Research Paper C: Endnote Documentation*

Though abandoned by the Modern Language Association in 1984 in favor of the documentation style that we examined in Chapters **19** and **20**, endnote documentation remains in wide use in other humanities fields. This method of documentation inserts superior numbers (numbers raised a half-line) into the text to refer to citations that are then collected together on pages at the end of the paper. (A more complicated alternative that we will not consider here is to place the appropriate notes at the bottom of each page; in that case they are called footnotes.)

In this chapter we discuss the key features of endnotes, provide a list of note forms for various kinds of citations, and offer a sample student research paper documented with endnotes.

23a Using endnotes

Anyone who is familiar with the current style of MLA documentation will find the transition to using endnotes an easy one.

1. Features of endnotes

In place of the parenthetical citation in the text prescribed in MLA documentation, the writer using endnotes inserts a slightly raised number in the text corresponding to a citation given on note pages that follow the paper. The raised numbers inserted in the text do not start over with *1* on each page but run consecutively throughout the paper. Content notes, if any, do not appear on a separate note page but are intermingled with citations to sources.

Endnote forms differ from MLA Works Cited forms in five major ways.

1. The first line of an endnote is indented five spaces; subsequent lines are not indented (the reverse of Works Cited citations).
2. Authors' names are always presented in normal rather than inverted order.
3. Publication information for books is enclosed in parentheses.
4. In general, where MLA Works Cited forms separate elements with periods, endnote forms connect them with commas. However, no punctuation ever comes before parentheses unless the word before the parentheses is an abbreviation that ends in a period.
5. An endnote always ends with a page citation, unless (1) the note refers to the entire work being cited, or (2) the source is one without pages (for example, computer software, a film, an interview, or a lecture).

23a

2. Features of the endnote page

In the center of the endnote page, one inch from the top, type the word *Notes,* not underlined or in quotation marks. Double-space, indent five spaces, and type a slightly raised *1*. Leave a space after the raised number before beginning the note; do not indent the second and subsequent lines of the note. Continue in the same manner with the rest of the paper's notes, double-spacing within and between notes. A bibliography page following the page or pages of endnotes is optional; if included, it is arranged like an MLA Works Cited page but given the heading "Bibliography."

In citations to a source for which full publication information has been given in an earlier note, provide only the author's last name (or a shortened form of the title, if it is an anonymous work) and the page number:

First citation

> [1] Alice Walker, The Color Purple (New York: Harcourt, 1982) 44.

Subsequent citation

> [2] Walker 70–71.

If the endnotes include citations to two works by the same author, subsequent citations include a shortened form of the appropriate title to distinguish between them.

First citations

> [1] Alice Walker, The Color Purple (New York: Harcourt, 1982) 23.

> [2] Alice Walker, The Temple of My Familiar (San Diego: Harcourt, 1989) 101.

Subsequent citations

> [3] Walker, Temple 34.

> [4] Walker, Color Purple 70–71.

The abbreviations *ibid.* (Latin *ibidem,* "in the same place") and *op. cit.* (Latin *opere citato,* "in the work cited") are no longer used with endnotes.

23b Endnote forms

On the following pages are endnote forms corresponding to the MLA Works Cited forms given in **19b**. A hypothetical page citation has been added to the end of each note to illustrate the positioning of page numbers in endnotes.

Table of endnote forms

Books

1. Book by one author
2. Book by two or more authors
3. Book by a committee, commission, association, or other group
4. Anonymous book
5. Later or revised edition of a book
6. Edited book (*author's work is being cited*)
7. Edited book (*editor's work is being cited*)
8. Translated book (*author's work is being cited*)
9. Translated book (*translator's work is being cited*)
10. Book in more than one volume
11. Republished book
12. Book that is part of a series
13. Book published by a division of a press
14. Book published before 1900
15. Book with incomplete publication information

Parts of books

16. Introduction, preface, foreword, or afterword in a book
17. Essay in a collection of essays by various authors
18. Poem, short story, or other work in an anthology
19. Journal or magazine article reprinted in a collection of essays by various authors

23b

Articles in journals and magazines

20. Article in a journal paginated by the volume (*continuous pagination*)
21. Article in a journal paginated issue by issue
22. Article in a journal with issue numbers only
23. Article in a weekly or biweekly magazine
24. Article in a monthly or bimonthly magazine

Articles in newspapers

25. Article in a newspaper
26. Editorial in a newspaper
27. Letter to the editor

Other print sources

28. Abstract in *Dissertation Abstracts International*
29. Book review
30. Dissertation, unpublished
31. Encyclopedia article (*or article in similar reference work*)
32. Government document
33. Interview, published
34. Map
35. Pamphlet
36. Proceedings of a conference

Nonprint sources

37. Computer software
38. Film
39. Interview, personal
40. Lecture
41. Microfilm or microfiche
42. Recording
43. Television program
44. Videotape

23b

Books

1. Book by one author

[1] David Novarr, The Lines of Life: Theories of Biography, 1880–1970 (West Lafayette: Purdue UP, 1986) 113.

2. Book by two or more authors

[2] Robert Scholes and Robert Kellogg, The Nature of Narrative (London: Oxford UP, 1966) 27.

3. Book by a committee, commission, association, or other group

³ Ground Zero, <u>Nuclear War: What's in It for You?</u>
(New York: Pocket, 1982) 66–67.

4. Anonymous book

⁴ <u>Kodak Guide to 35mm Photography</u> (Rochester:
Eastman Kodak, 1980) 12.

5. Later or revised edition of a book

⁵ Casey Miller and Kate Swift, <u>The Handbook of
Nonsexist Writing</u>, 2nd ed. (New York: Harper, 1988)
98.

6. Edited book (*author's work is being cited*)

⁶ Elizabeth Gaskell, <u>The Life of Charlotte
Brontë</u>, ed. Alan Shelston (Harmondsworth: Penguin,
1975) 254–55.

7. Edited book (*editor's work is being cited*)

⁷ Frederick Garber, ed., <u>The Italian</u>, by Ann
Radcliffe (London: Oxford UP, 1968) 201.

8. Translated book (*author's work is being cited*)

⁸ Ursula Brumm, <u>American Thought and Reli-
gious Typology</u>, trans. John Hoaglund (New Brunswick:
Rutgers UP, 1970) 107–08.

23b

9. Translated book (*translator's work is being cited*)

[9] L. R. Lind, trans., The Aeneid, by Vergil (Bloomington: Indiana UP, 1962) 76.

10. Book in more than one volume

[10] Luigi Sturzo, Church and State, 2 vols. (Notre Dame: U of Notre Dame P, 1962) 1: 67.

11. Republished book

[11] William L. Shirer, Berlin Diary: The Journal of a Foreign Correspondent 1934–1941 (1941; Harmondsworth: Penguin 1979) 198.

12. Book that is part of a series

[12] Virginia L. Radley, Samuel Taylor Coleridge, Twayne's English Authors Ser. 36 (New York: Twayne, 1966) 34–36.

13. Book published by a division of a press

[13] Barbara Ehrenreich and Deirdre English, For Her Own Good: 150 Years of the Experts' Advice to Women (Garden City: Anchor–Doubleday, 1979) 333.

14. Book published before 1900

[14] Brainerd Kellogg, A Text–Book on Rhetoric (New York, 1897) 22.

15. Book with incomplete publication information

15 George S. Marr, The Periodical Essayists of
the Eighteenth Century (London: Clarke, n.d.) 40–
44.

Parts of books
16. Introduction, preface, foreword, or afterword in a book

16 J. Hillis Miller, introduction, Bleak House,
by Charles Dickens, ed. Norman Page (Harmondsworth:
Penguin, 1971) 12.

17. Essay in a collection of essays by various authors

17 Richard E. Young, "Concepts of Art and the
Teaching of Writing," The Rhetorical Tradition and
Modern Writing, ed. James J. Murphy (New York: Modern
Lang. Assn., 1982) 133.

23b

18. Poem, short story, or other work in an anthology

18 Walter Raleigh, "The Advice," The Anchor Anthology of Sixteenth-Century Verse, ed. Richard S.
Sylvester (New York: Anchor-Doubleday, 1974) 330.

19. Journal or magazine article reprinted in a collection of essays by various authors

19 Richard Harter Fogle, "The Abstractness of
Shelley," Philological Quarterly 24 (1945): 362–79,

rpt. in Shelley: A Collection of Critical Essays,
ed. George M. Ridenour, Twentieth Century Views (Englewood Cliffs: Prentice, 1965) 28–29.

Articles in journals and magazines

20. Article in a journal paginated by the volume (*continuous pagination*)

[20] Jerome A. Miller, "Horror and the Deconstruction of the Self," Philosophy Today 32 (1988): 287.

21. Article in a journal paginated issue by issue

[21] George Butterick, "Charles Olson's 'The
Kingfishers' and the Poetics of Change," American
Poetry 6.2 (1989): 28–29.

22. Article in a journal with issue numbers only

[22] Paul Jacobson, "Temperature and Your Guitar's Health," Guitar Review 75 (1988): 17.

23. Article in a weekly or biweekly magazine

[23] Barbara Rudolph, "Adrift in the Doldrums,"
Time 31 July 1989: 33.

24. Article in a monthly or bimonthly magazine

[24] Mary Kay Blakely, "Coma: Stories from the
Edge of Death," Life Aug. 1989: 82.

Articles in newspapers

25. Article in a newspaper

[25] Denis Donoghue, "Does America Have a Major Poet?" <u>New York Times</u> 3 Dec. 1978, late city ed., sec. 7: 9.

26. Editorial in a newspaper

[26] "'Restraint' Spurs Terrorists," editorial, <u>Chicago Sun-Times</u> 3 Aug. 1989: 42.

27. Letter to the editor

[27] Lavonna Hayden, "Broadway Blues," letter, <u>Village Voice</u> 28 Feb. 1989: 4.

Other print sources

23b

28. Abstract in *Dissertation Abstracts International*

[28] Susan Ellen Krantz, "The First Fortune: The Plays and the Playhouse," <u>DAI</u> 47 (1986): 189A (Tulane U).

29. Book review

[29] Norma Pettit, rev. of <u>American Puritanism: Faith and Practice</u>, by Darrett B. Rutman, <u>New England Quarterly</u> 43 (1970): 504-05.

30. Dissertation, unpublished

[30] James Vernon Rauff, "Machine Translation with Two-Level Grammars," diss., Northwestern U, 1988, 29.

31. Encyclopedia article

[31] "Phonetics," Encyclopaedia Britannica: Micropaedia, 15th ed., 1986.

32. Government document

[32] United States, Superintendent of Documents, Poetry and Literature (Washington: GPO, 1978) 7–8.

33. Interview, published

23b

[33] Margaret Drabble, interview, Interviews with Contemporary Novelists, by Diana Cooper-Clark (New York: St. Martin's, 1986) 72–73.

34. Map

[34] Southeastern States, map (Falls Church: American Automobile Assn., 1988).

35. Pamphlet

[35] Dennison I. Rusinow, Yugoslavia's Muslim Nation (Hanover: Universities Field Staff Intl., 1982) 3.

36. Proceedings of a conference

[36] Stephen W. Rousseas, ed., Inflation: Its Causes, Consequences and Control, Symposium Held by the Dept. of Economics, New York U, 31 Jan. 1968 (Wilton: K. Kazanjian Economics Foundation, 1968) 77.

Nonprint sources

37. Computer software

[37] Thomas Etter and William Chamberlain, Racter, computer software, Mindscape, 1984.

38. Film

[38] Casablanca, dir. Michael Curtiz, with Humphrey Bogart, Ingrid Bergman, and Claude Rains, Warner Bros., 1942.

23b

39. Interview, personal

[39] Teresa Toulouse, personal interview, 31 Mar. 1985.

40. Lecture

[40] James V. Catano, "The Paradox Behind the Myth of Self-Making: Self-Empowerment vs. the Power of the Academy," Conference on College Composition and Communication, Seattle, 17 Mar. 1989.

41. Microfilm or microfiche

When citing a publication reproduced on microfilm or microfiche, simply use the ordinary note form appropriate for that publication.

42. Recording

42 Fred W. Friendly and Walter Cronkite, eds.,
The Way It Was: The Sixties, narr. Walter Cronkite,
CBS, F3M 38858, 1983.

43. Television program

43 Nightline, ABC, WLS, Chicago, 23 Jan. 1990.

44. Videotape

44 The Beggar's Opera, videocassette, by John
Gay, prod. and dir. Jonathan Miller, with Roger Dal-
trey and Carol Hall, BBC-TV/RM Arts, 1985 (135 min.).

23c Sample student paper

The student research paper that follows, Emmet Geary's "Recovery from the Florence Flood: A Masterpiece of Restoration," is an excellent example of an informative report that is tightly focused around a precise thesis statement. As we explained in Chapter **17**, Geary drew on his reading about the effects of the 1966 flood in Florence, Italy, to define a narrow subject for his paper—the efforts of professionals and volunteers to rescue and restore the city's valuable art. The thesis statement in which he introduces this focusing idea comes at the end of his first paragraph, a paragraph that compactly provides all the background needed by the reader to understand the rest of the paper.

Perhaps the best feature of this paper is Geary's skillful integration of his sources. A glance at his endnotes page shows that he has not relied too heavily on any one source; instead he moves back and forth among his sources, pulling together related pieces of information from different sources and weaving them into a coherent and well-developed narrative. Excellent transitions between paragraphs help to unify the paper, and Geary's clear explanations of occasionally technical information hold the reader's interest.

From start to finish, this paper is another example of the way in which the researcher's vision of his or her subject can shape the diverse products of reading and note taking into a unified and original whole.

23c

Note the effective movement of Geary's introductory paragraph. It begins with a brief but specific survey of the flood's devastating impact on Florence, then moves to the damage done to the city's art, then (with the Batini quotation) shifts to the narrower subject of art restoration, the focus of Geary's paper.

Compare the version of the Batini quotation given in the paper with the original, on Geary's note card:

23c

> Batini, p. 90
>
> "Despite the various complex restoration methods briefly explained above, the havoc played by the flood among works of art in Florence presented many new problems. For example, never before had so many and diverse works of art been damaged at the same time, all of which needed to be restored at once by an army of specialists, unfortunately a rarity today."

In Geary's paper, the bracketed capital *N* at the start of the quotation and the ellipses at the end indicate that only part of the original sentence is quoted here.

Emmet Geary

Professor P. L. Herrold

History 100

March 28, 1990

Recovery from the Florence Flood:

A Masterpiece of Restoration

On November 4, 1966, the swollen Arno River in-
undated Florence, Italy. Nineteen inches of rain had
fallen in two days, causing floodwater to reach
depths of twenty feet in some parts of the city. The
damage was devastating: six thousand of the city's
ten thousand shops were destroyed, five thousand
families were left homeless, and more than a hundred
people drowned. But the primary reason that most out-
siders grieved for Florence was the damage to its
unique collection of Renaissance art treasures and
rare books. As Giorgio Batini noted, "[N]ever before
had so many and diverse works of art been damaged at
the same time, all of which needed to be restored at
once. . . ."[1] The story of this restoration is a
story of commitment and ingenuity. Though the Florence flood destroyed some priceless masterpieces
and heavily damaged others, it inspired valiant
efforts among professional restorers and untrained

If we compare Geary's paraphrase of Horton (note 3) with the original text, we see that he has effectively and accurately summarized the source in his own words:

23c

A few days after the disastrous floods that occurred in Italy on November 4, 1966, a group of art lovers in the United States organized the Committee to Rescue Italian Art (CRIA). One of their first acts was to send, on November 8, two art historians to Florence and Venice, the areas where the art losses were reported to be the greatest, to assess the damage and to find out what could be done to help. Word was received from them by transatlantic telephone that restoration experts and materials were urgently needed. By November 14, there were 16 conservators on their way to Florence. Within the next week, they were joined by four more conservators. This group of 20, headed by Lawrence Majewski, acting director of the Conservation Center, Institute of Fine Arts, New York University, included: a chemist; 13 conservators of paintings, frescoes, mosaics, and furniture; two conservators of prints and drawings; one librarian; and three bookbinders, specializing in the restoration and conservation of books, manuscripts, and other library materials.

2

volunteers alike, and even occasioned some discoveries in the field of art that would otherwise never have been made.

As the floodwater rose, the first demonstration of dedication to art was shown by fourteen members of the staff of the Uffizi Gallery, who risked their lives to rescue twenty-four paintings stored in the museum's basement.[2] When the floodwater had subsided, generous contributions from all over the world arrived in Florence, and hundreds of volunteers—mainly students from throughout Europe and North America—came to undertake the messy cleanup that would return Florence to normal and salvage the city's damaged treasures. The volunteers were led by an international team of art historians and conservators. Within only a few days of the flood, for example, one group of American art lovers had organized the Committee to Rescue Italian Art and two weeks later had dispatched to Florence a team of twenty experts, including specialists in paintings, mosaics, furniture, prints, bookbindings, and manuscripts.[3]

Two distinct types of damage to art had resulted from the flood: that due to submersion, and that due to water pressure, turbulence, and friction.

23c

By inserting the citation to Ricci (note 5) in the middle of his sentence, Geary makes it clear that only the information in the first half of the sentence—the specific data about the size and speed of the floodwater—comes from this source.

Geary found his information about the damage to Ghiberti's baptistry doors in many sources; consequently, it could be considered common knowledge and did not require specific documentation.

3

Submersion caused the flood's most significant artistic loss—the great <u>Crucifix</u> by Giovanni Cimabue, painted at the end of the thirteenth century—as well as most of the other damage to paintings and books. Compounding the problem of submersion was oil, which had spilled from ruptured fuel tanks around the city, and which rode the top of the floodwater, coating everything it touched. Having never before worked on paintings stained by fuel oil, restorers were forced to experiment with a number of solvents, including benzene and carbon tetrachloride.[4] Water pressure and turbulence created a different kind of devastation. Sweeping through the city at forty to fifty miles an hour, the twelve-foot wave of water[5] knocked sculptures from their pedestals and damaged the altarpieces of churches. The famous baptistry doors of the city's cathedral, cast by Lorenzo Ghiberti in the fifteenth century, were violently battered by the water, which dislodged five of the doors' bronze panels.

23c

The first task that restoration workers faced was collecting the objects to be restored. Since the last serious threat to Florence's art had come from German artillery bombardment during World War II,

In his paragraph describing the flood's damage to Florence's libraries, note Geary's effective integration of related material from different sources.

23c

A quotation of more than four typed lines is set off by indenting ten spaces. Double-space between the last line of the text and the first line of the quotation, and double-space the quotation itself. No quotation marks are used when a quotation is set off in this way.

4

many valuable books and manuscripts had been stored
below ground for safety.[6] Now these books had to be
pulled from library basements full of water and mud.
In the Biblioteca Nazionale alone, more than 300,000
volumes were damaged; in the library of the Gabinet-
to Vieusseux, 250,000 more had been under water and
needed immediate attention.[7] All told, nearly two
million books were damaged by the flood.[8]

Not only the floodwater but the subsequent
growth of destructive mold spores threatened Florence's priceless books. As Carolyn Horton explains,
mold endangered even books that had escaped direct
damage from the flood:

> Books are hygroscopic, i.e., have the
> capacity for absorbing water from the
> air around them. Therefore any books
> stored in conditions of high humidity are
> in danger of being damaged by mold. We
> had received reports that the flooded
> area of Florence had become, in effect, a
> huge humidity chamber. The wet books in
> rooms that were ony partially flooded were
> humidifying the dry books on the upper
> shelves.[9]

23c

Again, the information given here about methods of restoring and drying books was available in several sources and therefore did not require documentation in Geary's paper.

Note Geary's smooth transition between the last two paragraphs, which deal with salvaging books, and this one, which moves on to consider damage done to paintings on wooden panels: "Like books. . . ."

Compare Geary's version of the quotation from the anonymous article "The Florentine Flood Disaster" (note 10) with the original text:

23c

> The situation regarding panel paintings has not changed much since the preliminary reports. The return to health will be slow and laborious. As is well known, when the water has soaked into the wood, the priming layer of glue and gesso dissolves, and the colours dissolve with it. This is not only the case with panels that were entirely submerged, as at Santa Croce (Fig. I). Even in cases where a few inches along the bottom were submerged, those parts buckle, and crack the part that seemed safe. More unexpected still, some panels which seemed quite undamaged when the flood subsided, developed blisters two or three days later, and the paint began to fall.

Note the editorial changes that Geary has made: (1) he has enclosed the initial *W* of his quotation in brackets to indicate that the first words of the original quotation have been omitted; (2) he has inserted the word *plaster* in brackets to define the unfamiliar term *gesso* for the reader; (3) he has inserted ellipsis marks to indicate an omission after his third sentence (note that the usual three periods follow a fourth period—the period of the sentence); and (4) he has inserted the word *only* in brackets to make the sense of the original quotation clearer. Geary has retained the unorthodox punctuation and the British spelling ("colours") of the original text.

5

Salvaged books, covered with mud and oil and soaked
with water, were first washed with mild soap and then
treated with fungicides and antibiotics that would
inhibit the growth of mold and bacteria. Then came
the drying, by any means available: heating in tobacco ovens and brick kilns, interleaving pages with
absorbent paper, spraying with powder.

Like books, paintings on wooden panels were particularly susceptible to damage from submersion in
water. As one observer described the problem:

> [W]hen the water has soaked into the wood,
> the priming layer of glue and gesso [plas-
> ter] dissolves, and the colours dissolve
> with it. . . . Even in cases where [only]
> a few inches along the bottom were sub-
> merged, those parts buckle, and crack the
> part that seemed safe. More unexpected
> still, some panels which seemed quite un-
> damaged when the flood subsided, devel-
> oped blisters two or three days later, and
> the paint began to fall.[10]

To prevent wooden panels from drying too fast and
shrinking, thus causing the pigment to flake off,
restoration workers had to reduce the humidity around

23c

Another excellent transition links these two paragraphs: "Even more difficult to restore. . . ."

6

the panels gradually. Within twelve days of the
flood, the Limonaia, a large greenhouse in one of
Florence's public parks, was converted to a sophisticated drying facility complete with an elaborate
humidity-control system. Initially set at ninety
percent, the humidity level inside was gradually low-
ered, and the panels were constantly checked to
ensure sufficiently slow drying.[11] Only after complete drying, a process that sometimes took many
months, could the painted panels be moved to labora-
tories for further restoration, which usually involved planing down the back of the panels until only
the pigment and priming layers remained, and then
attaching a laminated, shrink-proof panel to the
back of the painting.[12]

Even more difficult to restore were Florence's
frescoes, paintings originally executed directly on
damp plaster, so that the pigment fused with the surface of the wall. Besides damage from submersion and
floating fuel oil, frescoes were affected by dampness, which caused the plaster layers to separate
from the wall,[13] and by salt contained in the floodwater, which penetrated the plaster and caused "tiny
explosions" in the painted surface as the wall

23c

When parts of a sentence derive from different sources, insert references to the appropriate notes in midsentence, as Geary has done here, for accurate documentation. Consider the following two note cards.

"Florentine Flood Disaster," p. 193

Damage to frescoes more serious than people thought at first: dampness penetrated plaster even above the level of the floodwater, causing [4] "a breaking down of the adhesion between the plaster layers and the wall."

23c

"Slow Art Restoration," p. 42

Salt dissolved in the floodwaters "had become lodged inside and under wood panels and frescoes, causing tiny explosions to tear the paint."

7

dried.[14] To save frescoes, restorers used a technique called "strapo," which involves applying a
coating of glue and a canvas sheet to the wall. After
the glue has dried, the painting can be pulled from
the wall intact on the canvas. Difficult as this process is, it yielded an unexpected reward: when the
painted surfaces were removed, more than three hundred sinopias, or preliminary drawings for the frescoes, were uncovered on the walls.[15]

Surprisingly, sculpture seems to have received
more benefit than harm from the flood. Some statues
were actually cleaned by the swirling water, whose
mud acted as a gentle abrasive, removing the grime
of hundreds of years. The restorers themselves used
mud to clean sections of statues that were untouched
by the floodwater.[16] Fuel oil, on the other hand,
did pose a serious threat to sculpture. Since marble
is a porous stone, the oil penetrated beneath the
surface and had to be drawn out and absorbed by
talc applied to the statues. But such thorough
cleaning of these statues actually left them cleaner
than they had been before the flood and led to a few
surprises. For example, the restoration revealed
for the first time that Donatello's statue The Magda-

23c

The Ricci quotation provides the foundation for an effective concluding paragraph. It not only echoes ideas from the paper's introduction but also gives Geary the opportunity to reiterate one of his main ideas— the importance of the volunteer efforts to save Florence's art.

23c

8

<u>len</u> had originally had gilded hair.[17]

Only a few months after the floodwater had devastated Florence, as the frantic restoration work
continued, Leonardo Ricci aptly described the
world's reaction to the disaster. "Many floods indeed and natural tragedies have happened everywhere
in the world," he wrote. "But never have we heard
such a cry as for Florence. As if, instead of a city
it were a person, a loved one who in a way belongs to
everybody and without whom it is impossible to
live."[18] In a real sense, the rescued art of Florence
does belong to everyone: without generous contributions of money from around the world and the tireless
efforts of an international corps of volunteers,
Florence's treasures could not have survived.

23c

One hallmark of a successful research paper is the writer's ability to integrate his or her sources—that is, to avoid dependence on a single source for large sections of the paper and to draw instead from many different sources as he or she composes. A glance at the sequence of Geary's notes shows how well he has integrated material from his research.

23c

Subsequent references to a source for which full publication information has been given consist only of the author's last name and the page number. Do not use the abbreviations *ibid.* and *op. cit.*

The March 12, 1967, issue of the *New York Times* is a Sunday edition divided into sections; the section number must therefore be included in the citation. The August 9, 1967, issue—a weekday issue—is paged continuously without section divisions; no section number is necessary, since there is only one page 42 in the issue.

Notes

[1] Giorgio Batini, <u>4 November 1966: The River Arno in the Museums of Florence</u>, trans. Timothy Paterson (Florence: Bonechi Editore, 1967) 90.

[2] Eric Rhode, "Good News from Florence," <u>New Statesman</u> 6 Jan. 1967: 20.

[3] Carolyn Horton, "Saving the Libraries of Florence," <u>Wilson Library Bulletin</u> 41 (1967): 1035.

[4] Joseph Judge, "Florence Rises from the Flood," <u>National Geographic</u> July 1967: 39.

[5] Leonard Ricci, "Exploratory Research in Urban Form and the Future of Florence," <u>Arts and Architecture</u> Feb. 1967: 25.

[6] Horton 1036.

[7] "The Florentine Flood Disaster," <u>Burlington Magazine</u> 109 (1967): 194.

[8] Horton 1036.

[9] Horton 1035.

[10] "Florentine Flood Disaster" 193.

[11] Batini 90–91.

[12] "Road Back is Long for Florentines," <u>New York Times</u> 12 Mar. 1967, late city ed., sec. 1: 80.

[13] "Florentine Flood Disaster" 193.

23c

Ricci's article begins on page 25 but continues on nonconsecutive pages later in the magazine.

10

[14] "Slow Art Restoration Continues in Florence," New York Times 9 Aug. 1967, late city ed.: 42.

[15] "Church Found Under Basilica in Florence," New York Times 4 Nov. 1967, late city ed.: 35.

[16] Batini 103–05

[17] "Florentine Flood Disaster" 194.

[18] Ricci 25, 32.

23c

Grammatical Usage

24 *Sentence Structure*

25 *Agreement*

26 *Case of Pronouns and Nouns*

27 *Adjectives and Adverbs*

28 *Verbs*

29 *Sentence Fragments, Comma Splices, Fused Sentences*

PART
VI

24 *Sentence Structure*

We all know that a sentence in grammar is a series of spoken or written words that forms the grammatically complete expression of a single thought. On the page, such a unit of discourse begins with a capital letter and ends with the appropriate end punctuation mark. Spoken aloud, the sentence is marked by voice inflection and pauses, the longest of which signals its completion. We have a well-developed, intuitive sense of the sentence because we have been hearing, speaking, writing, and reading sentences most of our lives.

If we look up the word *sentence* in the *Oxford English Dictionary*—that historian of our language—we find that it is one of those words that have contracted over the centuries: it had more meaning in Shakespeare's time than it has in ours. Some of these meanings, such as "opinion" and "way of thinking," are listed in the dictionary as obsolete and are not available to contemporary writers. Nevertheless, they point the way back to the Latin origin of the word, *sentire,* to feel, to be of the opinion, to perceive, to judge. The word *sentence* shares the same root as *sentiment* and *sense,* and appropriately so, for the construction of a sentence, even the simplest two-word kind, requires sensing and thinking, perceiving and judging. Good sentences are written by a vigilant observer prepared to consider and to declare.

24a

24a Elements of a sentence

For any kind of grammatical analysis, we need to classify the words and groups of words that make up a sentence. To *classify* means simply to group together words that are alike in some respects and to give names to those groups.

Let's start with a kind of classification you may never have thought of. *Pen, telephone, tax,* and *fluid* are alike in that they often appear after words like *the, a,* or *this: a pen, the telephone, this tax.* Words of this class also take inflectional endings to indicate the plural, usually a suffix including the letter *s: telephones, taxes, fluids.* Another class of words is made up of those to which inflectional suffixes like *-ed* can be added: *ask, asked; cry, cried; walk, walked.* A third class consists of words to which *-er* and *-est* can be added: *happy, happier, happiest; swift, swifter, swiftest.*

Let's adopt as names for these classes the ones used by traditional grammar: we'll call the first class **nouns,** the second class **verbs,** and the third class **adjectives.** As we go on to classify more and more words, it will become apparent that these classes must be broadened. Traditional grammar will suggest that a word like *child* should be put in the first class, even though the plural is *children,* not *childs.* Similarly, in the second class we will want to put such a word as *weave,* even though, instead of taking an *-ed* ending, it is inflected *wove.* The third class will be widened to include some words that do not add *-er* and *-est,* like *beautiful,* which is inflected *more beautiful, most beautiful.*

In broadening the classification of words, traditional grammar makes use of another set of similarities: it puts words into classes not merely by their forms (the way they can be inflected), but by their functions in a sentence. That is, traditional grammar says that *pen* and *tax* belong together in a class because they name something, *ask* and *cry* belong together in another class because they assert something, and *happy* and *swift* belong together in still another class because they modify (that is, describe or limit) something.

24a   Modern linguists have proposed alternative classifications that may well provide a more accurate and complete analysis of grammatical structures and relationships than the categories of traditional grammar do. But for the limited sort of analysis needed in a handbook, which tries merely to explain why certain constructions are "grammatical" without offering a complete system of grammar, the traditional classifications and the old names have the advantage of simplicity, familiarity, and reasonable consistency.

In the rest of this chapter, we will be examining the four functions of words in sentences: to name things, to assert things, to modify (describe or limit) other words, and to connect parts of a sentence.

Function	Class	Examples
to name	substantive	nouns, pronouns, gerunds, infinitives
to assert	predicative	verbs
to describe or limit	modifier	adjectives, adverbs, participles
to join elements	connective	conjunctions, prepositions

Note that groups of words (what linguists call **constructions**) may have the same functions as single words; such groups are called **phrases** or **clauses.**

1. Subject and predicate

A statement says something about something; to make a statement you need to *name* what you are talking about and *assert* something about it. The grammatical term for the word or words that name what you are talking about is the **subject.** The **predicate** is the assertion you make about the subject.

subject	predicate
Edison	invented the light bulb.
The storm	cut off our electricity.
A coyote	howled all night.
I	like spices.
My younger sister	does not like spices.

The subject is usually a noun or **pronoun** (a word used in place of a noun), though it may be a phrase or clause, as we will see below. The predicate may contain a number of different words used in different ways, but the essential part is a verb, a word that asserts.

2. Modifiers

It is possible to make a complete sentence of only two words, a subject and a verb:

Rain fell.

24a

Few sentences, however, are as simple as this one. We usually add other words whose function is to describe the subject or the verb:

A gentle rain fell steadily.

Here *gentle* describes *rain,* and *steadily* describes how it fell. Such words are called **modifiers,** and they may be attached to almost any part of a sentence. Although modifiers usually describe, they may also indicate how many (*three* books, *few* books), which one (*this* pencil, *my* pen), or how much (*very* gently, *half* sick).

Modifiers are divided into two main classes: **adjectives** and **adverbs.** Any word that modifies a noun, pronoun, or gerund is an adjective in function; an adverb is any word that modifies a verb, an adjective, or another adverb.

Very hungry people seldom display good table manners.

In this sentence, *hungry, good,* and *table* are adjectives, describing or indicating what kind of people and manners. *Very* is an adverb that modifies the adjective *hungry; seldom* is an adverb modifying the verb *display.*

Adjectives and adverbs have different forms to indicate **relative degree.** In addition to the regular, or **positive,** form (*slow, comfortable, slowly*), there are the **comparative** (*slower, more comfortable, more slowly*) and **superlative** (*slowest, most comfortable, most slowly*) **degrees.** The examples illustrate the rule: adjectives with more than two syllables form the comparative and superlative degrees by addition of the words *more* and *most,* instead of the suffixes *-er* and *-est.* All adverbs ending in *-ly* use *more* and *most* to indicate degrees of comparison. (For further discussion of adjectives and adverbs, see Chapter **27.**)

24a

3. Identifying subject and verb

The analysis of any sentence begins with the identification of the simple subject and the verb. Look first for the verb: often a word or group of words that states an action or happening. Some forms or tenses of a verb are really phrases, including one or more **auxiliary verbs**—he *was hit,* he *has been hit;* you *had taken,* you *will have taken.* Verbs that do not add *-ed* to form the past tense are called **irregular** verbs—for example, *swim, swam, swum; eat, ate, eaten*. (For a longer list of irregular verbs, see Chapter **28**.)

> I *sprained* my wrist.
>
> Joe Miller *wrote* me a letter.
>
> The fire *burned* out.
>
> He *has* never *painted* landscapes before.

Some verbs merely assert, with varying degrees of certainty, that something is—or looks or sounds like or seems or appears to be—something. These verbs are called **linking verbs,** or **copulas.**

> She *is* a talented athlete.
>
> He *seems* intelligent and dependable.
>
> You *sound* angry.
>
> The troops *looked* weary.

Once you have found the verb in a sentence, put it in the blank in the following question: "Who or what _____?" The answer to the question is the subject, and if you strip away the modifiers you have the **simple subject.**

> A long, dull speech *followed* the dinner.
> **[What followed the dinner? *A long, dull speech. Long* and *dull* are adjectives describing *speech;* the simple subject is *speech.*]**

This method of identifying the subject is especially helpful when the normal order of the sentence is inverted (that is, when the subject comes after the verb).

24a

> Half a mile away *rose* the spires of the cathedral.
>
> "No," *said* his father firmly.
> **[What rose half a mile away? The answer is the subject, *spires.* Who said "No"? The answer is the subject, *father.*]**

In a sentence that asks a question, the subject often follows some form of the verb *have* or *be,* or a form of an auxiliary verb.

verb	subject	
Have	*you*	the time?
Is	*he*	qualified?

auxiliary	subject	verb	
Have	*you*	read	this novel?
Did	*she*	write	it?
May	*they*	borrow	it?

	auxiliary	subject	verb
What kind of story	did	*he*	tell?

In an imperative sentence—one that commands or requests—the subject is not expressed. Since a command is addressed directly to someone, that person need not be named.

	subject	verb	
	( )	Come	in.
	( )	Return	the book no later than Monday.
Please	( )	take	these books to the library.

Since we can make one assertion about several persons and things, a sentence may have several nouns as its subject. Such a construction is called a **compound subject.**

The *trees* and *plants*	were dying.
Jane Austen, George Eliot, and *Emily Brontë*	are my favorite novelists.

Similarly, we can make several assertions about one subject. Such a construction is called a **compound predicate.**

She *wrote, revised, typed,* and *proofread* the manuscript.

Exhausted, she *went* to bed and *slept* for twelve hours.

24a

EXERCISE 1

Pick out the simple subjects and the verbs in the following sentences. Note that either the subject or the verb may be compound.

1. After locking the door, the flight attendant sat down at the rear of the plane.
2. Invisible to us, the pilot and copilot were checking the instruments.
3. Signs warning passengers not to smoke and to fasten their seat belts flashed on.
4. Directly beneath the signs was a door leading to the pilot's compartment.
5. Altogether there were about sixty passengers on the plane.

6. In a few moments the plane moved, slowly at first, and then roared into life.
7. After taxiing out to the airstrip, the pilot hesitated a moment to check the runway.
8. Then with a sudden rush of speed the plane roared down the runway and gradually began to climb.
9. Below us, at the edge of the airport, were markers and signal lights.
10. The football field and the quarter-mile track enabled me to identify the high school.

4.   Complements

Some verbs, called **intransitive** verbs, require nothing to complete them; that is, in themselves they make a full assertion about the subject.

After meeting all the relatives, my cousin *left*.

In a heavy rain, cabbage *may explode*.

Transitive verbs, in contrast, are incomplete by themselves. If one says only "I bought," the reader is left hanging in midair and is likely to ask "What did you buy?" Words that answer such a question, and thus complete the assertion, are called **complements** of the verb.

subject	verb	complement
I	bought	*a scarf.*

The commonest type of complement is the **direct object** of a transitive verb, illustrated in the sentence above. The direct object is usually a noun or pronoun, though it may be a phrase or a clause, and it usually names the thing acted upon by the subject.

subject	verb	direct object
My niece	built	*a water clock.*
They	chased	*whoever came near them.*

24a

The easiest way to identify a direct object is to say the simple subject and verb and then ask the question "What?" My niece built what? The answer, *clock,* is the direct object of the verb *built.* Note that the direct object may be a compound object.

subject	verb	direct object
I	borrowed	*a tent, a sleeping bag,* and *a gas stove.*

In addition to the direct object, certain verbs (usually involving an act of giving or telling) may take an **indirect object,** a complement that receives whatever is named by the direct object.

> The award gave the young photographer encouragement.
> **[What did the award give?** *Encouragement* **is the direct object.**
> **Who received the encouragement?** *Photographer* **is the indirect**
> **object—the receiver of what is named by the direct object.]**

The same meaning can be expressed by a phrase beginning with *to:*

> The award gave encouragement *to* the young photographer.
> He offered me his pen.
> He offered his pen *to* me.

Direct and indirect objects are called **object complements. A subject complement,** in contrast, follows a linking verb and completes the predicate by giving another name for the subject or by describing the subject.

> My mother was the *mayor* of our town.

Mayor cannot be called the direct object of the verb, since it is merely another name for my *mother,* and it can be made the subject of the sentence without changing the meaning: "The mayor of our town was my mother." To appreciate the difference between object and subject complements, substitute a transitive verb.

> My mother *criticized* the mayor.

The direct object, *mayor,* now names a person other than the subject, one who is acted upon by *my mother.* Making *mayor* the subject of this sentence would completely change the meaning.

A noun that serves as a subject complement of a linking verb is called a **predicate noun.** Linking verbs may also be completed by an adjective that describes the subject. Such a subject complement is called a **predicate adjective.**

> The mayor was *articulate* and *popular.*

Articulate and *popular* describe the subject, *mayor,* but instead of being directly attached to the noun ("an articulate, popular mayor"), they are joined to it by the linking verb *was* and become predicate adjectives.

24a

Pick out the subjects and verbs in the following sentences. Identify direct objects, indirect objects, predicate nouns, and predicate adjectives.

1. As a wedding present, my uncle gave us a picture.
2. It was an original sketch by Dufy.
3. The technique was interesting, since Dufy had used only a few simple lines.
4. It seemed an early work, according to a friend to whom I showed it.
5. We hung it in the living room and it looked good.
6. I wrote my uncle a note and thanked him for the picture.
7. We enjoyed it for several months, until my friend told us its value.
8. Then we worried about burglars, and we wrote my uncle again asking if he would give us a less valuable picture.

5. Phrases

A group of words may have the same function in a sentence as a single word. For example, in the sentence "The train to Boston leaves in ten minutes," the group of words *in ten minutes* modifies the verb *leaves* in exactly the same way as an adverb like *soon*. Similarly, *to Boston* functions like an adjective: it describes and identifies *train*. Such groups of words, which do not make a complete statement but which function like a single word, are called **phrases.** Phrases may be named for the kind of word around which they are constructed—prepositional, participial, gerund, or infinitive. Or they may be named by the way they function in a sentence—as adjective, adverb, or noun phrases.

24a

Prepositional phrases

A **prepositional phrase** consists of a preposition joined to a noun or a pronoun, which is called the object of the preposition. Such phrases usually modify nouns or verbs, and they are described accordingly as adjective or adverb phrases.

	adjective		**adverb**
The leader	*of the band*	swayed	*in the sun.*
The procession	*from the church to the cemetery*	continued	*for an hour.*

Verbal phrases

A **verbal** is a form of a verb that functions as some other part of speech. It is important to distinguish between verb forms ending in *-ing* and *-ed* when they function as part of the verb, as in "I was turning around," and such forms when they function as adjectives to modify a noun, as in "a turning point" or "a turned ankle." A verbal that modifies a noun is called a **participle.** Note that a participle may be in the past or in the present tense—"*a used* [past] car with *splitting* [present] upholstery."

A verb form that functions as a noun is called a **gerund:** "Writing is his passion." In this sentence, *writing* is the subject of the sentence. Gerunds may also be used as the objects of verbs or of prepositions.

		object of preposition
object of verb	
He loves	*writing*	and amuses himself by *scribbling dull verses.*

A third type of verbal is the **infinitive,** the present form of the verb preceded by the preposition *to: to write, to scribble.* Infinitives are frequently used as nouns—as subject or object of the verb.

| subject | | object |
| *To err* | is human, but remember | *to apologize.* |

Since they are verb forms, participles, gerunds, and infinitives may take objects, and they may be modified by adverbs or by prepositional phrases. A verbal with its modifier and its object, or subject, makes up a verbal phrase and functions as a single part of speech, but it does not make a full statement.

24a

| **Participial phrase** | *Moved by my mother's life of selfless dedication to the disadvantaged,* the townspeople voted to build a monument to her.
[Here the participle *moved*, modified by a prepositional phrase, describes the townspeople.] |
| **Gerund phrase** | *Selecting an inexpensive and appropriate site* took considerable time.
[Here the phrase—gerund, object, and the modifiers of the object—is the subject of the sentence.] |

Infinitive phrase   The task required *us to walk for hours.*
[The infinitive has a subject, *us,* and a modifying prepositional phrase, *for hours.*]

Absolute phrases

An **absolute phrase** is a group of words that has a subject but no verb and is not grammatically connected to the rest of the sentence. The subject of an absolute phrase is frequently followed by a participle.

The site having been selected, we met to choose a sculptor.

A tree, *all things considered,* is a better monument than a statue.

His brow creased with anger, his hands clenched on the table, the speaker insisted on having his way.

The subject of an absolute phrase may also be followed by an adjective or a prepositional phrase:

She recounted the incident, *her voice angry, her face pale.*

We listened quietly, *our hearts in our mouths.*

We left the room, *all hopes of a peaceful settlement in shambles.*

Because absolute phrases are formed by the suppression of connecting elements—prepositions ("*with* our hearts in our mouths") or subordinating conjunctions and finite verbs ("*when* all things *are* considered")—they have a toughness and economy that can be a virtue in writing.

24a

Appositive phrases

An **appositive** is a noun, or noun substitute, added to explain another noun: "My mother, *the mayor,* was the subject of controversy all her life." Appositives with their modifiers make up phrases, since they function as a unit to give further information about a noun.

The memorial she wanted, *a grand magnolia tree,* now stands in the center of town.

The townspeople, *wise and practical citizens,* made the decision, *a radical one for that time and place.*

Appositives, like absolute constructions, compress connections by eliminating words. The last sentence could have been written, "The townspeople, who were wise and practical citizens, made the decision, which was a radical one for that time and place," but the result would be a less economical and far less effective sentence.

EXERCISE 3

Pick out the phrases in the following sentences. Identify them as prepositional, participial, gerund, infinitive, or appositive, and be ready to describe their function in the sentence.

1. On Tuesday I came home expecting to drive my car, a shiny new convertible, into the garage.
2. To my surprise, I found a ditch between the street and the driveway.
3. A crew of workers had begun to lay a new water main along the curb.
4. Hoping that I would not get a ticket for overnight parking, I left the car in the street in front of the house.
5. For three days a yawning trench separated me from my garage.
6. Finding a place to park was difficult, since all the neighbors on my side of the street were in the same predicament.
7. By Friday the workers had filled up the ditch, but my car, stained with dust and dew, looked ten years older.
8. I had to spend the weekend washing and polishing it.
9. My brother, a strong advocate of justice, suggested sending the city a bill for the job.
10. But by this time my anger had dissipated, and I decided to forget the inconvenience I had endured.

24a

6. Clauses

A **clause** is a group of words that contains a subject and a predicate and that makes a statement. Except for elliptical questions and answers, every sentence must contain at least one clause.

Independent and dependent clauses

Although all sentences must contain a clause, not all clauses are sentences. Some clauses, instead of making an independent statement, serve only as a subordinate part of the main sentence. Such clauses, called **dependent** (or **subordinate**) **clauses,** perform a function like that of adjectives, adverbs, or nouns. **Independent clauses,** on the other hand, can stand alone as complete sentences. They provide the framework to which modifiers, phrases, and dependent clauses are attached in each sentence. Any piece of connected discourse is made up of a series of independent clauses.

"She heard the news" is a clause because it has a subject, *she*, and a verb, *heard*. It is an independent clause because it is complete in itself and can stand alone as a sentence. "When she heard the news" is also a clause because it has a subject and a predicate, but it is a dependent one. The addition of the word *when* creates a condition of incompleteness, or dependency. Any reader will expect to be told what happened when she heard the news.

dependent clause	independent clause
When she heard the news,	she was delighted.

Dependent clauses are usually connected to the rest of the sentence by **relative pronouns** (*who, which,* and *that*) or by **subordinating conjunctions** (such as *although, because, if, since, when,* and *while*). The terms *relative* and *subordinating* remind us that clauses introduced by these words are not self-sufficient; they are related or subordinated to the main or independent clause of the sentence. Written separately, they are fragments. (For more on relative pronouns and subordinating conjunctions, see **8a**. For further discussion of sentence fragments, see Chapter **29**.)

Dependent clauses function as parts of speech. Like nouns, they can be subjects and objects, and, like adverbs and adjectives, they can be modifiers.

Noun clauses

A **noun clause** functions as a noun in a sentence. It may be a subject or a complement in the main clause, or the object of a preposition or of a gerund.

Noun clause as subject of the sentence

That Lauren was considered for the position at all is remarkable.

Noun clause as direct object of the verb

She said *that she would accept only under certain conditions.*

24a

Noun clause as object of the preposition

We will give the job to *whoever is best qualified.*

Noun clause as object of a gerund

We do best for ourselves by asking *what we can do for others.*

Adverb clauses

An **adverb clause** is a dependent clause used to modify a verb, an adjective, or an adverb in the main clause.

Adverb clause

We ate *whenever we felt like it.*
[The clause *whenever we felt like it* modifies the verb *ate.*]

Adverb clause

The trip was as pleasant *as we had hoped.*
[The clause *as we had hoped* modifies the adjective *pleasant.*]

Adverb clause

The train arrived sooner *than we expected.*
[The clause *than we expected* modifies the adverb *sooner.*]

Adjective clauses

24a

A dependent clause used to modify a noun or pronoun is called an **adjective clause.**

Adjective clauses

The detective *whom we met yesterday* showed us his library, *which includes all the first editions of Dorothy Sayers.*
[The adjective clause *whom we met yesterday* modifies the noun *detective;* the adjective clause *which includes all the first editions of Dorothy Sayers* modifies the noun *library.*]

Adjective clauses are usually introduced by relative pronouns, which serve both as pronouns and as subordinating conjunctions. The following sentences illustrate how relative pronouns work.

Dorothy Sayers wrote many books; the books were widely read.
[This sentence consists of two independent clauses. It would be more idiomatic, however, if we substituted a pronoun for the second *books*.]

Dorothy Sayers wrote many books; *they* were widely read.
[If, instead of using the pronoun *they*, we now substitute the relative pronoun *that*, the second clause becomes dependent, and the sentence itself becomes more tightly subordinated.]

Dorothy Sayers wrote many books *that* were widely read.
[*That were widely read* no longer will stand as an independent sentence. Joined to the first clause, it functions as an adjective, modifying *books*.]

The relative pronouns *who* (and *whom*), *which*, and *that* always have two simultaneous roles: (1) they serve as subordinating conjunctions, connecting dependent clauses to independent ones, and (2) they function like nouns, as subject or complement in the dependent clause. Often, relative pronouns can be omitted: "She is a person I cherish." But sometimes they need to be expressed. "Hers is the kind of writing other writers envy" is awkward and confusing, but "Hers is the kind of writing *that* other writers envy" is not.

EXERCISE **4**

Find the simple subject and verb of each clause in the following sentences. Point out the main clauses and the dependent clauses, and be prepared to state the function in each sentence of each dependent clause.

24a

1. The movie director who did much to perfect the one-reel Western as a distinct genre was D. W. Griffith.
2. Shortly after he entered filmmaking in New York, Griffith achieved immediate success with his first film, which he directed in 1908.
3. Between 1908 and 1913, while he was directing Westerns, Griffith continually worked with techniques that others had introduced but that he gradually refined and perfected.
4. Griffith was delighted by the Western because it offered opportunities for spectacle and scope.
5. He found that the Western was an ideal genre in which to experiment with close-ups and with cross-cutting, the techniques he employed to build narrative suspense.
6. Some critics have pointed out that Griffith was more interested in

dramatic situations that lent themselves to lively visual treatment than he was in the details of plot or conventional justice.

7. He would willingly let the villains go free whenever he felt the dramatic situation warranted it.

8. The close-up of the outnumbered settlers grimly hanging on and the panoramic view of the battle seen from afar were characteristic Griffith shots.

9. In 1915, Griffith produced *The Birth of a Nation*, the first great spectacle movie.

10. It made use of many of the techniques he had developed while he was making one-reel Westerns.

24b Types of sentences

Sentences ask questions or answer them, issue commands or requests, express strong feeling, and, most often, make statements. The **syntax** of the sentence, its arrangement of words, tells us immediately what kind of sentence it is.

Exclamatory	What a ridiculous assignment!
Imperative	Write the paper.
Interrogative	Are you writing the paper?
Declarative	I have written the paper.

From the standpoint of structure, sentences are traditionally classified as simple, compound, complex, and compound-complex.

24b

1. Simple sentences

A **simple sentence** consists of one independent clause with or without modifying words or phrases but with no dependent clauses attached.

                   subject   **verb**
Simple   Harvey   despaired.

                         modifying phrase   **subject**   **verb**
Simple   Nervously biting his fingernails, Harvey   despaired

                     modifying phrase
of ever learning grammar.

modifying phrase
Simple   Nervously biting their fingernails,

compound subject
Harvey and his friend Zelda,

modifying phrase
puzzled once more by the red marks on their papers,

compound predicate with modifying phrase
despaired of ever learning the fine points of grammar and
longed for the simple beauty of differential calculus.

Obviously, simple sentences can be quite elaborate when the subject
or the verb is modified with verbals and appositives. Still, such sentences
can be reduced to a simple kernel and, as such, are limited in expressing
complicated ideas or showing the relation of one idea to another.
Moreover, simple sentence following simple sentence leads, at best,
to tedious writing, and, at worst, to what in writing is called a primer
style. The straightforward thrust of the simple declaration should be
modulated by the careful use of other types of sentences.

2. Compound sentences

The **compound sentence** consists of two or more independent
clauses joined by a coordinating conjunction or by a semicolon. There
are seven **coordinating conjunctions:** *and, but, for, nor, or, so,* and
yet.

24b

independent clause   **independent clause**
Compound   He wrote for hours,   and   his hunger vanished.

independent clause   **independent clause**
Compound   His style was graceful;   his sentences were lively and
                                          varied.

independent clause
Compound   His roommate left the shower running,   but

independent clause
Al did not notice.

The compound sentence offers the advantage of possible balance and antithesis. Skillfully used, it creates effective parallelism and coordination (see **8a** and **8c**).

3. Complex sentences

A **complex sentence** contains one independent clause and one or more dependent clauses that express subordinate ideas.

<table>
<tr><td></td><td align="center">dependent clause</td></tr>
<tr><td>**Complex**</td><td>Because he was tired and hungry and discouraged,</td></tr>
</table>

<table>
<tr><td></td><td align="center">independent clause</td></tr>
<tr><td></td><td>he did not want to rewrite the paper.</td></tr>
</table>

<table>
<tr><td></td><td align="center">independent clause</td><td align="center">dependent clause</td></tr>
<tr><td>**Complex**</td><td>Still, ideas for writing come</td><td>when we least expect them.</td></tr>
</table>

<table>
<tr><td></td><td align="center">independent clause</td><td align="center">dependent clause</td></tr>
<tr><td>**Complex**</td><td>Reluctantly, he put pen to paper,</td><td>while his roommate sang in the shower.</td></tr>
</table>

The complex sentence has the advantage of flexibility; it can be arranged to produce a variety of sentence patterns and to indicate subtle relationships between ideas. It also provides selective emphasis, since the subordination of dependent clauses throws the weight of the sentence onto the main clause. Understanding when and how to subordinate is a fundamental writing skill (see **8a**).

24b

4. Compound-complex sentences

When a compound sentence contains one or more dependent clauses, the whole is described as a **compound-complex sentence**.

<table>
<tr><td></td><td align="center">independent clause</td></tr>
<tr><td>**Compound-complex**</td><td>He was surprised</td></tr>
</table>

<table>
<tr><td></td><td align="center">dependent clause</td><td></td></tr>
<tr><td></td><td>when the water rose above his shoes,</td><td>but</td></tr>
</table>

<table>
<tr><td></td><td align="center">independent clause</td></tr>
<tr><td></td><td>he went on writing.</td></tr>
</table>

dependent clause

Compound-complex   Although he was drenched to the bone,

independent clause
he typed up the paper,   and

dependent clause
while his roommate bailed out the room,

independent clause
he read the finished manuscript with undampened satisfaction.

EXERCISE 5

Classify the following sentences as simple, compound, complex, or compound-complex. Identify the subject, verb, and complement, if any, in each clause. Describe the function of each dependent clause.

1. When Renaissance physicians began to study human anatomy by means of actual dissection, they concluded that the human body had changed since the days of antiquity.
2. Galen, a physician of ancient Greece, was generally accepted as the authority on anatomy and physiology.
3. His theory of the four humors—blood, phlegm, bile, and black bile— was neat and logical, and authorities had accepted it for centuries.
4. Similarly, his account of the structure of the human body, revised by generations of scholars and appearing in many printed editions, was generally accepted.
5. If dissection showed a difference from Galen's account, the obvious explanation was that human structure had changed since Galen's time.
6. One person who refused to accept this explanation was Andreas Vesalius, a young Belgian physician who was studying in Italy.
7. Asked to edit the anatomical section of Galen's works, Vesalius found many errors in it.
8. Galen's statement that the lower jaw consisted of two parts seemed wrong to Vesalius, who had never found such a structure in his own dissections.
9. He finally concluded that Galen was describing the anatomy of lower animals—pigs, monkeys, and goats—and that he had never dissected a human body.
10. When he realized that Galen could be wrong, Vesalius began a study that came to be recognized as his major work: a fully illustrated treatise on the human body based on actual observation.

24b

25 *Agreement*

As in many other languages, most of the nouns, pronouns, and verbs in English have different forms that indicate their relation to one another in a sentence. Most nouns and all verbs, for example, have different singular and plural forms; for a sentence to make grammatical sense, singular verbs must be used with singular subjects, and plural verbs with plural subjects. Pronouns, too, have separate forms to indicate number (singular or plural) and person (first person: *I, we;* second person: *you;* third person: *he, she, it, they*). The matching of subjects and verbs, pronouns and nouns, according to person and number in a sentence is called **agreement.**

The rules of agreement sound simple enough in theory, but in practice they can sometimes be a bit confusing. One reason for this confusion is that most speakers of English are not very sensitive to questions of agreement, because English has relatively few inflections, or different forms, to begin with. The verb *walked,* for example, remains the same whether its subject is singular or plural, or first, second, or third person:

I walked   you walked   they walked

A more unusual grammatical construction may therefore momentarily puzzle even the most meticulous user of English:

Either Susan or Alan is?/are? going to be nominated.

Athletics is?/are? in danger of being cut from the school budget.

To complicate matters further, dialectical variations among speakers of English often affect the rules of agreement, since various dialects may form singulars and plurals in different ways. Speakers of such dialects have two sets of rules to keep in mind: those that apply in

536

their dialect and those that operate in what is called Edited English, the English commonly used in business, journalism, academics, and professional life.

25a Agreement of subject and verb

The subject and verb of a sentence must agree in person and number. For example, if the subject is in the first-person singular (*I*), the verb must be also (*am*). The only highly inflected verb in English, that is, the only verb with several different forms, is *be:*

I *am*	we *are*
you *are*	you *are*
he/she/it *is*	they *are*

In most other English verbs, the only inflection is the *s* or *-es* added to the third-person singular in the present tense:

I know	we know
you know	you know
he/she/it knows	they know

What may be confusing here is the fact that plural nouns and singular verbs in the third-person-singular present usually end in *s,* whereas singular nouns and plural verbs usually do not:

Singular (verb ends in *s*)

The clock ticks loudly.

The star shines faintly.

That contestant has talent.

Plural (noun ends in *s*)

The clocks tick loudly.

The stars shine faintly.

Those contestants have talent.

This rule holds most of the time, but English includes some nouns whose singular *and* plural forms end in *s,* as well as a few irregular

25a

nouns whose plural forms do *not* end in *s* (for example, *man, woman, child, tooth, sheep, goose, criterion*). These unusual noun forms do not affect the correct form of the verb.

Singular (some nouns end in *s*)

That bus looks unreliable.

Gas sells for less now than it did last month.

Plural (some irregular nouns do not end in *s*)

Her feet feel tired.

Those phenomena seem to be inexplicable.

These, then, are the basic rules for subject-verb agreement in English. But we must also consider several grammatical situations that are sometimes puzzling. Note that these are not exceptions to the rules above; they are simply cases where it may be difficult at first to see how to apply those rules.

1. Modifying phrases after the subject

Uncertainty about which word is the subject of the sentence can result in an agreement error. A modifying phrase placed between the subject and verb may seem to change the number of the subject, but it does not.

Incorrect   A program of two Bergman films were shown last night.

Correct   A *program* of two Bergman films *was shown* last night.
[Because *films* is the noun closest to the verb, it may appear at first that the verb in this sentence should be plural. But *films* is simply the object of the preposition *of*. The subject of the sentence is *program*, and the verb must always agree with its subject no matter what words or phrases come between them.]

Phrases such as *accompanied by, as well as,* and *together with* suggest a plural idea, but they do not change the number of the subject. When you are determining whether your verb should be singular or plural, disregard these phrases and remember what your subject is.

25a

Incorrect	The prisoner, accompanied by guards and her lawyer, were in the courtroom.
Correct	The *prisoner,* accompanied by guards and her lawyer, *was* in the courtroom.
Incorrect	The mansion, along with the guest house and garages, were up for sale.
Correct	The *mansion,* along with the guest house and garages, *was* up for sale.

2. Compound subject

When two subjects are joined by *and,* they are usually considered plural.

Science and *math are* my best subjects.

The *screening, hiring,* and *training* of each applicant *are* left to the Personnel Department.

Sometimes, though, two nouns are used together to indicate a single idea; in those cases the verb is singular.

Bacon and eggs *is* a typical American breakfast.

Similarly, when the two nouns of a compound subject both refer to the same person or thing, the verb is also singular.

This young bachelor and man-about-town *was* finally discovered to be an impostor.

Finally, when *each* or *every* is used to modify a compound subject, a singular form of the verb is also used.

25a

Each soldier and sailor *was* given a complete examination.

Every camera and light meter *has* been reduced in price.

3. Collective nouns

Collective nouns, such as *class, committee, team, family,* and *number,* are treated as singular when they refer to the group as a unit. But if you want to emphasize the individual members of the group, you may use the plural form of the verb.

The committee *was* unanimous in its recommendation.

The team *were* unable to agree on a date for the party.
[Many writers would find this sentence awkward, even though it is correct, and would rephrase it, *The members of the team were unable to agree. . . .*]

The number of correct answers *was* small.

A number of papers *are* overdue.
[*Number* is singular when preceded by *the*, plural when preceded by *a*.]

4. Nouns ending in *s*

Some nouns that are plural in form are grammatically singular—for example, *aesthetics, economics, linguistics, mathematics, news, physics, semantics.*

Physics *was* the hardest course I had in high school.

The news *is* better than we had expected.

Note that certain other nouns ending in *s* have no singular form and are always plural—for example, *trousers, scissors, measles, forceps.* Finally, some nouns ending in *-ics*—such as *athletics, politics,* and *statistics*—may be either singular or plural, often with a distinction in meaning.

Athletics [the collective activity] *builds* the physique.

Athletics [particular activities] *are* her favorite pastime.

Statistics [the academic subject] *is* my most difficult course.

Statistics [the collected data] *suggest* that his argument is weak.

5. Linking verbs

When two nouns in a sentence are connected by some form of the verb *to be*, remember that the first noun is the subject and that the verb always agrees with it.

Incorrect The first thing visible on the horizon were the tuna boats.

Correct The first *thing* visible on the horizon *was* the tuna boats.

Correct The tuna *boats were* the first thing visible on the horizon.

25a

6.   Inverted sentence order

Sometimes the subject of a sentence follows the verb. In these cases of inverted word order, the subject and verb still agree.

Incorrect   Beyond the old mud fort was the endless sands of the desert.

Correct   Beyond the old mud fort *were* the endless *sands* of the desert.
[*Fort* **is the object of the preposition** *beyond* **in this sentence. The subject is** *sands,* **and the verb must therefore be plural,** *were.*]

In sentences beginning with *there is* or *there are, there* is an element called an **expletive** and is not the subject. The real subject of the sentence always follows the verb in these cases.

There *is* only one correct *solution* to this problem.

There *are* a million *laughs* in that movie.

There *is* a long *list* of jobs to be done before we leave.

There *are* many *jobs* to be done before we leave.

7.   Or/nor

When two singular subjects are joined by *or* or *nor,* the verb is singular if both subjects are singular and plural if both are plural.

Neither the *manufacturer* nor the *consumer was* treated fairly.

Poor testing *procedures* or inadequate safety *standards were* responsible for the accident.

When one subject is singular and one is plural, the verb agrees with the subject nearer it.

Neither Sam nor his *sisters have* ever been abroad.

Either good grades or an outstanding *recommendation is* needed for admission to the honors program.

8.   Indefinite pronouns

Some indefinite pronouns are always singular in number: *anybody, anyone, each, either, everybody, everyone, neither, nobody, no one,*

25a

one, somebody, someone. They are always correctly followed by singular verb forms.

> *Anyone* not admitted *is* guaranteed a refund.
>
> *Each* of the students *was* tested.
>
> *Somebody is* quietly walking up the stairs.

Other indefinite pronouns may be singular or plural: *all, any, more, most, none, some.* To determine whether the pronoun is singular or plural, look at the noun that it refers to.

> *All* of the food *has* been eaten.
>
> *All* of the hamburgers *have* been eaten.
>
> *None* of the money *was* lost.
>
> *None* of the coins *were* lost.

A few indefinite pronouns are always plural: *both, few, fewer, many, others, several.*

> *Others are* still waiting to apply, even though *fewer* than half *are* likely to be interviewed.

9.   Relative pronouns as subjects

The relative pronouns *who, which,* and *that,* when used as subjects of subordinate clauses, take a singular verb when their antecedent in the sentence is singular and a plural verb when it is plural.

> Betsy is a *woman* who *loves* life in the country.
>
> The school was destroyed by high *winds,* which *are* unusual at this time of year.

25a

The correct number of the relative pronoun may be a bit harder to determine when the sentence contains the phrase *one of the* or *one of those.*

> This is one of those inexpensive quartz *watches* that *are* made in Japan.
>
> **[The pronoun *that* refers to the group of watches.]**
>
> I selected the only *one* of the watches that *is* guaranteed for ten years.
>
> **[The pronoun *that* refers to just one of the watches, the one with the ten-year guarantee.]**

EXERCISE 1

Choose the correct verb forms in the following sentences.

1. The McCarthy hearings, held during 1953 and 1954, (represents, represent) a dark era in American history.
2. Senator Joseph R. McCarthy of Wisconsin had claimed as early as 1950 that there (was, were) more than two hundred Communists in the State Department.
3. McCarthy offered no proof for this claim, but people's concern that Communists were infiltrating various government offices (was, were) strong enough to give rise to a period of national hysteria.
4. The tool that McCarthy used to support his charges (was, were) public hearings before the Senate Investigations Subcommittee, which he chaired.
5. Each of the people who (was, were) called before the committee (was, were) confronted by several equally unpleasant choices.
6. A witness could admit his or her affiliation with the Communist party, could expose a friend or an associate who (was, were) linked to the party, or could take the Fifth Amendment.
7. The last of these options (was, were) almost as good as an admission of guilt.
8. Many of the people who (was, were) branded Communists by McCarthy's committee (was, were) "blacklisted"—that is, denied employment—after testifying.
9. Among the more famous of those who suffered blacklisting (was, were) the writer Dashiell Hammett and the musician Pete Seeger.
10. McCarthy's political influence, together with the waves of hysteria it spawned, (was, were) finally ended in December 1954, when the Senate voted to condemn his conduct.

25a

EXERCISE 2

Choose the correct verb forms in the following sentences.

1. Fads are phenomena that (touches, touch) almost every area of contemporary life.
2. Fashion, food, recreation, music—any of these fields (is, are) likely to be affected by fads.
3. One of the many clothing fads that (seems, seem) ridiculous when we look back at them (was, were) disposable paper dresses.
4. In the 1980s, Cajun cooking, including dishes like jambalaya and

blackened redfish, (was, were) suddenly popular in cities far away from the rural Cajun towns of Louisiana.

5. Among college students, the number of fads that (has, have) involved setting new records (is, are) high.

6. Sitting on flagpoles, swallowing goldfish, and packing people into phone booths (was, were) fun partly because of the publicity that such activities attracted.

7. Neither those tie-dyed T-shirts in the back of your closet nor that Hula-Hoop collection in your basement (is, are) likely to see daylight again.

8. But the skeptic or critic who (denounces, denounce) all fads will occasionally be surprised to discover that what once seemed a fad has found a permanent place in American culture.

9. (Was, Were) any of the people who scoffed at the jogging craze of the 1970s prepared to see this activity become so widespread and respectable two decades later?

10. Rock and roll (is, are) still more proof that some fads are here to stay.

25b Agreement of pronoun and antecedent

Pronouns agree in number with their antecedents, the words in a sentence that they refer to.

Many *people* pay a genealogist to look up *their* ancestry.
[*People*, the antecedent, is plural, so the pronoun *their* must also be plural.]

My *uncle* paid a genealogist to look up *his* ancestry.
[*His* agrees with *uncle*.]

Like subject-verb agreement, the basic principle of agreement between pronouns and antecedents is easy enough to understand. But again, a few unusual constructions may at first seem puzzling.

1. Compound antecedents

Compound antecedents, like compound subjects, are usually considered plural when joined by *and* and singular when joined by *or* or *nor*.

25b

My father encouraged *Henry* and *David* to postpone *their* trip.

Neither the *dog* nor the *cat* had touched *its* food.

2.   Collective nouns as antecedents

When the antecedent is a collective noun, the singular pronoun is used to emphasize the cohesiveness of the group, the plural to emphasize the separate individuals.

The *audience* showed *its* approval by applause.

The *audience* were on *their* feet, booing and whistling.

Note that in the second sentence the verb *were* is also in the plural form. Be consistent. If the verb form indicates that the antecedent is singular, the pronoun must also be singular. If the verb is plural, the pronoun must be plural too.

Incorrect	The panel is ready to give their opinions.
Correct	The panel *is* ready to give *its* opinions.
Correct	The panel *are* ready to give *their* opinions.

The second sentence here suggests that the panel members all hold the same opinions; the last sentence suggests that various members of the panel have different opinions to offer.

3.   Indefinite antecedents

In informal usage, indefinite pronouns like *anybody, anyone, each, either, everybody, everyone, neither, nobody, no one, somebody,* and *someone* are often treated as if they were plural.

25b

Informal	Almost *everyone* eats some fruit as part of *their* basic diet.

Strictly speaking, though, all of these pronouns are singular, and pronouns that follow them in Edited American English must also be singular. The problem is that English lacks singular personal pronouns that can refer to both males and females. Consequently, sentences such as the following, while grammatically correct, illogically exclude half the human population.

Illogical	*Anyone* returning merchandise must present *his* sales receipt.
Illogical	*No one* in line for the canceled tennis match got *her* money back.

Women, as well as men, may need to return merchandise, and men, as well as women, attend tennis matches. One solution to this problem is to use two pronouns, one masculine and one feminine, when the antecedent can be either male or female.

Correct	*Anyone* returning merchandise must present *his or her* sales receipt.
Correct	*No one* in line for the canceled tennis match got *his or her* money back.

However, some writers might consider this construction awkward, and most writers would probably reject the following similar sentence as unacceptably clumsy:

Correct but awkward	For once, *everyone* in the class saw *himself or herself* as *he or she* really was.

For all of these cases, a second correct—and less awkward—alternative is simply to rewrite the sentence with plural, rather than singular, nouns and pronouns.

Customers returning merchandise must present *their* sales receipts.

None of the people in line for the canceled tennis match got *their* money back.

For once, the class *members* saw *themselves* as *they* really were.

25b

Agreement problems similar to those involving indefinite pronouns as antecedents may arise when the antecedent is a singular noun that is not intended to refer to a specific person, place, or thing:

Incorrect	When a client calls the office, do not leave them on hold for more than a minute.
Incorrect	A person who fails to keep their dog on a leash will be ticketed.
Incorrect	If a customer isn't satisfied with their purchase, we will happily refund their money.

The agreement error can be corrected by using singular forms for the pronoun:

Correct   When a *client* calls the office, do not leave *him or her* on hold for more than a minute.

Again, though, the most graceful way of solving the agreement problem in such sentences may be to change the antecedents to the plural. Remember to make other nouns in the sentence plural if logic demands that you do so.

Correct   When *clients call* the office, do not leave *them* on hold for more than a minute.

Correct   *People* who *fail* to keep *their dogs* on *leashes* will be ticketed.

Correct   If any *customers aren't* satisfied with *their purchases,* we will happily refund *their* money.

(For additional advice on avoiding sexism in writing, see **13f**.)

4. Demonstrative pronouns

When demonstrative pronouns (*this, that, these, those*) are used as adjectives, they must agree in number with the words they modify. *This* and *that* are used with singular nouns, *these* and *those* with plural nouns.

Incorrect   These kind of vegetables are grown in the valley.

Correct   *This kind* of *vegetable is* grown in the valley.

Correct   *These kinds* of *vegetables are* grown in the valley.

25b

EXERCISE 3

Determine the causes of faulty agreement in the following sentences and correct the errors.

1. Cramped seating, unappealing food, long airport delays, lost baggage—because of these kind of problems, many people have come to dislike traveling by plane.
2. In contrast, a person who boards a long-distance train can expect to enjoy the trip ahead of them as much as the arrival at their destination.
3. Anybody who believes that train travel is obsolete should test their belief by traveling on one of Amtrak's scenic routes.
4. No one who takes the *Pioneer* from Chicago to Seattle, for example,

will be disappointed by the views from their window when the train crosses through the Rocky Mountains.

5. Because every car in the train is a double-decker, they offer passengers a spectacular view of the canyons and rivers.

6. These kind of cars are used only on Amtrak's western trains, because it could not fit through the low, nineteenth-century tunnels that are found along many eastern routes.

7. Eating your dinner as the scenery flies by outside your window is a delight, and the courteous dining-car staff is ready to do what they can to make your meal enjoyable.

8. Some people are able to sleep soundly in the wide coach seats, but the compact sleeping compartments, each of which can sleep two, has its advantages.

9. Anyone interested in history will appreciate the brochure they receive highlighting some of the historical events that occurred along the train's route.

10. The typical Amtrak passenger is someone who is less interested in arriving at their destination quickly than in enjoying the experience of traveling.

25b

26 Case of Pronouns and Nouns

Case refers to the changes in form of noun or pronoun that show how it is used in a sentence. Englis nouns used to have many case forms, but today the only case ending remaining are those that indicate possession (*child's, woman's, year's* Most pronouns, however, have three case forms: the **nominative** (o **subjective**) case when the pronoun is the subject of a verb; the **posses sive** (or **genitive**) case to show possession; and the **objective** cas‹ when the pronoun functions as the object of a verb or preposition.

Nominative	I	you	he	she	it	we	they	who
Possessive	my	your	his	her	its	our	their	whose
Objective	me	you	him	her	it	us	them	whom

As with agreement, we usually get the case right without consciously thinking about it. But a few constructions can occasionally cause writers trouble.

26a Compound constructions

A noun and a pronoun used together in a compound construction should be in the same case; the same principle applies to constructions like *we citizens* and to appositives. In most of these situations, you can easily check to determine that you have the pronoun in the right case by reading the sentence without the noun. It should still sound correct.

Correct   My *mother* and *I* have a good relationship.
[*Mother* and *I* are both in the nominative case because they are the compound subject of the verb *have*.]

Incorrect   The doctor asked my *mother* and *I* to come in together.
[Because a construction like *my mother and I* is so common, one can easily slip into it even in this sentence, where the objective pronoun is needed. The correct case of the pronoun becomes clear when we delete the noun *mother* from the compound direct object: *The doctor asked . . . I?/me? . . .*]

Correct   The doctor asked my *mother* and *me* to come in together.

Correct   *We children* always tried to please our parents by getting good grades.
[The fact that the pronoun is correctly in the nominative case is clear when we read the sentence without the noun *children: We . . . always tried. . . .*]

Incorrect   Our parents always rewarded *we children* for getting good grades.
[The correct case of the pronoun becomes clear when we delete the noun *children* from the sentence: *Our parents always rewarded we?/us? . . .*]

Correct   Our parents always rewarded *us children* for getting good grades.

Incorrect   Most of the float was designed by only two members of the class, Howard and *I*.
[Again, deleting the nouns *members* and *Howard* makes it clear that the objective case of the pronoun is needed here because the pronoun is in apposition with the object of the preposition *by: Most of the float was designed by . . . I?/me? . . .*]

26a

Correct   Most of the float was designed by only two members of the class, Howard and *me*.

Incorrect   Between *you* and *I*, this essay hasn't got a chance of winning the contest.
[Both pronouns are objects of the preposition *between*, and both must therefore be in the objective case.]

Correct   Between *you* and *me*, this essay hasn't got a chance of winning the contest.

26b *Who* and *whom* in dependent clauses

When in doubt about the case of the relative pronouns *who* and *whoever*, try a personal pronoun (*he/him, she/her, they/them*) in its place in the sentence. If *he, she,* or *they* sounds right, use the nominative, *who;* if *him, her,* or *them* fits the grammatical context, *whom* is correct.

Here is the woman *who?/whom?* can explain eclipses.
[We could say *she can explain eclipses,* but not *her can explain eclipses.* Thus, *who* is correct in this sentence; as the subject of the clause, it is in the nominative case.]

Marshall is the man *who?/whom?* I told you about.
[In this sentence, the pronoun is not the subject of the clause; instead, the clause means *I told you about. . . . Him,* rather than *he,* fits this context; the correct pronoun is thus *whom,* the object of the preposition *about.*]

Here are the extra blue books for *whoever?/whomever?* needs them.
[We could say *he needs them* or *she needs them,* but not *him needs them* or *her needs them.* The correct pronoun is thus *whoever.* It is in the nominative case because it is the subject of the verb *needs.*]

The awards will be presented to *whoever?/whomever?* the council nominates.
[We could say *the council nominates them,* but not *the council nominates they.* The correct pronoun is thus *whomever.* It is in the objective case because it is the object of the verb *nominates.*]

26b

Note that the case of the pronoun *who* or *whom* is unaffected by the insertion of phrases like *I think* or *we know* into the dependent clause.

The artist *who?/whom?* I thought would design the awards has changed her mind.
[The sense of the dependent clause is *I thought [that] she/her would design the awards.* Only *she* fits into this clause, so *who* is the correct pronoun. It is in the nominative case because it is the subject of the verb *would design.*]

We trust the advice of friends *who?/whom?* we know can be objective.
[The sense of the dependent clause is *we know [that] they/them*

**can be objective. Only *they* fits this clause, so *who* is again
the correct pronoun. It is in the nominative case because it is
the subject of the verb *can be*.**]

But compare the following different situation, where the phrase *we
know* constitutes the subject and verb of the dependent clause:

> We trust the advice of the friends *who?/whom?* we know best.
> **[Here the dependent clause means *we know they/them best*.
> Only *them* fits into this sentence, so the correct pronoun is *whom*,
> the object of the verb *know*.**]

26c *Who* and *whom* in interrogatives

To determine the correct case of the interrogative pronouns
who and *whom*, apply the same test described above for dependent
clauses. If the answer to the question includes the nominative form
of the personal pronoun, *who* is the correct interrogative; if the answer
includes the objective form, *whom* is correct.

> *Who* is coming to the party? [*They* are coming.]
>
> *Whom* are you expecting at the party? [I am expecting *them*.]

In speech and in much informal writing, the tendency is to use *who*
as the interrogative form, no matter what its grammatical place in
the sentence. Formal, edited English requires *whom* when the pronoun
is in the objective case.

> **Informal**   *Who* are you expecting for dessert?
> **Formal**   *Whom* are you expecting for dessert?
>
> **Informal**   *Who* are you leaving with?
> **Formal**   With *whom* are you leaving?

26d Reflexive and intensive pronouns

A special type of pronoun is used to refer to a noun or pronoun
mentioned earlier in a sentence. These pronouns are called **reflexive
pronouns.**

Nominative form	Reflexive form
I	myself
you (singular)	yourself
he	himself
she	herself
it	itself
we	ourselves
you (plural)	yourselves
they	themselves

Note that the following forms do not exist except in nonstandard usage: *hisself, themself, theirselves.*

The reflexive form of the pronoun is used instead of the objective form whenever the actor in a sentence and the recipient of the action are the same.

Reflexive *Scott* accidentally cut *himself* with the knife.

Reflexive *We* had never seen *ourselves* on television before.

Since a reflexive pronoun by definition refers back to another noun or pronoun, it may appear in a sentence only if the noun or pronoun to which it refers also appears.

Incorrect Gina and *myself* are flying to Des Moines tomorrow.

Correct Gina and *I* are flying to Des Moines tomorrow.

Incorrect The plane tickets arrived in an envelope addressed to my mother and *myself.*

Correct The plane tickets arrived in an envelope addressed to my mother and *me.*

26d

When the pronoun forms above are used to emphasize a noun or another pronoun in a sentence, rather than to designate the recipient of an action, they are known as **intensive pronouns:**

Intensive *Scott himself* was responsible for the accident.
[No one else was to blame.]

Intensive *We* found the television studio by *ourselves.*
[No one assisted us.]

26e Pronouns after *than, as,* and *but*

After *than* or *as,* the case of a pronoun is determined by its use in the shortened clause of which it is a part.

My cousin is taller than *I* [am].

They take more photographs than *we* [do].

I can type as well as *he* [can].

Sometimes a comparison involving *than* or *as* can be completed in two possible ways. In such situations, the case of the pronoun will determine how the reader understands the sentence:

They like Kelley more than *I* [do].

They like Kelley more than [they like] *me.*

Kelley cares about them as much as *I* [do].

Kelley cares about them as much as [she cares about] *me.*

The word *but* is sometimes used as a preposition meaning "except." A pronoun that follows *but* in such constructions is the object of the preposition and should therefore be in the objective case.

| Incorrect | All the guests at the party had a good time but Judy and *I.* |
| Correct | All the guests at the party had a good time but Judy and *me.* |

26f Pronouns with linking verbs

The subject complement of a linking verb, such as a form of the verb *be,* is in the nominative case (see **24a**). Despite the widespread tolerance in spoken English of forms like "It is me" and "I thought it was her," the correct, nominative form of a pronoun should be used when the pronoun follows a linking verb in writing.

| Incorrect | When the voice on the telephone asked for Dr. Kim, I said, "This *is her.*" |
| Correct | When the voice on the telephone asked for Dr. Kim, I said, "This *is she.*" |

Incorrect	I expected the caller to be Richard Markson, but it *was* not *him*.
Correct	I expected the caller to be Richard Markson, but it *was* not *he*.
Incorrect	It appears that the members of the delegation *will be* Mr. Rosen, Ms. Kowalski, and *me*.
Correct	It appears that the members of the delegation *will be* Mr. Rosen, Ms. Kowalski, and *I*.

26g Pronouns with infinitives

Both the subject and the object of an infinitive (usually a verb form preceded by *to*) are in the objective case. The objective form of a pronoun must be used when the pronoun is in either of these positions in the sentence.

| Subject of infinitive | The company president wanted *me to lie* when I testified before the committee. |
| Object of infinitive | I would not like *to be him* when the company's wrongdoing is revealed. |

26h Pronouns and nouns with gerunds

In grammatical terms, gerunds function in a sentence like nouns (see **24a**). Therefore, a noun or pronoun modifying a gerund, like a noun or pronoun modifying any noun, must be in the possessive case.

26h

Incorrect	Alan's parents disapproved of *him traveling* alone in Greece.
Correct	Alan's parents disapproved of *his traveling* alone in Greece. **[The first sentence erroneously suggests that Alan's parents disapproved of *him*. In the second sentence, the possessive pronoun *his* identifies the gerund *traveling* as the actual object of the preposition *of*.]**
Incorrect	They also objected to his *sister bicycling* through Canada.
Correct	They also objected to his *sister's bicycling* through Canada. **[The first sentence suggests that they found his *sister***

objectionable. In the second sentence, the possessive noun *sister's* identifies the gerund *bicycling* as the actual object of the preposition *to.*]

Choose the correct case for the pronoun in each of the following sentences.

1. John Fitzgerald Kennedy, the man (who, whom) we remember as America's thirty-fifth President, was born in Massachusetts in 1917.
2. For decades, his family and (he, him) figured prominently in the news.
3. Political observers were consequently not surprised by (him, his) deciding to run for President in 1960.
4. Whatever people thought of Kennedy's politics, they agreed that few presidential candidates had been as charismatic as (he, him).
5. The presidential debates between the two candidates, Richard Nixon and (he, him), were the first ever to be televised.
6. It was Kennedy (who, whom) the analysts declared to be victor.
7. After the debates Kennedy's support grew, and although the election was one of the closest ever in terms of the popular vote, the winner was finally determined to be (he, him).
8. Kennedy's administration was marked by idealism from the beginning; after all, it was (he, him) who said, "And so, my fellow Americans, ask not what your country can do for you; ask what you can do for your country."
9. Kennedy was the leader (who, whom) a new generation of Americans looked to for inspiration.
10. In his short lifetime, he left his mark on American politics—indeed, on all of (we, us) Americans.

26h

Choose the correct case for the pronoun in each of the following sentences.

1. Gertrude Stein, (who, whom) critics continue to regard as one of the great creative figures in modern literature, was born in Pennsylvania in 1874 but spent most of her life abroad.
2. (Who, Whom) would have guessed that this Radcliffe undergraduate would go on to influence art and literature in the early decades of the twentieth century?
3. After moving to Paris in 1903, Stein used her personal wealth to support young artists; indeed, no one of the time was a more dedicated patron of art than (she, her).

4. Pablo Picasso and (she, her) became friends soon after he moved to Paris in 1904.

5. Stein's experiments in literary form propelled her into the world of literature and made her a writer (who, whom) dazzled and inspired her contemporaries in the 1920s.

6. Ernest Hemingway, F. Scott Fitzgerald, and Ezra Pound were among the authors (who,whom) she encouraged and influenced.

7. It was (she, her) who coined the now-famous phrase *a lost generation* to describe such writers after World War I.

8. Stein's witty autobiography, *The Autobiography of Alice B. Toklas* (1933), has remained popular among readers (who, whom) want to understand (she, her) and her times.

9. Stylistic innovations established Stein as a major literary figure, and it is largely because of (they, them) that her reputation has endured.

10. Admittedly, though, Stein's often difficult style can sometimes be as puzzling to (we, us) readers today as it was to her contemporaries.

26h

27 *Adjectives and Adverbs*

Adjectives and adverbs are similar types of modifiers with slightly different functions. **Adjectives** modify nouns and pronouns; they provide such information as the color, size, type, or manner of the words they describe.

> The car came to a *sudden* stop.

> The performers began an *elegant* dance.
> **[In these sentences, *sudden* describes the kind of stop that the car made, and *elegant* describes the dance done by the performers.]**

Adverbs, on the other hand, modify verbs, adjectives, and other adverbs. They answer questions like *when? where? why? in what way? to what degree?*

> The car *suddenly* stopped.

> The performers began an *unusually* elegant dance.
> **[In the first sentence here, the adverb *suddenly* modifies the verb *stopped*. In the second, the adverb *unusually* modifies the adjective *elegant* (not the dance, but its elegance, was unusual).]**

Most adverbs are formed by adding *-ly* to the adjective: *clear, clearly; immediate, immediately*. But like other rules of English, this one has its exceptions. Some adjectives and adverbs have the same form: the *far* corner, *much* pleased, I *little* thought, do it *right*, run *fast*. And a few adjectives and adverbs have completely different forms: a *good* job, a job done *well*. Finally, some adjectives already end in *-ly*: a *friendly* gesture, a *manly* appearance, a *leisurely* vacation. In some of these cases, the adverb form is the same; in others, there is no corresponding adverb in English. A dictionary is your best guide.

27a Comparative and superlative forms

For establishing comparisons, most adjectives and adverbs have three different forms: the **positive** (or dictionary) form, the **comparative** form, and the **superlative** form.

1. Comparative and superlative forms of adjectives

Adjectives usually form the comparative by adding *-er* and the superlative by adding *-est*.

tall	taller	tallest
lively	livelier	liveliest

Many adjectives of two syllables and all longer adjectives form the comparative and superlative by adding *more* and *most*.

alert	more alert	most alert
ambitious	more ambitious	most ambitious

All adjectives indicate lesser degree by adding *less* for the comparative and *least* for the superlative.

lively	less lively	least lively
ambitious	less ambitious	least ambitious

2. Comparative and superlative forms of adverbs

Adverbs nearly always form the comparative and superlative with *more* and *most*.

slowly	more slowly	most slowly
beautifully	more beautifully	most beautifully

A few adverbs that do not end in *-ly* form the comparative and superlative by adding *-er* and *-est*.

fast	faster	fastest
near	nearer	nearest

27a

All adverbs indicate lesser degree by adding *less* for the comparative and *least* for the superlative.

slowly	less slowly	least slowly
beautifully	less beautifully	least beautifully

3. Irregular comparative and superlative forms

A few adjectives and adverbs form the comparative and superlative irregularly.

Irregular adjectives

bad	worse	worst
good	better	best
little	less	least
many	more	most
much	more	most
some	more	most

Irregular adverbs

badly	worse	worst
well	better	best

4. Adjectives and adverbs without comparative and superlative forms

Some adjectives and adverbs, like *unique/uniquely*, *perfect/perfectly*, *infinite/infinitely*, and *chief/chiefly*, cannot logically take comparative or superlative forms. Since unique means "one of a kind," no object can be more unique than another. Similarly, a thing is either perfect or not perfect; strictly speaking, no degree of perfection is possible.

Formal writing, therefore, tends to avoid expressions like *more perfect* or *most unique*, although you may use modifiers like *nearly* and *almost* that indicate an approach to the absolute.

Correct   Records are disappearing from the shelves of music stores now that compact discs offer *more nearly perfect* sound reproduction.

27a

Correct The brilliance of this diamond makes it an *almost unique* gem.

In informal writing, the comparative and superlative forms *more perfect* and *most perfect* are occasionally tolerated.

Acceptable informally This is the *most perfect* pumpkin in the field.

The forms *more unique* and *most unique,* however, remain unacceptable in any context to the vast majority of users of English.

Unacceptable That abstract painting is the *most unique* representation of the New York City sky-line that I have seen.

5. Correct use of comparative and superlative forms

In formal writing, the comparative is used for comparisons involving two persons or things, and the superlative for comparisons involving three or more persons or things.

Of my two brothers, Jack was the *taller*.

She was the *quickest* person on the team.

In speech and informal writing, this distinction is not always observed, and the superlative is often used even when only two things are being compared: "Of the two styles offered, the first was the *most* popular."

Be careful to avoid double comparisons—that is, constructions that combine *more* or *most, less* or *least* with an adjective or adverb that already ends in *-er* or *-est.*

27a

Incorrect I prefer this *more darker* shade of green paint.

Correct I prefer this *darker* shade of green paint.

Incorrect The salesperson says that of all the paints on the market, this one dries *most fastest*.

Correct The salesperson says that of all the paints on the market, this one dries *fastest*.

For advice on avoiding incomplete comparisons, see **12g**.

27b Adjectives with linking verbs

Linking verbs such as *be, become, seem,* and *appear,* as well as verbs associated with the five senses (*look, feel, taste, sound, smell*) and certain other verbs suggesting development (*become, grow, prove*), are often used to link a subject and a modifying adjective, the subject complement (see **24a**).

The swimmer
$$\begin{cases} \text{was} \\ \text{seemed} \\ \text{looked} \\ \text{felt} \\ \text{sounded} \\ \text{became} \end{cases}$$ *cold.*

Note that a subject complement can never be an adverb, because adverbs modify only verbs, adjectives, and other adverbs, not nouns or pronouns.

Incorrect	I felt *badly* about Carolyn's accident.
	[Since the only word in this sentence that the adverb *badly* can modify is the verb *felt*, the sentence seems to suggest that the writer's ability to feel was deficient.]
Correct	I felt *bad* about Carolyn's accident.
	[The adjective *bad* correctly modifies the subject, *I*.]
Incorrect	George looks *well* in a tuxedo.
	[Since the only word in this sentence that the adverb *well* can modify is the verb *looks*, the sentence seems to suggest that wearing a tuxedo enhances George's vision.]
Correct	George looks *good* in a tuxedo.
	[The adjective *good* correctly modifies the subject, George.]

27b

Of course, a verb in the list above may be followed by an adverb, but in such a case it ceases to function as a linking verb. Consider the following examples:

Adjective and linking verb	The *gong* sounded *hollow.*
	[It seemed to be hollow.]
Adverb	The gong *sounded hollowly.*
	[It made a hollow sound when it was rung.]

Adjective and linking verb	*Gail* looked *weary* to me. **[I thought she appeared weary.]**
Adverb	Gail *looked wearily* to me. **[She turned to me in a weary manner.]**
Adjective and linking verb	My opponent's *argument* proved *convincing*. **[It turned out to be a convincing argument.]**
Adverb	My opponent's argument *proved convincingly* that she had not adequately prepared for the debate. **[It offered convincing proof that she was unprepared.]**

27c Nouns used as adjectives

Nouns in English frequently function as adjectives modifying other nouns.

> *Contract negotiations* are stalled over the issue of *salary increases* for the *night shift.*

Our lives are full of concrete things and abstract concepts identified by such noun-plus-noun combinations: *light bulb, sofa bed, turkey sandwich, gas station, movie review, smog alert, computer literacy, investment opportunity.* The main point to remember in using nouns as adjectives is that more than three nouns in a row can make for a dense, confusing sentence:

Confusing	The spring office softball tournament preparations are proceeding smoothly.

Such a sentence can be clarified by breaking up the cluster of nouns and by using possessive nouns where possible:

Clearer	Preparations for the office's spring softball tournament are proceeding smoothly.

27d Compound adjectives

When a compound adjective is formed from two nouns, from an adjective and a noun, or from two adjectives, the compound is hyphenated when it precedes the noun that it modifies.

The *locker-room* brawl left six players injured.

My favorite *high-school* teacher was Ms. Resnick.

Marcia looked out over the *blue-green* waters of the gulf.

All the elements of a phrase used as an adjective are also hyphenated.

I wish I had her *never-say-die* attitude.

Peter knew the invitation was a *once-in-a-lifetime* opportunity.

Remember, though, that *-ly* adverbs used with adjectives are a different grammatical situation. Such adverbs are modifiers, not parts of a compound, and they are not hyphenated.

Their first apartment was in an *exceptionally decrepit* building.

However, similar constructions with the term *well* usually *are* hyphenated when they precede the modified noun: *a well-managed business, a well-done steak* (but *a steak well done*).

27e Colloquial forms

In some spoken contexts, the following pairs of modifiers may be used interchangeably: *real/really, sure/surely, almost/most.* Written English demands more careful distinctions between them.

Real is an adjective; in writing, it should not be used in place of the adverb *really* ("truly") to modify verbs, adverbs, or other adjectives.

Acceptable in speech	Ever since our house was burglarized, we haven't been sleeping *real* well at night.
Preferred in writing	Ever since our house was burglarized, we haven't been sleeping *really* well at night.

Sure, another adjective, should not take the place of the adverb *surely* ("certainly") in writing.

Acceptable in speech	Steve *sure* feels bad about having left the back door unlocked.
Preferred in writing	Steve *surely* feels bad about having left the back door unlocked.

When *most* functions as an adverb, it means "very" or "to the greatest extent": "Last quarter's sales report is *most* encouraging." It

27e

should not be used in writing to mean "nearly," a sense reserved for the adverb *almost*.

Acceptable   *Most* every night since the burglary he's gone downstairs
in speech   to recheck the locks.

Preferred   *Almost* every night since the burglary he's gone downstairs
in writing   to recheck the locks.

EXERCISE 1

Correct the use of adjectives and adverbs in the following sentences so that it conforms to the standards of formal written English.

1. Learning to write is a bit like learning to play a musical instrument such as the piano. You can spend hours listening to records or tapes and still play bad, for only practice will bring real results.
2. In the same way, you may study a composition textbook and grasp all of its abstractest principles, but they will remain abstract until you actually write.
3. If you pick up a little piano playing on your own and then study the instrument more formal, you will experience the difficulty of overcoming bad habits.
4. By the same token, in a college writing class you are not really a beginner, since you have had years of high school practice, but you may have been writing without consciously paying attention to details.
5. As a sophisticated writer, you will need to discover a more unique voice, a self projected onto the page, just as a musician finds a style that seems real natural.
6. In addition, you will need to develop a more subtler understanding of the audiences you write for.
7. There's room for developing your technical expertise as well. Just as the novice pianist masters the keyboard by practicing drills and scales, you will find that the college composition textbook grammar exercises that your instructor assigns will contribute to your mastery of the language.
8. In this comparison of the pianist and the writer, does the latter's task seem to be the most difficult?
9. In one way, at least, it is: unlike the pianist, the writer most always has to find his or her own subject. That challenge is a great one, for readers expect a writer to avoid run of the mill topics and to strive for originality.
10. For many writers, finding an original perspective is the most infinitely difficult part of the writing process.

27c

11. Some writers read widely, some keep journals, some use a variety of brainstorming strategies—all in the hope that they will see the world fresh.
12. Writers do enjoy one advantage denied to musicians, though: they are free from the terror of a live, one time performance.
13. As a writer you can work in private as slow as you wish.
14. You can revise your essay over and over, and your audience will not see it until it is fixed firm on the page exactly as you want it.
15. In contrast, pianists never know how their performances will turn out, and they do not have the opportunity to take back their less perfect ones.

27e

28 *Verbs*

At the center of every sentence stands a verb, a word describing an action or a condition. In Chapter **24** we examined the syntactic relationship between the verb and other elements in a sentence. Here we turn our attention to verb forms—in particular, the forms that indicate tense, voice, and mood.

28a Verb forms

Verbs not only present an action or a condition, but also indicate a time frame within which that action or condition occurs—at present, in the past, in the future. This indication of time depends on verb forms known as **tenses,** which in English are constructed from the five verb forms illustrated in the tables below. The first three of these forms—base, past, and past participle—are known as the **principal parts** of a verb. Depending on how they form their principal parts, verbs are classified either as **regular** or as **irregular.**

Regular verbs

Base	Past	Past participle	Present participle	-s form
trust	trusted	trusted	trusting	trusts
agree	agreed	agreed	agreeing	agrees
deny	denied	denied	denying	denies

As these examples illustrate, the past and past participle of regular verbs are both formed by adding -*ed* or (when the verb already ends in *e*) -*d.*

Irregular verbs

Base	Past	Past participle	Present participle	-s form
sing	sang	sung	singing	sings
have	had	had	having	has
cut	cut	cut	cutting	cuts

By definition, irregular verbs form their principal parts in unpredictable ways. As these examples indicate, some change an internal vowel, others change an ending, and still others retain the same spelling in all three principal parts. For examples of some of the additional variations among irregular verb forms, see **28b** below.

One irregular English verb, *be,* is exceptional in that it has eight different forms rather than five:

Forms of *be*

Base	Past	Past participle	Present participle	-s form	Additional forms
be	was	been	being	is	am
	were				are

Be in the present and past tenses

	Present	Past
I	am	was
you (singular)	are	were
he/she/it	is	was
we	are	were
you (plural)	are	were
they	are	were

28b Irregular verbs

As noted above, a number of frequently used English verbs form their principal parts in irregular ways. Below are some of the most common and most commonly confused of these irregular verbs. Remember that your dictionary is a more complete guide. You can find the principal parts of any irregular verb in a desk dictionary by looking under its base form.

Base	Past	Past participle
arise	arose	arisen
awake	awoke, awaked	awaked, awoken
become	became	become
begin	began	begun
bid (offer)	bid	bid
bid (command)	bade	bidden
bite	bit	bitten
blow	blew	blown
break	broke	broken
bring	brought	brought
build	built	built
burn	burned, burnt	burned, burnt
burst	burst	burst
buy	bought	bought
catch	caught	caught
choose	chose	chosen
cling	clung	clung
come	came	come
cost	cost	cost
creep	crept	crept
deal	dealt	dealt
do	did	done
draw	drew	drawn
drink	drank	drunk
drive	drove	driven
eat	ate	eaten
fall	fell	fallen
fight	fought	fought
find	found	found

281

Base	Past	Past participle
fling	flung	flung
fly	flew	flown
forget	forgot	forgotten, forgot
freeze	froze	frozen
get	got	got, gotten
give	gave	given
go	went	gone
grow	grew	grown
hang (suspend)	hung	hung
hear	heard	heard
hide	hid	hidden, hid
hit	hit	hit
know	knew	known
lay (put)	laid	laid
lead	led	led
leap	leaped, leapt	leaped, leapt
lend	lent	lent
lie (recline)	lay	lain
plead	pleaded, pled	pleaded, pled
rid	rid, ridded	rid, ridded
ride	rode	ridden
ring	rang	rung
rise	rose	risen
run	ran	run
see	saw	seen
shake	shook	shaken
show	showed	shown, showed
shrink	shrank, shrunk	shrunk, shrunken
sing	sang	sung
sink	sank	sunk
sit	sat	sat
slay	slew	slain

28b

Base	Past	Past participle
speak	spoke	spoken
spin	spun	spun
spring	sprang, sprung	sprung
steal	stole	stolen
strike	struck	struck, stricken
strive	strove, strived	striven, strived
swear	swore	sworn
swim	swam	swum
swing	swung	swung
take	took	taken
teach	taught	taught
tear	tore	torn
think	thought	thought
throw	threw	thrown
wake	woke, waked	waked, woken
wear	wore	worn
weave	wove	woven
wed	wedded	wed, wedded
wind	wound	wound
wring	wrung	wrung
write	wrote	written

The following *regular* verbs are sometimes confused with similar irregular verbs:

1. dive/dived/dived

   The past form *dove* is widespread in speech, but it remains unacceptable in writing to many users of English. *Dived* is the safer choice.

2. hang/hanged/hanged

   In the sense "to execute," *hang* is a regular verb: "Despite protests from opponents of the death penalty, the convicted murderer was *hanged* at dawn." Compare with *hang* ("to suspend") above.

3. lie/lied/lied

In the sense "to tell an untruth," *lie* is a regular verb. Compare with lie ("to recline") above.

4. weave/weaved/weaved

In the sense "to move in and out," *weave* is a regular verb: "The car ahead of me *weaved* recklessly through the heavy traffic." Compare with *weave* ("to make cloth") above.

28c Verb tenses

As we explained above, by *tense* we mean variations in the form of a verb that indicate differences in time. English verbs have six principal tenses.

1. Present tense

The present tense designates a current act or condition, or an act that is regularly repeated. It is expressed with the base form of the verb or, in the third person singular, with the -*s* form.

> Some scientists *believe* that the so-called greenhouse effect *is* already apparent.
>
> The earth's average temperature *rises* slightly each year because of increased amounts of carbon dioxide in the atmosphere.

The present tense is also used in discussions of literary and artistic works.

> When Hamlet *is* alone, he *contemplates* suicide.

Combined with modifiers that indicate time, the present tense can assert that an act or condition will occur in the future.

> *Are* you available for tomorrow's staff meeting?
>
> No, my flight *leaves* tonight at eight o'clock.

2. Past tense

The past tense designates an act or condition that occurred at a specific time in the past. It is expressed with the past form of the verb.

On September 7, 1940, the German Luftwaffe *began* its night bombing of London.

The British people *were* ready for the attacks.

The past tense also indicates recurrent actions in the past that have not continued into the present.

Every night for two months, Londoners *took* refuge from the bombs in the city's vast network of subway stations.

3. Future tense

The future tense designates an act or condition that will occur at some time in the future. It is formed by preceding the base form of the verb with *will* or *shall*. Note that earlier differences in meaning between *will* and *shall* have largely disappeared, and *shall* is rarely used today in American English except in questions: "Shall we eat out tonight?"

The doctor *will see* you first thing tomorrow morning.

She *will be* pleased to hear that your condition has improved.

4. Present perfect tense

The present perfect tense designates an act or condition that occurred at an indefinite time in the past, or one that began in the past and continues in the present. It is formed by preceding the past participle form of the verb with *have* or *has*.

Professor Maguire *has finished* his most recent novel.

Several publishers *have been* interested in the manuscript since he began it.

28c

5. Past perfect tense

The past perfect tense designates an act completed or a condition existing in the past before some other specific time in the past. It is formed by preceding the past participle form of the verb with *had*.

I *had* already *composed* my letter of resignation when the telephone rang.

My supervisor wanted to know why I *had seemed* so unhappy during the previous weeks.

6. Future perfect tense

The future perfect tense designates an act that will be completed or a condition that will exist before some other specific time in the future. It is formed by preceding the past participle form of the verb with *will have*.

By March 1, the state transportation department *will have submitted* its plans for the new highway to the airport.

Unfortunately, projected increases in airport traffic suggest that the highway *will* already *have become* obsolete by the time it is completed next year.

7. Progressive forms

Each of the verb tenses in English also has a so-called **progressive form** to indicate that an act extends continuously over a period of time. The progressive form is created by substituting the present participle for the form of the verb used in each tense and adding a form of the verb *be*. Compare the following sentences in the progressive tense with their counterparts above.

Present progressive	The earth's average temperature *is rising* slightly each year because of increased amounts of carbon dioxide in the atmosphere.
Past progressive	The British people *were preparing* for the attacks.
Future progressive	The doctor *will be seeing* more patients this afternoon than she expected.
Present perfect progressive	Professor Maguire *has been finishing* his most recent novel for several months.
Past perfect progressive	I *had been composing* my letter of resignation for two hours when the telephone rang.
Future perfect progressive	By March 1, the state transportation department *will have been planning* the new highway to the airport for two years.

28c

28d Sequence of tenses

Almost any extended passage of English prose contains verbs in different tenses:

> I suddenly *remembered* [past] that Chris *is* [present] often late for business meetings and *wished* [past] that I *had called* [past perfect] to make sure he *was* [past] on his way. If he *fails* [present] to show up, I *thought* [past], the client *will* probably *drop* [future] us from the project and we *will have wasted* [future perfect] a month of work.

The trick is determining which tenses can logically follow one another, particularly in a sentence containing one or more dependent clauses. As the following sentences indicate, the relationships among tenses can sometimes be more complicated than they first appear:

Incorrect When the mayor died, her fellow citizens realized how much she contributed to the community, and since then they collected money for a memorial.

Correct When the mayor died, her fellow citizens realized how much she *had contributed* [before her death] to the community, and since then they *have collected* [from that time to the present] money for a memorial.

1. Sequence of tenses in dependent clauses

There are no absolute rules governing the correct sequence of tenses in sentences that contain dependent clauses. Instead, you have to let the sense of the sentence be your guide. The examples below illustrate some, but not all, of the possibilities.

28d

Main verb in present tense

The motor *starts* when I *press* this button.
[Present + present. The verbs in both the independent clause and the dependent clause are properly in the present tense because the sense of the sentence is to describe two recurring actions: "The motor starts *every time* I press this button."]

Main verb in past tense

The motor *started* when I *pressed* this button.
[Past + past. When the verb in an independent clause is in the past tense, the verb in a dependent clause is often in the past tense as well. In this sentence the two verbs designate actions that occurred approximately simultaneously in the past and that have not continued into the present.]

The motor *started* after I *had pressed* this button.
[Past + past perfect. When the verb in an independent clause is in the past tense, the verb in the dependent clause may be in the past perfect tense. In this sentence the verb in the dependent clause designates an action in the past that occurred before the action designated by the verb in the independent clause.]

The motor *started* even though it *is* old.
[Past + present. When the verb in an independent clause is in the past tense, the verb in the dependent clause may be in the present tense. In this sentence the verb in the dependent clause designates a condition that is true without respect to time: the motor was old yesterday, it is old today, and it will be old tomorrow. This use of the present tense is sometimes called the *timeless present.*]

Main verb in future tense

The motor *will start* when I *press* this button.
[Future + present. When the verb in an independent clause is in the future tense, the verb in the dependent clause may be in the present tense, because the present tense, as we have seen, may in some contexts refer to the future. The sense of this sentence is: "The motor will start *if* I *will press* this button."]

The motor *will start* once I *have pressed* this button.
[Future + present perfect. When the verb in an independent clause is in the future tense, the verb in the dependent clause may be in the present perfect tense. In this sentence, the verb in the dependent clause designates an action that will occur before the action designated by the verb in the independent clause.]

28d

Main verb in present perfect tense

The motor *has started* because I *pressed* this button.

[Present perfect + past. When the verb in an independent clause is in the present perfect tense, the verb in a dependent clause is usually in the past tense. In this sentence the verb in the dependent clause designates a past action that has not continued into the present, whereas the verb in the independent clause designates a past action that has continued into the present.]

Main verb in past perfect tense

The motor *had started* before I *pressed* this button.

[Past perfect + past. When the verb in an independent clause is in the past perfect tense, the verb in a dependent clause is usually in the past tense. In this sentence the verb in the independent clause designates an action in the past that occurred before the action designated by the verb in the dependent clause.]

Main verb in future perfect tense

The motor *will have started* by the time I *press* [or *have pressed*] this button.

[Future perfect + present or present perfect. When the verb in an independent clause is in the future perfect tense, the verb in a dependent clause is usually in the present or present perfect tense. In this sentence the verb in the independent clause designates an action in the future that will occur before the action designated by the verb in the dependent clause.]

2. Sequence of tenses with infinitives

28c

Use an infinitive in its present-tense form (*to* + base form of verb) unless it represents an action earlier than that of the sentence's main verb. In that case, the correct infinitive form is the perfect infinitive (*to* + *have* + past participle of verb).

Incorrect   July 14, 1789, was a thrilling day to have been alive in Paris.

Correct   July 14, 1789, was a thrilling day *to be* alive in Paris.
[The sentence discusses the thrill of being alive on July 14, 1789, not before that date. The present infinitive is correct.]

Incorrect	Many modern historians would like to witness the events of that day.
Correct	Many modern historians would like *to have witnessed* the events of that day.

[Witnessing events in the eighteenth century would necessarily precede desiring to do so in the twentieth. The perfect infinitive is correct.]

3. Sequence of tenses with participles

When the action designated by a participle occurs at the same time as the action designated by the main verb in the sentence, the present participle is correct.

Believing the defendant to have been a victim of circumstances, the jury found her not guilty.

[The jury's belief and their decision occurred at the same time, so the present participle is correct. The perfect infinitive *to have been* appears in the sentence because the defendant's status as a victim preceded the jury's belief about her (see "Sequence of Tenses with Infinitives" above).]

When the action designated by a participle occurs before the action designated by the main verb, the present perfect participle (*having* + past participle) is correct.

Having announced their verdict, the jury members felt relieved.
[First they announced their verdict; then they felt relief. The present perfect participle is correct.]

28d

EXERCISE 1

Choose the correct tenses of verbs, infinitives, and participles in the following sentences.

1. Thomas Edison (1847–1931), America's most prolific inventor, (had, had had) only three months of formal education as a child.
2. Before he (became, had become) a telegraph operator at the age of sixteen, Edison (sold, had sold) newspapers and candy on trains in Michigan.
3. By the time he was twenty-two, Edison (patented, had patented) his first two inventions, an electric vote recorder and an improved stock ticker.

4. In 1870, (selling, having sold) his interest in an electrical engineering firm that he (helped, had helped) to found, Edison (went, had gone) into business manufacturing his new stock ticker.

5. The research laboratory that he (established, had established) in Menlo Park, New Jersey, a few years later was the first such lab (to bring, to have brought) together a creative team of full-time researchers.

6. (Working, Having worked) in his New Jersey lab, Edison invented the phonograph, a device that (will always be, had always been) associated with the man known as the Wizard of Menlo Park.

7. The apex of Edison's accomplishments in the field of electric lighting was his design for the Pearl Street power plant in New York City, which was the first electric-light power plant in the world when it (opened, had opened) in 1892.

8. Edison's light-bulb manufacturing company (evolved, has evolved) into the corporation that we (know, have known) today as General Electric.

9. When Edison died in 1931, he (held, had held) more than a thousand patents and (established, had established) himself as the leading technological genius of his era.

10. To honor Edison, President Hoover (planned, had planned) to turn off the country's electrical power for a few minutes during the inventor's funeral, until his advisers warned that (to do, to have done) so would throw the nation into chaos.

28e Auxiliary verbs

We have already seen how forms of the verbs *have* and *be* are combined with the principal parts of verbs to create the tenses of verbs, infinitives, and participles. When used in this way, *have* and *be* are called **auxiliary verbs.** A few other auxiliary verbs remain for us to discuss.

1. *Do*

Like the verbs *have* and *be, do* may function both as a main verb ("I *did* the laundry this morning") and as an auxiliary verb. In the latter role, it has three functions: to form negative constructions, to form interrogatives, and to add emphasis to a verb. The auxiliary *do* is always combined with the base form of a verb.

Negative construction	Kate's religion *does not permit* her to receive blood transfusions.
Interrogative	*Did* she *share* her belief with the doctor?
Emphasis	I *do try* to see both sides of an issue like this, even when I find it perplexing.

2. Modal auxiliaries

Nine verbs in English are known as **modal auxiliaries.** Each adds a specific shade of meaning to the main verb that it is used with.

1. **Can** expresses ability: "Since my car is fixed, I can leave for California tomorrow."
2. **Could** expresses condition: "If my suitcases were packed, I could leave for California tomorrow."
3. **May** expresses possibility ("I may leave tomorrow, but I may not") or permission: "May I leave for California tomorrow, or would you prefer that I stay?"
4. **Might** expresses weaker possibility than *may:* "Depending on the weather, I might leave for California tomorrow."
5. **Must** expresses necessity: "I must leave for California tomorrow if I expect to get there by Friday."
6. **Ought to** expresses obligation: "Jon called from Los Angeles to say that he needs my help. I ought to leave for California tomorrow."
7. **Should** expresses obligation: "I should stop procrastinating and leave for California tomorrow."
8. **Will** expresses intention: "I've put this trip off long enough. Tomorrow I will leave for California."
9. **Would** expresses condition: "If I were to leave for California tomorrow, would you come with me?"

28e

Note that unlike the other auxiliary verbs *have, be,* and *do,* each modal auxiliary has only one form. It is therefore unaffected by the person or number of the subject:

I *should* leave tomorrow.

She *should* have left yesterday.

They *should* be leaving soon.

EXERCISE 2

Insert a modal auxiliary into each of the following sentences to create the meaning indicated.

1. Anyone who has gratefully reached for a candy bar during a long afternoon of work or an evening of tedious study (   ) thank the ancient Aztecs. [Obligation]
2. If it seems strange that we owe chocolate to the Aztecs, we (   ) remember that the cacao tree, on which the cocoa bean grows, is native to South America. [Necessity]
3. Even the word *chocolate* (   ) be traced to the Aztec word *xocolalt*, meaning "bitter water." [Ability]
4. You (   ) understand that origin of the word *chocolate* if you tasted an unprocessed cocoa bean. [Condition]
5. Credit for introducing chocolate to Europe (   ) be given to the sixteenth-century Spanish explorers who first tasted it in the New World and returned with it to their native land. [Necessity]
6. It (   ) be hard for us to believe, but as recently as the seventeenth century, chocolate was a luxury in England, commanding prices that put it out of reach of all but a few. [Possibility]
7. If you were asked about the origins of the chocolate industry in North America, (   ) you know that chocolate was not produced here until 1765? [Condition]
8. Milk chocolate came still later; for that we (   ) be grateful to the Swiss, who perfected its formula at the end of the nineteenth century. [Obligation]
9. A century later, the Food and Drug Administration continues to stipulate that only chocolate containing milk or cream (   ) be sold in the United States under the label "milk chocolate." [Permission]
10. Chocolate (   ) not be addictive, but chocolate lovers know how difficult it is to decide that they (   ) reduce their consumption of the sweet. [Possibility/Intention]

28f

28f Voice

Transitive verbs in English have two forms, called **voices,** to indicate whether the subject of the sentence is the actor in the sentence or is acted upon. In a sentence whose verb is in the active voice, the subject does the action that the verb describes:

Active verbs

actor ⟶ action ⟶ recipient
New Orleans *has inspired* writers for more than two centuries.

actor ⟶ action ⟶ recipient
A writer *cannot escape* the city's influence.

By contrast, in a sentence whose verb is in the passive voice, the subject is acted upon by an actor that may or may not be named in the sentence:

Passive verbs

recipient ⟵ action ⟵ actor
Writers *have been inspired* by New Orleans for more than two centuries.

recipient ⟵ action
The city's influence *cannot be escaped*.

1. Forming passive verbs

The passive voice is created by combining appropriate forms of *be* and the past participle. Notice how the passive verb in each of the following tenses reverses the meaning of the corresponding active sentence:

	Active	Passive
Present	I trust you.	I *am trusted* by you.
Past	I trusted you.	I *was trusted* by you.
Future	I will trust you.	I *will be trusted* by you.
Present perfect	I have trusted you.	I *have been trusted* by you.
Past perfect	I had trusted you.	I *had been trusted* by you.
Future perfect	I will have trusted you.	I *will have been trusted* by you.

Passive verbs form the progressive by adding the appropriate progressive form of *be* to the past participle. Among the progressive forms in the passive voice, the present and past progressive are the most common:

28f

Present progressive passive   I *am being trusted* by you.
Past progressive passive   I *was being trusted* by you.

2. Using active and passive verbs

We need passive verbs to express actions when the actor is unimportant or cannot be identified. In the following sentence, for example, the passive verb effectively focuses attention on the action and the recipient of that action and de-emphasizes the unknown actors:

recipient ◄──────── action
Our apartment *was burglarized* yesterday.

The corresponding active sentence would in this case be ludicrously redundant: "Burglars burglarized our apartment yesterday."

But when the actor in a sentence is known and may be significant, the active voice is usually preferable for two reasons. First, a passive verb always requires more words than an active verb to express the same idea; when overused, passive verbs thus result in a wordy writing style. Second, a passive verb may de-emphasize or obscure an actor that should in fact be identified in a sentence, as in the following case:

Passive verb obscures actor   It *has* long *been asserted* that cigarette smoking is not necessarily harmful to your health.

Active verb indicates actor   Tobacco companies *have* long *asserted* that cigarette smoking is not necessarily harmful to your health.

Who does the asserting here makes all the difference. Without an active verb and an expressed actor, we can't adequately evaluate the claim. For more on the stylistic advantages of the active voice, see **8b**.

28f

EXERCISE 3

Identify passive verbs in the following sentences. If a sentence would be improved by using the active voice instead, revise it, making up likely actors if necessary.

1. Carmen was working for the state government when she discovered that important tax records were apparently being removed from the office at night.
2. Sometimes records would be missing for days; then suddenly, mysteriously, they would be returned to their file cabinets.

3. The decision was finally made by Carmen to determine who was responsible.
4. She would conceal herself in the office at night, and the culprit would be caught in the act.
5. An empty cabinet large enough to sit in was selected as her hiding place.
6. One Monday afternoon at five o'clock, Carmen slowly straightened her desk until the office had been vacated by her co-workers.
7. Into the cabinet she crawled, making sure that a crack was left through which the thief could be seen.
8. After an hour, Carmen realized that her left leg had been positioned in a way that cut off circulation to her foot.
9. As her legs were untangled, she bumped the cabinet door, which clicked shut, trapping her inside.
10. As the long night wore on, Carmen consoled herself by reflecting that she had been hired for her expertise as an accountant, not as a sleuth.

28g Mood

Verbs express a speaker's or writer's attitude by what is called their mood. English verbs have three possible moods: indicative, imperative, and subjunctive.

1. Indicative mood

The indicative mood is by far the most frequently encountered in English. It is used to state a fact or ask a question.

I *was sitting* next to Nancy.

Were you *sitting* nearby?

2. Imperative mood

The verb in a command is said to be in the imperative mood.

Sit next to Nancy, please.

3. Subjunctive mood

The subjunctive mood is used to express conditions contrary to fact and to state certain demands and requests. In modern English, subjunctive verb forms differ from indicative forms in only two cases:

1. The present subjunctive uses the base form of the verb for all persons and numbers, *including the third-person singular,* where indicative verbs use the *-s* form.
2. The past subjunctive form of the verb *be* is *were* for all persons and numbers.

Though used much less today than formerly, the subjunctive mood still surfaces in a number of idiomatic expressions ("*Be* that as it may," "Far *be* it from me") and in the three specific situations described below.

Clauses beginning with *if, as if,* or *as though* and stating a condition contrary to fact

If I *were* [not *was*] you, I would pay no attention to Steve's investment advice.
[In reality, I am not you.]

Steve confidently offers advice *as if* he *were* [not *was*] an experienced investor.
[In reality, he is not experienced.]

He talks *as though* the stock market's future *were* [not *was*] predictable.
[In reality, it is not predictable.]

Clauses expressing a wish or desire

I wish that your Hungarian cooking class *weren't* [not *wasn't*] already full.

If only I *were* [not *was*] able to enroll!

28g

Clauses beginning with *that* and stating a demand, a request, a recommendation, or a requirement

I demand *that* I *be* [not *am*] allowed to address the council!

May I ask *that* my friends *be* [not *are*] recognized as well?

We suggest *that* the council *take* [not *takes*] immediate action to preserve the historic Pelham Building on Market Square.

The legislation we are proposing stipulates *that* developers *be* [not *are*] prohibited from demolishing the building under any circumstances.

<u>EXERCISE</u> 4

Correct the following sentences by changing verbs in the indicative mood to the subjunctive mood where necessary.

1. If the winter in Alaska was less harsh, the state's population would probably increase dramatically.
2. My friends Tom and Lori, who live outside Anchorage, talk about the state as if it was the only place on earth to live.
3. They wish my home was closer to Alaska, so that I could visit them more often than I do now.
4. Like many other Alaskans, they feel they have a right to demand that every tourist respects the pristine condition of the state's wilderness lands.
5. Together with a group of their neighbors, they are collecting signatures on a petition requiring that all future plans to drill for oil in Alaska's wilderness areas are reviewed by environmental experts.

29 *Sentence Fragments, Comma Splices, Fused Sentences*

Sentences broken into fragments or incorrectly joined together should be avoided not simply because they violate rules of grammatical usage, but because they distract and confuse any reader. An eye trained to spot subjects and verbs and an ear tuned to the intonations of speech are usually sufficient to catch fragmented and run-together sentences. To strengthen your feel for complete sentences, read your writing aloud. Listen to the accents, pitch, and rhythms of the words on the page. Notice the different breath pauses for different marks of punctuation, the rising and falling pitch at different points in the sentence. Read aloud the sentences of other writers for cadence and intonation. Remember that grammar and the human voice often coincide in remarkable ways.

29a Types of sentence fragments

When part of a sentence is punctuated as if it were a complete sentence, it is called a **sentence fragment.** A sentence fragment is typically either a dependent clause or a phrase lacking a finite verb.

> **Fragment** The network newscasts on television each night provide only twenty-three minutes of news coverage. Thereby making superficial reporting almost inevitable.

Though its opening capital letter and concluding period at first make it look like a sentence, the second group of words here is a fragment—in this case, a participial phrase without a subject or a finite verb. It should be joined to the sentence that precedes it.

> **Correct** The network newscasts on television each night provide only twenty-three minutes of news coverage, thereby making superficial reporting almost inevitable.

Most fragments result from inadvertently punctuating one of the following constructions as a sentence.

1. Dependent clause as fragment

A dependent clause must either be joined to the sentence of which it is logically a part or be rewritten as an independent clause.

> **Fragment** Often I stay up late in my room, studying, writing, or thinking about the future. While all the other people in the dorm are asleep.
>
> **Correct** Often I stay up late in my room, studying, writing, or thinking about the future while all the other people in the dorm are asleep.
>
> **Fragment** I was grateful to learn of the college's loan funds. Because I didn't know where I could turn for help or see how I could take a part-time job.
>
> **Correct** I was grateful to learn of the college's loan funds, because I didn't know where I could turn for help or see how I could take a part-time job.

The fragments above might have been eliminated by omitting the conjunctions *while* and *because* to change the dependent clauses into independent clauses. Note, however, that without the conjunction the precise connection between the two clauses in each case is lost.

> **Correct but weak** Often I stay up late in my room, studying, writing, or thinking about the future. All the other people in the dorm are asleep.

29a

| **Correct but weak** | I was grateful to learn of the college's loan funds. I didn't know where I could turn for help or see how I could take a part-time job. |

2. Participial phrase as fragment

A participial phrase functions as an adjective and must be joined to the sentence containing the noun or pronoun that it modifies.

| **Fragment** | I was surprised at the commotion in the magazine's office. Reporters and secretaries were rushing all over the place. Running up and down the aisles, conferring with the editors, and talking in little groups. |
| **Correct** | I was surprised at the commotion in the magazine's office. Reporters and secretaries were rushing all over the place, running up and down the aisles, conferring with the editors, and talking in little groups. **[*Who* are *running, conferring,* and *talking?* Those three participles describe the reporters and secretaries, so they cannot be separated from the second sentence in this passage.]** |

| **Fragment** | I stepped into the chaotic room in search of a desk with my name on it. Having already decided that working here would be an adventure. |
| **Correct** | Having already decided that working here would be an adventure, I stepped into the chaotic room in search of a desk with my name on it. **[A phrase constructed around the participle *having decided* cannot stand by itself. It must be joined to the sentence that names the decision maker. In this case it is *I.*]** |

29a

A participial phrase may also be rewritten as an independent clause, though the result is often a somewhat less economical style:

| **Correct** | I was surprised at the commotion in the magazine's office. Reporters and secretaries were rushing all over the place. *They were* running up and down the aisles, conferring with the editors, and talking in little groups. |

3. Infinitive phrase as fragment

An infinitive phrase, a group of words constructed around *to* plus a verb form, does not convey a complete thought and cannot stand alone.

Fragment After a long discussion, I finally received permission from my parents. To spend the summer and fall with El Centro de Paz, a work project in Mexico.

Correct After a long discussion, I finally received permission from my parents to spend the summer and fall with El Centro de Paz, a work project in Mexico.

4. Prepositional phrase as fragment

A preposition (such as *at, for, in, over, through, with*), its object, and any modifiers constitute a prepositional phrase. A prepositional phrase modifies another word in a sentence and must always be joined to the sentence containing that word.

Fragment Many people, seeking a perfect carpet of green grass, pour chemicals on their lawns each summer. Without a thought about the possible hazards of these concoctions.

Correct Many people, seeking a perfect carpet of green grass, pour chemicals on their lawns each summer without a thought about the possible hazards of these concoctions.
[*Without a thought about the possible hazards of these concoctions* is a prepositional phrase modifying the verb *pour* and must be joined to the sentence in which that word appears.]

29a

In some cases, it may be possible to expand a prepositional phrase into a full sentence:

Correct Many people, seeking a perfect carpet of green grass, pour chemicals on their lawns each summer. *They don't think* about the possible hazards of these concoctions.

5. Appositive phrase as fragment

An appositive phrase is typically a noun phrase that describes or explains another noun or a pronoun. Such a phrase cannot stand alone, but must be linked to the word it describes, usually with a comma or dash.

Fragment The emergency-room physician recognized the signs of shock in the accident victim. Elevated pulse rate, low blood pressure, and clammy skin.

Correct The emergency-room physician recognized the signs of shock in the accident victim—elevated pulse rate, low blood pressure, and clammy skin.
[**The appositive phrase *elevated pulse rate, low blood pressure, and clammy skin* explains the word *signs*.**]

An appositive phrase may contain within it a dependent clause, but the phrase remains incomplete and must be connected to the sentence containing the word that it describes.

Fragment No one could identify the victim. A woman in her late twenties who had staggered into the hospital before collapsing.

Correct No one could identify the victim, a woman in her late twenties who had staggered into the hospital before collapsing.

Sometimes an appositive can be rewritten as an independent clause without any loss of conciseness:

Correct No one could identify the victim. A woman in her late twenties, *she* had staggered into the hospital before collapsing.
[***A woman in her late twenties* is now in apposition with the pronoun *she*.**]

29b Acceptable incomplete sentences

Professional writers sometimes use sentence fragments deliberately to create specific effects. In the following description of a London

29b

railway station, for example, the series of fragments re-creates the way in which impressions bombard the arriving traveler:

Acceptable fragments for effect

> Waterloo Station: big, bustling, not sepulchral like today's American termini. Numerous stalls for magazines, flowers, tea, and every other railway-station vendible; direction signs everywhere, plain, explicit, always helpful—no traveler who can read is in danger of being misled in Britain. To the taxi stand, and another gratifyingly authentic touch of London, the high-slung, dignified taxi with its pipe-smoking, tweed-jacketed, cloth-capped driver.
>
> —Richard D. Altick, *To Be in England*

Fragments are acceptable, even desirable, when they are used in such a self-conscious and effective way.

Fragments are also acceptable in speech and in some informal writing when the speaker's or writer's full meaning is clear. Permissible fragments include those in the categories below.

Elliptical expressions

> Just wanted to thank you for dinner last night.
>
> Hope to see you soon.

Questions and answers

> Why not? Because it's late.
>
> How much? Two dollars.

29b

Exclamations

> No way!
>
> At last!

Requests

> This way, please.
>
> If I could have your attention for a moment.

Informal transitions

So much for the first point.

Now to consider the next question.

EXERCISE 1

Some of the passages below contain sentence fragments; others do not. Locate each sentence fragment, identify its type, and revise the passage in order to eliminate it.

1. Surgery apparently has its roots in prehistoric times. Archaeological evidence suggests that the prehistoric surgeon's tool for making incisions was a sharpened piece of flint. Amputations seem to have been performed with crude saws made out of bone.

2. In ancient Greece and Rome, surgery was a highly developed art. Greek and Roman surgeons operated with great skill and with surprising concern for cleanliness, thanks to the teachings of Hippocrates. The influential Greek physician who lived about 400 B.C.

3. But the ancient tradition of excellence in surgery was short lived. The advances made by the Romans were lost when the Roman Empire collapsed and the world entered the Dark Ages.

4. Lacking the understanding of surgery that the Romans had possessed. Most medieval physicians wanted nothing to do with it. Surgery thus became part of the practice of barbers.

5. Surgery remained distinct from, and subordinate to, the practice of medicine until well into the nineteenth century. And for patients, surgical procedures remained experiences in terror. In the absence of any effective anesthetic. The surgeon's assistants would position themselves around the operating table to hold the patient down.

6. Perhaps the most important attribute that a nineteenth-century surgeon could possess was speed. The best surgeons performed an amputation in little more than a minute and a half. To minimize the patient's agony.

7. One of the most dramatic advances in surgery came in the 1840s with the development of ether. An anesthetic that allowed the surgeon to work more slowly and carefully. Without the distraction of the patient's screaming and thrashing.

8. But infection remained a serious—and baffling—problem. Until Joseph Lister discovered in the 1860s that operating in a room full of carbolic acid mist greatly reduced the occurrence of postoperative gangrene.

29b

9. The first surgical gloves were not intended to protect the patient from germs on the surgeon's hands. But to protect the hands of the surgeon and the nurses from irritation caused by the carbolic acid spray.

10. Blood transfusions were another mystery to nineteenth-century physicians. Some transfusions were successful. Whereas others had disastrous results. It was not until the turn of the century, when blood typing was finally understood, that transfusions could be performed safely.

29c Comma splices

A **comma splice**—sometimes called a **comma fault**—occurs when two independent clauses are joined only with a comma. Comma splices are distracting to a reader, and they can often lead to misreading.

> **Comma splice** My nephew stood in the doorway, soaked from the rain, the stray dog lay at his feet.

Is it the nephew who is soaked from the rain, or the stray dog? The confusion results because the comma by itself is not a strong enough punctuation mark to indicate the end of an independent clause. Two stronger punctuation marks are the period and the semicolon; note how they can be used to interpret the incorrectly joined clauses above:

> **Correct** My nephew stood in the doorway, soaked from the rain. The stray dog lay at his feet.
> **[The nephew is soaked.]**

> **Correct** My nephew stood in the doorway; soaked from the rain, the stray dog lay at his feet.
> **[The dog is soaked.]**

29c

You can sometimes catch comma splices in revision by reading your paper aloud. If you naturally drop your voice or pause substantially at a comma, check to see whether you have mistakenly used the comma to connect independent clauses. To correct a comma splice, try one of the strategies below.

1. Use a period to divide the clauses into separate sentences

Correct the comma splice by making each main clause a sentence punctuated with a period. This strategy works well when a transitional word, phrase, or clause is present to express the relationship between the two sentences that you create.

Comma splice	There was an extremely heavy rain on Monday night, after the storm had passed, the streams were overflowing.
Correct	There was an extremely heavy rain on Monday night. After the storm had passed, the streams were overflowing. **[The adverbial clause *after the storm had passed* links the two new sentences chronologically.]**

2.   Use a semicolon to connect the clauses

Correct the comma splice by replacing the comma with a semicolon. A semicolon may be used by itself or together with a conjunctive adverb or a transitional phrase.

Semicolon by itself between independent clauses

A semicolon alone can connect two independent clauses when the two clauses are so closely related that their relationship does not need to be stated explicitly with a conjunction or transitional phrase.

Comma splice	Gambling is like a drug, after a while the gambler finds it impossible to stop.
Correct	Gambling is like a drug; after a while the gambler finds it impossible to stop.

Note that a semicolon must be preceded *and* followed by an independent clause. If it is not, a sentence fragment results.

Fragment	Gambling is like a drug; *after a while, impossible to stop.*

Semicolon with conjunctive adverb or transitional phrase

When two independent clauses are linked by a conjunctive adverb such as *consequently, however, moreover, nonetheless, then,* or *therefore,* or by a transitional phrase like *as a result, for example,* or *on the other hand,* a semicolon is required. A comma used with a conjunctive adverb or transitional phrase creates a comma splice.

29c

Comma splice	To most of the economists at the conference, a rise in inflation seemed inevitable, however, three of the experts predicted the opposite.
Correct	To most of the economists at the conference, a rise in inflation seemed inevitable; however, three of the experts predicted the opposite.
Comma splice	The three optimists came with evidence to support their prediction, for example, they cited a slight decline in the gross national product during recent months.
Correct	The three optimists came with evidence to support their prediction; for example, they cited a slight decline in the gross national product during recent months.

As an alternative, of course, two independent clauses linked by a conjunctive adverb or by a transitional phrase may be divided into separate sentences.

Correct	To most of the economists at the conference, a rise in inflation seemed inevitable. However, three of the experts predicted the opposite.
Correct	The three optimists came with evidence to support their prediction. For example, they cited a slight decline in the gross national product during recent months.

29c   Note that a conjunctive adverb, unlike a coordinating conjunction or subordinating conjunction, need not come first in a clause but may be inserted in a number of places. It is preceded by a semicolon *only* when it comes at the beginning of a clause and serves as the connective between two independent clauses.

Incorrect	The paint remover was difficult to apply. Its fumes; moreover, irritated our eyes and throats.
Correct	The paint remover was difficult to apply. Its fumes, moreover, irritated our eyes and throats. **[The conjunctive adverb *moreover* is not preceded by a semicolon because it is not used as a connective between two clauses.]**

Correct   The paint remover was difficult to apply; moreover, its fumes irritated our eyes and throats.
[Here *moreover* is preceded by a semicolon because it begins the second clause and serves as a connective between the two clauses.]

3. Use a coordinating conjunction to connect the two clauses

Use a coordinating conjunction—*and, but, for, nor, or, so, yet*—to connect two independent clauses when you wish to give them equal emphasis. A coordinating conjunction is usually preceded by a comma.

Comma splice   The parks in this city are very poorly maintained, the two public swimming pools are in bad condition as well.

Correct   The parks in this city are very poorly maintained, *and* the two public swimming pools are in bad condition as well.

Comma splice   We would be willing to pay higher taxes, we just want some assurance that the city will use our money wisely.

Correct   We would be willing to pay higher taxes, *but* we just want some assurance that the city will use our money wisely.

When a coordinating conjunction joins two independent clauses that are punctuated internally with commas, a semicolon rather than a comma may be used with the coordinating conjunction to show the main division of the sentence more clearly.

29c

Comma splice   As the development of the atomic bomb, of computer systems, and of guided missiles shows, technology, indeed basic scientific research itself, is often determined by political and military considerations, many people do not recognize this interdependence and instead regard changes in technology as changes that simply "happen."

Correct   As the development of the atomic bomb, of computer systems, and of guided missiles shows, tech-

nology, indeed basic scientific research itself, is
often determined by political and military considerations; *but* many people do not recognize this interdependence and instead regard changes in technology as changes that simply "happen."

For more on using coordination effectively, see **8a**.

4. Use a subordinating conjunction or a relative
   pronoun to subordinate one clause

If a comma joins two independent clauses that are unequal
in importance, you may be able to correct the comma splice by subordinating one clause with a subordinating conjunction (such as *after,
although, because, since, while, whereas,* and *when*), or with a relative
pronoun (such as *that, which,* and *who*).

Comma splice	Marjorie has stopped lending her nephew money, she doesn't trust him any longer.
Correct	Marjorie has stopped lending her nephew money, *because* she doesn't trust him any longer.
Comma splice	Last week he asked her for a loan of $200, he said he needed it for car repairs.
Correct	Last week he asked her for a loan of $200, *which* he said he needed for car repairs.

For more on using subordination effectively, see **8a**.

29d

29d Acceptable comma splices

A few minor exceptions to what we have said about comma
splices should be mentioned here. Short parallel independent clauses
are sometimes joined only with commas, particularly in narratives.

Acceptable	The sky darkened, the wind blew, the cold rain began to fall.

Also, an elliptical question is attached to the end of a related independent
clause with only a comma.

| **Acceptable** | You told Sam to meet us at three o'clock, didn't you? |
| **Acceptable** | Sam's not very reliable, is he? |

29e Fused sentences

A **fused sentence** is one in which two independent clauses are joined with no punctuation between them.

| **Fused** | The Senate passed the bill only after long hours of debate both sides had strong feelings about the measure. |

The fused sentence is an even more serious error than the comma splice because it makes the reader's task of deciphering the sentence's meaning extremely difficult. To correct a fused sentence, use any of the strategies that we have discussed for correcting comma splices.

Use a period

The Senate passed the bill only after long hours of debate. Both sides had strong feelings about the measure.

Use a semicolon

The Senate passed the bill only after long hours of debate; both sides had strong feelings about the measure.

Use a semicolon and a conjunctive adverb

Both sides had strong feelings about the bill; *consequently,* the Senate passed it only after long hours of debate.

29e

Use a semicolon and a transitional phrase

Both sides had strong feelings about the bill; *as a result,* the Senate passed it only after long hours of debate.

Use a comma and a coordinating conjunction

The Senate passed the bill only after long hours of debate, *for* both sides had strong feelings about the measure.

Use a comma and a subordinating conjunction

The Senate passed the bill only after long hours of debate, *because* both sides had strong feelings about the measure.

EXERCISE 2

Correct comma splices and fused sentences wherever they appear in the following sentences.

1. The 1960s are remembered as a time of idealism, protest, and change in America, however, the first year of the next decade was no less turbulent.
2. On May 2, 1970, President Richard Nixon expanded the war in Vietnam by ordering American troops into Cambodia, it was a neutral country in the conflict.
3. A storm of protest broke out around the nation even many people who had not opposed the role of the United States in Vietnam felt that this step was wrong.
4. A million and a half college students nationwide responded by walking out of classes and joining massive protests, President Nixon publicly referred to the protesters as "bums."
5. On May 4, 1970, edgy National Guard troops protecting the campus of Kent State University in Ohio fired into a crowd of unarmed students and killed four persons two were protesters, two were bystanders.
6. Many of the year's movies reflected the nation's social and political concerns, *Woodstock* and *M*A*S*H*, for example, were popular films.
7. The former was a documentary account of the massive three-day rock concert that had been held a year earlier in upstate New York, the latter was the satirical antiwar film that gave rise to the popular television series of the same name.
8. The year also brought the drug-related deaths of two talented musicians, Jimi Hendrix and Janis Joplin, both of them were twenty-seven years old.
9. Perhaps to escape from such serious concerns, people were buying books with other themes the two best-sellers in 1970 were *Love Story* and *Everything You Always Wanted to Know about Sex but Were Afraid to Ask*.
10. An August 26 celebration of the fiftieth anniversary of women's suffrage focused attention on equal rights, nonetheless, the campaign for an Equal Rights Amendment that began in 1970 ended in failure more than a decade later.

29e

11. The major early issues of the women's movement were child care and job discrimination, they are among the issues that remain important to many women and men today.
12. Jobs in particular were on the minds of all Americans, in 1970 almost two million more people were out of work than in 1969.
13. The nation's unemployed reached four million, it was the highest number since the Great Depression of the 1930s.
14. Many people forget that it was during the Nixon administration that concern for the environment was institutionalized in July of 1970 the Environmental Protection Agency, commonly known today by its initials EPA, was formed.
15. The twelve months of 1970 brought changes that would be felt for years, their wounds, too, would take longer to heal than most people realized.

29e

Punctuation, Spelling, Mechanics

30 *Punctuation*

31 *Spelling*

32 *Mechanics*

PART
VII

30 *Punctuation*

Punctuation is to writing what notation is to music: it allows the eye to re-create from the page the sounds the author of the composition had in mind. Both are necessary and exacting systems. Just as musicians know the crucial difference between a quarter note and a half note, so writers know the crucial difference between a comma and a semicolon, between brackets and parentheses. The brief, moderate, or extended pauses noted by punctuation give cadence and rhythm to prose, but, more important, they signal meaning. Only a person who understands punctuation knows how the drop in the voice signaled by the commas makes one of these sentences mean something quite different from the other.

> The students who have worked diligently and completed all the assignments on time will not have to take the final.

> The students, who have worked diligently and completed all the assignments on time, will not have to take the final.

If you have come to believe that correctly punctuating sentences is a mysterious art, we hope this chapter will demystify punctuation for you. In the following sections, we explain rules that specify the main places where punctuation marks are needed, as well as some places where those marks should be avoided. If you are in doubt about whether or not to punctuate and cannot identify a rule that applies, use your best judgment, but keep in mind that modern usage tends toward less punctuation rather than more.

30

30a The period

Periods are used as end punctuation in several types of sentences. They also are part of many abbreviations, and they have some special functions in quotation and dialogue.

1. Period after a declarative or mildly imperative sentence

Use a period after a sentence that makes a statement or issues a mild command.

A declarative sentence, like this one, ends with a period .

Don't forget to end a mild command with a period, too .

A period at the end of the sentence is never combined with another punctuation mark. For example, if a statement ends with an abbreviation that includes a period, a second period to end the sentence is not necessary.

Incorrect   Amtrak's *Crescent* leaves New Orleans every day at 7:25 A.M..

Correct   Amtrak's *Crescent* leaves New Orleans every day at 7:25 A.M .

Similarly, if a declarative sentence ends with a quotation, the final punctuation within the quotation marks suffices for the entire sentence.

Incorrect   Michael looked at me oddly and said, "I never received your letter.".

Correct   Michael looked at me oddly and said, "I never received your letter."

Incorrect   I gasped, "What!".

Correct   I gasped, "What!"

30a

See also **30f**.

2.   Period after an indirect question or a polite request

Use a period, not a question mark, to end an indirect question, that is, a question that has been rephrased as a statement.

> I wonder how many people would know that this is an indirect question .

Similarly, use a period, not a question mark, to end a request that has been phrased as a question for the sake of politeness.

> Will you please remember to use a question mark only after a direct question, not after an indirect one .

3.   Periods with abbreviations

Many abbreviations include or are followed by periods.

Mr .	D .V .M .	B .C .
Ms .	M .B .A .	etc .
Rev .	Ph .D .	Inc .

However, note that some abbreviations, like the U.S. Postal Service abbreviations for states, are not followed by periods: *IL, LA, NY, WA.* Many organizations and agencies, also, are represented by their initials without periods: *CBS, FAA, NAACP.* Finally, periods are not used with acronyms, abbreviations spoken as words: *DOS* (disk operating system), *ERIC* (Educational Resources Information Center), *SADD* (Students against Drunk Driving).

See also **32d**.

4.   Periods with ellipses

Three periods—with spaces before, after, and between them—are called ellipsis marks; they are used to indicate the omission of a word or words from a quoted passage. If the omitted words come at the end of a sentence, do not leave a space before the first period, but add a fourth period to end the sentence.

30a

> "I pledge allegiance to the flag . . . and to the country for which it stands. . . ."

5.   Periods in dialogue

Three (or at the end of a sentence, four) periods are sometimes used in writing dialogue to indicate hesitation and pauses.

> "I've been around. Went to that Tom Petty concert at the **. . .** Forum. He sang that song, oh, you know, that song we always used to listen to**. . . .**" Julian closes his eyes and tries to remember the song.
> —Bret Easton Ellis, *Less Than Zero*

30b   The question mark

Question marks close questions and indicate doubtful information.

1.   Question marks after direct questions or questions in a series

A direct question ends with a question mark.

Isn't this the kind of question that must end with a question mark **?**

Short questions in a series also end with question marks, whether or not they are complete sentences.

Shouldn't you use a question mark at the end of this question **?**
And this one **?** And what about this one **?**

If a question ends with an abbreviation that includes a period, the question mark does not replace the period, but follows it.

Incorrect   Did the invitation say R.S.V.P?
Correct   Did the invitation say R.S.V.P **. ?**

In other situations, though, a question mark is not combined with other punctuation marks. For example, if a question ends with a quoted declarative sentence, the period that would ordinarily end the sentence is omitted.

Incorrect   Did you say, "I'm not going to the party."?
Correct   Did you say, "I'm not going to the party"**?**

30b

2. Question mark indicating doubtful information

You may use a question mark in parentheses to indicate that the information you provide in a sentence is of doubtful accuracy.

> Hippocrates, the renowned Greek physician for whom the Hippocratic oath is named, was born on the island of Cos in 460 (**?**) B.C.

However, don't use a question mark in parentheses to be sarcastic; find words to convey your feelings instead.

Avoid   The prize I won in the drawing was a lovely (?) landscape painted on black velvet.

Better   The prize I won in the drawing was a tacky landscape painted on black velvet.

30c The exclamation point

An exclamation point is appropriate only after statements, commands, or interjections that would be given unusual emphasis if spoken.

I will *not* go to this party with your cousin !

Don't try to make me !

No !

If an emphatic statement ends with an abbreviation that contains a period, the exclamation point does not replace the period, but follows it.

Incorrect   I refuse to leave for the party before nine p.m!

Correct   I refuse to leave for the party before nine p.m . !

In other situations, though, an exclamation point is not combined with a period. For example, if an emphatic statement ends with a quoted declarative sentence, the period that would ordinarily end the sentence is omitted.

Incorrect   All right! I said, "I'll go."!

Correct   All right! I said, "I'll go"!

30c

Use exclamation points sparingly, and never use them in parentheses for an attempt at irony.

Avoid   Your cousin's personality is just a little (!) bland.

Better   Your cousin has the personality of a potato.

30d The comma

The comma is perhaps the most used and, consequently, the most abused punctuation mark. It separates coordinate elements within a sentence and sets off certain subordinate constructions from the rest of the sentence. Since it represents the shortest breath pause and the least emphatic break, it cannot separate two complete sentences.

A primary function of the comma is to make a sentence clear. Use commas to prevent misreading—to separate words that might be erroneously grouped together by the reader.

1. Comma with a coordinating conjunction to separate independent clauses

Two independent clauses joined by a coordinating conjunction (*and, but, for, nor, or, so, yet*) should be separated by a comma. Note that the comma is always placed *before* the conjunction.

I failed German in my senior year of high school , *and* it took me a long time to regain any interest in foreign languages.

I went through the motions of studying , *but* my mind was elsewhere.

Very short independent clauses need not be separated by a comma if they are closely connected in meaning.

The bell rang and everyone left.

30d Coordinating conjunctions are often used to join the parts of a compound predicate, that is, two or more verbs with the same subject. In such a sentence a comma is not required to separate the predicates but may be used for clarity or emphasis.

Mr. Cowan *demonstrated* the difference between preserving wood with oil and with shellac , *and advised* the use of oil for durable tabletops.

To our dismay, the suede *could not be washed* at home or *dry-cleaned* at an ordinary place **,** *but had to be sent* to a specialist.

When the clauses of a compound sentence are long and are also subdivided by commas, a semicolon rather than a comma may be used with the coordinating conjunction to show the main division of the sentence more clearly.

For purposes of discussion, we will recognize two main varieties of English, Standard and Nonstandard **;** and we will divide the first type into Formal, Informal, and Colloquial English.

2. Comma to set off an introductory element

An introductory element is a clause or phrase that precedes the subject of the sentence. An introductory dependent clause is almost always set off from the sentence with a comma.

dependent clause
Whenever I read about the nineteenth century **,** I am struck by the sufferings of the poor.

An introductory verbal phrase (participial, gerund, or infinitive) is usually followed by a comma. A prepositional phrase of considerable length at the beginning of a sentence may be followed by a comma for clarity.

participial phrase
Suffering from disease, overcrowding, and poverty **,** the people of Manchester were prime victims of the early Industrial Revolution in England.

gerund phrase
After seeing the poverty and unfair treatment of the working-class people **,** Elizabeth Gaskell wrote several protest novels.

infinitive phrase
To understand Hemingway's uneasy friendship with F. Scott Fitzgerald **,** one must know something of Hemingway's attitude toward Fitzgerald's wife, Zelda.

30d

long prepositional phrase
Soon after his first acquaintance with Fitzgerald **,** Hemingway took an intense dislike to Zelda.

Even an introductory element consisting of a single word or two may need to be set off from the sentence by a comma in order to prevent misreading.

Incorrect	Ever since he has devoted himself to athletics.
Correct	Every since **,** he has devoted himself to athletics.
Incorrect	Inside the house was brightly lighted.
Correct	Inside **,** the house was brightly lighted.
Incorrect	Soon after the minister entered the chapel.
Correct	Soon after **,** the minister entered the chapel.
Incorrect	To elaborate the art of flower arranging begins with simplicity.
Correct	To elaborate **,** the art of flower arranging begins with simplicity.

3. Commas to separate elements in a series

Separate words, phrases, or clauses in a series by commas. However, if *all* the elements of a series are joined by coordinating conjunctions (*a and b and c*), no commas are necessary to separate them.

Series of nouns

Books **,** *papers* **,** and *photographs* were strewn about the room.

Series of adjectives

The shy devilfish blushes in *blue* **,** *red* **,** *green* **,** or *brown.*

Series of prepositional phrases

30d

Water flooded *over the riverbanks* **,** *across the asphalt road* **,** and *into the basements* of nearby homes.

Series of verbal phrases

Running a mile or two **,** *swimming laps* **,** and *playing tennis* are all excellent ways to improve one's aerobic conditioning.

Series of predicates

The bear *jumped away from the garbage can* , *snarled at the camper* , and *raced up the tree.*

Series of dependent clauses

If you feel faint , *if your vision becomes blurred* , or *if you have difficulty breathing,* then discontinue this medication.

Series of independent clauses

Greek revival architecture swept through this country from 1820 until about 1860 , *the Italianate style was popular well into the 1870s* , and *the Romanesque revival dominated the last decades of the century.*

The comma before the last item in a series is omitted by some writers, but its use is generally preferred because it can prevent misreading.

Misleading	The three congressional priorities are nuclear disarmament, the curtailment of agricultural trade and aid to underdeveloped countries. **[Without the comma before *and*, *agricultural trade* and *aid to underdeveloped countries* can be read as compound objects of *curtailment of*, and the reader reaches the end of the sentence still waiting for the third priority. No such misreading occurs if the comma is included.]**
Clearer	The three congressional priorities are nuclear disarmament, the curtailment of agricultural trade , and aid to underdeveloped countries.

4. Comma with coordinate modifiers

Adjectives modifying the same noun should be separated by commas if they are coordinate in meaning. Coordinate adjectives are those that could be joined by *and* without distorting the meaning of a sentence.

30d

Bus lines provide *inexpensive* , *efficient* transportation.
[The adjectives are coordinate: transportation that is *inexpensive* and *efficient*.]

Sometimes an adjective is so closely linked with the noun that it is thought of as part of the noun. Such an adjective is not coordinate with a preceding adjective.

> The Paynes bought a *spacious summer* cabin.
> [This does not mean a cabin that is *spacious* and *summer*. *Summer* indicates the kind of cabin; *spacious* describes the summer cabin.]

Note that numbers are not coordinate with other adjectives and are not separated by commas.

> They screened in *two large , airy* outdoor porches.
> [*Two* and *large* should not be separated by a comma. But since the two outdoor porches were *large* and *airy,* a comma is used to separate these two coordinate adjectives.]

5.   Commas to set off a nonrestrictive modifier

A dependent clause, participial phrase, or appositive is **nonrestrictive** when it can be omitted without changing the main idea of the sentence. A nonrestrictive modifier gives additional information about the noun to which it refers. A **restrictive** modifier, on the other hand, provides *required* information about the word it modifies. If it is omitted, the main idea of the sentence is changed.

Nonrestrictive clause

> My faculty adviser , *who had to sign the program card* , was hard to
>   find.
> [If the clause were omitted, some information would be lost, but the sentence would make the same point: that my adviser was hard to find.]

Restrictive clause

> Faculty advisers *who are never in their offices* make registration difficult.
> [Omitting the clause here changes the sense completely. The purpose of the clause is to limit the statement to a certain kind of faculty adviser—those who are never in their offices.]

Two commas are required to set off a nonrestrictive modifier in the middle of a sentence; one comma is used if the modifier is at the beginning or end of the sentence.

30d

nonrestrictive clause
I found the letter under the door , *which had been locked.*

restrictive clause
The letter *that I found under the door* was a mystery.
[Note that in relative clauses beginning with *that* or *which*, *that* is used in restrictive clauses, *which* in nonrestrictive clauses.]

nonrestrictive phrase
Uncle Sid's letter , *lying unclaimed in the dead-letter office* , contained the missing document.

restrictive phrase
We have had many complaints about letters *undelivered because of careless addressing.*

Notice how the meaning of a sentence may be altered by the addition or the omission of commas:

The board sent questionnaires to all members , who are on Social Security.
[Nonrestrictive clause. The sentence implies that all members are on Social Security.]

The board sent questionnaires to all members who are on Social Security.
[Restrictive clause. The questionnaire is sent only to some members, those on Social Security.]

Appositives are usually nonrestrictive and hence are set off by commas. If, however, an appositive puts a necessary limitation upon its noun, it is restrictive and no punctuation is used.

Nonrestrictive appositive

Scientists working with cryogenics have produced temperatures within a thousandth of a degree of absolute zero , *approximately 459.7 below zero Fahrenheit.*

Restrictive appositive

The noun *cryogenics* comes from a Greek word meaning "icy cold."

An appositive used to define a word is often introduced by the conjunction *or.* Such appositives are always set off by commas to distinguish

30c

them from the common construction in which *or* joins two coordinate nouns.

> The class found a fine specimen of pyrite , *or fool's gold.* [appositive]
>
> At first it was difficult to tell whether the specimen was *pyrite* or *genuine gold.* [coordinate nouns]

An abbreviated title or degree (*K.C.B., USMC, M.D., Ph.D.*) is treated as an appositive when it follows a proper name.

> He was introduced as Robert Harrison , *LL.D.* , and he added that he also held a Ph.D. from Cornell.

6. Commas to set off parenthetic elements

Parenthetic is a general term describing explanatory words and phrases that interrupt the normal sentence pattern to supply additional, but not essential, information. Parenthetic elements are set off by commas, or in some cases by parentheses or dashes (see **30h**). In the widest sense of the term, parenthetic elements include the nonrestrictive modifiers discussed above. Any other sentence element may also become parenthetic if it is removed from its regular place in the sentence and inserted so that it interrupts the sentence's normal order—for instance, by falling in between the subject and verb.

Notice in the following case how adjectives are moved from their normal position before the noun they modify to become parenthetic elements that must be set off by commas.

Adjectives in normal position

> Two *tired and hungry* boys wandered into camp.

Adjectives as parenthetic element

> Two boys , *tired and hungry* , wandered into camp.

In the same way, the parenthetic elements in the following sentences must be set off by commas.

Prepositional phrase as parenthetic element

> Placing a powerful telescope in orbit may , *in the opinion of some astronomers* , radically change our conception of the galaxy.

Clause as parenthetic element

> Space research **,** *I am convinced* **,** should remain one of this nation's highest priorities.

Conjunctive adverbs (such as *consequently, furthermore, however, moreover, nonetheless,* and *therefore*) and transitional phrases like *as a result, for example,* and *on the other hand* frequently function as parenthetic elements and are set off with commas when they occur in the middle of a sentence and with a single comma when they appear at the end.

> Beef should be bright red and marbled with pure white fat. Packaged meat may appear fresher than it is because of tinted lighting in a supermarket **,** *however.*

> Shoppers should **,** *as a result* **,** take care to examine meat packages carefully.

7. Commas to set off absolute phrases

An absolute phrase typically consists of a noun and a participle or complement. It is not gramatically part of the sentence in which it appears and is set off with commas.

> *The hurricane having passed* **,** workers began to clear trees and debris from the roads.

> Residents of the town **,** *their faces sorrowful* **,** slowly returned to their damaged homes.

8. Commas in comparative and contrastive constructions

Commas are used to separate some idiomatic coordinate constructions involving a comparison of adjectives or adverbs. Such constructions include the formulas *the more . . . , the more . . .* and *the more . . . , the less. . . .*

30d

> *The older* the tree **,** *the weaker* its resistance to disease.

> *The more* I study forestry **,** *the less* I understand what role human beings should play in forest management.

Coordinate words or phrases that are contrasted are also separated by a comma.

We are *a contentious group* , not *a belligerent one.*

Our aim is to encourage *question and debate* , not *criticism and personal attacks.*

9. Commas with interjections, direct address, and tag questions

Interjections and nouns used as terms of direct address are set off by commas.

Oh , is it my turn to talk?

Yes , I am prepared to address the assembly.

Ms. Kuhn , may I speak frankly?

This absurd budget proposal , *ladies and gentlemen* , raises questions about the school board's competence.

An elliptical question, or tag question, attached to the end of a related statement is set off by a comma.

You can't defend this proposal , *can you?*

10. Commas with dates, addresses, place names, and numbers

If only one element in a date (month and day, or month and year), place name, or address (number and street) appears in a sentence, no comma is required.

April 4 is Sandy's birthday.

She has lived in Bloomington since June 1989.

She recently bought the house at 15 Center Street.

30d

But multiple elements in dates, place names, and addresses are set off by commas. (Exception: no comma appears between the state and the zip code in an address.)

Sandy was born on *Monday* , *April 4* , *1960* , in *Scranton* , *Pennsylvania.*

She has lived in *Bloomington* **,** *Indiana* **,** for several years.

Her new address is *15 Center Street* **,** *Bloomington* **,** *Indiana 47401.*

A comma is not included when a date is written in inverted style: *7 December 1941.*

Commas are used to divide numbers of more than four digits into groups of three in order to designate thousands, millions, billions, and so on.

About *110* **,** *000* people live in Tempe, Arizona.

It's part of the Phoenix metropolitan area, whose population exceeds *1* **,** *500* **,** *000.*

Four-digit numbers may include commas as well.

There are *5* **,** *280* feet in a mile.

But do not use commas in numbers referring to pages, years, or addresses.

On page 2522 of my almanac is a calendar for all the years from 1801 to the present.

11. Commas with direct quotations

The words used to identify the speaker of a quotation—such as *he said, she asked, they exclaimed*—are set off by commas when used with a direct quotation.

"When I was in Africa **,**" *Brad said* **,** "I learned a great deal about the plight of elephants."

"The poaching of elephants for their tusks is decimating herds **,**" *he explained.*

When the quotation contains two independent clauses, use a semicolon after the words identifying the speaker when they occur between the clauses, in order to prevent a comma fault.

"The future of African elephants depends on the world outside Africa," *Brad pointed out* **;** "we have to insure that the market for ivory trinkets disappears."

30d

Do not use a comma in an indirect quotation.

> Brad said that most countries have now banned the importation of ivory.

For additional rules regarding the punctuation of direct quotations, see **30f**.

12.   Misuse of the comma

Since modern practice is to use less rather than more punctuation in expository and narrative prose, a good working rule for beginning writers is to use no commas except for those required by the preceding conventions. Be especially careful to avoid the incorrect use of commas illustrated below.

Comma erroneously separates subject and verb

> Ted's ability to solve the most complicated problems on the spur of the moment **,** never failed to impress his co-workers.

Comma erroneously precedes first element of a series

> For lunch I usually have **,** a sandwich, some fruit, and milk.

Comma erroneously follows last element in a series

> New Jersey, Rhode Island, and Massachusetts **,** were the most densely populated states as of the last census.

Comma erroneously divides indirect quotation

> During chapel the minister announced **,** that the choir would sing Handel's *Messiah* for Easter.

Comma erroneously splits idiomatic construction

> Joy is so tall **,** that she may well break the school's record for rebounds.

30d

EXERCISE 1

In the following sentences, insert commas where they are needed to set off nonrestrictive modifiers. In doubtful cases, explain the two possible meanings of the sentence.

1. Many people who have never been to the United States think of it as a country of luxury and ease for all.

2. My friend Theodore who lives in Brooklyn knows better.
3. Theodore who is in his late twenties never finished high school.
4. His friends who did graduate got jobs or went on to college.
5. But Theodore's reading ability which is at the third-grade level makes it difficult for him to find a job which is worthwhile.
6. Theodore lives at home with his mother and sister who work in Manhattan.
7. He rarely sees his old high-school friends who are working during the day.
8. But Theodore has now enrolled in a literacy education program which operates out of his local public library.
9. Already the progress which he has made is remarkable.
10. Theodore's first goal which is to obtain a driver's license now seems within reach.

EXERCISE 2

Add commas to the following sentences where they are needed, and be prepared to justify your punctuation according to the rules discussed in the preceding section.

1. I have some fond memories of high school but playing the cornet in my high-school marching band is not one of them.
2. Though I wasn't much of a musician I could at least march in step and that put me ahead of most of the others.
3. My high-school marching band was to tell the truth among the worst in the state of Pennsylvania.
4. I still remember our morning practice sessions which were held in a playground near a doughnut factory.
5. We had to report at seven o'clock each morning a full ninety minutes before the school day began.
6. The weather was bitter the field was frozen and the instruments were icy but somehow the smell of doughnuts baking across the street made the long tedious practice sessions bearable.
7. Everyone having arrived Mr. Bell our band director would sketch out the marching routine we were to learn.
8. His explanations of course could just as well have been delivered to us in Greek.
9. Marching in step was difficult enough for most members of the band but simultaneously marching playing music and avoiding holes in the uneven field usually proved impossible.
10. We were terrible not just bad and everyone knew it.

11. Mr. Bell's philosophy however was "the more you practice the better you become."
12. Well that wasn't quite true in our case.
13. On one particularly memorable occasion we were practicing a routine that required the sousaphone players to bow to the audience at the end of the song.
14. Having done the routine over and over for nearly an hour the sousaphonists were becoming tired and dizzy for the instrument is heavy.
15. Mr. Bell frustrated and tired himself asked us to try the routine one final time.
16. Across the field we marched a sousaphone leading each column.
17. The music ended and the time came for the sousaphonists to bow.
18. Exhausted they all toppled over in different directions.
19. One tipped sideways and landed on Mr. Bell another went face first into the ground and a third fell backward into the startled woodwind section.
20. After a long cold morning on the drill field the marching routine was no better than it had been when we started and now six people were injured.

30e The semicolon

The semicolon indicates a greater break in the sentence than the comma does, but it does not have the finality of a period.

1. Semicolon to connect independent clauses not linked by a coordinating conjunction

When the independent clauses of a compound sentence are not joined by a coordinating conjunction, a semicolon is required. Use a semicolon in place of a comma and coordinating conjunction when the relationship between two clauses is so clear that it does not need to be stated explicitly.

> I'm not saying that these stories are untrue ; I'm just a bit doubtful about your source.
>
> You trust Terry ; I don't.

A semicolon used in this way must be preceded *and* followed by an independent clause. If it is not, a sentence fragment results (see **29a**).

30e

Fragment   I'm not saying these stories are untrue ; *just doubtful, perhaps.*

A semicolon is also necessary when two independent clauses are linked by a conjunctive adverb such as *consequently, however, moreover, nonetheless, then,* or *therefore.* A comma used with a conjunctive adverb creates a comma splice (see **29c**).

> Our plan was to sail from Naples to New York ; *however,* an emergency at home forced us to fly back instead.

> We were understandably tense on the flight back ; *moreover,* when we landed, we learned that our bags were lost.

2. Semicolon to separate independent clauses with internal punctuation

When two independent clauses with internal punctuation are joined by a coordinating conjunction and a comma, the dividing point between the clauses may at first be difficult to perceive. In such a case, a semicolon instead of a comma may be used with the coordinating conjunction to show the main division of the sentence more clearly.

Confusing   In recognition of her years of service, the principal received a farewell dinner, a framed picture of the student body and the faculty, and a compact edition of the *Oxford English Dictionary,* and later the library in the elementary school, after considerable discussion by the school board, was named for her.
[The list of gifts for the principal at first seems to include the elementary-school library.]

Clearer   In recognition of her years of service, the principal received a farewell dinner, a framed picture of the student body and the faculty, and a compact edition of the *Oxford English Dictionary* ; and later the library in the elementary school, after considerable discussion by the school board, was named for her.

30c

3. Semicolon to separate elements in a series

When elements in a series contain internal commas, a comma is not a strong enough mark of punctuation to separate those elements clearly. In this case, use semicolons instead.

Confusing	The parents' day discussion was led by Mr. Joseph, the chaplain, Ms. Smith, a French instructor, the dean, and his assistant. **[How many people in all participated?]**
Clearer	The parents' day discussion was led by Mr. Joseph, the chaplain **;** Ms. Smith, a French instructor **;** the dean **;** and his assistant.

Do not use a semicolon to *introduce* a list or series; the proper punctuation for that purpose is a colon or dash.

Incorrect	The guest list included the following distinguished citizens; the mayor and her husband, the members of the city council, and the president of the school board.
Correct	The guest list included the following distinguished citizens **:** the mayor and her husband, the members of the city council, and the president of the school board.

EXERCISE 3

Some of the following sentences are correct as they stand. In the others, insert semicolons where they should appear.

1. In 1871, Chicago was the nation's railroad, livestock, and grain center, then the great fire erupted.
2. Only forty years earlier, Chicago's population had been barely 100, now it was more than 300,000.
3. After the fire had finally burned itself out, four square miles of the city lay devastated, moreover, 100,000 people were homeless.
4. The rubble from the fire was plowed into Lake Michigan, on top of it today sits beautiful Grant Park.
5. Rebuilding the city was complicated by the fact that the fire had destroyed deeds and other key documents, therefore, it was difficult at first to determine who rightfully owned the burned-out but still-valuable land.
6. The city council acted swiftly, if belatedly, to ban frame buildings in the downtown area, and as a result architects streamed into Chicago to help design the new city.
7. Among the technological innovations that affected the new buildings erected in Chicago after the fire were elevators, which had been introduced in the 1860s, new, stronger foundations, which could support

30e

taller, heavier buildings, and the skeletal frame, which made the modern skyscraper possible.

8. By the 1890s, Chicago was home to the tallest office buildings in the world, rising sixteen, even seventeen, stories above street level.

9. During this decade the word *skyscraper* was applied to buildings for the first time, previously it had referred only to ships' sails, big horses, and tall tales.

10. Many of Chicago's famous early skyscrapers remain in use as desirable office buildings, others have been converted into chic apartments and condominiums.

30f Quotation marks

Quotation marks are used primarily to indicate dialogue, the word-for-word citation of printed material, and certain types of titles.

1. Quotation marks to enclose direct quotations

Use quotation marks to enclose a direct quotation, but not an indirect quotation. A direct quotation gives the exact words of a speaker; an indirect quotation is the writer's paraphrase of what someone said.

Indirect quotation   He said that he would call.

Direct quotation   He said, " I will call. "

Expressions like *he said* and *she explained* are never included within the quotation marks. If the actual quotation is interrupted by such an expression, both halves must be enclosed by quotation marks.

"I am interested, " he said, "so let's talk it over. "

" It all began accidentally, " Jackson said. " My remark was misunderstood. "

If a quotation consists of several sentences, uninterrupted by a *he said* or *she said* expression, use one set of marks to enclose the entire quotation. Do not enclose each separate sentence.

Barbara replied, " Right now? But I haven't finished my paper for economics. Call me in a couple of hours. "

30f

If a quotation consists of several paragraphs, put quotation marks at
the beginning of each paragraph and at the end of only the last paragraph.

> Poor Richard has a number of things to say about diet: " They that
> study much ought not to eat so much as those that work hard, their
> digestion being not so good.
>   " If thou art dull and heavy after meat, it's a sign thou hast exceeded
> the due measure; for meat and drink ought to refresh the body and make
> it chearful, and not to dull and oppress it.
>   " A sober diet makes a man die without pain; it maintains the senses
> in vigour; it mitigates the violence of the passions and affections. "

Quotation marks and other punctuation

At the end of a quotation, a period or comma is placed inside
the quotation mark; a semicolon or colon is placed outside the quotation
mark.

"Quick ," said my cousin, "hand me the flashlight ."

The bride and groom in the film said, "I do" ; the audience in the
theater cheered.

I have only one comment when you say, "All people are equal" : I
wish it were true.

A question mark or exclamation point goes inside the quotation mark
if it applies to the quotation only, and outside the quotation mark if
it applies to the whole sentence.

"Did you arrive on time ? " asked my mother.

Did the invitation say "R.S.V.P." ?

He called irritably, "Move over !"

Above all, don't let anyone hear you say, "I give up" !

Quotations within quotations

A quotation within a quotation is enclosed with single quotation marks. Be sure to conclude the original quotation with double
marks.

The lecture began, " As Proust said, ' Any mental activity is easy if
it need not take reality into account. ' "

In the rare instance when a third set of marks must be included within a quoted passage, they become double:

> In her edition of Flannery O'Connor's letters, Sally Fitzgerald comments: " Anything but dour, she never ceased to be amused, even in extremis. In a letter after her return from the hospital and surgery, in 1964, she wrote: ' One of my nurses was a dead ringer for Mrs. Turpin. . . . Her favorite grammatical construction was " it were. " . . . I reckon she increased my pain about 100%. ' "

Long quotations

When a borrowed quotation runs more than four typed lines, it should be set off by indenting ten spaces and double-spacing. Quotation marks are not used to set off such material, though they may be required within the quotation.

```
T. S. Eliot begins the essay "Tradition and the Indi-
vidual Talent" as follows:

            In English writing we seldom speak of tra-
        dition, though we occasionally apply its
        name in deploring its absence. We cannot
        refer to "the tradition" or to "a tradi-
        tion"; at most, we employ the adjective
        in saying that the poetry of So-and-so is
        "traditional" or even "too traditional."
         Seldom, perhaps, does the word appear ex-
        cept in a phrase of censure. If otherwise,
        it is vaguely approbative, with the impli-
        cation, as to the work approved, of some
        pleasing archaeological reconstruction.
```

30f

For information on documenting such a quotation, see **20c**.

2. Quotation marks to enclose verse quotations

A quotation of one line of verse, or part of a line, should be enclosed in quotation marks and incorporated into the text.

> Lytton disliked the false heroics of Henley's " My head is bloody but unbowed. "

If two or three lines of verse are run into the text, indicate the line breaks by a slash (/):

> Stark Young and Rex Stout both found book titles in Fitzgerald's " never grows so red **/** The rose as where some buried Caesar bled. "

A quotation of more than three lines of poetry should be set off by indenting and double-spacing, without quotation marks. Be sure to keep the line lengths exactly as they are in the original.

```
Blake characterizes this freshness of perception at

the beginning of "Auguries of Innocence":

        To see a World in a Grain of Sand

        And a Heaven in a Wild Flower,

        Hold Infinity in the palm of your hand

        And Eternity in a hour.
```

3. Quotation marks to indicate titles

Use quotation marks for titles of articles, short stories, short poems, songs, chapters of books, lectures and speeches, and individual episodes of radio and television shows.

30f

" Sharp Drop in Unemploy-ment " (newspaper article)

"Doris Lessing's Heroines " (journal article)

" Young Goodman Brown " (short story)

" Mending Wall " (poem)

" Jane Austen and the Dance " (lecture)

" Summertime " (song)

" Fictions " (chapter)

" Prelude to Tragedy " (episode of the television show *The Spanish Civil War*)

When one of the titles above (for example, the title of a short story) appears in a title that would itself be enclosed in quotation marks (for example, the title of an article), the shorter title is enclosed in single quotation marks:

> " Understanding the Misfit in Flannery O'Connor's ' A Good Man Is Hard to Find ' "

The titles of books, plays, long poems, pamphlets, periodicals, films, radio and television programs, and major works of opera, dance, and music are represented by italics or, on a typewriter, by underlining (see **32e**). Note that the titles of books of sacred scripture and the names of books of the Bible are neither underlined nor enclosed in quotation marks.

Exodus	Vedas	Koran
Old Testament	Talmud	Upanishads

4. Quotation marks to enclose words defined in the text

Use quotation marks to enclose an unfamiliar word or phrase that you define in your writing. Do not repeat the quotation marks in subsequent uses of the term in your text.

> When people speak of " modernist " architecture, they are usually thinking of the style popularized in this country by Ludwig Mies van der Rohe.

> Not surprisingly, the architectural style that has followed modernism is known as " postmodernism. "

To refer to a word as such, use italics (on a typewriter, use underlining) rather than quotation marks: the word *word*.

5. Misuse of quotation marks

Quotation marks enclosing a borrowed text signal to the reader that the material is being quoted word for word from the original source. Be careful not to make any changes in a text that you enclose in quotation marks, and never use quotation marks to enclose material that you have paraphrased (see **19c** and **20b**).

30f

Finally, avoid using quotation marks as an implicit apology for slang or other questionably appropriate language:

Avoid   That comedian's monologue really " slayed " me.

If you have to apologize for a word, don't use it.

30g The apostrophe

The chief uses of the apostrophe are to indicate the possessive case of nouns and indefinite pronouns, to mark the omission of letters in a contracted word or date, and to indicate the plurals of letters and numerals.

1. Apostrophe to indicate the possessive case

All singular nouns and indefinite pronouns, including those that already end in -*s*, form the possessive by adding -'*s*.

a child ' s toy	Agnes ' s clarinet
someone ' s wallet	Charles Dickens ' s novels
day ' s end	the bus ' s exhaust

An exception to this rule exists only when the addition of -'*s* would create an awkward-sounding proper name. In those few cases, the singular possessive may be formed by adding the apostrophe alone.

Moses ' life
Xerxes ' conquests
Euripides ' plays

All plural nouns that do not end in -*s* also form the possessive by adding -'*s*.

children ' s games	two deer ' s tracks
men ' s and women ' s clothes	two moose ' s antlers

All plural nouns that end in -*s* form the possessive by adding the apostrophe alone.

boys ' and girls ' games	the Kennedys ' estate
in two hours ' time	the Douglases ' party
both babies ' cries	the two buses ' engines

Compound nouns and pronouns form the possessive by adding -'s to the final word.

the team captain's decision
someone else's book
my sister-in-law's visit

In a phrase that indicates joint possession, the last noun takes the possessive form; in a phrase that indicates individual possession, each noun takes the possessive form.

Marshall and Ward's Minneapolis branch
John's, Pamela's, and Harold's separate claims

Note that personal pronouns *never* take an apostrophe, even though their possessive forms end in -*s*.

his	ours
hers	yours
its	theirs

2. Apostrophe to form contractions

Use an apostrophe to indicate omissions in contracted words and dates.

it's = it is	o'clock = of the clock
I'm = I am	class of '94 = class of 1994
let's = let us	doesn't = does not
we're = we are	haven't = have not

3. Apostrophe to form the plurals of letters and numerals

30g

The plurals of letters and numerals are formed by adding -'s.

Her *w*'s were like *m*'s, and her *6*'s resembled *G*'s.

Form the plural of a word considered as a word in the same way.

His conversation is too full of *you know*'s punctuated by *well*'s.

EXERCISE 4

Insert quotation marks, apostrophes, and other appropriate punctuation where necessary in the following sentences.

1. Has anyone downstairs seen my calculus book called Louis from the second floor, where he was searching his room unsuccessfully.
2. Whats it called responded his sister Toni, looking up from a tabloid article whose headline was Martians Told Me to Live the Rest of My Life in Belgium.
3. I cant remember said Louis. All I know is that its cover is green and that its not where I left it.
4. Louiss cry hadnt attracted anyone elses attention.
5. In the kitchen, his father was engrossed in a cookbook chapter entitled Chocolate and You; somewhere in it he hoped to find a dessert to make for that evenings dinner.
6. In the garden, his mother wasnt noticing anything except the curious disease that was rapidly withering both of her prize rosebushes leaves.
7. In two days time said Louis as he walked down the stairs Ive got to know a lot more about solving integrals with algebraic substitutions than I do now.
8. Yesterday he explained to Toni my math professor unexpectedly said I'm sorry, but were going to have to have our midterm exam a week earlier than Id planned, since the examination day on my original syllabus is a holiday.
9. Louis had barely finished speaking when Bruno, the family collie, came into the room, dropped the moist shreds of a green book at his feet, raised its eyes proudly, and said Woof!
10. It looks as if my calculus grade has literally gone to the dogs said Louis weakly.

30h Other punctuation marks: colon, dash, parentheses, brackets

1. The colon

The colon is used primarily to introduce a formal enumeration or list, a quotation, or an explanatory statement.

Consider these three viewpoints : political, economic, and social.

Tocqueville expresses one view : "In the United States we easily perceive how the legal profession is qualified by its attributes . . . to neutralize the vices inherent in popular government. . . ."

I remember which way to move the clock when changing from Daylight Savings Time to Standard Time by applying a simple rule : spring ahead, fall backward.

Note that a list introduced by a colon should be in apposition to a preceding word; that is, the sentence preceding the colon should be grammatically complete without the list.

Incorrect	We provide : fishing permit, rod, hooks, bait, lunch, boat, and oars.
Correct	We provide the following items : fishing permit, rod, hooks, bait, lunch, boat, and oars.
Correct	We provide the following : fishing permit, rod, hooks, bait, lunch, boat, and oars.
Correct	The following items are provided : fishing permit, rod, hooks, bait, lunch, boat, and oars.

The colon may be used between two principal clauses when the second clause explains or develops the first.

Intercollegiate athletics continues to be big business, but Robert Hutchins long ago pointed out a simple remedy : colleges should stop charging admission to football games.

A colon is used after a formal salutation in a business letter.

Dear Sir or Madam :   Dear Mr. Harris :   Ladies and Gentlemen :

A colon is used to separate hour and minutes in numerals indicating time.

The train leaves at 9 : 27 A.M. and arrives at Joplin at 8 : 15 P.M.

It also separates the title and subtitle of a book.

Winifred Gérin's *Charlotte Brontë : The Evolution of Genius*

The Kings and Queens of England : A Tourist Guide, by Jane Murray

In bibliographical references, a colon is used between the place of publication and the name of the publisher.

New York : Oxford UP

30h

Finally, a colon is often used to separate chapter and verse in a biblical citation.

> Proverbs 28 : 20

2. The dash

The dash, as its name suggests, is a dramatic mark. Like the comma and parentheses, it separates elements within the sentence, but what parentheses say quietly the dash stresses. Note that on a typewriter, a dash consists of two hyphens with no spaces before, after, or between them.

The dash is an essential punctuation mark in three situations. First, when an appositive or parenthetic element contains commas, it should be set off with dashes, rather than commas, to avoid confusion.

Confusing	Three works of art, a watercolor, an oil, and a silk-screen print, hung on the west wall. **[Are there three—or six—pieces in all?]**
Clearer	Three works of art — a watercolor, an oil, and a silk-screen print — hung on the west wall.

Second, when a parenthetic element consists of an independent clause, it must be set off with dashes (or parentheses) rather than commas.

> By the time the speech was over — it lasted two hours — most of the audience members were in a stupor.

Third, when a sentence begins with a series or list, a dash is commonly used to link the list with the statement of summary or comment that follows it.

> The soldier in combat who sees his friend killed twenty yards away while he himself is unhurt, the pupil who sees another child get into trouble for copying on a test — they don't wish their friends ill, but they can't help feeling an embarrassing spasm of gratitude that it happened to someone else and not to them.
>
> —Harold S. Kushner, *When Bad Things Happen to Good People*

30h

Beyond these situations, dashes function to create mild or intense dramatic effect. Frequently a dash is used to indicate a sharp and perhaps unexpected turn of thought in a sentence.

> He suffered from claustrophobia. He wanted to run away — either to run away or to smash the place up.
>
> —Doris Lessing, *The Grass Is Singing*

> She had a strong impulse to get up, walk across the rug, and slap his face. That'll make him wink, she thought, rising, dizzy, half out of her seat — and then subsiding in horror at the idea of the spectacle she had nearly created.
>
> —Alison Lurie, *The Nowhere City*

A parenthetic element set off with dashes gets special emphasis.

> An intellectual weakness — and saving grace — of American students has always been that they are unable to sit still for ideology and its tight flemish-bonded logics and dialectics.
>
> —Tom Wolfe, *From Bauhaus to Our House*

To introduce a list, the dash is more informal and dramatic than the colon.

> They hugged the memories of illnesses to their bosoms. They licked their lips and clucked their tongues in fond remembrance of the pains they had endured — childbirth, rheumatism, croup, sprains, backaches, piles.
>
> —Toni Morrison, *The Bluest Eye*

Use the dash cautiously. Its flashy interruption can create energy and drama in a sentence, but its overuse weakens rather than intensifies that effect.

3. Parentheses

Like commas and dashes, parentheses are used to enclose or set off parenthetic, explanatory, or supplementary material. But unlike commas, parentheses usually enclose material than is less closely related in thought or structure to the rest of the sentence. And unlike dashes, parentheses reduce rather than increase dramatic effect.

Parentheses are often used to include material of the sort we might

30h

expect to find in a footnote—useful information that is not essential to the sentence.

> He commonly had more important things to think about than his shortness (and average height then was less than it is now) but the chief references in his letters . . . suggest that it was often in his mind.
>
> —Douglas Bush, *John Keats*

They also provide opportunities for the writer's comments and asides.

> Acting out of volition and necessity he had "chosen" (to the extent that it was a matter of choice) his distinctive mode, muckraking.
>
> —Justin Kaplan, *Lincoln Steffans: A Biography*

Parentheses are also used to enclose numbers that mark an enumeration within a sentence.

> The types of noncreative thinking listed by Robinson are (1) reverie, or daydreaming; (2) making minor decisions; and (3) rationalizing, or justifying our prejudices.

Finally, parentheses are used in the formal documentation of research. For more information about that function, see Chapters **19 to 23**.

When a passage in parentheses is part of a sentence element that is set off by a comma, the comma is placed outside the parentheses. If the material within parentheses is an exclamation or question, appropriate punctuation goes inside the parentheses.

> If we are willing to commit ourselves to a true war on drugs (and shouldn't we be willing to do so?) , then we need to begin not with drugs, but with poverty and lack of opportunity in our inner cities.

4.   Brackets

Square brackets are used to enclose a word or words inserted into a quotation by the person quoting. Such insertions typically comment on the quotation or provide an explanation of a word or phrase in the quotation that would otherwise be unclear.

> "Everyone in the metropolitan area [the company's report claimed] will welcome the opening of City Waste Disposal's newest incineration facility."

> "In a typical Chicago building of the turn of the century, the spandrels [horizontal panels under the windows] are recessed and discontinuous so that the building's uninterrupted vertical piers dominate the viewer's perception."

Sometimes a noun in brackets replaces a pronoun in a quotation whose antecedent does not otherwise appear in the quoted passage. In the following passage, for example, the bracketed material has been substituted for the pronoun *its*.

> "We know more about [the English language's] state in the later Middle Ages than earlier, and from the time of Shakespeare on, our information is quite complete."

The word *sic* (Latin for "thus"), enclosed in brackets, is inserted into a quotation after a misspelling or other error to indicate that the error occurs in the original text.

> He sent the following written confession: "She followed us into the kitchen, snatched a craving [sic] knife from the table, and came toward me with it."

Finally, if one parenthetical expression falls within another, brackets replace the inner parentheses. (Avoid this situation when possible. Usually [as here] it is distracting to the reader.)

EXERCISE 5

Insert appropriate punctuation where it is needed in the following sentences. The punctuation that has already been supplied to guide you is correct.

1. No one is certain about the origins of the blues a black American music form but historians believe that it grew out of two earlier forms of music from the rural South the field holler and the choral work song.
2. As John Stropes writes in his book Twentieth-Century Masters of Finger-Style Guitar When W. C. Handy published St. Louis Blues in 1914, the great commercialization of the blues had begun, and the guitar was an important instrument in this style.
3. To distinguish this music from the more jazz-oriented style of entertainers such as Louis Armstrong and Bessie Smith its also called country blues.

30h

4. The most common variety of country blues is known as twelve-bar blues it consists of three lines of eight measures each.
5. The first line is sung it is repeated and then a new line is sung.
6. An example of twelve-bar blues is these three lines from one of Robert Wilkins songs: Look like I can see trouble in the air, Look like I can see trouble in the air, But it aint all here friend—trouble everywhere.
7. Lacking formal musical training gifted blues artists began playing and singing in the streets during the early decades of this century.
8. In the 1960s, a number of black blues performers many in their sixties and seventies by then were popular on the college concert circuit.
9. Among the finest guitarists were Blind Blake a southeastern guitarist who was a master Rev Gary Davis who played with a ragtime flavor Blind Lemon Jefferson and Mississippi John Hurt.
10. There have been fewer women blues guitarists but Memphis Minnie is one fine example.
11. Another variety of country blues is called Chicago blues it originated among rural blacks who moved to Chicago in the 1940s.
12. At least two of these performers Elmore James and Muddy Waters greatly influenced rock and roll.
13. Even if you do not listen to the blues though you might want to begin chances are that some of the music you enjoy wouldnt exist in its present form without the groundwork laid by these amazing musicians.
14. Blues enthusiasts however are concerned about the future of this art.
15. The countrys legendary blues musicians are rapidly reaching old age many are now in their eighties and there are few younger musicians interested in continuing the tradition they have established.

EXERCISE 6

30h

Insert appropriate punctuation where it is needed in the following paragraphs. The punctuation that has already been supplied to guide you is correct.

I could tell without turning who was coming. There wasnt a big flatfooted clop-clop like horses make on hard-pack but a kind of edgy clip-clip-clip. There was only one man around here would ride a mule at least on this kind of business. That was Bill Winder who drove the stage between Reno and Bridgers Wells. A mule is tough all right a good mule can work two horses into the ground and not know it. But theres something about a mule a man cant get fond of. Maybe its just the way a mule is just as you feel its the end with a man whos that way. But you cant make a mule part of the way you live like your horse is its like he had no insides no soul. Instead of a partner youve just got something else to work on along with the steers. Winder didnt like mules either but thats why he rode them. It was against his religion to get on a horse horses were for driving.

Its Winder Gil said and looked at Davies and grinned. The news gets around dont it?

I looked at Davies too in the glass but he wasnt showing anything just staring at his drink and minding his own thoughts.

—Walter Van Tilberg Clark, *The Ox-Bow Incident*

30h

31 *Spelling*

The word *orthography*, meaning the art of correct spelling, is derived from two Greek roots: *ortho* (straight) and *graphy* (write). Spelling right, then, is writing straight. Since the time of Aristotle, correct spelling has distinguished the scholar from the dolt. Indeed, Lord Chesterton could write in the eighteenth century that one false spelling would fix ridicule on a writer for life: "I know many of quality," he claims, "who never recovered from the ridicule of having spelled *wholesome* without the *w*." In the next century, such American rebels as Walt Whitman and Mark Twain could ridicule the English aristocratic passion for correctness. "Morbidity for nice spelling," Whitman scolded, "means . . . impotence in literature," and Twain pouted, "I don't see any use in spelling a word right, and never did. . . . We might as well make all our clothes alike and cook all dishes alike." No impotence in literature for Twain, who then wrote one of the greatest works in the language in which many of the words are (intentionally) misspelled.

In *The Adventures of Huckleberry Finn,* Twain catches by means of misspellings the sound of Huck speaking a dialect that is not Standard English. Our language, which scholars began to standardize in the late seventeenth century, grows out of hundreds of dialects such as the one Huck spoke, and that variety of origins accounts for many of the peculiarities of English spelling. English is not an easy language to spell, and it is in the American spirit to chafe at the propriety of good spelling. Still, many readers expect accurate spelling, and fairly or not, they regard a writer's spelling mistakes as indications of a general sloppiness of mind. Like so many other aspects of writing, then, good spelling has a *rhetorical* function: it helps a writer to establish a persona characterized by precision and carefulness.

31a Trouble spots

Learn to look for trouble spots in words and concentrate on them. If you can remember the correct spelling of the trouble spot, the rest of the word will often take care of itself. *Receive,* like *deceive, perceive,* and *conceive,* is troublesome only because of the *ei* combination; if you can remember that it is *ei* after *c,* you will have mastered these words. To spell *beginning* correctly, all you need to remember is the double *n.*

Careful pronunciation may help you to avoid errors at trouble spots. In the following words, the letters in boldface are often omitted. Pronounce the words aloud, exaggerating the sound of the boldface letters:

accidentally	liable	recognize
candidate	library	sophomore
everybody	literature	strictly
February	occasionally	surprise
generally	probably	temperament
laboratory	quantity	usually

Many people add letters incorrectly to the following words. Pronounce the words, making sure that no extra syllable creeps in at spots indicated by boldface type.

athletics	entrance	mischievous
disastrous	height	remembrance
drowned	hindrance	similar
elm	lightning	umbrella

Trouble spots in the following words are caused by a tendency to transpose the boldface letters. Careful pronunciation may help you to remember the proper order.

31a

children	perform	prejudice
hundred	perspiration	prescription
irrelevant	prefer	tragedy

31b Similar words frequently confused

Learn the meaning and spelling of similar words. Many errors are caused by confusion of such words as *effect* and *affect*. It is useless to spell *principal* correctly if the word that belongs in your sentence is *principle*. The following list distinguishes briefly between words that are frequently confused.

accept	receive	breath	noun
except	aside from	breathe	verb
access	admittance	capital	city
excess	greater amount	capitol	building
		choose	present
advice	noun	chose	past
advise	verb	clothes	garments
affect	to influence (verb)	cloths	kinds of cloth
		coarse	not fine
effect	result (noun)	course	path
effect	to bring about (verb)	complement	to complete
		compliment	to praise
aisle	in church	conscience	sense of right and wrong
isle	island		
all ready	prepared	conscious	aware
already	previously	corps	group
allusion	reference	corpse	dead body
illusion	misconception	costume	dress
altar	shrine	custom	social convention
alter	change	council	governmental group
angel	celestial being		
angle	corner	counsel	advice
ascent	climbing	dairy	milk supplier
assent	agreement	diary	daily record
berth	bed	decent	proper
birth	being born	descent	slope
boarder	one who boards	desert	wasteland
border	edge	dessert	food

31b

device	noun	quiet	still
devise	verb	quite	entirely
dual	twofold	respectfully	with respect
duel	fight	respectively	in the order named
formally	in a formal manner	shone	from *shine*
formerly	previously	shown	from *show*
forth	forward	stationary	not moving
fourth	4th	stationery	writing supplies
ingenious	clever		
ingenuous	frank	than	comparison
its	of it	then	at that time
it's	it is	their	possessive
later	subsequently	there	in that place
latter	second of two	they're	they are
lead	metal	to	as in *go to bed*
led	past tense of the verb *lead*	too	as in *too bad, me too*
loose	not tight	two	the number 2
lose	misplace	weather	rain or shine
peace	not war	whether	which of two
piece	a portion	who's	who is
personal	private	whose	possessive
personnel	work force	you're	you are
principal	most important	your	possessive
principle	basic doctrine		

31c Spelling rules

The available spelling rules in English apply to a relatively small number of words, and unfortunately almost all rules have exceptions. Nevertheless, some of the rules may help you to spell common words that cause you trouble, especially those words formed with suffixes.

31c

It is as important to learn when a rule may be used as it is to understand the rule itself. Applied in the wrong places, rules will make your spelling worse, not better.

1. Final silent *e*

Drop a final silent *e* before suffixes beginning with a vowel (*-ing, -age, -able*). Keep a final silent *e* before suffixes beginning with a consonant (*-ful, -ly, -ness*).

arrange + ment = arrangement	nine + teen = nineteen
bale + ful = baleful	pale + ness = paleness
dote + age = dotage	plume + age = plumage
guide + ance = guidance	sincere + ly = sincerely
hope + ful = hopeful	stone + y = stony
hope + ing = hoping	white + wash = whitewash
late + ly = lately	white + ish = whitish
love + able = lovable	write + ing = writing

Note the following exceptions:

awful	dyeing	judgment	truly
duly	hoeing	ninth	wholly

The *e* is retained in such words as the following in order to keep the soft sound of *c* and *g:*

courageous	outrageous
noticeable	peaceable

EXERCISE 1

Following the rule above, write the correct spelling of each word indicated below.

use + ing	pale + ing
use + ful	manage + ment
argue + ment	write + ing
nine + ty	refuse + al
pale + ness	waste + ful
immediate + ly	hope + less
please + ure	absolute + ly
manage + able	sure + ly

31c

2.   Double the final consonant

When adding a suffix beginning with a vowel to words ending in one consonant preceded by one vowel (*red, redder*), notice where the word is accented. If it is accented on the last syllable or if it is a monosyllable, *double* the final consonant.

*bén*efit + ed = benefited   pre*fér* + ed = preferred
*díf*fer + ence = difference   *pró*fit + ing = profiting
oc*cúr* + ence = occurrence   *réd* + er = redder
o*mít* + ing = omitting   *trá*vel + er = traveler

Note that in some words the accent shifts when the suffix is added.

re*fér*red   *réf*erence
pre*fér*ring   *préf*erence

There are a few exceptions to this rule, such as *transferable* and *excellent*; and a good many words that should follow the rule have alternative spellings—for example, *worshiped* or *worshipped; traveling, traveler,* or *travelling, traveller.*

EXERCISE 2

Make as many combinations as you can of the following words and suffixes. Give your reason for doubling or not doubling the final consonant. Suffixes: *-able, -ible, -ary, -ery, -er, -est, -ance, -ence, -ess, -ed, -ish, -ing, -ly, -ful, -ment, -ness, -hood.*

occur	equip	man	expel
happen	commit	defer	rival
begin	equal	sum	glad
shrub	ravel	stop	profit
scrap	kidnap	clan	level
red	rid	libel	jewel

31c

3.   Words ending in *y*

If the *y* is preceded by a consonant, change the *y* to *i* before any suffix except *-ing.*

lady + es = ladies   lonely + ness = loneliness
try + ed = tried   accompany + es = accompanies
study + ing = studying

The *y* is usually retained if it is preceded by a vowel:

valleys   monkeys   displayed

Note the following exceptions: laid, paid, said, ladylike.

EXERCISE 3

Add suffixes to the following words. State your reason for spelling the word as you do.

mercy	relay	hardy	bounty	medley
duty	study	wordy	jockey	galley
pulley	essay	fancy	modify	body

4. *ie* or *ei*

When *ie* or *ei* is used to spell the sound *ee*, Put i *before* e, *except after* c.

achieve	grieve	retrieve	ceiling
belief	niece	shield	conceit
believe	piece	shriek	conceive
brief	pierce	siege	deceit
chief	relief	thief	deceive
field	relieve	wield	perceive
grief	reprieve	yield	receive

Note the following exceptions: either, leisure, neither, seize, weird.

31d Hyphenation

Compound words, entities formed by combining two or more individual words, are written in three ways: as one word (*townspeople*), as separate words (*city hall*), or as words joined by a hyphen (*city-state*). In general, the hyphen is used in recently made compounds and compounds still in the process of becoming one word. Because usage varies considerably, no arbitrary rules can be laid down. When in doubt, consult the latest edition of a good desk dictionary. The following guidelines represent the usual current practice.

1. Compound adjectives

Words used as a single adjective *before* a noun are usually hyphenated.

air-conditioned office   three-quarter binding
high-school prom   matter-of-fact statement
no-win situation   twenty-first-century technology
well-informed leader   old-fashioned attitude

When these compound adjectives *follow* the noun, they usually are not hyphenated.

The *snow-covered* mountains lay ahead.

The mountains were *snow covered*.

When the adverb ending in *-ly* is used with an adjective or a participle, the compound is not hyphenated.

highly praised organization
widely advertised product

See also **27d**.

2. Prefixes

When a prefix still retains its original strength in the compound, use a hyphen. In most instances, however, the prefix has been absorbed into the word and should not be separated by a hyphen. Contrast the following pairs of words:

ex-president, excommunicate   pre-Christian, preconception
vice-president, viceroy   pro-British, procreation

Note that in some words a hyphen indicates a difference in meaning.

She *recovered* her strength.

She *re-covered* her sofa.

31d

3. Numbers

A hyphen is used when the numbers 21 through 99 are written out.

twenty-six

one hundred sixty-three

The numerator and denominator of a fraction are also hyphenated.

two-thirds

ten and one-half

4. Suspensive hyphen

When two compound words are connected by *and* or *or* and the second word in both compounds is the same, you may indicate the first compound by writing just its first word followed by a hyphen and a space.

four- and six-cylinder engines

full- or part-time employment

The same principle applies when two prefixes are joined to the same word.

pre- and postgame activities

EXERCISE 4

Should the compounds in the following sentences be written solid, with a hyphen, or as two words? Consult a recent edition of a good dictionary, if necessary.

31d

1. We need an eight foot rod.
2. All the creeks are bone dry.
3. She gave away one fourth of her income.
4. The United States is a world power.
5. Who was your go between?
6. He is extremely good looking.
7. The younger son was a ne'er do well.
8. Let us sing the chorus all together.
9. They are building on a T shaped wing.

10. She is getting a badly needed rest.
11. Are you all ready?
12. The leak was in the sub basement.
13. He was anti British.
14. She does her work in a half hearted manner.
15. I don't like your chip on the shoulder attitude.
16. They always were old fashioned.
17. A high school course is required for admission.
18. I do not trust second hand information.
19. He is as pig headed a man as I ever knew.
20. She will not accept anything second rate.

31e Words commonly misspelled

Below is a list of some ordinary words that are often misspelled.
Have a friend test you on these words—fifty at a time. Then concentrate
on the ones you miss. To help you remember correct spellings, trouble
spots are indicated by boldface type in most of the words.

absence	airplane	appropriate
absorption	allotment	arctic
absurd	allotted	argument
abundant	all right	arithmetic
academic	already	arrangement
accidentally	altogether	article
accommodate	always	ascend
accumulate	amateur	association
accurate	among	athletic
achievement	analysis	attacked
acquainted	annually	attendance
acquire	apology	audience
across	apparatus	available
additionally	apparent	awkward
address	appearance	bargain
adequately	appetite	basically
aggravate	appreciate	becoming

31e

31c

beginning
believe
benefited
boundary
brilliant
Britain
business
calendar
candidate
career
category
cemetery
certain
challenge
changeable
changing
Christian
column
coming
commission
committee
comparatively
competent
competition
conceit
concentrate
condemn
confidence
conqueror
conscientious
conscious
consider
consistent

contemporary
continuous
controlled
convenience
coolly
copies
courteous
criticism
dealt
deceive
decision
definitely
descendant
describe
description
desirable
despair
desperate
dictionary
different
difficult
dining room
disappear
disappoint
disastrous
discipline
disease
dissatisfied
dissipate
divide
doctor
dying
effect

eighth
eliminate
embarrass
emphasize
entirely
entrance
environment
equipped
especially
etc. (et cetera)
exaggerate
exceed
excellent
exceptionally
exercise
existence
exorbitant
expense
experience
explanation
familiar
fascinate
feasible
February
fictitious
finally
foreign
forty
friend
gauge
government
grammar
guard

harass	lose	parallel
hardening	luxury	paralyzed
height	magazine	parliament
hindrance	maintenance	particularly
humorous	manufacturer	partner
hurriedly	marriage	pastime
hyprocrisy	mathematics	perform
illiterate	mattress	perhaps
imagination	meant	permanent
imitation	medieval	permissible
immediately	merely	persistent
incidentally	miniature	personnel
incredibly	municipal	persuade
independent	murmur	physical
indispensable	mysterious	pleasant
infinite	necessary	politician
initiative	neither	possess
intelligence	nineteen	possible
interest	noticeable	practically
involve	nowadays	preceding
irrelevant	nuclear	predominant
irresistible	obstacle	prejudice
itself	occasionally	preparation
jealousy	occurred	prevalent
knowledge	occurrence	primitive
laboratory	omission	privilege
laid	omitted	probably
led	opinion	procedure
leisure	opportunity	proceed
library	optimism	profession
license	origin	professor
literature	paid	prominent
loneliness	pamphlet	pronunciation

31e

prove	seize	syllable
psychology	sense	sympathize
pursue	separate	temperament
questionnaire	sergeant	tendency
quizzes	severely	thorough
really	shining	together
receive	siege	tragedy
recognize	similar	transferred
recommend	sincerely	truly
reference	soliloquy	typical
referred	sophomore	tyranny
religious	specimen	undoubtedly
reminisce	speech	unnecessary
repetition	stopping	until
representative	strenuous	using
rhythm	stretch	usually
ridiculous	studying	vengeance
sacrifice	succeed	village
safety	suppress	villain
schedule	surprise	weird
secretary	susceptible	writing

EXERCISE **5**

Write the present participle and the past participle of each of the following verbs (e.g., *stop, stopping, stopped*).

prefer	begin	acquit	equip
profit	hop	commit	recur
slam	differ	drag	confer

EXERCISE **6**

31e

Write the following words together with the adjectives ending in *-able* derived from them (e.g., *love, lovable*).

dispose	prove	console	imagine	measure
move	compare	blame	cure	

EXERCISE 7

Write the following words together with their derivatives ending in -*able* (e.g., *notice, noticeable*).

trace	change	charge	damage	manage
service	marriage	place	peace	

EXERCISE 8

Write the plural of the following nouns (e.g., *lady, ladies*).

baby	remedy	treaty	turkey
hobby	enemy	delay	decoy
democracy	poppy	alley	alloy
policy	diary	attorney	corduroy
tragedy	laundry	journey	convoy

EXERCISE 9

Write the third-person present and the first-person past of the following verbs (e.g., *he/she cries, I cried*).

fancy	spy	vary	worry
qualify	reply	dry	pity
accompany	occupy	ferry	envy

EXERCISE 10

Study the following words, observing that in all of them the prefix is not *diss-* but *dis-*.

dis + advantage	dis + obedient
dis + agree	dis + orderly
dis + approve	dis + organize
dis + interested	dis + own

EXERCISE 11

Study the following words, observing that in all of them the prefix is not *u-* but *un-*.

un + natural	un + numbered
un + necessary	un + named
un + noticed	un + neighborly

31e

EXERCISE 12

Study the following words, distinguishing between the prefixes *per-* and *pre-*. Keep in mind that *per-* means "through," "throughout," "by," or "for," and that *pre-* means "before."

perform	perhaps	precept
perception	perspective	precipitate
peremptory	perspiration	precise
perforce	precarious	precocious
perfunctory	precaution	prescription

EXERCISE 13

Study the following adjectives, observing that in all of them the suffix is not *-full*, but *-ful*.

peaceful	graceful	grateful	pitiful
dreadful	forceful	faithful	thankful
handful	shameful	healthful	plentiful

EXERCISE 14

Study the following words, observing that in all of them the ending is not *-us*, but *-ous*.

advantageous	specious	fastidious
gorgeous	precious	studious
courteous	vicious	religious
dubious	conscious	perilous

EXERCISE 15

Study the following words, observing that in all of them the suffix *-al* precedes *-ly*.

accidentally	terrifically	exceptionally
apologetically	specifically	elementally
pathetically	emphatically	professionally
typically	finally	critically

EXERCISE 16

Study the following words, observing that the suffix is not *-ess*, but *-ness*.

31e

clean + ness	plain + ness	stern + ness
drunken + ness	stubborn + ness	keen + ness
mean + ness	sudden + ness	green + ness

EXERCISE 17

Study the following words, observing that the suffix is not *-able*, but *-ible*.

accessible	horrible	legible
admissible	imperceptible	perceptible
audible	impossible	permissible
compatible	incompatible	plausible
contemptible	incredible	possible
convertible	indefensible	reprehensible
discernible	indelible	responsible
eligible	intelligible	sensible
feasible	invincible	susceptible
flexible	invisible	tangible
forcible	irresistible	terrible

EXERCISE 18

Study the following groups of words.

-ain	*-ain*	*-ian*	*-ian*
Britain	curtain	barbarian	guardian
captain	fountain	Christian	musician
certain	mountain	civilian	physician
chieftain	villain	collegian	politician

EXERCISE 19

Study the following groups of words.

-ede	*-ede*	*-eed*
accede	precede	exceed
antecede	recede	proceed
concede	secede	succeed

31e

EXERCISE 20

Fill the blanks with *principal* or *principle*. *Principle* is always a noun; *principal* is usually an adjective. *Principal* is also occasionally a noun: the *principal* of the school, both *principal* and *interest*.

1. The _____ will be due on the tenth of the month.
2. Her refusal was based on _____ .
3. This is my _____ for going.
4. The _____ has asked that we hold our meeting tomorrow.
5. He did not even know the first _____ of the game.
6. Can you give the _____ parts of the verb?

EXERCISE 21

Fill the blanks with *affect* or *effect:*

1. I do not like his _____ed manner.
2. An entrance was _____ed by force.
3. The _____ upon her is noticeable.
4. The law will take _____ in July.
5. It will be an _____ive remedy.
6. The hot weather will _____ the crops.
7. There was no serious after_____ .
8. She _____ed ignorance of the whole matter.

EXERCISE 22

Fill the blanks with *passed* or *past*. *Passed* is the past tense or past participle of the verb *pass; past* can be an adjective, noun, adverb, or preposition.

1. We _____ your house.
2. She went _____ me.
3. They whistled as they _____ by.
4. He is a man with a _____ .
5. My cousin is a _____ master at the art of lying.
6. That vocalist is _____ her prime.
7. Many years _____ before he returned.
8. It is long _____ bedtime.

EXERCISE 23

31e

Fill the blanks with:

1. *Its* (pronoun in the possessive case) or *it's* (contraction of *it is*).
   a. _____raining.
   b. The cat has had _____ supper.
   c. The clock is in _____ old place again.
   d. _____now six years since the accident.
   e. I think that _____ too late to go.

2. *Your* (pronoun in the possessive case) or *you're* (contraction of *you are*).
   a. _____mistaken; it is _____ fault.
   b. _____ position is assured.
   c. _____ to go tomorrow.
   d. I hope that _____ taking _____ vacation in July.
3. *There* (adverb or interjection), or *their* (pronoun in the possessive case), or *they're* (contraction of *they are*).
   a. It is _____ turn.
   b. _____ ready to go.
   c. _____ , that is over with.
   d. _____ car was stolen.
   e. _____ back from _____ trip.
4. *Whose* (pronoun in the possessive case) or *who's* (contraction of *who is*).
   a. _____ turn is it?
   b. There is the woman _____ running for mayor.
   c. _____ responsible for this?
   d. _____ book is this?
   e. He is one _____ word can be trusted.
   f. Bring me a copy of _____ *Who*.
   g. _____ ready to go?

EXERCISE 24

Choose the correct italicized word in each of the following sentences. Consult section **31b** if necessary.

1. Everyone is going *accept, except* me.
2. People came to her every day for *advice, advise*, and she was always ready to *advice, advise* them.
3. At so high an altitude it was hard to *breath, breathe*.
4. His *breath, breathe* came in short gasps.
5. One of the sights of Washington, DC, is the *Capital, Capitol*.
6. Albany is the *capital, capitol* of New York.
7. Before dinner I had time to change my *clothes, cloths*.
8. The tickets were sent with the *complements, compliments* of the manager.
9. The country was as dry and dreary as a *desert, dessert*.
10. The shack in which we *formally, formerly* lived is still standing.
11. It's *later, latter* than you think.
12. The winners were *lead, led* up onto the stage.
13. Button the money in your pocket so you won't *lose, loose* it.

31e

32 *Mechanics*

The appearance of a paper, like the appearance of a person, indicates regard for self and for the world at large. Accurate typing, a clean page, observance of editing conventions—all of these suggest a writer's confidence and authority. Wise writers use any available means—including care with mechanics—to win the favor and attention of their readers.

32a Manuscript preparation

Unless your instructor specifies otherwise, you should prepare your essays on standard 8½-by-11-inch white paper. Typed papers—which are preferable—should be double-spaced on unruled white bond. If your instructor permits handwritten papers, use wide-ruled paper, write legibly in black or dark blue ink, and skip lines. An instructor or an editor grows weary with a manuscript that has to be puzzled out one word at a time. Give your thoughts and sentences a fair chance by presenting them neatly on the page.

1. Format

Below are some widely accepted conventions for arranging the text on your page. Your instructor may have additional, or different, requirements.

1. Type or write on one side of the sheet only.
2. Leave a margin of one inch on the top, bottom, and sides of typed papers, slightly more for handwritten essays.
3. On four double-spaced lines in the upper left corner of the first page, give your name, your instructor's name, the course number,

32a

and the date. Double-space again (or skip another line) and center your title. Do not use quotation marks or underline your title unless it includes words that require such punctuation (see **32e**). Capitalize all words in the title except articles, short conjunctions, and short prepositions. Double space after your title and begin the first line of your essay.

4. Indent paragraphs five spaces when you type. In handwritten manuscripts, indent about an inch.

5. Number all pages with Arabic numbers in the upper right corner, one-half inch from the top of the page.

2. Quotations

When you reproduce quotations in your text, observe the following conventions. (For an extended discussion of the correct use of quotations, see **20c**. For detailed instructions on the use of quotation marks, see **30f**.)

1. A quotation of only a few words should be incorporated into your sentences:

In Childhood and Society, Erik Erikson notes that

the young adult, "emerging from the search for

and insistence on identity," has become "ready

for intimacy."

2. A quotation of more than four typed lines of prose, or more than three lines of verse, should be set off from the main text without quotation marks by indenting. Introduce the quotation with a colon unless the quotation begins in the middle of a sentence that grammatically continues your own sentence of introduction; in that case, use no punctuation. Indent the quotation ten spaces from the left margin, double-spacing between the last line of your text and the first line of the quotation, and between the lines of the quotation itself.

3. A quotation of poetry should be divided into lines exactly as the original is divided. If an entire line of verse does not fit on one

32a

line of the page, the words left over should be indented on the next line:

> Allons! the inducements shall be greater,
>
> We will sail pathless and wild seas,
>
> We will go where winds blow, waves dash,
>
>> and the Yankee clipper speeds by
>>
>> under full sail.

4. When quoting dialogue from a story, novel, or play, be sure to reproduce the paragraphing and punctuation of the quotation exactly as in the original.

> "Are you better, Minet—Chéri?"
>
> "Yes. I can't think what came over me."
>
> The grey eyes, gradually reassured, dwelt on mine.
>
> "I think I know what it was. A smart little rap on the knuckles from Above."
>
> I remained pale and troubled and my mother misunderstood:
>
> "There, there now. There's nothing so terrible as all that in the birth of a child, nothing terrible at all. It's much more beautiful in real life. The suffering is so quickly forgotten, you'll see! The proof that all women forget is that it is only men——and what business was it of

32a

```
Zola's, anyway?--who write stories about

it."
```

Note, incidentally, that British writers and publishers commonly use a single quotation mark (') where American convention requires double quotation marks(").

3.   Manuscript corrections

If a reading of your final draft shows the need for minor corrections, make them unmistakably clear. It is not necessary to recopy an entire page for the sake of one or two small insertions or alterations, but recopying is called for if the number of corrections would make the page difficult to read or messy in appearance. Words to be inserted should be typed or written above the line, and their proper position should be indicated by a caret (ˏ) placed below the line.

```
         other
On the hand, Nightingale's books on the nursing pro-
        ^
fession remained influential for years after her

death.
```

Inserted words should not be enclosed in parentheses or brackets unless these marks are required by the sentence. Cancel words by drawing a neat line through them, not by enclosing them in parentheses or brackets.

32b Capital letters

The general principle governing capitalization is that proper nouns are capitalized and common nouns are not. A proper noun is the name of a particular person, place, or thing:

Richard Wright	Alaska	the Capitol
Virginia Woolf	New Orleans	the Golden Gate Bridge

A common noun is a more general term that can be used as a name for a number of persons, places, or things:

author	state	building
woman	city	bridge

Note that the same word may be used as both a proper and a common noun.

> Of all the *peaks* in the Rocky Mountains, *Pike's Peak* is the mountain I would most like to climb.

> Our beginning *history* class studied *legislative* procedure and the part our *representatives* play in it. When I took *History 27,* our class visited the *Legislative* Committee hearing in which *Representative* Cella expressed his views on the Alliance for Progress.

Abbreviations are capitalized when the words they stand for would be capitalized: USN, ROTC, NBC.

1. Proper nouns

Capitalize proper nouns and adjectives derived from them. Proper nouns include the following:

1. Days of the week, months, and holidays:

Sunday	Thanksgiving
October	New Year's Eve

2. Organizations such as political parties, governmental bodies and departments, societies, institutions, clubs, churches, and corporations:

Socialist Party	Boston Public Library
U.S. Senate	Optimist's Club
Department of the Interior	Greek Orthodox Church
American Cancer Society	Raytheon Company

3. Members of organizations:

Republicans	Buddhists
Lions	Girl Scouts

4. Historical events, periods, and documents:

Battle of Hastings	Declaration of Independence
Middle Ages	Stamp Act
Baroque Era	Magna Carta

5. Specific places and geographical areas:

Latin America	Colorado River
Ellis Island	the Far East
Sahara Desert	the Midwest

6. Names of races, ethnic groups, and languages (but not the words *white* and *black* when used to refer to races):

Caucasian	Japanese
African-American	Italian

7. Names of religions, religious figures and holidays, and sacred books:

the Lord	the Bible
the Son of God	the Book of Mormon
Allah	Day of Atonement
Lutheran	All Saints' Day

8. Registered trademarks:

Coca-Cola	Volvo
Tide	Sony

9. Terms identifying family members only when such words are used in place of proper names:

My sister and brother both received letters from Grandmother and Grandpa.

10. Titles of persons when they precede proper names. When titles are used without proper names, only those of high rank should be capitalized:

Senator Marsh   Professor Stein   Aunt Elsa

Both the Governor and the Attorney General endorsed the candidacy of our representative.

The postmaster of our town appealed to the Postmaster General.

32b

11. In biological nomenclature, the names of genera but not of species:

> *Homo sapiens*   *Equus caballus*
>
> *Salmo irideus*   *Aquila heliaca*

12. Stars, constellations, and planets, but not the words *earth, sun,* or *moon* unless they are used as astronomical names:

> Sirius   Taurus
>
> Arcturus   Jupiter

2. Titles of works

Capitalize the first word and the important words of the titles of books, plays, articles, musical compositions, pictures, and other literary or artistic works. Unimportant words in a title are the articles *a, an,* and *the;* short conjunctions; and short prepositions.

> *I, Claudius*   *Summer in Williamsburg*   Beethoven's *Third Symphony*
>
> *Childhood and Society*   *Measure for Measure*   *Friar Felix at Large*
>
> Brancusi's "Bird in Space"   Bruce Springsteen's "Born in the U.S.A."

3. Sentences and quotations

Capitalize the first word of every sentence and of every direct quotation in dialogue. Note that a capital letter is not used for the part of a quotation that follows an interpolated expression like *he said,* unless that expression begins a new sentence.

> "Mow the lawn diagonally," said Mrs. Grant, "and go over it twice."
>
> "Mow the lawn twice diagonally," said Mrs. Grant. "It will be even smoother if the second mowing crosses over the first one."
>
> Mrs. Grant said, "Mow the lawn twice."

Following a colon, the first words in a series of short questions or sentences may be capitalized.

> The first-aid questions were dull but important: What are the first signs of shock in accident victims? Should they be kept warm? Should they eat? Should they drink?

32b

Capitalize the first word of every line of poetry except when the poem itself does not use a capital letter.

> I'll walk where my own nature would be leading:
>   It vexes me to choose another guide:
> Where the grey flocks in ferny glens are feeding;
>   Where the wild wind blows on the mountain-side.
>
> —Emily Brontë

> last night i heard
> a pseudobird;
> or possibly
> the usual bird
> heard pseudome.
>
> —Ebenezer Peabody

32c Numbers

In general, treat all numbers in a particular context similarly; in the interest of consistency, do not use words for some and figures for others. The following additional guidelines for writing numbers are widely accepted.

1. Numbers from one to ten and round numbers that can be expressed in one or two words are usually written out.

> *three* people in line
> *twenty-five* flavors
> *seven hundred* reserved seats

Adjectival forms of numbers are also written out when they can be expressed in one or two words.

> *second* chance
> *thirty-fifth* floor
> the *ten-thousandth* customer

All numbers that begin a sentence are written out, even though they would ordinarily be represented by figures.

> *Four hundred sixty* dollars was too much.

32c

2. To indicate a range of numbers, use the complete second number up to 99.

> 33–34 90–99

For larger numbers, use the last two digits of the second number unless more are required.

> 123–25 100–09
> 399–401 12,500–13,000

3. Use figures to express the day of the month and the year in a date.

> December 7, 1941 14 July 1789

References to centuries and decades are usually written out in lowercase letters but may be expressed in figures. In the latter case, the figures are followed by an *s* without an apostrophe.

> the *nineteenth* century the 1800s
> the *sixties* the 1960s, the '60s

Write out the names of centuries when they are used as adjectives.

> a *twentieth*-century invention

4. Use figures for numbers in street addresses; long numbers; chapter and page numbers; time citations followed directly by *A.M.* or *P.M.*; and decimals.

> 525 Spring Street page 33
> 11337 Palm Boulevard 9:00 P.M. [but *nine o'clock*]
> 1,275 gallons 7:25 A.M.
> Chapter 12 8.5 percent

32c Use figures with abbreviations and symbols.

> 80 lbs. 66%
> 55 mph 6'1"

5. Use figures after a dollar sign.

> $12.50 $1,000

If the amount of money in question can be expressed in one or two words, it may be written out.

fifty-five cents   *sixteen* dollars

Amounts of money in the millions, billions, or trillions of dollars may be expressed with a combination of figures and words when a dollar sign is used.

$12 million (but *twelve million dollars*)

32d Abbreviations

Minimize the use of abbreviations in expository prose. As a general rule, spell out the first names of people, the words in addresses (*North, Street, New Jersey*), the days of the week and the months of the year, and units of measurement (*ounces, pounds, kilometers, hours, quarts*).

Elliott Brodie of 327 *West* 27th *Avenue*, Kenosha, *Wisconsin*, died on *December* 16, 1989.

Abbreviations cannot be avoided entirely, however, and it is important to be familiar with the most important conventions governing their use.

1. Some abbreviations are always written with periods.

Mr.	Ph.D.
etc.	i.e.
A.D.	P.M.

Others, such as the U.S. Postal Service abbreviations for states and the abbreviations for many organizations and agencies, are written without periods.

CA	DAR
TX	FAA

Acronyms (abbreviations spoken as words) are also written without periods.

NATO	UNICEF
MADD	OPEC

32c

Still other abbreviations may be written with or without periods.

mph or m.p.h.	USA or U.S.A.
rpm or r.p.m.	PTA or P.T.A.

Your best guide to the proper punctuation of an abbreviation is a good desk dictionary. Many such dictionaries conveniently collect all abbreviations in a separate appendix.

2. Civil, religious, military, and academic titles are usually written out.

Senator Kennedy	Governor Cuomo
Secretary Baker	Colonel Mason
Father O'Malley	Professor Meyer

Such titles may be abbreviated only when they are followed by a person's full name: *Sen. Edward Kennedy,* but not *Sen. Kennedy.* The titles *Reverend* and *Honorable* must be followed by a full name *and* preceded by the word *the.*

the Reverend Thomas Jones (not *the Reverend Jones*)

the Honorable Alice Simpson (not *the Honorable Simpson*)

The word *the* is dropped if these titles are abbreviated, but the abbreviated forms must also be followed by a full name.

Rev. Thomas Jones (not *Rev. Jones*)

Hon. Alice Simpson (not *Hon. Simpson*)

3. The titles below are abbreviated when they precede names.

Mr.	Mrs.
Messrs.	Dr.
Ms.	St. [Saint]

32d

Titles and degrees such as the following are also abbreviated after names.

Sr.	Ph.D.
Jr.	M.A.
M.D.	LL.D.
D.D.S.	Esq.

Do not duplicate a title before *and* after a name.

Incorrect   Dr. Rinard Z. Hart, *M.D.*

Correct   Rinard Z. Hart, *M.D.*, or
Dr. Rinard Z. Hart

4. The words *volume, chapter, edition,* and *page* should be written out in references within a text, but abbreviated in parenthetical citations and bibliographies.

I found this quotation on *page* 267 of the third *edition.*

For further information on proper terms for addressing dignitaries, consult the Appendix of your style manual (*pp.* 664–80).

5. In technical writing, directions, recipes, and the like, terms of measurement are often abbreviated when used with figures.

32° F	½ tsp.
5 cc	32 mpg
12 ft.	4 hrs

6. When referring to corporations, use the ampersand (&) and abbreviations such as *Co., Inc.,* and *Bros.* only when a company uses such an abbreviation in its official title.

Incorrect   D.C. Heath & Co.

Correct   D. C. Heath and Company

7. Abbreviations that end in a period form their plurals by adding -'s.

two *Ph.D.'s*   *M.A.'s* in several disciplines

Abbreviations that do not end in a period usually form their plurals by adding -*s* without an apostrophe.

the *PTAs* of both schools

a fraternity house full of *BMOCs*

32e Italics

Italics are used for certain titles, unnaturalized foreign words, scientific names, names of ships and aircraft, and words used as words.

32e

To italicize a word in a manuscript, draw one straight line below it, or use the underlining key on the keyboard: King Lear.

1. Italicize all words in the titles of books and monographs; plays and motion pictures; magazines, journals, and newspapers; paintings and sculpture; and long poems and long musical compositions. The article *the* preceding the title of a newspaper is not italicized or capitalized.

> Stephen Crane's *The Red Badge of Courage*
> Arthur Miller's *Death of a Salesman*
> *The Wizard of Oz*
> *Newsweek*
> the *Southern Review*
> the *Chicago Tribune*
> the *Mona Lisa*
> Michelangelo's *David*
> Alexander Pope's *The Rape of the Lock*
> Ravel's *Bolero*

Titles of parts of published works and articles in magazines are enclosed in quotation marks.

> The assignment is "Despondency" from William Wordsworth's long narrative poem, *The Excursion.*
> In the *New Yorker,* I always read filler material entitled "Letters We Never Finished Reading."
> She hoped to publish her story entitled "Nobody Lives Here" in a magazine like *Harper's.*

32e

2. Italicize foreign words that have not yet become accepted in the English language. If you are not certain whether a foreign word has become naturalized, consult a dictionary. Be sure to consult the dictionary's explanatory notes to see how foreign words are indicated. Italicize the Latin scientific names for plants and animals.

A feeling of *gemütlichkeit* pervaded the hotel we stayed at in Munich.

The technical name of Steller's jay is *Cyanocitta stelleri.*

3. Italicize the names of ships, planes, trains, and spacecraft.

The S.S. *Constitution* sails for Africa tomorrow.

We saw Lindbergh's *Spirit of St. Louis* when we visited Washington last month.

I'm going to Baltimore on Amtrak's *Yankee Clipper.*

Voyager 2 is still sending back information from deep space.

32f Syllabication

Dividing a word at the end of a line is mainly a printer's problem. In manuscripts it is not necessary to keep the right-hand margin absolutely even, so it is seldom necessary to divide a word at the end of a line. If such a division is essential, observe the following principles, and mark the division with a hyphen (-).

1. Divide words only *between* syllables—that is, between the normal sound divisions of a word. When in doubt as to where the division between syllables comes, consult a dictionary. One-syllable words, such as *though* or *strength,* cannot be divided. Syllables of one letter should not be divided from the rest of the word. Nor should a division be made between two letters that indicate a single sound. For example, never divide *th* as in *brother, sh* as in *fashion, ck* as in *Kentucky, oa* as in *reproaching,* or *ai* as in *maintain.* Such combinations of letters may be divided only if they indicate two distinct sounds: *post-haste, dis-hon-or, co-au-thor.*

> **Incorrect**   a-dult, burg-lar-ize, co-ord-in-a-tion, li-mit, ver-y
> **Correct**   adult, bur-glar-ize, co-or-di-na-tion, lim-it, very

2. A division usually comes at the point where a prefix or suffix joins the root word.

> anti-dote, be-half, con-vene, de-tract, sub-way
>
> fall-en, Flem-ish, lik-able (or like-able), like-ly, place-ment, tall-er, tall-est

This rule does not hold when it contradicts the normal pronunciation of the word.

> bus-tling, jog-gled, prej-u-dice, prel-ate, res-ti-tu-tion, twin-kling

32f

3. When two consonants come between vowels (me*m*ber), the division is between the consonants if pronunciation permits (*mem-ber*). If the consonant is doubled before a suffix, the second consonant goes with the suffix (*plan-ning*).

> at-tend, bur-lesque, clas-sic, dif-fer, fas-ten, fit-ting, hin-der, im-por-tant, laun-der, nar-rate, pas-sage, rab-bit, rum-mage, ser-geant, ten-don
>
> BUT NOTE: knowl-edge

4. The division comes after a vowel if pronunciation permits.

> devi-ate, modi-fier, ora-torical, oscilla-tor

EXERCISE 1

Correct any errors in capitalization, numbers, abbreviations, and italics.

1. The 1st bridges on the Earth were natural ones, formed by rocks and fallen trees.
2. The romans built incredible bridges out of rocks and concrete—some still stand 1,000 yrs. later.
3. Many bridges were built by 12th-century christians who wanted to carry their message all over europe.
4. According to the book Great Bridges of the World, bridge building, already sophisticated in many ways, became a Science in the seventeen hundreds.
5. Iron was introduced in bridges in seventeen seventy-nine, and in the last ½ of the 19 cent. bridge-builders began using steel.
6. There are 4 main kinds of bridges—beam, arch, suspension, and canti-lever—and 2 types of moveable bridges, pivot and vertical lift, which are a far cry from the drawbridges of Medieval Times.
7. The longest cantilever bridge, 3,239 ft. overall, is the quebec bridge over the saint lawrence river in Canada.
8. The lake pontchartrain causeway in La., called the longest bridge in the world, is 23.87 mi. long.
9. Bridges are technically fascinating, but a person doesn't have to be a Prof. of Engineering to appreciate their beauty.
10. Many bridges—such as the golden gate bridge in San Francisco, CA, and the famous london bridge, which was dismantled and moved to Ariz.—are Tourist attractions.

32f

EXERCISE 2

Correct any errors in capitalization, numbers, abbreviations, and italics.

1. Because movies are a reliable gauge of the Country's social attitudes, analyzing images of native americans in films can reveal a great deal.
2. Early images of native americans were of Savages, 100s of Godless warmongers who attacked small groups of innocent Settlers, and an occasional indian who recognized the value of the White Man's ways.
3. In some movies, at least a few of the Whites were equally bad, stealing land and carrying off indian women, but the larger evils of Government exploitation and genocide were never suggested.
4. One of the 1st movies to break this trend was Broken Arrow, which appeared in nineteen fifty.
5. In the 1957 movie Run of the Arrow, Rod Steiger played an outcast who considered becoming a sioux, but became an american citizen instead.
6. Over the next 15 yrs., movies began to recognize the existence of nat. am. cultures beyond the stereotypical tepees and peace pipes.
7. For ex., eighty % of the dialogue in A Man called Horse is in sioux.
8. It was not until Little big man in 1970 that a native american, chief Dan George, was cast in a lead role in a major motion picture.
9. The nineteen-eighty film Windwalker also stands out; even though a Brit. actor played the lead, the entire movie was done in the cheyenne and crow languages, with subtitles in english.
10. Perhaps these changes indicate that Mainstream American Culture is recognizing that the role of native americans in this country transcends cowboy-and-indian games.

32f

Special Writing Situations

33 *Writing Business Letters*

34 *Composing Résumés and Job Applications*

35 *Writing under Pressure*

36 *Writing with a Word Processor*

PART
VIII

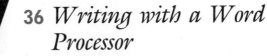

33 *Writing Business Letters*

The process of composing a business letter involves many of the same issues that are important in other writing tasks. What is your main point, and what do you wish to accomplish? How much do you know about your readers and their probable response? What tone should you adopt? How much specific detail must you include? But beyond these matters of content, the appearance of a business letter is also critical. An effective business letter *looks* like a business letter; it wins its reader's attention partly by following the conventions that characterize business correspondence. This chapter, therefore, deals not only with questions of content but also with important matters of form.

33a The rhetoric of business correspondence

We write business letters for many reasons—to request information, to place orders, to voice complaints, to offer thanks. Each business letter takes shape in a unique rhetorical situation, a specific relationship to be developed between writer and reader. The best letters build on that relationship to accomplish their writers' purposes.

1. Consider your reader

Whenever possible, address your letter by name to a specific person rather than to a mere job title such as "Personnel Director" or "Customer Relations Manager." Particularly for application letters or letters of complaint, it may well be worth the small cost to telephone a company and ask the name of the person to whom you should write. Letters addressed impersonally to a mere title will eventually land on the correct desk, but they lack the impressive sense of direct contact conveyed by letters written to a specific individual.

Think carefully about your reader, and try to strike an appropriate tone. A snarling letter of complaint may offer a temporary outlet for your frustrations, but it is less likely to resolve your problem than a letter that suggests your patience and reasonableness. As you organize the contents of your letter, keep in mind the suggestions for effective writing discussed elsewhere in this book. Provide your reader with specific information, and arrange it in paragraphs that are coherent and complete; no reader making his or her way through a stack of incoming correspondence will be willing to puzzle over your intended meaning. Give your letter the attention to style that suggests a sophisticated writer, and proofread the final copy with professional accuracy.

2. Consider your form

Business letters, even short ones, are usually typed, single-spaced, on one side of 8½-by-11-inch paper. Neat centering on the page is more important than adherence to standard margins. In what is called **block style,** all the parts of a letter are typed flush against the left margin, and the first lines of paragraphs are not indented (see sample on page 687). In the less formal **indented style,** by contrast, the inside address and the close are typed on the right side of the page and the first line of each paragraph is indented five spaces (see sample on page 682). The **modified block style** follows the general arrangement of the indented style, but without indentation of the first lines of paragraphs (see sample on page 681).

33b Parts of a business letter

A typical business letter has five parts.

1. The heading

The heading consists of your address and the date, usually typed on three lines, and placed either flush against the upper left margin (block style) or in the upper right corner (indented style). It is included so that the person who receives your letter will be able to respond to you even if your envelope is lost or discarded.

The first line of the heading contains your street address; the second, your city, state, and zip code; the third, today's date. If you abbreviate your state, use the standard two-letter abbreviation (without periods) prescribed by the U.S. Postal Service. Double-space or quadruple-space after the last line of the heading.

2. The inside address

The inside address is identical to the address that you type on the envelope. Including it inside the letter ensures that your letter will reach its addressee even if it is opened by someone else in an office and becomes separated from its envelope.

On the first line of the inside address, use the appropriate abbreviated title with the full name of the person you are writing to: Mr. David Hunt, Dr. Elizabeth Aikers, Ms. Harriet Sweeney, Rev. Stephen Jules. If the person has an official position within a company, the title of the position and the name of the company are given on the second line, separated by a comma, or on the second and third lines.

```
Mr. Robert O'Malley
Editor in Chief, The Indianapolis Courier

Ms. Margaret Wilson
Vice President
Blindex Corporation
```

The next line of the inside address contains the street address, followed on the concluding line with the city, state, and zip code. Again, if you abbreviate the state, use the U.S. Postal Service abbreviation. Double-space after the inside address.

3. The salutation

The salutation repeats the name given on the first line of your inside address, omitting the person's first name. In business letters the salutation is followed by a colon:

33b

```
Dear Mr. O'Malley:

Dear Ms. Wilson:
```

If you are unable to obtain the name of the person to whom your letter should be addressed, use one of the following salutations:

```
Dear Sir or Madam:
```
[used when you are writing to a specific person whose name you do not know—for example, the editor of a newspaper or the chief of surgery in a hospital]

```
Ladies and Gentlemen:
```
[used when you must address your letter to a company or organization rather than to a specific person]

If you know the sex but not the name of the person to whom you are writing, you may use the salutation *Dear Sir* or *Dear Madam.*

Avoid the salutations *Dear Sirs* and *Gentlemen,* both of which illogically exclude women. And never open a standard business letter with the phrase *To Whom It May Concern;* this salutation is used only in letters such as personal recommendations that are intended for distribution to various people unknown to the writer.

Double-space after your salutation.

4. The body

Clearly state your purpose for writing—to apply for a job, to order a replacement part, or to express a complaint—as early as possible in your letter. Major corporations and large government offices receive hundreds—if not thousands—of letters every day, and your correspondence will get the fastest possible treatment if the person who opens your letter can immediately determine what you want. For the same reason, be concise, specific, and clear.

5. The close

Double-space or quadruple-space after the last line of the body of your letter, and type an appropriate close: very formal ("Very truly yours,"), formal ("Yours truly," "Sincerely yours," "Sincerely,"), or relatively informal ("Best wishes,"). The close is positioned under the inside address, either flush left (block style) or at the right side of the page (indented style). Capitalize only the first word, and follow the close with a comma. Leave room for your signature by quadruple-spacing, and type your name exactly as you will sign it:

Sincerely yours,

William A. Quinn

William A. Quinn

Business letters are usually mailed in long (9½-inch) envelopes. Type your name and address in the upper left corner, and center the name and address of your correspondent, just as they appear in your letter's inside address:

```
Maureen Brown
218 East 10th Street
Columbus, OH 43202


              Mr. Stephen Hernandez
              Circulation Manager
              Book Collectors' Digest
              2121 Peachtree Plaza
              Atlanta, GA 30309
```

Sample business letter (modified block style)

```
                              218 East 10th Street
                              Columbus, OH 43202
                              February 8, 1990

Mr. Stephen Hernandez
Circulation Manager
Book Collectors' Digest
2121 Peachtree Plaza
Atlanta, GA 30309
```

33b

Dear Mr. Hernandez:

For the second consecutive month, I have not received my issue of Book Collectors' Digest. Since my address has not changed, I am inclined to think that a mailing problem exists somewhere in your office, and I would appreciate your looking into the matter. My subscription number is B2184–886.

Because I have missed two issues of my subscription through this delivery problem, may I ask that you extend my subscription by two months, until October of this year? I enjoy your magazine and look forward to remaining one of your subscribers.

Sincerely,

Maureen Brown

Maureen Brown

Sample business letter (indented style)

90 North Thomas Avenue
Kingston, New York 12401
May 16, 1990

Catalog Department
Gillespie Furniture Creations
3101 Fontaine Road
Denver, CO 80203

Ladies and Gentlemen:

On April 26 I ordered a chrome–and–glass coffee table (model C261/LY) from your spring 1990 catalog. When it arrived yesterday, I discovered that several pieces of hardware needed for assembly were missing. Would you please send me the following missing parts:

33b

                6—#17 metal screws
                1—connecting rod "B"
                2—chrome finishing caps

     For your information, I have enclosed a copy of
the shipping invoice. I appreciate your assistance
and look forward to hearing from you.

                          Yours truly,

                          Mark Wallace

                          Mark Wallace

Encl.

34 *Composing Résumés and Job Applications*

Job applications are among the most important letters that anyone writes. When you compose a résumé and write an accompanying letter of application, you must rely on your writing to persuade a potential employer that your qualifications, personality, and interests make you the best candidate for the job.

34a Designing a résumé

A **résumé,** sometimes called a vita (the Latin word for *life*), lists chronologically the activities of your life that qualify you for a job. It is an essential part of every job application.

1. Format

There is no fixed format for a résumé, but you should keep in mind a few general guidelines. Above all, make the content of your résumé clear and easy to follow, and arrange it attractively. Make headings and subheadings stand out by underlining or using boldface type. Leave wide margins and sufficient white space between the major sections of your résumé. Don't feel that you have to crowd everything onto a single page, but don't pad your résumé with needless detail or trivial facts simply to extend its length.

2. Content

Every résumé should begin with your full name (avoid nick-names), your current address, and your telephone number (include both a home and an office number if you are willing to receive calls from potential employers at your present place of work). Typically, the major categories under which the remaining material on a résumé is placed are "Education" and "Experience." List items in reverse chronological order, and provide accurate dates, so that a reader can see what you have done in each recent year of your life. A résumé usually ends with the names, addresses, and telephone numbers of several references, persons whom the reader can contact for more information about you. Some employers also like to find something about a candidate's outside interests on a résumé; others consider such information irrelevant padding. Use your best judgment, based on what you can learn and surmise about your reader. In any case, you should not include such personal information as height, weight, or marital status unless it has direct bearing on the job you are applying for. (See the sample résumé on page 688.)

34b Letters of application

A résumé is usually accompanied by a cover letter personally addressed to a potential employer. Such a cover letter should be complete but normally should not exceed one page. We can summarize the essential contents of a **letter of application** by considering its main parts.

1. Introduction

Use your introductory paragraph (which may be no longer than a sentence or two) to accomplish three things. First, make it clear that you are writing a letter of application. Businesses receive many kinds of letters every day, and you want to be sure that yours is immediately grouped with those of other job applicants. Second, state the specific job that you are applying for. Often a company will advertise several positions at once; it is to your advantage, obviously, to be sure that your letter correctly places you in competition for the

34b

job you want. Finally, indicate how you learned of the opening you are applying for—whether you read a newspaper advertisement, for example, or were referred by a friend who knew of the company's hiring plans.

2. Body

The body of your letter should summarize your qualifications clearly and specifically. Don't simply repeat all the facts on your résumé; instead, use your letter to *comment* on the résumé, emphasizing your most important qualifications and providing additional information about your background where appropriate.

At the same time, let the style of your writing reveal something about your personality. Ideally, the tone of an application letter should be businesslike but not stuffy, natural but not chatty. Be positive, but without being pushy or insistent; most employers, like most general readers, are impressed by confidence but not by raw aggressiveness. Don't make insupportable assertions about your suitability for the job in question ("I am unquestionably the candidate you are looking for"). Similarly, don't offer glowing evaluations of your accomplishments ("My course work in economics has given me outstanding mastery of the field"). Take a more objective stance instead, and let the facts in your background speak for themselves ("At my graduation I was named Outstanding Student in Economics on the basis of the 4.00 grade-point average that I earned in my economics course work"). Finally, avoid a highly idiosyncratic style or an unorthodox approach in your letter unless you are certain that it is appropriate for your potential employer.

3. Conclusion

Use the brief conclusion of your letter to direct the reader's attention to the résumé that you have enclosed, to state your willingness to be interviewed for the position, and to provide information about when and where you would be available for a possible interview. Some employment counselors recommend that a letter of application end with the applicant's offer to call the reader in the near future in order to arrange an interview; others argue that such calls are presumptuous and will only alienate a potential employer. You much decide which approach is suitable for the employers you address.

Sample cover letter (block style)

```
2094 Neil Avenue, Apt. 45
Des Moines, Iowa 50312
June 17, 1990

Mr. William Prewett
Personnel Director, A&G Associates
1212 Milliken Drive
Cedar Rapids, Iowa 52401

Dear Mr. Prewett:

I wish to apply for the position of Public Relations
Assistant that you advertised in the Des Moines
Register last week.

I received my B.A. in May from the University of Iowa
with a major in history and a minor in communications.
My major field has given me not only the broad intel-
lectual background of a liberal arts curriculum, but
also substantial experience in research and report
writing. Through my minor in communications, more-
over, I have gained experience in the areas of inter-
personal communication, group dynamics, and organi-
zational and small-group communication.

From my extracurricular work, I have gained practical
experience in publications and editing. As managing
editor of the University of Iowa student literary
magazine for the past two years, I shared responsi-
bility for all editorial decisions with the maga-
zine's editor in chief. In addition, I had primary
responsibility for overseeing the actual production
of each semester's issue. During my junior year, I
was one of two student assistants employed by the Of-
fice of the Dean of Students to prepare office memo-
randa for distribution throughout the campus.

My résumé is enclosed. Although I am currently living
in Des Moines, I would be happy to come to Cedar Rapids
```

34b

at any time for an interview. I appreciate your consideration and look forward to hearing from you.

Sincerely,

Phyllis   Wainwright

Phyllis Wainwright

Sample résumé

RÉSUMÉ

Phyllis Wainwright
2094 Neil Avenue, Apt. 45
Des Moines, Iowa 50312
(515) 555-6682

Education   B.A., cum laude, University of Iowa, 1990.
             Major: History
             Minor: Communications

Experience   Managing Editor, Iowa Literary Journal,
             1988–90.
                Solicited student submissions of fic-
                tion and poetry; shared responsibility
                for all editorial decisions; supervised
                proofreading, design, and layout of mag-
                azine.

             Student Assistant, Office of the Dean of Stu-
             dents, University of Iowa, 1988–89.
                Responsible for preparing and dis-
                tributing office memoranda, dis-
                tributing incoming mail, and helping to
                maintain office files.

             Host, Macmillan's Restaurant, Des Moines,
             Iowa, Summer, 1988.

             Peer Tutor, Department of History, Uni-
             versity of Iowa, 1987–88.
                Tutored students in History 121, 122 (Eu-
                ropean History I, II).

34b

References   Dr. Rosemary Eddins
              Faculty Adviser, Iowa Literary Journal
              Department of English
              University of Iowa
              Iowa City, Iowa 52240

              Mr. Nathaniel Robinson
              Dean of Students
              University of Iowa
              Iowa City, Iowa 52240

              Dr. Alice Voros
              Chair, Department of History
              University of Iowa
              Iowa City, Iowa 52240

35 *Writing under Pressure*

We don't always have the time to plan, write, and revise with the leisure we would prefer. Pop quizzes, short-answer essays, the hour-long test with two questions to be covered, the three-hour final with four questions to be covered—these examples should remind us of the limits often imposed. Here, we will stress the techniques for effective economizing, that is, working intelligently to one's best advantage within such restrictions. And because the paragraph, *not* scattered sentences, is the usual form expected of the writer for essay examinations, it helps to know some techniques for writing under pressure.

A few preliminary words about these techniques follow. First, none of them are substitutes for having mastered the material; they will not conceal the fact that a writer has little to say, given ten minutes or two hours, one page or five. Second, although some of these aids may seem obvious or general, *that* is their value. Because they are obvious, they are often ignored or forgotten; because they are general, they can be applied to a number of writing situations. Third, although several of them may seem like formulas, that also is a value: while being learned, they may help give confidence; once mastered, they can be modified by experience.

35a Preparing for the essay examination

Last-minute cramming may work for some students, but it won't for most. Plan your time so that you can review systematically and fully. Begin by going over your class notes and your underlinings in your text or texts. In doing so, pay special attention to the concepts and ideas that your instructor has stressed and the information or key examples that flesh out these primary ideas. For instance, in an introductory film course you would need to know the concept of "shooting angle" and to be able to illustrate it by a concretely detailed reference to Hitchcock or some other master. Take the time to work through any methods of analysis you are uncertain about. For instance, in a course on educational tests and measurements, you would want to be able to explain *how* to determine the validity and reliability of a test. Start, then, by reviewing the major course topics, techniques of analysis, and key illustrations.

You can also prepare by trying to anticipate the kind of question you are likely to be asked. One way of doing this is to pose such questions for yourself and to think through how you would answer them. For example, if you had just finished a long unit on the Civil War in an American history course, you could easily frame questions on the Civil War's early roots, its more immediate causes, and its major phases. Posing such questions is excellent preparation in two ways: it facilitates your reviewing, and it enables you to synthesize the materials into your own understanding of them. Many students have found it helpful to work together in framing and answering possible essay examination questions.

35b Reading the examination

Once the examination has been handed out, *read it through carefully*. As you read, keep in mind the number of questions you are expected to answer and the suggested time limits, if any, for each question. If the instructor has not indicated the weight of each question by suggesting time limits, you will have to make these choices yourself. Usually, you will have a pretty good idea of which questions are harder and therefore require more time, and which are easier and require less.

1. Understand the directions

After having read the examination and tentatively allocated your time, go back and reread the questions you plan to answer with *special attention to the directions* for each. If you don't understand what is called for, ask the instructor. Your doubts or bewilderments may be shared by other students. Further, in reading the topic, note the verb that tells you what you are required to do:

Explain = Spell out the reasons, causes, connections.

("Explain why Britain adopted the VAT" = spell out the reasons Britain adopted the value-added tax.)

Analyze = Break up, separate, segment into parts, steps, phases, sections, causes.

("Analyze the effects of the Cold War on French foreign policy" = separate into phases the effects of the Cold War on French foreign policy.)

Compare = Place side by side and **point out** significant similarities, differences, or both.

("Compare the role of the government in Keynesian and monetary economic theory" = place the roles of government in Keynesian and monetary economic theory side by side.)

Summarize = Reduce, abbreviate to the major aspects, features, events, arguments, without distortion.

("Summarize Hume's views on causation" = abbreviate Hume's major arguments on causation.)

Evaluate = Judge, take a position on the merits of, adequacy of, reasons for or against, consequences of.

("Evaluate Piaget's views on how children learn" = judge the merits or adequacy of Piaget's views on how children learn.)

But what about *discuss,* that open-ended verb so often used for exam questions? Broadly, *discuss* means to open up, reflect on, show that you know about and have thought about the subject. Sometimes, the context makes clear what is called for. "Discuss the pros and cons of federal intervention in abortion," for instance, means "Summarize, compare, and evaluate the case for and against federal intervention in abortion." If you are in doubt, try turning the command into a question

35b

in order to discover which analytic skills are called for. To take a few examples:

1. Discuss the plausibility of Jung's doctrine of the collective unconscious = How convincing is Jung's doctrine? = **Evaluate.**
2. Discuss the major therapies in the treatment of autistic children = What are the major therapies? = **Summarize** and **compare.**
3. Discuss the significant changes in Hester Prynne's attitude toward her sin in *The Scarlet Letter* = What are the major changes? = **Analyze.**

2. Plan your answer

Once you are clear on what is called for, *plan your answer.* This is the most important step you can take before you begin writing. Except for brief quizzes, you always have at least a few minutes to think before answering; take them. Strategies for planning answers vary: some students jot down an informal outline, with major headings and subheadings; others simply list key terms, phrases, names, or details, and then look for a pattern or case; still others reflect, work out a thesis, a case to argue, and then dive in. Any of these techniques are valuable. The point is to get *inside* the topic *before* writing, so that you don't use up half your time in desperate false starts or chewing on your pen and vaguely wondering what to say. By planning you not only gain focus; you also make yourself a searcher in pursuit of an answer, instead of remaining a spectator waiting for something to happen.

35c Writing the essay

In writing your answer, you should strive for the same qualities of effective exposition that are expected in papers written out of class. Obviously, though, time won't always allow you to polish and review your answer as fully as you and your teacher would like. Sometimes, you will be pushed just to finish and to have a few minutes for proofreading. Nevertheless, while writing you should try to keep the following principles in mind, a minimal list of the characteristics of an effective answer.

1. Start briskly

Don't begin with long, prefatory remarks, but *go quickly and directly to the question*. Answers that begin with sentences like "This is a very controversial issue on which people hold many different viewpoints" or "This is a very complicated subject and solutions are hard to find" and that run on this way for a whole paragraph are mere throat-clearing. If the issue is controversial, your analysis should make that fact clear in its treatment of the viewpoints; if the issue is complex, your analysis should reflect that complexity. Similarly, don't begin with a long digression on something you haven't been asked about. If, for instance, you were asked to discuss the effects of the Vietnam War on America in the 1960s, you would simply be avoiding the question if you started with a long paragraph on French colonial policy or the history of the Monroe Doctrine. Such false starts are rather like the complaint of one of Saul Bellow's characters in *Seize the Day:* "If you wanted to talk about a glass of water, you had to start back with God creating the heavens and earth."

2. Respond to the question

Your beginning is a promise to yourself and the instructor about your intended direction. Often, your opening will be framed by the terms of the topic: "Discuss three causes of," "Compare Tweedledum's and Tweedledee's theories of," "Summarize the symptoms of," and the like. Go directly *to* the causes, theories, or symptoms, in an orderly enumeration and discussion. In cases where the wording of the topic is more open-ended, try turning the directions into a question. Thus, for example, if you were directed to "Write an essay on some significant aspect of Cézanne's achievement as a painter," you could easily ask yourself "What *is* a significant aspect of his achievement as a painter?" If, as sometimes happens, you do find yourself off to a false start, stop immediately. Return to the question and redirect your thinking to it.

3. Be analytical

The body of your essay is the heart of your answer. Your instructor will, naturally, look for coherent connections and transitions

35c

and for adequate development and relevant detail. One of the more common but easily avoidable failures in essay answers is the substitution of summary for analysis. If, for instance, you are asked to compare two major historical figures, a mere description, which only outlines each, will not do: you are asked to bring prominent similarities and differences together—to highlight these features. Similarly, if you are asked to analyze or evaluate a case, a plot, or an event, don't give a summary. A sure sign that thought is absent is the writer's stating what happened without shaping an argument, making connections, or offering an interpretation—the summary that all too often runs: "This was said and that happened and this was the result, so thus and such also was said and led to another result, and. . . ."

4. Provide specific evidence

The crucial choices you face in the body of the answer concern examples: what kind? how many? how thoroughly discussed? First, unless asked to give all examples, be selective, not exhaustive. Pick the most telling or typical ones. For instance, if you were discussing Huck Finn's essential decency, his humaneness, you couldn't list all cases—the novel is full of them—but you could focus on his growing awareness of how much he cares for Jim and his resolve to help Jim escape, and you could point to the risks Huck takes to help the Wilks girls. Perhaps other examples interest you more—Huck's shock at the feud or pity for the tarred-and-feathered Duke and King, despite their treachery. Whatever the case, *limit* your choices to a few pointed ones.

Second, *do* something with your evidence. Merely mentioning an example or two in a sentence is not enough. Until you show by concrete development how the example applies, how it makes your point, *how it fits the terms of the question,* you have no depth. For instance, if you were discussing why German and more recently Japanese car manufacturers have taken over a significant part of the American market, you couldn't merely drop the names Volkswagen and Toyota. What about them—better engineering and design? quicker anticipation of the demand for small cars and flexibility in planning and retooling? lower cost to the consumer because of gas economy and cheaper production costs? better marketing and servicing? Any or several of these may be relevant. However, until you specifically discuss, say, what is better

35c

in the engineering of a major foreign model, you haven't done anything with your evidence or answered the question "Why?"

5. Review what you have written

As you come to the end of your essay, look over what you have written to determine whether you need a conclusion or not. Usually, a short summary paragraph that restates your argument or recapitulates your main points will serve well enough. Finally, when finished take a few minutes to proofread, not just skimming for obvious errors but considering changes in wording, insertions, even the renumbering of paragraphs. You haven't really finished until you turn the blue book in.

35d Two sample essays

We will conclude by illustrating the differences between an ineffective answer and an effective answer. Here are two examples in miniature as answers to the following question:

> What did William James mean by "the moral equivalent of war" and how does his idea illustrate pragmatism as a philosophy?

First, consider this answer:

Ineffective essay

> William James was the brother of the novelist Henry James and was Gertrude Stein's teacher. James taught at Harvard for many years, along with such other notables as Santayana and Royce. James was one of the founders of pragmatism, a philosophy that judges ideas by their practicality. By "the moral equivalent of war," James meant something to replace war with. James speaks of war as "a school of strenuous life and heroism." He believed war was destructive and hardened soldiers. He also believed war promoted discipline and was a universal model of heroism. He wanted to discover a peaceful equivalent of war. That was what he meant by "the moral equivalent of war."

You can easily see why this answer is ineffective. The opening two sentences are a false start; they have nothing to do with the question. The third sentence—on pragmatism—is brief, unclear, and left dangling,

35d

unrelated to the question or the answer. The rest of the paragraph consists of choppy, disconnected sentences that lack focus. And except for the quotation from James, there isn't much concreteness.

Now, by contrast, a more successful answer:

Effective essay

> By "the moral equivalent of war," James means a spiritual or social equivalent that would appeal as universally to our capacity for discipline and bravery as war does, but without its terrible destructiveness. Defining war as "a school of strenuous life and heroism," James recognizes how it hardens soldiers but also how it is the only model of selflessness available to the mass of humanity. He observes that voluntary poverty might be one example of a disciplined life that does not rely on hurting others. Pragmatism, a philosophy that tests concepts by looking at their actual consequences in life, is clearly expressed in James's suggestion. In effect, he looks at the facts—the consequences—and says that if something as vicious as the idea of war can still draw out heroic qualities, then we ought to be able to find a noble idea—"a moral equivalent of war"— that brings out the best in us.

This effective answer begins by defining James's idea and develops it clearly and coherently. This second answer is much more tightly organized and precisely worded than the first. And it *connects* James's idea to pragmatism, as directed by the question, while also defining pragmatism more adequately than the first answer defines it. Finally, the second answer closes strongly with a firm restatement of James's idea. The second paragraph isn't much longer than the first, but it contains far more information and is much easier to follow. It answers the question.

35d

36 *Writing with a Word Processor*

The writing process has been transformed during the past decade or so by the widespread availability of personal computers and computer programs known as word processors. If you have never used a word processor, or if you have tried word processing but did not feel comfortable with it, this chapter is for you. In the pages that follow, we will discuss some of the capabilities common to all word processors and suggest ways of making the best use of them as you compose and revise your manuscript.

36a Understanding word processing

A word processor is a computer program that allows a writer to create and manipulate a text on an electronic screen, called a **monitor,** and then send it to a printer to be reproduced on paper. Word processing offers two key advantages over other methods of composing and revising. First, the electronic text is infinitely flexible; a writer can add, delete, and move words in the document at the touch of a keyboard key. Second, since the text is stored on a computer disk after each working session, the writer needs to type it only once; after making whatever changes are necessary, he or she prints the paper electronically without further retyping.

If you find it difficult to get started on a writing assignment, or if you have trouble finding ways to revise your writing once you've put a draft down on paper, then word processing could make your writing sessions easier and more productive. Don't put off learning

36a

698

word processing because you are intimidated by computers; you don't need to know anything about how a computer works to use a word processor. And don't be concerned about damaging the computer you're working on by inadvertently striking the wrong keys on the keyboard; it's impossible to harm a computer that way (though it's true that you can damage or even lose the document you are working on).

On most campuses, computer labs are staffed by assistants who will be happy to get you started on the equipment available there—usually microcomputers like IBM PCs or Apple Macintoshes. If that's not the case where you are, ask a friend to show you how to turn the computer on, how to use a computer disk, and how to begin working with whatever word-processing program is available. All of us who now use word processing effortlessly started out feeling stupid and clumsy; it's a feeling that quickly passes.

1. Basic word-processing functions

Word-processing programs differ in their capabilities and complexity, but all such programs share the features that we describe below, and the basic functions of many are so easy to use that even a novice can begin to compose and edit a text during his or her first working session.

Word wrap

Unlike a typewriter, a word processor does not force you to hit a carriage-return key at the end of each line. Instead, by a function known as **word wrap,** the program automatically advances you to a new line. As a result, you are free to type continuously, without ever thinking about how close you are to the right margin.

Backup and save

When you create a text (usually referred to as a **document** or a **file**) on a word processor, it is held electronically in the computer's memory as you work on it. However, should the power go off while you are writing on a computer, or should a surge of electricity cause the computer to malfunction, the document you are working on may be lost. All word-processing programs, consequently, enable to you make electronic **backup copies** of your document while you are working

36a

on it—copies that will be preserved on a disk even in the event of a power outage. When you finish a word-processing session, you **save** the final version of your work on a disk; with most word processors, this last version replaces all the interim backup copies that you made as you were composing.

Insert and delete text

All word processors allow you to make additions to a text by a command called **insert.** The additions can be as small as a letter or a word, or as large as a paragraph or a page or more of text. When you activate the insert command, the existing text moves aside to make space for whatever you wish to add. Conversely, the **delete** command is used to eliminate part of a text that you no longer want. The rest of your text then automatically moves up to fill in its place.

Move text

A word processor lets you electronically mark a portion of your text—a word, a phrase, a paragraph, or more—and move it to a different position in the text. When you use the **move** command, the first sentence in a paragraph can become the last, or your concluding paragraph can become your introduction, all with just the touch of a key.

Copy text

A word processor allows you to **copy** a passage in your text and insert it at another point in the text as well, or to copy it into an entirely separate document.

2. Basic formatting functions

Besides enabling you to manipulate the words of your text on the screen, every word-processing program allows you to format your final printed document in a number of ways.

Spacing and margins

You can print out your text single-spaced or double-spaced, with margins of any size that you wish (many word processors allow other line spacing as well). Moreover, you can change the margins or

36a

spacing within a document as often as you want. Word processors also permit automatic centering of part of a text (for example, a title) and automatic indenting of blocks of text (such as long quotations in a research paper).

Automatic headers and page numbers

With a word processor, you can create a **header**—that is, a repeated heading—that will automatically print out at the top of each page of your final text (an example of such a header is the short title required on the pages of a research paper prepared according to APA style [see Chapter **22**]). If you wish your header to include the page number, the word processor will also consecutively number your pages when it prints them—and it will automatically renumber them if you make additions to or deletions from the original text.

Hyphenation and right justification

To even up the text's appearance on the page, some word-processing programs automatically break and hyphenate words at the end of the line; most others allow you to insert hyphens manually. Most word processors also allow you to print your text with what is called a **right-justified** margin; that is, they will automatically space out the words in each line so that all the lines of print extend evenly to the right margin. Check with your instructor to see whether he or she prefers a right-justified text or the usual uneven right margin, known as a **ragged right** margin.

Special fonts

In addition to underlining words, some word processors allow you to print words in boldface, or even in a variety of **fonts,** or type styles. The range of possibilities will depend not only on your word-processing program, but on the kind of printer you are using.

36b Getting the most out of word processing

When you sit down at the computer for your first session of word processing, you should bring with you a real project that you are about to begin—for example, an essay assignment due in a few weeks in one of your classes. Without such a task to focus your efforts, you may find that your first few sessions of word processing amount only to aimless experimentation. In contrast, if you begin by working on a genuine assignment, you will more quickly learn the word processor's most important commands, and your working sessions will give you a greater feeling of accomplishment.

1. Planning your paper on a word processor

All of the planning strategies that we discussed in Chapter **2** work effectively with a word processor. Indeed, you may discover that a word processor makes you more efficient and more creative as you plan and organize a paper.

Brainstorming

Instead of brainstorming with paper and pen, try filling your computer screen with the ideas that occur to you as you think about your subject. Because a word processor lets you shift words and phrases around on the screen, you can finish a brainstorming session by rearranging the ideas you've generated, moving the best ones to the top of your list. In subsequent brainstorming sessions, you can go back and add new ideas to this list, or delete those that no longer seem important. And when you are ready to begin serious work on a paper, you can print out a copy of all the ideas that you accumulated in several sessions of brainstorming, organized in any way that you wish.

Free writing

Some people who freeze up when they confront a blank sheet of paper have just the opposite reaction when they sit down before a blank computer screen. The blinking cursor on the screen seems to invite them to compose, and the ease with which the text goes up on the screen somehow dissolves their writer's block. If you want to try free writing without the distraction of the computer screen, simply turn the monitor off as you write; you may discover that writing without seeing what you write helps you focus on what you really want to say.

36b

Keeping a journal

If you have access to a word processor on a regular basis, you might consider keeping a journal on a floppy disk. If you decide that parts of your journal might be the core of a good paper, you don't need to copy them out by hand; instead, you can electronically copy them out of the journal and into a separate document that will become the genesis of your paper.

Using structured methods of discovery

To use the structured approach to discovery that we discussed in **2b**, simply type onto the screen each of the questions to be answered, and add underneath each one as many responses as you can produce. You can save the results of one working session on disk, and then come back the next day and add to it. When you've completely answered all the questions, print out your responses and circle those you might use in your paper. If you go back to the original document and copy out all the responses you've circled into a separate file, you'll have the beginnings of your paper.

Outlining

If you like to write from an outline, the flexibility that word processing offers can be particularly useful. As your ideas change, you can easily modify the outline that you create on a word processor by adding new ideas, deleting those you've discarded, and moving ideas around to different places. You can also print the outline at the beginning of each draft of your paper to guide you as you revise. When you're ready to print the final version of the paper, simply delete the outline before sending the text to the printer. (For a review of outlining, see **5g**.)

2. Writing with a word processor

Don't feel that you have to give up your preferred method of composing when you write on a computer; instead, use the computer in a way that is compatible with the composing process that's most natural to you. Here, for example, are three alternative ways of getting your text onto a computer disk.

36b

Composing on the screen

Some people like to compose directly on the screen. Fast writers like this approach because it's easier than writing out a paper longhand; they can produce a rough draft in a fraction of the time that it would take to compose with pen and paper. Slower, more methodical writers often like composing on the screen as well; it enables them to pause and play with the wording of each sentence before going on to the next one.

Transferring a longhand draft to the computer

Many writers find that they simply cannot get a firm grasp on their ideas unless they begin with paper and pen. That's fine too. After you've composed a longhand draft, type it into the computer to begin your revising. Remember that you will never have to retype the entire paper again.

Alternating between computer composing and longhand composing

Some writers start with a partial handwritten draft and develop enough momentum while typing it into the computer to continue writing directly on the word processor. Others compose parts of a paper on the computer screen, print out their work, fill in the other sections by hand, and then return to the computer to type in the new handwritten portions.

3.   Revising with a word processor

As useful as word processing can be in the planning and drafting stages of the writing process, many writers find that it is even more valuable when they begin to revise. No longer do you have to stumble through a draft attempting to decipher the changes that you penciled in between the lines last night, or last week. Now, after each revising session, you can print out a new copy of your text that incorporates all the changes you have made. Reading such a clean copy of each version of your paper will make your revising more efficient by helping you to evaluate the revisions you have made and to spot opportunities for other changes.

36b

To revise effectively with a word processor, though, you have to take advantage of the features that set word processing apart from mere typing—especially the insert, move, and copy commands.

Insert

The ease with which you can add new material to your draft should make you more willing to consider substantial changes in your original version. Have you thought of a new example to use in one of your paragraphs? Have you realized that your introduction needs to be expanded? With a typed or handwritten page, you may feel that the additions you can make to your draft are restricted by the amount of white space available between lines or in the margins. But the situation is vastly different when you add new material to the text that appears on a computer screen. At the touch of the insert key, the text moves aside, creating as much room as you need for your new ideas.

Move

In a handwritten or typed draft, the parts of the paper are fixed in a rigid order. That's not so with the electronic version of a paper created on a word processor. By touching the key that activates your program's move function, you can effortlessly switch sentences around within paragraphs or move whole paragraphs to different positions in the paper. Print out a copy of the changes you've made and decide whether the new arrangement of ideas is an improvement. If not, it's an easy matter to move elements back to their original places.

Copy

Some writers are hesitant to make major changes when they revise because they are afraid that the new version of a draft will be worse than the original and that they will never be able to reconstruct the text they started with. But you needn't have that fear with word processing, which invites experimentation. If you think you'd like to try a drastic revision of your draft, simply copy the entire draft into a new file and try out the changes you have in mind. If you decide that they don't work, you can delete this new file and go back to the original version of the paper.

36b

4. Editing with a word processor

Revising involves rethinking the contents, organization, and phrasing of a paper; editing, in contrast, is a matter of correcting small errors that slipped into a paper while it was being drafted. Two supplementary computer programs that are available with many word processors can help you spot and correct at least some of the errors that should be edited out of your final text.

Spelling checkers

Many word processors include a special program called a **spelling checker,** which compares the words in your text against a large number of correctly spelled words held in the program's memory and then highlights any of your words that it is unable to match. A spelling checker is a handy device; it not only alerts you to incorrectly spelled words but also picks out typographical errors that you may have overlooked. One caution is in order, however. A spelling checker will not identify a correctly spelled word that you have accidentally used incorrectly—*it's* in place of *its,* for example. Thus you can't rely on a spelling checker alone to make your spelling free of errors, though it will help you take a major step in that direction.

Style checkers

Another kind of auxiliary computer program analyzes certain stylistic features of a text and prints out comments and suggestions for revision. Typically, **style checkers** flag such matters as errors in agreement (for example, plural pronouns used with singular antecedents), unusual sentence length (for example, very long sentences), weak verbs (for example, linking verbs and passives), and inappropriate diction (for example, clichés and slang). Some style checkers can also produce a statistical analysis of your prose (average sentence length, average paragraph length, and so on). A style checker is an intriguing aid, but because its analysis is often inexact, you have to be ready to overrule its advice when you have a good reason for doing so. The style checker can't tell, for example, when a long sentence or a passive verb is appropriate, but by marking those features in your text it at least gives you one last opportunity to reflect on what you have written and to make a deliberate choice.

36b

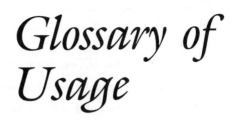

Glossary of Usage

This Glossary discusses a number of commonly misused words; for more complete advice on questions of usage, you should rely on a good college dictionary (see Chapter **9**).

a, an Indefinite articles. *A* is used before words beginning with a consonant sound, *an* before words beginning with a vowel sound. Before words beginning with *h,* use *an* when the *h* is silent, as in *hour,* but *a* when the *h* is pronounced, as in *history.*

accept, except Different verbs that sound alike. *Accept* means "to receive," *except* "to leave out."

I **accepted** the diploma.

When assigning jobs, the dean **excepted** students who had already worked on a project.

A.D. An abbreviation of the Latin *anno Domini,* "in the year of the lord." It is properly placed *before* the date in question. See **B.C.**

adapt, adopt To *adapt* is to change or modify to suit a new need, purpose, or condition.

Human beings can **adapt** to many environments.

The movie was **adapted** from a novel.

To *adopt* something is to make it one's own, to choose it.

The couple **adopted** a child.

Our club **adopted** "Opportunity knocks" as its motto.

adverse, averse Often confused, but important to distinguish. *Adverse* means "antagonistic" or "unfavorable."

Adverse weather forced postponement of the regatta.

707

gl

Averse means "opposed to"; only sentient beings can be *averse.*

She was **averse** to sailing under such conditions.

advice, advise   *Advice* is a noun, *advise* a verb.

He gave me some good **advice.**

I **advise** you to listen carefully.

affect, effect   Words close in sound and therefore often confused. *Affect* as a verb means "to influence." *Effect* as a verb means "to bring about."

Smoking **affects** the heart.

How can we **effect** a change in the law?

As a noun, *effect* means "result."

One **effect** of her treatment was a bad case of hives.

aggravate   Means "to intensify" or "to make worse."

The shock **aggravated** his misery.

Colloquially, it means "to annoy," "irritate," "arouse the anger of."

ain't   A nonstandard contraction of *am not, is not,* or *are not.* Not to be used in most writing.

all ready, already   Not synonyms. *All ready* refers to a state of readiness.

The twirlers were **all ready** for the halftime show.

Already means "by or before the present time."

Has the game **already** started?

all together, altogether   *All together* refers to a group with no missing elements.

If we can get our members **all together,** we can begin the meeting.

Altogether means "completely."

You are **altogether** mistaken about that.

allude, refer   To *allude* is to make an indirect reference.

Did her letter **allude** to Sam's difficulties?

gl

To *refer* is to call attention specifically to something.

The instructor **referred** us to Baudelaire's translations of Poe.

allusion, illusion, delusion   An *allusion* is a brief, indirect reference.

Anyone who speaks of "cabbages and kings" is making an **allusion** to *Alice in Wonderland*.

An *illusion* is a deceptive impression.

He enjoyed the **illusion** of luxury created by his imitation Oriental rugs.

A *delusion* is a mistaken belief, implying self-deception and often a disordered state of mind.

She fell prey to the **delusion** that she was surrounded by enemy agents.

alot, a lot   The only correct spelling is *a lot*.

alright, all right   The only correct spelling is *all right*.

among, between   *Among* always refers to more than two.

He lived **among** a tribe of cannibals.

Between is used to refer to two objects or to more than two objects considered individually.

The scenery is spectacular **between** Portland and Seattle.

The governors signed the agreement **between** all three states.

amoral, immoral   Anything *amoral* is outside morality, not to be judged by moral standards.

The behavior of animals and the orbits of the planets are equally **amoral.**

Anything *immoral* is in direct violation of some moral standard.

Plagiarism is generally considered to be an **immoral** act.

amount, number   *Amount* is used as a general indicator of quantity; *number* refers only to what can be counted.

An immense **amount** of food was prepared for the picnic, but only a small **number** of people came.

an   See **a.**

ante, anti As a prefix, *ante* means "before": *ante*date, *ante*cedent. *Anti* means "against": *anti*war, *anti*knock.

anxious, eager *Anxious* refers to worry about the future.

> He was **anxious** about the outcome of his exam.

> *Eager* indicates hopeful excitement.

> She was **eager** to meet her relatives from Ohio.

anyone, any one *Anyone* is an indefinite pronoun and means "any individual at all." *Any one* designates a particular person or thing.

> **Anyone** could see the obvious error.

> **Any one** of us could have pointed out the error.

> *Everyone, every one* and *someone, some one* follow this pattern.

> **Everyone** enjoyed the Olympics, and **every one** of the events was well attended.

> **Someone** should do the job. **Some one** person will have to be responsible.

> Also see **everybody, every body.**

apt See **liable.**

as Dialectal when used in placed of *that* or *who*.

> I don't know **that** (not **as**) we can go.

> There are some **who** (not **as**) trust him.

> *Because* and *since* are clearer than *as* for introducing clauses showing causal relationship.

> **Because** (or **since**) I was late, I missed the opening curtain.

at about Prefer *about* in writing; *at about* is overworked and redundant.

> **Preferred in writing** It happened **about** three o'clock.

awhile, a while *Awhile* is an adverb.

> I'm tired so I'll sit **awhile.**

> *A while* consists of a particle and a noun, often used as the object of a preposition.

> I'm tired so I'll sit for **a while.**

bad, badly   Formal usage employs *bad* as an adjective with linking verbs like *feel* and *look*.

I feel **bad** (not **badly**) because of my headache.

Badly is an adverb used with most verbs.

I served **badly** during the tennis match because of my headache.

barely   See **hardly.**

B.C.   Abbreviation of "before Christ," placed after the date in question. See **A.D.**

between   See **among.**

but   Often used colloquially in such idioms as *I can't help but think.* In writing, *I can't help thinking* is preferred. If the nonstandard expression *I don't know but what he wants it* leads to confusion (does he or doesn't he?), it should be avoided in speech, too.

can, may   In formal speech and in writing, *can* is used to indicate ability, *may* to indicate permission.

If you **can** open that box, you **may** have whatever is in it.

In informal questions, *can* is often used even though permission is meant.

Can I try it next? Why **can't** I?

censor, censure   To *censor* something (such as a book, letter, or film) is to evaluate it on the basis of certain arbitrary standards to determine whether it may be made public.

All announcements for the bulletin board are **censored** by the department secretary.

Censor is often used as the equivalent of "delete."

References in the report to secret activities have been **censored.**

Censure means "to find fault with," "to criticize as blameworthy."

Several officers were **censured** for their participation in the affair.

compare to, compare with, contrast with   *Compare to* is used to show similarities between different kinds of things.

Sir James Jeans **compared** the universe **to** a corrugated soap bubble.

gl

Compare with means to examine in order to note either similarities or differences.

Compare this example **with** the preceding one.

Contrast with is used to show differences only.

Contrast the life of a student today **with** that of a student in the Middle Ages.

complementary, complimentary *Complementary* means "serving to fill out" or "to complete."

His tenor and her soprano are **complementary**.

Complimentary means "freely given" or "giving praise."

Members of the audience were quite **complimentary** about the couple's recital.

concur in, concur with *Concur in* refers to agreement with a principle or policy.

She **concurred in** their judgment that the manager should be given a raise.

Concur with refers to agreement with a person.

She **concurred with** him in his decision to give the manager a raise.

conscious, conscience *Conscious* is an adjective meaning "aware of."

She was **conscious** of the others in the room.

Conscience is a noun meaning "the sense of moral goodness or badness."

Her **conscience** told her to leave.

contact The use of *contact* as a verb meaning "to get in touch with" has gained wide acceptance, but a more exact term such as *ask, consult, inform, meet, see, telephone,* or *write* is generally preferable.

continual, continuous The first is widely used to indicate an action that is repeated frequently, the second to indicate uninterrupted action.

We heard the **continual** whimpering of the dog.

The dog kept a **continuous** vigil beside the body of his dead master.

contrast with   See **compare to.**

data, criteria, phenomena   Latin plural, not singular, forms, and hence used as English plurals in formal writing. But the use of *data* (rather than *datum*) with a singular form is widespread.

These **data** have been taken from the last Census Report.

Criteria and *phenomena* are always plural. The singular forms are *criterion* and *phenomenon.*

Scientists encountered a **phenomenon** that could not be evaluated under existing **criteria.**

delusion   See **allusion.**

different from, different than   *Different from* is the acceptable form.

College is **different from** what I had expected.

Different than is not acceptable in formal writing.

dilemma, problem   A *dilemma* is a choice between two equally distasteful alternatives.

We faced the **dilemma** of paying the fine or spending three days in jail.

A *problem* is wider in meaning, referring to a difficulty or a question that must be solved.

The United States must soon resolve the **problem** of guaranteeing an energy supply for the twenty-first century.

disinterested, uninterested   *Disinterested* means "unbiased," "impartial." *Uninterested* means "without any interest in," or "lacking interest."

Although we were **uninterested** in her general topic, we had to admire her **disinterested** treatment of its controversial aspects.

don't   A contraction of *do not.* Not to be used in formal writing with a subject in the third person singular.

Nonstandard   He **don't** know.

Standard   He **doesn't** know.

due to   In writing, *due to* should not be used adverbially to mean *because of.*

gl

Colloquial	I made many mistakes **due to** carelessness.
Preferred in writing	I made many mistakes **because of** carelessness.

Due is an adjective and usually follows the verb *be*.

His illness was **due** to exhaustion.

each other, one another   When two individuals are involved in a reciprocal relationship, *each other* is used.

My sister and I respected **each other.**

When more than two individuals are mutually related, *one another* is appropriate.

The sheep rubbed against **one another** in the chill.

eager   See **anxious.**

effect   See **affect.**

either, neither   As subjects, both words are singular. When referring to more than two, use *none* rather than *neither.*

Either (Neither) red or (nor) pink **is** appropriate.

I asked Leahy, Mahoney, and another colleague, but **none** of them **were** willing.

eminent, imminent   *Eminent* means "prominent," "well known."

She was an **eminent** judge.

Imminent means "impending," "menacing," "about to occur."

The jury's verdict is **imminent.**

enthused   Either as a verb (he *enthused*) or adjective (he was *enthused*), the word is strictly colloquial. In writing, use *showed enthusiasm* or *was enthusiastic.*

equally as good   A confusion of two phrases: *equally good* and *just as good.* Use either of the two phrases in place of *equally as good.*

Their TV set cost much more than ours, but ours is **equally good.**

Our TV set is **just as good** as theirs.

-ess   A feminine ending that is now widely considered unacceptable because it implies that women are functioning in roles defined

gl

by men and must be distinguished from their male counterparts: *poetess, authoress, sculptress, stewardess, hostess. Actress,* one of the last such terms still in wide use, shows signs of giving way to *actor,* and *waiter* and *waitress* have been replaced in some restaurants by the sex-neutral *table server.*

etc.   Abbreviation of the Latin *et cetera* ("and others"). Avoid the vague use of *etc.*; use it only to prevent useless repetition or informally to represent terms entirely obvious from the context.

Vague	The judge was honorable, upright, dependable, **etc.**
Preferred	The judge was honorable, upright, **and** dependable.
Standard	Use even numbers—four, eight, ten, **etc.**

Avoid *and etc.,* which is redundant.

everybody, every body   *Everybody* is an indefinite pronoun.

Everybody is welcome.

Every body consists of a noun modified by *every.*

We could see every lake and **every body** of land as we flew north.

Somebody and *some body* are similar to *everybody, every body.*

Somebody did this inaccurate sketch.

The drawing should be redone to give it some shading and **some body.**

Be careful of *every* in other contexts.

Every day that I waited seemed longer.

Everyday events soon become habitual.

everyone, every one   See **anyone.**

except   See **accept.**

expect   Colloquial when used to mean "suppose" or "presume."

Colloquial	I **expect** it's time for us to go.
Preferred	I **suppose** it's time for us to go.

factor   Means "something that contributes to a result."

Industry and perseverance were **factors** in her success.

Avoid using *factor* vaguely to mean any thing, item, or event.

gl

Vague   Ambition was a **factor** that contributed to the downfall of Macbeth.
[Since *factor* includes the notion of "contributing to," such usage is redundant as well as vague and wordy.]

Preferred   Ambition contributed to the downfall of Macbeth.

farther, further   In careful usage *farther* indicates distance; *further* indicates degree and may also mean "additional." Both are used as adjectives and as adverbs: *a mile farther, further disintegration, further details.*

faze, phase   *Faze* is a colloquial verb meaning "to perturb," "to disconcert." *Phase* as a noun means "stage of development" (a passing *phase*); as a verb it means "to carry out in stages."

fewer, less   *Fewer* refers to number, *less* to amount. Use *fewer* in speaking of things that can be counted and *less* for amounts that are measured.

Fewer persons enrolled in medical schools this year than last.

Less studying was required to pass chemistry than we had anticipated.

flaunt, flout   Commonly misspelled, mispronounced, and, therefore, confused. *Flaunt* means "to exhibit arrogantly," "show off."

He **flaunted** his photographic memory in class.

Flout means "to reject with contempt."

They **flouted** the tradition of wearing gowns at graduation by showing up in blue jeans.

former, latter   Preferably used to designate one of two persons or things. For designating one of three or more, write *first* or *last*.

further   See **farther.**

get, got, gotten   *Get to* (*go*), *get away with, get back at, get with* (something), and *got to* (for *must*) are acceptable in colloquial usage but should be avoided in writing. Either *got* or *gotten* is acceptable as the past participle of *get*.

good   An adjective. Should not be used in formal writing as an adverb meaning "well."

Colloquial	She plays tennis **good.**
Standard	She plays tennis **well.**
	She plays a **good** game of tennis.

had of Nonstandard when used for *had.*

Nonstandard	If he **had of** tried, he would have succeeded.
Standard	If he **had** tried, he would have succeeded.

had ought Nonstandard as a past tense of *ought.* The tense of this verb is indicated by the infinitive that follows.

He **ought to go;** she **ought to have gone.**

hanged, hung When *hang* means "to suspend," *hung* is its past tense.

The guard **hung** a black flag from the prison to signal the execution.

When *hang* means "to execute," *hanged* is the correct past tense.

After the flag was **hung,** the prisoner was **hanged.**

hardly, barely, scarcely Since these words convey the idea of negation, they should not be used with another negative.

Nonstandard	We **couldn't hardly** see in the darkness.
	We **hadn't barely** finished.
Standard	We **could hardly** see.
	We **had barely** finished.

hopefully Although widely used in speech to mean "it is to be hoped," or "I hope" ("*Hopefully*, a check will arrive tomorrow"), the adverb *hopefully* is used in writing to mean "in a hopeful manner."

They spoke **hopefully** of world peace.

illusion See **allusion.**

imminent See **eminent.**

immoral See **amoral.**

impact Used colloquially (and in bureaucratic writing) as a verb meaning "to have an effect on": "Will this power plant *impact* the environment negatively?" Not yet well-enough established for use in most writing.

gl

imply, infer   *Imply* means "to suggest" or "hint"; *infer* means "to reach a conclusion from facts or premises."

> His tone **implied** contempt; I **inferred** from his voice that he did not like me.

incredible, incredulous   Both are adjectives, or, more rarely, nouns, but *incredible* means "unbelievable," "unlikely," while *incredulous* means "skeptical," "unbelieving."

> The ad made **incredible** claims for the product, but I remained **incredulous.**

inside of   Omit the superfluous *of* when *inside* is used as a preposition.

> I'll meet you **inside** the station.

> See **outside of.**

insupportable, unsupportable   Often confused, but not synonymous. *Insupportable* means "unable to be endured."

> The noise of bulldozers during the lecture was **insupportable.**

> *Unsupportable* means "not capable of support."

> The building program, though imaginative, is financially **unsupportable.**

inter, intra   As a prefix *inter* means "between" or "among": *international, intermarry; intra* means "within" or "inside of": *intramuscular, intramural.*

irony   See **sarcasm.**

irregardless   A nonstandard combination of *irrespective* and *regardless.*

> **Regardless** (or **irrespective**) of the minority opinion, we included the platform in the campaign.

is when, is where   Avoid using these phrases as parts of a definition.

> Smog is polluted air (rather than "Smog **is when** the air is polluted").

> Literacy is the ability to read and write (rather than "Literacy **is where** a person can read and write").

its, it's   Often confused. *Its* is the possessive form of *it.*

> My suitcase has lost one of **its** handles.

> *It's* is the contracted form of *it is* or *it has.*

It's a good day for sailing.

It's been a month since I mailed the check.

There is no such form as *its'*.

kind, sort, type   Singular nouns that must be used with singular pronouns and verbs.

Incorrect	These **kind** of books **are** trash.
Correct	**This kind** of book **is** trash.
	These kinds of books **are** classics.

In questions, the number of the verb depends on the noun that follows *kind* (or *sort* or *type*).

What kind of **book is** this?

What kind of **books are** these?

kind of, sort of   Colloquial when used to mean "rather."

| Colloquial | I thought the lecture was **kind of** dull. |
| Standard | I thought the lecture was **rather** dull. |

later, latter   *Later* designates time; *latter* designates the second of two items, choices, or objects.

I'll see you **later** in the day.

The pound had a young poodle and a young terrier. I chose the **latter**.

Also see **former**.

latest, last   *Latest* means "most recent"; *last* means "final."

I doubt that their **latest** contract proposal represents their **last** offer.

lay, lie   Often confused. *Lay* is a transitive verb meaning "to put" or "place" something. It always takes an object. Its principal parts are *lay, laid, laid*. *Lie* is intransitive; that is, it does not take an object. It means "to recline" or "to remain." Its principal parts are *lie, lay, lain*. When in doubt, try substituting the verb *place*. If it fits the context, use some form of *lay*.

Present tense	I **lie** down every afternoon.
	Every morning I **lay** the paper by his plate.
Past tense	I **lay** down yesterday after dinner.
	I **laid** the paper by his plate two hours ago.

gl

> **Perfect tense** I **have lain** here for several hours.
> I **have laid** the paper by his plate many times.

lend See **loan.**

less See **fewer.**

let's Contraction of *let us*. In writing, it should be used only where *let us* can be used.

> **Colloquial** Let's **don't** leave yet. Let's **us** go.
> **Standard** Let's **not** leave yet. Let's **go.**

liable, likely, apt In careful writing, the words are not interchangeable. *Likely* is used to indicate a mere probability.

They are **likely** to be chosen.

Liable is used when the probability is unpleasant.

We are **liable** to get a parking ticket.

Apt implies a natural tendency or ability.

She is **apt** to win the musical competition.

lie See **lay.**

like The use of *like* to introduce a clause is widespread in informal English, especially that used by advertising agencies. In edited writing, *as, as if,* and *as though* are preferred.

> **Colloquial** This rose smells sweet, **like** a flower should.
> **Standard** This rose smells sweet, **as** a flower should.
> This perfume smells **like** roses.

literally Means "precisely," "without any figurative sense," "strictly." It is often inaccurately used as an intensive, to emphasize a figure of speech: "I was *literally* floating on air." (This construction makes sense only if one is capable of levitation.) Use the word *literally* with caution in writing.

loan, lend Traditionally, *lend* is a verb, *loan* a noun, but *loan* is also used as a verb, especially in business contexts.

The company **loaned** us money for the down payment.

loose, lose *Loose* is usually an adjective meaning "unfixed," "unattached." *Lose* is a verb meaning "to misplace," "forget."

The screws are **loose** and the door wobbles.

Don't **lose** patience and don't **lose** your temper.

may   See **can.**

moral, morale   As an adjective or noun, *moral* refers to ethical conduct or values. As noun, *morale* refers to a prevailing mood or level of confidence.

She is a **moral** person.

He always looks for the **moral** of the novel.

His last three failures have hurt his **morale.**

most   As a noun or adjective, *most* means "more than half."

Most of us plan to go to the dance.

Most people admire her paintings.

As an adverb, *most* means "very."

His playing was **most** impressive.

Most is sometimes used colloquially to mean "almost" or "nearly."

Colloquial   **Most** everyone was invited.

Preferred in writing   **Almost** everyone was invited.

much   See **very.**

myself   Correctly used as a reflexive: I cut *myself,* sang to *myself,* give *myself* credit. Colloquial when used as an evasive substitute for *I* or *me.*

Colloquial   She spoke to my brother and **myself.**

Preferred in writing   She spoke to my brother and **me.**

neither   See **either.**

notorious   Means "of bad repute": a *notorious* gambler. Not to be used for "famous," "celebrated," or "noted."

number   See **amount.**

of   *Could of, may of, might of, must of, should of,* and *would of* are slurred pronunciations for *could have, may have, might have, must have, should have,* and *would have;* they are nonstandard in writing.

off of   A colloquial usage in which *of* is superfluous.

gl

| **Colloquial** | Keep **off of** the grass. |
| **Preferred in writing** | Keep **off** the grass. |

one another   See **each other.**

outside of   Correct as noun: "He painted the *outside of* the house." Colloquial as a preposition: "He was waiting *outside of* the house." Omit the *of* in writing. Colloquial as a substitute for *except for, aside from.*

over with   *With* is superfluous.

The regatta is **over** (not **over with**).

part, portion   A *part* is any piece of a whole; a *portion* is that part specifically allotted to some person, cause, or use.

We planted beans in one **part** of our garden.

She left a **portion** of her estate to charity.

party   Colloquial when used to mean "person," as in "The *party* who telephoned left no message." Write *person.*

percent   In formal writing use *percent,* or *per cent,* only after a numeral—either the spelled-out word (six) or the numerical symbol (6). The sign (%) is used only in strictly commercial writing. The word *percentage,* meaning "a part or proportion of a whole," is used when the exact amount is not indicated.

A large **percentage** of the city's residents were government employees.

Thirty-one **percent** of the city's residents were government employees.

phase   See **faze.**

phenomena   See **data.**

portion   See **part.**

principal, principle   As a noun, a *principal* is the head or leading figure in an institution, an event, or a play.

The **principals** in the contract negotiations met with the press to discuss their progress.

Used as an adjective, *principal* refers to a leading feature or element in a group.

The **principal** types of telescopes are the refracting and the reflecting, or Newtonian, telescope.

A *principle* is a rule.

The main **principle** in skiing is to keep on one's feet.

problem   See **dilemma.**

raise, rise   Often confused. Remember that *raise* means to "cause something to rise." Therefore *raise* must always have an object. Remember the principal parts of each verb:

Standard	I rise	I rose	I have risen
	I raise	I raised	I have raised
	(something)	(something)	(something)

Standard   I **rise** at six o'clock every morning.
I **raise** flowers for sale.

I **rose** at six o'clock.
I **raised** flowers for sale.

I **have risen** at six o'clock for years.
I **have raised** flowers for years.

real   Colloquial when used for *very.* Write *very* hot (not *real* hot).

reason is because, reason why   Both of these expressions are wordy. Eliminate *is because,* or *why,* or *reason is.*

Wordy   The **reason** we came **is because** we knew you needed help.

Concise   We came **because** we knew you needed help.

refer   See **allude.**

regarding, in regard to, with regard to, in relation to, in terms of   These windy phrases are usually dispensable. Replace them with concrete terms.

Wordy   **With regard to** grades, she was very good.

Concise   She **got** very good grades.

sarcasm, irony   *Sarcasm* is not interchangeable with *irony. Sarcastic* remarks, like *ironic* remarks, convey a message obliquely, but sarcasm contains the notion of ridicule, of an intention on the part of the writer to wound. Events are *ironic* when they are different from what had been expected.

> The sergeant inquired **sarcastically** whether any of us could tell time; it was **ironic** that his watch turned out to be ten minutes fast.

sarcely See **hardly.**

sensual, sensuous Both words refer to impressions made upon the senses. Their connotations, however, are widely different. *Sensual* often carries unfavorable connotations. It is frequently applied to the gratification of appetite and lust.

> **Sensual** delights are often considered inferior to spiritual pleasures.

Sensuous, on the other hand, is used literally or approvingly of appeals to the senses (the *sensuous* delight of a swim on a hot day), even such abstract appeals as those found in poetry.

> Milton's **sensuous** imagery calls upon sight, touch, and smell to form the reader's impression of Eden.

set, sit *Set* is a transitive verb meaning "to put" or "place" something. It should be distinguished from *sit,* an intransitive verb.

Present tense	I **sit** in the chair.
	I **set** the book on the chair.
Past tense	I **sat** on the chair.
	I **set** the book on the table.
Perfect tense	I **have sat** in the chair.
	I **have set** the book on the table.

shall, will The distinction between these words is rapidly fading. Most writers now use *will* almost exclusively. *Shall* may still be used for emphasis ("He *shall* be heard"); since it is less common than *will,* it has a formal tone.

should, would *Should* substitutes for "ought to" ("He *should* go on a diet"), *would* for "wanted to" ("He could do it if he *would*"). *Should* indicates probability ("I *should* be finished in an hour"); *would* indicates custom ("He *would* always call when he got home").

so, such Avoid using *so* and *such* as vague intensifiers: "I am *so* glad." "I had *such* a good time." *So . . . . that,* however, is an acceptable idiomatic construction.

I was **so** glad to find this print **that** I bought copies for all my friends.

some   Colloquial when used as an adverb meaning "somewhat" ("I am *some* better today") or when used as an intensifying adjective ("That was *some* dinner").

> **Preferred in writing**   I am **a little** (or **somewhat**) better today.
> That was **an excellent** dinner.

somebody, some body   See **everybody.**

someone, some one   See **anyone.**

sort   See **kind, sort, type.**

sort of   See **kind of.**

such   See **so.**

sure   Colloquial when used for "certainly" or "surely," as in "He *sure* can play poker."

that, which   *That* is used to introduce restrictive clauses, which limit or define the antecedent's meaning and are not set off by commas.

The law **that** gave women the right to vote was passed in 1920.

Which is used to introduce nonrestrictive clauses, which do not limit or define the meaning of the antecedent. Nonrestrictive clauses are always set off by commas.

The Nineteenth Amendment, **which** gave women the right to vote, was passed in 1920.
[The amendment is already identified by number; the clause *which gave women the right to vote* merely provides additional information.]

that, who   Use *that* in relative clauses that refer to things, but *who* in clauses that refer to people.

> **Incorrect**   I can't tolerate being around people **that** smoke.
> **Correct**   I can't tolerate being around people **who** smoke.
> **Incorrect**   There's the clerk **that** overcharged me.
> **Correct**   There's the clerk **who** overcharged me.

their, there   Often confused. *Their* is the possessive form of *they*.

Their time will come.

gl

There refers to place.

Put the book **there.**

this here, these here, that there, those there Nonstandard. Say *this, these, that,* or *those.*

to, too, two Sometimes confused. *To* is a preposition.

We went **to** the late show.

Too is an adverb meaning "more than enough" or "also."

He has made the same mistake **too** many times.

She **too** shares this feeling.

Two is an adjective or a noun designating number.

Two people were early.

We found only **two** of the people who had been there.

toward, towards Interchangeable. *Toward* is more common in America, *towards* in Britain.

transpire In formal writing, where the word properly belongs, *transpire* means "to become known." It is colloquial in the sense of "happen," or "come to pass."

try and Often used for "try to," but should be avoided in writing.

I must **try to** (not **try and**) find a job.

type See **kind, sort, type.**

uninterested See **disinterested.**

unique Since *unique* means "one of a kind," the colloquial—but illogical—forms *very unique* and *most unique* remain unacceptable to most writers.

unsupportable See **insupportable.**

up Do not add a superfluous *up* to verbs: "We opened *up* the box and divided *up* the money." Write: "We opened the box and divided the money."

very, much (with past participles) A past participle that is a part of a verb form, rather than an adjective, should not be immediately preceded by *very* but by *much, greatly,* or some other intensive. A past participle that can be used as an adjective may be preceded by *very*.

Colloquial	He was **very** admired by other students. He was **very** influenced by the teacher.
Preferred in writing	He was **very much** admired by other students. He was **greatly** influenced by the teacher. He was a **very** tired boy.

wait on   Colloquial for *wait for*.

Colloquial	I can't leave yet; I have to **wait on** my cousin.
Preferred in writing	I can't leave yet; I have to **wait for** my cousin.

ways   Colloquial in such expressions as *a little ways*. In writing, the singular is preferred: *a little way*.

where . . . to, where . . . at   Colloquialisms whose prepositions are redundant or dialectal.

Colloquial	**Where** are you going **to**? **Where** is he **at**?
Preferred in writing	**Where** are you going? **Where** is he?

who, whom   For extended discussion of the difference between these forms, see **26b**.

whose, who's   *Whose* is a possessive pronoun.

Whose book is this?

Who's is a contraction of *who is* or *who has*.

Who's at the door?

will   See **shall**.

-wise   Commercial jargon when attached to nouns in such combinations as *taxwise, languagewise, timewise,* and *moneywise*. To be avoided in serious writing.

would   See **should**.

would have   Colloquial when used in *if* clauses instead of *had*.

Colloquial	If he **would have stood** by us, we might have won.
Preferred in writing	If he **had stood** by us, we might have won.

gl

write-up   Colloquial for "a description," or "an account," as in "a *write-up* in the newspaper."

you was   Nonstandard. Use *you were* in writing.

your, you're   Often confused. *Your* is the possessive of *you*.

Your train is late.

You're is a contraction of *you are*.

If **you're** ready, we can leave.

Grammatical Terms

absolute construction, absolute phrase   An absolute phrase consists of a participle with a subject (or, occasionally, a subject followed by an adjective or a prepositional phrase). It is grammatically unconnected with the rest of the sentence but usually tells when, why, or how something happened. See also **24a**.

> **The floodwaters having receded,** people began returning to their homes.

> I hated to leave home, **circumstances being as they were.**

abstract language   Words expressing general ideas, states, or conditions: *generosity, love, goals.* See **concrete language.** See also **13c**.

active voice   See **voice.**

adjective   A part of speech used to describe or limit the meaning of a substantive. See also Chapter **27**.

Descriptive	a **true** friend, a **poor** man
Limiting	**an** apple, **the** woman, **two** boys

Notice that many kinds of pronouns regularly perform the function of an adjective.

Possessive	**my** book, **his** sister, **your** house
Demonstrative	**this** chair, **these** papers
Interrogative	**whose** hat? **which** one?
Indefinite	**any** card, **each** boy, **some** candy

adjective clause   See **clause.**

adverb   A part of speech used to modify a verb, an adjective, or another adverb. An adverb answers the questions *Where? When? How? Why?* or *To what extent?* See also Chapter **27**.

gr

He bowed **politely.**
[*Politely* **modifies the verb** *bowed.*]

A **very** old woman came in.
[*Very* **modifies the adjective** *old.*]

He was **too** much absorbed to listen.
[*Too* **modifies the adverb** *much.*]

Substantives may also be used adverbially:

He walked **two miles.**
[*Two miles* **modifies the verb** *walked.*]

He walked **two miles** farther.
[*Two miles* **modifies the adverb** *farther.*]

adverb clause   See **clause.**

agreement   The correspondence in number and person between the subject and verb in a sentence and the correspondence in number, person, gender, and case between a pronoun and its antecedent. See also Chapter **25.**

antecedent   A word, phrase, or clause to which a pronoun refers.

I saw the **house** long before I reached **it.**
[*House* **is the antecedent of** *it.*]

This is a **problem that** cannot be solved without calculus.
[*Problem* **is the antecedent of** *that.*]

appositive   A substantive attached to another substantive and denoting the same person or thing. A substantive is said to be **in apposition** with the substantive to which it is attached. See also **24a, 29a.**

Alice, my **cousin,** was enjoying her favorite sport—**sailing.**
[*Cousin* **is in apposition with** *Alice; sailing* **is in apposition with** *sport.*]

article   The word *the* is called the **definite article;** the words *a* and *an* are called the **indefinite articles.** In function, articles can be classed with adjectives.

auxiliary   When the verbs *be, have, do, shall, will, may, can, must, ought to,* and *should* assist in forming the voices, modes, and tenses of other verbs, they are **auxiliaries.** See also **28e.**

A message **was** given to me.

He **should have** known better.

He **has been** gone a week.

cardinal number   Any of the numbers *one, two, three, four,* and so on, denoting quantity, in distinction from *first, second, third,* and so on, which are **ordinal numbers** and show sequence. Cardinal and ordinal numbers can function as adjectives or as nouns.

gr

case   The inflection of a noun (*girls', friend's*) or pronoun (*she, her, hers*) to show its relationship to other words. In English, pronouns are classified into three cases. See also Chapter **26**.

Nominative (or subjective)	I spoke; **they** listened; **she** dozed. **[The inflected pronouns function as subject.]**
Objective	John tossed **me** the ball. I collided with two other players and knocked **them** down. **[The inflected pronouns function as indirect object and direct object of the verbs.]**
Possessive (or genitive)	**His** score and **mine** were identical. **Our** scores were higher than **theirs.** They wondered **whose** grade was the highest. **[The inflected pronouns show possession.]**

In modern times, English nouns are inflected only to indicate the possessive case: *Jerry's* money and *Sarah's* money was invested at their *parents'* advice; this plan allayed the *relatives'* fears about the *boy's* future and the *girl's* education.

clause   A group of words containing a subject and predicate. Clauses that can stand alone as complete sentences are **independent** (or **main**) clauses. Clauses that are not by themselves complete in meaning are **dependent** (or **subordinate**) clauses. Subordinate clauses are used as nouns, adjectives, or adverbs. They are usually introduced by subordinating conjunctions or relative pronouns. See also **24a**.

We heard him **when he came in.**

gr

[*We heard him* is the main clause; *when he came in* is the subordinate clause.]

That she will be late is certain.
[Subordinate clause used as a noun.]

The woman who spoke to us is our sheriff.
[Subordinate clause used as an adjective.]

He will come in when he is ready.
[Subordinate clause used as an adverb.]

Independent clauses connected by a coordinating conjunction are called **coordinate clauses.**

The bell rang, and everyone stood up.

collective noun   A noun that is singular in form (*class, crowd, orchestra*) but that denotes a group of members. See also **25b.**

colloquial language   Language appropriate to speech but not to formal writing, unless a relaxed and casual tone is intended. See also **9b.**

comma splice   A sentence error in which two independent clauses are joined by a comma with no coordinating conjunction. See also **29c.**

> **Comma splice**   The car was an ancient model, it made the trip successfully.
>
> **Revised**   The car was an ancient model, **but** it made the trip successfully.

comparison   Inflection of an adjective or adverb to indicate an increasing degree of quality, quantity, or manner.

> **Positive degree**   Our house is **cold.**
> **Comparative degree**   Their house is **colder.**
> **Superlative degree**   Their house is the **coldest** in town.

When adjectives have one or two syllables, the comparative degree is usually formed by adding *-er* to the positive, and the superlative degree is usually formed by adding *-est* to the positive. To form the comparative degree of adverbs and of adjectives with more than two syllables, place *more* before the positive form; the superlative degree is usually formed by placing *most* before the positive. Some adjectives have irregular comparison—for example, *good, better, best; bad, worse, worst.* See also **27a**.

complement   Traditionally, a word or phrase added to a verb to complete the sense of the statement. The complement may be the direct object of a transitive verb, an indirect object, or a predicate noun or adjective. See also **24a**.

Direct object	A big wave swamped our **boat.**
Indirect object	I paid **him** the money.
Predicate noun	Our destination was **Corsica.**
Predicate adjective	The waves were **enormous.**
	A limber branch made the tree house **shaky.**

complex sentence   See **24b**.

compound sentence   See **24b**.

concrete language   Words describing specific things, perceptible by the senses: *smooth, bitter, yellow, creaky, shrill.* See **abstract language.** See also **13c**.

conjugation   The inflected forms of a verb that show person, number, tense, voice, and mood. Below is a conjugation of the indicative mood of the verb *see*. See also **28a**, **28b**, **28c**, **28f**.

		Active voice	Passive voice
		Present tense	
singular	1.	I see	I am seen
	2.	you see	you are seen
	3.	he/she/it sees	he/she/it is seen
plural	1.	we see	we are seen
	2.	you see	you are seen
	3.	they see	they are seen
		Past tense	
singular	1.	I saw	I was seen
	2.	you saw	you were seen
	3.	he/she/it saw	he/she/it was seen
plural	1.	we saw	we were seen
	2.	you saw	you were seen
	3.	they saw	they were seen

gr

	Active voice	Passive voice

Future tense

singular	1. I will see	I will be seen
	2. you will see	you will be seen
	3. he/she/it will see	he/she/it will be seen
plural	1. we will see	we will be seen
	2. you will see	you will be seen
	3. they will see	they will be seen

Perfect tense

singular	1. I have seen	I have been seen
	2. you have seen	you have been seen
	3. he/she/it has seen	he/she/it has been seen
plural	1. we have seen	we have been seen
	2. you have seen	you have been seen
	3. they have seen	they have been seen

Past perfect tense

singular	1. I had seen	I had been seen
	2. you had seen	you had been seen
	3. he/she/it had seen	he/she/it had been seen
plural	1. we had seen	we had been seen
	2. you had seen	you had been seen
	3. they had seen	they had been seen

Future perfect tense

singular	1. I will have seen	I will have been seen
	2. you will have seen	you will have been seen
	3. he/she/it will have seen	he/she/it will have been seen
plural	1. we will have seen	we will have been seen
	2. you will have seen	you will have been seen
	3. they will have seen	they will have been seen

conjunction   A part of speech used to connect words, phrases, and clauses. There are the following kinds:

Coordinating   Pure, or simple, conjunctions: **and, or, nor, but, for, so, yet.** Correlatives: **either . . . or, neither . . . nor, both . . . and, not only . . . but [also].**

Subordinating Conjunctions introducing noun clauses, adjective clauses, or adverb clauses: **that, when, where, while, whence, because, so that, although, since, as, after, if, until.**

Coordinating conjunctions connect sentence elements that are logically and grammatically equal; that is, they may connect two subjects, two verbs, two clauses, and so on. Subordinating conjunctions connect subordinate (or dependent) clauses with their principal (or independent) clauses. See also **8a**, **8c**, **24a**, **24b**.

conjunctive adverb An introductory adverb, or sentence modifier, that indicates the relationship between principal clauses. Conjunctive adverbs include the following: *besides, consequently, furthermore, however, instead, moreover, nevertheless, nonetheless, still, then, therefore,* and *thus.* Between independent clauses a conjunctive adverb must be preceded by a semicolon or by a coordinating conjunction. See also **29c**.

connotation The associations, suggestions, and feelings that a word brings to mind, as opposed to its literal, dictionary meaning. For example, both *baby* and *infant* denote, or mean literally, a small child, but *baby* connotes coddling, affection, and tender protection. See **denotation.** See also **13b**.

coordinate Sentence elements that are parallel in grammatical construction are coordinate. In the sentence *He and she talked lengthily and earnestly and at last agreed, he* and *she* are coordinate; *talked* and *agreed* are coordinate; and *lengthily* and *earnestly* are coordinate. See also **8a**, **8c**.

dangling modifier A word or phrase that does not modify another word or phrase or that cannot be easily linked to the sentence. See also **12b**.

Dangling Dashing out the door, the mat caused me to stumble.

Revised Dashing out the door, *I* stumbled on the mat.

declension See **inflection.**

demonstrative See **adjective** and **pronoun.**

gr

denotation The literal or dictionary definition of a word. See **connotation**. See also **13b**.

diction Choice of words, especially as those words affect the tone of the writer's voice, depending on their formality or informality, the range of which is suggested below. See also Chapters **4**, **9**, and **13**.

highly formal ◄─────────────────────────► highly informal			
residence	home	house	pad
affluent	wealthy	rich	loaded
obtuse	ignorant	stupid	dumb

direct address A grammatical construction in which the speaker or writer addresses a second person directly.

Mary, wait for me.

Friends, Romans, countrymen, lend me your ears.

direct object See **object**.

double negative A nonstandard form consisting of two negatives.

> **Double negative** He **doesn't** have **no** place to go.
>
> **Correct** He **doesn't** have **any** place to go.

elliptical expression An expression that is grammatically incomplete, but whose meaning is clear because the omitted words are implied. See also **12b**.

> **Elliptical** **If possible,** bring your drawings along.
>
> **Complete** **If it is possible,** bring your drawings along.
>
> **Elliptical** To me he gave his watch; **to Mary,** [he gave] **his favorite painting.**

euphemism The substitution of an often trite and sentimental expression for one considered to be unpleasant or indelicate: *in an interesting condition* or *in the family way* are old-fashioned euphemisms for *pregnant*. See also **13f**.

finite verb A verb that makes an assertion and can serve as a predicate—as distinguished from infinitives, participles, and gerunds.

> **Finite verb** The alarm **rang** and I **got** up.

Verbal   The **ringing** alarm awoke me and I hurried **to get** up.

fused sentence   A sentence error in which two independent clauses are joined without any punctuation or conjunction. See also **29e**.

Fused   The car stalled at the corner it was out of gas.

Revised   The car stalled at the corner. It was out of gas.

gender   In grammar, the division of nouns (*man, woman, book*) and pronouns (*he, she, it*) into sexual categories: masculine, feminine, and neuter.

genitive   See **case**.

gerund   A verb form ending in *-ing* and used as a noun. The gerund should be distinguished from the present participle, which also ends in *-ing* but is used as an adjective. See **participle**. See also **12b, 24a, 26h**.

Subject of verb   Fishing is tiresome.

Object of verb   I hate **fishing**.

Object of preposition   I have a dislike of **fishing**.

Predicate noun   The sport I like least is **fishing**.

Like a noun, the gerund may be modified by an adjective. In the sentence *They were tired of his long-winded preaching, his* and *long-winded* modify the gerund *preaching*. A noun or pronoun preceding a gerund is normally in the possessive—in this case, *his* preaching. Since a gerund is a verb form, it may take an object and be modified by an adverb.

He disapproved of our **taking luggage** with us.
[*Luggage* is the object of the gerund *taking*.]

Our success depends upon his **acting promptly**.
[*Promptly* is an adverb modifying the gerund *acting*.]

idiom   An expression that is understood and used by speakers of a particular language or region, but whose meaning cannot be determined from the literal meaning of the individual words. See also **13d**.

She **was taken in** by the practical jokes.

Every now and then, I have a mind to tell her off.

He is, **after all,** my brother, and I have to **stick up for him.**

He was **out of his head** for a while, but he finally **pulled himself together.**

imperative   See **mood.**

indicative   See **mood.**

indirect object   See **object.**

infinitive   That form of the verb usually preceded by *to. To* is called the "sign of the infinitive." Since it is a verb form, the infinitive can have a subject, can take an object or a predicate complement, and can be modified by an adverb.

They wanted **me to go.**
[*Me* **is the subject of** *to go.*]

They asked **to meet him.**
[*Him* **is the object of** *to meet.*]

We hope **to hear soon.**
[*Soon* **is the adverbial modifier of** *to hear.*]

The infinitive may be used as a noun (*To meet her* is a pleasure. He wanted *to buy my car.*), or as an adjective or adverb (He gave me a book *to read.* He waited *to see you.* We are happy *to help.*). See also **12b, 12d, 24a, 26g, 28d, 29a.**

inflection   A change in the form of a word to show a change in meaning or use. Nouns may be inflected to show number (*man, men*) and the possessive case (*dog, dog's*). Pronouns may be inflected to show case (*he, him*), person (*I, you*), number (*I, we*), and gender (*his, hers*). Verbs are inflected to show person (I *go,* he *goes*), number (she *is,* they *are*), tense (he *is,* he *was*), voice (I *received* your letter, your letter *was received*), and mood (if this *be* treason). Adjectives and adverbs are inflected to show relative degree (*strong, stronger, strongest*). The inflection of substantives is called **declension;** that of verbs, **conjugation;** that of adjectives and adverbs, **comparison.**

intensive pronoun   When the pronouns *myself, himself, yourself,* and so on, are used in apposition, they are called **intensives** because they serve to emphasize the substantives that they are used with: *I myself will do it. I saw the bishop himself.* When one of these words is used as the object of a verb and designates the same person or thing as the subject of that verb, it is called a **reflexive pronoun:** *I hurt myself. They benefit themselves.* See also **26d**.

interjection   An exclamation that has no grammatical relation with the rest of the sentence: *oh, alas, please.*

intransitive   See **verb.**

irregular verb   A verb that does not form its past tense by adding *-ed* or *-t: sing, sang, sung; drink, drank, drunk.* Such a verb is sometimes called a **strong verb.** See also **28a, 28b.**

jargon   Specialized, technical language that is used by a profession, class, group, or discipline, but that is obscure to the general public. See also **13f**.

linking verb   A verb like *be, seem, appear, become, feel,* or *look* that acts mainly as a connecting link between the subject and the predicate noun or predicate adjective. See also **13f, 24a, 26f, 27b.**

misplaced modifier   A modifier that is awkwardly placed—usually too far from the term it modifies—so that its relation to rest of the sentence is confusing. See also **12c.**

> **Misplaced**   I sped across the river that was frozen **on skates.**
>
> **Revised**   I sped **on skates** across the river that was frozen.

mixed construction   The fusion within a sentence of two parts that do not fit together grammatically or semantically. See also **12f.**

> **Mixed**   Because she was early is the reason she found a seat.
>
> **Revised**   Because she was early, she found a seat.

modifier   A word or group of words that functions as an adjective or an adverb to limit, define, or qualify another word or group of words. In the sentence *I dislike these sour oranges, sour* describes *oranges,* and *these* limits them to a nearby group. They are adjectival modifiers. In the sentence *She sang for half an hour,* the phrase *for half an hour,* which tells how long she sang, is an adverbial modifier.

mood   Inflection of a verb to indicate whether it is intended to make a statement or command or to express a condition contrary to fact. See also **28g.**

gr

The **indicative mood** is used to state a fact or to ask a question.

The wind is blowing.

Is it raining?

The **imperative mood** is used to express a command or a request.

Do it immediately.

Please answer the telephone.

The **subjunctive mood** is used to express a wish, a doubt, a concession, or a condition contrary to fact. In speech and in all but formal writing, the subjunctive mood has largely been replaced by the indicative.

Wish	I wish that I **were** able to help you.
Condition contrary to fact	If she **were** older, she would understand.

nominative   See **case.**

nonrestrictive modifier   A dependent clause or phrase that adds information without limiting the meaning of the word it modifies. See also **30d.**

noun   A part of speech: a noun names a person, place, thing, or abstraction. There are the following kinds:

A **common noun** refers to any member of a group or class of things, or to abstract qualities—for example, *village, book, courage.* Common nouns are not usually capitalized.

A **proper noun** or **proper name** is the name of a particular person, place, thing, or event—for example, *Jane Austen, Chicago, Domesday Book, War of Independence.* Proper nouns are capitalized.

A **collective noun** is the name of a group or class considered as a unit—for example, *flock, class, group, crowd, gang, team.*

Nouns may also function as modifiers: *town hall.* Such constructions are sometimes called **compound nouns.** See also **25b, 32b.**

noun clause   See **clause.**

number   Inflection of verbs, nouns, and pronouns to indicate singular or plural.

object   The **direct object** of a verb names the person or thing that completes the assertion made by a transitive verb. It answers the question *what* or *whom*.

Father dried the **dishes** and broke a **plate**.

I trusted **him** and followed his **advice**.

The **indirect object** of a verb is the person or thing to which something is given or for which something is done. The indirect object can usually be made the object of the preposition *for* or *to*. See also **24a**.

I built my **wife** a shelf. = I built a shelf **for my wife**.

I wrote **him** a letter. = I wrote a letter **to him**.

objective (accusative)   See **case**.

objective complement   Either a noun or an adjective that completes the predicate by telling something about the direct object. See also **24a**.

noun
They call him a **fool**.

adjective
I like my coffee **hot**.

ordinal number   See **cardinal number**.

parallelism   The stylistic device of putting equal ideas into equivalent structures in a sentence. See also **8c**.

She wants **fame, prestige,** and **power**.
[The boldface words are equally weighted as objects of the verb *wants*.]

That she must work hard, that many obstacles stand in her way, that few encourage her endeavors—these facts do not affect her pluck one bit.
[Clause is balanced against clause to create parallel structure.]

participle   A verb form used as an adjective. The present participle ends in *-ing: eating, running*. The past participle ends in *-ed, -d, -t, -en,* or *-n,* or is formed by vowel change: *stopped, told, slept, fallen, known, sung*. See also **12b, 24a, 28d, 29a**.

gr

gr

Since a participle is a verbal adjective, it has the characteristics of both a verb and an adjective. Like an adjective, it modifies a substantive.

The **inquiring** reporter stopped him.

Encouraged by his help, she continued her work.

Having just **returned** from my vacation, I had not heard the news.

Like a verb, the participle may take a direct or an indirect object and may be modified by an adverb:

Wishing us success, he drove away.
[*Us* is an indirect object, *success* a direct object, of the participle *wishing*.]

Stumbling awkwardly, he came into the room.
[*Awkwardly* is an adverb modifying the participle *stumbling*.]

parts of speech   The classification of words according to the special function that they perform in a sentence: *nouns, pronouns, verbs, adjectives, adverbs, prepositions, interjections,* and *conjunctions.* See also **24a**.

passive voice   See **voice**.

person   Inflection of verbs and personal pronouns to indicate the speaker **(first person)**, the person spoken to **(second person)**, and the person spoken of **(third person)**.

> **First person**   I am, we are; I go, we go.
> **Second person**   you are; you go.
> **Third person**   she is, they are; he goes, they go.

phrase   A group of words without a subject and predicate, used as a single part of speech—as a *substantive, verb, adjective,* or *adverb.* See also **24a**.

predicate   A group of words that makes a statement about, or asks a question about, the subject of the sentence. Thus in the sentence *Jim drove the car, drove the car* is the predicate, because it tells what the subject (*Jim*) did. The predicate always contains a finite verb—for example, *drove, had driven.*

The **simple predicate** is the verb alone. The **complete predicate** is the verb and its modifiers and complements. See also **24a**.

Jim drove the car into the garage.
[*Drove* **is the simple predicate.** *Drove the car into the garage* **is the complete predicate.**]

predicate adjective, predicate noun   See **complement.**

prefix   Letters added before a word's base to form a new word: *pre-, re-, com-*. See **suffix.**

preposition   A part of speech that shows the relationship between a substantive and another word in the sentence—for example, *in, on, into, to, toward, from, for, against, of, between, with, without, before, behind, under, over, above, among, at, by, around, about, through*. The word that completes the meaning of the preposition is called the **object of the preposition.** In English, many words may be used as either prepositions or adverbs, their classification depending on their function in the sentence. If they are followed by a substantive that, with them, forms a phrase, they are prepositions; if by themselves they modify a verb, they are adverbs. See also **24a, 29a.**

He stood **behind** the chair. [**Preposition**]

The money is **in** the bank. [**Preposition**]

They came **in** while we were there. [**Adverb**]

principal parts   In English, the three forms of a verb from which all other forms are derived. They are (1) the base form, (2) the past form, and (3) the past participle: *send, sent, sent; choose, chose, chosen; swim, swam, swum*. All present- and future-tense forms, including the present participle, are derived from the first principal part: I *send*, he *sends*, we *will send*. The second principal part is used for the simple past tense: he *sent*, I *chose*, you *swam*. Compound past tenses and the forms of the passive voice employ the third principal part: he *has chosen*, they *had swum*, the package *was sent*, or *may be sent, is being sent, will be sent*. The verb *be* is too irregular to be reduced to three principal parts. See also **28a, 28b.**

pronoun   A part of speech—a word used to refer to a noun already used (or implied). The types of pronouns are listed below. See also **25b,** Chapter **26.**

> **Personal**   **I, you, he, she, it,** and their inflectional forms
> I listened to **her.**

Demonstrative	this, that, these, those **This** is my favorite book.
Interrogative	who, which, what **Who** can answer this question?
Relative	who, which, that, and compounds like **whoever** This is the house **that** Jack built.
Indefinite	any, anyone, some, someone, no one, nobody, each, everybody, either, and so on **Someone** has my pen.
Reflexive	myself, yourself, and so on I hurt **myself.**
Intensive	myself, yourself, and so on He **himself** is to blame.
Reciprocal	each other, one another John and Mary looked at **each other.**

reflexive pronoun   See **intensive pronoun.**

regular verb   A verb that forms its past tenses by adding *-ed,* or *-t: start, started; dream, dreamed* or *dreamt.* Also called a **weak verb.** See also **28a.**

relative pronoun   A pronoun (*who, which,* or *that*) used with a double function: (1) to take the place of a noun and (2) to connect clauses the way a subordinating conjunction does. See also **25a, 26b.**

restrictive modifier   A dependent clause or phrase required in a sentence to define or limit the word it modifies. See also **30d.**

                    restrictive
The students **who come regularly to class** do better work and earn

                    restrictive
higher marks than the students **who attend only periodically.**

run-on sentence   See **fused sentence.**

sentence   An independent utterance, usually including a subject and predicate, that can stand by itself and is set off by capitalization of its beginning and a period or other terminal punctuation at its end. A sentence may range in length from one word (*Why?*) or short phrases (*What an absurd idea!*) to a main clause (*I saw him sitting on the fence*).

gr

From the point of view of structure, sentences are classified as **simple, compound, complex,** or **compound-complex.**

From the point of view of meaning or function, sentences may be classified as follows:

A **declarative sentence** asserts something about a subject.

> The man felt ill and called the doctor.

An **interrogative sentence** asks a question.

> When is she coming?

An **imperative sentence** expresses a command.

> Call him again.

An **exclamatory sentence** expresses strong feeling.

> What a fool he was!

See also Chapters **8**, **12**, **24**, **29**.

sentence fragment   Dependent clauses or phrases that are punctuated as sentences but that should be joined to an independent clause or made into one. See also **29a**, **29b**.

> **Fragment**   I accepted jury duty. **Since I was free.**
> **Revised**   I accepted jury duty **since I was free.**

subject   The part of the sentence or clause naming the person or thing about which something is said. The subject of a sentence is usually a noun or pronoun, but it may be a verbal, a phrase, or a noun clause. See also Chapter **24**.

> **Noun**   Beyond the ridge lay a high **plateau.**
> **Verbal**   Nowadays **flying** is both safe and cheap.
> **Phrase**   **To fear the worst** oft cures the worse.
> **Clause**   **That she will be promoted** is certain.

The **simple subject** is a substantive, usually a noun or pronoun. The **complete subject** is the simple subject and its modifiers.

The young trees that we planted last year have grown tall.
[*Trees* is the simple subject. *The young trees that we planted last year* is the complete subject.]

subjunctive   See **mood.**

subordination   Making one element of a sentence grammatically dependent on another in order to show the relationship of ideas. See also **8a**, Chapter **24**.

> **When the party was over,** I left.
> **[The subordinate clause *when the party was over* limits the time of the action.]**

gr

substantive   Any word or group of words used as a noun. A substantive may be a noun, a pronoun, a clause, an infinitive, or a gerund.

suffix   Letters added at the end of a word's base to form a new word: *-tion, -ship, -ing.* See **prefix.**

syntax   The way in which words are put together to make phrases, clauses, and sentences.

tense   Different forms of a verb that indicate distinctions in time. In English there are six tenses: the present tense, the past tense, the future tense, the perfect (present perfect) tense, the past perfect tense, and the future perfect tense. See also **28c**, **28d**.

verb   A part of speech whose function is to assert that the subject exists, acts, or has certain characteristics. (The man who *is* on my left *wrote* the book; he *is* very difficult to talk to.) The verb may be a word or a group of words, but in either case its form changes to indicate time, person, or mood. (He *was saying* that I *am* too young but *should have* a chance next year.) See also Chapter **28**.

A **transitive verb** is a verb that requires a direct object (a noun or another substantive) to complete its meaning.

He **shut** the **door.**

They **greeted her.**

An **intransitive verb** is a verb that does not require a direct object.

After a heated argument, he **left.**

The child **sat** near the fire.

A **linking verb** acts mainly as a connecting link between the subject and the predicate noun or predicate adjective.

That **is** correct.

He **seems** sleepy.

She **felt** warm.

verbals   Forms of a verb (*stealing, stolen, to steal*) used as nouns, adjectives, or adverbs. See **gerund, participle, infinitive.**

voice   Inflection of a verb to indicate the relation of the subject to the action expressed by the verb. A verb is in the **active voice** when its subject is the doer of the action. A verb is in the **passive voice** when its subject is acted upon. See also **28f**.

Active voice	I **rang** the bell. **[The subject *I* did the act of ringing.]**
Passive voice	The bell **was rung** by me. **[The subject *bell* was acted upon by me.]**

weak verb   See **regular verb.**

word order   The ordering of words in a sentence, a major determinant of meaning in English.

The Cubs beat the Reds.

The Reds beat the Cubs.

gr

Index

Section numbers are in **boldface;** page numbers are in regular type. Thus **30d:**616 refers to Section 30d, page 616.

a, **gl:**707
A.D., **gl:**707
a lot, **gl:**709
abbreviation
  as appositive, **30d:**616
  in bibliography, **32d:**669
  in citation, **32d:**669
  with figures, **32d:**669
  period with, **30a:**607, **32d:**667
  plural of, **32d:**669
  of title, **32d:**668–69
absolute construction, **gr:**729
absolute phrase, **24a:**527, **gr:**729
  beginning sentence with, **8f:**154
  comma with, **30d:**617
abstract, dissertation
  endnote citation of, **23c:**489
  MLA citation of, **19b:**370
abstract language, **13c:**231–33, **gr:**729
abstract page, APA form for, **22d:**454
  sample, **22e:**457
accept, **gl:**707
acronym, **32d:**667

active voice, **8b:**131–34, **28f:**581–83, **gr:**747
ad hominem argument, **15d:**281
adapt, **gl:**707
address
  in business letter, **33b:**678–79, 681
  comma with, **30d:**618–19
  direct. *See* direct address
adjective, **24a:**518, 520, **gr:**729
  comparison of, **27a:**559–60, 561, **gr:**732
  compound, **27d:**563–64, **31d:**647
  coordinate, **30d:**613–14
  defined, **27:**558
  irregular, **27a:**560
  lacking comparative forms, **27a:**560–61
  with linking verb, **27b:**562–63
  noun used as, **27c:**563
  parenthetic, **30d:**616
  placement of, **12c:**214
  predicate, **24a:**524, **gr:**733
adjective clause, **24a:**530–31

748

adopt, **gl:**707
adverb, **24a:**520, **gr:**729–30
  colloquial forms of, **27e:**564–65
  comparison of, **27a:**559–60, 561,
    gr:732–33
  conjunctive, **29c:**595–97,
    29e:599, **30d:**617, **gr:**735
  defined, **27:**558
  formation of, **27:**558
  irregular, **27a:**560
  lacking comparative forms,
    27a:560
  placement of, **12c:**214, 215
adverb clause, **24a:**530
  beginning sentence with, **8f:**154
  misuse of, **12f:**222
adverse, **gl:**707–8
advice, **gl:**708
advise, **gl:**708
affect, **gl:**708
aggravate, **gl:**708
agreement
  defined, **25:**536
  pronoun-antecedent, **25b:**544–
    47, **gr:**730
  subject-verb, **25a:**537–42,
    gr:730
ain't, **gl:**708
all ready, **gl:**708
all right, **gl:**709
all together, **gl:**708
allude, **gl:**708
allusion, **13e:**239
allusion, **gl:**709
already, **gl:**708
alternating comparison, **7f:**109
altogether, **gl:**708
among, **gl:**709
amoral, **gl:**709
amount, **gl:**709

ampersand, **32d:**669
an, **gl:**707
analogy, **13e:**238
  defined, **15c:**279
  developing paragraph with,
    7g:111–13
  false, **15c:**280
  use of, **15c:**279–80
analyze, examination direction,
  35b:692
ante, **gl:**710
antecedent, agreement with,
  25b:544–47
  indefinite, **25b:**545–47
anthology
  endnote citation of, **23b:**487
  MLA citation of, **19b:**367
anthropology, reference works for,
  18b:343–44
anti, **gl:**710
anxious, **gl:**710
anyone, any one, **gl:**710
APA documentation
  characteristics of, **22a:**432–33
  sample research paper illustrating,
    22e:455–79
APA paper format, **22d:**452–54
APA reference forms, **22b:**433–45
APA source citation, **22c:**445–52,
  22e:460
apostrophe
  forming contraction, **30g:**631
  forming certain plurals, **30g:**631
  indicating possessive case,
    30g:630–31
application letter
  body of, **34b:**686
  conclusion of, **34b:**686–87
  introduction of, **34b:**685–86
apposition, defining by, **7d:**105

in

appositive, **24a:**527–28, **gr:**730
    beginning sentence with, **8f:**153
    nonrestrictive vs. restrictive,
        30d:615–16
appositive phrase, **24a:**527–28
    as sentence fragment, **29a:**591
apt, **gl:**720
architecture, reference works for,
    18b:337
argument
    assumptions of, **14b:**260–62
    structure of, **14a:**258–60
art
    APA citation of, **22b:**444–45
    reference works for, **18b:**337
article (part of speech), **gr:**730
article (written)
    APA citation of, **22b:**439–41
    endnote citation of, **23c:**487–89
    MLA citation of, **19b:**367–70
as, **gl:**710
    pronoun after, **26e:**554
at about, **gl:**710
atlas, **18b:**337
audience, **3a:**33–**3b:**38
    analyzing, **3b:**34–38
    background of, **3b:**35, 36
    and relation to subject and writer,
        3b:35–37
    voice and, **4c:**42–46
audiotape, APA citation of,
    22b:444–45
authorities, evaluation of, **14c:**268
authority, of sources for research,
    19d:380–81
auxiliary verb, **24a:**520, 522,
    28e:579–80, **gr:**730–31
    modal, **28e:**580
    omission of, **12g:**223
averse, **gl:**707–8
awhile, a while, **gl:**710

B.C., **gl:**711
backup file, **36a:**699–700
bad, badly, **gl:**711
barely, **gl:**717
be, **24a:**521–22
    principal parts of, **28a:**568
begging the question, **15d:**280–81
believability, **14d:**270–72
between, **gl:**709
bibliography, working, **19a:**357–59
bibliography page, **23a:**481
biography, reference works for,
    18b:337–38
block style, of business letter,
    33a:678, **34b:**687–88
body, of letter, **33b:**680, **34b:**686
book
    APA citation of, **22b:**435–38
    endnote citation of, **23c:**484–87
    italics with title of, **32e:**670
    MLA citation of, **19b:**361–66
book part
    APA citation of, **22b:**438–39
    endnote citation of, **23c:**487
    MLA citation of, **19b:**366–67
book review
    APA citation of, **22b:**441–42
    endnote citation of, **23c:**489
    MLA citation of, **19b:**370
brackets, **19c:**376, **21:**426,
    22e:472, **30h:**636–37
brainstorming, **2a:**16–20
    on word processor, **36b:**702
business letter, **33a:**677–**33b:**683
    form of, **33a:**678
    parts of, **33b:**678–81
    reader of, **33a:**677–78
    salutation of, **30h:**633
    sample, **33b:**681–83, **34b:**687–
        88

but, **gl:**711
  pronoun after, **26:**554

can, **28e:**580, **gl:**711
capitalization, **32b:**661–65
  of proper nouns, **32b:**662–64
  of sentences and quotations,
    32b:664–65
  of titles of works, **32b:**664
card catalog, **18a:**333–36
cardinal number, **gr:**731
caret, **32a:**661
case, **gr:**731
  compound constructions and,
    26a:549–50
  with linking verbs, **26f:**554–55
  of noun or pronoun modifying a
    gerund, **26h:**555–56
  of subject and object of infinitive,
    26g:555
  than, as, but affecting, **26e:**554
  who versus *whom,* **26b:**551–52
causality, errors in, **15b:**277–79
cause and effect, developing
  paragraph with, **7h:**113–14
CD-ROM data-base search,
  18e:351–54
censor, censure, **gl:**711
centering, on word processor,
  36a:701
chart, APA citation of, **22b:**444–45
chronology, developing paragraph
  with, **7b:**102–3
classics, reference works for,
  18b:338
classification, developing paragraph
  with, **7e:**107–8
clause, **24a:**519
  coordinate, **8a:**124, **gr:**732
  defined, **24a:**528, **gr:**731–32

main, **8a:**124
parallel, **8c:**137
as parenthetic element, **30d:**617
relative, **8a:**125
See also adjective clause, adverb
  clause, noun clause
cliché, **13f:**245–46
close, of letter, **33b:**680–81
coherence, revising for, **11b:**196–
  201
collective noun, **gr:**732, **gr:**740
  as antecedent, **25b:**545
  and subject-verb agreement,
    25a:539–40
colloquial English, **9b:**166
colloquial language, **gr:**732
colon, **30h:**632–34
  capitalization after, **32b:**664
  introducing long quotation with,
    20c:399, **21:**428, **22c:**446
  outside quotation mark, **30f:**626
comma, **30d:**610–20
  with absolute phrase, **30d:**617
  in comparative and contrastive
    constructions, **30d:**617–18
  with coordinate modifiers,
    30d:613–14
  with coordinating conjunction,
    30d:610–11
  with date, address, place name, or
    number, **30d:**618–19
  with direct quotation, **30d:**619–
    20
  with elements in series, **30d:**612–
    13
  with interjection, direct address,
    or tag question, **30d:**618
  with introductory element,
    30d:611–12
  misuse of, **30d:**620

in

comma (*continued*)
  with nonrestrictive modifier,
    30d:614–16
  with parenthetic element,
    30d:616–17
  inside quotation mark, **30f**:626
comma splice or fault, **29c**:594–98,
  gr:732
  acceptable use of, **29d**:598–99
commerce, reference works for,
  18b:339
common knowledge, plagiarism vs.,
  20b:396–97
common noun, **32b**:661–62,
  gr:740
communication triangle, **1b**:5–6
comparative degree, **24a**:520,
  gr:732
  adjective forms, **27a**:559, 561
  adverb forms, **27a**:559–60,
    561
*compare to, compare with, contrast
  with,* **gl**:711–12
compare, examination direction,
  35b:692
comparison
  alternating, **7f**:109
  comma with, **30d**:617–18
  degrees of, **24a**:520, **27a**:559–
    61, **gr**:732–33
  developing paragraph with,
    7f:109–11
  divided, **7f**:110
  incomplete, **12g**:224–25
  unidiomatic, **12f**:222
complement, **24a**:523, **gr**:733
  object, **24a**:524
  subject, **24a**:524, **27b**:562
complementary, complimentary,
  gl:712

complete predicate, **gr**:742–43
complete subject, **gr**:745
complex sentence, **24b**:534
compound adjective, **27d**:563–64,
  31d:647
compound antecedent, **25b**:544–45
compound construction, **26a**:549–
  50
compound noun, **gr**:740
compound predicate, **24a**:522
compound sentence, **24b**:533–34
compound subject, **24a**:522
  subject-verb agreement and,
    25a:539
compound-complex sentence,
  24b:534–35
computer software
  APA citation of, **22b**:444
  endnote citation of, **23c**:491
  MLA citation of, **19b**:373
concrete language, **13c**:231, 233–
  34, **gr**:733
concur, **gl**:712
conference, proceedings of
  APA citation of, **22b**:443–44
  endnote citation of, **23c**:491
  MLA citation of, **19b**:372–73
conjugation, **gr**:733–34
conjunction
  coordinating, **8a**:123, 124,
    8c:140, **24b**:533, **29c**:597–98,
    29e:599, **30d**:610–11, **gr**:734–
    35
  correlative, **8c**:143–45
  subordinating, **8a**:123, **24a**:529,
    29c:598, **29e**:600, **gr**:735
conjunctive adverb, **29c**:595–97,
  29e:599, **gr**:735
  as parenthetic element, **30d**:617
connectives, wordy, **8b**:130–31

connotation, **13b:**229–31, **gr:**735
conscious, conscience, **gl:**712
construction
  compound, **26a:**549–50
  defined, **24a:**519
contact, **gl:**712
content note, **20c:**406–7, **21:**430,
  22d:454, **22e:**464, 479
continual, continuous, **gl:**712
contraction, apostrophe to form,
  30g:631
contrast, developing paragraph with,
  7f:109–11
coordinate sentence elements,
  gr:735
coordinate clause, **8a:**124, **gr:**732
coordinating conjunction, **8a:**123,
  124, **8c:**140, **24b:**533, **30d:**610–
  11, **gr:**734–35
  correcting comma splice with,
    29c:597–98
  correcting fused sentence with,
    29e:599
coordination, faulty, **8a:**122–25,
  8c:140, 141
copula, **24a:**521
copy, word processing function,
  36a:700, **36b:**705
correlative, **8c:**143–45
could, **28e:**580
cover letter, **34b:**687–88
criteria, **gl:**713
critical reading, **14a:**257
critical thinking, **14a:**257–**14d:**272
cumulative sentence, **8d:**148–
  149
currency, of sources for research,
  19d:380
current events, reference works for,
  18b:338

dance, reference works for, **18b:**341
dangling modifier, **12b:**210–14,
  gr:735
  permissible, **12c:**213–14
dash, **30h:**634–35
data, **gl:**713
data-base search
  CD-ROM, **18e:**351–54
  on-line, **18e:**349–51
date
  comma with, **30d:**618–19
  in inverted style, **30d:**619
declarative sentence, **24b:**532,
  30a:606, **gr:**745
definite article, **gr:**730
definition
  by apposition, **7d:**105
  developing paragraph with,
    7d:104–7
  extended, **7d:**105–6
  misuse of, **7d:**106–7
degrees of comparison, **24a:**520,
  27a:559–61, **gr:**732–33
delete, word processing function,
  36a:700
delusion, **gl:**709
demonstrative pronoun, **gr:**744
  as adjective, **gr:**729
  as antecedent, **25b:**547
denotation, **13b:**229–31, **gr:**736
dependent, **gr:**731–32
dependent clause, **24a:**528–29
  misuse of, **12f:**221–22
  as sentence fragment, **29a:**588–
    89
  sequence of tenses in, **28d:**575–
    77
details
  conveying writer's attitude toward
    subject, **4b:**40–42

details (*continued*)
developing paragraph with,
7a:100–102
revising paragraph with,
11a:192–95
Dewey Decimal System, 18a:335
dialect, 9b:167–68
agreement in, 25:536–37
dialogue
capitalization with, 32b:664
paragraphing of, 6c:95–96
periods in, 30a:608
quoting, 32a:660–61
diction, gr:736
abstract, 13c:231–33
concrete, 13c:233–34
pretentious, 13f:249–50
problems with, 13f:239–50
dictionary
abbreviations in, 9a:159–61
abridged, 9a:158–59
elements of entry in, 9a:161–62
idioms in, 13d:235
symbols in, 9a:159–61
unabridged, 9a:157–58
value of, 13b:230–31
different, gl:713
dilemma, gl:713
direct address, gr:736
comma with, 30d:618
direct object, 24a:523, gr:733, 741
noun clause as, 24a:529
direct quotation
accuracy of, 20b:393
beginning an introduction with,
5d:62–63
capitalization in, 32b:664–65
citation of, in research paper,
20c:399–404, 22c:446–51
comma with, 30d:619–20
manuscript form for, 32a:659–61

in notes, 19c:376
quotation marks with, 30f:625–
28
discovering ideas
structured methods of, 2b:28–32
unstructured methods of, 2a:15–
27
discuss, examination direction,
35b:692–93
disinterested, gl:713
dissertation
APA citation of, 22b:442
endnote citation of, 23c:490
MLA citation of, 19b:371
distance between writer and reader,
4c:43–45
dive, 28b:571
divided comparison, 7f:110
do, 28e:579–80
documenting sources, in research
paper
in APA style, 22a:432–33,
22c:445–52
in endnote style, 23a:480–82
in MLA style, 20c:397–407
dollar sign, 32c:667
don't, gl:713
double negative, gr:736
draft, revising. *See* revision
due to, gl:713–14
dummy subject, 15d:281

-e, spelling rules for words ending
in, 31c:644
each other, gl:714
eager, gl:710
economics, reference works for,
18b:339
Edited English, 9b:165

education, reference works for, **18b**:339

effect, **gl**:708

either, **gl**:714

either/or fallacy, **15e**:281–82

elements in a series, **8c**:142, **30d**:612, **30e**:623–24

ellipses, **19c**:376, **21**:416, 426, **22e**:462, **23c**:494

   period with, **30a**:607

elliptical clause, **12c**:213

elliptical expression, **29b**:592, **gr**:736

elliptical question, **29d**:598–99

   comma with, **30d**:618

eminent, **gl**:714

emphasis, in body of essay, **5e**:64–65

encyclopedia

   APA citation of, **22b**:442–43

   endnote citation of, **23c**:490

   MLA citation of, **19b**:371

endnotes, **23a**:480–**23c**:513

   citation forms in, **23b**:482–92

   features of, **23a**:481

   page, **23a**:481–82

   sample research paper documented with, **23c**:492–513

enthused, **gl**:714

equally as, **gl**:714

-ess, **gl**:714–15

essay

   APA citation of, **22b**:438–39

   body of, **5e**:64–65

   conclusion of, **5f**:65–67

   controlling paragraphs in, **6d**:96–98

   endnote citation of, **23c**:487

   evidence in, **35c**:695–96

   introduction of, **5d**:62–64

   MLA citation of, **19b**:366

   organization. *See* organizing an essay

   revising. *See* revision

   sample, **5h**:74–79, **6d**:96–98, **10b**:176–84, **16c**:303–7, **35d**:696–97

Essay and General Literature Index, **18d**:348–49

etc., **gl**:715

etymology, **13a**:229

   in dictionary, **9a**:161

euphemism, **13f**:250, **gr**:736

evaluate, examination direction, **35b**:692

everybody, every body, **gl**:715

examination

   planning answer for, **35b**:693

   preparing for, **35a**:690–91

   reading directions for, **35b**:691–93

   sample answers for, **35d**:696–97

   writing, **35c**:693–96

examples, developing paragraph with, **7c**:103–4

except, **gl**:707

exclamation, **29b**:592

exclamation point, **30c**:609–10

   quotation mark and, **30f**:626

exclamatory sentence, **24b**:532, **30c**:609, **gr**:745

expect, **gl**:715

explain, examination direction, **35b**:692

explication, of literary work, **16d**:310–14

fact

   defined, **14c**:264–65

   use in argument, **14c**:267–68

   versus judgment, **14c**:265–67

in

factor, **gl:**715–16

false alternatives, **15e:**281–82

false analogy, **15c:**280

farther, **gl:**716

faze, **gl:**716

fewer, **gl:**716

figurative language, **13e:**236–39
  misuse of, **13f:**246–47

film
  APA citation of, **22b:**444–45
  endnote citation of, **23c:**491
  MLA citation of, **19b:**373
  reference works for, **18b:**339

finite verb, **gr:**736–37

flaunt, **gl:**716

flout, **gl:**716

fonts, on word processor, **36a:**701

footnote, **23:**480
  in APA documentation, **22d:**454,
  22e:464, 479

foreign words, italics with, **32e:**670

formal English, **9b:**165–66

former, **gl:**716

fragment, sentence. *See* sentence
  fragment

free writing, **2a:**20–24
  on word processor, **36b:**702

further, **gl:**716

fused sentence, **29e:**599–600,
  gr:737

future perfect tense, **28c:**574,
  28d:577

future tense, **28c:**573, **28d:**576

gazetteer, **18b:**337

gender, **gr:**737

general reference works, **18b:**337

generalization
  hasty, **15a:**276–77

unqualified, **15a:**277

valid, **15a:**273–76

genitive case, **26:**549, **gr:**731

gerund, **24a:**526, **gr:**737
  dangling, **12b:**212
  idiomatic use of, **13d:**235
  noun clause as object of, **24a:**530
  possessive case with, **26h:**555–56

gerund phrase, **24a:**526
  beginning sentence with, **8f:**153–
  54

glossary of usage, **gl:**707–28

good, **gl:**716–17

got, gotten, **gl:**716

government document, **18f:**354–55
  APA citation of, **22b:**443
  endnote citation of, **23c:**490
  MLA citation of, **19b:**371

grammatical terms, list of, **gr:**729–
  47

had of, **gl:**717

had ought, **gl:**717

hang, hanged, **28b:**571, **gl:**717

hardly, **gl:**717

hasty generalization, **15a:**276–77

have, **24a:**521–22

he, generic use of, **13f:**241–42

header, word processing function,
  36a:701

heading, of business letter,
  33b:678–79

history, reference works for,
  18b:339–40

hopefully, **gl:**717

hung, **gl:**717

hyphen, **31d:**646–48
  in compound adjective, **27d:**563–
  64, **31d:**647
  with numbers, **31d:**648

with prefix, **31d:**647–48
suspensive, **31d:**648
with syllabication, **32f:**671–72
hyphenation, word processing
function, **36a:**701

ibid., **23a:**482
idiom, **13d:**234–35, **gr:**737–38
ie, ei, spelling rules for, **31c:**646
illusion, **gl:**709
image, in literary work, **16b:**295–96
imminent, **gl:**714
immoral, **gl:**709
impact, **gl:**717
imperative mood, **28g:**584, **gr:**740
imperative sentence, **24a:**522,
    24b:532, **30a:**606, **gr:**745
implied topic sentence, **6b:**91–92
imply, **gl:**718
in regard to, **gl:**723
in relation to, **gl:**723
in terms of, **gl:**723
incomplete comparison, **12g:**224–25
incomplete construction, **12g:**223–25
incredible, incredulous, **gl:**718
indefinite article, **gr:**730
indefinite pronoun, **gr:**744
    as adjective, **gr:**729
    as antecedent, **25b:**545–47
    possessive case of, **30g:**630
    subject-verb agreement and,
        25a:541–42
indented style, of business letter,
    33a:678, **33b:**682–83

independent clause, **24a:**529,
    gr:731
    conjunctive adverb and semicolon
        with, **29c:**595–97, **30e:**623
    coordinating conjunction with,
        29c:597–98, **30d:**610–11
    as elements in a series, **30d:**613
    in fused sentence, **29e:**599–600
    as parenthetic element, **30h:**634
    rewriting as subordinate clause,
        29c:598
    rewriting sentence fragment as,
        29a:588–91
    semicolon with, **29c:**595,
        30e:622–23
indicative mood, **28g:**584, **gr:**740
indirect object, **24a:**524, **gr:**733,
    741
indirect quotation, **30d:**620,
    30f:625
infer, **gl:**718
inference, **14a:**259
infinitive, **24a:**526, **gr:**738
    case and, **26g:**555
    dangling, **12b:**212–13
    idiomatic use of, **13d:**235
    sequence of tenses with,
        28d:577–78
    split, **12d:**216
infinitive phrase, **24a:**527
    as sentence fragment, **29a:**590
inflected forms, in dictionary,
    9a:161
inflection, **gr:**738
insert, word processing function,
    36a:700, **36b:**705
inside address, of business letter,
    33b:679
inside of, **gl:**718
insupportable, **gl:**718
intensive, **13f:**247

in

intensive pronoun, **26d**:553,
gr:738–39, 744
inter, **gl**:718
interjection, **gr**:739
comma with, **30d**:618
interrogative pronoun, **gr**:744
as adjective, **gr**:729
case of, **26c**:552
interrogative sentence, **24b**:532,
30b:608, **gr**:745
interview
APA citation of, **22b**:443
endnote citation of, **23c**:490,
491
MLA citation of, **19b**:372, 373
intimacy between writer and reader,
4c:45–46
intra, **gl**:718
intransitive verb, **24a**:523, **gr**:746
introduction, writing an, **5d**:62–
64
related to conclusion, **5f**:66
introductory element, comma with,
30d:611–12
inverted word order, **24a**:521
beginning sentence with, **8f**:153
subject-verb agreement and,
25a:541
irony, **gl**:723–24
irregardless, **gl**:718
irregular verb, **24a**:520–21,
28a:568, **28b**:568–72, **gr**:739
is when, is where, **gl**:718
it, misuse of, **12a**:207
it is, **8b**:134–35
italics, **32e**:669–71
added to quotation for emphasis,
22e:466–67
its, **gl**:718–19
it's, **gl**:718–19

jargon, **13f**:247–49, **gr**:739
journal (personal)
keeping, **2a**:24–27, **16d**:307–8
keeping on computer, **36b**:703
journal (published)
APA citation of, **22b**:439–40
endnote citation of, **23c**:488
MLA citation of, **19b**:367–68
judgment
defined, **14c**:265–67
use in argument, **14c**:267–68
versus fact, **14c**:265–67

kind, **gl**:719
kind of, **gl**:719

language, reality and, **1a**:4
last, **gl**:719
later, **gl**:719
latest, **gl**:719
latter, **gl**:716, 719
lay, **gl**:719–20
lecture
APA citation of, **22b**:445
endnote citation of, **23c**:491
MLA citation of, **19b**:373
lend, **gl**:720
less, **gl**:716
let's, **gl**:720
letter (of alphabet), plural of,
30g:631
letter, business. *See* business letter
letter of application, **34b**:685–88
liable, **gl**:720
library
card catalog in, **18a**:333–36
data-base searches in, **18e**:349–54

Essay and General Literature Index,
  18d:348–49
government documents in,
  18f:354–55
locating books in, **18a**:335
on-line catalog in, **18a**:335–36
periodical indexes in, **18c**:344–48
reference works in, **18b**:343–44
Library of Congress System,
  18a:335
lie, **28b**:572, **gl**:719–20
like, **gl**:720
likely, **gl**:720
limiting a subject, **5a**:53–56
linking verb, **24a**:521, **gr**:739, 746–
  47
  adjective with, **27b**:562–63
  case and, **26f**:554–55
  subject-verb agreement with,
    25a:540
literally, **gl**:720
literature
  false assumptions about,
    16a:288–92
  productive questions to ask about,
    16b:293–303
  reference works for, **18b**:340–41
  sample student essay analyzing,
    16c:303–7
  strategies for thinking about,
    16d:307–14
  writing about, **16a**:288–**16d**:314
loan, **gl**:720
loose, lose, **gl**:720–21

macro revision, **10a**:174
magazine
  APA citation of, **22b**:440
  endnote citation of, **23c**:488
  MLA citation of, **19b**:368–69

main clause. *See* independent clause
man, alternatives to use of, **13f**:240–
  41
manuscript
  corrections in, **32a**:661
  format of, **32a**:658–59
  quotation in, **32a**:659–61
map
  endnote citation of, **23c**:490
  MLA citation of, **19b**:372
mapping diagram, **2a**:17, 18
margins, on word processor,
  36a:701
may, **28e**:580, **gl**:711
meaning, in dictionary, **9a**:161
metaphor, **13e**:236–38
micro revision, **10a**:174
microfilm or microfiche
  endnote citation of, **23c**:492
  MLA citation of, **19b**:374
might, **28e**:580
misplaced modifier, **12c**:214–15,
  gr:739
mixed constructions, **12f**:221–25,
  gr:739
mixed figures of speech, **13f**:246–
  47
MLA documentation
  characteristics of, **20c**:397–98
  sample research paper illustrating,
    21:413–31
MLA paper format, **20d**:407–8
MLA source citation, **20c**:397–407
MLA Works Cited forms, **19b**:359–
  74
modal auxiliary, **28e**:580
modified block style, of business
  letter, **33a**:678, **33b**:681–82
modifier, **24a**:519–20, **gr**:739; *see
  also* adjective; adverb
  beginning sentence with, **8f**:152

in

modifier (*continued*)
    dangling, **12b:**210–14, **gr:**735
    misplaced, **12c:**214–15, **gr:**739
    nonrestrictive, **gr:**740
    restrictive, **gr:**744
    squinting, **12c:**215
mood, of verb, **28g:**584–85, **gr:**739–40
    shift in, **12e:**219–20
moral, morale, **gl:**721
most, **27e:**564–65, **gl:**721
move, word processing function, **36a:**700, **36b:**705
much, **gl:**726–27
music, reference works for, **18b:**341
must, **28e:**580
myself, **gl:**721

narration, developing paragraph with, **7b:**102–3
negative, double, **gr:**736
neither, **gl:**714
newspaper
    APA citation of, **22b:**441
    endnote citation of, **23c:**489
    MLA citation of, **19b:**369–70
nominalization, **8b:**129–30
nominative case, **26:**549, **gr:**731
non sequitur, **15f:**282
nonrestrictive clause, **30d:**614–15, **gl:**725
nonrestrictive modifier, **30d:**614–16, **gr:**740
nonstandard English, **9b:**167–68
nor, subject-verb agreement and, **25a:**541
note card, **19c:**375–76, **23c:**494, 506

notes
    content, **20c:**406–7, **21:**430, **22d:**454, **22e:**464, 479
    identifying connections among, **20a:**389–90
    note cards, **19c:**375–76, **23c:**494, 506
    organizing, **20a:**390–91
    selectivity in taking, **19c:**379–80
    types of, **19c:**376–78
notorious, **gl:**721
noun, **24a:**518
    collective, **25a:**539–40, **gr:**732, 740
    common, **32b:**661–62, **gr:**740
    compound, **gr:**740
    ending in -*s,* **25a:**540
    formed from verb, **8b:**129–30
    predicate, **24a:**524, **gr:**733
    proper, **32b:**661–64, **gr:**740
    singular and plural forms of, **25a:**538, 540
    used as adjective, **27c:**563
noun clause, **24a:**529–30
number, **gr:**740
    shift in, **12e:**218–19
number, **gl:**709
numbers
    cardinal, **gr:**731
    comma in, **30d:**618–19
    hyphen in, **31d:**648
    ordinal, **gr:**731
    writing out, **32c:**665–67
numeral, plural of, **30g:**631

object
    direct, **24a:**523, **gr:**733, 741
    indirect, **24a:**524, **gr:**733, 741

noun clause as, **24a:**529–30
  of preposition, **gr:**743
object complement, **24a:**524
objective case, **26:**549, **gr:**731
objective complement, **gr:**741
objectivity
  of sources for research, **19d:**381
  in writing, **4b:**42
of, **gl:**721
off of, **gl:**721–22
on-line catalog, **18a:**335–36
on-line data-base search, **18e:**349–51
one, use of, **12a:**209
one another, **gl:**714
op. cit., **23a:**482
or, subject-verb agreement and, **25a:**541
ordinal number, **gr:**731
organizing an essay
  body, **5e:**64–65
  conclusion, **5f:**65–67
  introduction, **5d:**62–64
  limiting a subject, **5a:**53–56
  organizing ideas, **5c:**59–62
  outlines in, **5g:**67–74
  sample essay, **5h:**74–79
  thesis statement, **5b:**56–59
orthography, **31:**640
ought to, **28e:**580
outline
  conventions of, **5g:**71–74
  for research paper, **20a:**391
  subdivisions of, **5g:**72–74
  types of, **5g:**68–71
  uses of, **5g:**67–68
  on word processor, **36b:**703
outside of, **gl:**722
over with, **gl:**722
oversimplification, **15a:**277, **16b:**303

pagination, word processing function, **36a:**701
pamphlet
  endnote citation of, **23c:**490
  MLA citation of, **19b:**372
paragraph
  analogy to develop, **7g:**111–13
  cause and effect to develop, **7h:**113–14
  classification to develop, **7e:**107–8
  coherence between paragraphs, **11b:**200–201
  coherence in, **11b:**196–200
  combined methods of development, **7i:**114–15
  comparison or contrast to develop, **7f:**109–11
  definition to develop, **7d:**104–7
  details to develop, **7a:**100–102
  dialogue in, **6c:**95–96
  within essay, **6d:**96–98
  examples to develop, **7c:**103–4
  inadequate development of, **11a:**190–95
  length of, **6c:**93–96
  narration to develop, **7b:**102–3
  recognizing, **6a:**82–84
  revising, **11a:**190–**11b:**201
  rhetorical function of, **6a:**84
  topic sentence of, **6b:**87–93
  transitions in, **7c:**104, **11b:**197–98
paragraph outline, **5g:**68
parallel
  clauses, **8c:**137
  sentences, **8c:**138–40, **11b:**199–200
  words and phrases, **8c:**137
parallelism, **8c:**136–47, **gr:**741
  faulty, **8c:**140–47

in

paraphrase, **19c:**378, **23c:**496
 accuracy of, **20b:**395–96
 APA citation of, **22c:**451–52
 MLA citation of, **20c:**404–6
parentheses, **30h:**635–36
parenthetic element, **30d:**616–17
 dash with, **30h:**634
part, **gl:**722
participial phrase, **24a:**526
 beginning sentence with, **8f:**153–
 54
 dangling, **12b:**211–12
 as sentence fragment, **29a:**589
participle, **24a:**526, **gr:**741–42
 sequence of tenses with, **28d:**578
parts of speech, **gr:**742
 in dictionary, **9a:**161
party, **gl:**722
passive voice, **8b:**131–34, **28f:**582–
 83, **gr:**747
past perfect tense, **28c:**573–74,
 28d:577
past tense, **28c:**572–73, **28d:**576
peer editing, **10c:**183–84
 group, **10c:**184–85
 worksheet for, **10c:**185–88
percent, **gl:**722
period, **30a:**606–8
 with abbreviation, **30a:**607,
 32d:667
 correcting comma splice with,
 29c:594–95
 correcting fused sentence with,
 29e:599
 in dialogue, **30a:**608
 with ellipses, **30a:**607
 ending indirect question, **30a:**607
 ending sentence, **30a:**606
 inside quotation mark, **30f:**626
periodic sentence, **8d:**149–50
periodical index, **18c:**344–48

person, **gr:**742
 shift in, **12e:**218–19
personal pronoun, **gr:**744
 possessive case of, **30g:**631
phase, **gl:**716
phenomena, **gl:**713
philosophy, reference works for,
 18b:341
phrase, **24a:**519, 525, **gr:**742. *See
 also* absolute phrase; appositive
 phrase; gerund phrase; infinitive
 phrase; participial phrase;
 prepositional phrase; verbal phrase
place name, comma with, **30d:**618–
 19
plagiarism, **17d:**331, **19c:**376, 378
 avoiding, **20b:**392–97
political science, reference works for,
 18b:342
portion, **gl:**722
positive degree, **24a:**520, **27a:**559,
 gr:732
possessive case, **26:**549, **30g:**630–
 31, **gr:**731
possessive pronoun, as adjective,
 gr:729
post hoc, ergo propter hoc fallacy,
 15b:278
predicate, **24a:**519, **gr:**742
 compound, **24a:**522
predicate adjective, **24a:**524, **gr:**733
predicate noun, **24a:**524, **gr:**733
prefix, **gr:**743
 hyphen with, **31d:**647–48
premise, **14a:**259, **14b:**261
preposition, **gr:**743
 idiomatic use of, **13d:**234–35
 noun clause with, **24a:**530
 omitted, **12g:**223–24
prepositional phrase, **24a:**525
 beginning sentence with, **8f:**152

parenthetic, **30d:**616
as sentence fragment, **29a:**590
present perfect tense, **28c:**573,
 28d:577
present tense, **28c:**572, **28d:**575
pretentious diction, avoiding,
 13f:249–50
principal, **gl:**722–23
principal parts, of verbs, **28a:**567–
 68, **gr:**743
principle, **gl:**722–23
problem, **gl:**713
proceedings of a conference
 APA citation of, **22b:**443–44
 endnote citation of, **23c:**491
 MLA citation of, **19b:**372–73
progressive forms, of verbs, **28c:**574
pronoun, **24a:**519
 as adjective, **gr:**729
 ambiguous reference of,
  12a:204–5
 case of, **26:**549–**26h:**555, **gr:**731
 demonstrative, **255b:**547, **gr:**744
 indefinite, **25a:**541–42,
  25b:545–47, **30g:**630, **gr:**744
 intensive, **26d:**553, **gr:**738,
  gr:744
 interrogative, **26c:**552, **gr:**744
 it, they, you, **12a:**207–9
 linking sentences in paragraphs
  with, **11b:**198
 one, **12a:**209
 personal, **30g:**631, **gr:**743
 reciprocal, **gr:**744
 reference of, **12a:**204–9
 reflexive, **26d:**552–53, **gr:**744
 relative, **8a:**123, **24a:**529, 531,
  25a:542, **26b:**551–52,
  29c:598, **gr:**744
 remote reference of, **12a:**205
 this, that, which, **12a:**206–7

pronoun-antecedent agreement
 collective noun and, **25b:**545
 compound antecedent and,
  25b:544–45
 demonstrative pronoun and,
  25b:547
 indefinite pronoun and, **25b:**545
pronunciation, in dictionary, **9a:**161
proper name, **gr:**740
proper noun, **32b:**661–64, **gr:**740
psychology, reference works for,
 18b:342
punctuation, **30a:**606–**30h:**637. *See
 also* individual punctuation marks

question, **24a:**521, **29b:**592,
 30a:607
 elliptical or tag, **30d:**618
 method of discovering ideas,
  2b:28–30
 punctuation of, **30b:**608
question mark
 indicating doubtful information,
  30b:609
 after question, **30b:**608
 quotation mark and, **30f:**626
quotation
 accuracy of, **20b:**393–94
 APA citation of, **22c:**446–51
 beginning introduction with,
  5d:62–63
 capitalization in, **32b:**664–65
 comma with, **30d:**619–20
 direct. *See* direct quotation
 indirect, **30d:**620, **30f:**625
 long, **20c:**399, **30f:**627
 in manuscript, **32a:**659–61
 MLA citation of, **20c:**399–404
 in notes, **19c:**376

in

quotation (*continued*)
quotation marks with, **30f:**625–28
verse, **30f:**628
within quotation, **30f:**626–27
quotation marks, **20b:**393–94, **32a:**659
defined term in, **30f:**629
with direct quotation, **30f:**625–28
misuse of, **30f:**629–30
other punctuation with, **30f:**626
single, **30f:**626, **32a:**661
title in, **30f:**628–29, **32e:**670

raise, **gl:**723
reader
of research paper, **17c:**329–30
subject and, **5a:**55
writer and, **4c:**43–46
real, **27e:**564, **gl:**723
reason is, **gl:**723
reasoning, **14a:**257–**14d:**272
analogy, **15c:**279–80
errors in, **15a:**273–**15f:**282
reciprocal pronoun, **gr:**744
recording
endnote citation of, **23c:**492
MLA citation of, **19b:**374
reductive fallacy, **15b:**278–79
redundancy, **8b:**128–29
refer, **gl:**708
reference list, APA
characteristics of, **22a:**432–33
citation forms in, **22b:**433–45
format of, **22d:**454
sample, **22e:**477–78
reference works, **18b:**336–44
reflexive pronoun, **26d:**552–53, **gr:**744

regarding, **gl:**723
regional English, **9b:**167
regular verb, **28a:**567, **gr:**744
relative clause, **8a:**125
relative pronoun, **24a:**529, 531, **gr:**744
case of, **26b:**551–52
correcting comma splice with, **29c:**598
list of, **8a:**123
as subject, **25a:**542
religion, reference works for, **18b:**342
repetition, **8b:**131
for clarity in parallel construction, **8c:**142–43
for paragraph coherence, **11b:**198–99
report, **17a:**322–24. *See also* research paper
APA citation of, **22b:**444
reporting, objective, **4b:**42
research
identifying subject for, **17b:**327–29
planning, **16b:**302–3
preparing for, **17a:**322–27
recursiveness of, **17d:**332
understanding, **17d:**331–32
research paper
APA documentation of, **22a:**432–**22c:**452
APA format for, **22d:**452–54
assessing subject for, **19e:**381–82
considering reader of, **17c:**329–30
endnote documentation of, **23a:**480–**23b:**492
features of, **17a:**326–27
finding subject for, **17b:**327–29

MLA documentation of,
  19b:359–74, **20c:**397–407
MLA format for, **20d:**407–8
notes for, **19c:**375–80, **20a:**389–91
organization of, **20a:**388–91
outline of, **20a:**391
paraphrasing in, **20b:**395–96
plagiarism in, **20b:**392–97
planning, **17d:**330–32
quoting in, **20b:**393–94
revision of, **20a:**392
sample, APA documentation,
  22e:455–79
sample, endnote documentation,
  23c:495–513
sample, MLA documentation,
  21:413–31
sources of information for. *See*
  source, for research paper
subheadings in, **22e:**460
title page of, **20d:**408, **22d:**453
types of, **17a:**322–26
working bibliography for,
  19a:357–59
writing, **20a:**391–92
researched argument, **17a:**324–26
restricting phrase, in thesis
  statement, **5b:**56–57, 58
restrictive clause, **30d:**614–15,
  gl:725
restrictive modifier, **30d:**614–16,
  gr:744
résumé
  content of, **34a:**685
  format of, **34a:**684
  sample, **34b:**688–89
review
  APA citation of, **22b:**441–42
  endnote citation of, **23c:**489
  MLA citation of, **19b:**370

revision
  defined, **10a:**173
  of diction, **13a:**228–**13f:**250
  guidelines for effective, **10a:**173–75
  to improve paragraph coherence,
    11b:196–201
  to improve paragraph
    development, **11a:**190–95
  instructor's role in, **10b:**175–83
  peer editing and, **10c:**183–88
  peer editing worksheet for,
    10c:186–87
  sample essay illustrating,
    10b:176–83
  of sentence, **12a:**204–**12g:**225
  types of, **10a:**173–74
rhetoric, defined, **3a:**33
rhetorical situation, **3a:**33–34
right-justification, word processing
  function, **36a:**701
rise, **gl:**723

salutation, of business letter,
  30h:633, **33b:**679–80
sarcasm, **gl:**723–24
save, word processing function,
  36a:700
scarcely, **gl:**717
sciences, reference works for,
  18b:343
semicolon
  connecting independent clauses,
    30e:622–23
  correcting comma splice with,
    29c:595–97
  correcting fused sentence with,
    29e:599
  with elements in series, **30e:**632–24

in

semicolon (*continued*)
   outside quotation mark, **30f**:626
   separating independent clauses
      with internal punctuation,
      30d:611, **30e**:623
sensual, sensuous, **gl**:724
sentence
   capitalization in, **32b**:664–65
   comma splice in, **29c**:594–
      99
   complex, **24b**:534
   compound, **24b**:533–34
   compound-complex, **24b**:534–
      35
   concise, **8b**:127–35
   cumulative, **8d**:148–49
   declarative, **24b**:532, **gr**:745
   defined, **24a**:517, **gr**:744
   elements of, **24a**:517–22
   exclamatory, **24b**:532, **gr**:745
   faulty coordination in, **8a**:122–
      25, **8c**:140, 141
   faulty subordination in, **8a**:122–
      23, 125, **8c**:145–46
   fused, **29e**:599–600, **gr**:737
   imperative, **24a**:522, **24b**:532,
      gr:745
   incomplete. *See* sentence fragment
   interrogative, **24b**:532, **gr**:745
   inverted word order in, **8f**:153,
      24a:521, **25a**:541
   mixed constructions in, **12f**:221–
      25
   parallelism in, **8c**:136–47
   periodic, **8d**:149–50
   revising, **12a**:204–**12g**:225
   simple, **24b**:532–33
   syntax of, **24b**:532
   topic. *See* topic sentence
   unified, **8a**:119–25

   varying first element in, **8f**:152–
      54
   varying length of, **8e**:150–51
sentence fragment, **29a**:587–88,
   gr:745
   acceptable use of, **29b**:591–93
   appositive phrase as, **29a**:591
   dependent clause as, **29a**:588–89
   infinitive phrase as, **29a**:590
   participial phrase as, **29a**:589
   prepositional phrase as, **29a**:590
sentence outline, **5g**:69–71
sequence
   of ideas in parallel construction,
      8c:146–47
   of tenses, **28d**:575–78
series
   comma with elements in, **30d**:612
   parallel elements in, **8c**:142
   semicolon with elements in,
      30e:623–24
set, **gl**:724
sexist language
   definition of, **13f**:239–40
   examples of, **13f**:240–43
   ways to avoid, **13f**:240–43,
      25b:545–47
shall, **gl**:724
shift
   in mood or tense, **12e**:219–20
   in person or number, **12e**:218–
      19
   in sentence structure, **12e**:217
   in voice or subject, **12e**:218
should, **28e**:580, **gl**:724
sic, **30h**:637
simile, **13e**:238
simple predicate, **gr**:742–43
simple sentence, **24b**:532–33
simple subject, **24a**:521, **gr**:745

single quotation marks, **30f:**626, **32a:**661
sit, **gl:**724
slang, **9b:**168–69
slash, **21:**418, **30f:**628
slides, APA citation of, **22b:**444–45
so, **gl:**724
sociology, reference works for, **18b:**343–44
software
  APA citation of, **22b:**444
  endnote citation of, **23c:**491
  MLA citation of, **19b:**373
some, **gl:**725
sort, **gl:**719
sort of, **gl:**719
source, for research paper
  assessing quality and appropriateness of, **19d:**380–81
  books as, **18a:**333–36, **18d:**348–49
  citing, APA style, **22a:**432–33, **22c:**445–52
  citing, endnote style, **23a:**480–82
  citing, MLA style, **20c:**397–407
  in data base, **18e:**349–54
  government documents as, **18f:**354–55
  periodicals as, **18c:**344–48
  reference works as, **18b:**336–44
spacing, on word processor, **36a:**700
spelling, **31:**640–57
  in dictionary, **9a:**161
  frequently confused words, **31b:**642–43
  hyphenation and, **31d:**646–48
  rules for, **31c:**643–46
  trouble spots in, **31a:**641
  words commonly misspelled, **31e:**649–52

spelling checker, on word processor, **36b:**706
split infinitive, **12d:**216
square brackets, **19c:**376, **21:**426, **22e:**472, **30h:**636–37
squinting modifier, **12c:**215
Standard English, **9b:**164–65
stereotype, **15a:**276–77
structured approach, to discovering ideas
  defined, **2b:**28
  example of, **2b:**30–32
  questions to use with, **2b:**29–30
  with word processor, **36b:**703
style checker, on word processor, **36b:**706
subheadings, in APA manuscript style, **22e:**460
subject (of essay)
  assessing, **19e:**381–82
  discovering ideas for, **2a:**15–**2b:**32
  of research paper, **17b:**327–29
  strategies for limiting, **5a:**53–56
  in thesis statement, **5b:**56–58
  voice and, **4b:**40–42
subject (of sentence), **24a:**519, **gr:**745
  compound, **24a:**522, **25a:**539
  dummy, **15d:**281
  noun clause as, **24a:**529
  shift in, **12e:**218
  simple, **24a:**521
subject complement, **24a:**524, **27b:**562
subject-verb agreement
  collective noun and, **25a:**539–40
  compound subject and, **25a:**539
  indefinite pronoun and, **25a:**541–42
  inverted word order and, **25a:**541

in

subject-verb agreement (*continued*)
    linking verb and, **25a:**540
    modifying phrases and, **25a:**538–39
    noun ending in *-s* and, **25a:**540
    with *or* and *nor,* 25a:541
    relative pronoun and, **25a:**542
    rules governing, **25a:**537–38
subjective case, **26:**549, **gr:**731
subjunctive mood, **28g:**584–85, **gr:**740
subordinate clause. *See* dependent clause
subordinating conjunction, **24a:**529, **gr:**735
    correcting comma splice with, **29c:**598
    correcting fused sentence, **29e:**600
    list of, **8a:**123
subordination, **gr:**746
    faulty, **8a:**125, **8c:**145–46
    upside-down, **8a:**125
substantive, **gr:**746
such, **gl:**724–25
suffix, **gr:**746
summarize, examination direction, **35b:**692
summary, in notes, **19c:**378
superlative degree, **24a:**520, **gr:**732
    adjective forms, **27a:**559, 561
    adverb forms, **27a:**559–60, 561
superscript, **20c:**406, **21:**414, **23a:**480
sure, **27e:**564, **gl:**725
suspensive hyphen, **31d:**648
syllabication, **32f:**671–72
    in dictionary, **9a:**161
synonyms, in dictionary, **9a:**162
syntax, **gr:**746

tag question, comma with, **30d:**618
television program
    endnote citation of, **23c:**492
    MLA citation of, **19b:**374
tense, **28a:**567–68, **28c:**572–74, **gr:**733–34, 746
    sequence of, **28d:**575–78
    shift in, **12e:**219–20
than, pronoun after, **26e:**554
that, **gl:**725
    misuse of, **12a:**206
theater, reference works for, **18b:**344
their, there, **gl:**725–26
there is, **8b:**134–35
thesis statement
    beginning introduction with, **5d:**62
    components of, **5b:**56–57
    ending introduction with, **5d:**63–64
    formulating, **5b:**56–59
    placement of, **5b:**59
    precision in, **5b:**57–58
they, misuse of, **12a:**207–8
this, misuse of, **12a:**206–7
this here, that there, **gl:**726
time, colon with, **30h:**633
title
    abbreviation of, **32d:**668–69
    capitalization of, **32b:**663, 664
    italics with, **32e:**670
    of literary work, **16b:**294
    in quotation marks, **30f:**628–29
title page
    APA format for, **22d:**453, **22e:**456
    MLA format for, **20d:**408, **21:**415
to, **gl:**726

tone. *See also* voice
    of literary work, **16b**:296–98
    vehement versus moderate,
        14d:270–72
too, **gl**:726
topic outline, **5g**:68–69
topic sentence
    formulating, **6b**:87–88
    implied, **6b**:91–92
    position of, **6b**:88–92
toward, towards, **gl**:726
transitional phrase
    list of, **11b**:197
    semicolon with, **29c**:595–97,
        29e:599
transitive verb, **24a**:523, **gr**:746
translation
    APA citation of, **22b**:437
    endnote citation of, **23c**:485–86
    MLA citation of, **19b**:364
transpire, **gl**:726
try and, **gl**:726
two, **gl**:726
type, **gl**:719

unclear pronoun reference,
    12a:204–9
uninterested, **gl**:713
unique, **27a**:560–61, **gl**:726
unqualified generalization, **15a**:277
unstructured approach, to
    discovering ideas
    brainstorming as, **2a**:16–20
    defined, **2a**:15–16
    free writing as, **2a**:20–24
    journal as, **2a**:24–27
    mapping diagram as, **2a**:17–18
    with word processor, **36b**:702–3
unsupportable, **gl**:718
up, **gl**:726

upside-down subordination, **8a**:125
usage
    glossary of, **gl**:707–28
    levels of, **9b**:164–69
usage labels, in dictionary, **9a**:161–
62

verb, **24a**:518
    auxiliary, **24a**:520, **28e**:579–80
    conjugation of, **gr**:733–34
    defined, **gr**:746
    finite, **gr**:736–37
    intransitive, **24a**:523, **gr**:746
    irregular, **24a**:520–21, **28a**:568,
        28b:568–72, **gr**:739
    linking, **13f**:244, **24a**:521,
        25a:540, **26f**:554–55,
        27b:562–63, **gr**:739, 746
    modal auxiliary, **28e**:580
    mood of, **28g**:584–85, **gr**:740
    number of, **gr**:740
    person of, **gr**:742
    principal parts of, **28a**:567–68,
        gr:743
    progressive forms of, **28c**:574
    regular, **28a**:567, **gr**:744
    sequence of tenses of, **28d**:575–
77
    singular and plural forms of,
        25a:537
    strong versus weak, **13f**:243–45
    tense of, **28a**:567–68, **28c**:572–
74, **gr**:746
    transitive, **24a**:523, **gr**:746
    used to form noun, **8b**:129–30
    voice of, **8b**:131–34, **28f**:581–
83, **gr**:747
    weak, **gr**:744
verb phrase, split, **12d**:215–16

in

verbal, **gr:**747
 defined, **24a:**526
verbal phrase
 beginning sentence with, **8f:**153–
 54
 idiomatic use of, **12c:**213–14
verse, quoting, **30f:**628
very, **gl:**726–27
videotape
 APA citation of, **22b:**444–45
 endnote citation of, **23c:**492
 MLA citation of, **19b:**374
vita. *See* résumé
voice (in writing), **4a:**39–**4c:**46
 audience and, **4c:**42–46
 subject and, **4b:**40–42
voice (of verb), **8b:**131–34,
 28f:581–83, **gr:**747
 shift in, **12e:**218

wait on, **gl:**727
ways, **gl:**727
weak verb, **gr:**744
weave, **28b:**572
where, **gl:**727
which, **gl:**725
 misuse of, **12a:**206
who, **gl:**725
who, whom, **gl:**727
 in dependent clause, **26b:**551–52
 in interrogative clause, **26c:**552
whose, who's, **gl:**727
will, **28e:**580, **gl:**724
Wilsearch, **18e:**351–53
-wise, **gl:**727
with regard to, **gl:**723
word order, **gr:**747
word processing
 benefiting from, **36b:**701–6
 brainstorming with, **36b:**702

definition of, **36a:**698
 editing with, **36b:**706
 equipment for, **36a:**698–99
 formatting functions of,
 36a:700–701
 free writing with, **36b:**702
 functions of, **36a:**699–700
 keeping a journal with, **36b:**703
 on-screen composing with,
 36b:704
 outlining with, **36b:**703
 planning paper with, **36b:**702–3
 revising with, **36b:**704–5
 spelling checker, **36b:**706
 using structured approach to
 discovering ideas with, **36b:**703
 style checker, **36b:**706
word wrap, **36a:**699
wordiness, **8b:**127–35
working bibliography, **19a:**357
 assembling, **19a:**358
 recording information in,
 19a:358–59
Works Cited page, **19a:**358,
 20c:398–407
 sample, **21:**431
would, **28e:**580, **gl:**724
would have, **gl:**727
writer
 background of, for limiting
 subject, **5a:**54–55
 distance from reader, **4c:**43–45
 intimacy with reader, **4c:**45–46
writing
 believability in, **14d:**270–72
 of examination, **35a:**690–
 35c:696
 idiosyncratic nature of, **1c:**9–10
 importance of, **1:**3